The Rise of Guardian Democracy

HARVARD POLITICAL STUDIES

Published under the direction of the
Department of Government in Harvard University

Ward E. Y. Elliott is an associate professor of political science at Claremont Men's College.

**ELLIOTT, Ward E. Y. The rise of guardian democracy; the Supreme
   Court's role in voting rights disputes, 1845–1969. Harvard, 1975
   (c1974). 391p tab bibl 73-90611. 15.00. SBN 674-77156-7**

CHOICE   SEPT. '75
Political Science

This is more than the standard discussion of how and why the Supreme
Court became involved with voting rights reforms. The major thrust
of the book involves a critical analysis of "the effect the Court's involvement [in voting rights cases] has had on the quality of American democracy." In Elliott's view, these reforms have weakened representative institutions by demanding too much of them. The motivating
force behind these changes in reapportionment, residency, and age
requirements has been an intellectual-elitist "Guardian Ethic" that
unites knowledge and power through the rule of experts. In developing
this theme Elliott provides a highly controversial yet fascinating analysis of the power linkages that exist between policy-making institutions
and the professional social scientist. Highly recommended for a graduate level or advanced undergraduate audience.

The Rise of Guardian Democracy

The Supreme Court's Role in Voting Rights Disputes, 1845–1969

WARD E. Y. ELLIOTT

Harvard University Press   Cambridge, Massachusetts

1974

A.M.D.G.

Preface

This is a book of perspectives. It is also a book about perspectives. It offers theories as to how voting rights reforms came about in the old days, how they have come about in the modern era (since the "Court revolution" of 1937), how and why the Supreme Court became involved in the reform process, and what effect the Court's involvement has had on the quality of American democracy. The book also touches more than lightly on the mystique of standardization, expertise, crisis, and progress, which I call the Guardian Ethic and which I believe played a predominant role in intellectuals' reformist thoughts in the modern era. Few, if any, of the facts presented here are new discoveries, though I suppose some readers might be surprised at the implications I attach to material already known. If there is any novelty in this book, it is its reinterpretation of modern facts and beliefs in the light of much older perspectives which I fancy to have more staying power than many of those in vogue in the last generation.

By these old perspectives words were supposed to mean something, and that something was supposed to be tolerably stable. Democratic governments were supposed to be responsive to the will of the governed. Laws were supposed to last until changed by proper authority. Political affections and institutions which supported these ends were supposed to be cherished. Today, if we are sophisticated, we know that the old perspectives were imperfect and often misleading, their followers too credulous of their own premises. We know that there is considerable plasticity and ambiguity in words, that laws shift and stretch in response to changing political pressures. We recognize transiency as a necessary and even desirable aspect of the natural order of things (though in opening ourselves to things that do not last we tend to close ourselves to things that do). More and more, we have come to judge in terms of immediate results, first flattering our institutions with elevated expectations, then killing them with demands which they cannot possibly meet. By the newer perspectives institutional virtues are ignored, while shortcomings that bothered very few in the old days now appear as damning indictments of the entire system, calling for its prompt and radical reconstruction. Curiously, the most confirmed recon-

structionists have been highly sophisticated social scientists, often the
most knowledgeable and articulate available—men who should have known
better than to rate governments by the same absolute, abstract standards
they use for rating graduate students. Eminent social scientists have zeroed
in with distressing regularity on this or that "intolerable" anomaly of
the political system—big city machines, gerrymanders, low voter turnout,
political appointments, Constitution worship, and so forth—calling for
their abolition and replacement with something less imperfect but usually
less workable. The dismal record of social scientists in the matter of policy
recommendations should suggest both to social scientists and to politicians
that we should be more cautious about imposing our professional paradigms on the body politic.

It seems to me that there is more to the older perspectives than is commonly conceded today in intellectual circles, and less to the newer. Words and
laws are plastic, yes, but not infinitely plastic. The Constitution is not a
blank check to posterity. Democracy is not the same thing as total mobilization of the electorate. I am sure that there are institutional reasons that
the "urban problem" is yet "unsolved," the German mine safety record
is better than ours, Swedish babies are healthier, Japanese trains are faster, and
Russian rockets beat us into space. I am less sure, however, that any or all
of these amount to a mandate for change, far less for the wholesale super-
cession of representative institutions so loudly called for in the 1960's.
Despite the Knowledge Explosion, the Technetronic Age, and the Global
Village, despite its mystique of diffusion of innovation (or was it because of
these?), the Warren era was a rather narrow-minded one. Warren-era intellectuals who followed the Guardian Ethic were toughminded about the
old perspectives but often softheaded about the new. They doted on novelty,
they fought for universal equality in form, but also for special privileges in
substance for those with expertise; they scoffed at the bumbling, com-
promising efforts of legislatures and political parties, but their faith in
management by the executive or judiciary knew no bounds. Their mixture
of cynicism and faith was the central component of the Warren Court's great
decisions on civil and political rights, bearing considerable responsibility
for the Court's high prestige in the early 1960's and perhaps also for its
declining prestige in the late 1960's.

Though the Guardian Ethic was humane in inspiration and supported by
the most enlightened people we had, I consider it no less exaggerated in
its "pragmatic" orthodoxy than the old faith in lasting laws and institutions.
It was heedless of the informal affections and ties which make democracy
work effectively; it was oblivious to past and future; it was keenly sensitive
to the most minute transgression of formal equality but blind alike to considerations of practical equality and to freedom of political choice for individual citizens and their elected representatives. Though moderns hailed its

triumphs in the 1960's as victories for democracy, the same triumphs from
the older perspective look more like a series of steps away from the representative democracy Tocqueville described in America toward something
resembling the administrative bureaucracy Tocqueville thought he had
left behind in France.

The great voting rights decisions of the Warren era, characterized by Chief
Justice Warren himself as the principal accomplishment of his court, represent more than just a quaint reversal of old perspectives about democracy.
Though their overall political impact was less than most people had been
led to expect, they are notable for the ease with which the Court bypassed
almost all known tests of constitutional logic and still managed to rout
utterly the platoons of objecting senators, congressmen, and state legislators
who sought to stem its will. Nothing (so they say) is so powerful as an idea
whose time has come, but political ideas were much more rigorously tested
in the traditional political arenas, where they had to win acceptance by
one of the dominant parties and then win at the polls before becoming law.
American history is littered with the remains of ideas whose time came
and then went away, fortunately, without doing serious harm. The Anti-
Masonic, Know-Nothing, Greenback, and Populist movements all had to
face the old, stern test of party and public acceptance, as did the movements
for Henry Wallace and the Dixiecrats in the 1940's, Joseph McCarthy in
the 1950's, and Eugene McCarthy and George Wallace in the 1960's. Some
movements, such as abolitionism, progressivism, and prohibitionism, did
succeed in passing the test (though not always for the "right" reasons);
but modern reforms like reapportionment and abolishing the poll tax were
tried in a different arena which exempted them from the old tests. The
modern reforms did have to win the acceptance of scholars and professional
associations, but this test turned out to be a pushover, owing to the scholar's
own perceptual weaknesses in matters of public policy. A nod from the
experts, a nod from the national press, law professors, and the solicitor
general, a word from seven justices on the Supreme Court, and reapportionment was in.

Surely this was a casebook lesson in diffusion of innovation, but also a
hint of fundamental changes in the American political universe strengthening the administrative and the expert but weakening the representative and
the layman he represents, not to mention the integrative agencies (political
parties) that hitherto have filtered out ill-considered innovations, guarded
against the most pernicious forms of polarization, and kept the system
stable and responsive for the longer run. The conventional wisdom of experts,
no matter how scholarly in appearance, is a poor substitute for the practical
skills of professional politicians, who have very strong incentives not to
make policy mistakes. Scholars have strong professional incentives to produce
bold and innovative ideas and to avoid mistakes in technique, but they have

almost no political, and very little professional incentive to avoid mistakes in areas of policy which are normally too broad to be decided with professional technique alone. Many a scholar looks back with appreciation to the days of John Marshall, when the Court played the role of educator to the nation. We might look back with some misgivings to the 1960's, when educators came close to becoming the court of the nation and, in some few instances, a shortcut equivalent of a constitutional convention as well.

I am much in debt to my first critics, several of whom have read the manuscript almost entirely: my father, William Y. Elliott, who first turned my thoughts to the distinction between organicism and mechanism; my friend and colleague Charles A. Lofgren, who tightened up a number of loose historical allusions in the early chapters; Martin Shapiro, whose hard-nosed critique produced a number of changes for the better; and two gentle, cultured and judicious scholars, Robert McCloskey and Arthur Sutherland, who are no longer alive to accept my thanks and whose passing is a great loss to the profession. Robert McCloskey first introduced me to constitutional law and later guided me through the formative stages of the manuscript with exactly the right blend of criticism and encouragement. I fear that I have only partially fulfilled his hope that I would trim my long sentences to make them less reminiscent of Gibbon and more of Macaulay. Arthur Sutherland patiently sharpened and focused numberless imprecisions in several drafts of the manuscript and moderated some of its bombast. He was a devoted supporter of reapportionment to the end, but a tolerant one.

Robert Dixon, Henry Salvatori, and James Q. Wilson gave me much needed commentary on the most difficult part in the book, Chapter I. Benjamin F. Wright helped with early drafts of Chapters II and II. George Blair and Alan Heslop added light to a prior draft of Chapter VII that appeared in the *Chicago Law Review.*

My typists, Lorraine McElroy, Fröke Blessum, Linda Barnard, and Lynn Weatherman, and my indexer, Mary Eiland, were models of industry, My wife, Myrna, has been very quiet about the manuscript, but she is the light of my eyes and the flower of my heart. I am sure the book would have had an even more somber tone had she not come along.

Finally, I owe special thnks to my special backers: my parents, William Y. and Louise Ward Elliott; George Benson, Henry Salvatori, and Arthur Smithies. Each one offered encouragement well beyond the call of duty at critical times when there was no assurance that this book would ever see the light of day. Without their support the book would surely have come out later and weaker, if indeed it came out at all. I am most grateful to these, and also to the Henry Salvatori Center for the Study of Individual

Freedom in the Modern World, which supported the project generously for a period of three years.

Ward E. Y. Elliott
Claremont, California,
New Years Day 1974

Contents

I. Introduction: The Dynamics of
Democracy and the Guardian Ethic

Trace Science then, with Modesty thy guide;
First strip off all her equipage of Pride;
Deduct what is but Vanity, or Dress,
Or Learning's Luxury, or Idleness;
Or tricks to shew the stretch of human brain,
Mere curious pleasure, or ingenious pain:
Expunge the whole, or lop th'excrescent parts
Of all, our vices have created arts:
Then see how little the remaining sum
Which serv'd the past, and must the times to come.

—Alexander Pope

The Dynamics of Democratic Reform

Not so long ago, in the days of what Alexander Bickel called the "Heavenly City of the Justices,"[1] American intellectuals seemed remarkably agreed that the country had attained, through enlightened management, an unprecedented level of democratic well-being. This happy consensus dated from about 1960, when Seymour Martin Lipset announced that the fundamental problems of the Industrial Revolution had been solved and hinted that the democracy of the day was rather close to being "the good society itself in operation."[2] It lasted in full bloom till the winter of 1968, when President Lyndon Johnson declined to run for reelection, and intellectuals found deep differences among themselves—and also between themselves, the government, and the public at large. The 1960's were an age of democratic ideology and rhetoric; they were also a time when the government was exceptionally sensitive to rhetoric, and when intellectuals were peculiarly inclined to believe that the rise of democracy in American history was the product of rhetoric.

Today, with the consensus of the 1960's in tatters and the work of political historians like William Gillette, Alan Pendleton Grimes, and Chilton Williamson in hand, both the older expansions of democracy and the more recent ones appear in a more sober light.[3] It now seems that most democratic re-

1

forms before 1937, when the Supreme Court acceded to the Roosevelt Revolution, were primarily (though by no means exclusively) motivated by hopes of partisan advantage. It also seems that reforms since 1937, while less partisan in inspiration than the older reforms, were also less democratic in that they were typically imposed administratively from the top, rather than representationally from the bottom. The old reforms won or lost in "input" agencies devoted to the consultation and aggregation of political interests: parties, state legislatures, and Congress. Their success or failure often depended on their perceived promise of reward to some powerful interest. Modern reforms have normally issued from "output" agencies like the executive or the judiciary, devoted to the promulgation, interpretation, and enforcement of rules. The success or failure of modern reforms was more likely to depend on their perceived consonance with abstract principles of justice and sound administration. Older reforms were not particularly democratic in inspiration, but they were democratic in origin and effect; modern reforms were highly democratic in inspiration, but undemocratic in origin and not always very democratic in effect.

One of the main influences for modern reforms was what I call the Guardian Ethic, the bureaucratic, elitist ideology of action-minded intellectuals in the modern age, most of whom thought they were beyond ideology. Most intellectuals and well-educated people believed, without really thinking about it, that anything new must be better than anything old, that action must be better than inaction, expert better than amateur, standard better than special, and administered better than unadministered. This Guardian Ethic was democratic in its stress on equality, but it was antidemocratic in its stress on administration and intellectual elitism—a distinction important because the Warren Court followed the Ethic in most of its decisions involving voting rights (and other civil rights). The Ethic tended to extend equality in form while debasing it in substance. It granted equal access to representative institutions, in a sense, but it also treated the institutions as though they were unfit to decide the main questions.

There have been many extensions of suffrage in American history. Few, if any, of these before the time of Franklin Roosevelt resulted primarily from solicitude by the franchised for the rights of the unfranchised. Few, if any, were the primary result of a struggle for representation by the unfranchised. Suffrage extensions were usually brought about by an already dominant party or faction seeking to perpetuate its control by strategic enlargement of the electorate. The post-Civil War Radical Republicans, as a group, cared very little for the black vote until they came to believe that it would help secure their position in the South, and then in the North, against a Democratic resurgence. Once convinced that they would profit from the black vote, they passed the Fifteenth Amendment. Yankee Protestant voters likewise sought their own advantage when they enfranchised women in the early 1900's to help protect "the ideals that won independence" from corruption at the hands of immigrant ethnic and religious minorities. Property qualifications were dropped in the states, in the early days, less because of sympathy for the unpropertied than because the qualifications were hard to enforce and produced constant wrangling and fraud in the parties; moreover, party leaders feared what might happen if the other party should get the jump in cultivating a new market of votes.[4]

The Supreme Court got involved with voting rights, first because of a transfer of voting rights disputes from state to federal arenas, and then because of a change within the federal arena from the input side (parties and Congress) to the output side (president, Justice Department, Supreme Court). Before the passage of the Fifteenth Amendment, voting rights were recognized as almost exclusively of concern to the states; major reforms were made in state legislatures. Since the Fifteenth Amendment, voting rights have been both of state and federal concern, but the states have had little reformative influence since the 1930's. Since 1940, the Supreme Court, with some help from the solicitor general, has been the major instigator of voting rights reform.

Types of Voting Rights

Voting rights, which are used here in their broadest sense, include four major subheadings:[5]

(1) *Rights against administrative abuses*, such as ballot box stuffing, fraud, intimidation, and so on;
(2) *Suffrage qualification rights*, such as property, literacy, and other tests for voters;
(3) *Rights involving problems of the district system*, including what we have been taught to call malapportionment, and multi-member districts, and gerrymanders, with their attendant problems of wasted and excess votes,[6] and, finally,
(4) *Rights involving checks and balances*, or limits on the power of majorities.

These categories are listed in ascending order of complexity; they are also approximately in the order in which they were addressed by the Supreme Court, which first decided not the oldest ones but the simplest ones. It then went on to build up a basis of doctrine which enabled it later to attack the more difficult categories, more and more under constitutional authority of its own manufacture. Unequal districts and gerrymanders have been the subject of fierce political contests since the earliest days of the Republic—as literacy tests, white primaries, and grandfather clauses have not—but it would have been unthinkable for the Supreme Court to have attacked the older and more complex issues without the help of doctrines it had devised to deal with simpler and more recent issues.

3

Three Periods in the History of Voting Rights Reform

The Supreme Court learned the rudiments of intervention in voting rights disputes as a player in the new federal arena, applying the principles of the Fifteenth Amendment to techniques of disfranchising blacks, techniques themselves devised only after 1890. It took the Court fifteen years even to warm up for the task, as it did in *Guinn v. United States*, outlawing a grandfather clause in one state, and another three decades to get into it seriously, which it finally did in 1944 by outlawing white primaries in *Smith v. Allwright*.[7] The ratification of the Fourteenth Amendment in 1868 provides a convenient dividing line between the Pre-Intervention period of Marshall and Taney, when the Court would have nothing to do with voting rights, and the period of Intervention by Interpretation, when the Court had fresh constitutional authority, fresh issues, and growing power to intervene. Likewise, in *Baker v. Carr* (1962), the Court's passage back from its concentration on black voting rights under the Reconstruction amendments, to concentration on issues which antedated the Civil War, marks the end of interpretive intervention and the beginning of legislative intervention.[8] These dividing lines form three periods, the Pre-Intervention period, from the Revolution to 1868, the period of Intervention by Interpretation, 1868 to 1962, and the period of Legislative Intervention, 1962 to Chief Justice Earl Warren's retirement in 1969. I also refer to the modern era of the Supreme Court, a common usage among Constitutional scholars to separate the post-1937, civil-rights-conscious Court from its predecessors.

The period of Intervention by Interpretation encompassed three separate lines of development which ultimately made it possible for the Court to intervene against malapportionment with almost no constitutional authority in the traditional sense and almost no explicit consideration of policy issues, which would be necessary to make a constitutional case in the modern sense. The first of these lines of cases was the black voting rights progression, in which the Court itself developed a bold, broad mode of constitutional interpretation, piercing through legal forms and dealing with the substance of disfranchisement under the Fifteenth Amendment. The second line of cases was the equal districts progression, decided mostly by state courts, which, unlike the Supreme Court, enjoyed explicit authority under state constitutions to intervene against unequal districts. The main difficulty facing these state courts was finding ways to enforce equal district requirements without embroiling the courts in a battle with the legislatures or precipitating a deadlock of state government. The Supreme Court had to face the same kind of problem, but the state courts had done a lot of the work for it in their efforts to develop enforcement techniques. The third line of cases, which will only be mentioned in this book, was the laissez faire progression, deriving from the Court's war on economic regulation. This line of cases gave the Court some notion of its own political power to read ideological doctrines into the Constitution. Though the Court ultimately had to back down to an aroused executive, the justices could not have failed to notice how five of their number, in an unpopular cause, could stymie the other branches in areas of major concern. Such power in a waning cause portended even greater powers in causes with more promise, as the Court has more than proved since the Second World War.

Intervention Factors: Will, Authority, Power, and Technique

To intervene successfully in matters of political importance, the Court must have four elements, which will hereafter be called the intervention factors, in its favor: will, authority, power, and technique.

Will may not be very helpful as an explanatory concept since one does not always know what a justice's will is till after he has expressed it, but it is important to account for will, even if one cannot predict it, since it is now widely accepted that courts do have force and will, as well as judgment. If constitutional authority can be found, judges can be expected to do things they want to do and to avoid things they do not want to do.

Authority is the traditional focus of constitutional attention; it is basically a legal concept, and it can derive from several sources: explicit provision in the Constitution or laws; implied provision; historical understanding of the meaning of a provision; or, more recently, a consensus that an act is just, independent of any written provision or understanding.

Power is a political concept, more related to whether an act is feasible than to whether it is authorized or just. Most of us have a general notion of what power is, which tends to become misty and elusive when we try to pin it down in the specific. We know it has something to do with the ability to get your way, but we are vague as to whether it means actual control or only potential for control, and nobody knows quite how to measure it.[9] We might dismiss such a vague concept as meaningless, or we might attempt to define our way out of vagueness, or we might follow the example of Don Quixote and push on with an analytical tool which looks usable though it may not be foolproof. I have chosen the third course. *Power* in this book generally refers to the Court's ability (or anyone else's ability) to have its way, sometimes with reference to its actual influence, sometimes with reference to its potential influence, most often with reference to estimates which attempt to take both actual and potential influence into account. The reader may best understand the concept of power as common currency, but soft.

The fourth intervention factor, *technique*, has to do with tools of litigation and adjudication necessary to put the other three factors to use.

Sources of the Court's Power

The perennial problem of political theory, the relationship between power and authority, between "is" and "ought," is particularly acute in the case of the Supreme Court, whose power is supposed to derive primarily from its authority. The judicial power granted by Article III of the Constitution is secured and preserved by popular acceptance of the Constitution as the supreme law of the land and of the Court as an impartial interpreter of the Constitution. The reader will find recurrent references to the Court's "long-term power base," which could as well apply to the Court's authority as to its power, because it refers both to the Court's legal authority under the Constitution and public acceptance of that authority. "Short-term power base" refers to the Court's resources as a contender in day-to-day or year-to-year politics and is more distantly related to its authority.

Although the Supreme Court did not enter the 1970's in the fullest flush of power, no one looking back on the Warren years could fail to marvel at the accomplishments of a body with no purse, no sword, no staff, no assigned constituency, and no patronage, insulated from party politics and deployed far back of the political front lines. Observers of the Court's battle against the Roosevelt Revolution in the 1930's could see that the Court had special resources of its own. It possessed a mystique, an authority to speak the law which the president lacked, but it was not hampered by the local party orientation and parliamentary encumbrances which kept Congress from being a leader of national action. But the wise men of the 1930's assumed that these resources were negative ones, useful only for the counterrevolution by a body inextricably tied to the symbols of the old ruling class. Max Lerner concluded, just as the "Court Revolution of 1937" was taking place, that "the path toward . . . a reshaping of the Constitutional symbol lies necessarily through the decline and fall of the symbol of the divine right of judges."[10]

Today we know that the judges have long since given up the counterrevolution and pushed their way into the vanguard of the revolution. The Court has taken so much of the main action since 1940 that by the end of the Warren era one could easily agree with Adolf A. Berle that "ultimate legislative power in the United States has come to rest in the Supreme Court."[11] Looking back on the Warren years we may well ask how this transformation came about and how permanent is the Court's role as revolutionary intendant?

A proper answer must recur to the Roosevelt revolution, which created the institutional basis for an interventionist Court. Roosevelt broke through the political stagnation of monopolistic, regional parties, which had dominated the nation since 1896. He replaced it not with national parties, such as are found in Great Britain, but with a battery of federal administrative bureaus dedicated to standardizing and centralizing control of the economy and eventually, with the help of the judiciary, to extending federal standards to many other areas of society as well. Leaving aside the question of whether the regulatory agencies have succeeded in standardizing and centralizing federal control (this seems doubtful)[12] few people would dispute the conclusion that the Roosevelt revolution has shifted power away from Congress, away from the states, toward the executive and toward the judiciary. It strengthened the Court's power base in two ways: by strengthening national power relative to local power, and by increasing the Court's share of national power relative to the other branches by virtue of its ability to represent the views of the Guardians more faithfully than either of the other branches in certain key areas of policy, of which voting rights were one.

In our system political power has tended to lodge itself in the hands of those most representative of dynamic new social forces. In a pluralistic government with representative functions divided among different political bodies, power has tended to shift from one body to another according to each body's success or failure in responding to powerful demands from society.[13] George Washington and Thomas Jefferson were strong because they were representative of the strongest currents of public opinion. When Jefferson's successors faltered in serving the demands of the growing western states in the era of Henry Clay, power passed from the executive to the more representative House of Representatives till Andrew Jackson won it back for the White House by appealing to a wider and more participatory electorate. The Senate took its turn as ruling power in the 1870's and 1880's by aligning itself with emergent industrial capitalism and party machines. Since the turn of the century, as the nation has become more and more involved in world politics and the economy apparently too large and complex to handle with laws of the nineteenth century stamp, laws have been overshadowed by policies, and the legislative branch has been overshadowed by the executive. Theodore Lowi's capsulization of twentieth-century American government as "the rise of delegation and the decline of law" bespeaks the rise of the president who operates through delegation and the decline of Congress, which could only make laws—and also attests to a basic shift in the representative structure of the country from one where people and interests sought expression in the legislature to one where they seek it primarily in the executive or the judiciary.[14]

In the nineteenth century, legal relationships were well defined, or at least almost everybody but the Marxists thought they were, or could be made so with a little attention. The efforts of men as disparate as John Marshall, Jeremy Bentham, Sir Henry Maine, Auguste Comte, Herbert Spencer, the abolitionists, the Grangers, the Radical Republicans, the American Progressives, David Dudley Field, and perhaps Napoleon himself cannot be understood save in the light of a general faith, far surpassing our own, that good laws can bring the good life. Today we know from the Legal Realists and the Behavioralists that laws are really only policies: ritual emanations from the

political process representing temporary resolutions of conflict between interest groups rather than universal principles expected to govern future conflicts.
As Lowi pointed out, the nineteenth-century view of law and the nineteenth-
century political system, with few and simple regulations and unobtrusive
central rule, were ideally suited for congressional government, while the twentieth-century concept of law-as-policy and the twentieth-century political system, with lots of government involvement and stacks of complicated and discretionary regulations, demands resources of organization and staff which the
executive has, but Congress lacks.

Obviously *modern law has become a series of instructions to administrators
rather than a series of commands to citizens.* If at the same time (1) public
control has become more positive, issuing imperatives along with setting
limits, and if at the same time (2) application of laws and sanctions has become more discretionary, by virtue of having become more indirect as well as
more abstract, why should we assume we are talking about the same governmental phenomena in 1968 as in 1938 or 1908? The citizen has become an
administré, and the question now is how to be certain he remains a citizen.[15]

What has this meant for the Supreme Court? In general, the Court has so far
profited from the rise of policy, for it has had far more running room as a
policymaking body than it would have had as a body more strictly confined
to rule interpretation, and the Warren Court used its running room to great
advantage.[16] Throughout most of its earlier history, the Court usually succeeded in making decisions which would enhance its own powers in both the
short run and the long run. Like the other branches, it was usually strongest
in the short run where it was most representative and weakest where it got
out of line with changing patterns of power and opinion (as in the Dred Scott,
legal tender, and income tax cases, and in its war with Franklin Roosevelt).
These blundering decisions, however, also weakened the Court's long-run
power base by exposing it as a partisan body; they were "self-inflicted
wounds" from both long-run and short-run points of view.

In the Warren era, however, a curious partial reversal took place: the Court
waxed strong by aligning itself with the Guardians, often leading the other
branches in this representative role, yet it was extremely careless of maintaining the two traditional foundations of its long-term power—public respect for
the Constitution and public confidence in the Court as an impartial arbiter.
When the Court went into eclipse at the end of Warren's tenure, some wondered if it had not undermined its long-run power while adding to its power in
the short run. Several events indicated that public confidence in the Court was
running uncommonly low by the late 1960's: the election of Richard Nixon
on a pledge to curb judicial activism; Justice Abe Fortas's resignation under
heavy fire; and then, at the turn of the decade, senatorial rejection of Nixon's
two southern nominees, Clement Haynsworth and G. Harrold Carswell, together with talk of impeaching Justice Douglas. By 1970 the Court was look-

8

ing remarkably like a political football. Had it lost from the decline of law what it had gained from the rise of policy?

The 1970's are early enough to ask such questions, but too early to try to answer them, as the events of 1968 to 1970 may be as well explained by short-run factors as by long-run. Chief among the short-run explanations might be these: (1) the American public had lost faith in the Guardians for having led the country into costly and frustrating wars against poverty and the Viet Cong; or (2) the Guardians themselves had lost faith in the Supreme Court's ability to come across with more and bigger reforms. No one doubts that the handiwork of the Warren Court will have a lasting place in the American political landscape. No one expects future Supreme Courts, however thoroughly staffed with strict constrictionists, to lead the way back to crazy quilts, rotten boroughs, segregated schools, and indigent defendants unrepresented by counsel. On the other hand, the Warren Court's decisions had far less impact on practical life than friends or enemies of the Court would have had us believe in the 1960's. Moreover, there is some question whether even a Court of activists could continue to break ground at the Warren Court's rate without overtaxing its resources. The Warren Court pushed most of its reforms close to their natural limits for convenient judicial administration. Successor Courts of whatever political persuasion may be for a while in the position of the Taney Court in the 1830's and 1840's: custodians by inheritance of a juridical framework three-quarters finished, which offers some opportunity for minor alterations but very little opportunity for demolition or radical restructuring.

The Guardian Ethic

An Attempted Union of Knowledge and Power. More than at any time since the founding of the Republic, intellectuals and intellectual values influenced the politics of the modern era (post-1937). The Warren era (1953-1969) saw the zenith of this influence. At that time the Supreme Court, of all branches of government, was most receptive to dominant strains of academic opinion, particularly regarding voting rights reforms. The Court was sensitive to the opinions of law review writers and political scientists whose conclusions were winnowed and distilled by the national press, panels of experts, foundation studies, and the solicitor general. The justices looked for the best scholarly authority they could find; they sometimes followed professional scholars' recommendations more closely than they followed the Constitution. They borrowed the ideas, the conclusions, and often the very words of obscure political scientists to support their opinions. They relied heavily—too heavily —on conventional wisdom in the professions.

The general reader might not be familiar with the names of the scholar-

9

experts whose views shaped the reapportionment controversy, but, if he traced the origins of his own words and ideas on the matter, he would quickly see the truth of Lord Keynes's dictum: "The ideas of economists and political philosophers, both when they are right and when they are wrong, are more powerful than is commonly understood." Words and phrases like "malapportionment," "devaluation of urban vote," and "people, not trees and acres, vote" derive from the lucubrations of men like Ralph David and Paul Eisenberg, Manning Dauer and Robert Kelsay, or Gordon Baker or Anthony Lewis —names well enough known to other scholars but not household words. These men's words and ideas found their way to national acceptance through the sponsorship of the right people and the right groups: the Twentieth Century Fund, the American Political Science Association (APSA) the Brookings Institution, John F. Kennedy, the United States Advisory Commission on Intergovernmental Relations, the *New York Times*, the United States solicitor general, and finally the Court itself. The road to reapportionment was paved with what looked like blue-chip recommendations suggesting that reapportionment would strengthen federalism, invigorate representative government, help solve the urban problem, secure the Fundamental Principle of the Constitution of equal representation for equal numbers, and banish public cynicism, disillusionment, and apathy, besides producing a new breed of legislator. These suggestions were almost universally accepted outside the world of political science, as they were accepted by the APSA's own Committee on State Legislatures,[17] although they rested more on conventional wisdom than on hard evidence. As far as we can judge from the experience of the first decade since *Baker v. Carr*, they were mostly mistaken. Like most of the rest of us, the Court followed the guidance of the most eminent scholarly authorities, guidance which, in retrospect, was not very reliable. Unreliable guidance is always an embarrassment to professional scholars who claim to know their subject better than ordinary men, but it is more than an embarrassment if ordinary men are willing to honor the claim, as so often they were in the sixties, and act on half-empty rhetoric. Shoddy counsel is harmless when ignored, but potentially disastrous when followed.

It is hard to escape the conclusion that the Supreme Court and other voting reform agencies of the modern era did, in fact, follow the conventional policy wisdom of the period, nor that the conventional policy wisdom followed certain assumptions accepted by academics of the time, and by others, without adequate critical evaluation. There was very little interest in the traditional reform constituencies—parties, legislatures, dominant coalitions of interest groups—in abolishing white primaries, malapportionment, poll taxes, or blatant racial gerrymanders.[18] The political price of these reforms was too high, the return too low. Southern Democrats did not want open primaries; Northern Democrats did not want to split the party with a fight over opening the primaries. Republicans saw little reason to encourage black voters to become

10

active Democrats. Politicians normally shunned radical reapportionment as excessively disruptive to the status quo and threatening to their own tenure of office. Almost everyone but the Supreme Court and a handful of doctrinaire academic civil rightists treated the poll tax with the indifference it deserved. Prior to *Baker v. Carr*, the public, like the parties and groups dependent on public support, was apathetic about voting rights reform and sometimes hostile to it. It voted against reapportionment more often than not in pre-*Baker* referenda. Once the Court had acted, the public approved of reapportionment; on the other hand, 65 percent of Wisconsin voters polled in 1966, after *Baker v. Carr, Reynolds v. Sims*, and a highly publicized reapportionment within the state, could not recall whether the Supreme Court had made any recent decisions on reapportionment or thought it had not.[19] Of course, politicians and public opinion do exert some constraint on what the Court can do. The justices' discretion is ultimately limited by the tolerance of the elected branches. But, for the voting rights decisions, these constraints favored inaction, not action. Politicians showed their antipathy toward reapportionment in mustering thumping majorities in Congress and state legislatures to reverse *Reynolds v. Sims* with the Dirksen Amendment or the Tuck Bill. In some cases these majorities exceeded, and in others they fell only a few votes or states shy of, the two-thirds required to initiate action to amend the Constitution. I think it is true that the Court had a mandate for reform, but the mandate did not originate with the apathetic general public, nor with its foot-dragging elected representatives.[20]

The mandate may be more credibly traced by its wording, its timing, and the sequence and path of its implementation to the men I call Guardians—liberal, sophisticated university professors, a few of them specializing in voting rights studies; deans of law schools; editors and commentators of the national press (for example, of the *New York Times*, the *Washington Post, Newsweek*), enlightened lawyers and businessmen; and foundation managers. These "guardians of the civilized, humane values" were the principal expounders of a non-Marxist species of "correct thought."[21] They had no particular group interest or feeling of group identity, no name, no one organization or party; nevertheless, they did enjoy a loose community of principles. They shared a mystique of momentum which had great political influence in the 1960's, especially with the executive, and above all with the Supreme Court.

The momentum they felt and sought was away from the traditional, toward the modern; away from inaction, toward action; away from the special and toward the standard; away from the unadministered and toward the administered; and away from the amateur and toward the professional. I call this mystique of momentum the Guardian Ethic, the ideology of an age whose most eminent social theorists had proclaimed the end of ideology.[22] This ideology provided a link between professional (especially academic) values and conventional wisdom regarding sound public policy as espoused by the most articulate sectors of the general public. In the first show of its influence, in the 1940's and 1950's, the Guardian Ethic promised at least a partial fulfillment of the Platonic dream of uniting knowledge and power through the rule of experts. In some regards, I suppose it played a vital role in an age which saw an enormous expansion of both knowledge and power, multiplying opportunities for manipulation, but also making them more complex, less comprehensible to laymen, more plainly to be reserved for specialists.[23] At the same time, the knowledge explosion, the exponential expansion of the number of available facts and theories that has marked the modern era, also widened the gap between the layman and the expert. It enhanced the specialist's claim to special authority while diminishing the claims of amateurs, including those of the general public and its political representatives. The net political implications of expanded knowledge and power were more opportunities of manipulation, fewer people qualified to manipulate, more power to those with special knowledge and less to ordinary people.

The Guardian Ethic may have been indispensable under the conditions of the age, and something like the Guardian Ethic may likewise be indispensable to future generations faced with the continued expansion of knowledge and power. On the other hand, during the zenith of its influence in the 1960's, the Guardian Ethic revealed some signs of political and intellectual weakness. It lacked much of the moderating, prudential discipline of the political world, where power renews itself as much by following public opinion as by leading it. It also tended to slough off the cautions and reservations of careful scholarship, a hazardous proclivity in the case of the social sciences. The 1960's were a heady time for the sciences generally. The moon race, heart transplants, miracle wheat, super pesticides, think tanks, systems analysis, computers, huge budgets—in the rosy dawn of the technetronic age the land rang with calls for more Ph.D.'s to win all the wars we were fighting with a grand mobilization of expertise. The social sciences were not untouched by the general euphoria. Economists, sociologists, psychologists, and political scientists intimated that they had discovered how to embark "underdeveloped" countries on "journeys toward progress," through "diffusion of innovation," "nation-building," or "counter-insurgency techniques." Strategy planners proposed conceptual models for maximizing deterrence of the Soviet Union and winning the war in Vietnam at minimum cost; they planned with an abstract, Cartesian rigor not seen in military circles since the days of Vauban. Homefront, academic nation-builders, singly or in professional concert—or often in presidential commissions—planned with like clinical rigor ways to win the war on poverty, solve the urban problem, cut crime, inflation, and unemployment, stop riots, and prevent public cynicism, disillusionment, and apathy through the mobilization of professional talent.

Almost invariably the Guardians sought *administrative* implementation of

12

their nation-building recommendations, from the top down. No doubt they recognized that their abstract, paradigmatic prescriptions would be compromised and obscured if they had to be carried up from the bottom by the processes of horsetrading and coalition-building characteristic of successful politics on the input side. The Guardians were quite hard-nosed about their principles (despite their pragmatic rhetoric), and quite impatient with existing, functioning political personalities and institutions that did not measure up to the paradigm—and never could, for that matter, for the judgment was not between two practical alternatives but between one practical alternative and an abstract, disembodied norm. Their insistence on administered, abstract norms was incongruous in the light of their professed pragmatism, and particularly incongruous in the light of their professed, democratic, egalitarian aims. The greatest incongruity, however, was the vast apparent predominance of the Guardian Ethic among the most qualified political scientists, who of all people should have been best able to detect the contradictory assumptions of the Ethic, to balance its limitations and weaknesses against its promises and strengths, and to temper the public's exaggerated confidence in salvation of the body politic by conforming it to professional models of good governance. I am afraid that the needed cautions were not very loud within the profession, especially at the beginning, and were next to inaudible to the outside world. The clamor for reform prevailed within the profession and doubly prevailed in the national press and the world of general intellectual convention, stripped of even the meager caveats and qualifications attached to the professionals' original recommendations.

"Informed Opinion" Backs Reapportionment. Prior to 1954 reapportionment was mainly backed by urban political lobbies, such as the National Municipal League and the United States Council of Mayors, with some help from sharp-penned urban pressmen such as H.L. Mencken of the *Baltimore Sun*, and from individual political scientists such as Kenneth Colegrove, plaintiff in the first, landmark reapportionment case, *Colegrove v. Green*.[24] From 1954 to the eve of *Baker v. Carr*, and, indeed, for years afterward, a succession of skilled professional scholars and consultants, backed by the most prestigious foundations and institutions and even by the APSA itself, called for reapportionment to wipe out anomalies of democratic representation, ameliorate the "urban problem" by ending rural dominion of legislatures, and rejuvenate state government by introducing a "new breed of legislator" attuned to the values and needs of modern urban life. In 1954 the APSA's Committee on American Legislatures, after a four-year study commissioned by the Association, recommended equal numbers of population in each electoral district; no gerrymandering; district lines to permit a "wide representation of interests"; and reapportionment every ten years by a special administrative agency outside the legislature. The Committee further recommended "disregard of

13

counties and other areas of local government in laying off representative districts insofar as is consistent with efficient election administration," since the "unitary character" of American state governments would seem to have rendered representation of local political units "unnecessary." Representing local units was "unsatisfactory," since the local units no longer had "independent and distinctive interests of their own." Multi-member districts were also considered desirable in one house, "with or without proportional representation," to produce a "more vital bicameralism." All of these rearrangements were supposed to bring about compliance with the "fundamental principles" of our democratic tradition.[25]

From the other side of the 1960's some of these recommendations look prophetic, but, taken as a whole, they were astonishingly naïve for the work of political scientists, especially for the apparently unanimous recommendation of twelve specialists sponsored by the Association. Of the seven recommendations, two—equal districts and independent districting commissions—looked harmless and probably were widely endorsed within the profession as needed reforms. The other five were highly vulnerable to professional challenge, for they followed, implicitly or explicitly, the goals of proportional representation (PR): abolition of gerrymanders, repudiation of territorial politics, substitution of a logical, paradigmatic, academically certified system for the existing anomalous system created by politicians. "No gerrymandering" was an impossible and self-contradictory requirement for a system retaining winner-take-all districts, owing to the fluidity of political effectiveness of votes within a district. No such district (except one with only one voter) can be drawn to guarantee equal effective voting power to all voters on all issues. Gerrymandering is an intrinsic flaw of the existing district system. Multi-member districts without some form of PR are a form of gerrymander. They are used in some cases to submerge minorities, in others to spread the power of strategic majorities. PR, however, has been widely rejected within the profession since its vogue in the 1920's, owing to its tendency to produce volatile, schismatic, ineffective governments. The idea that counties and towns had no independent and distinctive interests of their own appeared to be an article of faith, a peculiarly bizarre one from a panel of political scientists for whom the detection of independent and distinctive interests is the staff of life. No evidence was adduced to support it, or to support the notion that PR and the partition of existing political units would vindicate the fundamental principles of our democratic tradition in anything other than a definitional sense. Nor, for that matter, was any evidence adduced to support the potentially more defensible notion that more equal districts would make for better government. The report's innocence of evidentiary backup or contention of any sort with opposing views within the profession should have marked its recommendations as dubious to anyone with an introductory exposure to political science, even in the easy old days before the Association became self-conscious about taking stands on issues of general public policy.

Yet there was not a murmur of qualification from any of the committee members, all specialists in the legislative process, nor any disclaimer from the Association. The report was eulogized by reviewers in the *Nation*, the *Annals of the American Academy of Political and Social Science*, and the *Christian Science Monitor*.[26] APSA president-to-be Charles Hyneman of Northwestern University, reviewing the report in the *American Political Science Review*, did raise an eyebrow over the report's unsubstantiated dismissal of local government representation, its unconcern for the helpful functions of local party organization, and its neglect of the question of urban bloc voting. However, he saluted the qualifications of the Committee and accepted its views as according with those of the profession generally.

This book reports the findings, conclusions, and proposals for action of twelve people who constituted the Association's Committee on American Legislatures. Two of the members have long been directors of research for state legislative committees. One is an officer of the Legislative Reference Service of the Library of Congress. Still another for many years had occupied positions in a state capital which permit close observation of a legislature at work. The other eight members of the committee are in academic life and have written about legislation and lawmakers. No doubt we may safely presume that what these twelve persons thought most important to say about American State Legislatures is essentially what American political scientists generally believe ought to be said on that subject . . . If this book comes to have an honored place in our literature, I am sure it will be because people like the reforms which are proposed, and not because people think the committee's research efforts are noteworthy.[27]

Better research efforts were already underway by the time Hyneman wrote, and more were to come. Later scholars concentrated on reapportionment, ignoring the most dubious of the Committee's recommendations. They showed no special desire to obliterate local units of government, or institute PR, or abolish gerrymanders, though they did suggest (probably erroneously) that gerrymanders would be much reduced by reapportionment. Far from scrapping existing political structures, the new scholars sought to strengthen them by ridding them of anomalies for which there was little remedy in input politics. Nevertheless, the new scholars seldom budged very far from the Committee's easy assumption that better-looking forms meant better government. More often, in a few pages, they would complain about urban decay, flourish a few grisly figures showing how powerless were urban voters (on paper) compared to rural, and cite each others' opinions, bolstered by indignant declarations by a few disgruntled urban officials, to show how everyone could see that the one (urban decay) followed from the other (malapportionment). The scholars would then proceed to perform various duller but safer professional exercises for the rest of the book. The exordial suppositions—that reapportionment would greatly ameliorate the urban problem, strengthen federalism, cut gerrymanders, and end barnyard government—were the weakest aspect of scholarly discussion of reapportionment, being scarcely more supported by evidence than the recommendations of the APSA Committee on American Legislatures. Yet these ill-supported suppositions, together with bold but unsubstantiated language about rotten boroughs, barnyard government, second class urban citizens, new breeds of legislator, and malapportionment, were the simplest, most vivid, comprehensible, and arousing portion of the scholarly works, and the most readily picked up by the press and transmitted to the reading public. This public quickly adopted both the terms and the suppositions as received wisdom.

Among the most influential scholarly works of the pre-*Baker* period were the Kestnbaum Commission *Report* (1955), Gordon Baker's *Rural versus Urban Political Power* (1955), Anthony Lewis's "Legislative Reapportionment and the Federal Courts" (1958), and Paul David and Ralph Eisenberg's *Devaluation of the Urban and Suburban Vote* (1961).[28] All of these strongly favored reapportionment. Baker and the Kestnbaum Commission suggested that malapportionment was responsible for the weaknesses of cities and states, having made state legislatures incapable of responding to urban needs. David and Eisenberg popularized the term *devaluation* for city votes and backed it with nationwide statistics. Lewis, following the others' exaggerated understanding of the evils of malapportionment and their correct conclusions that legislatures were unlikely to remedy the matter, prepared an excellent brief for intervention by federal courts.

Dissents. Among political science literature in the 1950's, only one uncertain trumpet was sounded about equalizing districts: David Derge's "Metropolitan and Outstate Alignments in Illinois and Missouri Legislative Delegations."[29] Derge actually counted eight years of roll-call votes in two states where reapportionist complaints about stagnation under barnyard government rang loudest. He discovered that nonmetropolitan delegates in both states very seldom voted as a bloc; metropolitan delegates voted as a bloc far more frequently, and with great effectiveness. The findings suggested that the reapportionist doctrine of rural suppression was a myth, while metropolitan bloc voting was a force to be reckoned with. Derge's labors with statistical evidence, however, were little noted within the profession and ignored altogether in the national press.

One more cautionary note appeared in 1961, Robert Friedman's "The Urban-Rural Conflict Revisited." Friedman was dissatisfied with the modest evidence supporting the by then widely held belief that cities and countryside were at war with each other. He suspected (correctly) that further investigation would show both so-called blocs much less monolithic than was commonly supposed in the profession.[30] Friedman's article attracted little attention. Some further professional dissent appeared after *Baker v. Carr*, too late to avert Court intervention but not too late to have moderated its course had the Court or its constituencies been disposed toward moderation. Very distinguished constitutional scholars joined Felix Frankfurter in questioning the workmanship and statesmanship of *Baker v. Carr,* and *Reynolds v. Sims.*[31] New York University political theorist Alfred De Grazia, in a thoughtful but widely ignored book, aired a number of philosophical and practical doubts about reapportionment.[32] Several political scientists in the mid-1960's (after *Reynolds v. Sims)* could find little or no relationship between malapportionment and the various evils attributed to it in the 1950's.[33] In 1968, Robert G. Dixon, a law professor with a Ph.D. in political science, published his massive *Democratic Representation.* Dixon's book, highly critical of the Court, is still the most comprehensive and scholarly available discussion of judicial intervention in voting rights disputes.[34] These dissenters were in the minority in the 1960's (as they probably still are in the 1970's); nevertheless, I believe they had the heavier weight of scholarship, and they may ultimately prevail.

However, they did not prevail in the 1960's, either in the political science profession, which relished all the action in its own bailiwick, or among the Guardians generally, who shared the political scientists' dream that reapportionment would fulfill the promises of their Promethean rhetoric. The exuberant conformists had gotten there first (if not always with the most), leaving the dissenters to come puffing along a decade later with their deflationary studies, too late to have any influence on the decisive events of the reapportionment revolution. Perhaps the dissenters, running against the grain of Guardian perception, were slowed down by having more to prove (or disprove). Even after *Baker v. Carr*, the conformists were ready almost immediately with a spate of books welcoming the new era and offering advice to hasten its progress.[35] Only one dissenting political scientist fielded an early book (De Grazia, 1963). The other major dissenters were not political scientists specializing in the legislative process, but constitutional jurists writing for law reviews.[36] These men might not have been as well versed as the conformists in advanced political science methodology, but they may have been more accustomed to marshalling logic and evidence to survive examination from different points of view in an adversary process. The skeptical constitutional lawyer may not have been at home with roll-call analysis, but he could detect weak spots in a brief. He could not do much, however, to counter a brief whose case was already won, as was true by the mid-1960's and is still true in a sense in the 1970's. To understand the doctrinal background of the reapportionment revolution, however, we must forget for a moment the rejoinders of the mid-1960's and go back to the much less qualified discourse of the late 1950's.

Propagation by Foundations and National Press. For most thinking (or at least reading) people, this discourse was articulated by experts and propagated, in simplified form, by foundation reports and the national press. The most enlightened foundations and the best newspapers, besides being urban-based, were highly sensitive to trends of intellectual opinion. As a rule, they snapped up the prevailing (and largely erroneous) political science lore that there was "no justification in our democratic heritage, in logic or in the practical requirements of government" for any other system than one man, one vote, and that reapportionment would remove the crushing and unfair burden of barnyard government that was preventing the cities and states from solving the latest problems. They paid little attention to tedious scholarly cautions like those of Derge and De Grazia. In 1958, Senator John F. Kennedy published a simplified version of Gordon Baker's views in the *New York Times Magazine*, arguing that malapportionment had reduced urban voters to "second-class citizens."[37] In 1960, the *Times*'s senior Washington correspondent, Arthur Krock, attacked the "gross inequity" of Tennessee's crazy quilt districts, calling for congressional action or action in the Supreme Court under the equal protection clause.[38] At the beginning of 1961, *Times* constitutional commentator Anthony Lewis, a scholar in his own right, cited the Kestnbaum Commission Report to "show that unfair apportionment was responsible for the declining power of state governments." He feared, however, that state legislatures would not act on the matter, and that federal courts might follow the noninterventionist rule of *Colegrove v. Green* rather than the interventionist policy he had recommended in his *Harvard Law Review* article. "Unless the courts change their hands-off attitude or politicians suddenly become saints," he fretted, reapportionment would remain "only a marrow bone for political scientists to chew on."[39] At the end of 1961, *Times* junior Washington correspondent James Reston complained that overrepresentation of rural conservative districts in the House of Representatives was blocking progressive legislation backed by President John F. Kennedy.[40] Many of these arguments found their way into Solicitor General Archibald Cox's brief in *Baker v. Carr*, argued in 1961.

Finally, in March 1962, three weeks before the Court announced its decision in *Baker*, Cornell political scientist Andrew Hacker, in the *New York Times Magazine*, took note of Kennedy's implication (following the House defeat of his bill to establish a Department of Urban Affairs) that an "undeclared civil war between rural and urban" interests was taking place in the "malapportioned" House of Representatives. "Most newspaper columnists and virtually all professors of political science," Hacker added, "join in agreeing that the procedures, practices, and folkways of the legislative branch are unwieldy and irrational—in short, unsuited to our fast-moving times." However, he felt that the rurally dominated House might be defended as a needed shield for provincial America to prevent "real social and psychological deterioration" from the country's rapid progress into the Space Age.[41] Even this concession was too much for aroused *Times* readers, by now impatient for the promised benefits of reapportionment. "Must recognition of the needs of our urban population," demanded one reader, "wait until frustrated mobs of city dwellers burst into the Capitol, strangle the rural legislators, and toss their bodies into the Potomac?"[42] As it turned out, of course, the city dwellers did not have long to wait. A week later the Court handed down its decision in *Baker v. Carr* that something had to be done about state legislatures. Three months later, In June 1962, the Twentieth Century Fund brought together a Conference of Research Scholars and Political Scientists to decide what it was that had to be done. Conference reporter Anthony Lewis, vindicated by *Baker* and inspired to yet greater feats, prepared a pamphlet representing the next-to-unanimous agreement of the scholars that the thing to do was push on boldly and soon. "The fundamental principle upon which any proper system of legislative representation must be constructed," wrote Lewis, "[is that] one man's vote must be worth the same as another's"; moreover, the principle "is equally applicable in both houses of a state legislature," as well as in the federal House of Representatives. There was "no justification in our democratic heritage, in logic or in the practical requirements of government" for any other course. The notion that state senates with territorial representation were without justification in our democratic heritage was a bit novel for the time, but the Supreme Court adopted it two years later in *Reynolds v. Sims*, as it also adopted Lewis's much-quoted line that "acres do not vote; nor do trees."[43] It also equalized the House of Representatives within a year of the pamphlet's appearance, holding in close paraphrase of the pamphlet that "as nearly as is practicable one man's vote in a congressional election is to be worth as much as another's."[44]

Concurrently with the conference of scholars, Lewis hailed the Court, in the *New York Times Magazine*, as the "keeper of the national conscience."[45] Columbia political scientist Alan Westin, also an eminent constitutional scholar, applauded the Court again in the *New York Times Magazine* for reflecting the "dominant opinion" and the "passionate truths" of the time. "The justices are listening," Westin beamed, "and is this not as it should be in a constitutional democracy?"[46]

Westin's rhetorical question needs a much more qualified answer than Westin and other scholars were seeking to elicit at the time. Whether the justices' listening was "as it should be in a constitutional democracy" depends on whom and what they were listening to, and what they proposed to do about it. If they were following the wishes of the elected representatives of the people, or even, somehow, of the people at large, in a matter which the people, adequately informed, had seriously considered, then one could say the Court was acting democratically. If the justices were following the text and intent of the Constitution, whether broadly or narrowly construed, then one could say the Court was acting constitutionally. But if the justices were following passionate truths of the time, as espoused by the most professionally knowledgeable and informedly altruistic people they knew—but not the Constitution or the will of the people or their representatives—then they may have been acting nobly, but not constitutionally or democratically.

Scholarship or Professional Exuberance? Pursuit of passionate truths, I believe, describes the Court's behavior more accurately than pursuit of constitutional intent or popular will. The Court followed the Guardian Ethic more closely than it did the other two, perhaps with the confidence (at the time well-founded) that popular will would eventually follow the Ethic, and that elected representatives would follow popular will. The Court would lead this procession, while being itself led by the Guardians. Following passionate truths, however, has its drawbacks when the truths turn out to be more passionate than true—a point which should be of particular concern to political scientists who, like many other specialists, did little to discourage the public's exaggerated confidence in their ability to make better policy recommendations than the public's elected representatives. Where the public is unduly credulous of professional paradigms, members of the profession should be especially aware of the limits of paradigms.

Some of the profession's indifference to this issue may be traced to a general tendency in the modern ear to treat *intellectual* and *expert* as interchangeable terms. In an era in which knowledge was an entrée to power, many intellectuals aspired to be experts, and many experts aspired to be intellectuals, perceiving little difference between knowledge as a means and knowledge as an end.[47] Terms like *technetronic society, technocracy*, and *meritocracy* adorned the pages of the highbrow press, suggesting that the essence of good government was good staffing, and good staffing meant rule by experts.[48] But when knowledge is most likely to guide power, it is also most likely to be guided by power, above all in the social sciences.

In the social sciences, as perhaps in most sciences, there are two sets of rules: rules of scholarship and rules of professional exuberance. Rules of scholarship command the practitioner to find solid ground by mastering the accepted paradigms of his profession and by learning which questions can be answered with professional techniques and which cannot.[49] Having once found solid ground, the practitioner must also learn to stick to it by asking only the kind of questions which can be answered with technique. In uneasy and often contradictory coexistence with the rules of scholarship is another set of rules, the rules of professional exuberance. These acknowledge some kind of solid ground but insist that it should be expanded by treating every possible social situation as if it were a problem which could be solved by the application of a certain kind of technique. Because the world is wide and scholarly reason often narrow, there is usually a tension between cautious rules of scholarship and the spacious claims of professional exuberance. In this tension lie the best hopes of social scientists to break new ground, but the divided authority is also one of our most persistent sources of error. In thoughtful periods the two sets of rules could moderate each other, guarding the understanding against the possible extremes of intellectual self-seclusion and delusions of grandeur. In less thoughtful periods, however, it is just as possible to see both extremes represented concurrently.

We know from Max Weber, the classical exponent of the rules of scholarship, that certain questions are forbidden to us as professionals: questions like "what shall we do?" or "how shall we live?"[50] We have learned to wince when laymen naïvely ask who is going to win the next election, or what to do about poverty, happily unaware that they have asked us to straddle the forbidden line between what we can know and what we cannot know. If we are conscientious, we shall teach them to ask some other question, or redefine the original so that it cannot be answered for policy purposes, if indeed it can be answered at all.

There is a word for the questions we are still permitted to ask, and the word is "bite-sized." Both in and after graduate school we learn to bite off manageable projects since we know that our work will be professionally acceptable only if it is in our field and specialty, shows a reasonable level of technical rigor, is duly respectful of the current paradigms, and is finished in time for the pertinent deadline. No department could wait around today for the likes of Immanuel Kant, who published nothing of consequence till he was fifty-seven, or Socrates, who never published anything at all. With limited time and heavy insistence on production, the pressure on scholars to cut corners is overpowering, except in the case of professional corners, which are sacrosanct, if sometimes petty. The corners we cut are the scope of our projects or their pertinence, their anchorage in the real world. If we are well stamped in the graduate schools, we have learned to crank out slathers of microstudies (say, "Tearoom Trade: Impersonal Sex in Public Places") or macrostudies ("The Desired Political Entropy"), but we have also learned to shun the difficult task of pulling the two together, because the costs in time and methodological rigor are too high. Microstudies call for a different kind of rigor from macrostudies. A case study or statistical exercise calls for the rigor of using observational evidence, while a macrotheory calls for definitional or logical rigor. Although it is not hard to think of important questions in a field (such as "Why did the Supreme Court get involved in voting rights questions?") which would require both kinds of consideration, we try to avoid such questions because they are not bite-sized. They set us to the wearying and messy task of relating two or more different approaches between which there is no necessary relationship. Instead, we have case studies, statistical analyses, grand theories about what the Court is up to, and critical analyses of the Court's logic, but very little to pull them all together and that little either conveniently ideological, or embarrassingly miscellaneous, or both.[51]

One might conclude from our professional insistence on bite-sized questions and answers that we can properly offer our expertise only to solve bite-sized problems, which regrettably would exclude the big problems which we most dearly want to get our hands on. Because of our rule-imposed difficulty in pulling things together, professional wisdom seems most reliable where least relevant for policy guidance, and least reliable where most relevant. This, however, is not a palatable conclusion for professionals, least of all for the confident, outgoing practitioner with the most exalted and expansive view of his discipline's proper place in society. In spite of Karl Mannheim's attempt to exempt intellectuals from his general rule that social conditions determine consciousness,[52] professional intellectuals do not reason entirely independently from their social position as intellectuals. Intellectuals are trained to objectivity, to be sure, but there are many points, especially in the policy area, where objectivity can go only so far. At these points one must choose between folding his tent and slinking away, or following some rationale like the rules of professional exuberance, which bid him to try to treat every problem as if it could be solved with professional technique on the convenient but false assumption that all ground should be solid for those trained in the master science. The rules of professional exuberance permit the professional to claim a grander role in the world than the modest one implied by the rules of scholarship; they provide an explanation for his habit, paradoxical for the professed rule skeptic, of uncritically embracing the rules of his own and his colleagues' conventional wisdom, while painstakingly exposing the contradictions and weaknesses of the rules of other men.

When he examines society, the intellectual is scarcely less inclined than ordinary men to see it as most properly dealt with with his own special skills. When he chooses between an interpretation which permits him to deploy his talents and one which does not, he will be biased toward the one which gives him the more important role. This bias is reinforced at every stage of his professional career: recruitment, professional advancement, and response by the outside world by giving or withholding grants, enthusiastic reviews, or policy adoption. One does not normally join a profession he deems fit only for narrow-minded or falsely posturing scholastics. If he does join, he is not likely to advance himself by belittling his own and his colleagues capabilities. The outside world is understandably more likely to reward someone who claims he knows how to solve the latest social problem than it is to reward someone else who claims the problem (if it is one) is beyond quick technical solution. In every case, regardless of who has the correct understanding from an objective point of view, the professionally correct understanding is apt to be the one that follows the rules of professional exuberance.[53]

It seems to me that there is more resemblance than we care to admit between the world view of social scientists and those funny little maps of the United States, as seen from Massachusetts, where the perceived Cape Cod dwarfs everything else. For the social scientist, the world accessible to his paradigms dominates everything else. We demand of the world that it answer to our technical models, and we are not comfortable with its abundance of special, anomalous things that do not meet the standard model. We resent their exemption from professional rules and tried to subjugate or ignore them, following the dictum of Lord Kelvin: only that is real which can be weighed or measured—in terms of a specialist's schema. If individual social scientists exhibit a somewhat paradigmatic, narrowly professional outlook, groups of professionals do so doubly, thanks to the rules of professional exuberance which tend to come to the fore in collective undertakings like conventions, commissions, and panels: "expand the solid ground." Even where professionals disagreed on what solid ground was, they could, and generally did agree that, whatever it was, it should have been bigger. Thus, the APSA's Committee on State Legislatures could and did unanimously and unqualifiedly call for more funds and more research, and also for certain legislative reforms which would occupy political scientists and remake the government in the image of professional paradigms.[54] The stress on generating more jobs for political scientists and conforming the government to political science models was overwhelming, while the stress on conforming the models to the actual nature and needs of government was much weaker. Professional consensus on these matters was so strong as to make scholarly reconsideration of the recommendations superfluous. As indicated earlier, the national press, transmitting the apparent professional consensus to its readers, seldom reduced the perceptual bias but often made it more extreme.

Paradigms and Policy. The Guardians' paradigmatic orientation lent a note of abstract, and therefore qualified absolutism, to their recommendations. "Equality" was the catchword of the Warren era, along with "progress," and the Guardians demanded it with special vehemence, but in a rather restricted, almost symbolic sense, generally applying to measurables only. Everyone, for instance, was equally and absolutely entitled to a lawyer, but not equally entitled to a good defense. Everyone was equally and absolutely entitled to be informed of his constitutional rights, but not equally entitled to an effort to make certain he understood his rights. Everyone was supposed to have a right to go to a desegregated school, but not everyone could go to an integrated school. Everyone was entitled to almost absolutely equal districts, but not to equal opportunity for his group to gain power. When it appeared by the beginning of the 1970's that more students were reciting school prayers than in 1962, and more (by some measures) going to nonintegrated schools than in 1954, with the most vocal elements of the black communities calling for more segregation, and when *Miranda v. Arizona* seemed to have had even less effect on criminal convictions and techniques of interrogation than *Baker v. Carr* had had in revitalizing state governments, the equality conferred by the Warren Court came to look more like a gift of form than a gift of substance. Constitutional scholar Alexander Bickel concluded that the two greatest accomplishments of the Warren Court—school desegregation and reapportionment—were "heading toward obsolescence and abandonment."[55]

Finally, there was always the proviso that equalization and standardization would not deny intellectuals our rightful place of leadership. Our rhetoric was resoundingly democratic, but in practice we tended to go along with Zbigniew Brzezinski, professor of political science at Columbia, in reserving special powers for the right people. "Fortunately, American society is becoming more conscious not only of the principle of equal opportunity for all but of special opportunity for the singularly talented few."[56]

In the reapportionment cases the singularly talented few were the tiny handful of experts who laid the groundwork for the controversy, the professional associations, foundations, and national newspapers that appeared to certify the groundwork, and finally the Supreme Court, which read it into the Constitution to thunderous and almost universal hosannas for its vindication of equality and representative government. But was it a victory for equality and representative government? Or was it a victory for intellectual elitism and administrative intervention? The Court and the Guardians succeeded in bypassing the representative branches entirely, and also the Constitution, to substitute the new higher law, inspired by Jeremy Bentham, for the old higher law, as we knew it from James Madison. We accord the Court some right to fudge on us and the Constitution by legislating on its own in certain emergency situations, but, when it does so, it must risk the same kind of criticism for shortsighted laws as we would give to any other legislative body. Likewise the Guardians. We accord special political influence to those with special understanding of a subject, above all to those who have no partisan axe to grind. But knowledge of professional paradigms is not necessarily equivalent to understanding of a political need, because professional paradigms are usually simple and narrow and political needs are broad and complex. Political scientists have added enormously to our understanding of political processes, but political scientists' efforts to reform government paradigmatically have often been attended by a low level of discernment as to what practical results the reforms might have. Thus, around the turn of the century, political scientists (and the thinking public) appeared to share the mistaken notion of the eminent political historian Moisei Ostrogorski that various devices to create more direct democracy would end the rule of the "machines," the "bosses," and the "interests."

Their preconceptions [wrote Alfred De Grazia] forced them to look always down the straight road to direct representation. Any problem would have a formula applied to its solution. First, demand a demagogic candidate. If an officer misbehaves, his term should be shortened; if appointive, he should be made elective; if elective, he should be recalled, or his legislation should be referred to, if not initiated by, the people. It was everyone's duty to vote, even if no issues existed and he did not know who was running for office or what the party issues were. If the parties' oligarchies have caused trouble, make the oligarchies elective—and so on. For every problem there was a solution readily provided from the bag of populist tricks.[57]

Progressive reformers followed Ostrogorski in calling for more direct democracy. They wanted direct primary elections, initiative, referendum and recall, compulsory voting, long ballots, weakening the dominance of the Speaker of the House of Representatives, and, later, direct popular election of senators and woman suffrage. Being tinged with a strong streak of Yankee nativism, the progressives may not have been as pure in motive as the Guardians, but much of their thinking pointed in the Guardian direction of encouraging total voter mobilization as much for its own sake, or for some vague but compelling notion that it would solve social problems, as to consolidate the power of a particular political group.

The progressives' expectation that their reforms would solve social problems, or even encourage voter participation, were ill-founded. Some of their reforms (for example, initiative, referendum, and recall) were merely ineffectual. Others (for example, direct primaries, weakening the Speaker) weakened the parties who had been the chief instrument to encourage voter participation and coordinated action in Congress. Voting turnout dropped; blacks were barred from effective political citizenship in the South; control of the House was decentralized; the House Rules Committee, liberated from the Speaker's control, eventually became a graveyard for progressive, liberal legislation. Still other reforms (for example, compulsory voting) were never adopted—fortunately, for their premise that educated, responsible voters tend to stay home, while the ignorant, idle, and vicious flock to the polls, has turned out to be the reverse of the truth.

Woodrow Wilson, our one political scientist president, attempted unsuccessfully to impose a different paradigm, responsible party government, to solve the problems left by the progressives' direct participation paradigm.[58] Other political scientists looked to yet another paradigm, proportional representation, to do the job. Elegant in its logic, symmetry, and representational accuracy, PR was the cornerstone of the disastrous German Weimar Constitution, the first to which political scientists made a major contribution. In retrospect, it seems plain that our contribution was the kiss of death, for PR was all too successful in reflecting every nuance of political difference, while discouraging the compromise and coordination necessary to permit political action.

Against this background of repeated exaggerated hopes of paradigmatic reforms, political scientists' inflated notions of what reapportionment would accomplish seem comparatively modest in their mistaken pretensions. True, reapportionment does not seem to have done much on a national basis to solve the urban problem, invigorate the states, reduce gerrymanders, or un-leash thitherto bottled-up forces for progress. Still, in three or four deep-South states, it probably has been a substantial force (among others) for more equitable representation; moreover, it has not seriously harmed representative institutions as, say, PR might have done had it been adopted. Reapportion-ment was not unique for the misguided exuberance of its professional apolo-gists, for this has always been with us, nor was it dangerous for anything it did to existing political institutions, for these, on the whole, were very little affected by the reapportionment revolution. However, it was unique, and also dangerous, because of the country's willingness to swallow it whole—to toler-ate its imposition without going through the usual political tests of adoption by elected representatives of the people or demonstrated consonance with the Constitution. The progressives may have been mistaken in many of their ex-pectations from their reforms, but at least they went to the trouble of con-vincing legislators to go along with them. They did not win out by bypassing the representative institutions they sought to reform. Advocates of PR gener-ally, and fortunately, lost out for having to submit their paradigms to the test of politics. But reapportionment was excused from the usual political tests, as it had been excused from effective scholarly testing, because it happened to fit the "passionate truths" of the 1960's embodied in the Guardian Ethic. The reapportionists did bypass the institutions they purported to strengthen with their reforms, and the representative bodies were unable to stop them. The net implication, despite claims to the contrary, was a marked preference for quick, administrative imposition of various modish innovations, unhamp-ered by any discipline but that of executive convenience.

The Spirit of the Times. I have taken my own discipline to task for mis-placed perspectives, too broad for the most careful scholarship, too narrow to serve practical political needs. Political scientists get special critical attention here because voting rights are our field and we *should* know better, and com-municate better to the outside world, the true extent of our own strengths and weaknesses, as well as those of the outside world. But political scientists were only a small segment of the thinking public, whose hopes, perceptions, and delusions we largely shared. The Guardian Ethic was a national intellec-tual and political obsession which might very well have brought off the reap-portionment revolution without any help at all from political scientists. Its insistence on modernity, action, standardization, expertise, and administra-tion, which was generally benign in moderate doses in the 1940's and 1950's, grew increasingly hazardous when fueled by the Promethean and paradig-matic dreams of the 1960's. If an ounce of modernization was good in the 1940's, then surely a ton of it would be even better in the 1960's. If ending a surgical racial gerrymander in the deep South was a good thing, then surely equalizing every district in every state and local body of government must be even better. If political scientists were right in condemning the evils of white primaries (as we were, though the issue was pushed much harder in the law reviews than in political science literature), then we surely must be right about ending public cynicism, disillusionment, and apathy with equal districts. If black voter participation made southern governments more responsive, then surely the following incentives for voter participation, seriously advocated by intelligent and dedicated men in the 1960's and 1970's, should make all governments even more responsive:

(1) "Maximum feasible participation" by the poor in administering poverty programs[59]
(2) Elective leadership of administrative agencies; government funding of all election campaigns for all parties; PR, but with gerrymandering "to reduce the number of outvoted minorities"; "majority rule on second step" (that is, if 25 percent of legislators want something, it must be discussed until a majority approves or 76 percent reject [!]); one man, one vote to stockholders of large corporations[60]
(3) Collective resolutions by university professors, students, and professional associations on burning issues of general interest[61]
(4) Representation of women, blacks, and young people in presidential nominating conventions in proportion to their numbers in the population at large[62]
(5) Compulsory voting[63]

All of these followed assumptions now understood by most political scientists to be false: that if participation is good, total participation must be better, even if it has to be forced on the participants, and that if one set of representative institutions is tolerably responsive to the will of the governed, several sets, or hundreds of sets of separately constituted representative institutions should be several times as responsive.

Even as these men of intelligence and dedication were calling for ultrapopulism, to solve society's problems, other men of at least comparable motivation and skill were calling for mobilization of unfettered managerial talent to the same end. Taking their lead from John F. Kennedy's affirmation that the times called for more management, not less, they variously proposed:

(1) An up-to-the-minute new Constitution full of appointive positions for planners, administrators, and staffers, with long, nonrenewable terms of office and liberal retirement benefits for the few elected officers. The Constitution would come up for self-destruction after one generation, or "whenever its time shall have come," whichever came first[64]
(2) A Council of Social Advisors to help the executive solve social problems too tough for Congress[65]

(3) A strong input of "technocrats" trained in computer-based analysis techniques to meet the political needs of the electronic age[66]

(4) A Council of Constitutional Advisors to help the Supreme Court take charge of the Revolution before the masses made a mess of it[67]

One might suppose that the populist reformers and the managerial ones would be at swords points with each other, but this was seldom so, for they otherwise shared the same narrow Guardian perspectives. They tended to be contemptuous of existing political institutions, certain that they could be much improved or supplanted with a few simple, radical innovations. They shared a faith in salvation through expertise matched in no nation save possibly the Soviet Union, but they also demanded that the experts follow the rules of the Ethic. Recommendations to leave things alone, tolerate traditional anomalies, recognize the limits of scholarly perception, and so on were suspect. The Guardians were pragmatic, but in a rigid way, too insistent on providing abstract solutions to perceived problems of bite-sized dimensions.[68]

In one sense political scientists could afford to snicker at the narrow perspectives of both the populist and the managerial reformers, who were mostly badly advised political figures or academicians from other disciplines repeating various follies which political scientists have played with in the past but since outgrown. We know that too much required response to raw popular will can incapacitate governments, while too much reliance on administrative discretion, however, enlightened, cuts off the government from the governed. In the strongest and best governments (and perhaps also in the strongest and worst) one or more political party bridges the gap between popular will and sustained leadership, focusing, cultivating, and thereby strengthening the one, while guiding, disciplining, and thereby strengthening the other.

Democracy Without Consent

In another sense, however, there is less cause for amusement. The country no longer shrugs off ill-supported intellectual fancies as it did before the 1930's. On the contrary, it has shown itself potentially sensitive to intellectual vogues as never before, even though intellectual paradigms are no more reliable than they have ever been as policy guides.[69] Such paradigms do bridge the gap between popular will and political leadership, but in usually a formal, abstract way with little regard to the informal mechanisms of representation which make American democracy work. The various calls for more technocracy at least made no pretense of strengthening democracy; the apparent intent was to scrap it, at least in part, as unsuited to the needs of the space age. The populist Guardians, though they used democratic rhetoric, were scarcely less elitist than the managerial ones, for they typically invoked

28

the mystique of management to "improve" popular representation by command from the top. Their pleasure was more in applying neat, egalitarian rules than in accommodating the actual desires of the public, which were often crassly attached to the status quo. They were vitally interested in the forms of democracy, but not its substance; in fact, there was more than a little of the spirit of the Animal Rescue League in these men, who tended to express their devotion to their clientele by having them politically spayed. Like the managerial Guardians, the populist ones were genuinely concerned for social welfare, but they entertained a coldly impersonal approach to common people, sometimes verging on contempt, and much the same may be said of their attitude toward institutions which responded to the wishes of common people. There seemed to be a general impression among the hard-nosed (but sometimes soft-minded) activists of the 1960's that democracy and total mobilization were pretty much the same thing, and that thing was so precious that the government should stuff it down people's throats. Andrew Hacker, the reapportionist Cornell political scientist, spoke for the hard-noses in dismissing the desires of voters who defeated reapportionment in popular referenda: "Citizens should be given the blessings of equality whether they want them or not."[70] The Supreme Court, of course, followed just this view in *Lucas v. Colorado.*[71] Ramsey Clark, attorney general under Lyndon Johnson and chairman of the Democratic National Committee Task Force on Freedom to Vote, thought that compulsory voting might be a good way to strengthen democracy. "You don't like to think about it," he mused, "until you see a 40-percent vote in an important election. We've just got to involve people in our political processes if we're going to make our institutions really effective and responsive."[72]

The Guardian Ethic's tinge of authoritarian elitism is not proof that the Ethic was intrinsically evil, or even intrinsically authoritarian. All principles have an authoritarian tinge if you push them hard enough, and the major flaw of the Ethic in the 1960's is that it was pushed a bit too hard.[73] The proper lesson for the 1970's is not to repudiate the Ethic, but to keep it in better perspective. The Ethic was no more intrinsically evil than it was intrinsically good. It should properly be judged in the light of its effects in securing other, more fundamental goals, such as freedom of political choice, and stable, effective, just government, responsive to tides of public opinion, but not to ripples.[74]

The Guardian Ethic has contributed to these goals on more than one occasion. It mobilized the country to meet a real crisis, World War II, and also to face the Cold War with some semblance of a sense of direction. It also broke the white primary, a difficult and commendable accomplishment, and motivated the needed civil rights acts of the 1950's and 1960's—conceivably with the same sort of steel-nosed activist intellectuals pushing to get rid of the bad institutions and meet real crises as were pushing to get rid of the good institutions and meet manufactured crises. The circumstances of the last generation have offered ample justification for judicious application of some kind of meritocratic, managerial principle like the Guardian Ethic, and the next generation may need it even more—but that is a long way from saying that we needed or need the Guardians' longed-for preemptive strike on our representative institutions, much less that we should have to swallow their assertion that it will "make our institutions really effective and responsive."

Our very need for something like the Guardian Ethic should keep us aware of the risks of letting it get out of perspective, because the modern, paradigmatic notion of voting rights reform has demonstrated impressive strength in Congress (which passed the eighteen-year-old vote amendment and came within a hair of restructuring the electoral college) and also in the Democratic party, which actually tried something resembling proportional representation in the 1972 presidential nominating convention. The eighteen-year-old vote will probably be harmless; the others carry somewhat more risk of weakening the integrative capacity of the party system. When future debates arise over pushing this or that democratic principle one step closer to its logical extreme (as will surely happen in the 1970's), we should be more aware of the trade-off between the form of democracy and the substance, and the substance of democracy should get more attention than it did in the 1960's. The Guardian Ethic is not a satisfactory universal guide to reform. It was useful in a few specifics, but it was as anti-democratic in its general operating principles as it was democratic in its rhetoric. Its purported aim of expanding the electorate was vitiated by its insistence on overriding the legislatures to whom access was granted. Its democratic largesse resembled, in some ways, that of the Roman emperors who extended the hollow shells of Roman citizenship throughout the empire even as they continued to debase it in Rome. The triumph was for management, not democracy.[75]

Questions for the Court

Even if we work from the convenient but debatable Warren-era assumption that equality is the main standard of a just political order, every fresh insight into the varieties of political influence must make us despair of dividing it all into equal parts. In political encounters, the side which is more interested, better organized, better financed or entrenched, or more militant prevails over the side which lacks such enhancements, without much regard to whether or not it has more adherents than the losing side. Although 95 percent of the professional discussion of reapportionment was about technique (for example, how to measure malapportionment, how to use courts and commissions to reapportion, and how to classify state constitutions), almost all of it started from the dubious assumption that if you equalize the measurable (electoral districts), you thereby tend to equalize the unmeasurable (political power). Most of us accepted this assumption, as the Supreme Court did, be-

cause Gordon Baker, Anthony Lewis, and the APSA accepted it. Certification
by these technical authorities in this case proved to be harder currency for
buying policy than the text and intent of the Constitution and the desires of
most of the people affected.

This is not to say that the Guardian Ethic, of itself, made bad law or bad
policy. The Court's two greatest ventures in securing voting rights—the touted
reapportionment cases, and the white primaries cases, which are normally
packed away in the footnotes—both showed the inspiration of the Guardian
Ethic. They both denied claims to special privilege through usage and intervened to standardize rights in a manner favored by the intellectuals and the
establishment. But the white primary cases showed the Guardian Ethic at its
best, while the reapportionment cases showed it at its worst. The Court's
arduous campaign to outlaw white primaries by direct assault pierced through
the subterfuge of functional substitutes for disenfranchisement and helped
give the blacks a right of representation in fact such as had been intended for
them in law by the passage of the Fifteenth Amendment. *Smith v. Allwright*
and *Terry v. Adams*[76] were strong decisions in the traditional sense of being
rooted in the text and original understanding of the Constitution; they were
also strong in the modern sense of removing a comparatively bald discrimination against one class of citizens. One measure of their strength is the great
increase in the percentage of blacks registered to vote in the South (from 5
percent in 1940 to 64 percent in 1969). Another is the fallout of major constitutional decisions, including *Shelley v. Kraemer*[77] and the school segregation cases, which followed the principles of interpretation laid down in the
white primary cases.

By contrast, the reapportionment cases were tactically much stronger than
the white primary cases, and strategically much weaker. In less than half a
decade,[78] with hardly a shred of traditional constitutional authority, they
seized all the states but Oregon by the scruff of the neck and made them toe
a very hard line, while all right-thinking people hooted at the states' ineffectual efforts, led by Senator Dirksen, to resist. Yet the very limited perspective
we have on the effects of reapportionment indicates that, outside of a dozen
or so states that had been egregiously malapportioned, reapportionment has
contributed very little to state politics but disruption, while maintaining the
effectiveness of gerrymanders by requiring the parties to redraw the old ones
every ten years to keep them abreast of changes in the population. Reapportionment did not do what the experts told us it would do. It neither revitalized state and local government nor diminished public cynicism and apathy.
It added little to equal representation because it brought with it a resurgence
of gerrymandering, and in many cases further strengthened elements already
disproportionately strong by virtue of representational quirks like bloc voting, multi-member districts, and strategic majorities, which the Court could
not regulate with simple rules.

The problem of regulating complex political problems with simple rules put off-limits most of the new areas of constitutional development opened up by the reapportionment cases. The Court could equalize districts, but it could not equalize effective legislative representation without resorting to PR, which had itself gone out of vogue with the Guardians for its failure to produce action, or even permit it. The Court wisely declined to rule on gerrymanders less blatant than that involved in *Gomillion v. Lightfoot* because the rules of political advantage and disadvantage were too relative to other considerations, too unstable to be regulated by the kind of order which an appellate court can hand down.[79] The reapportionment cases did not generate the kind of major constitutional developments that the white primary cases generated, and it is not likely that they will do so in the future without seriously eroding the Court's authority.

Justices Stewart and Clark properly described the Court's intervention in the reapportionment cases as "heavy-handed," because it was administrative in inspiration and draconian in effect, substituting the Court's standards for those of the people affected. The leading theorists of reapportionment managed to interpret the Court's intrusion as a triumph of representative government, perhaps because the modern notion of representation equated it with "standardization by a higher body of experts"—a shocking transformation to those of us who had thought that representative government was supposed to be influenced by the desires of the governed. Standardization and hierarchy of expertise were the essence of the new higher law; the Guardians were thoroughly at home with the notion of a blue-ribbon panel of philosopher kings charting new avenues of revolutionary action from the Supreme Court Building, but they grew very nervous at the prospect of Senator Dirksen's threatened constitutional convention of men whose only qualification to rule would have been election by the public.

The popularity of the reapportionment cases reflected the prevalence of the Guardian Ethic among those who concerned themselves with the Supreme Court and its doings and stressed the importance of intellectuals in the Court's constituency. What could be wrong with a program which had been approved with apparent unanimity by the most knowledgeable and least partisan authorities in the country? But there were things wrong with reapportionment, and there were things very wrong with a Court which tied itself too closely to an ideological vogue. The Guardian Ethic was indeed a vogue. In spite of all its followers' assertions that it was "transvaluational," we are beginning to see its limits in the light of other, higher values. The Court must be aware of vogues, but it must beware of committing itself so thoroughly to one vogue that the next one makes it look silly, and it must particularly beware of encouraging the notion that constitutional authority is largely a question of fashion, because it relies too heavily for its own authority on our disposition toward Constitution-worship and our desire for stable institutions to prosper in the long run from the rise of constitutional atheism.

All of us are prisoners of ideology; so was the Warren Court, and so were most of its predecessors; but the Court's inheritance of extraordinary powers from the Warren era triples the dangers of rash excursions and intrusions based on fleeting and often superficial consensus among the Court's clientele. The Warren Court showed us that such intrusions could clear away older institutions, but did not always show us that they could offer something better in their place. The reapportionment cases required a sacrifice of self-government, such as people might make to keep constitutional stability, but they also required a sacrifice of constitutional stability, such as we sometimes make to maintain effective self-government. The net result was a loss for both objectives. The Warren Court left us a new set of standards that has greatly increased the risk of trading birthright institutions for a mess of pottage. For us who are heirs to the Guardian Ethic, it is vitally important to try to examine the question of voting rights from a viewpoint that goes beyond the Guardian Ethic.

II. Voting Rights in the
Pre-Intervention Period, 1776–1868

The newly enfranchised had about as much to do with the extension of the suffrage as the consuming public has had to do with the expanding market for toothpaste. The parties, assisted by some excited minorities, were the entrepreneurs, took the initiative, and got the law of the franchise liberalized.
—E.E. Schattschneider

Motives for Reform

Democracy did not make its way in this country by any command of the Constitution. Neither did it come by the force of equalitarian ideals among the franchised, nor by the demands of the unfranchised, though these often played a secondary role in producing reforms. The main force behind virtually every major democratic reform from the earliest days of the Republic to the time of Franklin D. Roosevelt was partisan advantage. Reforms which were thought to favor the party or parties in power passed; other reforms were shelved till they offered more political return. All parties thought for various reasons to profit by dropping property qualifications; the Republicans sought to consolidate the power they won in the Civil War by enfranchising blacks; Yankee Protestants hoped to curtail the power of urban ethnic and religious minorities by enfranchising women. But other reforms like proportional representation, compulsory voting, equal districts, and abolition of gerrymandering and white primaries offered little advantage to either party and met with little success in legislatures. The Supreme Court has enacted some of these reforms left undone by default of the state and national legislatures—under political inspiration of its own which shall be considered in later chapters—but the political inspiration today is primarily administrative, not representative in the older sense; it differs qualitatively from political inspiration as it was understood in the last century, and it must be examined by different rules.

When the framers drafted the Constitution to meet the needs of governing a federal union, they carefully skirted the most divisive issues of representation by leaving them in the hands of the states. The Constitution nowhere conferred at its drafting, nor does it confer now, any right to vote to any person.[1] The Pre-Intervention period, from the Revolution to the Civil War, saw the rise of the broadly based political party and was filled with hot debate on many aspects of representation: gerrymandering, apportionment, financial and religious qualifications for voting, the secret ballot, and voting by aliens and free blacks. The United States experienced during this period a transformation of its political structure, but the transformation was more the sum of developments in the states than an implementation of principles embodied in the text of the federal Constitution.

To understand the policies of the modern interventionist Supreme Court, it is important to ask how and why the earliest voting reforms took place in the states and why the Court of those days could not and did not intervene. What did people do about voting questions before they could take them to court? In Pre-Intervention days they fought them out in state legislatures and state conventions, doggedly, patiently, for their political attention span was longer than ours—"for want of other diversions" Morison says, but perhaps also because they expected more of their representatives and representative institutions.[2] Reformers like Thomas Dorr tried to keep their causes out of courts which were not expected in those days to sponsor reforms, and the courts were happy to oblige by refusing to consider the merits of Dorr's cause when he was brought to trial. The Supreme Court of those days lacked the will, the power, the authority, and the technique to intervene in voting questions.

The main events of the Pre-Intervention period were the dropping of property requirements and subsequent adjustments to make sure that the wrong people, for example, women, aliens, and blacks, did not rush in to fill the gap. What factors produced these developments? Answers could help distinguish the real grievances from the rhetoric they generated; they help put today's invocations of "fundamental principles" into a more realistic perspective; and they provide a basis for contrast with the ineffectuality of representative bodies today to settle questions like apportionment and gerrymandering out of court.

Democratic values were undoubtedly a factor in bringing about the reforms of the Pre-Intervention period, but not as determinative a factor as one might conclude from the fact that democracy turned out to be the common denominator of the revolts against property qualifications. Wars, taxes, economic dislocations, and especially party rivalries had a more immediate and telling effect in producing reforms than democratic values alone. The Revolution and its economic aftermath cut deeper into people's lives than any secular act of government had done before, packing citizens off to war and then taxing them to pay for it. Veterans and others who felt the burden of political mobilization demanded more representation, and most of them got it.

The Revolution itself made little change in the basic character of local and state politics, which had been democratic since colonial times. The earliest colonial charters had had little to say about voting rights; later restrictions were far less exclusive in practice than they now look on paper. Franchises limited to church members excluded few in most of the colonies, as religious diversity was exceptional; moreover, religious qualifications were largely abolished or ignored after the Revolution. Property qualifications, which were yielded after the Revolution much more grudgingly than religious qualifications, were of small significance in colonial times when land was cheap and the suffrage restrictions very casually observed. Even where the restrictions were enforced, freehold qualifications could be legally avoided by so-called fagot voting: voting by ad hoc freehold grantees, who returned the deeds to the grantor after the election, or even kept them as a reward for voting the grantor's ticket. A generous, though incomplete, scattering of figures in different local elections in the latter half of the eighteenth century gives the impression that most people could vote, since most of them did vote. Typical percentages of white, resident males voting in Chilton Williamson's collection of elections ranged from fifty to eighty-five, comparing very favorably with local elections today. Unenforceable qualifications like those of Connecticut at the time of the Revolution—"maturity in years, quiet and peaceable behavior [and] a civil conversation"—characterized an era when qualifications did not make much difference.

After the Revolution, the franchise was not so much extended as revised to fit a more differentiated electorate and a more lively climate of political contests, which moved the states to pay closer attention to the rules and to change them where they chafed. New divisions developed with immigration and the industrial revolution; it became more and more important to distinguish or protest distinctions between merchants, bankers, manufacturers, native Protestants, immigrant Catholics. Moreover, old divisions, like country and town, freeholder and nonfreeholder, rich and poor, widened, and the old rules were more and more rigorously observed and more and more bitterly fought over in the context of partisan rivalry for people's votes. Reforms developed most rapidly where the rivalry was keen but not intransigent; they were most delayed in states such as Virginia, where genteel and affable elections generated little effective pressure for change, and Rhode Island, where embattled Yankee freeholders could tolerate no voting outside of what they called "the sound part of the community."

No one can deny that the ideology of the Revolution helped focus attention on voting rights. It was fought for representation, and it got people to thinking in terms of representation. How many times had they been told that taxation without representation is tyranny? The words seemed to apply as readily to the unfranchised citizens of the states as they had to the colonies themselves—the more so when landless veterans were turned away from the polls, while Tory freeholders got to vote.

One may agree that those who share the burdens of the state should also share in its direction, however, without agreeing with the Supreme Court that the Fundamental Principle of the Revolution and the Constitution was one man, one vote. The Revolution contributed its share of democratic slogans, and it was followed by generally democratic trends in the states, but the trends seldom show a clear connection with the slogans, let alone with the federal Constitution. Although the slogans were always prominent in the arguments of the reformers, action on the reforms usually awaited more direct and less ideological incentives.

The Revolution, like the War of 1812 and almost any war, did supply such direct incentives in two ways: it mobilized people for military service, and it taxed them to pay for the fighting, stirring up by its exactions demands for representation more insistent than those generated by its battle cries. The Revolution called more than a quarter of a million men to the colors on the American side alone; more than half a million took arms in the War of 1812. Veterans of these wars never formed a permanent or national lobby, but they frequently provided a nucleus for expressions of transient, local grievances, such as the "Newburgh Conspiracy" of 1782, in which disgruntled officers of the Continental Army threatened "to change the milk-and-water style of the veterans' petitions to Congress, while weapons are still in hands that know their use." Another early, but transient, instance of military men organizing for the redress of grievances was the Revolt of the Pennsylvania Line in 1783, in which a company of enlisted men encircled the state house in Philadelphia, inducing the congress to flee to Princeton. Veterans figured prominently in the leadership of Shays's Rebellion in Massachusetts in 1787 and swelled the ranks of the Whiskey Rebellion in Pennsylvania in 1794; veterans' prominence in these dramatic efforts to influence policy reflected a like influence in everyday politics. Long before the day of organized interest groups like the American Legion and the Veterans of Foreign Wars, veterans demanded redress for their grievances within the system as well as outside of it. One such grievance was the freehold qualification, which excluded many veterans while welcoming every ex-Tory with fifty acres of land. The outrage of the veterans was soon translated into the overthrow of the freehold vote in a majority of the states. Of the original thirteen states, five relaxed or dropped their property qualifications within ten years after the Revolution; two more joined the list prior to the War of 1812; three more states made the change in the seven years following the War of 1812. Five states had special provisions for former militiamen to vote.[4] New states did not have property qualifications.

Wars thrust the hands of government deeper than ever into the public's pockets. The Revolution and the War of 1812 each cost the federal government $100 million, and the states only slightly less, burdening the people with a huge public debt, heavy taxes, and ruinous inflation. Repeated issues of paper money produced inflation ranging from fortyfold to a thousandfold,

37

driving specie, already scarce, wholly out of circulation in 1780 and again in
1814. Federal tax revenues rose from nothing before the Revolution to $3.7
million in 1792 (90 percent of which went to service the federal debt), then
to $8.4 million in 1796 to pay for undeclared wars with France, Spain, and
Indians.[5] Heavy taxes and painful economic disruption inspired the Whiskey
Rebellion and Shays's Rebellion; they also inspired less dramatic but equally
pointed demands of underrepresented people who found the most pressing of
economic reasons to want a full voice in government: government policies put
too many people into debtor's prison, at the same time enriching too many
others, to be safely ignored.

Heavy state investments in public improvements and services by the 1820's
and 1830's continued in peacetime the economic pressures for representation.
Vast expenditures on schools, hospitals, jails, roads, railroads, and canals
could confer or deny prosperity according to how they were spent; they also
added to the states' appetite for more taxes and to state public debts, which
grew from nothing in 1800 to $175 million in the 1830's.[6] These expendi-
tures nourished fierce antagonisms between various potential beneficiaries
and tax sources, especially between tidewater and upcountry factions in the
South Atlantic states.

Party rivalry provided much of the force behind efforts to apply the old
franchise requirements more strictly, and then for extending representation
to groups formerly excluded. When the Federalists attempted to stifle the
emerging Republicans, they found a temporary advantage in enforcing property requirements with a zeal little known in colonial times. Republicans
fought property qualifications with equal zeal and for like reasons, though
the parties were seldom unanimous in supporting or opposing reforms. It was
no easier to predict the political consequences of a reform in 1800 than it is
today; moreover, the political benefits and ideological appeal of general rules
were varied then, as they are today, in specific application. Democrats were
usually more reformist than Federalists and Whigs, but such arch-Democrats
as James Madison, James Monroe, and John Randolph, in the Virginia Convention of 1829-30, opposed reforms which threatened their power base.[7] By
the same token, practical-minded Federalists, Whigs, and others understood
the dangers of holding aloof when reform was in the wind. They knew that in
politics, as in business, the first one to invade a new market is often the one
who keeps that market, and many of them swallowed their ideological misgivings and backed reforms to try to avert a Republican monopoly of newly
franchised voters.

The very fact of party and sectional rivalry, particularly with the rise of
mass-based parties in the 1820's and 1830's, was decisive in producing reforms, even without reference to the parties' expectation of specific advantage. The freehold qualification raised questions of title and appraisal beyond
the competence of an ordinary voting registrar to settle. Even with modern

registration facilities no one today would think of buying a freehold without consulting experts—lawyers, surveyors, appraisers, title insurance companies—and partisans of the last century rightfully protested the difficulties of administering a franchise whose freehold basis required experts to evaluate. The freehold qualification lent itself too readily to manipulation, fraud, and fagot votes to be tolerated. Such a sloppy standard was all right for the local politics of the eighteenth century, but it no more fitted the game of nineteenth-century politics than stickball rules would fit the world series today. The authorities dropped the freehold qualification much as later authorities dropped the amateur qualification at Wimbledon—not so much for discriminating against professionals or nonfreeholders as for being impossible to enforce effectively.

The parties' impatience with the ambiguities and vulnerabilities of the freehold rules joined with pressures from veterans, debtors, city people, people from places whose population growth outstripped their representation, and others who wanted a bigger voice in government to produce several major conventions in the northern states: Connecticut in 1818; New York in 1821; Massachusetts in 1822; and Rhode Island in 1828 and 1834. Franchise reform was the major concern of these conventions, and it called forth on both sides the full range of grand arguments that are remembered today, while the less inspiring but more operative details of party interest are forgotten. The reformers invoked the Revolution, the Englightenment, Locke, and even Native Americanism; they assailed the freehold vote as a relic of the Dark Ages which provided fertile ground for fraud and sham.[8] They called, not for universal suffrage, but for taxpayer suffrage, on the basis of their most telling argument, that those who share in the burdens of government should also share in its direction. They also thought the tax rolls were harder to manipulate than the property records. However alien it may have been to the American political tradition in the eyes of the Warren Court, taxpayer suffrage was the main aim of the reformers of the Pre-Intervention period, for it gave them a stronger argument for reform than universal manhood suffrage while correcting the difficulties of administering the property qualifications that preceded it.[9]

Conservatives countered, to little avail, with Aristotle, Blackstone, and their own variety of Native Americanism. What man could be expected to vote responsibly in a state in which he lacked a permanent interest? Was not the man who lacked the muniments of success and industry in his own business destined to become the dependent instrument of more ambitious souls? What man's property would be safe in a state run by the plundering instincts of the mob? The freehold vote had the additional attraction of being thoroughly American, as it was thought to exclude new foreigners as well as other urban workers; it also was comfortingly English, being free of the odor of Jacobinism which clung to the arguments of the reformers.

It is customary to dismiss these arguments with an indulgent chuckle at their pretense of stemming the tide of democracy, but it is also important to remember the very limited nature of the desired reforms. Neither the northern states nor the new western states, which uniformly shunned property qualifications, were prepared to push democracy past the point where it would meet the complaints of the parties and the veterans. Apart from a few midwestern states, hungry for settlers, no one was very warm to the prospect of aliens and immigrants at the polls; all the states but Maine, Massachusetts, Vermont, New Hampshire, Rhode Island, and New York explicitly barred free blacks from voting, and New York imposed special property requirements on blacks which, while repeatedly challenged, were repeatedly upheld in popular referenda. Even in the tiny handful of northern states that did not exclude blacks by law, social pressures tended to accomplish the same end.[10] New Hampshire and Vermont in 1857 and 1858 had to pass special laws against excluding blacks from voting. Chancellor Kent concluded that only in Maine could the black man participate equally with the white man in civil and political rights.[11] Women were universally denied the vote.

In the South pressures for reform led to a rash of constitutional conventions in the 1830's: Virginia in 1829-30; Mississippi in 1832; Georgia in 1833 and 1839; Tennessee in 1834; North Carolina in 1835; and Maryland in 1836. These conventions differed from those of the prior decade in the northern states in that, while they touched on freehold and other franchise requirements, the main issue was reapportionment.

Heavy planting of cotton after 1793 had exhausted the soil of eastern plantations, driving hordes of people from the tidewater; at the same time western, upland counties had grown by leaps and bounds. Thomas Jefferson had long since called for equal representation for growing upstate counties with an anti-urban gusto that would have shocked modern reapportionists. Jefferson had praised the farmers as the chosen people of God, warning that the mobs of great cities added "not so much to the support of pure government as sores do to the strength of the human body." Upcountry people had taken up Jefferson's cry in earnest in the early nineteenth century when they found that the enormous expenditures on public works and services seemed to flow like rivers into the tidewater—perhaps a natural course from an engineering standpoint, but one bound to rankle upcountry taxpayers who got more bills than benefits.

As in the North, the southern reformers were selective in their desires for democracy. They wanted more equal apportionment, broader suffrage, direct election of the governor, smaller legislatures with less frequent elections, and more local control of the judiciary. But they also wanted to settle doubts as to whether free blacks should vote, and in every case they joined the rest of the country in barring blacks from the polls. Table 1 shows that the reformers were not uniformly successful in achieving more popular government.

Table 1. Reforms in Four South Atlantic States, 1830's

State and Date	More Equal Apportionment	Wider Franchise	Reforms			Religious Qualifications for Office
			More Streamlined Legislature	Direct Election of Governor	Judiciary Reform	
Virginia 1829–30	yes	taxpayer heads of families, yes; blacks, others, no	no	no	yes	yes
Georgia 1833, '39	no[a]	b	yes[a]	yes[a]	yes[a]	
North Carolina 1835	yes	house, yes; senate, no; blacks, no	yes	yes	yes	Protestants, Catholics, yes; others, no
Maryland 1836	yes	blacks, no b	yes	yes	no	

Source: Adapted from Fletcher M. Green, *Constitutional Development in the South Atlantic States, 1776–1860* (New York: Norton, 1966), pp. 221–253.

[a]Both Georgia draft constitutions were rejected by popular vote for increasing existing inequalities of apportionment; however other reforms passed by separate amendment.

[b]Georgia and Maryland had already abolished property requirements.

Table 1 gives only a partial picture of the difficulties of reform. It omits South Carolina, which was too taken up with national politics to bother with local reforms, and it does not touch on the fortunes and misfortunes of reform in convention and preconvention maneuvering. Virginia reformers got their desired grand convention only after a quarter century of badgering the legislature and convening abortive lesser conventions; despite the presence of Madison, Monroe, John Randolph, John Marshall, and a host of other luminaries at the convention, it produced a compromise constitution which fell so far short of the desires of the western counties (which had called for the convention) that these voted against it five to one. The constitution passed only on the votes of the eastern counties that had opposed the convention. Maryland, North Carolina, and Georgia reformers got action only by threats of calling extralegal conventions, and Georgia's two legal conventions produced constitutions so reactionary as to be rejected by popular vote. Even with apportionment, the main concern of the reformers, action was almost as difficult in the 1830's as it was a century later. Extending the franchise, a secondary concern in the South, found very limited acceptance in Virginia and North Carolina, their few grudging departures from property qualifications being balanced by their decision to bar free blacks from voting. Virginia and North Carolina did not drop property qualifications altogether till the 1850's, almost a half century after the first serious agitation for reform, and did so then only under pressure from both parties to simplify the election rules and heal internal disputes "in contemplation of the ominous and threatening state of our relations with our Northern brethren upon the subject of slavery."[12] Nat Turner's rebellion (1831) evoked in Virginia a reaction precisely opposite to that aroused in Rhode Island by Thomas Dorr's rebellion; the lesson of Dorr's rebellion was to draw the unfranchised into the system, while the lesson of Turner's rebellion was to draw the whites together into a solid front to exclude blacks from politics and thwart the schemes of the North to interfere with slavery.

In all of the states but Delaware, North Carolina, Pennsylvania, and Rhode Island, the taxpayer qualification was either never adopted, or, having been adopted to extend and simplify the franchise, was dropped by the time of the Civil War. Taxpayer qualifications were attacked with the same arguments originally used to procure their adoption: the tax rolls apparently still left room for argument as to who had paid; voters complained of wrongful granting or denial of the vote by election officials with inaccurate records; taxes were either undemocratic in excluding the very poor, or too nominal in amount to be worth the bother—or, however inconsistently, both.

For whatever reason, the taxpayer qualification in this period seems to have been more significant as a wedge toward abolishing property qualification than as a lasting instrument of state policy. When the ideological need dropped away, the taxpayer qualification generally dropped away as well. In this respect, it is far from unique. In a sense, the various stages of property qualifications were stepping stones away from religious qualifications or non-qualifications like "a civil conversation." The ideological stepping stone is a time-honored instrument of development in the field of voting rights, as in other fields, and the very intensive use it has gotten from the modern Supreme Court is not wholly alien to the spirit of state politics in the Pre-Intervention period.

Not all of the stepping stones, however, led toward greater democracy. The secret ballot was adopted in some places, rejected in others. The original gerrymander appeared in 1812, when the Democrats, under Governor Elbridge Gerry, divided Essex County, Massachusetts, into a dragon-shaped district, isolating Federalist strongholds in Boston and the North Shore and augmenting the Democrats' majority in the state senate by 50 percent—even though the Federalists got more votes in the election![13] The constitutional systems were no more able to stop gerrymandering in 1812 than they are today. Moreover, abolishing property and tax tests revealed that they had served a number of indispensable functions, such as holding down the voting strength of free blacks, women, infants, criminals, mental incompetents, unpropertied immigrants, and transients, besides providing an up-to-date reference as to who was qualified to vote. Most of the categories mentioned were not represented on the tax rolls in any great numbers, still less on the property rolls, and many states were shocked to find, on extending the suffrage, that a multitude of people far less attractive than the militiamen were threatening to vote. New Jersey, which had unwarily extended her franchise to "all free inhabitants" in 1797, expressly barred women in 1807 and blacks in 1820.

New Jersey followed the national pattern of adjustment to suffrage reforms: sweeping egalitarian principles would be enlisted to effect a specific reform, such as franchising the militiamen or the taxpayer; then the principle could be seen to apply in logic to species of equality not contemplated by those who enacted it. The reform would be followed by a period of reaction to the new doors opened. The states tolerated some new voters but barred others permanently (for example, mental incompetents) and yet others temporarily (for example, women), while the public was becoming accustomed to a wider view of equality than that which had prompted the reform.

Other states joined New Jersey in closing loopholes in the new franchise laws against the threat of participation by unfavored groups. Blacks were barred by law everywhere except in New York and New England, where their negligible numbers permitted the whites to indulge an egalitarian sentiment which they did not always extend to other more numerous groups, such as women and recent immigrants. Even in New York, blacks had to meet a property requirement stiffer than the one which had been abolished for whites; attempts to remove this restriction were defeated by referenda in 1846, 1850, and 1867.[14] Between 1792 and 1838, Connecticut, Kentucky, and all the Middle Atlantic states changed their constitutions to exclude blacks, all of the new states in the West excluded blacks, and they were universally excluded in the South.

America may have welcomed the wretched refuse of Europe's teeming shores when it arrived in force in the 1840's, but the states with the greatest influx of immigrants were less than eager to welcome them to the polls. Much of the opposition to the reforms demanded in the 1842 Dorr Rebellion in Rhode Island was grounded in the fears of rural-based Yankee Protestants that abolishing the freehold requirement would also abolish their near-monopoly of political representation by extending the vote to urban Catholic immigrants. The Native American, or Know-Nothing party, founded in Philadelphia in 1847, expressed a hostility toward foreigners harking back to the famous tirades in the Pennsylvania constitutional convention of 1837 against attempts to "place the wandering Arabs, the Tartar hordes of our large cities on the level with the virtuous and good man." The states with the most immigrants developed a special interest in residency, citizenship, language, and literacy tests. The Know-Nothings suggested that twenty-one years of continued residence be required for naturalization.[15] The New York Constitutional Convention of 1846 saw efforts to strike out the terms *born* or *naturalized* from the franchise qualifications, leaving the state free to substitute its own more stringent qualifications for residence for the five years required by the federal government. These efforts, and efforts to establish a literacy test with special dispensation for natives, proved too cumbrous to attract a majority of delegates.[16] Similar efforts failed in Maryland, but Connecticut and Massachusetts adopted literacy tests in 1855 and 1857, Rhode Island retained its freehold requirement for naturalized citizens in 1842, and Massachusetts added a special residency requirement for naturalized citizens in 1859.[17]

Why the Court Stayed Out

Late though it was, and less generously endowed with the thoughts of the founders than earlier state disputes, the Rhode Island suffrage controversy, which raged from 1828 to the defeat of Thomas Dorr in 1842 rates special attention. This controversy is more thoroughly documented than most; it was unusually comprehensive, capitulating much of the experience in other states. Taken by itself, it affords as good a picture of the forces, motives, tactics, and issues involved in a fight for suffrage reform as one could hope to find in the Pre-Intervention period. Moreover, it exemplifies, through the political events which brought it before the Supreme Court in *Luther v. Borden*,[18] the overwhelming array of factors which led the Court to stay out of the dispute. It also exemplifies the great gulf which is often found between the rhetoric of voting and representation questions and the forces which actually settle them in court. The Court had nothing to build on—no substantive right, no interpretive rules as bold as those later developed for the white primary cases, no power base, no techniques of enforcement. Much of the doctrine of political questions now associated with *Luther v. Borden*, including the rejection of the guarantee clause as a basis of court jurisdiction, is aimed at straw targets. Luther's counsel claimed jurisdiction under the diversity-of-citizenship rules applicable to all civil cases and mentioned the guarantee clause only to maintain that it was not relevant to the case. The Court ignored Luther's arguments and devoted many of its own arguments to obscuring the considerations—the intervention factors—which really decided the case.

Rhode Island was no different from the other states in its exposure to influences which brought about voting reforms elsewhere. Its people had had to fight and pay taxes like the rest; it suffered more than its share of financial upheaval during the Revolution; by the time of Thomas Dorr it had a differentiated citizenry and two-party rivalry. But it also had in those days (as it has had since) a stronger political polarity than most states, and a weaker capacity for concerted political action. Rhode Island had boycotted the Constitutional Convention of 1787, being caught in the grip of the paper money faction; it was the last of the thirteen states to ratify, in 1790; it had never bothered to change its colonial charter; it had dragged its feet in the War of 1812, joining Massachusetts and Connecticut in the Hartford Convention of 1814 to consider seceding from the Union. Why? Did it fear engulfment because it was so small? Undoubtedly the smallness of its hinterland lent a special urgency to the efforts of its rural Yankee freeholders to stifle the votes of Providence immigrants. For whatever reason, Rhode Island, with the blessings of both parties, clung to property qualifications for two decades after the other northern states had laid them by and resisted reapportionment with a zeal matched only by Georgia.

Thomas Dorr started in politics a Whig and a moderate reapportionist with only a peripheral interest in broader suffrage, falling well short of universal manhood suffrage. Frustrated by repeated rebuffs to his moderate reforms, he became more and more radical, first switching to the Democratic party, and then, in 1841, organizing his own People's party to bring about more thoroughgoing reforms than either party had been willing to tolerate in the 1830's. Dorr's rhetoric on behalf of underrepresented urban citizens sounds very familiar to modern ears, in contrast to Jefferson's anti-urban pleas for upcountry representation. Dorr talked about rotten boroughs, the great foundations of republican liberty and equality, population trends, the industrial revolution, horribly unequal districts; he even threw in a Dauer-Kelsay score.[19] He also invoked a splendid phalanx of miscellaneous authority for wider suffrage, such as might grace the pages of the Supreme Court Reporter today: Dorr said that political participation is a natural right rooted in the federal Constitution, the Declaration of Independence, the ordinances of the pilgrim fathers, the "most valuable portion of the Constitution of England," voting traditions from the earliest days of Rhode Island's Royal Charter, "the institutions of our remote progenitors in the forests of Germany," and ultimately the hand of God.[20] This natural right "cannot be abridged, nor suspended any farther than the greatest good of the greatest number imperatively requires."[21]

In 1841, without permission from the legislature, Dorr called a People's Convention, which produced a People's Constitution. This constitution was approved by popular vote with only 46 out of 14,000 dissenting.[22] The legislature countered with a Freeman's Constitution, which was narrowly defeated in a second popular vote, leaving the government in dispute between the General Assembly, which proposed to continue under the old charter, and the Dorrites, who claimed that the charter would become void when a government elected under the People's charter was inaugurated in May 1842.

When the Dorrites scheduled elections under the People's Constitution, the General Assembly passed the Algerine laws (so called by the suffragists for their fancied resemblance to the despotic practices of the Dey of Algiers), prescribing heavy penalties for assuming state offices on the basis of elections not authorized by the Royal Charter. Both parties held elections in April and met for inauguration in May—Dorr and his legislature in Providence, Samuel Ward King and his legislature in Newport. Neither party was anxious to take action in Rhode Island because the even division of allegiance in the state offered little prospect of strong support for either side. Instead, each government resolved that the other government was illegal and called for help from President Tyler and Congress, neither of whom was anxious to take sides.

Dorr's People's government attracted a lot of sympathy throughout the country, especially in the Democratic party. Leaders of Tammany Hall promised him several companies of New York militia and presented him with a sword which had seen service in the Revolution. Dorr flourished the sword and marched his supporters to seize the Providence arsenal; however, his two cannon failed to fire, and his troop dissolved, President Tyler, despite his sympathy with the Democrats and his onetime support of nullification in South Carolina, cautiously indicated that he would probably support the charter government. With no effective support inside the state or outside of it, Dorr's government collapsed, and Dorr was eventually convicted of treason to the state. The charter government then hastened to enact most of the reforms Dorr had demanded.

In the course of these excursions, Tocqueville's assertion that political questions in the United States resolve themselves into judicial questions was more than borne out of the posturings and rhetoric of the participants, however feebly it later fared in the courts. The justices of the state supreme court had entered the fray without hesitation during the controversy in March 1842 which preceded the vote on the Freeman's Constitution, explaining that they felt free to point out the unlawful character of the People's Constitution because it was not a question "which might be presented to us officially."

We have ever held it our duty, as Justices of the Supreme Judicial Court, not to intermeddle with party politics, nor to volunteer our opinion on questions of law which might be presented to us officially. The questions submitted to us . . . do not seem to us to be of such class, nor are they such, under all the circumstances of the case, as we feel at liberty to decline answering. We state, then, as our opinion, that . . . the 'People's Constitution' . . . is of no binding force whatever . . . and that any attempt to carry it into effect by force will be treason against this State if not against the United States.[23]

Dorr and his friends had answered with the Nine Lawyers' Opinion, contending that sovereignty had passed into the hands of the people at the time of the Revolution; and that the People's Convention, being called by the people, derived from an exercise of sovereignty of no less dignity than that of the General Assembly in calling the Freeman's Convention, since the Royal Charter made no provision for the mode of establishing a constitution; moreover, the People's Constitution established a republican form of government as required by the guarantee clause of the federal Constitution. Chief Justice Durfee of the state supreme court admonished a grand jury immediately prior to the vote on the Freeman's Constitution that allegiance to constituted authority was the first duty of every citizen and that armed support of the People's Constitution was treasonous.[24]

Dorr's rebellion aroused, if anything, a superabundance of lawyers, inside the state and out, who asserted that the controversy could and should be settled with reference to fundamental legal principles—as if it were, in fact, a "judicial question"—though the Dorrites were not so confident of their principles as to trust them to the interpretation of the hostile supreme court of Rhode Island when their chances seemed better in the arenas of arms and politics. When Dorr was tried for treason in May 1844, he asserted that he had been elected governor under a duly adopted constitution—the People's Constitution—and offered to prove his case by calling in the 13,944 voters who had voted for the constitution in 1841.[25] The court refused to consider the question, Chief Justice Durfee pointing out: "The fact is, the prisoner asks leave to bring into this Court a political question, which cannot be settled here . . . We can recognise the Constitution under which we hold our places and no other . . . If such proceedings (as the adoption of the People's Constitution) should be tolerated in a court of law, and be accounted to hold any man justifiable for the violation of it, then law is at an end, and general anarchy would ensue."[26] Justice Staples added: "Can we permit such a proceeding as this—to have our own existence drawn into question? The acts set up by the prisoner in his justification were revolutionary in their character, and success was necessary to give them effect."[27]

Thus, the court invoked the doctrine of political questions, questions which it declined to decide by reason of constitutional mandate but also by reason of the logic of its position. If Dorr had won and his enemies had come to trial for treason, the same arguments which the court had used to sidestep the issue of the People's Constitution's validity could as well have been used to sidestep the issue of the validity of the charter. The court's refusal to consider the validity of the People's Constitution could hardly be based solely on the charter, which did not specify how it was to be amended. Nor could the court have refused to consider the "political question" on the sole basis of its stated principle of noninterference with politics, because the court had been in the thick of politics from the beginning, having expressed its members' unanimous opinion in March of 1842 on the very political question they refused to consider in 1844. In this context, the term *political* seems to mean "inconvenient or impossible for the court to decide" more than "related to party politics." The court's decision hinged not so much on choosing or refusing to choose between the doctrines of both sides as in recognizing that the charter side had won. Justice Staples came to the point of the matter in saying of Dorr's doctrines, "success was necessary to give them effect."

Though the Supreme Court of the United States was not so tightly bound to refuse to choose between the two Rhode Island governments when the issue came before it, since it was not the judicial arm of one of the parties, the members of the Court were no more anxious to face the choice than President Tyler and his Congress and the Rhode Island Supreme Court had been. As with the Rhode Island court in Dorr's treason trial, the outcome of *Luther v. Borden* undoubtedly depended much more on factors, many of them unstated, outside of the judicial principles advanced than it did on the principles themselves. On the other hand, the Court's use of the doctrine of political questions deserves consideration because it has been the first point of reference for much of its subsequent treatment of questions of political representation.

Along with Dorr and others, the charter government indicted Luther, a town official elected under the People's Constitution, for violation of the Algerine laws. Pursuant to this indictment, Borden broke into Luther's house to arrest him. Luther, having fled and established residence in Massachusetts, sued Borden for trespass in the United States circuit court in Rhode Island, claiming that Borden was not acting under valid public authority since the charter government was illegal. The circuit court refused to entertain Luther's attack on the charter government, the jury accordingly found for Borden, and Luther appealed to the Supreme Court.

The Supreme Court had escaped having to rule on the legitimacy of the charter government when it rejected Dorr's habeas corpus petition, submitted in 1847 after his conviction for treason.[28] The Court then postponed hearing the appeal in *Luther v. Borden*, also received in 1845, pending the filling of

48

vacancies.[29] The case was argued in the 1848 term, Benjamin F. Hallett of Boston and former United States Attorney General Nathan Clifford of Maine for the plaintiff Luther, and Daniel Webster of Massachusetts and John Whipple of Rhode Island for Borden. These counsel offered the Court four different arguments to choose from to settle the case: Hallett's contention that the People's Constitution had been legally adopted; Whipple's and Webster's that it had not; Webster's alternative argument that the question was one of sovereignty, not susceptible to judicial determination; and Clifford's that the trespass was illegal, regardless of the sovereignty question, because its martial law authorization was invalid in Luther's part of the state, where there had been no hostilities.

The Court chose the political question point to dispose of the case. Webster had devoted only five of his twenty pages of argument to the political question point, reiterating the arguments of the Rhode Island Supreme Court that "sovereignty is above courts or juries, and the creature cannot sit in judgment upon its creator" and stressing the difficulty of proving the validity of every vote cast by testimony in court. Such arguments, decisive for a state court, were less so when addressed to the Supreme Court, which was not being asked to sit in judgment on its own creator or to rule on the validity of anyone's votes.

Webster tried to close the gap by invoking the guarantee clause,[30] suggesting that it barred the Supreme Court from sitting in judgment on matters committed by the Constitution to the other branches. Had not the president committed the federal government to support the charter government?[31] What confusion might not be expected if the judiciary should back one of two rival governments and Congress and the president the other?[32] This argument is plausible but not compelling. The president's message had been highly tentative, insisting that the guarantee clause did not apply to the Rhode Island controversies, which had not become an actual insurrection. Even a positive commitment, moreover, need not have barred intervention by the Court. The guarantee clause does prescribe that the United States shall guarantee to every state a republican form of government and protect them against domestic violence, but the power granted was not necessarily exclusive to the president or Congress any more than the power to regulate interstate commerce is exclusive to the federal government.[33] If Congress had chosen to protect the charter government against the Dorrites by taxing exports from Dorr's part of Rhode Island—a power denied it by Article I, section 9—the Court might easily have found that the discretion conferred by the guarantee clause was not exclusive at all, but subject, like most other powers, to judicial review, and hence no bar to Hallett's arguments.

Webster's brief, like the opinion of the Court and most other arguments addressed to the subject, left it a matter of conjecture whether the political question was not for the Court to consider by reason of a constitutional mandate, or because of policy considerations. He would have had some difficulty in finding in the words of the guarantee clause anything that forbade the Court to decide what a republican form of government might be. Luther was not asking the Court to guarantee a republican form of government; nor was he asking it to assist in putting down an insurrection. He was asking the Court to rule on the legitimacy of the charter government—a decision which Congress and the president had carefully tried to avoid—but his case, apart from Clifford's arguments on the martial law point, rested solely on the concepts of sovereignty embodied in the Revolution. Hallett relied on Article II, section 2 to show jurisdiction over suits between citizens of different states, assuming that the question of legitimacy could be settled under the principles of common law.[34] His arguments bristled with invocations of the Declaration of Independence, the Virginia Declaration, and the Bill of Rights, of Locke, Madison, Algernon Sydney, James Burgh, John Taylor, and many others, and of every species of natural law as it was understood in the eighteenth century.[35] Hallett referred to the guarantee clause only to insist that it had no bearing on the case.[36]

As a rule, all of the intervention factors—will, authority, power, and technique—must be present before the Court can step in to protect a voting right; in *Luther v. Borden* virtually all of the factors were lacking, and the Court, perforce, refused to intervene. Although all of the Justices except John McLean had been appointed by Democratic administrations, and although the Dorr war had in retrospect aligned the Democrats with Dorr, the Court unanimously accepted Webster's urging that the legitimacy issue was a political question. Only Levi Woodbury of New Hampshire dissented, following Clifford's argument that Borden's claimed authority under martial law was beyond the powers granted in the charter, especially at the scene of the trespass, where there had been no fighting. It might strike a modern observer as odd, in the light of the reapportionment and poll tax cases of the 1960's, that a Court of Democratic appointees, which might be presumed to have a political affinity with the Dorrites, was so backward about asserting its views as the command of the federal Constitution.[37] Could anyone imagine the Warren Court as unresourceful on behalf of its favored clients and causes as Taney's Court was with Dorr? The flaw in the Taney Court's will to intervene was the antifederalist cast of Democratic opinion, which in conjunction with the other factors made them more reluctant to try to impose a national rule on the states than they were anxious to chastise enemies of the party in Rhode Island, especially when the enemies had granted the substance of Dorr's demands.

Constitutional authority for intervening was lean by the standards of the day, though not irremediably so. Hallett's natural law argument was tenable, and a case could be, in fact, has been made for the guarantee clause as authority for the Court to intervene in voting questions.[38] The Ninth and Tenth

Amendments, which emphasize residual rights in the people, could have been pressed into service. The Court could easily have used Clifford's martial law argument to chasten the anti-Dorrites and still avoid the legitimacy question.[39]

The crucial missing factors were power and technique. The Court's antifederalist views were more than matched by an antifederalist balance of power in national politics. The states threatened continually to contravene the powers of the whole federal government; they had no difficulty in flouting the desires of the Court unsupported by the other branches. The Court did not have to look very far back to be reminded of its own impotence against the states, as demonstrated in the *Cherokee Nation* and *Missionary* cases, where even John Marshall had feared to match the unaided power of the Supreme Court against the power of the state of Georgia.[40] Marshall had dismissed with misgivings a Cherokee suit to enjoin Georgia from exercising its authority over the Cherokee nation, ostensibly on the ground that it did not constitute a state or a foreign state within the meaning of Article III, section 2. The real reason was Andrew Jackson's refusal to countenance the Indians' attempt to form an independent government. Marshall, thrown upon his own resources, admitted " a serious additional objection . . . to the jurisdiction of the court . . . The bill requires us to control the legislature of Georgia, and to restrain the exertion of its physical force. The propriety of such an interposition by the court may well be questioned. It savors too much of the exercise of political power to be within the proper province of the judicial department."[41] The Court was able to achieve a stand-off with Georgia in the *Missionary* case, where the confrontation was not so direct, only because Jackson, challenged by Nullificationists in the States, had undertaken to "meet treason at the threshold," thereby committing himself to a firmer policy of federal control. The uneasy confrontation between the nation and the states had not been resolved by Dorr's time, and the same barriers of power and philosophy which stayed the president and Congress from intervening in Rhode Island—wholly without reference to the written provisions of the Constitutions—served also to stay the Court. The real difference between the interventions of the Warren Court in suffrage questions and the nonintervention of the Taney Court is not so much the adoption of the Fourteenth Amendment as the victory of the Union in the Civil War, which gave the Court a federal power base without which its additional jurisdiction would have been useless.

Lack of technique confronted the Court with the insoluble problem of retroactive intervention. The Warren Court, powerful as never before and able to manufacture its own authority for the right causes, could hardly have decided *Luther v. Borden* differently from the Taney Court because the decision in *Luther* was so tightly wrapped up in the posture of the case. Taney properly complained that a decision for Luther threatened to invalidate every

51

act of the charter government—its laws, its contracts, its financial obligations, funds paid to its officers, official acts of its employees—because that was precisely the remedy Luther wanted; an invalidation of Borden's authority to have trespassed because it derived from the charter government. Such a holding would have produced hideous disruption in Rhode Island and certainly among its creditors, far out of proportion to the comfort it might have given to Luther.[42] The modern Court has studiously avoided retroactive holdings in the reapportionment cases and would have been bound, no less than Taney's Court, by the facts of *Luther v. Borden.*[43]

That is not to say, however, that the modern Court could not intervene in the kind of voting rights controversy that led to *Luther v. Borden.* The difference between the Warren Court and the Taney Court in this regard was the Warren Court's possession of techniques which permitted it to intervene prospectively and avoid the problem of retroactivity. A plaintiff today has more ways of getting into a federal court and can demand a wider range of remedies than he could in Taney's day. Much of this widening reflects judicial techniques, decades in the making, for circumventing constitutional objections to jurisdiction which existed in Taney's day. A basic difficulty of Taney's time was the Eleventh Amendment, which barred suits by individuals against states and placed a jurisdictional block on the only direct avenue of assault on franchise abuse by the persons most aggrieved. The Eleventh Amendment was not circumvented until 1908, when it became possible to sue to enjoin a state official from acting outside of constitutional bounds.[44] The federal Declaratory Judgments Act of 1934 now provides another judicial technique unavailable in Taney's time.[45] It was long thought that an action seeking a declaratory judgment was not a case or controversy within the meaning of Article III, section 1; these doubts were not resolved till 1937.[46] Finally, a body of legislation relative to federal elections, plus a half-dozen civil rights acts passed since 1870, have greatly increased the means by which one can protest abridgements of representation in court.

Lacking these techniques, Taney could not have intervened effectively in Rhode Island, even if he had wanted to do so and even if he had had more backing from the other branches. A modern Dorr could go to a federal court, sue the charter government officer responsible for elections, as was done in most of the apportionment cases, and ask for a declaration that the charter was unconstitutional, together with an injunction from holding elections until the offending situation was rectified. If he found the charter government slow to comply, he could also ask that the legislature be enjoined from passing any laws till his demands were met. More important, he could start action the minute he had a case—January, April, or May 1842, or even 1834 or 1824—instead of waiting six years till the charter government had long since prevailed on the field of battle and then having to suggest indirectly, through a trespass action, that it would have been more proper if the charter government had lost.

The availability of means to get into Court and enjoin state officials made the difference between night and day in enabling the Warren Court to address itself to issues like those urged but not reached in *Luther v. Borden* without having to face the insuperable obstacles to enforcement inherent in the indirect and retrospective way the issues had to come before the Taney Court. The procedural posture of the case carried with it, if not the specific outcome which Taney chose, at least a virtually absolute bar to deciding the legitimacy issue in favor of Luther and the Dorrites. The Court's purchase on the issue was too clumsy, too lacking in leverage on the many difficult questions a judgment adverse to the charter would raise to warrant so bold a holding, regardless of what substantive constitutional authority might have supported such a move.

If any lesson may be drawn from *Luther v. Borden* and the politics of the Pre-Intervention period, it is this: the major voting disputes could not be settled in the courts of the time, but they could be, and usually were settled through representative institutions. Neither the Supreme Court nor the state courts had enough support in the intervention factors to stand in independent judgment on the major issues of representation, as the Supreme Court does today. The major disputes of the period, property qualifications and apportionment, were vulnerable to political pressures and could usually be settled with a simple change in the rules. The states succeeded in setting suffrage disputes, though not always without a long struggle for reform, nor with the thoroughgoing inclusiveness of modern fashion. With only a few exceptions, such as Georgia, they were more successful in satisfying demands for reapportionment than they have been in the twentieth century. We owe the regional focus of our representative institutions to patterns set largely in the Pre-Intervention period: single-member districts, plurality elections, and the two-party system, with the attendant strengths of inclusiveness and compromise in the parties and the weakness of submerging and dispersing nonregional interest groups. The problems of gerrymanders and multi-member districts are inherent in the district system and were no more disposable by representative bodies in Marshall's and Taney's time than they are by judicial bodies today.

The overall trend of voting laws after the Revolution was aptly described by Chilton Williamson as a progression "from property to democracy," but the triumph of democracy was the common denominator of a host of lesser triumphs whose connections with democracy were largely coincidental. The rhetoric of democracy, always in evidence, seldom brought reforms without the help of pressures generated by wars, big spending, bigger governments, more differentiated electorates, and more organized interest groups, reinforced by the inadequacies of property qualifications to meet the demands of party competition. The reforms of the period differed in several respects from the Supreme Court's current version of the Fundamental Principle of the Constitution: they were not rooted in the federal Constitution; they were related more to specific grievances than to democratic rhetoric; and they were often limited in scope, excluding women, blacks, nontaxpayers, and aliens.

Thomas Dorr's own career reflects the low priority of radical democratic measures in the politics of the great spokesman of radical democracy. Dorr sought his earliest support, not on the suffrage question which later produced most of the rhetoric, but on the apportionment question. His first target constituency was not the man in the street but the Providence merchants, his clients in his law practice. His apportionment arguments on their behalf stressed not so much the population of Providence as its share of tax payments; and his first political party was not the Democrats but the Whigs. These wanted a bigger voice for themselves, and Dorr's proposals at the 1834 convention reflected not only the moderation of his own desires, which fell well short of universal manhood suffrage, but also the greater political pulling power which he expected then, as politicians still do now, of a limited and specific reform backed by limited and specific interest groups. Only when Whiggery failed did Dorr turn to radicalism, and only when radicalism had failed in the field did Dorr fall back on radical principles in court.

For all their fair talk, the Dorrites invited the Court to the ball only as a last resort. They did not see it as a likely partner in reform, standing as it did on two wooden legs: a tenuous power base and shaky constitutional authority. Voting intervention is a modern kind of dance, and the Taney Court was neither empowered nor disposed to learn the steps, which would have been too late anyway by the time of *Luther v. Borden.* The federal Constitution's "plain objective" of equal representation for equal numbers, discovered by Justice Black in *Wesberry v. Sanders,*[47] dates from 1964, not 1788. Democratic rhetoric alone was as frail a motive for Court intervention as it was for reforms in the states. The modern Court could afford to join the dance in *Baker v. Carr* and its successor cases; it had the power, and it had mastered the wild new steps of our time, techniques of interpretation and enforcement as alien to Taney's time as the Boogaloo. In this forbidding context it is small wonder that Taney turned the Dorrites down.

III. Intervention by Interpretation, 1868–1962:
The Black Voting Rights Progression

The [Fifteenth] Amendment nullifies sophisticated
as well as simple-minded modes of discrimination.
—Felix Frankfurter

The Reconstruction Amendments

While political reforms in the period of Intervention by Interpretation continued to follow their old motivation of partisan advantage, in the South they also retained their tendency to exclude blacks. Though armed with the Fifteenth Amendment, the Supreme Court did not intervene effectively for seventy years. However, when it did intervene in 1944, it demonstrated that its power had in some respects outgrown that of the elected branches, and it unleashed an interpretive technique, summed up by Frankfurter in the epigraph above, which has been crucial to its boldest decisions of modern times.

The Civil War laid the groundwork for later intervention by giving the Court power and authority it had not known before. The victory of the Union added to the power of the Supreme Court, as it added power to every branch of the federal government. The prewar controversies over states' rights and black rights were not silenced, but they shifted from their former concern with slavery and nullification to new ground: Reconstruction. The political power and allegiance of blacks suddenly became a question of vital national concern, not only to preserve Republican power in the South, but also to increase it in the North.

Since both lines of the Supreme Court's intervention in voting rights—the black rights progression and the equal districts progression—purport to rest on the Fourteenth and Fifteenth Amendments, it is necessary to examine briefly the politics of their passage. The examination is needed not just to reinforce the thesis that democratic-looking reforms were not always passed for democratic reasons, but also to test two other conclusions of this book: that the black rights progression rests on solid constitutional ground (in the traditional sense of preserving the meaning of the constitutional authority invoked) because it applies a genuine voting rights amendment—the Fifteenth—to modern circumstances through interpretation, while the equal districts progression is much less secure because it reverses the original understanding of the Fourteenth Amendment by misapplying section one of that amendment to voting rights.

Sponsors of the Fourteenth and Fifteenth Amendments, like Thomas Dorr before them, were driven to bolder and bolder notions of equality in support of specific partisan aims and often in the face of their own antidemocratic sentiments. Popular sympathy for the black vote was low, as always, in the states. Voters in eleven northern jurisdictions rejected black suffrage from 1865 to 1869: Wisconsin, Minnesota, Connecticut, Colorado Territory, and the District of Columbia in 1865; Nebraska in 1866; Kansas and Ohio in 1867; Michigan and Missouri in 1868; New York in 1869. Only in Iowa and Minnesota, in 1868, did voters accept black suffrage; in Wisconsin the state supreme court ordered black suffrage in 1866, pursuant to an 1849 referendum.[1] Lincoln and Johnson were willing to see educated blacks enfranchised but feared that the enfranchisement of all blacks would be a catastrophe; Johnson campaigned against the Fourteenth Amendment; abolitionists working for the passage of the Thirteenth Amendment were at pains to point out that emancipation and enfranchisement were entirely separate;[2] the framers of the Fourteenth Amendment, after some initial equivocation, finally averred that equal protection of the laws and the privileges and immunities of citizens had nothing to do with the vote.

In contrast to other issues, such as incorporation of the bill of rights, state action, segregation, and corporations as persons, which have raised in retrospect questions about the "original understanding" of the Fourteenth Amendment,[3] the right to vote was of central concern to the framers, and they have left us a far clearer notion of the original understanding than we have of the other questions.

Republican control of the southern states depended on the army of occupation, a temporary prop whose removal would permit the Democrats to regain control of the states, take from southern blacks most of the fruits of emancipation, and emerge more powerful than ever to fill national offices with the "yelling of secessionists and the hissing of copperheads." The first Democratic majority in Congress might repudiate the Union war debt and pay off that of the Confederacy; moreover, the freeing of the slaves had added to the threat of such a majority by giving the South a prospective bonus of thirteen congressmen to "represent" the last two-fifths of the freed blacks, who as slaves had only entitled the South to the federal ratio of three-fifths of their numbers.[4] The Republicans had not bled for four years to swallow such bitter fruit when the armies withdrew. When President Johnson announced in December 1865 his wish for the speedy restoration of the southern states to the Union, Republican leaders responded at once to the threat to their hold on the South and the nation. "With the basis [of representation] unchanged," said Thaddeus Stevens, leader of the House section of the Joint Committee on Reconstruction, "the 83 southern members with the Democrats that will in the best times be elected from the North will always give them a majority in Congress and in the Electoral College."[5] Stevens wanted to thwart this majority with constitutional amendments to prohibit repudiation of the Union debt, bar assumption of the Confederate debt, protect blacks from the resurgence of white man's government in the South, and above all cut down southern representation by changing the congressional basis from population to actual voters. The South could then disfranchise its free blacks after Reconstruction, but it would thereby forfeit almost half its representation in Congress and the electoral college.[6]

The original understanding of the Fourteenth Amendment derives from these aims "to secure perpetual ascendancy to the party of Union." The Joint Committee on Reconstruction succeeded in writing the debt provisions, together with a conditional ban on certain ex-Confederates in public office, into sections three and four of the Fourteenth Amendment; it restricted white man's government in section one; it dealt with the black vote question in section two, which provides for a reduction of representatives for states which deny or abridge any adult male's right to vote in federal or state elections.[7] Stevens's idea of apportioning by actual voters was discarded when James G. Blaine pointed out wide variance in the percentage of qualified voters in different states which would favor new states, such as Democratic California, with 58 percent of its adult males voting, over older states, such as Republican Vermont, with 19 percent.[8] The Senate decisively rejected two attempts to ban racial voting discrimination outright;[9] it also rejected Blaine's proposal to subtract *all* blacks from any state's basis of representation where *any* black's right to vote was denied or abridged.[10] The Joint Committee also rejected Robert Dale Owen's proposal for black suffrage after 1876, with discrimination allowed under penalty till then. The Senate and the Joint Committee were well aware of northern opposition to black suffrage; it was written into most northern constitutions, ratified by almost every referendum prior to 1868, and re-emphasized by fresh protests from New York, Illinois, and Indiana congressional delegations.[11] The Senate and the Committee refused to tolerate black suffrage, present or future, and section two of the Fourteenth Amendment passed only after its backers removed every reference to race or color. The final version of section two leaves little question as to the original understanding of what it was supposed to do; namely, to confront the southern states, when they returned to southern white control, with a choice between enfranchising the blacks and losing almost half their votes in the House of Representatives and the electoral college. Jacob Howard, radical Republican Senator from Michigan, explained the Joint Committee's views on suffrage and the Fourteenth Amendment three weeks before its final passage by both houses: "The committee were of opinion that the states are not yet prepared to sanction so fundamental a change as would be the concession of the right to suffrage to the colored race. We may as well state it plainly and fairly, so that there shall be no misunderstanding on the subject. It was our opinion that three-fourths of the states of this Union could not be induced to vote to grant the right of suffrage even in any degree or under any restriction, to the colored race."[12]

Because the Supreme Court has relied on the equal protection clause of section one of the Fourteenth Amendment to decide the reapportionment and poll tax cases, it is important to look behind Howard's statement (which was addressed to the Fourteenth Amendment in its entirety) to see whether section one might not be interpreted to protect voting rights. Most of the Court's looking in the Warren period is contained in John Marshall Harlan's dissent in *Reynolds v. Sims*;[13] Harlan later amplified his thesis in *Oregon v. Mitchell*.[14] Harlan concluded that section one had nothing to do with voting rights, on the basis of many statements like that of Jacob Howard, already quoted, or of John A. Bingham, who wrote section one and declared: "The amendment does not give, as the second section shows, the power to Congress of regulating suffrage in the several states . . . The exercise of the elective franchise, though it be one of the privileges of a citizen of the Republic is exclusively under the control of the states."[15] Harlan could see no sense in passing section two, let alone the Fifteenth and subsequent voting rights amendments, if section one had already forbidden the states to abridge voting rights.[16]

During the Warren era the Court never got around to dealing with Harlan's highly damaging case against section one's having any bearing on voting rights, though Justice William Brennan did finally make his historical case for *Baker v. Carr* in *Oregon v. Mitchell*, a year after Warren's retirement and almost a decade after *Baker*. By 1970 many things had changed from the 1960's. Warren had retired; conservative Justices Burger and Blackmun had been appointed; and Brennan was writing in dissent. However, Guardian elements in Congress had claimed the authority of Warren-era voting rights decisions to base the eighteen-year-old vote provisions of the voting rights amendments of 1970 on the equal protection clause. By a curious reversal, the Warren Court's ideology, waning in the Court itself, had caught on in Congress to prod a newly cautious Court with its own old walking stick. That story will be told in more detail in Chapter V. For this chapter the important aspect of Brennan's dissent was the staff work on which it was based: William W. Van Alstyne's remarkable essay, "The Fourteenth Amendment, the Right to Vote, and the Understanding of the 39th Congress." Van Alstyne had rushed in to pick up Harlan's gauntlet where the justices of the majority had feared to tread; the only fault of his scholarly study was that it tried to prove the impossible.[17] Van Alstyne challenged Harlan for treating the Fourteenth

Amendment as a single text, when sections one and two had been written by different men and debated separately in Congress prior to their consolidation in April 1866.[18] In the course of the debates in January 1866 on what was to become section two, several members of Congress declared their belief that Congress already enjoyed power to regulate state suffrage under the guarantee clause, Article I, section 4, Article IV, section 4, the Thirteenth Amendment, or the Declaration of Independence and natural law.[19] Some of these men were worried that section two might be construed to forfeit Congress' existing powers; Bingham and Stevens abjured such a construction. "There cannot be such a construction," said Bingham; "we are not to be told that we confer a power to override the express guarantees of the Constitution. We propose the penalty in aid of the guarantee, not in avoidance of it."[20] "Now, Sir," added Stevens, "I venture to say that there is no good philogist who, upon reading this proposed amendment, will for a single moment pretend that it either grants a privilege or takes away a privilege from any State on that subject [regulating suffrage]. It does, however, punish the abuse of that privilege if it exists."[21]

With this kind of evidence, Van Alstyne was in a good position to assert that the framers of sections one and two—as of January 1866, when they were still exploring their political resources—did not expect the precursor of section two of itself to preempt whatever other voting regulatory powers the federal government may have enjoyed prior to the framing and passing of section one. Why, then, would it preempt any powers later conveyed by section one? Were not the later statements of Bingham, Howard, and the others that section one had nothing to do with the right to vote merely one permissible inference as to a question which could be resolved either way? Van Alstyne was able to dig up statements from several opponents of section one who, prior to Bingham's and Howard's disavowals, expressed fears that section one might threaten state control of suffrage.[22] He also found a murky statement made by Stevens two years later in the course of arguments over the Fifteenth Amendment that "since the adoption of the fourteenth amendment," he had "no doubt of our full power to regulate the elective franchise, so far as it regards the whole nation."[23] Stevens's statement gave no indication whether he was talking about section one or section two of the Fourteenth Amendment; the statement is far less pertinent evidence of his understanding of the meaning of the Fourteenth Amendment than that afforded on April 28, 1866, when, under pressure from northern opponents of black suffrage, he successfully moved to strike Robert Dale Owen's proposal for black suffrage after 1876.[24] Stevens's acts at the time of passage tell us more than his words of two years later.

Like most supporters of the Warren Court's expressionistic reading of the Fourteenth Amendment, Van Alstyne tried to break through awkward specifics to arrive at a longer-range general understanding of terms like *equal pro-*

tection and *due process* that can convert them for voting rights, as Alexander Bickel did with segregation,[25] into "blank checks for posterity." The technique for this is to show one of two situations: (1) disagreement in 1866 on the matter at hand today—not a difficult task for any question important enough to divide congressional and public opinion in 1866; or (2) failure in 1866 to consider the matter at hand today—an easy task for all remaining questions. Bickel was able to do both: to show that some opponents of the equal protection clause thought it might one day be used to attack segregation, but also to show that public education was in such an undeveloped state in 1866 that there really was no specific intent of the framers applicable to the problems of public education today. Having shown either that there was no original understanding on an issue, or that there was a difference of opinion as to what it was, the commentator could point to general-sounding language in the text, together with general-sounding language by its sponsors, thoughtfully separated from the specific grievance which prompted the language and gave it its original meaning. The process bore some resemblance to a heart transplant: the doctor destroyed the original protein antipathies of the text, carefully severed it from its old moorings, held it glistening for an instant between life and death, and asked: what is there now about this truncated mass of tissue to prevent me from stuffing it into a new patient?[26]

To those accustomed to the heart as it was in the old patient the doctor could then say, "We must never forget that it is a *constitution* we are expounding." Most of us now recognize this formula as a ritual throat-clearing for what we know will come next: "Therefore it says what I want it to say." Nevertheless, we must also recognize in it a grain of truth. Constitutions are written in general language intended to deal with situations past the framers' powers of anticipation. They are harder to change than ordinary laws, and people expected more latitude in their interpretation than they would expect of ordinary laws since constitutions are written for the ages. Thus, while nobody actually said that they understood the Fourteenth Amendment to be a blank check to posterity, the framers and the members of the state legislatures who ratified the amendment might not have been shocked to find language like "equal protection," "due process" and "privileges and immunities" extended to deal with problems like wiretapping, which they were in no position to anticipate.[27] Van Alstyne contrasted the 39th Congress's treatment of section one with its treatment of the Civil Rights Act of 1866 to show that the framers, without saying so, might have thought the amendment more open to free interpretation than the statute: in the face of objections that "privileges and immunities" in the one and "civil rights and immunities" in the other might be construed to invade state control of suffrage, sponsors of the statute actually deleted the broad language about civil rights.[28] Sponsors of the amendment, on the other hand, left in the language and contented themselves with denying that it had any application to suffrage. This treatment left the amendment open, in Van Alstyne's view, to later expansion which might protect suffrage and certainly might extend to apportionment, which was not considered by the 39th Congress.[29]

It is one thing to extend old words to cover new problems: it is quite another to reverse them to enact new views on what to do about old problems. Van Alstyne made an acceptable case for the first, but the reapportionment and poll tax cases are really examples of the second, as both reapportionment and taxpayer suffrage were issues long before the Fourteenth Amendment was passed. Black suffrage was the main issue of contention in the framing of the Fourteenth Amendment. The amendment's legislative history is a series of attempts to secure general federal protection for voting rights—all of which were rejected decisively—followed by a series of challenges by opponents of the amendment, complaining that its broad language might permit Congress to interfere with state control of the franchise. Sponsors of the amendment heatedly denied this construction. "The amendment does not give, as the second section shows, the power to Congress to regulate suffrage in the several states," said drafter John Bingham, assuring doubters that his coalition of radicals and moderates had agreed to confine voting rights questions to the provisions of section two. For Van Alstyne or anyone else to convert these repeated repudiations of voting rights as protected by section one into an original understanding that section one might one day be used to outlaw poll taxes and unequal districts would be an amazing *tour de force*. One could hardly derive such an understanding from Van Alstyne's evidence—opponents' fears, and sponsors' hopes expressed long before or long after, but not at the moment of passage—without making a special effort to suspend disbelief.[30]

Such an effort may yet be in order. What friend of law and liberty could cavil seriously at the efforts of people like van Alstyne, Goldberg, Brennan, and Bickel to give us the color of authority we need to support the long line of civil liberties and other cases based on section one? We owe too much to our tradition of free construction of section one to cut it back now; *s'il n'existait pas, il faudrait l'inventer*; we need a broad construction. But to say because we need a broad construction that we have a blank check is to say too much; it attempts to create something out of nothing. It jars even the most sophisticated among us by telling us, in effect, "We must never forget it is a *blank check* we are expounding." The same Madisonian urge which rallies us to the defense of the Supreme Court and the Constitution makes us gag at the Court's attempts to treat the Constitution as a source of unrestricted authority for its own views. The next four chapters will consider the need for a new reading of the Fourteenth Amendment on voting rights questions, as well as the Court's own handling of the problem of the original understanding. Need is far too big a factor in interpreting the Constitution to ignore, but attempts to derive constitutional authority from need alone lose track of what a constitution is: a set of assumptions which must limit court action as well as authorize it, and which can provide a coherent basis for distinguishing between needs to be indulged under federal constitutional authority and those which must be met, if at all, in other ways. If it is great enough, we may let a need rewrite the Constitution without all of the prescribed formalities and perhaps even help it out by historical speculation like Van Alstyne's. Nevertheless, it is not easy to escape the notion that we are being cozened on the bare strength of our own desires into bowing before a cleverly fabricated original understanding which is the precise reverse of the real one. We are being asked, in effect, to believe in the parthenogenesis of a voting right. If our faith in the Constitution be tied too closely to such miracles, we must also be more tolerant of the constitutional atheists among us, who are understandably fastidious about swallowing such doctrines.

In any case, it is not surprising that the Supreme Court's major attempts to protect voting rights during the Interpretive period relied not on the Fourteenth Amendment, but on the Fifteenth, which afforded much firmer ground for intervention. The Republicans had been unable to pass a voting rights amendment in the Fourteenth, owing to the unpopularity of the black franchise in their own ranks, but they still looked to black votes to secure the blacks and the party against a Democratic resurgence, in the North as well as in the South. After their great victories in the elections of 1866, Republicans of the 39th Congress experienced a change of heart. The same Congress which had repeatedly and decisively rejected black suffrage provisions in the Fourteenth Amendment and the Civil Rights Act of 1866 now mustered equally decisive majorities to override presidential vetoes and require black suffrage in all territory under its direct control: the District of Columbia, federal territories, Nebraska, as a condition of its admission as a state, and finally in the southern states as a condition for their readmission to the Union.[31] William Gillette aptly summarized the resulting climate of opinion as of the winter of 1867: "a substantial consensus among Republicans in Congress to enfranchise the Negro everywhere except back home in the North."[32]

Despite their fears that these gains for black suffrage would be only temporary unless protected by a constitutional amendment, the Republicans did not dare to risk the displeasure of their own constituents at having to share their votes with blacks. The Republicans, who suffered heavy losses in the 1867 state elections, cautiously took a double stand on black suffrage in their plank for the 1868 elections—equal vote in the South, state option in the North—and narrowly won the presidency in 1868 against a weak Democratic candidate, while losing seats in the House of Representatives. The threat of Democratic resurgence seemed closer than ever, and the need of quick preventative action great, though no one knew just what kind of action would be required. Two months of intense debate in the winter of 1869 produced in the Fifteenth Amendment, an answer somewhat the reverse of the consensus of 1867. The amendment was well suited to enfranchise blacks in the North, where they were not likely to be blocked by coercion, literacy tests, and property requirements. Lacking any bar to such tests, however, or to racial restriction on office holding, the Fifteenth Amendment omitted protections everyone knew were essential to preserving the black vote in the South.

The reversal of the Republican position on the black vote in 1869 from that of 1867 reflects a growing awareness of the importance of the black vote in close northern elections. Grant had won the election 1868 by only 300,000 votes. The southern black vote was more than 450,000—indispensible for his popular majority, though not for his majority in the electoral college. Gillette pointed out by comparing potential black voters with the presidential margin of victory in 1868 that the black vote could have been decisive in eleven major states: Maryland, Missouri, Pennsylvania, Ohio, New York, New Jersey, Indiana, Delaware, West Virginia, Connecticut, and California.[33] The point was not lost on Republican strategists of the time. "You need votes in Connecticut, do you not? [asked Charles Sumner.] There are three thousand fellow citizens in that state ready at the call of Congress to take their place at the ballot box. You need them also in Pennsylvania, do you not? There are at least fifteen thousand in that great state waiting for your summons. Wherever you most need them, there they are; and be assured that they will all vote for those who stand by them in the assertion of Equal Rights."[34] The Republicans had lost votes by alienating northern whites on the suffrage question; why not get them back and to spare by enfranchising northern blacks whose exclusion was in any case a barrier to effective enfranchisement of southern blacks?

This course proved possible only by a process of compromise which discarded protections for the southern black vote. The House of Representatives rejected proposed amendments to grant suffrage to all adult males except former rebels,[35] and all adult males including rebels,[36] besides shelving a bill to enfranchise the black nationally (that is, in the North) without additional constitutional authority.[37] In a tangled and often self-contradictory series of votes,[38] the House and Senate rejected amendments guaranteeing the right to hold office, as well as vote,[39] expressly enfranchising blacks,[40] and barring discrimination based on nativity, property, education, or religious belief.[41] The final version, passed in both houses by nearly straight party vote, represented a victory for the moderates and something of a defeat for radicals and southern Republicans who had wanted an office-holding guarantee and broader suffrage reforms which would keep the southern states from taking away with literacy and property tests most of what the amendment granted with its ban on racial discrimination. In the words of Republican Senator Willard Warner of Alabama, "the animus of this amendment is a desire to protect and enfranchise the colored citizens of the country; yet, under it and without any violation of its letter or spirit, nine tenths of them might be prevented from voting and holding office by the requirement on the part of the states or of the United States of an intelligence or property qualification."[42]

The ratification of the Fifteenth Amendment in 1870 completed the constitutional basis of Reconstruction, but the Framers' failure to protect the southern black vote was only the first of many signs of flagging interest in the problems of southern blacks, problems soon to be magnified by the obstruction of resurgent southern whites. President Johnson's amnesty proclamations of September 7 and Christmas 1868 restored suffrage to most former Confederates; the Democrats gained in the elections of 1869 and 1870; and the Ku Klux Klan had begun to block black voting with threats and violence. From 1870 to 1871 Congress passed three enforcement acts to protect black suffrage in the South. The first of these forbade state electoral officials to discriminate on the basis of race or color, barred various forms of private coercion, including deprivation of employment and going in groups in disguise on public highways or on the premises of another with intent to interfere with constitutional liberties.[43] The second enforcement act provided for voting supervisors where fraud was suspected;[44] the third forbade conspiracies to overthrow the United States government, or to prevent people from holding office, enjoying protection of the laws, or voting.[45]

For three years federal officials tried hard to enforce these laws in the face of formidable obstacles. The Fourteenth and Fifteenth Amendments say "no state" shall do the forbidden acts; could the enforcement acts forbid them also to private individuals? Many judges thought not, including Supreme Court Justice Joseph Bradley, who chilled federal counsel by sitting in at the trial stage of what became *United States v. Cruikshank*;[46] counsel described his presence as a "nightmare."[47] Others found their cases hampered by uncooperative white witnesses and dead black witnesses; one district attorney complained after the murder of his five key witnesses that he could find no more, "as all feel it is sure death to testify before the Grand Jury."[48]

State and local officials harassed federal officials by charging them with false arrest or prosecuting blacks for perjury in testifying to United States commissioners.[49] Defensive techniques like federal habeas corpus proceedings or removal to federal courts were authorized by statute but difficult to employ in practice.[50] Southern juries would not convict unless they were packed with blacks; federally ordered posses dragged their feet; federal officials in trouble were denied troops except in cases of actual riot.[51] The conviction rate dropped from 74 percent of federal actions brought in 1870 to 49 percent in 1872, 36 percent in 1873, and 10 percent or less in 1874 and after, reflecting the fact that Grant's attorney-general, George Williams, under heavy attack from North and South, had thrown in the towel in 1874.[52] Williams's withdrawal was followed shortly by Supreme Court decisions hostile to the enforcement acts,[53] the end of Reconstruction in 1877 pursuant to Rutherford B. Hayes's short-lived attempt to win southern conservatives to the Republican party,[54] a decade or so of black voting under white dominion, and then, in the 1890's, an all-out campaign to segregate and disfranchise southern blacks, endorsed in Congress by the repeal of most of the supervisory provisions of the enforcement acts.[55]

The Dawn of Intervention: Early Black Voting Decisions

By 1874, when the Supreme Court was called for the second time in its history to intervene in voting rights issues, the intervention factors had changed less than one might suspect from those which had prevailed twenty-five years before. The doctrinal cast of Morrison Waite's Republican Court, evenly divided between Lincoln Civil War Republicans and Grant Railroad Republicans,[56] was not unlike that of Taney's Democratic Court: generally favorable to the prosuffrage side, but not disposed to take difficult specific measures to enforce suffrage. Waite's Court had far more constitutional and statutory authority to intervene than Taney's, owing to the passage of the Fifteenth Amendment and the enforcement acts, but questions remained as to what might constitute state action under the amendment.[57] The Court's enforcement techniques were still in a very undeveloped state; its power and prestige were as low as at any time in its history. Too many of the Court's blunders and failures were fresh memories for it to share immediately in the augmented power of the federal government. The Court's self-reversal in the legal tender cases[58] and its inability to contend with obstruction from the president, Congress, or the states[59] did little to brighten its image, already tarnished in the *Dred Scott* case.[60]

In this context it is not surprising that the Court was far more circumspect about intervening than one accustomed to its later behavior would have expected. In *Minor v. Happersett,*[61] the Court denied relief to a woman who claimed the right to vote under the privileges and immunities clause of the Fourteenth Amendment, following the original understanding of section one: that it did not affect the right to vote. In the next year, however, the Court leaned over backward to void two convictions for violation of the enforcement acts in state elections, both on the narrowest of technical grounds. In *United States v. Reese,*[62] the defendant, a state electoral official, had refused to register a black's vote and was indicted under two sections of the enforcement acts. Section 2 of the acts required that administrative preliminaries to elections be conducted without regard to race, color, or prior condition of servitude; section 3 forbade wrongful refusal to register votes where a prerequisite act "required to be done as aforesaid" had been omitted. The Court voided the operative section, section 3, for vagueness, since it did not repeat the words about race, color, and servitude. In *United States v. Cruikshank,*[63] the Court had to deal with one of ninety-six indictments arising out of the massacre of sixty blacks in Colfax, Louisiana, 1873. After the riot-torn, cor-

rupt state elections in 1872 both parties claimed victory; the Grant administration seated the Republicans under William Pitt Kellogg but did not succeed
in quieting disputes over local offices. Cruikshank and other Democrats shot
down a posse of blacks which had seized the courthouse in Colfax under the
authority of Kellogg's government. For this they were indicted under the
enforcement acts for banding together to hinder the blacks in the free exercise and enjoyment of their constitutional rights, including the right to vote.
After two trials, another massacre, and a year of deliberation, the Court announced that the indictment was defective for failure to plead racial discrimination. "We may suspect that race was the cause of the hostility," said Chief
Justice Waite, "but it is not so averred." Cruikshank went free.[64]

In both of these cases, involving state elections, the rights invoked were
based on the Fourteenth or Fifteenth Amendment alone. The Court showed
more confidence in *Ex parte Siebold* its first intervention on behalf of voting
rights. *Siebold* involved a conviction for ballot-box stuffing in a federal election, permitting the Court to invoke Article I, section 4 as well as the Fifteenth Amendment, and freeing it to some extent from the state action problem since Article I, section 4 is not expressly limited to state action.

In the next three decades the Court developed a very narrow line of intervention under the enforcement acts, partly because Congress repealed important sections in 1894. Though the Court's constitutional authority to intervene would seem to require *either* state action under the Fourteenth or Fifteenth Amendments *or* a statute regulating congressional elections under Article I, section 4, the Court seldom intervened unless it had both. In criminal
prosecutions, it would intervene against fraud or ballot-box stuffing in federal
congressional elections,[65] but it found reasons not to intervene in presidential elections,[66] state elections,[67] or state voter registration disputes,[68] none
of which are covered by Article I, section 4. While willing in federal elections
to sustain convictions for conspiracy to intimidate black voters,[69] the Court
found conspiracies to deprive citizens of constitutional rights, in situations
not involving federal elections, to be "private action" which could not be
governed by the Fourteenth Amendment.[70] After the repeal, in 1894, of the
enforcement act sections forbidding voting bribery and fraud conspiracies,
the Court would not allow indictments for conspiracy to bribe, even in federal elections;[71] however, it did permit (as it still permits) the use of the general criminal conspiracy statute[72] to prosecute conspiracies by electoral officers to falsify election results or stuff the ballot-box,[73] in spite of the repeal
of the corresponding prohibitions of conspiracy under the enforcement acts
and over objections by Justices Douglas and Black, which might sound
strangely strict to readers of their reapportionment opinions: "I would leave
to Congress any extension of federal control over elections."[74]

In 1900 the Court indicated that it was willing to permit damages actions
against voting officials for refusing to count votes in federal elections,[75] but
it declined to grant relief by injunction, writ of mandamus, or award of dam-

ages in two suits against Alabama state officials for willful failure to register the black plaintiff.[76] Justice Holmes's reasoning denying the injunction was at least straightforward: he doubted the competence of courts to decide voters' qualifications individually or to enforce them once decided.[77] Justice Day in the other case was somewhat more circuitous, dismissing the black plaintiff's action for mandamus and damages as disposable under an "independent" point of state law: even assuming (the state court had said) that the statute creating the voting board was unconstitutional for racial discrimination, then "there would be no board" to sue, and plaintiff's action could not possibly lie against a nonexistent body. Justice Day concluded, "We do not perceive how this decision involved the adjudication of a right claimed under the Federal Constitution."[78]

The Supreme Court seemed only too anxious to embrace the state court's sleight of hand and even refine it with some quick technical work of its own. The state court had defined the issues to preclude the plaintiff from having any cause of action: if the electoral board was constitutional, the plaintiff had nothing to complain about; if unconstitutional, it did not exist, hence could not be sued. The Supreme Court, without saying so, implied a preclusive logic of its own: if the board's action was authorized by state law, then it was state action and the plaintiff had a case under the Fourteenth or Fifteenth Amendments, but he could not sue the state because the Eleventh Amendment forbids suits by individuals against states. If, on the other hand, the board's action was not authorized by state law, then the plaintiff could sue the board members as individuals but would have had no case against them because the Fourteenth and Fifteenth Amendments do not apply to private action. Such arguments sound cramped and hypocritical to modern ears, for the net of them is that individuals could not enforce the Fourteenth or Fifteenth Amendments, either against other individuals or against states; however, the Court's reasoning did reflect genuine technical uncertainties which it may have been unwilling to face on the black rights issue (which was out of favor by the turn of the century) nor on the as yet uncertain authority of the Fourteenth or Fifteenth Amendments as applied to individuals. The Court had not arrived at any way of dealing with an unconstitutional statute more sophisticated than to hold it "in legal contemplation, as inoperative as though it had never been passed";[79] moreover, it was four years away from circumventing the Eleventh Amendment by allowing individuals to sue state officials for unconstitutional acts under color of state authority, and it chose for that technical breakthrough a case based on the commerce clause rather than the Fourteenth or Fifteenth Amendments.[80]

"Legal" Disfranchisement of the Black

While these questions were being argued, southern politics had undergone a transformation which rendered the enforcement acts of secondary importance in protecting the voting rights of blacks or anyone else. The Civil War and Reconstruction had destroyed the two-party competition which had been the major catalyst of voting reforms before the war, though they had not destroyed the political differences between upcountry and plantation whites. These groups united under the aegis of the Democratic party to overthrow the Republicans, subdue the blacks, and end Reconstruction, all three of which aims had been accomplished by 1877. Southerners then had to face the task of settling the traditional regional differences without the traditional two-party mechanisms and without yielding to the blacks the balance of power between the old factions. The whites had three alternatives: to institutionalize the dominion of one of the regions, to form a new party to express regional differences, or to establish some kind of new institution like primary elections to settle regional differences, or to establish some kind of new institution like primary elections to settle regional differences without interparty competition. Southern politics today range between the first and third alternatives because the second alternative, formation of a new party, foundered under the threat of giving the blacks the balance of power.

The traditional sectional rivalries first asserted themselves in the form of the Populist party, which pressed hard to remedy the grievances of upcountry farmers, captured many counties throughout the South, and even succeeded—briefly, with the help of black votes and the Republicans—in capturing control of North Carolina.[81] In the heat of battle the Populists had shown themselves willing to bid for black support, and the strong showing of the Populists in the mid-1890's threatened to undo the South's hard-won victory over Reconstruction. In every case, by appropriating the Populist's programs, or by fraud, bribery, or coercion, the Democrats managed to put down the Populists, whose resources were too lean to sustain their counterefforts. By 1898 the Populist party was in ruins, and its upcountry backers were out of power in every southern state but South Carolina and Georgia, where they had seized control of the Democratic party.

Everywhere the Democrats won, a new species of reformer appeared, calling for measures to undo the awkward centralization tried in many states after 1876 to keep Black Belt counties from electing black sheriffs, and especially to settle the unstable and tumultuous electorate which seemed to breed savage rivalry among the whites, plainly fostered fraud and coercion at election time,[82] and threatened to throw power into the hands of the blacks. Surely a more manageable electorate would be less disruptive to everyone's peace and quiet than the unbridled, unpredictable factions of the 1880's and 1890's. Mississippi, in her constitutional convention of 1890, adopted Jim Crow voting laws to take the blacks and agrarians in hand in an orderly and legal fashion without contravening the Fifteenth Amendment. The new laws featured a two-year residency requirement, a poll tax, a registration requirement, disqualification for certain crimes, and a literacy-or-understanding test which fell naturally harder on blacks than whites and gave electoral officials discretion broad enough to admit most whites while rejecting most blacks. A Mississippian proudly announced: "Every provision in the Mississippi Constitution applies equally, and without any discrimination whatever, to both the white and the Negro races. Any assumption, therefore, that the purpose of the framers of the Constitution was ulterior, and dishonest, is gratuitous and cannot be sustained."[83]

The other southern states followed Mississippi's lead with reformist zeal, though some of the reformers, like Virginia's Carter Glass, entertained a somewhat bolder view of the purpose of the reforms than that professed by the Mississippi pioneers: "Discrimination! [Glass roared] Why that is exactly what we propose; that exactly is why this convention was elected, to discriminate to the very extremity of permissible action under the limitations of the Federal Constitution with the view to the elimination of every Negro who can be got rid of, legally, without materially impairing the white electorate."[84] South Carolina followed suit in 1895; Lousiana in 1898; North Carolina in 1900; Alabama in 1901; Virginia in 1902; Georgia in 1908.[85] Voting officials demonstrated by their reports to party officials their determination to secure a more literate electorate: "All right will sirtunly do my best to get the Dem voters to register & vita versa I am one of the registrars they seems to be verry little interest taken in the registrations but I think they are awakening to the necesity prety fast There wont be no negro registered that aint entitled to You bet."[86] Plantation whites hailed the new franchise restrictions as a triumph of statesmanship. The *Richmond Times* announced: "At the hour of noon today the dark cloud will be lifted, and peace and sunshine will come to regenerated Anglo-Saxon people as a result of the organic law made with its own hands."[87] Nevertheless, the reforms fell far short of expressing a unanimity of white opinion. Upcountry whites attacked them as a Bourbon scheme to break their power, along with that of the blacks. Prior to its final passage, disfranchisement was rejected in Virginia, Louisiana, and Alabama, with the strongest opposition coming from upcountry counties with the least blacks.[88] Only in Louisiana did the disfranchisement conventions get more than 61 percent of the votes, and the Virginia politicians who lifted the dark cloud were careful not to submit their work to a popular vote. In short, the antidemocratic reforms of the turn-of-the-century South were not less rooted in the reformers' political interests than the democratic reforms that had gone before. Interest, not ideology, was the guiding light.

What had become in the meantime of the northern liberals, the abolitionists, the radical Republicans, the quondam defenders of black rights? What of the national conscience embodied and enshrined in the Supreme Court? In truth, the Republicans had already abandoned their long-term hopes for the party in the South when they settled for a Fifteenth Amendment which left the states in control of the franchise. Cutting prosecutions under the enforcement acts in 1874, pulling out the army in 1877, and repealing major sections of the enforcements acts in 1894 represented further steps away from national concern with black rights. The nation had had its fill to trying to civilize the South; it had become more important to civilize the railroads and pacify the farmers, and by the 1890's the need of civilizing the natives of the Caribbean and Pacific Oceans called forth the rhetoric of the white man's burden, a rhetoric ill suited to rekindle national enthusiasm for black representation. The Spanish-American War and the acquisition of Pacific territories brought under United States jurisdiction some eight million people described by the *Nation* as "a varied assortment of inferior races which, of course, could not be allowed to vote."[89]

It is well known that Americans are a people of principle, though the principles may vary according to the needs of the moment. Spokesmen of the National Mission called in 1900, as they have many times since, for a domestic view of civil rights consistent with what we are trying to get across abroad— but in those days we were trying to get across the necessity for responsible administration of colored people by white people, and intellectual leaders in the North found fresh attraction (as they have many times since) in southern white doctrines. "If the stronger and cleverer race," asked the *Atlantic Monthly*, "is free to impose its will upon 'new-caught, sullen peoples' on the other side of the globe, why not in South Carolina and Mississippi?"[90] Had not Josiah Strong spoken a universal truth fifteen years before? "If I read not amiss, this powerful [Anglo-Saxon] race will move down upon Mexico, down upon Central and South America, out upon the islands of the sea, over upon Africa and beyond. And can any one doubt that the results of this competition will be the 'survival of the fittest?' "[91] With men like Strong, Alfred Thayer Mahan, John W. Burgess of Columbia University, and Senator Albert Beveridge of Indiana speaking for the mission of the race, it was hardly to be wondered that the *New York Times* found that "Northern men . . . no longer denounce the suppression of the black vote [in the South] as it used to be denounced in the reconstruction days. The necessity of it under the supreme law of self-preservation is candidly recognized."[92]

Southern politicians were not slow to see that racism in the North cleared the way for racist policies in the South. The two Senators from South Carolina, Pitchfork Ben Tillman and John J. McLaurin, declared that "The North has a bloody shirt of its own" and thanked Senator Hoar of Massachusetts for his "complete announcement of the divine right of the Caucasian to govern the inferior races," which "most amply vindicated the South." Hilary A. Herbert, supporting black disfranchisement in Alabama, noted that "we have now the sympathy of thoughtful men in the North to an extent that never before existed."[93]

The Supreme Court adhered to the national preference for letting the South segregate and disfranchise its blacks. While the Court had been willing to intervene to protect black rights in cases involving electoral crimes by state officials in federal elections,[94] and in cases where blacks were barred from jury panels,[95] it never wavered in defending segregation from legal attacks[96] it strictly limited the coverage of the enforcement acts, and it confined its constitutional objections to the Jim Crow voting laws to the permanent grandfather clause, leaving the main elements of disfranchisement untouched.[97]

The one exception to the Court's policy of nonintervention in southern disfranchisement is *Guinn v. United States,*[98] where the Court struck down a grandfather clause exempting persons who could vote in 1867 (that is, whites) and their descendants from a literacy requirement, leaving the full weight of the test to fall on nonwhites alone. The Court, having by 1915 lost all but two of the justices who declined to intervene against the literacy test itself from 1898 to 1904, was willing to recognize the racial inspiration of the grandfather clause but not to reconsider its earlier refusal to interfere with the Jim Crow voting laws. *Guinn v. United States* had small bearing on who got to vote in the South, since it applied only to Oklahoma and there only to the grandfather clause, but it is a milestone in the history of the Court's intervention in voting questions because it signaled, for the first time in a voting case, the Court's willingness to look through nondiscriminatory form to discriminatory substance.[99] The Court's strong stand on principle[100] at least marked a limit to its tolerance of racialism, and its willingness to discard its cramped prior interpretations of the Fifteenth Amendment and adopt the freer, modern mode of thought which brushes aside words and pierces through to facts, made *Guinn v. United States* the first really modern voting rights decision.[101] Broad, fact-oriented constitutional construction has been the life blood of voting rights decisions ever since; it is nowhere better distilled than in the words of Justice Frankfurter: "The [Fifteenth] Amendment nullifies sophisticated as well as simple-minded modes of discrimination."[102]

The *Guinn* case foreshadowed later cases in one other respect: the Court had access to law review articles testing the constitutional ground it would have to traverse. Law reviews were then barely out of their infancy, and the reader would search in vain for such landmarks for intervention as Anthony Lewis's "Legislative Reapportionment and the Federal Courts."[103] Nevertheless, a juridical lead for the Court's action was available in Julien C. Monnet's *Harvard Law Review* essay, "The Latest Phase of Negro Disfranchisement."[104] Monnet, an Oklahoman, was no friend of the Fifteenth Amendment. He entertained some doubts as to the validity of its passage and felt that its full enforcement would be a national calamity; however, he did feel that it had been violated by the grandfather clause.[105] The Court made no reference to Monnet's work, though it did follow his reasoning about the meaning of the Fifteenth Amendment. It rejected without discussion the contention of Monnet and Arthur Machen that the Amendment was itself void.[106]

White Primaries

The Jim Crow voting laws were less important for blocking black votes than the white primary and one-party rule. Recorded black disfranchisement in half the southern states did not run much above ten percent of blacks registered; actual disfranchisement for all southern blacks was higher than the recorded ten percent, but was still probably less than a third.[107] Although the percentage of blacks registered dropped from levels of 40 to 50 percent in Louisiana and Mississippi in the 1890's to less than 5 percent by the 1940's,[108] statements like Burke Marshall's that black nonvoting results "almost exclusively from racial discrimination by state officials and from fear among Blacks engendered by the attitudes and actions of white persons"[109] are misleading when applied to other states than the Cotton States. One-party government, isolated from national issues and less evocative of local issues than northern party systems, cut everyone's incentive to vote, black and white alike.[110] It is worth remembering that, if 95 percent of blacks in Virginia did not vote in primaries from 1920 to 1940, neither did 85 percent of the whites.[111] V. O. Key's analysis of voter turnout for general and primary elections for governor in Texas and Georgia from the 1880's to the 1940's shows the weakness of generalities like Burke Marshall's: total turnout in Texas plummeted from over 80 percent at the high tide of the Populist challenge in 1886 to less than 40 percent in 1902—before either the poll tax or the white primary laws were passed.[112] Georgia and other southern states followed a similar pattern, with a precipitous drop in turnout following the rout of the Populist and Republican parties in the 1890's. Like the Jim Crow voting laws, the white primary did not of itself defeat the Republicans and Populists, did not turn the tide against the blacks and upcountry whites, but consolidated a victory already won. The South's low voter turnout, which came into existence in some states before white primaries and Jim Crow voting laws, seems to derive more from the collapse of opposition parties than from laws to disenfranchise blacks.

Even if they were sometimes secondary in creating the political pattern of the twentieth-century South, the Jim Crow laws and especially the white primaries were of great importance in maintaining the status quo for the late 1890's, and the Supreme Court's thirty-year assault on white primaries probably worked a greater overall change in the political structure of the states affected than any of its other interventions, including reapportionment. Primary elections were something new in state politics; nationally they reflected the same progressive motives—impatience with bossism, party oligarchy, and undue influence from big business and immigrant minority groups—which led to other direct government reforms at the same time. The first two decades of the twentieth century saw a rash of such reforms—primary elections, direct elections of senators, initiative, referendum, recall, and woman suffrage—all reflecting Progressivism's aspiration to wipe out corruption with more direct representation of the people, as temperance laws and immigration restrictions reflected its less tolerant means to the same end. In the South, however, there was a special need of primary elections in the Democratic party to fill the function of a general election where the general election could return only the Democratic nominee.

Since blacks from their first enfranchisement had been Republicans, and the Democrats identified with white man's government, it went without saying that Democratic primaries would be white primaries; but as it became apparent that victory in the Democratic primary was tantamount to victory in the general elections, it became necessary to specify by state or local party rules, or by state legislation, that the primary was to be limited to whites. Paul Lewinson by 1930 found blacks barred from the primary by state party rule throughout the South except in a few counties in Florida and North Carolina, and in most of Tennessee. The Virginia party rule excluding blacks had been nullified by decision of a lower federal court.[113]

The Supreme Court's first brush with primaries was not a white primary case but a prosecution under the Corrupt Practices Act of 1910, which limited the expenditures of congressional candidates. The defendant, Senator Truman Newberry of Michigan, had spent more than the authorized amount in the primary election to win the Republican nomination from Henry Ford. The Supreme Court split 4-4 on Newberry's contention that a primary election was not an election within the meaning of Article I, section 4 because primary elections did not exist at the time that article was drafted; however the deciding vote reversed Newberry's conviction on a different point, leaving the question whether Article I, section 4 applied to primaries still in doubt.[114]

The Court invalidated white primary laws in its next two cases, *Nixon v. Herndon* and *Nixon v. Condon*,[115] but it again declined to say whether the voting rights provisions of the Constitution applied to primary elections. In these cases Dr. L. A. Nixon, an El Paso black, had attacked Texas statutes respectively barring blacks and letting the parties bar blacks from voting in Texas primaries. Although both counsel argued the Fifteenth Amendment,[116] Justice Holmes (speaking for a unanimous Court) confined his brisk opinion to the equal protection clause of the Fourteenth: "We find it unnecessary to consider the Fifteenth Amendment, because it seems to us hard to imagine a more direct and obvious infringement of the Fourteenth."[117] Holmes's reliance on the equal protection clause had some tactical advantages: it gave Dr. Nixon what he wanted, in the immediate litigation, without backing the Texans into a corner by threatening to abolish the white primary. It also avoided the awkward constitutional task of deciding whether a primary was an "election" within the meaning of the Fifteenth Amendment. On the other hand, it also avoided the more difficult task of supporting its own holding in the light of the text and intent of the equal protection clause, as neither of the parties to the case had any interest in arguing against the use of the clause, and there was no John Marshall Harlan on the Court to complain about lax constitutional workmanship.

Holmes's opinion in *Nixon v. Herndon* illustrates the strength and the danger of the proto-Guardian mode of thought pioneered in the grandfather clause case. Holmes was quick enough to recognize that the Texans were denying the substance of a voting right, while granting it in form by letting the blacks vote in the rubber-stamp general elections—but he was perhaps deliberately careless of the long-run consequences of his decision in two ways. He chose a weak constitutional foundation, and he looked through form to substance only so far as was administratively convenient. Convenience apart, he would have done better on both grounds to base Nixon's voting right on the Fifteenth Amendment instead of on the equal protection clause. Section one of the Fourteenth Amendment was not addressed to voting rights, as the Court had long since held in *Minor v. Happersett*,[118] and Holmes's reliance on it seems arbitrary and wrong unless one reads him to say that the right to vote in primaries is neither the "right to vote" pre-empted by the Fifteenth Amendment nor the "right to vote" at specified state and federal elections pre-empted by section two of the Fourteenth Amendment. Such an argument would be tenable, though strained, because primaries were not known to the framers and ratifiers of the Fourteenth and Fifteenth Amendments, but neither Holmes nor Cardozo, who wrote for a 5-4 majority in *Nixon v. Condon*, chose to wrestle with the problem of finding firm support in the equal protection clause for what looked like a voting rights case. Whether the omission was from inadvertence or prudence, or both, is not clear.

In any case, nobody got very excited about the *Nixon* cases, even in the South. Such interest as there was tended to focus on technical issues raised by the two cases. Texas Governor Dan Moody recognized that modest legislative adjustments would be needed to keep blacks out, but he saw no fundamental threat to the white primary. "Some legislation," he allowed, "will be necessary to protect the ballot and give that guarantee of good government which the voided statute was designed to offer."[119] *New York Times* coverage of both cases was noncommittal,[120] perhaps reflecting a continuance of the *Times*'s historical moderate Whig position, but no doubt also reflecting a neglect of northern moderates in those days to regard the white primary as inherently scandalous. Justice Holmes had shrugged off his own narrowly based decision for offering little real help to the blacks. He was reported to have said, in a wry aside after delivering his opinion, "I know that our good brethren, the Negroes of Texas, will now rejoice that they possess at the primary the rights which they heretofore have enjoyed at the general election."[121]

The law reviews dispatched the *Nixon* cases in brief, post-decision casenotes, sniffing at the narrow Fourteenth-Amendment holdings, wondering why the Court dodged the question raised in *Newberry v. United States* of whether the Constitution could govern primary elections, and noting that the Texas whites could easily circumvent the Court's restraints. The Court, observed the *Michigan Law Review*, "seems to be arguing for the discriminatory effect of the statute rather than the right of Negroes to vote in primaries."[122] The *Yale Law Journal* criticized the Court for "failing to take account of the realities of Texas politics" and leaving the Texans' way clear to exclude blacks by repealing all state laws pertaining to primary elections and leaving the task of exclusion to the party.[123] Three weeks after *Nixon v. Condon* was decided, the Texans followed just this strategy.

As the law reviews had noted, any trust the Court may have had in the Fourteenth Amendment to breach the white primary was misplaced. The Court's focus on "law" failed it in the mid-thirties when Texas revoked all its laws about qualifications to vote in primaries and left the question to the state party convention. Party officials continued to exclude blacks from the primaries, but the Court, by unanimous vote in *Grovey v. Townsend*,[124] forbore to intervene since it could find no state action, no state laws whose equal protection could be denied. Once again, the Court's willingness to tolerate white primaries seemed in line with the "public," as represented by those who followed the news and editorial positions of the *New York Times*. This public by 1935 was already in a furor over Franklin Roosevelt's economic policies and a few early civil rights causes like the Scottsboro cases, but it was still blasé about white primaries. The *Times*, which had reported *Nixon v. Herndon* on page one and *Nixon v. Condon* on page two, reported *Grovey v. Townsend* on page fifteen and noted equivocally that, while "better citizenship would be promoted by educating the Negro in the responsibilities of government," granting the vote would "afford opportunities for illiterate bloc voting."[125] The law reviews were only slightly less bland. They again issued cursory casenotes, if anything less committal than the ones for the *Nixon* cases, mildly chiding the Court for not giving the Fifteenth Amendment its due. The *Michigan Law Review* went so far as to predict that "the last chapter on this story has not yet been written," but not much farther.[126] None of the casenotes aspired even to the modest guiding role, say, of Monnet's work and Machen's in the teens, far less that of the mightly legal scenarios of the Warren era. Were law review editors less activist in those days than since? Or were they, like the rest of the country outside the South, more interested in other things than white primaries?

Like questions could be raised in regard to the Court itself. Why did liberal justices like Cardozo, Brandeis, and Stone join in the unanimous decision? Did they want to spare Roosevelt the threat of a southern revolt in the 1936 campaign? Had they made a deal with the conservatives to join in another unanimous landmark opinion handed down the same day? The Court seemed to be as united in striking down the white jury in the second Scottsboro case[127] as it was in averting its eyes from the white primary in *Grovey v. Townsend*. For the liberal justices the complex problems of constitutional interpretation and the lack of national interest in white primaries may have outweighed their interest in fighting one more losing battle in a Court already badly polarized.

Whatever the reasons for the justices' decision, *Grovey v. Townsend* was a serious setback for the Texas blacks. It was also a setback for the Supreme Court, which had temporarily abandoned its modern mode of interpretation and conceded to form a victory over substance, surrendering (in contrast to its previous refusals to intervene in voting disputes) ground it had already won. Texas blacks were still disfranchised in the one election that counted, and for six years it seemed that the "private" discrimination of the Democratic party was too sophisticated for the Court to nullify.

The six years, however, spanned the "Court revolution" of 1937, the Court's "switch in time" to forestall being packed by Roosevelt, a cease-fire in its war on economic regulation, accompanied by mothballing of juridical weapons like dual federalism, economic due process, and commerce power broad enough to block state economic regulation but too narrow to permit federal regulation. Crucial to the switch was Justice Owen Roberts's defection to the liberal wing of the Court, which converted the Court's 5-4 majority against economic regulation into a 5-4 majority permitting it. Since 1937 the Court has tended to give civil rights the same special protection it once gave business; voting rights shared this protection, and Justice Roberts played an important, though apparently unintended, part in this changeover, too.

The Court revolution was only one manifestation of the great transformation taking place in Court and country between *Grovey v. Townsend* and its reversal in *Smith v. Allwright*. The centralizing, managerial mystique of the Guardian Ethic was no longer just a gleam in Roosevelt's staffers' eyes; it had been hammered into the constitutional structure of the country to fight the Depression and then to fight the Axis powers. Roosevelt's college professors stayed on to manage one crisis after another, though it would be decades before the Kennedy School would coin and propagate the term *crisis management*. The Court blossomed with seven new liberal Roosevelt appointees. The war called for fresh feats of mobilization and participation.

The solvent effect of war on franchise limitations has been mentioned many times in this and the last chapter. Religious and property qualifications had dissolved in the wake of the Revolution and the War of 1812; the black vote (such as it was) had been a product of the Civil War; women suffrage had triumphed with the help of World War I. World War II proved no exception to this pattern. Voting rights, which had been a page-fifteen item in 1935, were all over the front page by 1944. A half-dozen major voting rights issues erupted between 1941 and 1945, reflecting the concern of any wartime democracy to balance the needs of national security with the needs of representative government, but also reflecting some special factors which the country had not seen since the Civil War, and then only in embryonic form. World War II was a long war spanning two elections. It involved an unprecedented mobilization of 12 million men, with improved communications that made overseas voting technically feasible. It also saw an unprecedented influence in sectors of the public that accepted and even demanded more national management. War-born voting rights issues included questions of whether elections would be held at all,[128] whether to abolish poll taxes,[129] presidential nomination conventions,[130] and white primaries,[131] and whether to require a direct, mandatory, presidential primary,[132] with eighteen-year-olds to vote,[133] if need be, under compulsion.[134] These questions flourished in the light of public attention generated by the biggest issue of them all: the soldier vote question.

The soldier vote issue had lain dormant in prior wartime elections since the Civil War, but it became one of the main bones of contention in the otherwise issue-poor elections of 1944. In 1942, with 5.7 million citizen soldiers under arms, Congress had passed P.L. 712, a limited soldier vote act which provided for the army and navy to distribute state-prepared ballots for federal offices. The act suspended poll tax and registration requirements for the federal ballot. P.L. 712 had little effect on the 1942 elections. Despite the triumphs of communications technology which made the soldier vote possible, only one half of one percent of the troops voted. Commentators saw the low turnout as fresh evidence that the old federalism would not work and should be replaced by national administration. The states had failed to standardize their absentee balloting procedures, weakening the war effort by burdening the services with the inconvenient task of handling forty-eight different kinds of ballots under forty-eight different kinds of state law. Besides the normal diversity in poll taxes, literacy, and residence requirements, some of the states had no provisions for absentee ballots. Those that did required the voter's timely initiative in applying for the ballot. Some states had September primaries, which made it difficult to get the ballots to the troops in time for the general elections. The *New York Times*, which had been blasé about organized disfranchisement of blacks in the 1920's and 1930's, was outraged at the disorganization which impeded the soldier vote in 1944. It demanded standardized federal administration to eliminate "48 kinds of confusion," concurrently noting that the poll tax was "an evil which must be dealt with sooner or later . . . The more nearly our citizenship turns in a 100 percent vote," it proclaimed, foreshadowing the total-mobilization concept of representation of the 1960's, "the better entitled we are to call ourselves a self-governing democracy."[135]

Roosevelt was not oblivious to the infringement of the Guardian Ethic, or to threats from southern politicans and northern black leaders[136] that they would bolt his coalition, or to polls that indicated he would get 61 percent of the service vote. By January 1944 his supporters had introduced a bill calling for federal control of the soldier vote. The bill was bitterly contested and eventually watered down by strong southern and Republican opposition—but not without shots fired by Roosevelt on its behalf. "Our men," he wrote, "cannot understand why the fact that they are fighting should disqualify them from voting."[137] The soldier vote question was contested all winter in Congress and then debated in the states almost till election time, the states-rights faction having prevailed in Congress. The *New York Times* Index, which registered only 18 items on the soldier vote in 1942, listed 400 items in 1944, more than one a day, including endorsements by the CIO Political Action Committee, the United Auto Workers, the United Steel Workers, the National Federation of Temple Sisterhoods, the Aluminum Workers of America, the National Negro Council, the NAACP, the Negro Newspaper Publishers Association, and Professor Kenneth Colegrove, who was shortly to become famous for bringing the landmark reapportionment suit, *Colegrove v. Green.*[138]

Of the many voting rights issues that boiled up along with the soldier-vote debate, the one of greatest lasting significance was the reconsideration of the white primary by the Supreme Court. The white primary per se had not attracted much separate public attention, and even less attention from the political branches, since neither party stood to gain by a battle over the primaries. However, the Court (with the help of powerful briefs by Herbert Wechsler, and later Thurgood Marshall and William Hastie, plus the initial concurrence of both voting survivors of the *Grovey* Court) had been quietly laying a foundation for intervention. In the *United States v. Classic,*[139] the Court had to consider a federal criminal prosecution for tampering with the returns in a Louisiana congressional primary. No question of racial exclusion was raised; Classic was, in fact, an overzealous member of a New-Orleans-based anti-Huey Long reform group; he had been convicted of falsifying election returns. The prosecution, under a general federal conspiracy law forbidding conspiring "to injure, oppress, threaten or intimidate any citizen in the free exercise or enjoyment of any right or privilege secured to him by the Constitution" raised the question of whether the right to vote in a primary was secured by the Constitution.[140]

The landmark *Classic* case was an uncommonly rich brew of influences and doctrines. The original prosecution had been brought by the new Civil Rights section of the Justice Department's criminal division, created by Attorney General Frank Murphy and then directed by Attorney General Robert Jackson, both later Supreme Court justices. It was argued before the Court by Justice Harlan Fiske Stone's former law clerk, Herbert Wechsler. Wechsler successfully persuaded his old chief, and a majority of the other justices, to sidestep *Grovey* and recur to first principles: that "if the machinery of choice involves two elections, primary and general, rather than one, the right to participate in the choice must include both steps."[141]

. The justices aligned themselves with an anomalous array of concurrences and dissents, presenting a curious spectacle of men and ideas in transition. By 1941 all but three of the justices who decided *Grovey v. Townsend* had been replaced by liberal Roosevelt appointees. The three were Charles Evans Hughes, Harlan Fiske Stone, and Owen Roberts. Chief Justice Hughes, on the eve of his own retirement, disqualified himself for having been counsel to Senator Newberry in *Newberry v. United States*. Owen Roberts, who had written the *Grovey* decision, joined a 5-3 majority in supporting principles which would shortly, over his bitter objections, be used to overthrow *Grovey*. Harlan Fiske Stone, the remaining *Grovey* survivor, without mentioning *Grovey*, wrote the Court's opinion in *United States v. Classic*, making several points which strongly suggested a rejection of *Grovey's* elevation of form over substance. Stone noted that the primary election was subject to comprehensive state regulation, that it was conducted at public expense, that it was the only stage in a one-party state where the voter had a significant choice, and that the primary election was therefore an "integral part of the procedure for choosing Representatives" subject to the provisions of Article I, section 4.[142] Stone's opinion was notable for its reliance on political science texts by Charles Merriam, Louise Overacker, and Paul Hasbrouck regarding the significance of primary elections.[143] Why Roberts went along with the decision is still unclear. He may have been oblivious to the "integral part of public choice" issue in the absence of a black rights claim, or he may have been confident that jurisdiction over primaries under Article I, section 4 (which is not expressly limited to state action) could be distinguished from jurisdiction over primaries under the Fourteenth or Fifteenth Amendments.

The point, however, was not lost on the law reviews, which noted with mild annoyance that the Court had neglected to discuss the question it raised regarding the status of primaries under the Fifteenth Amendment. "The rationale of the case," observed the *Columbia Law Review*, "goes farther than simply the right to vote and the right to choose. It gives the right to participate in the choice."[144] Nor was the question lost on the NAACP, whose two most celebrated lawyers, Thurgood Marshall and William Hastie, once again brought a Texas case before the Court, in hopes of using the logic of *United States v. Classic* to overturn *Grovey v. Townsend*. Their hopes were rewarded. In *Smith v. Allwright*,[145] over bitter objection from Roberts, the new justices (along with Stone, who changed his vote) settled the Court's score with the Texans by overruling *Grovey* on the basis of the "fusing by the Classic case of the primary and general elections into a single instrumentality for choice of officers," extended from Article I, section 4 to the Fifteenth Amendment. Justice Reed's reasoning was very much in the practical-minded tradition of the Court's boldest prior interventions;[146] he found state action in a battery of state laws applicable to primaries, and he found much firmer footing for attacking the white primary under the Fifteenth Amendment than Holmes and Cardozo had found under the Fourteenth:

The party takes its character as a state agency from the duties imposed upon it by state statutes; the duties do not become matters of private law because they are performed by a political party . . . If the state requires a certain electoral procedure, prescribes a general election ballot made up of party nominees so chosen and limits the choice of the electorate in general elections for state offices, practically speaking, to those whose names appear on such a ballot, it endorses, adopts and enforces the discrimination against Negroes . . . This is state action with the meaning of the Fifteenth Amendment.[147]

After twenty-three years of nibbling at the primary question (since *Newberry v. United States*) the Court had finally taken a firm bite, finding its proper authority in the Fifteenth Amendment. Would it have found the authority had it not found the will? The question is speculative, since the Court did find the will, but there is still some instruction to be had from asking where the will came from. *Times* Washington correspondent Arthur Krock, commenting on the overthrow of *Grovey v. Townsend*, thought he had the answer: "Neither he [Justice Reed] nor Justice Roberts mentioned the real reason for the overturn. It is that the common sacrifices of wartime have turned public opinion and the Court against previously sustained devices to exclude minorities."[148]

Southern states attempted in vain to preserve white primaries by dropping all laws related to primaries, requiring oaths of fealty to white supremacist party principles and splitting up primaries to isolate the black vote. Shortly after *Smith v. Allwright* was decided, Governor Olin D. Johnson of South Carolina asked his legislature to repeal all state primary laws, with this exhortation: "White supremacy will be maintained in our primaries. Let the chips fall where they may!"[149] The legislature obliged, and the voters in November 1944 expunged all reference to primaries from the state constitution. The Democratic state convention then required that membership in Democratic clubs (and eligibility to vote in Democratic primaries) be limited to white Democrats who could read, write, and interpret the state constitution. Barred from voting in the 1946 primary, a black plaintiff sued a county Democratic executive committee for damages; Federal District Judge J. Waties Waring of Charleston sustained the suit, branded the Democrats' attempted distinction between the situation before and after repeal as "pure sophistry," and rejected their contention that they were a private club not subject to federal control: "private clubs and business organizations do not vote and elect a President of the United States . . . Senators and . . . members of our national congress; and under the law of our land all citizens are entitled to a voice in such selections."[150]

Over objections from South Carolinians who agreed with Judge Waring that it was "time for South Carolina to rejoin the Union," the state Democratic convention devised a test oath: prospective Democrats had to swear to oppose communism, socialism, fascism, totalitarianism, nazism, F.E.P.C. laws, and racial integration. The test oath requirement, like a similar oath required by Arkansas in 1944,[151] had little but rhetorical significance. When some South Carolina Democratic party officials continued to drag their feet amid talk of impeaching Judge Waring, Waring threatened to throw them in jail and struck down the offending sections of the test oath.[152] Other states' efforts to keep white primaries were also bootless. Arkansas's attempt to hold separate primaries for federal and state offices proved too unwieldly to sustain; moreover it did not prevent blacks from voting—leading Key to dismiss it as "ceremonial."[153]

In 1953 the Supreme Court invalidated a curious form of double primary. In *Terry v. Adams*,[154] the Court had to deal with the Jaybird party, which had been excluding blacks from its own elections since 1889. Jaybird nominees almost always won in the Democratic primary and in the general elections as well. Though the specific logic of *Smith v. Allwright* (that a primary functioning as a final elections under substantial state regulation was a species of state action) did not strictly apply since the Jaybirds were not subject to state regulation, the Court acted on the strength of function plus membership to apply the Fifteenth Amendment. Once again looking through form to substance, the Court suggested three bases of state action, none of which really constituted an action by the state government, but all of which suggested that the Jaybird system amounted to the same thing as state action: the fact that the Jaybird primary was "the only effective part of the elective process";[155] that it was run by "those few in this small county who are politically active,"[156] that is, by the same people that run the general and primary elections; and because of "its role in the entire scheme to subvert the operation of the official primary."[157]

Thwarted in their defense of the white primary, white supremacists fell back on the Jim Crow voting laws in preference to the coercion, fraud, and bribery which preceded such laws, but there were signs that their ranks were thinning. Louisiana, Florida, and Georgia abolished their poll taxes. Of the eleven southern states only seven had enacted literacy tests in the first place,[158] and of the seven, four had substantially—but not completely— reduced discrimination in administering literacy tests.[159] Only in the Cotton States, Alabama, Mississippi, and Louisiana, was there still universal discrimination, and this was already under attack in the courts. A three-judge federal district court struck down Alabama's "Boswell Amendment" of 1946, which modified Alabama's existing literacy test by adding a requirement of "good character" and understanding of the "duties and obligations of good citizenship under a republican form of government" and eliminated a property alternative under which it had been difficult to exclude propertied blacks. "This amendment," said the court, "was intended to be, and is being used for the purpose of discriminating against applicants for the franchise on the basis of race or color."[160] The Supreme Court later used the same Fifteenth Amendment logic to invalidate literacy and good character tests in Louisiana and Mississippi;[161] it also struck down state poll taxes and property tests under the Fourteenth Amendment.[162]

Modern Civil Rights Acts

Starting in 1957 Congress joined in the assault on the Jim Crow voting laws with five civil rights acts and a poll tax amendment to the Constitution. The Twenty-Fourth Amendment barred poll taxes in federal elections. The Civil Rights Act of 1957 set up a Civil Rights Commission to protect against interference with constitutional rights by private persons; it empowered the attorney general to initiate civil actions in voting rights cases; and it gave federal courts jurisdiction in civil rights actions without the complainant's having exhausted all state remedies.[163] The Civil Rights Act of 1960 gave the attorney general power to examine voting records and provided for court-appointed referees to register voters in areas where the courts found discrimination.[164] Section 3 of the Civil Rights Act of 1964 provided for expediting voting rights trials; section 7 provided for keeping voting records and appointing federal voting registrars.[165] The Voting Rights Act of 1965, operative for five years in states and districts (mostly southern) where less than 50 percent of adult blacks were registered for the 1964 elections, authorized suspension of state tests and substitution of federal examiners to register blacks where discrimination was found; the act made a sixth-grade education in American schools presumptive evidence of literacy.[166] The Civil Rights Act of 1968 (P.L. 90-284, April 11, 1968) stiffened penalties for violation of previous civil rights laws. The voting rights amendments of 1970 extended the 1965 Voting Rights Act to 1975 and expanded its coverage to suspend literacy tests in all states during the period. It also called for more liberal residency requirements and the eighteen-year-old vote.[167] Of the Jim Crow voting laws, only the residence and criminal tests could retain even a claim to constitutional viability, and those were of little use for racial discrimination.[168] Literacy tests were still technically constitutional though suspended by the voting rights act amendments, but their usability for racial discrimination did not survive the 1960's.[169] Poll taxes had always been of tertiary importance in keeping people from the polls,[170] and they are now forbidden. Property alternatives had been permissive, not exclusive, had been almost universally abandoned by the 1960's, and, in any case, are no longer constitutionally viable.

Gomillion v. Lightfoot

Although the Supreme Court will no doubt always be deciding black voting rights cases, the major doctrinal developments of the black rights progression seem to have matured in the Jaybird case, *Terry v. Adams*. The last case in the progression, *Gomillion v. Lightfoot*,[171] looked backward to the white primary cases and forward to the reapportionment cases because it involved both racial and territorial abridgment of voting rights. *Gomillion* was the bridge between the Interpretive and Legislative periods, and, curiously, it was built by Felix Frankfurter, of all judges the least anxious to cross it. Frankfurter and an eight-man majority struck down an obvious racial gerrymander—a twenty-eight-sided redistricting of the city of Tuskegee, Alabama to exclude all but four or five of the city's 400 black voters while keeping every white voter—as a violation of the Fifteenth Amendment. Justice Whittaker, concurring, pointed out a weakness of the Fifteenth Amendment argument: as applied to the case, it seemed to guarantee not only the right to vote in the state, but also the right to vote in a particular district—a startling extension of the amendment from its words and prior application, and one which raised questions which Frankfurter had asserted in *Colegrove v. Green*[172] were beyond the competence of courts to decide.

Colegrove was an unsuccessful attack on unequal Illinois congressional districts; the plaintiff had demanded equal districts, hoping to get from the Court the same large reading of Article I, section 2 and the equal protection clause of the Fourteenth Amendment that the Court had adopted for the Fifteenth Amendment in *Smith v. Allwright*. Frankfurter had refused on two grounds: Article I, section 4 reserved the manner of elections of congressmen to the control of Congress and the states, not the Supreme Court, and a large reading of the equal protection clause, besides reversing the original understanding that it did not apply to voting rights, would raise problems too difficult for the court to settle with simple rules. If the Court were to "find" a constitutional right to equal representation, it would open the whole range of government to challenge in court—local, state, federal, legislative, executive, perhaps even judicial representation—exposing the most sensitive questions of balance of power to scrutiny by courts whose very existence presupposed that such issues had already been settled. Frankfurter raised the problem of "standards"—rules sophisticated enough to give real protection to the right claimed without treading on the toes of the political branches, but simple enough to guide the decisions of lower courts—and he did not believe that courts could make enforceable standards in an area as complex and politically sensitive as districting: "Courts ought not to enter this political thicket."[174]

Gomillion was a districting case no less than *Colegrove*, and it involved problems of standards which are inherent in any act of districting and undoubtedly led the Court not to intervene in its next racial gerrymandering case:[175] it is too hard to tell who wins and who loses from a gerrymander. Frankfurter attempted to distinguish *Colegrove* as involving involuntary nonracial disparities created by population shifts, while *Gomillion* was an act of intentional racial discrimination. Territorial divisions can and do discriminate, and the Court so held in *Baker v. Carr*, though it never came up with a sophisticated way of stopping territorial discrimination. *Gomillion* culminated the Court's progress from the simplest forms of electoral grievances, ballot-box stuffing, through the slightly more complicated realm of qualifications in the white primary, literacy test, and poll tax cases, and finally into the much more complicated realm of territorial grievances, thereby setting the stage for its breakthrough on reapportionment two years later.

The Black Rights Progression in Retrospect

Before going on to the reapportionment cases, it is important to consider what lessons might be drawn from the black rights progression. Why did the Court intervene as it did to protect black rights? Why did it wait so long? How effective was its intervention? What had it left undone? One must recur for answers to the intervention factors: will, authority, power, and technique. Authority has usually been the first question of scholars: could the Fourteenth and Fifteenth Amendments, or Article I, section 4 be extended to grant protection from fraud, intimidation, Jim Crow voting laws, white primaries, gerrymanders? All the argument over legislative history and original understanding has little changed what everyone knew in 1880: that the Fifteenth Amendment, though addressed mainly to enfranchising northern blacks, could be used to protect black voting rights anywhere; that section one of the Fourteenth Amendment had nothing to do with voting rights; and that both amendments applied to state action but probably not to most private action. The Court's major breakthroughs in the black rights progression—*Ex parte Siebold, Guinn v. United States*, and *United States v. Classic*—all involved federal congressional elections and permitted the Court to rely on Article I, section 4, which was not limited to controlling state action.

Though the basic elements of the Court's constitutional authority had not changed since the passing of the Fifteenth Amendment, the Court's pattern of intervention fluctuated considerably in response to questions of will and power. When Reconstruction lost favor in the North in the early 1870's, the Court was no more anxious than the attorney general to endure the opprobrium of imposing it on the South. Nor was it disposed to set itself against the combined racial doctrines of southern Democrats and McKinley Republicans from 1880 to 1915. It construed the enforcement acts as narrowly as it could and averted its eyes from the South's "legal" disfranchisement program embodied in the Jim Crow voting laws, with the single and late exception of outlawing one carelessly drafted grandfather clause after the fires of progressivism and reform had been lit for a dozen years.

Republicans and northern Democrats who had been fighting for initiative and referendum, direct elections of Senators, woman suffrage, and primary elections were not as closely wedded to the white man's burden doctrines as they had been in McKinley's time. Blacks fought in two world wars, bearing their own share of the burden, and whites throughout the nation drew from the Depression a different conclusion from that drawn by southern whites from the dislocations of the 1890's. The southern whites had found a scapegoat in enfranchised blacks, whom they blamed for the political and economic upheavals after Reconstruction; their solution was Jim Crow laws. By the 1930's there was very little action left that could have been taken to subdue blacks, and the whole nation sought its scapegoats in big business and Herbert Hoover and its remedy in Franklin Roosevelt and bigger government. Even the South turned to people like Huey Long, who was a Populist first and a racist second, in contrast to its earlier choice of people, like Pitchfork Ben Tillman of South Carolina, who had been a racist first and a Populist second.

The national retreat from racism, however, should not be mistaken for a national crusade against racism, in the Court or anywhere else. The new mood did find its way into the Supreme Court through the appointment of justices like Holmes, Brandeis, Stone, and Cardozo, yet even these men, pioneers of the Guardian Ethic, were stringently limited in their power, or disposition, to mobilize the Court effectively against voting rights discrimination. Fortunately for the civil rights movement, the Court's passivity was temporary. Roosevelt's reelection in 1936 and 1940, the Court revolution, the death or retirement of seven justices between 1937 and 1942, and a national concern with voting rights, kindled by the war, all helped bring about the first real breakthrough in re-establishing the protection of the Fifteenth Amendment. By the time of *Smith v. Allwright*, Roosevelt liberals, in the persons of Black, Frankfurter, Douglas, Murphy, and Jackson, dominated the Court, and the Court itself was incomparably more powerful than it had been after Reconstruction, both by the strengthening of the federal government relative to the states and by the strengthening of its own power relative to that of the other branches. The war surely limited the power of the Court in some race questions, like those involved in the Japanese internment cases,[179] but it strengthened the Court's hand immeasurably for intervening against white primaries because of national sympathy for the fighting man, including the black fighting man. It would be surprising if Roosevelt's appointees had not been disposed to help the blacks vote in primaries if a way could be found.

Such a way had been found long before in the grandfather clause case and preserved in the white primary cases. Despite its false start under the Fourteenth Amendment and the nine years sulking in its tent between *Grovey v. Townsend* and *Smith v. Allwright*, the Court had established a technique of constitutional interpretation—Holmes's technique of looking through words to the factual background that gives them meaning—which finished white primaries and would one day be used with a little fudging to finish unequal electoral districts as well.

In terms of their actual political impact, the white primaries cases are much the most important of the Court's interventions to protect voting rights. Black voting registrations tell the story: in 1940, 5 percent of voting-age blacks were registered in the South; *Smith v. Allwright* was decided in 1944; black registration by 1947 had risen to 12 percent despite efforts in Arkansas and the Deep South to evade the holding; by 1956, and still before any of the later civil rights acts, 25 percent of southern blacks were registered. By Warren's retirement in 1969, the figure had risen to 65 percent. Table 2 shows black registration in the South on a state-by-state basis, from 1940 to 1970.

Though the Jim Crow voting laws remained substantially unimpaired throughout and after the white primary cases, opening the primaries elicited a fivefold increase in black voters and forced the three diehard Cotton States, Alabama, Louisiana, and Mississippi, to fall back on the Jim Crow laws too blatantly for either Congress or the Court to tolerate. The five civil rights acts and a handful of federal court decisions quickly knocked out the discriminatory sections of the Jim Crow voting laws. It would be very hard to overrate the importance of *Smith v. Allwright* as a catalyst for subsequent civil rights action by the Court and Congress, for it was the first of many bold, fact-oriented, rights-conscious decisions, designed as much to educate and lead the public as to follow either the election returns or older understandings of the Constitution. Later landmark decisions of the modern Court—*Shelley v. Kraemer*, the school segregation cases, and the reapportionment cases, besides the poll tax and literacy test cases—bore the stamp of logic demonstrated in *Smith v. Allwright*, and the civil rights acts passed since 1957 reflected a concern with practical and sophisticated infringements of people's rights which Congress and the executive branch learned from the Court.

One might gain a better understanding of the importance of the Court's intervention against white primaries by speculating what might have happened if the Court had chosen not to intervene at all in black voting rights, or had attacked the Jim Crow voting laws without attacking the white primary, or had attacked the primary but left standing some instrumentality like the Jaybird party which could be used to serve the same discriminatory function as the white primary. It is a fair guess that the rest of the government would have been powerless to help the blacks except by appointing Justices who would attack white primaries as the Court has done in *Smith v. Allwright* and *Terry v. Adams*. Invalidating the Jim Crow voting laws would have been an empty victory if white primaries had been left standing, and neither party was well placed to attack white primaries—the Democrats for fear of splitting apart their own regional factions, the Republicans for fear that letting blacks vote in the Democratic primaries might bind them to the Democrats. One should remember that even Roosevelt was not so interested in black rights as to integrate the Army, his own command. He roared about the soldier vote but said nothing about the white primary. Truman neglected to integrate the schools in the District of Columbia. Eisenhower did take some steps to en-

Table 2. Estimated Percentage of Voting-Age Blacks Registered to Vote in the South, 1940–1970

State	1940	1947	1952	1956	1960	1964 (Nov.)	1966 (Oct.)	1970 (Summer)
Mississippi	a	1	4	5	6	7 (70)[b]	33 (63)	67.5 (86.9)
Alabama	a	1	5	11	14	23 (71)	51 (88)	64.0 (96.1)
South Carolina	a	13	20	27	—	39 (79)	51 (80)	57.3 (73.3)
Louisiana	a	2	25	31	31	32 (80)	47 (83)	61.8 (88.2)
Georgia	2	20	23	27	—	44 (75)	47 (77)	63.6 (89.6)
Arkansas	3	21	27	36	38	54 (72)	60 (70)	71.6 (80.3)
Florida	3	13	33	32	39	64 (84)	61 (80)	67.0 (94.2)
Virginia	5	11	16	19	23	46 (56)	47 (62)	60.7 (78.4)
Texas	9	17	31	37	30[c]	58 (53)	62 (53)	84.7 (73.7)
North Carolina	10	14	18	24	38	47 (93)	51 (82)	54.8 (79.6)
Tennessee	16	25	27	29	48[c]	69 (73)	72 (77)	76.5 (88.3)
Southwide	5	12	20	25	28	43 (73)	52 (70)	66.3 (83.3)

Sources: Data for 1940–1960: Testimony of James W. Prothro and Lewis Lipsitz, United States Commission on Civil Rights, *Hearings*, Jackson, Miss., Feb. 16–20, 1965 (Washington, D.C.: Government Printing Office, 1965), p. 243. Data for 1964, 1966, 1970: Estimates of the Voter Education Project of the Southern Regional Council, 24 *Congressional Quarterly Weekly Report* 2668 (28 Oct. 1966). 28 *Congressional Quarterly Weekly Report* 2952 (11 Dec. 1970).

[a]Less than 0.5 percent.

[b]Parentheses indicate percentage of voting age white registered.

[c]Incomplete data; the data for Tennessee are especially unreliable.

force school desegregation when he was driven to it by other people's initiative, but none of these presidents seem to have had the kind of concern with black rights that would have led them to undertake the heavy political risks of assaulting the white primary. John Kennedy was concerned about civil rights, but he was unable to get any of his civil rights legislation past Congress. Lyndon Johnson got the civil rights acts of 1964 and 1968 and the voting rights acts of 1965 past Congress, but even these were not independent of the judiciary because they presupposed a climate of opinion which was largely created by the Court's civil rights opinions.

Justice Holmes has told us that the life of the law is not logic but experience, but Holmes's own brand of logic, unleashed in the white primary cases, seems to have had a very full life of its own both in the Court's subsequent civil rights cases and in the attitudes of the public as expressed in Congress. This kind of logic is the essence of the modern Court's most revolutionary holdings, and it had in the hands of the Court a political leverage it could have had nowhere else. Though in retrospect it seems impossible that men like Frankfurter, Black, Douglas, Murphy, Jackson, and Stone could have decided not to intervene, even if they had not intervened it seems likely that the white primary and other instruments of racial discrimination would have yielded (if at all) not to the elected branches but to a later Court that changed its mind.

IV. Urbanism and the Equal Districts Progression:
From the Progressive Reformation to the Guardian Ethic

Scarcely any political question arises in the United States
that is not resolved, sooner or later, into a judicial question.
—Alexis de Tocqueville

The fundamental tendency of all bureaucratic thought is to
turn all problems of politics into problems of administration.
—Karl Mannheim

The Rise of the Cities

While the Court was struggling with the South over the black vote, the nation as a whole was changing from rural to urban. The change generated new
voting disputes and two successive new political ideologies. The first of these
was progressivism. It represented Yankee, Protestant America's desire to curb
big-city corruption and protect Yankee values by rationalizing city and state
electoral institutions. The second was the Guardian Ethic. It was also dedicated to rationalization, but on a national and administrative basis, not state/
local and electoral. Far from invoking to the old Yankee institutional mystique of the Progressives, the Guardians looked to a new and cosmopolitan
political order extending far beyond the bounds of the old national powers
and cleansed of old, interest-sensitive democratic impurities which even the
Progressives had been willing to tolerate. Both progressivism and the Guardian
Ethic found their way in due course into the Supreme Court's interpretation
of higher law.

Urban growth has been faster than rural in percentages since 1820, faster in
absolute growth since 1870. The growth of the cities reflected two social
factors of great political importance: mass immigration and mass organization. Immigrants by the millions flocked to factories in the cities; there they
were organized on a scale never known before, organized by financial and
manufacturing trusts, counterorganized by national labor unions and local
bosses. Politics, which had been highly regional since colonial times, were to

89

become more and more focused on class and economic interest groups, and the institutions set up in the 1820's and 1830's to settle regional antagonisms seemed unduly susceptible to pressure from the bosses and the trusts, and clumsy in their handling of labor unrest.

Progressivism

The Gilded Age (1865-1900) is remembered as the most corrupt in the nation's history. The growth of industry and finance after the Civil War made control of state and city governments a valuable prize for fortune hunters in and out of government. It was the era of the professional politician, the heyday of the boss. It was also probably the most intensely political era of an unusually political people. The Gilded Age saw the pinnacle of strength and discipline both in Congress and in the political parties. It saw the highest voting turnout in United States history and, in some respects, the strongest sense of popular participation in government.[1] No less than the new political groups which sought their favor, Congress and state and local legislative bodies were uniquely well organized, uniquely powerful, uniquely responsive to claims of interest. The modern observer may shrink from the corruption of the Gilded Age, but he must also marvel at its zestful spirit of participation and competition in the political arena, its approachable political leadership, and its ready accommodation of political demands. All of these seem somewhat remote in today's executive-judicial political universe, where the classical input institutions, legislature and parties, have fallen into a secondary role.

In any case, the flowering of Gilded-Age politics no doubt stimulated the professional study of politics, as evidenced by the founding of the American Academy of Political and Social Science in 1889 and the American Political Science Association in 1904. It also prompted the establishment of good government groups like the American Proportional Representation League, in 1893, the National Municipal League, founded in the early 1900's, and various state reform clubs. These professional and reform groups, largely city-based, were something new in politics. They wanted reform for its own sake, not for partisan advantages other than the reinforcement of their own claims, as enlightened reformers, to power. They were not conspicuously attached to either party. Their inspiration was proto-Guardian, managerial and principled, not result-oriented in the old sense. Like the later Guardians, they wanted formal, abstract justice, not concrete enhancement of their own power and convenience. They were at least vaguely associated with many of the most lofty aims of the Progressives—muckraking, trust-busting, conservation, and labor reform—and very directly involved with voting rights reforms. They called for every imaginable voting reform to fight corruption—compulsory voting,[2] the Australian ballot, proportional representation, corrupt practices acts, city councils and managers, initiative, referendum, and recall, primary elections (to replace party conventions), and direct election of senators.

These reforms, however, were implemented only where the not-so-partisan inspirational forces of progressivism coincided with the more partisan exec-utory forces of the same movement. These executory forces had a nativist, Protestant, Yankee, middle-class focus. They were aimed as much at protect-ing the old values against alien influences, as they were at establishing the abstract justice sought by the good government groups. Like their Democratic counterparts in the South, the Yankee Protestant majority in the North did not care for corruption and unrest, blamed the ambitions of cultural minori-ties for causing it, and called for reforms to protect the "native American" culture. Since the northern minority of immigrants and bosses was smaller but more powerful than the black minority in the South, northern reformers often found majoritarian measures more to their use than antimajoritarian ones. Instead of Protestant primaries and northern Jim Crow laws, they wanted direct government to prevent party bosses and interest groups from interfering with the will of their majority; they wanted woman suffrage to increase the strength of nativist votes. In a less egalitarian vein, but to the same end, they wanted limits on representation of the cities, literacy tests,[3] limits on immigration, and temperance laws.

If one could draw a self-interest scale for voting rights reforms, with arrant self-service at one pole and altruistic service of abstract ends of justice at the other, most of the progressive reforms would register toward the middle: more altruistic in inspiration than the Fourteenth and Fifteenth Amend-ments, but more self-serving than the Guardian reforms of the modern era. Alan P. Grimes outlined the self-interested side of progressive voting rights reforms by citing many examples of status-anxious Yankees voting concur-rently for pro-democratic and anti-democratic reforms whose common ground was not abstract justice but an apparent desire to curb the influence of urban ethnic minorities. For conservatives of the tradition of the Reverend Josiah Strong, a nineteenth-century enemy of Romanism, Mormonism, immi-gration, socialism, urbanization, and intemperance, and prophet of the civil-izing and Christianizing mission of the Anglo-Saxon race, Grimes argued, it was easier to swallow woman suffrage than to tolerate the continued rise of rum and Romanism.[4] Good-government altruism resulted in reforms only where it was reinforced by nativist self-interest. The heart of progressivism lay somewhere between the managerial axis of the good-government people and the status-anxious axis of the DAR, the WCTU, and the woman's suffrage organizations. Where the two axes coincided, reforms flourished. Where they did not coincide, reforms wilted.

From this rather conservative inspiration, from 1890 to 1920, flowed a freshet of organization and legislation, a Progressive reformation "to hold the nation to the ideals which won independence." Women played a special role in this reformation, being, as in most societies, carriers of the dominant cul-tural and status values and more conservative and religious than men.[5] In the Gilded Age and after, they organized with unprecedented vigor to protect public as well as family morality. The founding from 1890 to 1894 of the Colonial Dames, the Daughters of the American Revolution, the Daughters of 1812, and the Daughters of the Confederacy added to the moral force of the suffragist and temperance groups which existed already. Woman suffrage had started in Wyoming, where reformist elements in 1869 had tricked and cajoled the legislature into passing it to help repair the territory's national image as a barren way-station between better places for settling;[6] Utah adopted it in 1870 to double the Mormon vote and soften attacks in Congress on bigamy.[7] In other western states that lacked the special political motives of Wyoming and Utah, woman suffrage was repeatedly rejected in popular referenda[8] until after 1910, when it became identified with the national war on city power, ethnic minorities, and drink.[9] Bearing such banners, the suffragettes became an exceedingly powerful political force which had exacted some form of woman suffrage from twenty-nine states by the end of World War I.[10] Women's service to the nation in World War I added to their service in the war on urban corruption and won widespread sympathy for their cause, culminating in the passage of the Nineteenth Amendment in 1920.

The progressives also secured direct election of senators and Prohibition with the passage of the Seventeenth and Eighteenth Amendments in 1913 and 1919. Progressives and their precursors in Congress had been struggling for forty years to limit immigration, having barred criminals in 1875, idiots and paupers in 1882, Chinese in 1884, contract laborers in 1885, polygamists in 1891, and Japanese in 1907. Congress repeatedly passed literacy tests to stem the influx of immigrants from Asia and Southern and Eastern Europe; these were vetoed by Presidents Cleveland, Taft, and Wilson, passing only over Wilson's second veto in 1917 on a tide of anti-foreign war feeling.[11]

In the states the Progressives secured reforms for more direct government as a protection against the corrupt influence of interest groups and bosses and perhaps also as a reflection of the Protestant preference for more direct, less hierarchic links between individuals and authority. From 1903 to 1917 the party convention system of nomination in the states yielded almost universally to the direct primary system,[12] and from 1898 to 1914 more than twenty states adopted initiative, referendum, or recall.[13] However, the progressives' desire for direct, majoritarian government tended to evaporate when it came to giving full representation to city votes and ethnic minority votes. Western states that had been highly progressive in the matter of initiative, referendum, and recall, woman suffrage, and prohibition adopted literacy tests aimed at excluding Chinese and Japanese voters, and California, Idaho, Oregon, and Nevada banned native Chinese outright. Table 3 shows the concurrence of reforms involving woman suffrage, direct government, prohibition, and racial exclusion in the western states during the Progressive reformation. Urbanizing states across the country—California, Illinois, Michigan, New York, Ohio, and Pennsylvania—quietly abandoned the principle of equal ap-

Table 3. Progressive Reforms in Western States, 1869–1924

State	Woman Vote	Initiative, Referendum/ Recall	Prohi- bition	Literacy Test	Constitution Barred Chinese Vote
Wyo.	1869			1889[a]	
Colo.	1893	1910/1912	1914	1896[b]	
Ida.	1896	1912/1912	1915		1889
Utah	1870/1896[c]	1900	1917		
Wash.	1910	1912/1912	1914	1896[d]	
Calif.	1901	1911/1911		1894[d]	1879
Ore.	1912	/1908	1914	1924[d]	1914
Ariz.	1912	1911/1912	1914	1913[d]	
Mont.	1914		1916		
Nev.	1914	/1912			1880

Sources: Data for suffrage, literacy test, Chinese exclusion: Albert McCulloch, *Suffrage and Its Problems* (Baltimore: Warwick and York, 1929), pp. 57–58. Data for direct government and prohibition: Alan P. Grimes, *The Puritan Ethic and Woman Suffrage* (New York: Oxford University Press, 1966), pp. 115, 152.
[a]Read Constitution.
[b]May adopt by referendum after 1890.
[c]Federal government annulled woman suffrage in Utah while it was a territory.
[d]Read and write English.

portionment in their constitutions. Congress shortly followed suit, in practice if not in principle, by suspending its own reapportionment from 1910 to 1932.

Reapportionment is one of several reforms which progressivism passed by despite endorsement by intellectuals and good-government groups, others being protection of the black vote in the South, compulsory voting, and proportional representation (PR). None of these reforms had great popular appeal, least of all the kind of appeal that could be implemented through political parties; however, the continued and growing insistence of intellectuals on reapportionment and black rights led ultimately to their implementation by the Supreme Court. Compulsory voting and PR fell by the wayside because they lost their vogue with intellectuals. In 1891 it was possible for people like Frederick William Holls of New York to state as conventional wisdom in the *Annals of the American Academy of Political and Social Science* that "It is the well-to-do class, the refined and cultured gentlemen who shun . . . the polls," while the ignorant and vicious classes, "the men who regard a vote as property," flock to the polls.[14] Holls insured the doom of his plan by attacking the pillars of progressivism. He condemned rural polls as the chief seat of bribery, prohibition as "wrong and harmful," referenda as "sheer cowardice" by legislators who were supposed to "stand up manfully against public clamor."[15] Today it is conventional wisdom that the refined and cultured are more apt to vote than the ignorant and vicious, and the great turnout of normally stay-at-home extremist voters to support Hitler has dampened the intellectuals' enthusiasm for big turnouts.

PR had a more powerful appeal for intellectuals than compulsory voting, though it, too, was one of the many species of conventional wisdom that did not survive the 1930's. During the period of publication of the *Proportional Representation Review* (Chicago, 1893-1931), PR ranked with reapportionment as the intellectuals' palladium of free government and perhaps ahead of it, for PR was designed far more aptly than reapportionment to vindicate what Andrew Hacker, the Supreme Court, and most of the intellectual establishment insisted was the overriding issue, of representative policy and the Fundamental Principle of the Constitution: equal representation for equal numbers. If this were really so, we would have had PR long ago. PR bypasses the chronic complaints about the district system—gerrymandering and malapportionment—by representing every significant minority in proportion to its numbers. PR offered everybody an "effective" vote, gave candidates constituents whom they could represent "without straddling," represented majorities and minorities alike in proportion to their numbers, and killed gerrymanders, machines, and malapportionment.[16] Charles Beard spoke for many when he announced that "Co-operation is the great sign of the twentieth century . . . Proportional representation is the governmental instrument through which a co-operative democracy can realize its ideals and accomplish its purposes."[17]

The parties opposed PR because they stood to lose by any scheme to redistribute the votes; the Protestant majority mistrusted it as un-American and excessively focused on giving special representation to ethnic and religious minorities; ethnic and religious minorities entrenched in the existing political system saw no reason to change it; minorities outside the system had no leverage for changing it. It is not inconceivable that if the intellectuals had been able to hold out for another thirty years they might have gotten the Supreme Court to "find" that PR was the Fundamental Principle of the Constitution instead of equal districts, but even the intellectuals lost interest in PR after it was tried with disastrous consequences by Weimar Germany. PR encouraged schismatic, doctrinaire, ineffectual parties that were all too prone to represent "without straddling," willing enough to unite to block action but never willing to combine to take action—an unforgivable failure according to the Guardian Ethic, whose exponents quickly rallied to the standard of any Caesar who offered action where older institutions denied it. The rise and fall of the Fourth French Republic, which also tried PR, did little to revive its appeal. PR was tried in a few cities in the United States, notably Cincinnati and New York, and it has existed in highly diluted form in Illinois' cumulative voting system,[18] but, these minor exceptions apart, it was even more lacking in political appeal than in intellectual appeal. It was never a real alternative for intervention by the Supreme Court.

"Malapportionment" and the Guardians

After 1920, when progressivism had done its work toward making the country as safe and dry as laws could make it, reapportionment was the only one of the good-government schemes that had any political support, and its share of that was not sufficient to stem a long-term trend against equal districts. Progressivism had made substantial contributions to more direct and honest representation, and the Supreme Court had only to nod approval, as it did in cases like *Pacific States Tel. & Tel. Co. v. Oregon* (1912),[19] but the end of the Yankee Protestant majority which backed progressivism was in sight. The balance of political power was shifting to the cities, but the triumph of the cities was much less clear-cut than other triumphs, such as those of the North over the South or the southern Democrats over the Populists and Republicans, which had permitted the victor to consolidate his gains by changing the voting rules. Apportionment of representation in most states lagged behind population changes, to the growing outrage of intellectuals but seldom to the point of moving legislators to risk safe seats for equal districts.

In 1870 only one out of four persons lived in incorporated places with 2,500 or more inhabitants; by 1940 the ratio was three out of five; by 1960, seven out of ten. In 1900 there were 78 cities with more than 50,000 inhabitants; in 1960, 333; almost two-thirds (62.9 percent) of the population lived in such places and their suburban fringes. The influx to the cities far outstripped the states' capacity to reapportion themselves, even where their constitutions still required equal apportionment. For all its popularity with good-government groups, reapportionment was not the kind of reform legislators liked, even those whose constituencies were disadvantaged, because it threatened their tenure by reshuffling their constituencies. New constituencies entailed strange faces, unfamiliar issues, and a much greater prospect of return to private life. Moreover, serious attempts at reapportionment usually signaled a bloody, partisan war of all against all, endangering every man's seat as well as his peace of mind and diverting attention from more substantive demands of legislation. It is hardly to be wondered that before *Baker v. Carr*, most civilized legislators, including United States congressmen, confined their attention to redistricting to a diffident tinkering, save when an all-out power grab seemed advisable. In spite of federal apportionment acts which had required, at different times, that federal congressional districts be equal, contiguous, and compact, the requirements were never enforced and were subsequently dropped, with Supreme Court approval.[20] In many cases, the public matched and surpassed the legislatures in hostility to reapportionment, even in districts which stood to gain from it. Initiative propositions favoring urban voters in several urban states—Michigan, 1924, 1930, 1932, 1952; Colorado and Washington, 1962; California, 1926, 1928, 1948, 1960, 1962—were resoundingly defeated[21] amid grumblings by political scientists that the urban voters' actions "gave meager support for the dogma that man is a rational being" and that "citizens should be given the blessings of equality whether they want them or not."[22]

One can only speculate as to why it was so much more difficult to reapportion in the early twentieth century than it was in the early nineteenth. The public and legislative apathy of the later period about apportioning to match huge shifts of population to the cities contrasted sharply with the outrage of Jefferson's time at lesser shifts of population to the upcountry, perhaps because we retained Jefferson's notion that cities are cloacinae of human depravity, perhaps because we had less faith than he in legislatures' ability to undertake bold schemes on their own initiative, perhaps because legislatures had become more settled and routinized than they once were, or perhaps because twentieth-century population shifts were too big and too fast to permit of a legislative solution. The great reapportionments of the 1830's took as much as twenty-five years of hard political pressure to accomplish, and some states, such as Georgia, never reapportioned even then. Twenty-five years of wrangling would have been far too long to settle population shifts as rapid as those of this century.

For whatever reasons, although all but ten of the states had conducted some kind of redistricting between 1950 and *Baker v. Carr* (1962),[23] electoral districts by 1962 were considerably less proportional to population than they were in 1910. A study of the nation's 3,000-odd counties showed that the value of the big city vote dropped from .81 to .77 of the state average during the period. William J. Boyd's compendium on legislative apportionment[24] gave a state-by-state comparison of districts of extreme sizes with state averages. It also computed, by adding together the smallest districts until they represented a majority, the minimum percentage of population which could control the legislature. This method, pioneered by Manning Dauer, Robert Kelsay, and Thomas Dorr,[25] is more indicative of the overall

Table 4. Value of Vote for State Legislatures by Size of County, 1910, 1960, and 1962 (average statewide value of vote = 1)

Population of County	Value of Vote		
	1910	1960	1962
under 25,000	1.13	1.71	1.68
25,000–99,999	1.03	1.23	1.21
100,000–499,999	.91	.81	.83
500,000 and over	.81	.76	.77

Sources: Paul T. David and Ralph Eisenberg, *Devaluation of the Urban and Suburban Vote* (Charlottesville: Bureau of Public Administration, University of Virginia, 1961); Ralph Eisenberg, "Power of Rural Vote after Reapportionment," National Municipal League, *Reapportionment: A Year in Review* (New York, 1963), pp. 41 and 43.

equality of a state's districts than comparison of isolated extremes, for it averages out the eccentricities of geography, politics, and population distribution. These eccentricities can make a small number of variant districts in states otherwise equally apportioned (as with Massachusetts' allocation of representatives to the islands of Nantucket and Martha's Vineyard despite their small size) but with little prejudice to equal representation in the rest of the state. Boyd's compendium showed that in 1962 only five states—Massachusetts, New Hampshire, Oregon, West Virginia, and Wisconsin—had minimum majorities exceeding 40 percent in both houses. Only one state, Oregon, met the standard, 45 percent minimum majority selected by the APSA as the lowest limit of acceptability.

Perhaps the last word in sophisticated measurement of malapportionment was that of Glendon Schubert and Charles Press, who contributed an inverse coefficient of variations (ICV) to measure skewness and kurtosis of both houses in all state legislatures, followed with a joint variability scattergram of comparative House-Senate ICV scores. These permitted the assignment, with full accounting for bicameral integration, interstate comparability, political realism, and statistical adequacy, of "type II" apportionment scores.

Schubert and Press's original conclusions differed only in detail and vocabulary from what was generally understood from Boyd's figures: at the time of *Baker v. Carr*, Vermont was "unapportioned," Massachusetts, "well apportioned," Florida, "malapportioned," California and the United States as a whole, "misapportioned," and other states somewhere in between.[26]

The Myth of Barnyard Government

Schubert's adherence to political realism was too rigorous to permit him to inquire whether it made any difference whether a state was well apportioned or not, but other commentators were not so scrupulous. Academic opinion rallied around the concept of "barnyard government," a rural roadblock to effective (that is, urban) majority rule. Literature on the subject of apportionment blossomed with such terms as "tyranny of the minority," "veto," "stream polluted at its source," "courthouse gangs," "rotten boroughs," and "malapportionment" itself, all suggesting that unequal apportionment was responsible for many of the political evils of the pre-*Baker* era by overrepresenting conservative rural interests. The corporate wisdom of the country, including the National Municipal League, the Conference of Mayors, the American Assembly, the American Political Science Association, the Advisory Commission on Intergovernmental Relations, the Twentieth Century Fund, the Brookings Institution, and John F. Kennedy, seemed to be in substantial agreement that malapportionment had reduced urban dwellers to "second-class citizens" and hobbled the functioning of state governments.[27] Students of apportionment charged assemblymen with lack of sympathy for urban needs.[28] They declared that home rule, slum clearance, metropolitan transit, equal tax laws, and equal school and road expenditures "often fail because of the ignorance and indifference of rural legislators."[29] State government was weakened when the decaying central cities, slighted by the states, turned to the federal government for help.[30] State governments were further weakened by apportionment which favored the rural-based party over the urban-based party in state legislatures and tended to split control of the legislatures and the governorship.[31] "Public cynicism, disillusionment, and apathy" ensued in the states,[32] and even the national Congress languished, being "poorly equipped to handle the problems of an industrialized society" owing to the heavy concentration of its decision-making power in rural hands.[33]

These declarations were so universally accepted that hardly anyone bothered to try to document them, though they rested on dubious assumptions. No one knew quite what *urban* meant in practical terms; the Census Bureau had four or five different versions, none of which had any easily demonstrable political identification;[34] no one had undertaken the tedious analysis necessary to show whether urban-rural antagonism actually existed, or whether the cities' programs were really blocked by coalitions of rural legislators. Some people suspected that voters might be more divided by economic, party, and social allegiances than united by regional allegiances; moreover, where regional rivalries did exist, it seemed that the cities, being richer and more organized than the countryside, might also be more likely to wield disproportionate power.

Finally, the central cities had been losing population to the suburbs. By 1960 no city had a majority of the state's population. From 1950 to 1960 most of the big cities—New York, Chicago, Detroit, Baltimore, Cleveland, Minneapolis-St. Paul, Washington, St. Louis, Boston—actually lost population, and no reversal of the trend was in sight. The predictable gainer from reapportionment was the suburbs, which were at best an unknown quantity and in many respects a known enemy of the cities. Would the suburbs be politically "urban?" No one knew.

Moreover, few people seemed to care what the practical results of apportionment might be. Reapportionists would air a few paragraphs of suspicions, backed up, if at all, by nothing more than the grousing of frustrated city officials and a few figures showing that cities paid the states more than they got from them,[35] but in general they assumed that a bare and solemn display of unequal districts would be enough to settle the matter. Malapportionment was regarded without argument as a *malum in se*, evil by definition. The reapportionists concerned themselves neither with the question of whether equal districts were sound policy nor with the highly complicated question of whether equal districts contributed to or detracted from equal representation.[36] If unequal districts were evil by definition, then equal ones must have been good by definition, and apportionists could proceed with untroubled minds to their main concern over issues that could be settled with technique: measuring malapportionment, showing that the founders did not want malapportionment, and considering how good apportionment could be implemented. The field of "finding a better Yardstick" for measuring malapportionment was cratered with salvos in the professional journals;[37] the field of reapportionment as a "political question" was a smoking ruin;[38] the field of equal districts in original and current constitutions was littered with the debris of war;[39] the area of dispute over the original understanding of the Fourteenth and Fifteenth Amendments was like Verdun, and the Road to Equality (that is, from *Colegrove v. Green* to *Reynolds v. Sims*) could as well have run from Hiroshima to Nagasaki. John Roche did not miss the mark when he described reapportionment as afflicted with academic overkill.

Yet most of the countryside remained untouched, not for want of state summaries that listed what steps had been taken toward reapportioning each of the states,[40] but because the summaries had no bite; because they had no concern with what apportionment was doing to the states. Only a tiny handful of case studies allayed the suspicion that reapportionment at the village level had defied the weapons of modern intellectual warfare.[41] These case studies pointed to serious frustrations of majority rule in a few one-party southern states (Florida, Georgia, and Alabama)—where majority rule was already frustrated by other factors of more consequence than apportionment. They also showed fierce resistance to reapportionment in states such as Maryland, Illinois, Colorado, and California, usually with substantial backing from nonrural elements, but even in these northern and western states there was very little hard evidence of rural interests exercising disproportionate influence on any policy outside of reapportionment itself. Of all the case studies only one undertook a full-scale study of actual voting patterns in state legislatures, and its results did much more to undermine the myth of barnyard government than to support it.

In 1957 David R. Derge analyzed 19,000 votes in the legislature of Missouri and Illinois during a period when reapportionists were attacking both states as prime examples of governments paralyzed by intransigent rural legislators.[42] Derge's figures showed that "outstate" representatives (from outside of Chicago, St. Louis, and Kansas City) were hardly ever united enough to block anybody. Metropolitan representatives were much more likely to vote in a bloc, but even they were disunited in up to three-quarters of the contested votes (see Table 5).[43] Derge's figures showed that metropolitan legislators, on the average, were seven times more likely than outstate legislators to vote in a bloc (67 percent together) in the three legislatures studied.[44] What is more, when the metropolitan representatives voted together they crushed almost all opposition. Chicago and St. Louis-Kansas City lost only 20 percent and 15 percent of contested votes respectively, though Chicago had only half the state population and St. Louis and Kansas City together had only a third[45]—

Table 5. Cohesion of Rural and Urban Bloc Votes in Illinois and Missouri, 1949–1957

	Illinois		Missouri	
	House	Senate	St. Louis	Kansas City
Urban Bloc	25%	37%	25%	27%
Rural Bloc	3%	12%	.4%	0%

Source: David R. Derge, "Metropolitan and Outstate Allignments in Illinois and Missouri Legislative Decision," 52 *Am. Pol. Sci. Rev.*, 105, 1053 (December 1958). Figures are percent of contested votes in which 67 percent or more of bloc voted together.

and despite the fact that the cities in both states were weakened by party division.[46] The figures do seem to indicate that one faction was exercising influence out of proportion to its numbers, but the power was in the cities through bloc voting, not in the country through smaller districts.

Derge's study covered only eight years of votes in three legislative houses. It did not destroy the myth of barnyard government even for the states and period covered—after all, there was *some* cohesion of outstate representatives in Illinois. Still less did it destroy the myth of barnyard government in the same states at other times, or in other states at any time. But it was still the hardest evidence we had on regional bloc politics in any state, and its findings (which were supported by six other, more casual studies showing high city-vote cohesion relative to country-vote cohesion in other areas and times)[47] made it look as though the complaints of the reapportionists were far out of line with the facts of politics (outside the South), since the major practical threat of minority rule seemed to be much more in city bloc voting than in rural blocs.

After *Reynolds v. Sims* (1964),[48] several other studies appeared, attempting to find whether there was any overall relationship between unequal districts in the fifty states and their supposed consequences of reducing party competition, dividing governments between the parties, blocking public welfare measures, and short-changing the cities. Although the studies included the southern states where one would expect a relationship between unequal districts and low party competition, low public welfare, and anti-urban budgets (the South being noted for all four), the overall relationship varied from zero, in most cases, to "very low."[49] Since these studies appeared after the reapportionment cases (though based on data from before the reapportionment cases), they are mentioned only in passing in this chapter.

The barnyard government myth was, if anything, more vulnerable in Congress than it was in the states because Congress is much more accessible and visible than the state legislatures and many obscurities of state politics become more obvious when writ large in the federal government. Congressional districts reflected the same political pressures that made state districts unequal; they were unequal, too (see Table 6).

It was also plain that Congress was not passing the administration's bills as briskly as the reapportionists desired, but apportionment was not the roadblock. The real roadblock was the organizational tradition which divided the two parties into four, counting the executive and congressional wings of each party as a separate party.[50] This tradition has always hampered the national, progressive programs of the executive party by subjecting them to review by the locally oriented, conservative-leaning, congressional party. Rural congressmen have had disproportionate strength in both houses, not by virtue of their numbers, but by virtue of their seniority. Safe, rural seats have always produced a heavy preponderance of rural representatives in control of committees (see Table 7).

One can debate whether or not this quirk of representative power favoring rural interests is bad policy only if one is willing to undertake the arduous

Table 6. Urban, Suburban, and Rural Seats in House of Representatives, 1964[a] (average vote = 1)

	Percent Population	Actual Seats	"Ideal" Seats	Value of vote
Rural	46.8	203	187	1.08[a]
Urban	32.7	103	109	.95
Suburban	20.3	50	60	.83
Mixed	(not counted)	79	75	
Urban and Sub-urban total	53.2	153	169	.90

Source: Congressional Quarterly Census Analysis, Congressional Districts of the United States (August 21, 1964), p. 1784.
[a]"Urban" including cities with 50,000 or more inhabitants.

Table 7. House and Senate Committee Control, 1962 and 1964

House (1962):	Urban	Suburban	Rural
Chairmen (Democrats)	4	2	14
Ranking Minority (Republicans)	3	1	16

Senate (1964):	Urban-Suburban	Rural
Chairmen (Democrats)	3	12
Ranking Minority (Republicans)	7	8

Source: 20 *Congressional Quarterly Weekly Report*, 155–156 (February 2, 1962) (House); *Congressional Quarterly Census Analysis, Congressional Districts of the United States* (August 21, 1964) pp. 178–198 (Senate); *CCH Congressional Index*, Senate Committees, pp. 4001–4014 (1964).

task of trying to balance the prorural quirks against the possible antirural quirks, such as bloc voting, money, urban dominance in electing presidents and senators and appointing members of the Supreme Court, influence of primaries, and so forth, but such questions of checks and balances involve too many imponderables to try to settle with a show of intellectual force.[51]

Within Congress, however, it was possible to make an educated guess about the effects of unequal districts, and two studies of the 87th Congress (1960-1962) showed by different methods that reapportionment was not likely to produce a more liberal Congress and might well tend to produce a more reactionary one. The first study, a *Congressional Quarterly* analysis of urban, suburban, and rural seats in the 87th Congress, concluded that rural voters were indeed overrepresented in the House of Representatives, but that reapportionment would have no effect on liberal voting strength (*liberal* being defined as favoring greater federal control). Using this definition, the study analyzed ten roll-call votes and ranked the voting congressmen by party, section of the country, and character of constituency. The rank list showed wide variances between the parties and between the different sections of the country, but very narrow differences between urban and rural representatives of the same section and party.

Having thus established a liberal voting scale, the *Congressional Quarterly* then applied it to the changes its "ideal," equal-district Congress would require. The combined result of many local changes was no change at all in the national balance between liberals and conservatives and between Democrats and Republicans. Broadly speaking, Democratic gains in the cities would be offset by Republican gains in the suburbs. A projected gain of nine urban and suburban liberals of both parties would be offset by a loss of sixteen rural Democratic congressmen, a majority of them liberal.[52] A 1964 projection using the same techniques produced a similar forecast: equalizing the districts would little effect the party or philosophical balance of power.[53]

A second study of the same 87th Congress, using a different approach, even more dramatically contradicted the theory of rural obstruction—to the sur-

Table 8. Votes Favoring Increased Federal Control, Ten Roll Calls, 1961

Area	Urban		Suburban		Rural	
	G.O.P	Demo-crat	G.O.P.	Demo-crat	G.O.P.	Demo-crat
East	23.3%	96.9%	23.6%	92.7%	19.8%	88.0%
South	0.0	64.5	10.0	25.0	14.0	55.0
Middle West	4.0	98.8	5.1	97.5	5.2	91.0
West	8.3	98.9	0.0	98.3	20.2	92.2

Source: 20 *Congressional Quarterly Weekly Report* 153, 154 (Feb. 2, 1962).

prise of its apportionist author, Andrew Hacker. Hacker selected four roll calls on proposals with strong administration support, three of which had been defeated and one narrowly passed.[54] Then, testing the votes to determine whether the administration was being frustrated by an overrepresented minority, he recomputed the votes, weighing them first by district population and then by popular votes actually received by the voting representative: "In all four cases, with representatives' votes weighted by their districts' population, the Administration side would have fewer votes. It would have lost the urban affairs, education, and agriculture bills by greater margins than it actually did; and, most startling, the resolutions enlarging the Rules Committee would have been defeated . . . Does this exercise indicate that the conservatives in Congress are actually underrepresented?"[55] In asking this question, Hacker experienced for an instant the shock of discovery that his probe of the quagmire had found the wrong bottom. He fell back immediately on the Guardian Ethic, mumbling something about equal districts producing a "new breed of congressman" and representative government being "intended as much to lead the public in new directions as it is to reflect current sentiments."[56] He then concluded with a warning that his prior investigations and arguments "should not affect the overriding issue of equal votes for equal citizens,"[57] roadblock or no roadblock—which may explain his curious remark at the 1965 convention of the APSA: "Much of this discussion is really on aesthetic grounds."

Hacker deserves the greatest credit for asking questions penetrating enough to suggest embarrassing answers. He may have flinched, but he did not fudge. He also deserves credit for recognizing, even if in jest, the aesthetic character of the appeal of equal districts. Barnyard government may have been a myth; it did not matter; the districts had to be equal anyway because we should have equal votes for equal citizens. None of us could object to equal votes, but we can still question whether equal districts mean equal votes. Years after E-Day, the nearest answer to this question is yes, in some ways, but in others no, and in most, no difference.[58]

Perhaps the greatest lesson to be drawn from the reapportionment controversy is an insight into the aesthetics of the Guardian Ethic, with its impatience of authority, its stress on action, uniformity, equality, measurability, and expertise, its intensely intellectual outlook on life. Reapportionment was not pure in the sense that PR was pure (that is, by virtue of consistency between its program and its rhetoric), because it retained the district system's vulnerability to discrimination through gerrymanders and multimember districts. But it was pure in two other senses which distinguished it from prior voting rights movments: its sponsors desired it much more as an end in itself than as a means to other ends; and they were correspondingly unconcerned with what other ends it might accomplish. Prior voting rights reforms had been backed more as means than as ends. Reformers in Marshall's and Taney's time had little objection to property qualifications per se, but they did want veterans to vote and they did want to establish workable ground rules for party competition. The framers of the Fourteenth and Fifteenth Amendments were not so interested in black votes as they were interested in securing "the perpetual ascendancy of the party of Union"; the progressives wanted woman suffrage and direct government reforms only where and when it seemed useful for "holding the nation to the ideals which won independence."

Prospects for Court Intervention

Moreover, the old reformers sought their programs in legislatures. Reapportionment did not flourish in legislatures, and reapportionists, for all their talk about "reinvigorating" legislatures, were more likely to try to conquer legislatures from without than to persuade them from within. Frustrated by inaction in the legislatures, the reapportionists early developed the habit of trying to bypass them to achieve their desires through courts or referenda, and then, after repeated disappointments in referenda, almost exclusively through the courts.

Yet by means of the intervention factors as they were around 1930 (when reapportionment was beginning to supplant PR as the foremost concern of good-government intellectuals), intervention was not likely. Even the liberals on the Court, Holmes and Brandeis, had made such a fuss against the Court's meddling in politics to implement the economic doctrines of Herbert Spencer that they could not be expected to spearhead a move to implement the political doctrines of the National Municipal League. The conservatives, Van Devanter, McReynolds, Butler, Sutherland, and Roberts, had been barely touched by progressivism and regarded most post-progressive ideas as instruments of the devil. Although the Court had unanimously opposed blatant white primary laws in *Nixon v. Herndon* (1928), it mustered only a 5-4 majority against only slightly less blatant white primary laws in *Nixon v. Condon* (1932), and it withdrew from the field altogether, by unanimous vote, in *Grovey v. Townsend* (1935).[59] The will of such a Court to intervene in the much more difficult area of reapportionment could not have been great.

In the matter of constitutional authority, the Court faced several difficult barriers to intervention against unequal districts. A major problem in those days was the lack of any provision in the Constitution forbidding unequal districts. The Constitution forbade discrimination for race and sex; it guaranteed a republican form of government; it guaranteed equal protection of the laws and due process in civil rights, but not political. Far from guaranteeing equal districts, however, it seemed to enshrine unequal ones in the Senate and electoral college. Moreover, unequal districts were older than the republic, and no one had ever understood them to be offensive to the Constitution. In constitutional law it has long been possible, and even necessary, to put new wine in old wine bottles, as the Court has done with wiretapping, white primaries, and section one of the Fourteenth Amendment, but it is harder to stuff cod-liver oil, say, into the old bottle and then convince people that it had really been wine all along. Section one of the Fourteenth Amendment was understood to protect civil rights, but not to protect political rights, and the Court had to reckon with the arduous task of transubstantiating the original understanding if it wished to invoke the equal protection clause against unequal districts.[60]

No less difficult to overcome than the lack of specific constitutional authority was the political question problem, a mixed question of authority and policy involving the risk of clashing with other branches, and the problem of devising simple standards to deal fairly and effectively with complicated questions. All of these barriers the Court eventually overcame or bypassed, but the Court's breakthrough in reapportionment was possible only because of an elaborate buildup of its power and technique during its Interpretive period.

A third of this buildup was already underway in the black rights progression discussed in the last chapter. The Court was developing, by trial and error, a bold and broad technique of interpreting the Constitution to break through words and forms to apply the spirit of the Fifteenth Amendment to the facts of discrimination. The black rights progression was the Court's training ground in the Guardian Ethic, and it exemplified the Ethic at its best. This third of the Court's buildup might be called the authority third. The second third might be called the power third; it is embodied in the Court's judicial laissez-faire progression, which will not be treated in this book but certainly cannot be ignored. Edward Corwin properly diagnosed the Court's rigid and ill-founded opposition to government economic regulation as a self-inflicted wound, because it led ultimately to a confrontation with the rest of the government and a capitulation by the Court;[61] nevertheless, its battle against economic regulation in the 1930's also gave the Court a measure of its own immense power. Five justices on the Court held the entire country at bay for four years, not in some idle backwater of public policy, but in the very center of the political stage. From 1933 to 1937 the Court handed down twelve decisions voiding federal statutes and over thirty striking down state laws, usually over the bitter objections of a four-man minority.[62] The nation had never before seen such a judicial *tour de force*, and it really has not since because the Court has not since taken on the nation and the states at the same time. A court which could show such strength in a waning cause could look forward to even greater power in causes where it could make a better choice of allies and enemies.

The last third of the Court's buildup to intervention in reapportionment might be called the enforcement third, and it embraced many developments outside of the Court's own jurisdiction. If the black rights progression can be summed up as the development of sophisticated techniques of constitutional interpretation, and the laissez-faire progression as a test and demonstration of the Court's power, the equal districts progression can best be summed up as the development of sophisticated judicial techniques to enforce redistricting. By 1930 it was possible to sue state officials in a federal court, either for damages under the old enforcement acts, or, more importantly, for an injunction, under *Ex parte Young*[63] and the three-judge court acts.[64] The Eleventh Amendment was no longer an impregnable barrier to suits to stop state action. The passage of the federal Declaratory Judgments Act in 1934[65] and its endorsement by the Supreme Court in 1937[66] added another way to getting plaintiffs into federal courts, and with it another way for the federal courts to intervene *prospectively* in voting rights disputes. Voting rights complaints no longer had to be presented in the impossible posture, indirect and retroactive, which was all that the judicial techniques of Thomas Dorr's time would permit.

Reapportionment in State Courts

Although the federal Constitution gave the reapportionists very little to work with, they did enjoy the explicit authority of state constitutions and laws, and even, briefly, a federal congressional directive that districts in the House of Representatives should be of approximately equal population. Disgruntled voters and others sought relief in the state courts as early as the 1890's, and their efforts tested much technical ground which would have to be traversed to get relief from the federal courts. Whom do you sue for reapportionment? The legislature? Electoral officials? What do you ask them to do? What does the court do if the legislature balks? *New York Times* commentator Anthony Lewis, in an influential study, demonstrated that the states had produced a wide range of answers and nonanswers.[67] In the minority of states with nonlegislative apportionment bodies, it was possible to get reapportionment with a writ of mandamus to the apportionment committee,[68] though not always on the first try.[69] Plaintiffs had a much harder time trying to get courts to order legislatures to reapportion, although they showed great imagination in seeking ways to bring pressure on the legislatures. Reapportionists sought mandamus against the legislature itself,[70] injunction against the secretary of state to use the challenged districts,[71] restraint of payment of legislators' salaries till they would reapportion,[72] and even issuance of a writ of *quo warranto* to make the legislators show by what right they held office.[73] Other plaintiffs asked the courts in effect to do the redistricting themselves by ordering state officials to allocate more seats to populous districts and take them from smaller districts.[74] These efforts were not successful because they savored too much of the courts' sitting in judgment of their creator.

More successful in terms of getting court action were suits to invalidate current districts and return to an earlier and more equitable district system— or even to an inequitable earlier apportionment if it seemed likely to stir the legislature into action. This mode of attack was twice tried successfully in Kentucky against current malapportionment.[75] However, the Court would not allow attack on the earlier malapportionment, invoking the doctrine of laches: courts would deny relief to plaintiffs who had "slept on their rights."[76] This was not a very useful form of relief; it did solve the delicate problem of deciding how to redistrict when the current system was invalidated, but the solution was highly arbitrary and in most situations of little use to reapportionists, since older districts would normally have been more unequal in terms of current population than more recent ones. Reapportionists could threaten to go back to old districts, but only for nuisance value. They could make good the threat, but only at prohibitive cost to themselves.[77]

Perhaps the most promising of the techniques of compulsion developed in the state courts was that of ordering at-large elections until the legislature would redistrict. The Virginia Supreme Court of Appeals did this to force reapportionment of federal congressional districts;[78] when the legislature did not act, the state's representatives were ordered chosen at large; valid new districts were drawn before the next elections. An at-large election was far more uncomfortable for the candidates than older districts because it uprooted them all from their constituencies; at the same time, it was less uncomfortable for underrepresented areas because it did offer an equal vote, though it did not guarantee a very close relationship between the representative and his constituency. At-large elections are not a happy solution to the problem of apportionment, as the Illinois voters found out in 1964 when they had to face at-large elections for the state legislature, with long lists of unfamiliar candidates inscribed on what is known to history as the "bedsheet ballot." Congressional elections, however, posed less of a problem, as there were fewer names than in elections to the state legislatures. At-large elections, if inconvenient, were at least a feasible weapon for courts, for the threat to the legislators was greater and the risks for the reapportionists less than had been true of threats to go back to old constituencies.

A final contribution of the state courts to the future of reapportionment by federal courts was quieting fears that invalidating a legislature's mode of election might also invalidate the laws it passed. In Illinois, which had a particularly strong tradition of concern with good government and litigious resistance to malapportionment, a convicted criminal sought in vain, as Thomas Dorr had done eighty years before, to have his conviction reversed as based on a law passed by an invalidly elected legislature.[79] Another Illinois reapportionist, unable to get the Court to listen to a similar defense to a foreclosure action, shot the opposing lawyer.[80]

Early Supreme Court Reapportionment Cases

In 1932 the Supreme Court considered four cases involving reapportionment, all seeking prospective relief through injunction or mandamus, and it found ways to dispose of them all without having to consider reapportionment as a separate constitutional issue. In *Smiley v. Holm, Koenig v. Flynn*, and *Carroll v. Becker*,[82] the Court ruled that where state law required the concurrence of the governor in redistricting, Article I, section 4 did also, and redistricting without the governor's concurrence was invalid. *Wood v. Broom*[82] was the first case in which the Court faced a direct attack on apportionment; the plaintiffs challenged unequal federal congressional districts in Mississippi under Article I, section 4, the equal protection clause, and the Reapportionment Act of 1911.[83] Since Congress had repealed that act's requirements that congressional districts be as contiguous, compact, and equal as practicable, the Court dismissed the action on statutory grounds, paying no more attention to the constitutional claim than it had paid to the constitutional basis of *Nixon v. Condon*, decided in the same year. Justices Brandeis, Stone, Roberts, and Cardozo concurred in *Wood v. Broom* but believed the Court should have denied relief "for want of equity" in preference to deciding the case on its merits.

Colegrove v. Green *and Its Progeny*

Colegrove v. Green[84] presented the Court again with a demand to enjoin unequal congressional districts, this time without reference to any statute. The Court dismissed the action on two grounds, neither of which was supported by a majority of the justices: reapportionment was a political question not fit for judicial determination or enforcement, and the injunctive relief demanded in *Colegrove* "lacked equity"; that is, since injunctions have always been a discretionary form of relief, the Court should exercise its discretion and deny the injunction as a matter of policy. Three justices—Black, Douglas, and Murphy—felt that the action to restrain the Illinois Certifying Board from conducting elections without equal districts met every objection: that it did not present a political question, that the right claimed was protected by Article I, section 4 or the equal protection clause (a doubtful point little argued by either side), and that the situation was appropriate for the issuance of an injunction. Three justices—Frankfurter, Reed, and Burton—felt that the action was not justiciable because it presented a political question. Frankfurter's words have since been much quoted: "To sustain this action would cut deep into the very being of Congress. Courts ought not to enter this political thicket. The remedy for unfairness in districting is to secure State Legislatures that will apportion properly, or to invoke the ample powers of Congress. The Constitution has many commands that are not enforceable by

108

courts because they clearly fall outside the conditions and purposes that circumscribe judicial action."[85] Justice Rutledge cast the deciding vote against Colegrove,[86] believing that to grant the injunction would subject the Illinois voters to the excessive rigors of an at-large election. "The cure sought may be worse than the disease."[87]

Although Rutledge's concurrence, together with the opinion of the three dissenters in *Colegrove*, indicated that a majority of the Court thought relief in apportionment cases was at least discretionary with the Court, the Court seemed to follow Frankfurter's majority opinion in all its dealings with reapportionment for the next sixteen years, all *per curiam* opinions.[88] In *Colegrove v. Barrett*,[89] the Court dismissed a challenge to state legislative districts. In *MacDougall v. Green*,[90] the Court rejected a challenge to Illinois' requirement that new party candidates get nomination signatures from 50 of 102 counties in the state, against arguments that the requirement gave disproportionate power to voters in the smaller, rural counties:

To assume that political power is a function exclusively of numbers is to disregard the practicalities of government. Thus the Constitution protects the interests of the smaller against the greater by giving in the Senate entirely unequal representation to populations. It would be strange, indeed, and doctrinaire, for this Court, applying such broad constitutional concepts as due process and equal protection of the laws, to deny a State the power to assure a proper diffusion of political initiative as between its thinly populated counties and those having concentrated masses, in view of the fact that the latter have practical opportunities for expressing their political weight at the polls not available to the former.

In *South v. Peters*,[91] the Court dismissed a challenge of Georgia county unit system. "Federal courts consistently refuse to exercise their equity powers in cases posing political issues arising from a state's geographic distribution of electoral strength." Justices Douglas and Black dissented, feeling that race discrimination precedents were applicable: "I suppose that if a State reduced the vote of Negroes, Catholics or Jews so that each got only one-tenth of a vote, we would strike the law down."

The Guardians Make Their Case

Black and Douglas never relinquished their dissent in *Colegrove*; they nourished it for sixteen lean years between *Colegrove* and *Baker v. Carr*, gaining strength from the Court's pursuit of the Guardian Ethic in the black rights cases, from a small but growing body of very well-written legal, political, and statistical treatises favoring reapportionment, from Frankfurter's own opinion in *Gomillion v. Lightfoot*, and eventually from the endorsement of the United States solicitor general. Two years after *Colegrove* the United States

Conference of Mayors opened fire on *Colegrove*, announcing that "equal representation is not a mere theory or doctrine" but "a fundamental feature of democracy."[92] In 1954 the APSA entered the fray. Its Committee on American Legislatures called for equal districts, an end to gerrymanders, and "wide representation of interests." A special administrative agency outside the legislature was to reapportion every ten years.[93]

In 1955 two major appeals for reapportionment appeared: the Kestnbaum Commission report[94] and Gordon Baker's pioneering book, *Rural versus Urban Political Power.*[95] Both works made two arguments which were soon to be received as conventional wisdom: (1) that malapportionment was responsible for the "urban problem," having made state legislatures incapable of responding to urban needs; and (2) that it undermined the power of the states relative to the federal government by encouraging the cities to bypass state legislatures and seek help directly from Washington. In 1957, *New York Times* commentator Anthony Lewis spent a year at the Harvard Law School studying the legal problems of attacking malapportionment. He published his conclusions in the *Harvard Law Review* in 1958, making much the best case for reapportionment as an enforceable judicial policy that anyone had made before the federal courts proved it by enforcing *Baker v. Carr.*[96] Senator John F. Kennedy joined issue in the same year in the pages of the *New York Times Magazine*, presenting a simplified version of Gordon Baker's views for the wider, but still elite readership of the *Times.*[97]

In 1961 two more political scientists entered the fray with a new word to set beside *malapportionment, barnyard government*, and *rotten borough* in the growing list of loaded terms which the profession was supplying to the public to "assist their analytical understanding." The new word was *devaluation*, and it appeared in Paul David and Ralph Eisenberg's useful statistical study, *Devaluation of the Urban and Suburban Vote.*[98] Besides popularizing the term *devaluation*, this study armed the reapportionists for the first time with comprehensive statistics to give the term some backing. The backing, however, was purely statistical, and the study did not purport to draw any conclusions as to the effect of unequal districts on actual politics (though it has often been cited as if it did draw such conclusions). The urban vote was devalued only in a narrow, formal sense, and probably in practice a misleading one if the voting patterns David Derge found in Illinois and Missouri were prevalent in other northern states. But Derge's painstaking mode of examination never became popular—perhaps because it produced more qualified, less resounding results than studies which measured voter power only by district size, perhaps because the action-oriented intellectual interested in reapportionment was looking for go signs more than stop signs, or perhaps because none of us really wanted to spend a year collating and analyzing 19,000 votes in any state legislature.

However misleading they may have been, *devaluation* and *malapportion-*

ment had come into universal use by 1962, even by opponents of court intervention—a fatal concession, for, however much one may argue about such words, they carry their own verdict: whatever they describe must be evil. Such words may not have pacified the countryside in state legislatures, but they did disarm defenders of the countryside in forums such as the intellectual press, the federal executive branch, and the Supreme Court, which were more receptive to the urban point of view. When Felix Frankfurter in *Gomillion v. Lightfoot* committed the Court to ruling on a distracting case in spite of the standards problem, he filled yet another pothole in the road to reapportionment. This road had been charted by Black and Douglas in their *Colegrove* dissent, then graded and smoothed by the patient, though unheralded, efforts of political scientists and constitutional commentators, and finally metalled by John F. Kennedy, the *New York Times*, and the foundations. By 1962 Frankfurter's "road closed" sign was still posted, but many accredited and intelligent men had looked down the road since 1946, and most of these had declared the road less bumpy and the destination more alluring than Frankfurter had supposed.

Executive Adoption

The Justice Department furnished the final push for court-ordered reapportionment in March 1961 when it intervened in *Baker v. Carr* as an amicus curiae on the side of the urban interests. The decision to intervene had been made by the outgoing Republican administration of Dwight Eisenhower and adopted by the incoming Democratic administration of John F. Kennedy. Kennedy's solicitor general, Harvard Law Professor Archibald Cox, and his assistants were to become chief architects of the Court's interventionist voting rights decisions during the 1960's; Cox's argument and brief in *Baker v. Carr* set the tone for the rest of the Warren years. Cox and his men bolstered every aspect of the Court's willingness and capacity to intervene: will, authority, power, and technique. His amicus brief cultivated the Court's will through shrewd use of the arguments, and even the very words of Gordon Baker and the Kestnbaum Commission report. He saw in Tennessee's sprawling miscellany of districts and its sixty-year neglect to equalize the districts under its own constitution an illustration of nationwide shortcomings under the Guardian Ethic (though of course he did not use the name Guardian Ethic). Tennessee and other states were guilty of failure to modernize, both by their reluctance to redistrict and by their "refusal to meet the growing problems of our urban areas." They were also, of course, guilty of failure to standardize and to take action to implement the guidelines laid down by the Guardians. The result (echoing the words of Gordon Baker) was "public cynicism, disillusionment, and loss of confidence," and the solution, where representative action had been stymied, was administrative action by the courts.[99]

If the solicitor general mobilized Gordon Baker and the Kestnbaum Commission to create a will to intervene, the very fact of his intervention enhanced the Court's power to intervene by conveying the blessing of the executive branch. Moreover, he mobilized the arguments of Anthony Lewis and the "devaluation" language of David and Eisenberg and supplied arguments of his own to supply the Court with authority and technique. The *Baker* plaintiffs had already called for both injunctive relief and a declaratory judgment; they also asked for at-large elections to force action. The solicitor general's contribution was a much more straightforward argument for intervention under the Fourteenth Amendment than was provided either by the plaintiff's counsel or by the Court itself. "The Court has recognized that a voter has a constitutional right to have his vote counted without its being diluted by fraud," Cox argued. "The dilution of one's vote by gross malapportionment is just as unconstitutional. If the state legislatures violate the federal Constitution through discriminations against the voters, there must be a federal remedy—just as for other constitutional violations." Cox's argument was bold, and perhaps dubious in the light of the text and intent of the Fourteenth Amendment, but it gave the Court much more to go on than the plaintiffs' cautious and floundering efforts to argue that Tennessee's contravention of its own constitution—and not any substantive "inequality of representation under the Fourteenth Amendment"—denied equal protection of Tennessee's laws.[100] Cox recognized that the plaintiffs had tied their case not to the Constitution but to a species of vested status quo, itself far too miscellaneous and volatile to stand closer examination under the Guardian Ethic or any other constitutional standard. When Justices Frankfurter and Harlan demolished the Tennessee constitution argument, the majority was still free tacitly to adopt Cox's Fourteenth Amendment argument.

The solicitor general furnished two further critical aids to the Court: a loose "reasonableness" standard, and a very specific model for its application in Tennessee. He repeatedly stressed the broad discretion which his standard was supposed to leave the states, using language which would be enthusiastically echoed by concurring members of the majority in *Baker v. Carr*—though not followed in subsequent cases either by the majority or by the solicitor general himself. "Of course," Cox urged, "a wide range of discretion is left to the States in choosing units of representation. So long as the State legislature fairly represents the people of the State, there can be no violation of the Constitution. It does not follow, however, that merely because some degree of inequality from the nature of things must be permitted, gross inequality must be allowed."[101] The solicitor general gave no indication that his standard could mean diced cities, bedsheet ballots, and no more geographic representation in state senates, voters' wishes or no; if anything, his arguments were to the contrary.[102] As a matter of legislative policy, his suggested standard looked like one of the most sensible, and many, including the three concurring justices and the two dissenting justices in *Baker v. Carr*, took it to be the unstated position of the majority, to be praised or condemned for its great latitude. Its apparent flaw was not its rigidity but its flexibility, its vagueness as to what kind of inequality might be considered reasonable, and what kind of action the courts and the states were supposed to take to avoid gross inequality. This flaw the solicitor general boldly remedied in his *Baker* brief by submitting a suggested reapportionment decree meeting the requirements of the Tennessee constitution—not so much in hopes that the decree would be adopted as in hopes that it would show the task could be done.

We do not suggest that this is an ideal solution or even that it is free from substantial flaws. We outline it for the sole purpose of showing concretely the practicability of granting the complainants greater protection by easily administered judicial relief. If the court is forced to proceed to a final decree, the suggested decree would not be complex. Framing it would involve no nice choices. No political considerations could enter into the decision[!]. There is no wholesale remapping of the existing districts. And there is nothing nonjudicial or extra-judicial about such relief.[103]

In retrospect, the role of the executive in smoothing the way for the Court to implement the recommendations of the Guardians appears to have been a major one.

On the eve of *Baker v. Carr*, the Court, which had faced down the president in the steel seizure case in 1952, the states' massive resistance to school segregation between 1955 and 1960, and Congress' attempts to curtail its jurisdiction in 1958, did not lack political power to intervene in a question like reapportionment where public opinion did not run deep and politicians' objections would undoubtedly be matched by acclamation from the intellectuals. One might once have questioned the Court's will to intervene, considering its long line of per curiam opinions treating reapportionment as a political question, not to mention statements by the chief justice in his California politics days defending unequal districts—but by 1962 those who had expected Warren in court to hold to his former political views had long since folded their tents. The Court had become well versed in the Guardians' techniques of interpreting the Constitution from its pioneering work in black rights cases, and it could not have been deaf to rumors among the illuminati that Frankfurter himself had become "unsophisticated" in his old age for telling the reapportionists to seek relief in other branches[104]—the supreme opprobrium by the intellectual fashions of the time. From its fight against massive resistance, from the civil rights acts of 1957 and 1960, and from the trials and errors of state court apportionment decisions, the Supreme Court had available a wide range of techniques to enforce decisions against reluctant state political bodies. Of all the intervention factors it really lacked only one—express authority in the Constitution—and that it was shortly to manufacture by assumption in the reapportionment cases.

V. Political Questions, Wine, and Cod-liver Oil—the Tactics of Transubstantiation in the Legislative Period

> Whosoever hath an absolute authority to interpret any
> written or spoken laws, it is he who is truly the
> Lawgiver to all intents and purposes, and not the
> person who first wrote or spoke them.
> —Bishop Hoadley

> Equal is equal, isn't it?
> —John Veblen

> *Hoc volo, sic jubeo, sit pro ratione voluntas.*
> —Juvenal

An Overview of Baker v. Carr

Alexander Bickel, Harry Wellington, Herbert Wechsler, and Philip Kurland, among others, have noted in the efforts of the majority of the Court in the fifties and sixties to implement their concepts of social justice a failure to connect the results of their decisions with the claimed constitutional bases of the decisions.[1] Bickel's characterization is representative: "The Court's product has shown an increasing incidence of the sweeping, dogmatic statement, of the formulation of results accompanied by little or no effort to support them in reason; in sum, of opinions that do not opine—of per curiam orders that quite frankly fail to bridge the gap between the authority they cite and the results they reach."[2] The reapportionment cases bore this stamp, and they bore it for tactical reasons. Once the Court had decided to grant some sort of relief in *Baker v. Carr*[3] it had to devise a course of action and a rationale that would meet or avoid both traditional and modern objections to intervention: (1) the equal protection clause of the Fourteenth Amendment had nothing to do with the right to vote; and (2) even if it could be construed to affect voting rights, apportionment presented such risks of embroilment with the states and Congress and such difficulties of devising and enforcing fair standards that the Court should avoid it as a matter of policy—either as a

114

"political question" or in its discretion as a court of equity. The Court faced a difficult choice between rigid standards, equalizing every district (but short of imposing PR), or flexible standards, taking account of special circumstances—state senates, geographical political, or historical considerations, approval by referendum, and so forth. The looser standard might better fit the needs of the states, but it would also provide loopholes that might defeat the overall aim of equal districts, while adding to the lower courts' confusion as to what the Supreme Court wanted. The Court's approach to these problems has been justly criticized for its logical deficiencies.[4] A majority of the justices managed to get from *Baker v. Carr* to *Reynolds v. Sims* without ever facing either the Fourteenth Amendment issue or the standards question head-on. They uniformly avoided any attempt to prove their case either in the traditional sense or the modern sense. Instead, they assumed without argument that the equal protection clause and Article I, section 2 required equal districts, confining their argument to lesser points which they could prove without much trouble but which did not support the holdings. Justice Brennan in *Baker v. Carr* demonstrated that *Colegrove v. Green* did not preclude judicial consideration of reapportionment as a political question, which is true; Justice Warren demonstrated in *Reynolds v. Sims* that the Constitution does not require unequal districts in the states by analogy with the federal government, which is also true—but neither of these amounts to a showing that the Constitution does require equal districts.

The majority steadfastly declared their adherence to the principle of flexible standards while choosing in practice the most rigid standards possible. The Court followed the Guardian Ethic to the extent of ordering the states to undo discrimination that was easy to measure, but not to the extent of considering other means of discrimination, such as gerrymanders, multi-member districts, bloc votes, money, and organization, which are more important politically than apportionment but which cannot be settled with simple rules.

However doubtful its logic, the majority showed great tactical shrewdness. They picked an ideal series of cases to beat the dissenters, Frankfurter and Harlan. In Tennessee the districts were in such a mess that the majority had only to hint at what every citizen trained in the Ethic could see: the districts were unequal; the equal protection clause said something had to be equal; surely Tennessee's "crazy quilt" of districts, offensive as it was to the moral eye, must also have been offensive to the Constitution. The Court could say, as it did, that something must be done without embarrassing itself by saying what it was that had to be done. With the principle of intervention once established in *Baker*, well sugared with dictum about "leaving room for weighting," the Court could go on to successively tougher cases, each following the "command" of the Constitution as expressed in the holding or dictum of the last, until it could strike down state senates with unequal districts approved by a 2-1 majority of state voters—a holding "inevitable" in 1964 that would have been impossible in 1962. In the reapportionment cases, the Court accomplished with two years of tactics and indirection a *tour de force* of constitutional construction which in some ways eclipsed its accomplishment after seventeen years of arduous frontal assaults on the white primary. To deal with white primaries, the Court had expanded the coverage of the Fifteenth Amendment by a process of interpretation; to deal with unequal districts it had reversed the meaning of the equal protection clause by a process of interpretation; to deal with unequal districts it had reversed the meaning of the equal protection clause by a process of de facto constitutional amendment. Since 1962 the equal protection clause has said, in effect: "The right of citizens of the United States to vote shall not be denied or abridged by the United States or by any state on account of the size of their electoral districts. The Judicial shall have power to enforce this article through appropriate legislation."

Political Questions

Apart from the one cautious but crucial sentence at the end of *Baker v. Carr* stating that "the right asserted is within the reach of judicial protection under the Fourteenth Amendment," Justice Brennan's opinion for the Court was devoted entirely to showing that reapportionment was not a political question. By the time of *Baker v. Carr*, political questions were thought to include four subjects: matters expressly reserved for other branches than the judiciary, such as trial of impeachment; questions of war, foreign affairs, and Indian affairs, such as recognition of governments and commencement and termination of hostilities, which seemed to require unanimity among the branches and the resolution of which required resources not available to the Court; abstract questions of political power or sovereignty, such as taxpayer actions to enjoin an act of government using public funds to an allegedly unconstitutional purpose; and (most relevant to *Baker v. Carr*) questions of state organization and government, of which *Luther v. Borden* is the prototype.

Of these categories only the second and fourth—foreign affairs and state government—raise important, independent questions about judicial intervention. Only in a very few instances, such as impeachment, does the Constitution vest "sole power" outside of the judiciary; in most cases it omits the limiting term *sole*, leaving room to argue that the power expressly conferred is not necessarily confined to its stated recipient. Thus, Congress may make regulations for federal elections, choose its own officers, collect taxes, enforce the provisions of the Fourteenth Amendment, and so forth, but these powers are exclusive only insofar as they are protected by other considerations of power and logic. It is a safe guess that Congress's powers to coin money and raise and support armies will tend to remain exclusive, while other powers, although granted in much the same words, for example, declaring war and enforcing the Fourteenth Amendment, will remain shared in practice with other branches. Although the "expressly reserved" argument has often been invoked in political questions cases, it has almost no independent power to determine an issue because most of the powers expressly conferred to the nonjudiciary branches are not necessarily exclusive.

Questions of foreign and military policy have generated more pertinent arguments from the Court than questions under the other headings, perhaps because they seem to appeal more directly to the Court's discretion than the others and less directly to supposed mandates in the text of the Constitution. No provision of the Constitution binds the Court to rule on the legitimacy of foreign governments or the commencement and cessation of hostilities as specifically as, say, the Fifteenth Amendment and its implementing legislation bind the Court to rule on racial abridgements of the right to vote. The intervention factors, which are the real determinants of whether the Court acts or fails to act on claimed political questions, enter more openly into the deliberations of the Court. The Court could hardly be expected to intervene in situations where it lacked clear constitutional rules and the techniques for making such rules, or where it lacked a political power base and judicial techniques to exploit it. Thus, in *United States v. Palmer*[5] the Court refused to choose between belligerent factions fighting in Spain, lacking direction from the other branches, much as later, in *Luther v. Borden*, it refused to choose between the two domestic contenders in the Dorr War.

The risk of a confrontation with the other branches of government has always been a paramount consideration in this line of cases. The gains to be anticipated from the Court's taking sides in Spain or Rhode Island seem very small compared to the embarrassment it might expect if the other branches entertained a contrary view. In the great majority of cases before it involving war, foreign policy, and Indian questions, often in spite of deep misgivings of its own, the Court has acquiesced in the desires of the other two branches.[6]. In the very few cases in which it has tried to defy one of the other branches, it has succeeded only where the president and Congress were sharply divided.[7]

Most of the cases listed by Justice Brennan as involving "abstract questions of political power" really turn on the question of standing and are more immediately concerned with how much interest the plaintiff had in the desired holding than with whether the question raised belongs to a nonjudiciary decision-maker. A property-owner who has sold his property does not have standing to abate his former neighbors' nuisances; a parent with no children in school lacks standing to complain if other children have to salute the flag. These are political questions only in that the plaintiffs' only recourse is to the political branches, but that is true in any situation where relief in court is barred—sovereign immunity, running of the statute of limitations, and so on—without turning them into political questions. A taxpayer lacks standing to object to most expenditures from general funds not because such objection must be raised, if at all, in the political branches—this last is inherent in any denial of relief in court—but because his own interest in the expenditures is too tiny and remote to warrant a hearing in court. Although there was some language in *Frothingham v. Mellon*[8] suggesting that taxpayer challenges to public expenditures are political questions, the real focus is not on the subject matter but on the plaintiff's interest in the case, and the real issue was not whether such taxpayer actions are political, but whether the plaintiff had standing to object.[9] Lack of standing had never kept people claiming their right to vote had been infringed from seeking relief in court, either in the black rights cases, in the early reapportionment cases, such as *Wood v. Broom*,[10] or in *Colegrove v. Green*.

The final category of political questions which the Court had to distinguish in *Baker v. Carr* was questions of state organization and government, supposedly denominated political in *Luther v. Borden* and therefore avoided by the Court in subsequent decisions. By the time of *Baker v. Carr*, the Court had two hurdles to clear to show that apportionment was not a political question: case precedent, and the logic (especially that addressed to the problem of standards) which had supported the earlier decisions. Justice Brennan's majority opinion in *Baker* carefully avoided the second hurdle but cleared the first with no great difficulty.

Luther v. Borden, to be sure, did involve a question of state organization and government which the Supreme Court had refused to rule on for being political, but by 1962, the Court's many interventions to invalidate state economic regulations, criminal laws, and especially voting laws should have served notice that a bare connection with state government, however intimate, could not be relied upon to confer immunity from Court review. Moreover, the term *political question*, borrowed from the Rhode Island Supreme Judicial Court and properly used by that body to exclude argument on the legitimacy of the government from which the court drew its own powers, had been made to serve the purposes of the United States Supreme Court only by the subterfuge of Taney's guarantee-clause argument and by the analogy, more properly urged, with cases involving the legitimacy of foreign governments. The intervention factors ruled in *Luther v. Borden*, as they did in subsequent cases involving political questions, by confronting a relatively weak Court, itself probably ill-disposed to intervene, with an insuperable barrier to intervention in the indirect and retrospective way the legitimacy question was posed.

Most of the subsequent political questions cases involved attacks under the due process clause of the Fourteenth Amendment or under the guarantee clause on the validity of the enactment of state laws without reference to their substantive constitutional merits. These presented standard-making problems in the baldest way without appealing either to strong constitutional authority or to a strong Court disposition to intervene. Claims like that asserted in *Pacific States Tel. Co. v. Oregon*,[11] that a law passed by initiative and referendum violated the guarantee clause, ill-supported as they were by the text of the Constitution and the ideologies of the justices, could hardly hope to call forth the great effort at standard-making that Court intervention could be expected to require. Such claims raised too many hard-to-answer questions about what men and measures had been chosen in a "republican" manner—besides raising the spectre of retroactively invalidating all laws so passed—to inspire a warm reception even from a sympathetic Court, and the claimants might have expected scant sympathy for attacks on direct voter choice at the height of the progressive movement. The attacks on the enactment of laws asked too much of the Court; they called for judicial legislation too frank, too difficult, and too unpopular to raise any hope that the Court would intervene.

These difficulties did not bear so heavily on the black voting rights cases, where the Court had solid constitutional ground for intervention, or on the reapportionment cases, where the right claimed was democratic, egalitarian, and not unpopular with the Court's clientele. The reapportionment cases may have called for judicial legislation no less frank and not much less difficult than that called for by the antienactment cases, but the cause of reapportionment was much more in tune with the egalitarian temper of the sixties than the antienactment cases were with the ideals of the Progressive reformation.

Reapportionment had never been solidly accepted as a political question. Four of the seven justices in *Colegrove v. Green* agreed that reapportionment was not a political question, but Justice Rutledge, who cast the deciding vote, believed the Court in its discretion as a court of equity should not intervene, even though he thought the case was otherwise justiciable. Thereafter, without the explicit sanction of a full opinion, reapportionment actions were treated as though they presented a political question, being uniformly dismissed per curiam. *Colegrove*, with its split majority and its cryptic progeny of per curiam opinions, did keep the federal courts out of the apportionment business for fifteen years, but the logic of the reapportionment opinions prior to *Baker v. Carr* was not connected enough to bar subsequent intervention behind an integrated barrier of case law.

A Velitary Majority

Brennan in his *Baker v. Carr* opinion found little difficulty in showing that neither *Colegrove* nor its per curiam successors had conclusively held that reapportionment was a political question, still less that a citizen whose vote was denied or abridged lacked standing to object in court; but he refused to consider the main questions of the meaning of the equal protection clause and the standards problem. Justices Douglas and Clark, in separate concurrences, were not so cautious. Both of them essayed a few remarks on the standards question which seemed to suggest a more flexible position than either justice was later to take.

Douglas observed that "universal equality is not the test; there is room for weighting."[12] A year later he was to announce a much more rigid rule: the American conception of political equality "can mean only one thing—one person, one vote."[13] Clark felt that courts should not intervene in cases where there was a rational policy behind a nonproportional system, but that Tennessee's apportionment was "a crazy quilt without rational basis."[14] Clark cited the Georgia county unit system, upheld by the Court in *South v. Peters*,[15] as an example of rationality (though he later joined the majority in *Gray v. Sanders* in condemning it as irrational), and he believed that court intervention would be inappropriate if other relief, such as initiative and referendum, were available for state voters to use in correcting unequal districts if they wished to do so.[16]

A Frustrated Dissent

Apart from Douglas's and Clark's ill-fated dicta in *Baker v. Carr*, the Court scrupulously avoided tackling the policy questions raised in *Colegrove* and the textual and historical problems later raised in *Reynolds v. Sims*. The dissenting justices in *Baker v. Carr*, Frankfurter and Harlan, assailed the majority for this oversight and protested vigorously against the Court's venturing into an area of political dispute without a solid constitutional warrant, without adequate standards for judgment, and without adequate means of enforcing its decisions. Frankfurter warned that Court intervention in reapportionment would exceed the proper bounds of its rights and powers: "The Court's authority possessed of neither the purse nor the sword ultimately rests on sustained public confidence in its moral sanction. Such feeling must be nourished by the Court's complete detachment, in fact and in appearance, from political entanglements and by abstention from injecting itself into the clash of political forces in political settlements."[17] Citing many examples of representation not based on population at the time of the founding, at the time of adopting the Fourteenth Amendment, and since,[18] Frankfurter concluded that "there has never been a standard by which the place of equality as a factor in apportionment can be measured."[19]

Because the Court had said nothing about standards, Frankfurter had nothing concrete to attack. The Court was free to opt for rigid standards, subject to attack for being ill-suited to specific situations, or it could choose flexible standards, subject to attack for leaving the lower courts and the public in doubt as to what the law required. At the time of *Baker v. Carr* the second course seemed the more likely because the majority was talking much the way it had in the school segregation cases. With the Court's struggle against massive resistance in the South not yet over, observers like Jack Peltason had been criticizing the Court for giving no guidelines for desegregation: "What the district judges need—and what most of them want—is not the responsibility for making choices, but rigid mandates that compel them to act. The Supreme Court appears to have made a serious mistake when it delegated so much discretion to the district courts."[20] Yet now, ruling on a subject potentially more explosive than desegregation, the Court would not hazard even so vague a standard as "all deliberate speed." Instead, Brennan, perhaps tacitly relying on the solicitor's brief, declared that judicial standards under the equal protection clause were "well developed and familiar," leaving it open to courts "to determine, if on the particular facts they must, that a discrimination reflects *no* policy, but simply arbitrary and capricious action."[21] Douglas had said in *Baker* that "weighting" was permissible; Clark would permit "rational" systems. With this kind of guidance in the air Frankfurter chose to attack judicial reapportionment as a field not amenable to judicial standards. He characterized it as "a mathematical quagmire . . . into which this Court today catapults the lower courts of the country without so much as adumbrating the basis of a legal calculus as a means of extrication."[22]

A Fair Wind and a Full Sail

Both Frankfurter and the majority seem to have underestimated the resources of the lower courts and the favorable response of the public. Within two years of *Baker v. Carr*, cases were filed attacking unequal districts in forty-one of the fifty states; by March 1964, new apportionment plans had been approved in twenty-six states, often under heavy pressure from the courts. In Wisconsin, legislators were given nineteen days to reapportion, in Michigan thirty-three days, in Delaware twelve days.[23] Courts in Alabama, Oklahoma, and Tennessee drew up their own redistricting plans;[24] elsewhere courts threatened to enjoin all elections till reapportionment was carried out or to order at-large elections. The states made no effort to defy apportionment orders, and rapid compliance was almost universal. Enforcement of reapportionment was not nearly the problem in 1963 that most people expected it to be in 1962.[25]

If reapportionment was in the air in 1961, it was falling in showers of ink in law reviews and the public press from 1962 to 1965 under the stimulus of *Baker v. Carr*, with almost all of the commentary being favorable to reapportionment and much of it urging the Court to finish the job by ordering reapportionment in both houses of state legislatures.[26] The slogan *one man, one vote* was dragged out of the storerooms of the National Municipal League and splashed into headlines across the country. A few grumbles could be heard from conservative southern Democrats such as Strom Thurmond, John Stennis, Richard Russell, and Herman Talmadge, but these were largely drowned by the paeans of praise from the ADA, the American Municipal Association, the United States Conference of Mayors, and the Industrial Union Department of the AFL-CIO. Even Barry Goldwater, the embodiment of Republican conservatism, called *Baker v. Carr* "a proper decision."[27]

Once again, the solicitor general was ready to step in, with the warm glow of executive approval, to suggest the next step in converting the desires of a reform-minded public into the law of the land. This time, the vehicle was *Gray v. Sanders*,[28] where the plaintiffs had challenged the Georgia county-unit system as applied to the election of party candidates for statewide office. Since the case involved only elections within a single, statewide district, the case was not a reapportionment case, and the plaintiffs of record knew it. They insisted on the distinction in their brief, claiming an absolute, well-defined personal right of *suffrage*, while avoiding the pulpy, evasive questions of reasonableness raised by claims to a right of *representation*.[29] The solicitor general, by contrast, resolutely obscured the distinction, addressing himself not only to the single-district franchise issue at hand, but also to the "distinct, but related problem" of ending malapportionment throughout the country—perhaps a laudable goal, but one more tactically than logically related to the case at hand. He kept dwelling on items like "inevitable lack of mathematical precision," "extreme and invidious discrimination against any class of voters," and "defying any intelligible explanation." These items, as Robert Dixon pointed out, made sense only in the context of legislative apportionment of more than one district and had no real bearing on the issues of the case.[30] However, they did provide rhetorical cover for later attempts to nail down certain elusive questions of political representation by treating them as suffrage questions, and the Court took the hint so zestfully that one must wonder whether the solicitor's obscurity was by calculation or by oversight. It might have entailed a very slight risk of losing the battle in *Gray v. Sanders*, but it proved invaluable for winning the war in *Reynolds v. Sims*.[31]

Encouraged by favorable words from the solicitor general and the outburst of public reaction to *Baker v. Carr* the Court reacted much as the radical Republicans of the 39th Congress had reacted when they abruptly got tough on black suffrage after their great victories in the elections of 1866: the Court dropped the hedges and qualifications it had insisted on so strongly in *Baker v. Carr*, stoked its boilers with grandiose democratic rhetoric, much of it borrowed from reapportionist commentators, and steamed away at speed toward the passage of a constitutional amendment to embody the rhetoric. Frankfurter's fears that the Court could not produce simple and concrete standards were misplaced; the Court adopted the simplest and most concrete standard possible: every district must be equal in population. This standard may be criticized as cut from whole cloth; it may be criticized as draconian; but it can hardly be criticized as vague.

Frankfurter and Harlan's difficulty in countering the *Baker* majority's evasions and velitations tells something about the public's taste for measurable equality and the triumph of the Guardian Ethic, but it also attests to the shrewdness of the majority's timing and tactics. Timing was as crucial in the short run as it was in the long run; the Court could not have brought off the reapportionment revolution as it stood in 1962, say, in 1922; neither could it have brought off in 1962 what it brought off in 1964: a standard so strict that less than a half-dozen states could pass it. It picked the easiest target first—the Tennessee "crazy quilt," which violated Tennessee's own constitution and attacked only the vulnerable questions of standing and justiciability—ostensibly leaving the question of standards to lower courts on the grounds that they were "well developed and familiar," while confining its attention to its major premise to one sentence: "The right asserted is within the reach of judicial protection under the Fourteenth Amendment." Such cautious language gave the dissenters nothing to shoot at where the majority was weakest. Frankfurter and Harlan were obliged to construct and then attack their own notions of what the majority might mean; they had to join issue across a broad front of hypothetical points, most of them extremely abstruse, which might later be derived from the majority opinion. Unlike dissenters in cases where the majority had taken a stand, Harlan and Frankfurter had to assume a defensive posture for want of something concrete to attack. In this context the grotesque malapportionment which the dissenters were obliged to defend seemed all too concrete, while their objections to the majority opinion seemed all too abstract.

The majority in *Baker v. Carr* was able to lay the groundwork for its later draconian rule with the appearance of permitting the utmost flexibility to do justice in specific cases. A majority of the members of the Court had, in fact, gone on record against the inflexible equal-districts rule that the Court later adopted in *Reynolds v. Sims*. This majority consisted of Douglas and Clark,[32] Harlan and Frankfurter, and Warren, who had supported unequal districts when he was governor of California.[33] With all this flexibility and qualification in the air, however specious it may seem in retrospect, Harlan and Frankfurter may be forgiven for challenging the majority to lay down a rule concrete enough to be understood and applied by the lower courts.

The majority lost no time in taking up the challenge but did not depart from its policy of making its point in a tentative and qualified way in easy cases and then dropping the qualifications in harder ones. In *Gray v. Sanders* the Court followed the lead of the solicitor general. It invalidated the county unit system when applied to a statewide primary election on the narrow ground that there should be no discrimination between electors in a single district, but also with Justice Douglas's magniloquent rationale which could apply as well to electors in different districts: "The conception of political equality from the Declaration of Independence to Lincoln's Gettysburg Address, to the Fifteenth, Seventeenth, and Nineteenth Amendments can mean only one thing, one person, one vote."[34]

Douglas' opinion was the first of three salvos of thunderous rhetoric about fundamental principles of government, ungrounded in the Constitution and more securely rooted in the slogans of the Revolution, Lincoln, and the early reformers than in their actual politics. In the next blast, *Wesberry v. Sanders*,[35] the Court struck down unequal United States congressional districts as a violation of Article I, section 2 of the Constitution, joining issue with the minority for the first time on the textual meaning and intent of the relevant part of the Constitution. Article I, section 2 says that the House of Representatives "shall be composed of members chosen every second year by the people of the several States." Justice Black, writing for the Court, drew the dubious conclusion that election "by the people" implied a constitutional mandate for one person, one vote. This conclusion he attempted to support with a collection of statements by founding fathers that the House of Representatives should be elected "by the people"[36] and statements by James Wilson and James Madison suggesting that they thought the districts should be equal.[37]

This wispy authority could scarcely support the towering structure Black sought to place on it: "our Constitution's plain objective of making equal representation for equal numbers of people the fundamental goal of the House of Representatives."[38] A plainer objective appears in Article I, section 4, which says that the manner of holding congressional elections shall be prescribed by the state legislatures, subject to alteration by Congress—leaving little room for alteration by the Supreme Court. Justice Harlan observed, correctly, in his dissent that equality of representation *among* the states, even in the House of Representatives, ranked behind other aims, such as giving each state a congressman and allowing representation for three-fifths of the nonvoting slave population; moreover, such equality of apportionment as was required *among* the states hardly amounted to a requirement for equality *within* the states. The founders were too interested in creating an operable framework for national union to embroil the convention in disputes over representation in the states; the Court's historical conclusions had far more grandiloquence than truth.

Still, grandiloquence won, and the public loved it. Equality and democracy were on the march; all but a few of the states were in the throes of reapportionment; the great cities made ready to stand unshackled in the new breed of legislature. The Court discovered that it could make its own history in support of a popular cause and get away with it because its intellectual constituency was impatient of historical quibbles, niceties of textual interpretation, and abstruse questions of standards when it could get its teeth into a measurable inequality—and unequal districts were as measurable as anything could be. The democratic creed, feeble as it had been in producing reforms unaided in the field of politics, rallied behind the leadership of the Supreme Court, and thoughtful people across the land who had heard of the equal protection clause called for the Court to use it to equalize districts once and for all. "Equal is equal, isn't it?" they demanded, and the Court was happy to agree as it shed, one by one, the qualifications it had insisted on in *Baker v. Carr* and finally equalized state senates in the six *Reapportionment* cases of June 15, 1964.[39]

The solicitor general was as instrumental in obliterating the qualifications of *Baker v. Carr* as he had been in building them up in the first place. His architectural services in *Baker* and in *Gray v. Sanders* have already been mentioned:[40] he gave the Court executive support, a plausible-looking and flexible-looking constitutional rationale, a mandate for change from the Guardians, a concrete plan for redistricting, and a broad suggested "right to vote" which included both representational and suffrage questions. Now, with reapportionment unexpectedly popular with the political public and with the advent of the first indications that it could indeed be easily enforced, his momentum was away from flexibility and toward the simple, personal right to mathematical equality eventually adopted by the Court.

Robert G. Dixon's subchapter on the role of the solicitor general in co-ordinating the arguments of the plaintiffs in the six 1964 *Reapportionment* cases recalls Caesar's descriptions of his wars in Gaul, with Archibald Cox playing the part of Caesar and the several counsel for the defendants as Gauls. To be sure, the major theme was no longer the struggle of civilization with barbarism, that issue having been joined and largely settled in *Baker v. Carr* in favor of civilization. By 1964 the Guardians' strategic aims had been largely accepted, and the major theme was tactics. Dixon deftly outlined the confrontation between the Guardian plaintiffs, carefully coached, disciplined, united under seasoned expert leadership, and the defendant Gauls, well enough trained in feats of individual bravery and schooled in local jurisprudence, but uncoordinated, wasteful of their limited opportunities for effective communication, bewildered by the subtleties of constitutional litigation, no match for the Romans before the Supreme Court.

With the aid of the Solicitor General [said Dixon] nominally amicus curiae but more nearly plaintiffs' mentor and chief advocate, plaintiffs had an easy time in the "big six" reapportionment appeals. Plaintiffs also had held a planning session to learn each other's cases and to guard against shooting each other down in the course of making a point for their own state.

On the defendants' side there was no planning session, no detailed knowledge of each other's cases, no able co-ordinator of constitutional theory analogous to the Solicitor General on the plaintiffs' side. Too many of the defendants' counsel wasted many of their precious hours of oral argument. They dwelt on the varied topography and geography of their states, sounding like a misplaced chamber of commerce commercial; or they stressed history, which, to a Court that had decided the desegregation case on broad principles

125

of developing constitutionalism, was like trying to get Bertrand Russell to take Holy Communion; or they simply fell into the trap Justice Clark had constructed more neatly than he knew in Baker, by trying to establish how every interdistrict population disparity could be shown to be the result of some clear and "rational" formula, which is almost always an impossibility.[41]

The solicitor general prepared a consolidated argument for all six cases in his brief for Maryland (the most malapportioned of the six); separate briefs related the central argument to the other states in a total sequence of 530 pages. Once again the solicitor attacked the standards problem head-on, this time with a list of four constitutional tests for malapportionment.

1. The basic standard of comparison is the representation accorded qualified voters per capita.
2. The equal protection clause is violated by an apportionment that creates gross inequalities in representation without rhyme or reason.
3. The equal protection clause is violated by a discriminatory apportionment based upon criteria which are contrary to express constitutional limitations or otherwise invidious or irrelevant.
4. The equal protection clause is violated by an apportionment which subordinates the principle of popular representation to the representation of political subdivisions to such a degree as to create gross inequalities in the representation of voters and give control of the legislature to small minorities of the people.[42]

These tests, though somewhat more explicit than the tests recommended in the solicitor's *Baker* brief, still left the question: what does this mean? What kind of criteria for discriminatory apportionment are invidious or irrelevant? What kind of inequalities are gross? Without attempting a catalogue of examples, the solicitor general did urge intervention in all six cases to require equal apportionment of both houses of state legislatures. In five of the cases, he relied on the four standards listed. However, in the sixth case, *Lucas v. Colorado General Assembly,*[43] which was not briefed till after argument in the other five, he made two departures from his prior arguments: on the one hand, he admitted some hesitation about urging intervention under the "closely balanced" Colorado situation—where a 2-1 majority of the voters had approved the malapportioned state senate—but, on the other hand, while declining in words to urge the Court to adopt the rule of per capita equality in both houses,[44] he nonetheless strayed back to the tangled reasoning of his *Gray v. Sanders* brief, that the right to vote and the right to equal representation were pretty much the same thing. This reasoning added up to a demand for per capita equality despite all protestations to the contrary, for, as Dixon pointed out, "voting by a qualified voter does seem to be that kind of civil right which is an absolute and which cannot be 'balanced' and limited by other considerations."[45] It was this most dubious part of the solicitor's reasoning, however, that the Court adopted in the *Reapportionment* cases, and with far less embarrassment and reservation than that displayed by the solicitor.

E-Day

The *Reapportionment* cases raised in bold outline issues that had been inherent in *Baker v. Carr* but which the earlier opinion had carefully avoided or obscured. One of these issues was the problem of standards, the difficulty of devising simple and concrete rules to settle questions of enormous complexity. This is a question of the utmost importance which merits a chapter of its own. Only the concurring opinion of Justices Stewart and Clark addressed this question seriously. Surprisingly, but in line with its practice in prior reapportionment cases, the majority refused to join issue on the policy questions which constituted its strongest grounds. Instead, it concentrated, as it had in *Wesberry v. Sanders*, on textual and historical issues where it was weakest. Here it faced two grave difficulties: the equal protection clause was not addressed to the vote, either on its face or in the minds of those who wrote it and ratified it, and, even if it had been addressed to the vote, it had to proscribe as irrational and invidious in the states the same kind of representative structure the rest of the Constitution requires for the nation.

In logical terms the Court's solution was extremely risqué; in tactical terms it was tried and true. The Court again assumed that the equal protection clause required equal districts and went on to show that, this being so, the districts had to be equal in spite of the federal analogy. Once again the Court finessed the distinction between civil rights protected by the equal protection clause, and political rights, which had been understood to be a separate category not covered by the equal protection clause. Without saying so, the Court had quietly assumed that cod-liver oil had been transubstantiated into wine.

Justice Frankfurter having retired after *Baker v. Carr*, John Marshall Harlan was the only Justice left with the temerity to challenge the false assumption that voting was a civil right protected by the equal protection clause. Harlan's case was overwhelming. He showed that political rights were treated separately in section two of the Fourteenth Amendment, the Fifteenth, and all subsequent voting rights amendments, by the author and other sponsors of the equal protection clause, and by a unanimous Supreme Court in *Minor v. Happersett*.[46] Apportionment seemed to be understood as something other than a section one civil right by the twenty-one (of thirty-three) states ratifying the Fourteenth Amendment but retaining unequal districts in their own constitutions.[47]

Overwhelming though it may have been, Harlan's dissent still suffered from having nothing explicit to overwhelm. In all its apportionment opinions, the Court had added nothing but fluff about the Gettysburg Address and the Declaration of Independence to Brennan's one sentence in *Baker v. Carr* which had claimed without argument that "the right asserted" was "within the reach of judicial protection under the Fourteenth Amendment." The "Fundamental principle of equal representation for equal representation for equal numbers" promulgated by the Court was anchored in the contemporary vogue for equality in measurables, not in the Constitution.

However innocent of support in the Constitution the Court's fundamental rule may have been, the majority found it sufficient to carry the day for its arguments against the federal analogy. Even on the dubious assumption that there was a constitutional right to equal representation in the state legislatures, the Court could not strike down all forms of discrimination on the bare authority of the popular cry, "Equal is equal, isn't it?" Equal protection of the laws does not require that the same law be applied to everything. Though the Court has applied the equal protection clause to voting rights, no one takes it to extend the franchise to children and incompetents. What equal protection does require is that the same law apply to the same class of things, and that discrimination between different classes of things be "rational." All other discrimination is "invidious." In requiring equal districts in both houses of state legislatures the Court faced the disagreeable task of showing that the federal structure of representation was irrational and invidious in the states.

Given the Court's premise, unsupported, self-disavowed, but followed in rigid detail, that equal-sized districts were the only rational basis of representation, the federal analogy was untenable, unequal districts in the states being irrational by definition. Pursuant to its policy of concealing its premise, however, the Court took a different tack, purporting to show by the adoption of a population base in the original constitutions of some of the states and the Northwest Ordinance of 1787 that the federal system was not understood to be a model for the states, whose political subdivisions were never sovereign, as the states themselves had been. Apart from minor historical and logical overstatements which are treated in more detail elsewhere[48] the Court was correct in finding no constitutional obligation on the states to follow the federal system; however, such a showing fell far short of demonstrating an obligation on the states *not* to follow the federal system. This crucial gap the Court stuffed with invocations to prior reapportionment decisions and the "fundamental principles of representative government in this country" which required "equal representation for equal numbers of people."[49] This stuffing, where the strongest logical demonstration should have been, was a fabrication to support the Court's unstated major premise, not a showing of constitutional authority in either the traditional or the modern sense.

128

Voting or Representation?

There is some basis for believing that if the Court had not been so taken up with tactics it could have achieved the same results, or possibly better ones, without ducking the main issues of logic and policy. The policy questions, raised in concurring opinions by Justice Stewart, joined by Justice Clark, are treated separately in the next three chapters. The logical and historical issues could be attacked directly by separating the "right to vote," protected by section two of the Fourteenth Amendment and subsequent amendments using those words, from the "right to equal representation," protectable by the equal protection clause more conveniently than by the opposite but unused guarantee clause.[50] Apportionment was not considered by the 39th Congress, which drew up the Fourteenth Amendment. It can be distinguished generically from the suffrage questions so explicitly excluded from the coverage of the equal protection clause because it is more closely related to problems of the district system than to problems of qualifications.[51] Such a reading would be ahistorical, since most of the ratifying states would have been malapportioned under *Reynolds v. Sims*, but it would be no more ahistorical than the school segregation cases in giving the equal protection clause a meaning not contemplated by its framers and ratifiers. Such a reading is arguably authorized by a "larger intent" of the men who passed the Fourteenth Amendment, and it has come to be an acceptable mode of constitutional interpretation. It would have been a long step up from the Court's actual arguments in *Reynolds*, which were tied to the word *vote* and essentially antihistorical in trying to fob off a fabricated fundamental principle of "one person, one vote" that was exactly the reverse of the text and stated intent of the equal protection clause.

Speculation as to why the Court did not choose the stronger ground should touch on two possible limitations on what the Court could say or do: its own prior rhetoric, and Harlan's and Frankfurter's standing challenges to lay down a simple and workable rule. In a sense the Court was a prisoner of its prior interventions which relied so heavily on a broad interpretation of the right to vote guaranteed by the Fifteenth Amendment in preference to the shadowy right to equal protection of the laws guaranteed by the Fourteenth. Undoubtedly, the Court might have been embarrassed to take back the mighty words it had uttered in the white primary and Tuskegee gerrymander cases and read the right to vote under the Fourteenth Amendment as limited to the right to cast ballots. It had said too much about "effective participation" in the political process and "sophisticated modes of discrimination"; it had built too much on a sweeping, Fifteenth-Amendment right to vote to shift lightly to a lesser one when it switched to the Fourteenth. Such a shift could have been almost as jarring as basing the *Reapportionment* cases on the guarantee clause. In either case the Court would have had to shun, and perhaps even undermine, one of its most vigorous and popular lines of precedent and start a new line on different and untested ground. The public itself saw reapportionment as a voting issue, not a representation issue; it called for one man, one vote and demanded the end of "debased votes." Possibly such a public, riding the same intellectual new wave as the Court, would have been shocked to find that the whole business was not a question of voting at all, but of representation. Closer attention to constitutional logic might well have cost the Court some of the momentum it had painstakingly built up in the course of its prior interventions in voting questions.

On the other hand, the part of the public that is concerned about the Court's rationale is comparatively small, and a good share of this small part may have been more shocked by the Court's chosen misrepresentation than by the redefinition it spurned. For the rest the egalitarian results of the decisions were undoubtedly rationale enough, and the Warren Court was never noted for its hesitation to distinguish or reverse awkward precedent to arrive at a right-minded result. The threat of losing momentum by itself should not have been enough to make the Court cling to its broad definition of voting rights.[52]

A more pertinent threat arising from dropping voting in favor of representation is that representation raises more squarely the problems of standards and policy stressed by Frankfurter and Harlan. Representation is an issue even broader than voting in the modern understanding because it suggests the question of effectiveness which the Court had assiduously avoided. A man's vote may be scrupulously equal to the state average in terms of the fraction of a representative his vote commands, but he cannot be equally represented if his candidate never wins in his district, or, winning, is always in the minority in the legislature, or, winning and being in a majority, is frustrated by some quirk in the system—lobby pressure, filibustering, judicial intervention, bloc voting, and so on—which bars effective action by the majority. His vote may be equal in a technical sense, but his representation is hardly equal to that of the man or interest, voting or nonvoting, which gets action it wants from the state.

But the question of effectiveness, of who gets action and how much, is not answerable in simple, measurable terms. Political influence acts in different ways with different issues and at different times with the same issue; it is too volatile for any court to add it up and divide it evenly among all the voters in a state. The Court did indeed use the term *representation* in the *Reapportionment* cases, notably in its Fundamental Principle of equal representation for equal numbers, but it tried to show by many references to voting rights that *representation* was just another word for its broad use of *voting*. The retention of and stress on the term *voting* helped to keep the intangible elements of representation out of bounds, de-emphasizing all forms of influence which did not directly involve voting, and providing the basis of the simple and superficially egalitarian equal districts rule. This rule embodied a brave attempt by the Court to define itself out of the quagmire, but it also left open the question whether it did, in fact, secure equal representation for equal numbers.

VI. The Fundamental Principle

and the Quagmire

These are deep questions where great names militate against each other, where reason is perplexed, and an appeal to authorities only thickens the confusion; for high and reverend authorities lift up their heads on both sides, and there is no sure footing in the middle. This point is the great Serbonian bog, between Damiata and Mount Casius old, where armies whole have sunk.
—Edmund Burke

Simplicity v. Applicability

When the Warren Court "discovered" the Fundamental Principle of equal representation for equal numbers, it opened up many options for itself and for its successors to apply the Fundamental Principle to new situations. It had managed to skirt the quagmire in the reapportionment cases, but there is more to equal representation than equal districts. In the half-decade between *Reynolds v. Sims* and Warren's retirement in 1969, the justices repeatedly had to choose among applying the Fundamental Principle to new realms, renouncing it, and leaving it in abeyance for future courts to apply if they could get away with it. In general, the Warren Court was quite cautious about fresh adventures with the Fundamental Principle because most of its options seemed to verge on the quagmire.

Frankfurter's "mathematical quagmire" was a function of the difficulty of dealing with complex or sensitive political questions with simple rules such as can be laid down and enforced by a court of appeals. After the Supreme Court laid down its simple rule in the form of the Fundamental Principle of equal representation for equal numbers, as with prior voting reforms, the country had to face a period of adjustment of the new rhetorical principles to political facts. This chapter essays a chart of the quagmire, attempting to distinguish dry ground that can be policed with simple rules from boggy areas that resist rules. In general, although the Court's rhetoric could apply to the whole range of voting problems—administrative abuses, qualifications, districting problems, and checks and balances—most of the last two categories are quagmire which the Court could not traverse without going in over its head.

Throughout history, certain kinds of discrimination have been easy targets for reform by rule-making. Administrative abuses are simple and blatant, easily attacked by a rule. So are qualifications to vote: distinguishing felons, idiots, women, nonwhites, and even illiterates has presented no great conceptual problem. Reapportionment itself, if it is considered solely a question of relative district population, is easy to handle with a rule. A district is either equal or it is not.[1] Other forms of discrimination, however, have resisted rules. Tricks of the district system more complicated than the population of the districts, gerrymanders, multi-member districts, and so forth, present too many different versions of equality for one rule to impose them all. Organizational and constitutional quirks are even harder to reach. Who can measure the inequalities of representation deriving from the seniority system, from bloc voting, from party intrigue, arm-twisting in the hall, an interventionist court, or the chief executive's nagging wife? These forms of influence are lumped together as checks-and-balances questions with the Madisonian hope that they will cancel each other out but also with the conviction that they will never yield to a simple rule, no matter who promulgates it.

However hard it may be to measure these more complex forms of discrimination or to equalize them with simple rules, it is just as hard to ignore them, particularly for a public that has grown to accept the large reading of voting rights and representation rights already espoused by the Court. The Guardian technique of looking through forms to the realities they conceal has become too much the mode for the post-Warren Court to be wholly at ease with the formal rules laid down in the Warren era. The Court must still face the task of adjusting its rhetoric to deal with actual situations.

Voting for Federal Office

The Senate and the Electoral College.   At the federal level, the reapportionment cases raised questions about the legitimacy of the Senate under the equal districts rule.[2] It also raised questions about the electoral college, which had a numerical bias favoring the small states and an operational bias favoring the large ones. Both of these questions fell deep into the checks-and-balances category, besides entailing a threat of a head-on collision with the other branches. The Warren Court managed to avoid action on either question, despite efforts by Delaware to invoke the Court's original jurisdiction to abolish the unit rule which favored New York and other larger states in the electoral college.[3]

Although the Warren Court did not directly intervene to reform the electoral college, it did indirectly influence congressional reformers to take up the task by popularizing the one man, one vote slogan. Between the *Baker* decision in 1962 and the massive 1970 senatorial campaign for direct election of the president, the impetus for reform passed from conservatives, who thought the electoral college favored the large urban states excessively, to liberals, who were alarmed over various theoretical disasters, such as minority presidents, third-party threats, and resolution in the House of Representatives, which the electoral college could produce. There have been many attempts throughout the nation's history to replace the electoral college with a different system: either direct election, proportional division of state votes, or election through delegates from congressional districts. These were all revived after *Baker v. Carr*, but the strongest initial effort was for the two most conservative of the three options—districts or proportional election—and the initial sponsors were quite a different group from the urban-minded Guardians who had backed reapportionment. In general, the would-be electoral college reformers of 1963 were moderate or conservative senators from small states, desirous of taking down the big states a peg or two by altering the perceived structural bias of the electoral college, which favored big states.

In June 1963 two proposed amendments abolishing the unit rule were approved by the Senate Subcommittee on Constitutional Reform. One bill, introduced by Senator Karl Mundt (R, S. Dak.), called for electors from each congressional district, with two electors for each state. The district method divided state delegations, localized contests, and favored small rural states. Its cosponsors were mostly conservative: Strom Thurmond (D, S.C.), John McClellan (D, Ark.), Roman Hruska (R, Nebr.), Thurston Morton (R, Ky.), Hiram Fong (R, Hawaii), Caleb Boggs (R, Del.), John Stennis (D, Miss.), Winston Prouty (R, Vt.), and Barry Goldwater (R, Ariz.). The other bill, introduced by Estes Kefauver (D, Tenn.), called for proportional division of votes cast in each state. It also divided state delegations and benefited small, rural states, though not so much as the district method. It was cosponsored by a more moderate range of senators: Thomas Dodd (D, Conn.), Thomas Kuchel (R, Calif.), Jennings Randolph (D, W.Va.), Leverett Saltonstall (R, Mass.), John Sparkman (D, Ala.), and Claiborne Pell (D, R.I.). According to calculations of the *Congressional Quarterly*, either method would have given Richard Nixon the victory in the close election of 1960 over the urban man's candidate, John F. Kennedy, who, in 1956, two years before he attacked malapportionment in the *New York Times*, had solemnly and providentially warned Congress not to tamper with the electoral college for fear of producing unwanted effects in practical politics.

Kennedy's comparative indifference to perceived antirural discrimination was not unique. Other partisans of reapportionment, such as the American Political Science Association and the *New Republic*, were likewise unmoved over the electoral college's debasement of rural votes. The *New York Times* did, in 1966, advocate reform of the electoral college, but it insisted that the reform should be brought about by following the stern path set forth in Article V and not by wave of the judicial wand, as had been true of reapportionment. The solicitor general, the urban lobbies, and the establishment foundations that mobilized academic and political opinion against malapportionment appeared to share Kennedy's unconcern over the pro-urban bias of the electoral college. So, it seemed, did the Supreme Court. Since neither of the conservatives' amendments had made it out of the Senate Judiciary Committee, the anti-urban reformers took their case to the Supreme Court, which had just proclaimed the Fundamental Principle of equal votes for equal numbers and even, in *Gray v. Sanders*, proclaimed that the electoral college was based on a "conception of equality that belongs to a bygone day." In this case, however, the plaintiffs could not be classed with the warmest proponents of the Guardian Ethic; they had been rather far from the vanguard in the mobilization for reapportionment; moreover, they were asking for a rather vague and awkward remedy without the handy threat of imposing at-large elections, since at-large elections were just what they wanted to get rid of. Could it be that such non-Guardian personages as J. Harvie Williams of the American Good Government Society, James Kirby, chief counsel of the Senate Constitutional Amendments Subcommittee, John Gosnell of the National Small Business Association, law professor Robert Dixon, perhaps the foremost critic of the reapportionment cases, and the attorneys general of thirteen small states were trying to embarrass the Court? For whatever reason, the Court refused to hear the case (as it had every right to do in the exercise of its original jurisdiction) and sent the plaintiffs on their unanointed way, with the Guardians snickering at their barbarous attempt to invoke the Fundamental Principle for the wrong cause.

It was not many years, however, before the tables had turned, with the Guardians now pushing for reform of the electoral college—along with the normally conservative American Bar Association and the Chamber of Commerce of the United States—while the most conservative surviving sponsors of the 1963 reform proposals fought the 1970 reforms tooth and nail. The Guardian turnaround, which produced majorities for reform in both houses of Congress (though the amendment was ultimately defeated by filibuster in the Senate), may be ascribed to several factors. For one, the 1970 amendment called for direct nationwide election, rather than for proportional or district allocation of state votes. Direct election rewards voter turnout, not just bare population; hence, it might be expected to favor northern and western states with high turnout over southern states with low turnout, and also high-education, high-income, high-turnout voters. Liberals could thus expect some payoff from direct election not available from any of the other systems, including the existing electoral college. On the other hand, voter turnout in the South rose steadily during the 1960's, diminishing the payoff to northern liberals but also diminishing the penalty, and hence perhaps the determined opposition of southern conservatives who had traditionally rendered direct election impossible to pass. Southern turnout for the 1964 presidential election was almost 20 percent behind that of the rest of the country: 56.7 percent to 74.6 percent. But by 1968 the North and West were down to 71 percent and the South was up to 60.1 percent, narrowing the gap to 11 percent. Southern whites still stood to lose by virtue of the remaining gap, and also because many of the new southern votes were black; nevertheless, northern conservatives like Everett Dirksen (R, Ill.), and the American Bar Association, continued to support direct election as more likely to be adopted than the other two reform alternatives because of probable opposition by northern, urban liberals.

Despite its origin in the legislature under anti-Guardian sponsorship and despite the early coldness of the Guardians and the branches of government most attuned to the Guardian Ethic, the movement to reform the electoral college ultimately showed many signs of the Ethic's influence in Congress (and on the public) at the very time it was being repudiated by much the same public in the executive and the judiciary. By 1970 congressional support for reform was strong, broadly based, and not very partisan, and the reformers' motives appeared to be mostly of the modern sort: high-minded, managerial, egalitarian, sensitive to scholarly opinion, pursuant of an abstract, aesthetic justice, and with no great concern over political payoff, nor, in fact, for other political consequences of the reform in application. The 1968 elections focused attention on two lines of scholarly thought originating in the middle 1960's: John F. Banzhaf's mathematical demonstration that bloc voting in different-sized units (states) gave more choice to voters in the largest units, and Charles W. Bischoff's redoubtable statistical examination of elections from 1920 to 1964, suggesting that in very close elections (for example, 1960) there was no better than a 50-50 chance that the popular winner would win in the electoral college. The Country was experiencing a legitimacy crisis in 1968. The Roosevelt coalition (as happened from time to time) was falling to pieces. Intellectuals and others were having second thoughts about the Guardian Ethic in connection with the Vietnam War; on the other hand, they were horrified by all the inegalitarian and anti-Guardian threats posed by the election. Some of these were very real, for example, the threat that the parties might nominate candidates insufficiently eager to liquidate the obscenity in Vietnam on the spot and spend the proceeds to wipe out poverty. There was also a genuine threat that the less Guardian of the candidates so nominated might win the election.

Less justified by the facts, in my opinion, but no less disturbing to the intellectuals was the thought that the winner, already morally tainted by his policies, might owe his victory to quirks in the system which frustrated the will of the majority. When the Democrats nominated Hubert Humphrey (whom

polls showed to be the candidate most Democrats preferred), liberal intellectuals howled with outrage at the party's failure to "democratize" the nomination by representing youth, women, and blacks at the convention in accordance with their numbers in the population at large. The APSA, along with its
sister organizations in sociology, psychology, and history, blackballed Chicago for sheltering the convention that betrayed democracy, and the nomination was not the end of it. After the nomination came the possibilities that
the popular winner might not win in the electoral college, or that neither
candidate could get a majority in the college, leaving the balance of power in
the hands of the unspeakable segregationist third-party candidate, George
Wallace. Or that the electors might vote according to their own whims, or
that those eleven big states would all vote in a bloc, or that the little states
had too many electors or that John Banzhaf was right about voters in big
states having a mathematical advantage. Abstract statistical lucubrations of
scholars like Banzhaf and Bischoff, unknown to the public at large, figured in
the calculations and concerns of pertinent legislators and their staffs, suggesting that the Guardian Ethic, eclipsed in the executive and judiciary by the
events of 1968, was thriving in Congress. The 1968 elections once again raised
the old theoretical bogeys formerly affected by the conservatives, this time in
a manner better calculated to appeal to liberal reformers already sensitized by
the reapportionment cases to abstract, theoretical standards of democracy.

Besides focusing attention on new theories about the shortcomings of the
electoral college, the 1968 elections diminished the force of the old belief
that the unit rule favored the urban, liberal voter. In contrast to John F. Kennedy's narrow victory in 1960, in 1968 it was the not-so-urban, not-so-liberal
Richard Nixon who won 301 votes in the electoral college (to Humphrey's
191), with a popular edge of less than one percent of the votes. Applying
Bischoff's technique of assuming constant distribution of votes nationwide
and computing votes needed to win by adding them proportionally in every
state (rather than selectively by hindsight in two or three big states with close
votes), Carleton Sterling reckoned that Humphrey would not have won an
electoral college majority even if he had outpolled Nixon by a million popular
votes. By the distribution pattern of 1968, the liberal coalition would have
done better with a direct, popular election than with the electoral college.
Sterling concluded that bloc voting in the electoral college did not favor
urban, liberal, and ethnic groups, as the profession had long supposed it did.[4]

By the end of 1970, when it gathered the necessary two-thirds majority in
the House and was barely defeated in the Senate, direct election had attracted
strong support from the liberals with only a fragmentary loss of its accustomed conservative support. Among liberal opinionmakers, the *New York
Times* and the *Washington Post* supported the Bayh amendment, calling for
direct election with a popular runoff if neither candidate received more than
40 percent of the vote. Other liberal forces supporting direct election were

the AFL-CIO, Americans for Democratic Action, the American Civil Liberties Union, the B'nai B'rith Women, Allard K. Lowenstein, and Theodore C. Sorensen, special counsel, biographer, and speechwriter for John F. Kennedy. Sorensen initimated that Kennedy, had he lived, would have abandoned his former opposition to electoral college reform under the influence of the reapportionment decisions and come out for direct election of the president:

> Opponents of the direct election of Presidents often cite the words of Senator John F. Kennedy in opposition to this proposal in 1956. Inasmuch [said speechwriter Sorensen] as I had some connection with those statements, I should point out that Senator Kennedy, as a Senator from a populous State, was defending the big-State preference inherent in the present system; that he felt obligated to oppose all changes in order to maximize the opposition he was leading to the proportional and district division schemes which had a real prospect of passage that year whereas direct elections had none anyway; that he spoke of maintaining the balance of an entire "solar system" of advantages and disadvantages in our political system, in which the urban advantage in the electoral college was needed to offset the rural advantage in the House of Representatives, the latter not then having been emasculated by the Supreme Court's one-man, one-vote decision; and, finally, that he spoke before the 1960 and 1968 elections provided us not only examples of faithless and unpledged electors but electoral vote results so close as to bring us to the brink of constitutional crisis.[5]

As liberals like Sorensen and Lowenstein flocked to the once-conservative cause, a split took place in the ranks of the conservatives, with some groups, like the American Bar Association, the Chamber of Commerce of the United States, and the National Cotton Council, holding fast in some measure for direct election, while others, such as the American Good Government Society, opposed it. The ABA's rhetoric, heavy with scorn for the "archaic, undemocratic, complex, ambiguous, indirect, and dangerous" electoral college and well larded with invocations of the reapportionment cases, was strikingly Guardian. Opponents of the direct election included many of the conservative cosponsors of the district plan in prior sessions. Senators McClellan, Hruska, Fong, Thurmond, and Goldwater opposed direct election—correctly, I believe—for threatening to undermine the party system by raising the payoff for small parties and substituting a volatile, plebiscitary majority for the stable, party-structured majority which has traditionally governed the country.

The nearest the Senate came to a vote on the Bayh amendment was a vote to invoke cloture against the defecting conservatives and the southern senators who threatened to filibuster the bill to an overtimely demise. The cloture vote was 54 to 36, six votes short of the two-thirds the reformers needed. Support and opposition to the motion was bipartisan, with 33 Democrats and 21 Republicans favoring the reform, and 18 of each party opposing

it. The heart of the opposition was 19 southern senators, including 16 Democrats and 3 Republicans, voting the apparent interests of their constituents.
Two southern Democrats, Senators Gore of Tennessee and Yarborough of
Texas, supported the motion, along with one Republican, Senator Baker of
Tennessee. Senators from twenty-six small states with less than nine votes in
the electoral college, were divided almost evenly: 25 voted for cloture; 21
voted against; 6 abstained. To all appearances, reform of the electoral college,
which had started out looking like a traditional reform aimed at beefing up
the power of the conservatives, wound up a modern one, governed more by
abstract aesthetic than concrete partisan concerns. Had it succeeded, it would
no doubt have added to the symmetry of government; I suspect it would also
have subtracted from its operability.[6]

The House of Representatives: The Powell Case. The Warren Court, of
course, had no part in the debate over reforming the electoral college other
than to popularize the idea that one man, one vote was the Fundamental
Principle of the Constitution. However, Warren did lead the Court to a more
active role in settling Congressman Adam Clayton Powell's challenge to the
90th Congress for refusing to seat him. Asserting a somewhat modified version of the Fundamental Principle, Warren invalidated the Congress' act in his
last opinion before he retired. He concluded that Congress's authority to "be
the Judge of the Elections, Returns and Qualifications of its own Members"
(Article I, section 5) did not extend beyond the age, residence, and citizenship qualifications stipulated in Article I, section 2. Therefore, Congress could
not refuse to seat Powell for official misconduct and involvement in a civil
suit, as these were not covered by Article I, section 2. To support his narrow
reading of Article I, section 5, Warren relied on historical precedent, notes
and comments from the Harvard and Chicago law reviews, and "a fundamental principle of our representative democracy . . . in Hamilton's words,
'that the people should choose whom they please to govern them.' "[7]

Warren's position was logically and historically defensible (albeit a trifle out
of line with his reasoning in *Lucas v. Forty-Fourth General Assembly*), but
the Court was extremely circumspect about holding Congress accountable to
the new Fundamental Principle. Unlike Warren's successor, the then circuit
judge Warren Burger (whose decision was reversed in *Powell v. McCormack*[8]),
Warren and his colleagues were able to avoid a collision over reinstatement by
waiting until the 90th Congress had adjourned and the 91st Congress had
given Powell back his seat, though not the salary or the seniority denied him
by the 90th Congress. The Court did not rule on seniority, and, though it did
declare that Powell was entitled to his salary, it remanded the case to the trial
court for resolution of the hard question of how the salary payment was to
be enforced.

State Voting Questions: Qualifications

The Court had better prospects of intervening in state voting questions than federal for two reasons: the Court was stronger against the states than it was against the other branches, and the problems of rule-making were somewhat simpler. Nevertheless, even in the states the prospects of intervention were and are limited. In the most accessible area of potential reform, qualifications to vote, Congress entered the lists just after *Baker v. Carr*, passing what was to become the Twenty-Fourth Amendment to bar poll taxes in federal elections. The Supreme Court welcomed the idea but promptly rendered the new amendment something of a dead letter by reading an even broader amendment, abolishing poll taxes in state elections, into the equal protection clause.[9] Congress also attacked language and literacy tests in the Voting Rights Act of 1965, which received a warmer endorsement from the Court than the Twenty-Fourth Amendment.[10] It was shortly to attack certain age and residency requirements in the Voting Rights Act of 1970.

Age Qualifications

Eighteen-Year-Old Vote. Though the Warren Court did impose the same standards of due process for juveniles as adults in criminal actions,[11] it did not attack age requirements, or, for that matter, sanity requirements. Qualifications plainly related to competence should have been safe from judicial attack under the Guardian Ethic, which is amenable to the disfranchisement of the less competent and a fortiori amenable to disfranchising the incompetent. Just at the end of the Warren era, however, older notions of competence as a function of maturity in years were challenged in the scholarly press. Thomas Spencer's "Proposal for Voting Reform" appeared in a respected philosophical journal in July 1968, arguing that "the franchise should be extended to younger persons than now have it (*perhaps* seventeen- or sixteen-year-olds, but *certainly* eighteen-year-olds) and withdrawn from persons who are past sixty years of age," in order to "get the best possible electorate." Spencer cited a number of studies indicating that people over sixty were neither liberal nor future oriented and were undisposed and ill-equipped to learn new things, inclined to base their judgments "on attitudes rather than logical analysis," and possessed of "strong feelings of loyalty which might cause them to make decisions according to the recommendations of a trusted friend or group." Spencer wisely forbore to apply his reasoning to qualifications for office (say, membership on the Supreme Court) but assumed that younger people's greater ability to gain and retain new information, analogize, infer, and evaluate would add up to the *"special* mental endowments" necessary to produce a dynamic, liberal society.[12]

A month or so later, in Chicago, thousands of young people gathered to support their candidate, Eugene McCarthy, for the Democratic party nomination for president. McCarthy's candidacy had been a startling demonstration of the political power of youth outraged at the Vietnam War. McCarthy had relied heavily on young campaign workers, whose zealous efforts elicited strong support in primary elections, prompted the withdrawal of Lyndon Johnson from the race and the ill-starred entry of another peace-and-youth candidate, Robert Kennedy. By convention time, however, Kennedy had been shot, and most of the delegates had been cornered by Johnson's heir, Hubert Humphrey, who ran in none of the primaries but dominated the smoke-filled rooms. Hordes of young people converged on Chicago to protest, but their zeal was more than matched by that of the Chicago police. Threats, fists, cans of urine flew; billyclubs crunched; Humphrey won the nomination but lost the election to Richard Nixon, who favored gradual de-escalation of the war, but whose life style and values were an abomination to the Now Crowd.

Despite their success in reversing the trend of military involvement, the young people felt betrayed by a system which had not accorded them total victory. Agitation for the eighteen-year-old vote, a staple by-product of every war in this century, reached unprecedented proportions with a new rhetoric featuring educational credentials rather than military service. Both Nixon and Johnson had endorsed the eighteen-year-old vote in 1968 "not because they are old enough to fight, but because they are smart enough to vote." The Youth Franchise Coalition was founded in February 1969 to bring together twenty-three civil-rights-oriented groups which had flowered in the age of the modern Court: the groups included ADA, NAACP, SCLC, various kinds of Young Democrats and student groups, and YMCA.[13] The moment of truth, however, took place in March 1970, when the *New York Times* endorsed the eighteen-year-old vote, again in the light of the high educational attainments of modern college-age youths. "Young people presently in the affected age bracket are far better prepared educationally for the voting privilege than the bulk of the nation's voters have been throughout much of its history."[14]

This call was translated into law with startling rapidity, and not directly through judicial pronouncement either, but by a sequence of result-oriented maneuvers in the political branches, which some found reminiscent of the Court's treatment of voting rights in the 1960's. As with the reapportionment cases, most people liked the idea of a more extended, more equal franchise. Barry Goldwater joined with Edward Kennedy in endorsing the eighteen-year-old vote, and so did the post-Guardian president, Richard Nixon, though Nixon believed that the vote could not be conveyed by simple statute but required a constitutional amendment. Nationwide turmoil on college campuses in 1969 and 1970 lent a special sense of urgency to the movement, for many people supposed that lowering the voting age would calm the resentment of college-age youths over the prospect of bearing the burdens of the detested

Vietnam War under a system that seemed to ignore their desires while responding to those of the untutored but enfranchised Silent Majority.

Senate Majority Leader Mike Mansfield, with tactical adroitness rivalling that of the Supreme Court in the reapportionment cases, smuggled the eighteen-year-old vote through both Houses with almost no serious debate as to its merits or constitutionality. Mansfield's strategy was to tie the eighteen-year-old vote to other objectives so urgent as to stymie both effective opposition and serious discussion. The eighteen-year-old vote was attached as a rider to a bill extending the Voting Rights Act of 1965, along with three measures sponsored by the Nixon administration: extension of federal voting supervision to areas outside the South, suspension of literacy tests in all states for five years, and liberalized residency and absentee voting requirements for presidential elections. The combined bill was then brought to a quick vote, with the acquiescence of conservative and southern senators, who hoped (in vain, as it turned out) to get on with the confirmation of G. Harrold Carswell, Nixon's second southern nominee for the Supreme Court. From that moment, the passage of the eighteen-year-old vote provision was assured by the strong and widespread support for extending the Voting Rights Act of 1965, plus the press of finishing business before the end of the session. The Senate overwhelmingly endorsed the combined bill, despite complaints from New Yorkers Jacob Javits, Emmanuel Celler, and John Lindsay that the bill should not apply to the North (where there was supposed to be no discrimination) and despite a very widespread feeling among senators that the eighteen-year-old vote should be granted by constitutional amendment.[15]

Notwithstanding doubts of the bill's constitutionality both in Congress and among constitutional scholars,[16] the House of Representatives, in its anxiety to extend the Voting Rights Act of 1965, was obliged to take the Senate bill without alteration and with only one hour of debate on the floor and none in committee. Any changes in the bill would have sent it to conference committee too late in the season for it to have been enacted. Paradoxically, one of the main sponsors of the bill in the House was Emmanuel Celler, who had long opposed the eighteen-year-old vote in principle and admitted that he felt in his bones that the courts would declare it unconstitutional. Celler felt that the extension of the Voting Rights Act was of such overriding importance as to justify the passage of the unwanted and unconstitutional rider. By a large margin the House passed the bill unchanged and almost undebated; the president then signed the bill for the sake of extending the Voting Rights Act, giving concurrent instructions to his attorney general to start a case to test the doubtful constitutionality of the eighteen-year-old vote provision. From the moment of drafting, legislative and executive authorities charged with consideration of the bill chose to defer to the Court's judgment of its constitutionality, since neither the House of Representatives nor the president were in a position to exercise an item veto.

When Congress and the president had finished deferring to the Court, however, they left the Court some awkward questions as to how far it should defer to Congress. The Warren Court had been quite cautious about extending its Fundamental Principle to fields outside of reapportionment; however, it had invoked the equal protection clause to abolish poll taxes in state elections, and it also had upheld a provision of the Voting Rights Act of 1965 which overrode state requirements for literacy in English where the registrant had completed the sixth grade in Puerto Rico and was presumed literate in Spanish. This 1966 case, *Katzenbach v. Morgan,*[17] was the major authority cited by Harvard Professors Paul Freund and Archibald Cox to support Congress' power to regulate suffrage under the equal protection clause. The Court had invoked the clause, stating in the most deferential of terms, "It is enough that we be able to perceive a basis upon which the Congress might resolve the conflict as it did."[18]

The Court had also to reckon with the implications of the "compelling state interest" test, a powerful weapon of intervention propounded in several Warren-era cases to reverse the normal presumption that "a statutory discrimination will not be set aside if any state of facts reasonably may be conceived to justify it."[19] Where the statute was alleged to infringe certain "basic civil and political rights," this presumption was held inapplicable and the state had to justify the statute by showing that it was necessary to serve a compelling state interest, an exceedingly difficult task under the Court's narrow definition of the word "necessary." "The right to exercise the franchise in a free and unimpaired manner" was supposed to require such a showing,[20] a startling reversal of James Madison's and John Bingham's original understanding that the states retained control of the franchise.

This compelling-state-interest doctrine lent a special piquancy to the Guardian desire to probe the many issues the Court had opened up in the Warren years but avoided deciding. Did the states have to show "necessity" for the twenty-one-year-old vote to serve compelling state interest? Gerrymanders? Multi-member districts? Bloc voting in the electoral college? Residency requirements? Age requirements for holding office? Despite the compelling-state-interest test, the Warren Court ducked these questions for the best of reasons: most of them were either too subtle to be decided with simple rules, too blatantly legislative for the Court to risk, or both. They invited the Court into the quagmire, and, though many plaintiffs, emboldened by the grand language of the reapportionment and subsequent voting rights cases of the 1960's, had pressed for a decision, the Court always had found ways to avoid a ruling.

Between the Voting Rights Act's passage in June 1970 and January 1971, when the eighteen-year-old vote was to go into effect, the country was in a state of constitutional limbo. We may have been spared a crisis over the November elections only by the benign inaction of the lower courts. The problem was the self-effectuating nature of the Fourteenth Amendment, which the Warren Court had vigorously espoused since the school segregation case. If barring eighteen-year-olds violated the equal protection clause in January, why not also in November? And if eighteen-year-olds, why not sixteen-year-olds and all those other categories that the Court had managed to leave alone before Congress acted? Was not the system irrational which welcomed dotards with sixth-grade educations to the polls while excluding the best-educated tenth-graders in our entire history? As it turned out, the several cases pushing this point were stalled in the lower courts, hampered by long dockets, by plaintiffs who kept growing up while awaiting judicial relief, and no doubt also by sound judicial discretion. Had any of the cases been decided in favor of the young plaintiffs, there would have been enormous pressure on the Supreme Court to resolve the resultant perplexity about the 1970 elections and do it quickly to avert a crisis of confidence over the elections.[21]

Spared this difficult task, the Court divided almost perfectly in half over the validity of the eighteen-year-old vote provisions. In *Oregon v. Mitchell*[22] the justices divided almost perfectly on partisan lines over the eighteen-year-old vote, with all four Republicans, Harlan, Stewart, Blackmun, and Burger, holding the provision unconstitutional, and four of five Democrats, Brennan, Douglas, Marshall, and White, upholding the provision. The fifth Democrat, Justice Black, cast the deciding vote. He agreed with the Republicans that the equal protection clause did not empower Congress to regulate the voting age for state elections; however, he felt that Article I, section 4, which permits Congress to make or alter state regulations prescribing the "manner" of holding congressional elections, permitted it to require the eighteen-year-old vote in federal elections.[23] Of equal importance with the Republican justices' rejection of the Guardian Ethic for age qualifications in *Oregon v. Mitchell* was their acceptance of it for congressional regulation of literacy and residence tests in the same case. All four Republican justices joined the Democrats in upholding the 1970 Voting Rights Act's ban on literacy tests under the Fifteenth Amendment; all but Harlan endorsed the thirty-day residency requirement for voting in presidential elections, feeling that presidential elections were arguably of more exclusively federal concern than congressional elections.[24]

The Voting Rights Act of 1970, in the light of *Oregon v. Mitchell*, seems to have been a relatively innocuous example of the modern reform. Constitutional scholars no doubt welcomed it for making the Court furnish some specifics in the cloudy constitutional areas where the Warren Court had suggested the Fundamental Principle might apply. Not only did it tip the hand of the new justices, it also moved Justice Brennan, by now writing in dissent, to attempt to supply the constitutional foundation for judicial intervention under the equal protection clause he had so conspicuously omitted from his opinion of the prior decade, in *Baker v. Carr*. The act did not, as it turned out, produce a crisis over the 1970 elections. It did, as interpreted by the Court, put pressure on the states to adopt the eighteen-year-old vote for state elections to avoid having to maintain separate rolls for state and federal elections. With this additional impetus the states ratified the Twenty-Sixth Amendment in the summer of 1971, guaranteeing the eighteen-year-old vote on a nationwide basis.[25] Unlike contemporary proposals to reform the nominating conventions and the electoral college, neither the Voting Rights Act nor the Twenty-Sixth Amendment threatened to weaken the party system. If one may judge from the results of the 1972 elections, the political effects of enfranchising eighteen-year-olds have been negligible, apart from a few contests (such as that for the presidency) where one side took the youth vote too seriously and lost more heavily than it might have had it paid more attention to older voters.

The Rise and Fall of the Youth Bloc Myth. During the controversy over enfranchising eighteen-year-olds the questions of *cui bono* and *quantum bonum* were muted. Support for the Twenty-Sixth Amendment, though not always enthusiastic, was generally bipartisan. Most knowledgeable political scientists and veteran poll watchers believed on the basis of voting patterns and polls in prior elections that the eighteen-year-olds would not turn out in large numbers to vote and that those turning out would not vote as a bloc but would divide much like their elders—though with somewhat diminished party loyalty and slightly greater attraction to extremist candidates at both ends of the political spectrum. Centrist Democratic strategists Richard M. Scammon and Ben J. Wattenberg, writing after the 1968 elections but prior to the ratification of the Twenty-Sixth Amendment, spoke for this school. They sharply discounted the youth vote as an independent political force and warned their readers that the great majority of American voters were middle-aged, middle-class and middle-minded, and not fond of youthful extravagance in their politics. "Might not youth support," they asked, "be the kiss of death for any candidate who sought to appeal to the broad middle class of America?"[26]

On the other hand, many people in that image-sensitive time believed that the youth of the 1970's would be sui generis in its political behavior. Surely this of all generations the most highly educated in history, the only one to have lived in the World Village since infancy, and the possessor of its own (counter-) culture and consciousness (III), could hardly be expected to follow in the same routines as its dull, apathetic, ill-educated, and conformist predecessors.[27] These fancies were not wholly groundless. The 1960's had been a decade of unprecedented youth impact, both in numbers and tone. Adolescence began earlier and ended later than ever before. The cohort of fourteen-to-twenty-four-year-olds born during the baby boom of the 1940's and 1950's grew by a startling 13.8 million in the 1960's, more than the total increase for all of the preceding seven decades.[28] A growing percentage of this multitude went to college, necessitating the opening of one new institution of higher education per week during the 1960's. Educators, media people, frisbee makers, and others interested in the booming youth market (including politicians) looked with perhaps excessive awe on the new generation, the biggest, gaudiest, most lavishly cultivated, yet seemingly the most careless of traditional cultivation that had ever been seen.

The new youth culture was most conspicuous in the worlds of fashion and entertainment, but it had political dimensions also. It had heroes in John and then Robert Kennedy; it had dreams of making the world more like Camelot; it had rhetoric to show how and why the dreams had to come true; and it had enough organizational discipline and shrewdness to furnish effective campaigners for Robert Kennedy, Eugene McCarthy, and George McGovern. On the other hand, though the dreams were shared by many, the discipline was possessed by only a few, whose craving to save the world sometimes outweighed their tolerance of its inhabitants and their preferred institutions. It seemed a good idea in the early 1960's to send young Peace Corps people out to save other people from their archaic institutions. No one other than southerners worried when northern college students undertook the same task in the freedom marches of the mid-1960's on various southern cities. But there was less general public sympathy when the freedom marches gave way to peace marches on northern cities (including Chicago, 1968), and to student uprisings at the better campuses to show outrage at "unresponsive" institutions which did not move quickly enough to transfer legitimacy and funds away from the Vietnam war, ROTC, drug laws, the police, and the old politics and toward grape pickers, draft dodgers, black militants, and the new politics. The tone of these protests grew progressively more strident and imperious, and the protesters less patient.

> "Do this, or this," was their message;
> "Take in that kingdom and enfranchise that;
> Perform't, or else we damn thee."
> (*Antony and Cleopatra*)

These protests by small numbers of college students had enormous public impact. They were dramatic, mediagenic, heavily publicized, and even widely emulated by prison- and slum-dwellers, mostly young, who embarked on rampages of their own against "political oppression." The protests also heightened, by their similarity in inspiration and contrasting mode of execution, the impression of power and responsibility conveyed by the "children's crusade" campaigns of Eugene McCarthy in 1968 and George McGovern in 1972, even, as in both New Hampshire primaries, where they had not won majorities of their own. The youth candidates appeared to draw their strength from an erupting volcano of political power, yet their supporters, simply by behaving with ordinary civility and discretion, could make headline news and offer living proof that the eruption could be harnessed by a candidate who understood and responded to the youth mandate.

Much of the "McGovern phenomenon" of 1972 rested on the mistaken impression (if I may shift the analogy from fire to ice) that the young protesters and campaigners constituted the tip of the iceberg of a youth bloc of 25 million young world-savers, including 11 million freshly enfranchised eighteen-to-twenty-year-olds, which a sympathetic Democrat like McGovern could mobilize and add to his party base to win in November by 10 million votes.[29] The McGovern Commission reforms, designed to prevent a repeat of the "disaster" of the 1968 Democratic convention, purported to cultivate the youth bloc by requiring that young people (along with three other "alienated minorities," blacks, women, and chicanos) be represented on nominating delegations in proportion to their numbers in the nominating state and the Democratic party. McGovern succeeded only too well in securing the adoption of reforms to magnify the influence of the discontented, the disadvantaged, and the alienated in his party, as well as that of the indignant young intellectuals so professedly sympathetic to the outs in their own party and so hostile to the ins. The McGovern phenomenon, like the McGovern reforms, was a boon to those who burned to "strengthen" the party by cleaning out its main constituents—ethnic politicians, union bosses, and white southerners—and replace them with fresh young faces unspotted by the prior exercise of power.

The Miami Democratic Convention of 1972 reflected the force of McGovern's New Politics, not only in its abundance of fresh, young faces (which was further enhanced by a shortage of old ones), but also in its promulgation of a platform of chic, young intellectuals' causes: immediate pullout from Vietnam, amnesty for draft evaders, termination of "complicity" with oppression in South Africa, Portugal, and Greece, closer relations with Cuba, discreet use of busing, and further electoral reforms. The crowning victory, of course, was the convention's choice of George McGovern himself over two faltering centrist opponents and a crippled George Wallace. Idealism and youth had won a temporary victory over bread-and-butter politics and age, as dramatized by Chicago demonstrator Jerry Rubin's boast on the convention floor at Miami that he had three sets of credentials, while the despised (but popularly chosen) Mayor Daley could not get into the hall.

Despite this appeal to youth, which was bolstered by massive registration campaigns at colleges, beaches, and other youth haunts (many of which enrolled overwhelming Democratic majorities), McGovern's campaign was a failure of such proportions as to make the 1968 "disaster" look like a triumph by comparison. His youth image turned out to be as great a handicap for winning the election as it had been an aid in winning the nomination. Running against the uncharismatic Richard Nixon, who had beaten Hubert

Humphrey by less than one percent in 1968 and suffered from rising crime, inflation, unemployment, and the as-yet unended Vietnam war, not to mention a bumper crop of scandals, McGovern suffered the second-worst electoral drubbing of the twentieth century. He lost every state but one and lost the popular majority by a gaping 23 percent. His defeat was as bad in percentages as those of Republicans Alf Landon and Barry Goldwater in 1936 and 1964, but it was worse than Landon's and Goldwater's defeats in that these minority-party candidates at least carried the registered core of their own party. In 1972 Democratic regulars defected to Nixon in droves rather than vote for McGovern. Other droves refused to vote for either candidate. Most of the defectors objected to McGovern's perceived attachment to young intellectuals' causes (acid, amnesty, and abortion) or his appearance of inconstancy in disavowing many of these same causes (along with his first running mate, Thomas Eagleton) to broaden his appeal after nomination. McGovern did win about half of the under-twenty-five-vote—no doubt profiting more as anticipated from higher turnout among the sympathetic 30 percent of this group who were in school than among the probably more hostile 70 percent who were workers, housewives, soldiers and sailors, or jobseekers. On the other hand, estimated youth turnout, at 40 percent, was still lower by a third than the national participation rate of 55 percent, and winning half of the youth vote was a pitiful recompense for losing half of everyone else. McGovern's success with the youth vote was remarkable only in the same sense that his youthful supporters' disciplined behavior had been remarkable during the nomination campaign—that is, ordinary enough in itself but remarkable for one whose performance would otherwise have been even worse. Winning half of the youth vote was hardly a convincing demonstration of the existence of a youth bloc, much less a demonstration of its capacity to prevail over the contrary preferences of the majority of older voters.[30]

"Stake in the Community": Property, Tax Payment, and Residency Qualifications

The Warren Court's habitual preference of standardized, universal claims over special and local ones displayed itself in a series of cases involving efforts by states and communities to condition the franchise on tax payment, property ownership, parentage of school children in the community, or occupational status during residence. The court rejected these franchise restrictions, and the claims of community interest invoked in their defense, no less resolutely than it had rejected special regional considerations—geography, history, economic and cultural factors—to justify unequal districts in *Reynolds v. Sims*. In 1965 it struck down a Texas law barring military personnel entering the state from voting in the state as long as they were in the military; in 1966 it struck down a Virginia law conditioning the franchise on payment of a poll tax.[31] In 1969 it struck down New York and Louisiana laws limiting respectively the right to vote in school district elections to owners or lessees of real property and parents of children in the district's public schools, and the right to vote on municipal utility revenue bonds to property taxpayers.[32] The rationale in both of these last cases was the revolutionary compelling state interest test, requiring the state to justify any infringement of certain "basic rights" by showing that the infringement was "necessary to promote a compelling state interest." "Necessary," in this context (and contrary to John Marshall's classic broad construction of the word for the federal government in *McCulloch v. Maryland*) meant absolutely necessary and "tailored . . . with precision" to serve exactly the interest claimed and no other,[33] a requirement so strict as to make it almost needless to consider whether the interest claimed was "compelling."[34]

In its first years the Burger Court seemed inclined to follow the Warren Court's lead in cases where states attempted to limit the franchise to those whom they deemed to have a primary interest in the outcome of the election. In 1970 it unanimously invoked the compelling state interest test to strike down a Maryland law barring residents of the National Institute of Health, a federal enclave within the state, from voting in state elections.[35] In the same year, using the same test, it voided an Arizona law permitting only real property taxpayers to vote on general obligation bonds legally payable from real property taxes, though more than half of the debt service charges were expected to be paid from other tax sources. Justices Stewart, Harlan, and Burger himself dissented, describing the franchise limitation as "an entirely rational public policy."[36] In 1973, however, the Court threw off the lead and reverted to the easygoing old *McGowan v. Maryland* test to uphold a California law limiting the vote for directors of a water storage district to owners of land within the district. The law not only confined the vote to landowners (including nonresident ones) but also weighted it according to the assessed value of the land owned, a policy which, in effect placed control of the district in the hands of a single corporation. It nonetheless passed the *McGowan* test ("could any state of facts be reasonably conceived" to justify the law?) because the storage district did not have general governmental responsibilities and was supported entirely by taxes based on assessed land value. Justices Douglas, Brennan, and Marshall dissented, horrified at the resurrection of the old, soft test to permit a "corporate political kingdom undreamed of by those who wrote our Constitution."[37]

Whether or not the California water district case signals a general retreat from Warren-era standards is not clear. Nor is it clear whether any of the property or tax qualification cases have had practical impact in the scattered and usually low-salience local elections to which they applied (ironically, water districts in arid areas, where the Court chose not to intervene, may be the principal exception to the general rule of low salience and low impact). These cases, however, remain of interest as doctrinal barometers, valuable for what they tell us about the Court's premises which other cases of greater political importance may not. The New York school district case, for example, now serves as the Court's classic statement of the compelling state interest test. The Maryland enclave and Arizona bond cases were important for showing the considerable extent to which the Burger Court justices accepted the compelling state interest test in the early 1970's. If the water district case should have importance beyond its own, rather specialized facts, it will probably be doctrinal as well as practical, showing a boundary or a change in the temper of the Court.

Residency requirements are of somewhat greater practical and symbolic significance than whatever vestiges are left of property and tax qualifications. All of the states have residency requirements; many of them experienced heated controversy over residency requirements during the various turmoils of the late 1960's and early 1970's. The main contention was not over the idea of limiting voting to residents, which was generally accepted, at least in theory, but over questions of who should qualify as a resident. These questions involved state laws with requirements of duration or condition of residency to qualify to vote; specifically, could the states justify one-year residency requirements and laws providing that residency would not be deemed to be gained or lost by presence or absence on military service or to attend college?

Once again leaving aside the Constitution, which by the traditional canons of interpretation does not require the states to justify their voting laws, it is not hard to outline the principal considerations on either side of the residency law argument, nor to recognize which side better fit the standards of the Guardian Ethic. Though the Warren Court never ruled squarely on residency requirements, they were plainly vulnerable under the Ethic, more so than age requirements because they were founded not on a judgment as to the voter's personal competency but on a judgment as to his degree of attachment to the community. The idea that the "accident" of long or settled residency should convey a special qualification to share in the political affairs of a twentieth-century community was an affront to the Ethic. The virtues of residency requirements were the old, discredited kind, which had not sufficed to preserve the twenty-one-year-old vote, unequal districts, poll taxes, or, for that matter, male, white suffrage before the passage of the Fifteenth and Nineteenth Amendments: most people had accepted the restrictions without second thoughts; they had been chosen by a reasonably democratic process; they conveyed to the franchised special feelings of power and obligation; and they settled the question of who could vote with reasonable precision, protecting elections and elected government from unnecessary questioning of their legitimacy.

Moreover, they made a distinction between settled residents and transients, a distinction of special importance by the older perspectives in an unusually footloose era, when Alvin Toffler's "New Nomads" and "people of the future" had become wont to "use up places and dispose of them in much the same [way] that we dispose of Kleenex."[38] Public apprehension over the transient vote was compounded by its perceived correspondence in college and university towns with angry students eager to satisfy their political urges on whatever political body they could dominate. Young people were notoriously mobile, not only statistically for changing their residence twice as frequently as the average person,[39] but culturally for their well-publicized fondness for inundating places both nonpolitically (as at youth happenings at Woodstock, Altamont, Fort Lauderdale, and elsewhere) and politically (as with freedom rides, peace marches, mobilizations, and Resurrection Villages). None of these inundations involved the vote, but activist college students, once armed with the vote, looked forward to casting it at school where mass mobilization, registration, and access to the polls were most convenient. Other groups linked in the public mind with the youth phenomenon and the New Politics likewise dreamed of establishing dominion over some spot through planned political colonization. Black nationalists dreamed of establishing a Republic of New Africa in Mississippi; members of gay liberation planned to colonize sparsely populated Alpine County, California with homosexual voters.

Though the probability of any of these threatened or actual inundations becoming politically significant was not high, it seemed high enough in the case of college towns to worry the public and state and local officials. A Gallup poll taken just after the passage of the Twenty-Sixth Amendment showed a 2-1 majority of the general public opposed to college students voting at school. A *Newsweek* survey at the same time showed only twelve states officially permitting college students to register at college; others permitted married students, or those showing evidence of permanent residence, to register locally. Among politicians some of the reaction was partisan, with an eye to the heavy predominance of Democratic registrations among college students; much of the uneasiness, however, was based simply on a vision of the student as a nontaxpaying passerby whose disinterested idealism—perhaps more than his frivolity or radicalism—threatened the long-run stability of the community. "They float a bond issue and then move on, and who's left holding the bag?" asked one state official.[40]

The main flaw of these fears from the Guardian standpoint was not so much the improbability of their realization as the fact that they rested on the traditional concept of democracy which valued the vote for its expected political results, rather than for its psychological rewards to the voter. At least two strong proponents of expanded, nationally guaranteed suffrage rights have attacked this concept as outmoded. Paul R. Rentenbach, calling for liberal enfranchisement of college students, claimed that the importance of "self-interest," or concern with the results of the election, had become "discredited" by low turnout in local elections. The true prime motivator for voting, in his view, was a "general desire to participate," which should be gratified as a constitutional right under the compelling state interest test without regard to its impact on government action.[41] Richard Claude spoke of voting as part of "the inclusion process," functioning not so much to pick the voter's preferred candidate as to "legitimate" the winner through the application by courts of "nationalized standards" to "an increasingly unitary electorate."[42] These modern suffragists, in telling us that the main thing about voting is the sense of belonging it conveys to the voter, came close to telling us that the vote was a kind of opiate, more important for its effect on the user than for its effect on the government. Voting was seen as a civic ritual of self-expression, like wearing campaign buttons, reciting mantras, or whipping the Bosphorus with hot chains, and with about as much political impact.

From this standpoint, it was more important that everybody got the vote than that what they got amounted to anything. Distinctions between the settled resident and the passerby were of scant importance, since the voting experience would be equally therapeutic to either, though possibly not equally therapeutic to the community. The proper Guardian approach to the new nomads was to encourage them to stop wherever they were at election time and experience the vote before making the next scene. Constitutional justification from the Warren era was not lacking. The Court had laid down the directive: "the weight of a citizen's vote cannot be made to depend on where he lives"; it was not a radical or difficult extension of this basic principle to hold that a citizen's vote could not be made to depend on where he lived five months before the election.[43] The Court had also, as we have seen, rejected stake-in-the-community arguments to justify poll taxes and taxpayer, property, and schoolchild parentage qualifications for local elections. It had barred the exclusion of military personnel; moreover, it had invalidated a one-year residence requirement for eligibility for state welfare payments for infringing one of those "basic rights"—in this case, the right to travel—which activated the compelling state interest test.[44]

In *Oregon v. Mitchell*, with only Justice Harlan dissenting, the Burger Court upheld the residency provisions of the Voting Rights Act of 1970, permitting registration to vote in presidential elections as late as thirty days before the election.[45] In *Dunn v. Blumstein*, as with residents of federal enclaves and bond issue franchises, it zestfully applied the compelling state interest test to a Tennessee one-year-in-state/three-months-in-county residency law, this time over Chief Justice Burger's dissent. As always, the law was found insufficiently "tailored" to its stated objectives to pass the test. Tennessee had offered two objectives for the law: protecting against ballot-box fraud through colonization or plural voting, and securing knowledgeable voters with a genuine interest in the governance of the community. Justice Marshall found the durational requirement inappropriate to defeat fraud, since it relied on an oath of duration of residence, which he deemed just as vulnerable to fraud as an oath of intention to reside.[46] He failed to find an adequate rationale for "inconsistent" durational requirements of one year in the state and three months in the county; moreover, durational requirements which excluded some recently arrived but bona fide residents were "all too imprecise" in their classification to pass constitutional muster, settling the question of residency "by conclusive presumption, not by individualized inquiry." Likewise, the use of durational requirements to insure voter knowledge of, and interest in, the community, was "much too crude" in fencing out some persons more knowledgeable and interested than long-term residents.[47]

Narrowly read, *Dunn v. Blumstein* merely told states with laws like Tennessee's to be less stringent in their durational residence requirements. Shorter durations might be acceptable, or long ones with provision for bona fide residents to rebut the presumption of nonresidence. Broadly read, as it was broadly written and as it has been interpreted in most of the states, it was as hard-nosed and heavy-footed an application of the Guardian Ethic as any Warren-era voting rights decision, and as heavily freighted with embarrassing problems of further application. It was as contemptuous of local preferences as it was solicitous to expand national regulation and standardized justice. Though the Court did recognize, in an abstract way, a community's right to exclude outsiders from voting in its election, it did not offer satisfactory protection for this right in place of the durational residence requirements it struck down. Cross-checking each new registration with the former jurisdiction to avoid plural voting, if done seriously, is likely to require a substantial increase in centralized recordkeeping on all citizens which, besides being an additional burden to the registrant and an extra expense to both old and new jurisdictions, might be considered by some a greater threat to personal liberty and privacy than having to wait a few months to vote in a new jurisdiction.[48] Oaths of intent to reside, the Court's opinion to the contrary, are much easier to make lightly and falsely than oaths of duration of residence, since they cannot normally be verified or challenged by objective evidence.

For a community which fears inundation, whether rightly or wrongly, duration of residency requirements of a year or less are a gentle form of discrimination compared with other legal alternatives, such as stringent zoning laws (or with vigorous or selective enforcement of criminal sanctions, business discrimination, or other extra-legal sanctions), to which its leaders or members might be tempted to turn for protection. Durational requirements permitted hospitality to strangers by temporarily delaying the vesting of political rights, not by denying them altogether. The consequences of weakening residence requirements, if they include any of these more stringent defenses against feared inundation, may be particularly hard on colleges and universities.

Ironically, since university students and professors are responsible for almost all of the scholarly literature attacking residency requirements and most of the court actions filed to strike them down, no one has benefited more than academics from the political shelter of residency and age restrictions blocking the student vote. No one stands to lose more by their destruction. American higher educators and their students enjoy privileges which are not shared by the general American public, nor by academics in most other countries. They enjoy generous public support, but, within very broad limits, they are not held politically accountable for what they think, say, or do. Public universities are subsidized directly from the public treasury; private ones are subsidized indirectly by state scholarship funds, exemption from property taxes, and favorable tax treatment for donations. Tenured faculty are next to impervious to reprisals for all but the most blatantly improper behavior. Students are exempt from the economic obligations of adults. They pay no taxes other than those most tourists would pay. Some work part-time, but few have had to submit themselves to the career market. They need not accept the discipline of political accommodation, such as some careers and most forms of sustained political involvement require. In sum, both students and faculty live at substantial public expense protected by privileges analogous to those of foreign diplomats in an embassy compound or plants in a hothouse.

Though most of these privileges are vital to the health of higher education in America, as the Supreme Court has recognized in other contexts in the past, it is not likely that college people can enjoy simultaneously the fullest immunities of academic freedom and the fullest rights of political contestants in college-town areas. The essence of academic freedom has been a strict separation of scholarly agendas from political ones, both in principle and in practice, on the understanding that politics and scholarship operate under different rules. Every academic is familiar with the traditional requirements of academic freedom, aptly defined and justified by Felix Frankfurter: "These pages need not be burdened with proof, based on the testimony of a cloud of witnesses, of the dependence of a free society on free universities. This means the exclusion of governmental intervention in the intellectual life of the university. It matters little whether such intervention occurs avowedly or through action that inevitably tends to check the ardor and fearlessness of scholars, qualities at once so fragile and indispensable for fruitful academic labor."[49] No one expects scholarly ideas to be properly tested in the political arena. Politics aim at the marshalling of power, not the search for truth. Practices like log rolling, influence peddling, horse trading, issue dodging, and coalition building, which are virtues in the world of politics, are vices in the world of scholarship.

Not every academic, however, recognizes that the reverse is also true, that qualities which are virtues for scholarship can be vices for politics. Scholarship prizes novelty, pride of authorship, and doctrinal purity. It emphasizes the cosmic and the abstract over the immediate and the concrete. It prefers raising questions to laying them to rest or avoiding them where awkward. It glories in incessant debate, normally over principles (which are hard to compromise) rather than interests (which are easier to compromise). Compromise itself is a dirty word in the scholarly world, which values unyielding insistence on the most exacting standards and which tests ideas and institutions by striking them every morning at their roots. These preferences, which are well suited for expanding and sharpening knowledge, are ruinous for democratic politics, which depend for their operability on consensus, coalition, consultation, and compromise, and on the exclusion from their agenda of issues which are needlessly divisive, or whose resolution would be unduly hard on whoever lost. Academic values have sometimes been politically successful where adopted administratively by the executive or the judiciary, but in recent years, as typified by the 1972 presidential vote, they have been as much an irritant to most of the voting public as an inspiration. American colleges and universities have already been rebuffed for their largely rhetorical forays into the political arena since the Vietnam war. Their demands as self-appointed agents of change to stop the war, get rid of ROTC, suppress disfavored speakers, adopt the University of Hanoi as a sister, and so forth, did not strike a pleasing harmony with their *basso continuo* of requests for higher budgets for more of the same. Voters, legislators, and private donors who had been devoted supporters of higher education began to have second thoughts about further exerting themselves for such tart rewards. California, long a horn of plenty for universities and students, clapped a lid on state university faculty salaries, to popular acclaim. It also took a more pointed interest in matters of promotion and tenure, started charging tuition of in-state students, and appointed a number of get-tough administrators over faculty and student remonstrances that they "would not understand" about academic rights and needs. Police monitoring of campus activities took place in California and other states sharing California's uneasiness about political militance on campus.

Not all of these outside pressures can be laid to the campus vogue for political evangelism. Rising costs and leveling demand for academic services played a large and independent role in drying up financial support to education; rising public concern with law and order gave special impetus to efforts to monitor and control campus militants. Militance itself should be distinguished from evangelism, and the evangelism of a few students and faculty and the militance of a very few should be distinguished from the more moderate views of the majority of academics. On the other hand, such distinctions are harder to make in politics than they are in logic. A public which sees academic freedom defined to enable those wishing to hear Dan Ellsberg or George McGovern on campus to do so, and those wishing to prevent General Westmoreland, Arthur Jensen, or Richard Nixon from being heard on campus to do that also, might well see some resemblance to Anatole France's law which forbade rich and poor to sleep under bridges: a policy impartial in form and perhaps in intent, but biased in effect.

It is not likely that the dormitory vote will do much more to radicalize local politics than the unfranchised evangelism which preceded it. In most cases it will not be big enough, cohesive enough, or interested enough, let alone radical enough, to overcome a local public with contrary preferences.[50] Its prospects of inundating anyone *proprio vigore* in a local election seem more symbolic than real, and one should recall that many of the occasional triumphs of student sentiment, even on campus where it is most powerful, were more apt to be rhetorical ones like resolutions to get the United States out of Cambodia than practical ones like improving the quality of the food or lowering tuition. Conceivably, local bread-and-butter politicians could coexist amicably even with a powerful and united student vote simply by making the appropriate rhetorical gestures to satisfy the students, while pursuing their dull old interest politics, much as they always have, to satisfy their traditional constituencies.

On the other hand, such an accommodation is probably the least likely of all outcomes. Ordinary people are no less sensitive to symbolic issues than students; in some ways they are much more sensitive to symbols than students. Ordinary people are the ones who kneel before the Constitution; ordinary people are the ones most likely to knock you down for blowing your nose on their flag. Ordinary people are sensitive to assaults, symbolic or not, on the legitimacy and operability of their own institutions. The dormitory vote is likely, from time to time, to draw such assaults into local politics, moderated, perhaps, by the hope of winning extramural votes, but they are just as likely to be acts of sheer self-expression, like telling the city council to stop the war, for example, or telling the American public to elect George McGovern. The dormitory vote raises the possibility, which the old rhetoric did not, that the critical dissection of society which takes place in the classroom might actually be applied to local government—in other words, that the students might have to be taken seriously. The dormitory vote provides an outlet and a constituency for political evangelism that, while offering little prospect of winning, does present opportunities to lecture society and threaten to flunk it, which many academics may find difficult to resist and local politicians may find difficult to ignore. It invites students and faculty to try to load the local agenda with the kind of issues that have burdened faculty meetings and student governments in past years, some of them of the blowing-noses-on-the-flag variety, without considering the danger of anti-academic responses to such challenges. Local people and politicians might yield to student power in a few cases, attempt to minimize it or destroy it in others. The one thing they could no longer afford to do is leave the students alone.

The case of the Berkeley "April Coalition" provides an example of the hazards of putting intellectuals' causes on local political agendas, though it is by no means an example of an inundation of student power attributable to relaxed residency requirements. In April 1971, with no help from the Twenty-Sixth Amendment or liberalized residency laws, but with strong backing from students and street people, a radical coalition of angry blacks and women's libbers captured half the seats on the Berkeley City Council by a plurality victory over a divided opposition. Though the coalition was hailed by the *New York Times* for demonstrating that radicals could be brought within the system, the coalition's most radical member, D'Army Bailey—a black Yale Law School graduate who had moved into the city barely in time to qualify under the old ninety-day residency law—declared that his intention was just the reverse: to demonstrate that the system "can't be made to work from within."

In this goal he and his colleagues were remarkably successful. Berkeley political scientist Paul Seabury noted that city politics soon became "impacted with agenda items so numerous, shrill, and ideological that they would strain the stability of a moderate-sized Latin-American country."[51] A more sympathetic writer admitted two years later that the prevailing impression of radical rule in Berkeley was "quarrelsomeness, obstructionism, foul language in public debate, interminable post-midnight niggling over detail, and often a paralyzing standoff between black politics and women's lib politics."[52] Seabury thought that city council meetings "would resemble a Panmunjom truce negotiating session were it not for the presence of hundreds of jeering street people." His dour prediction of 1971, that "the city now hovers between disaster and chaos," was fulfilled in part by the resignations of the city manager, the assistant city manager, the city attorney, and the city librarian—all officials of long service and outstanding reputation—along with 70 of the city's 193-man police force, which had been known as one of the most sophisticated, best educated, and most tactful in the country. Despite the Twenty-Sixth Amendment and easier residency laws, the April Coalition did not succeed in expanding its membership on the council in the elections of April 1973. Its sex-balanced radical slate of a black sociology instructor, an antiwar schoolteacher, and two disgruntled graduate students lost to the Berkeley Four, a New Politics coalition of two blacks (one a law professor), a graduate student, and a liberal activist housewife whose "long blonde hair and granny spectacles" offered "visual proof of her close identification with campus attitudes."[53] The abundance of heart, soul, and mind on both tickets did not prevent an impression among organizers that students in 1973 had lost interest in local politics. Nor did radical D'Army Bailey's student following save him four months later from being ousted in a recall election held during summer vacation when 10,000 of the city's estimated 16,000 registered student voters were out of town. About half of the city's remaining 60,000 voters turned out to approve the recall by a margin of 18,569 to 11,548. The defeated Bailey announced, "I don't really consider this a defeat. If the elec-

157

tion had taken place when the university was in session, the results would
have been totally different." With pride (and no doubt with truth) he added:
"We left a mark on this town and it'll be a long time erasing."[54]

In a sense, the Berkeley experience tells us more about Berkeley than it
does about the generally realizable effects of liberalizing student voting laws.
Berkeley is uniquely magnetic not only to students but also to young drifters,
dabblers, communards, and militants attracted to the university scene. It has
been uniquely sympathetic to radical protest and even proud of its role as
birthplace of the Free Speech, Foul Speech, and Black Panther movements. It
does not present the picture of a horde of alien students erupting from their
dormitories to overwhelm the protesting native victims at the polls. On the
contrary, the coalition's plurality came from ordinary residents within the
meaning of the old duration-of-residency laws, voting, in effect, for their own
victimization. One can criticize the voters' choice of the coalition for crip-
pling the city government, and also for the coalition's desire (only partly successful) to use their positions to purge their enemies, but one cannot properly
criticize the election for contravening the chosen electoral laws of Berkeley or
of California. If radicalism could achieve no more than a stalemate in as New
Left a constituency as Berkeley, its prospects for triumph in most other college towns, despite the easy student vote, were not great.

The principal significance of the April Coalition is not so much the extent
of its success or failure as the kind of issues it placed on the political agenda.
Though some of its objectives, such as rent control, affirmative action, lowering tax load on the poor, and increasing public expenditures on child care,
public transit, low-cost housing, and bicycle paths were at least plausible and
negotiable, the overall tone of the agenda was one of caprice and disgruntle-
ment. Among its 307 items were mandates suitable for a children's crusade:
lowering the smoking and drinking age to ten, opening X-rated movies to
juveniles, lengthening the wires on public telephones to serve "small people,"
holding a referendum to legalize marijuana and psychedelic drugs (in which
everyone over sixteen would vote), and sending a delegation to Vietnam to
make peace. For the scholarly world, the coalition proposed a political overhaul, based on prosecution of professors engaged in research on war, insur-
gency, or Third-World politics, purge of "role-based" books repugnant to
women's lib from school libraries, and compulsory antiwar instruction in the
public schools. The *tout ensemble* of the April agenda was a more pretentious
version of the "issue politics" typical of student governments of the same
period: these were volatile, self-expressive, emphatic, and often united as to
what the students opposed, Briarean, vague, or trivial as to what they favored,
wavering always between apathy and ecstasy, principles and pranks, hampered at best, though blessed at worst, by the inexorable transiency of their
constituency of short-timers. Colleges, even the most communitarian ones
and the ones with the most mature and able student bodies available, have

repeatedly shrugged off the efforts of student governments to establish literal consumer sovereignty over the important areas of policy—wisely, because student governments do not have a long enough attention span to participate constructively in decisions with long-run implications. Where colleges themselves reject such governance, should college towns have to reckon with it?

We can tell from the Berkeley example that where college towns fall under the radical equivalent of student governance, colleges are less likely to be liberated from outside pressure than to be subjected to more of it. The April Coalition wanted to purge disfavored professors and books, and it actually succeeded in requiring antiwar instruction in the public schools. Four other possible voting outcomes may be divided between two which would have no practical impact and would not invite reprisals—students never voting at all, or students voting in consistent agreement with town majority—and two which might have practical impact and would probably invite reprisals—students voting in disagreement with town majority or students voting unpredictably. Even gentle, responsible disagreement can evoke prudential sanctions by politicians threatened with losing their seats. Local Republican legislators, for example, successfully spearheaded efforts to reduce the planned expansion of the University of California at Santa Cruz by two thirds; one motivator for their interest was a strong student turnout for the Democrats in the 1972 elections. The cut was a rulebook exercise of self-defense far harder on the university than the old residency restrictions on the vote had been. More pungent challenges could provoke other forms of reprisal which also make residency laws look mild by comparison: more vigorous intervention in questions of salaries, tenure, promotion, tuition, and admissions in the case of state colleges; putting conditions on state scholarships; attacking college tax immunities; taxing students; blocking college expansion with zoning laws; more ready use of the police or national guard in keeping order on campus— in short, attempting to curtail any or all of the privileges of an academic freedom bottomed on insulation from the political world, not dominion over it.

The reader may recall that these pages of speculation on the potential impact of the dormitory vote originated with the question of whether *Dunn v. Blumstein* would be broadly or narrowly construed. As far as the dormitory vote is concerned, though the Supreme Court has not ruled on the matter, all but about a dozen states by the summer of 1972 assumed a broad construction and removed all major obstacles to voting on campus—a polar reversal from the situation of 1971.[55] The Court itself, in four 1972-term cases, pointed tentatively in two directions. In *Marston v. Lewis* and *Burns v. Fortson*[56] it upheld fifty-day registration cutoffs in Arizona and Georgia in per curiam opinions which touched on peculiarities of registration practices within the two states but did not mention the compelling state interest test. The omission did not pass unnoticed or unlamented by Justices Marshall, Douglas, and Brennan, who considered it a substantial departure from the reasoning of

Dunn v. Blumstein. The Court's tolerance of the fifty-day period, its willingness to look at local circumstances, and its neglect to make the compelling state interest test all pointed to a narrow reading of *Dunn*, as did its holding in *Rosario v. Rockefeller*, a case which did not involve duration of residence but did involve an October registration deadline to vote in New York party primaries eight to eleven months later. Despite the long wait (which did not apply to new residents) the Court upheld the law, once again over the objections of Marshall, Douglas, and Brennan.[57]

In *Vlandis v. Kline*, however, the Court pointed toward a broad reading of *Dunn*, potentially capable of wounding state colleges and universities economically as badly as *Dunn* threatened to wound them politically. *Vlandis* involved a Connecticut law which required students who applied from out of state to pay higher tuition at the University of Connecticut than in-state applicants. The student plaintiffs were out-of-state applicants who objected that they had nonetheless come to school as bona fide residents of Connecticut and were entitled to the resident tuition rates, being domiciled in the jurisdiction without a fixed intent to go somewhere else. They had evidence, such as marriage to a resident, in-state auto registration and driver's license, and, of course, voting registration, to support their assertions. They complained that the conclusive presumption that out-of-state applicants, after arrival in the state, were nonresidents, denied them due process by denying them a chance to rebut the presumption. A number of the justices agreed that the law was unconstitutional, but they divided as to their rationale. Justice Stewart, writing for the Court, and Justice Blackmun, concurring, suggested a narrow rationale: if a state favors residents over nonresidents, it must, as a matter of due process, give people who think they are residents a chance to prove it.[58] Justices Marshall and Brennan, concurring, doubted that any one-year residence test could pass muster under the equal protection clause.[59] Justice White supposed that the equal protection clause would invalidate a residency test unequally imposed on different classes.[60] Dissenting Justices Burger and Rehnquist attacked the holding for its recurrence to the substantive due process notions of the bad old days, this time with the extravagant implication that the Court might extend the compelling state interest test to due process questions as well as to equal protection ones. To the surprise of some, Justice Douglas (the one university professor on the Court) joined the conservative dissenters in expressing sympathy for the parent taxpayers whose labor stood to be rededicated to support not only their own children's education, but also that of all out-of-state students who bothered to register to vote and drive in the host state.[61]

The dissenters' sympathy seems hardly misplaced. The old residency laws' merits were not those of mere nostalgia. They served psychological and institutional needs, on the whole, more effectively and gently than most conceivable alternatives. That these needs were not readily measurable and that they had not been reduced by national mandate to their lowest common denominator does not mean that they did not exist, nor that laws serving them were unjust, far less unconstitutional. A community should have some say as to whether it will be used like Kleenex by outsiders and transients. One cannot expect people to labor as hard to preserve rights that have been declared a national commons as they did to preserve rights which were once their own. The Court's premise that if a community allows anyone a privilege, it must grant it to all, if broadly construed, threatenes to overload economic as well as political agendas, telling taxpayers, in effect, that the fruits of their labors to provide quality public education for their own children must be offered impartially to other people's children who register themselves and their cars, and that the newcomers must be allowed the experience of political participation regardless of its risks of hampering the operability of both the university and its surrounding jurisdictions. Such a broad construction would have the Guardian-Ethic "advantages" of prior modern voting rights reforms: it would spread national standards yet farther and "strengthen" experiential democracy by making the voting experience available more equally to all people. Moreover, unlike many forms of discrimination under the district system and political checks and balances, franchise discriminations are not in the quagmire. They are simple and unequivocal, easily enforced for the most part, and easily attackable by Court ruling.

The broad, interventionist construction, however, would also share the disadvantages of prior modern voting rights reforms: lack of foundation in the Constitution, a risk of undermining the Court's authority, and a tendency to debase the right to vote in substance while purporting to strengthen it in form. The Court could, in a technical sense, make democracy in Sioux City "stronger" and "more meaningful" by enfranchising the sojourner from Grand Junction, but this kind of strength and meaning is credible only if you do not look too closely at its hidden premises: that the man from Sioux City is no more fit to share in his own government than somebody from Grand Junction—and neither one is as fit as the Supreme Court.

Problems of the District System: Preserving Community Representation

As noted earlier, it is much harder conceptually to equalize representation within the confines of the district system than it is to equalize discriminatory voting qualification laws. The Warren Court faced this problem with a simple policy: anything easy to equalize it would equalize with ferocious zeal; anything hard to equalize it would skip. Despite initial disclaimers in *Baker v. Carr* that mathematical equality was not the test and that the states would be left room for weighting factors other than population, the Court rapidly evolved standards of procrustean rigor for hacking and stretching districts

161

into near-perfect equality, at the cost of shredding and packing actual constituencies that did not quite fit the mold. The Court's zeal was excessive. In England, where politics were far less locally oriented than in the United States and where an equal-districts statute had been observed for decades, attempts to fit districts within a 25 percent range of variation from average had been abandoned as impractical, and, as of 1955, the largest district had twice as many people as the smallest.[62] The APSA, which might have been expected to choose a looser standard to fit American conditions, instead chose a stricter one more in keeping with the demands of the Guardian Ethic: no more than 15 percent variance from average and a Dauer-Kelsay score of at least 45 percent for all the districts.[63] An abortive 1967 attempt in Congress to set standards for congressional districts aimed to limit variance to 10 percent.[64] The Warren Court outdid all of these, refusing to tolerate apportionment systems with districts more than 3.1 percent greater or less than average,[65] even when the variance allowed for estimated population changes since the 1960 census, which in one case narrowed the maximum district variation from average to less than 1.9 percent.[66]

Standards as rigid as these made it hard to avoid jamming together constituencies that had little in common with each other and tearing pieces off constituencies that did have a community of interest, as occurred in the 1965 congressional redistricting of Texas, North Carolina, and Tennessee.[67] Dallas-Fort Worth, San Antonio, and Memphis were all torn to pieces and the pieces tied to rural districts. "Thus [concluded the *Congressional Quarterly*] urban voting power was severely diluted even though district populations were well within acceptable limits. Such districts often stretched for hundreds of miles, and sometimes were only one county wide—hardly fitting the definition of compactness and contiguous territory."[68] The Massachusetts islands of Nantucket and Martha's Vineyard were thrown together in a districting which in 1961 was one of the five most equal in the country but in 1968 was found to fall short of the requirements of the Fundamental Principle.[69] A three-judge court in Hawaii resisted the Fundamental Principle to the extent of forbearing to separate Keaukaha from Hilo, since it used Hilo's power, water, police, fire protection, schools, and public services, and since its native Hawaiian inhabitants worked in Hilo and had no community or ethnic bond with the sugar plantation workers of Japanese extraction in Puna, six miles away through a lava forest traversed by only one road—even though Hilo and Puna would be more equal with Keaukaha transferred to Puna. Delegates from Hilo wanted to keep Keaukaha despite the resultant so-called debasement of their constituents' votes.[70] The Court's decision on its face seemed to show an enlightened regard for the real basics of representative government—it gave the people in the three districts involved what they most wanted—but it was no less of a violation of the fundamental rule than the

162

"federal plan" preferred by Colorado voters but struck down by the Supreme Court for depriving individual voters of their personal right to equal representation.[71]

Whom to Count and How Much

Some questions arose as to whom to count in reckoning the size of electoral districts—total population, people eligible to vote, registered voters, or actual voters in the last elections. The Warren Court avoided a firm ruling on this question. It rejected a Virginia apportionment excluding transient military personnel from the population base,[72] but permitted a Hawaii apportionment based on registered voters (which thereby excluded tourist and military inhabitants).[73] It turned down a Florida apportionment which attempted to estimate total, between-census population on the basis of recent voter registration.[74] The question of whom to count, like the question of how equal the districts should be was not and is not in the quagmire category. The difference between different bases of reckoning is usually not great, and it seems likely that any of the four bases could be used if it did not discriminate against significant groups of eligible voters (for example, unregistered southern blacks).[75]

Related to the question of whom to count is that of how much to count. Did extraordinary majority requirements (for example, two-thirds) for the passage of certain kinds of laws "debase" the vote of proponents of change, in violation of the equal protection clause? The question was not seriously raised in the 1960's, but it was dredged up in 1970, occasioning differences among the lower courts before the Supreme Court laid the question to rest.[76]

Local Elections

Local elections presented more difficult problems, for they raised questions which could not be settled with simple rules.[77] A preliminary problem was the sheer weight of potential cases. As of 1967 there were 81,000 local government units, some elective, some appointive, some combining the two principles. These included 3,049 counties, 18,051 cities, 17,107 townships, almost all with general legislative powers, and 21,782 school boards, most of them popularly elected. The remaining 21,264 were special units, such as conservation, water, and sewage districts.[78]

Federal and state courts had been able to meet the demands of redistricting in the fifty states by taking extraordinary measures to expedite hearings, enforce compliance, and so on; by the end of Warren's tenure, after seven years of such litigation, it appeared that almost all of the states had been whipped into approximate compliance in time to start over again after the 1970 census. The burden of litigating the Fundamental Principle in fifty jurisdictions gave little comfort to courts anticipating litigating it in 80,000 jurisdictions, from the standpoint of caseload alone.

Moreover, there was so much overlapping of local districts as to make such litigation incomparably more complex than statewide apportionment cases. Everyone knows that the New York metropolitan area had 1400 "governments";[79] other areas offered similar examples of overlap on a smaller scale. The area drained by Lake Tahoe, for instance, covered portions of two states, five counties, a city, and fifty-nine local government districts, some overlapping, some with elected officials, some with appointed ones. Cities had been attempting for years to overcome the problems of fragmented, duplicated services by establishing regional planning, coordinating, and governing boards. Very often the price exacted by existing governments for submitting to the jurisdiction of such boards was equal representation with larger constituent units, despite differences of population,[80] much as was true of the "great compromise" of 1787, which Justice Warren in *Reynolds v. Sims* found irrelevant to the states.[81] This kind of consideration may be irrelevant in law, but it is not irrelevant in politics. Court imposition of the Fundamental Principle on local governments has not encouraged regional consolidation because the smaller governments must now choose between minority status or no consolidation. Before *Avery v. Midland County*[82] there was a third alternative, consolidation on the subunits' own terms, but this alternative seems to have been removed.

Local government remains a particularly incongruous domain for the Guardian Ethic, not only for weight of potential litigation, but also because of its profusion of special needs, which have called forth a rich mixture of special governmental powers. Regional boards with different powers and different authority in different parts of the region are not uncommon. A mandate for standardized government which would lump together people of different ethnic backgrounds, different financial resources, different attitudes toward taxation, zoning, schools, and other local services would be more jarring when applied to specific neighborhoods than when applied to the election of representatives to determine state or national policy. The inconsistencies between the abstract justice of the Fundamental Principle and the desires of most of the people affected would stand out more boldly when translated directly into neighborhood school or tax policies. The new breed of regional district had too little reference to local desires and too little concern with who pays for what benefits to commend itself to its constituents as anything other than a needless extravagance.

Nevertheless, by 1970, the Fundamental Principle seemed to have prevailed as the Court's preferred approach to the problems of local government. In *Avery v. Midland County* it held that the equal districts rule applied to the election of members of a county commissioners' court—once again following the lead of the solicitor general[83] but also following a consensus among state and lower federal courts that county boards of supervisors and municipal councils should be equally apportioned, if need be, over the objections of a majority of the people "represented."[84] Justice White, in the *Midlands County* case, did take care to stress the "flexibility" of the Court's approach to local government, asserting that "the Constitution and this Court are not roadblocks to innovation, experiment, and development among units of local government." At the time he had two prior local government cases, *Sailors v. Board of Education* and *Dusch v. Davis*, to suggest that the Court would not intervene promiscuously. In both cases, the Court had resisted the temptation to apply the Fundamental Principle. In *Sailors*, it found positions on a Michigan county school board to be "basically appointive, not elective" where the county school board members were chosen "pyramidally" by local school boards with one vote apiece, regardless of the size of the local electorate.[85] In *Dusch*, it permitted candidate residence requirements in unequal subdistricts where the overall elections of the multi-member district were at large.[86] Nevertheless, it is hard to imagine how anyone who could once have taken *Baker v. Carr* seriously, with its talk of flexibility and diversity, could have found much reassurance in Justice White's dictum. Though post-Warren Courts might wish to apply the Fundamental Principle more temperately to local government than the Warren Court had to state government, their choice of standards would still be influenced by the values and standards which produced the Warren Court's procrustean regime for the states: simplicity, universality, enforceability, administrative convenience, and bravos from the Guardians. The Burger Court, in its first major local government decision, *Hadley v. Junior College District*, strongly hinted that the old standards were still in force. Justice Black, writing for the majority, rejected arguments that junior college districts, as special purpose districts, should be exempt from the requirements of the Fundamental Principle. Invalidating a 1961 statute which encouraged school districts to cooperate to establish junior colleges, Black explained that elections of trustees by "unit vote" among the nonuniform districts violated the "general rule wherever a State government decides to select persons by popular elections to perform governmental functions" that votes must have equal weight.[87] With three dissenting Justices—Burger, Harlan, and Stewart—and with the full weight of Nixon appointments not yet registered on the Court, the Hadley decision might turn out to have been only a straw in the wind; nevertheless, the case suggested, a year after Warren's retirement, that the Court still believed that extremism in defense of equality could be no vice.[88]

Gerrymanders and Multi-Member Districts

Though Lenin once said that there are no fortresses which bolshevism cannot storm, the same is not true of the Fundamental Principle. Under present circumstances, the Fundamental Principle is helpless to solve the problem of wasted votes, inherent in the district system. As long as the country remains on the district system, even if the districts are meticulously equalized, there can be no guarantee, from the Court or anyone else, of equal *effective* representation. Size of districts is not a reliable measure of representation. The aesthetic elegance of equal districts, especially for a generation taught to look through form to substance, is scant consolation to the voter whose candidate is still denied an equal chance to win in his district, or, winning, is still denied an equal chance to win the day for his policies in the legislature. One's vote cannot be equal if it is not equal in effectiveness—but, as Robert Dixon insisted, *districting is gerrymandering.*[89] Discrimination against ineffective votes is an essential blemish of the district system, which cannot be eliminated by legislative or judicial tinkering. A more radical approach, wholesale conversion to proportional representation, could eliminate the blemish, but only at prohibitive costs in governmental effectiveness. It might also hurt the Court's image owing to the possibility that "finding" a Fundamental Principle of proportional representation in the equal protection clause or elsewhere in the Constitution might stretch the popular credibility of its "historical" arguments to the breaking point. Short of PR, courts can intervene only against exceptionally blatant manipulations of effective votes—perhaps one case in several thousand—because short of PR, equal effective representation is not amenable to simple rules.

Gerrymanders and multi-member districts, including such variants as at-large elections and floterial districts, are the familiar examples of conscious or unconscious manipulation of effective votes. All are forms of discriminatory districting, but the rules of discrimination vary diametrically from one situation to another. Some gerrymanders ineffectuate votes by dilution, others by concentration, leaving courts in understandable confusion in cases like *Wright v. Rockefeller*[90] about choosing between the claims of two groups of blacks, one correctly claiming that a gerrymandered district 80 percent nonwhite hurt blacks by cutting their strength in adjoining districts, the other correctly claiming that it helped them by guaranteeing a safe black seat. Partisan gerrymandering is often mixed with racial gerrymandering and is just as hard to reach.[91] Multi-member districts offer the same problem: everyone knows that they submerge minorities, but majorities and minorities are different for different times and different issues, and it is often difficult to show who is submerging whom in specific issues and doubly difficult to show who is submerging whom over the entire range of issues which can arise in a legislature from one term to the next.

Figures 1 through 6, each involving six compact and equal districts, illustrate some of the rule-making problems posed by gerrymandering and multi-member districts. Each system is divisible to represent a majority group, "white," and two minorities, "red" and "green." These could represent any kind of group—ethnic, religious, political, or a mixture of different categories—and the scoring rules for effective representation would vary according to what kind of groups and issues were involved. For simplicity it is arbitrarily assumed that possession of more than half a district is worth three points, half possession two, and less than half none. No court could make such a bold assumption, not only because real districts do not divide so easily, but also because of the fluid value of different degrees of possession. For party contests, half possession might be worth three points, electing a red representative over a divided opposition of white and green, while a 35 percent possession might be worthless. The same 35 percent, however, might be worth two or three points if it were a nonparty minority whom both parties had to please to have any chance at the polls. The Court refused to make this kind of evaluation in *Wright v. Rockefeller*, in which New York blacks claimed that an 80 percent concentration of black and Puerto Rican voters in Adam Clayton Powell's 18th district diluted the nonwhite minority in two adjacent districts. Powell and five other Harlem Democrats intervened, claiming that the division was nonracial and actually strengthened black representation in Congress by guaranteeing one black, Powell, a safe seat. The Court, claiming to find "no evidence of racial discrimination," declined to choose between the two parties' claims for equal representation, but the real reason for its decision was not so much lack of evidence as lack of a workable rule for interpreting the evidence.

Even if it were possible to assign values to different degrees of concentration, it would still be impossible in most cases to give equal effective representation to equal numbers without resorting to PR. Figures 1 through 4 show different configurations of equal districts with consolidated red and white populations with relative effective representation varying according to how the district lines divide red. Green, equal to red in numbers, is too scattered to get any effective representation at all under the district system without gerrymandering, as in Figure 5, which would take away effective representation from the other groups. Multi-member districting would strip red of whatever advantage it might have had from geographic consolidation, submerging it much as green had been submerged under the single-member district system. All of these systems are equally "rational" under the reapportionment cases, despite their wide variance in effective representation, because they observe the equal districts rule. Moreover, in all cases but Figure 5, they are contiguous and compact. Short of imposing PR, courts have no means of choosing between various forms of gerrymander, which relegates the gerrymander to the quagmire except in such clear-cut instances as *Gomillion v. Lightfoot*. The equal districts rule has narrowed the alternatives open to a redistricting authority, as shown in Figure 7, where red loses three points by confinement in a double-size district. This kind of gerrymander is forbidden by the equal districts rule, but the gerrymander in Figure 4, which is just as hard on red, cannot be touched.[92]

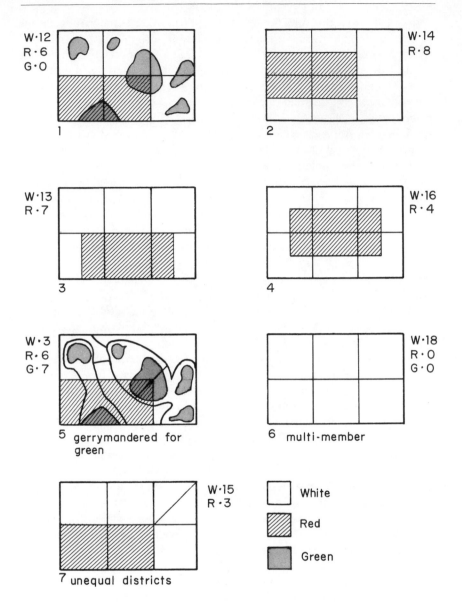

W·12
R·6
G·0

1

W·14
R·8

2

W·13
R·7

3

W·16
R·4

4

W·3
R·6
G·7

5 gerrymandered for green

W·18
R·0
G·0

6 multi-member

W·15
R·3

7 unequal districts

White

Red

Green

Multi-member districts and at-large elections, which are statewide, multi-member districts, obliterate minorities unless they are carefully contrived, like the 1964 at-large elections in Illinois, where the minority party was guaranteed 59 out of 177 seats, to preserve the loser. Properly manipulated multi-member districts can transfer the representatives of one territorial interest to adjacent territories. A city, for instance, might have excess votes (more than the 51 percent needed to carry elections within the city) of one group or party, that is, blacks and Democrats. These could be put to use by enlarging the city's voting boundaries till the favored city group can control as many representatives as possible without excess votes—at the expense of the adjacent areas. Such a city-dominated system was used in Denver to submerge Republicans until 1964, but the Supreme Court raised no objection.[93] By the same token, the adjacent areas could submerge the city, as may have been intended in Richmond and Atlanta—again without objection from the Court.[94] The Court found "no evidence of discrimination" in every multi-member district challenge it had to consider, giving the same reason it claimed for not ruling on gerrymander discrimination, which concealed the same true reason: the Court had no way under the district system of telling who has been discriminated against, or how much.

Multi-member districts of different size or used along with single-member districts—a situation prevailing in most of the states[95]—present a special problem of mathematical discrimination because a multi-member district voter's ability to influence the election of his representative decreases only as the square root of the increased population of his district, while he is normally overcompensated by the assignment of representatives in direct proportion to the population of the district.[96] Thus, a voter in a district with four representatives has half the voting power of a voter in a single-member district of proportionate size to influence the choice of each representative, but he gets to exercise this half power four times in choosing four representatives. His overall voting power is therefore double that of the voter in the single-member district. A voter in a nine-member district has three times the voting power of a voter in a single-member district, and the multiplier effect of multi-member districts is not limited to intrastate comparisons: New York voters profited from the same mathematical quirk compared with presidential voters in smaller states. With 64 delegates to the electoral college, New York voters had 2.3 times as much chance to affect the election as a Delaware voter, who had only three delegates.[97]

Against these mathematical ponderables one might try to balance (if such things could be balanced) the insulation of voters in multi-member districts from their representatives, the tendency in such districts to rubber-stamp party slates, often on the basis of absurdly small turnouts at primaries, their vulnerability to the alphabet effect (favoring candidates at the top of long ballots), their submersion of minorities, and their tendency toward long tenure in the hands of one party.[98] Special consideration, of course, should be given to the possibility that party control of legislators from the district might give them an influence as a bloc in the party and the legislature beyond what could have been expected from representatives of single-member districts.[99]

Floterial districts, which pool fractional population surpluses of several districts to equalize representation without breaking up existing units, presented additional problems. Madison County, Indiana, for instance, was a senatorial district that shared an additional senator in a floterial district which covered two other counties. With .7 of the population of the three counties, did it have 1.3, 1.7 or 2 senators? Howard Hamilton answered: "It all depends on how you look at things."[100] Even without floterial districts, formulas of representation can favor large or small units depending on whether they are reckoned by major, minor, or harmonic fractions.[101] Will courts one day have to resolve this kind of question also? The harmonic fractions controversy was only a tiny and elementary example of the many delicious technical wrinkles and esoteric controversies clamoring in the 1960's to be incorporated into the Fourteenth Amendment. Weighted votes, fractional votes, game theory, power indices, bargaining theory, coalition theory, probability theory, cubic proportions, model-building, Shapley-Shubik scattergrams, kurtotic indices, rank-order analyses, regressions—truly, the reapportionment revolution afforded the professions a decade of field days.[102]

Not the least of the technical frutescences of the 1960's was the computer. Computers held a special fascination for professionals of the day, for, in a sense, they were the embodiment of the Guardian Ethic: spanking new, Promethean in capacity, prodigious in production, speaking and understanding special standardized languages comprehensible only to themselves and a few highly qualified experts. Could these brooding omnipresences of the 1960's succeed, where traditional constitutional authorities had failed, in fulfilling the age-old dream of government unsullied by human intervention? Mathematicians, urban planners, science fiction writers, and a few lawyers and political scientists toyed fleetingly with the new concept of nonpartisan higher law: *res publica non debet esse sub homine, sed sub machina et sub lege expertorum.* But the idyll was, if anything, less substantial than the older concepts of the rule of law that the computers were supposed to replace. If the rule of law had meant rule by lawyers, then the rule of the computer meant rule by program-makers, and some wondered whether the federal bench was qualified to sustain such a heavy technical load. "Clearly," said law professor Robert Dixon, "before we entrust very much to mathematical formulae and computing machines, there is a need for a Supreme Court of Mathematics—as great a need as for a Supreme Court of Law."[103]

Computers cannot alter the inherent political imponderables of the district system; however, they can and do make it easier to handle the vast quantities of sophisticated data now becoming available. Moreover, computer technology made it very plain to the parties that gerrymanders from before the reapportionment revolution were clumsy, sandbox affairs compared to the equal-sized, computer-built models of the new era. After some computerized trial runs indicated that the Republicans could get twice as many seats from their own equal-districts program in the two California counties tested as from a Democratic program, members of the California Republican State Committee got this blunt revelation: "If the Democrats still control the Assembly in 1970, their apportioning of 1960 will look like child's play. But the chips in this game are anything but childish . . . This is a wallet-squashing reality. Republicans will have lost their last chance to regain the State."[104] The Republicans forthwith retained their own computer consultants and embarked on the California Plan, a special building effort to gain control of the legislature in time for the 1970 census, premised on the assumption that control of the 1970 redistricting might be translated into control of the legislature for at least a decade. The Democrats followed suit with their own building program and their own computer consultants. As each side jockeyed to invest its own programmers with the reapportionment, the idyll of nonpartisan legitimacy by the grace of the computer seemed to be but one more shattered dream of the 1960's, and the prospects of judicial rescue seemed remote.[105] With no sign of either a trend toward proportional representation or a Supreme Court of Mathematics, it seemed that regulation of the effective vote was indeed a fortress which the Fundamental Principle could not storm.

Party Organization and the Appointive Alternative: The Fundamental Principle in the Spectrum of Public Choice

Gerrymanders and multimember districts raised the question of *whether* the Fundamental Principle could be applied to equalize effective votes under the district system. The Warren Court also left many questions as to *what kind* of public choices the Fundamental Principles should control. It had applied the rule to these offices: United States senators and congressmen; state offices contested in general elections; single-district offices in primary elections; and county commissioners. The Court declined to apply the rule to the "pyramidal appointment" of county school board members. The Burger Court added one more category to be covered by the rule: trustees of a junior college district. These covered offices were only a small part of the spectrum of public choice, and would-be litigants across the land began to ask questions about the rest of the spectrum. What about party offices? What about nominating caucuses and conventions? What about delegates to constitutional conventions? What about elected judges? What about appointed positions? Table 9, "Categories of Public Choice," attempts to lay out varying kinds of public

Table 9. Categories of Public Choice

Area of constitutional protection (high perceived public involvement—"popular election to perform governmental functions")	Doubtful area (middling perceived public involvement)	No constitutional protection—yet (low perceived public involvement)
	A. PRE-NOMINATION	
Pre-primary elections (South)[d]	Membership, party committees[a] Delegates to constitutional conventions[b]	Semipublic choices: news, media law reviews, Guardians, lobbies,[c] advisory boards, drafting commissions
	B. NOMINATION-FOR-NOMINATION	
Filing fees (South)[f]	Designation by committees, juntas, machinations, acclaim, etc.[e]	
	C. NOMINATION	
Primary elections (South)[h]	Conventions, caucuses[g]	
	D. POSITION ON BALLOT/CAMPAIGN ADVANTAGES	
Petitions to run[i]	Access to line A[j] Equal time?	Equal campaign resources
	E. "FINAL CHOICE"	
General elections for legislative and executive positions, including local and some special-purpose offices.[k] Legislation by referendum	Elected judges[l]	

F. POST-FINAL CHOICES

Seating of elected delegates[m]

City managers
"Pyramidal appointment"[n]
Runoffs[o]
Executive appointments[p]
Interim appointments to elective offices
Civil service appointments
Advisers
Electoral college[q]
Legislative division of labor
Committee membership, leadership
Appointed judges

[a] Dahl v. Republican State Committee, 319 F. Supp. 682 (W.D. Wash. 1970) (NI = court did not intervene); Lynch v. Torquato, 228 F. Supp. 268 (W.D. Pa. 1964), aff'd, 343 F.2d 370 (3d Cir. 1965) (NI); Azvedo v. Jordan, 237 Cal. App. 2d 521, 47 Cal. Rptr. 125 (1965) (NI); Rogers v. State Committee of Republican Party, 96 N.J. Super. 265, 232 A.2d 852 (1967) (NI); Davis v. Sullivan, 47 Misc. 2d 60, 261 N.Y.S.2d 697 (Sup. Ct. 1965) (NI); Gallant v. LaFrance, 101 R.I. 299, 222 A.2d 567 (1966) (NI); State v. Bivens, 150 W. Va. 773, 149 S.E.2d 284 (1966) (NI).

[b] Livingston v. Ogilvie, 43 Ill. 2d 9, 250 N.W. 2d 138 (1969) (NI); West v. Carr, 212 Tenn. 367, 370 S.W. 2d 469 (6th Cir. 1963) (NI); Blount v. Board of Electors, 247 Md. 342, 230 A.2d 639 (1967) (NI).

[c] See New Jersey State AFL-CIO State Federation of Dist. Bds. of Education, 93 N.J. Super. 31, 224 A.2d 519 (Super. Ct. 1966) (NI).

[d] Terry v. Adams, 345 U.S. 461 (1953) (I = court intervened).

[e] Snowden v. Hughes, 321 U.S. 1 (1944) (NI).

[f] Bullock v. Carter, 405 U.S. 134 (1972) (I).

[g] See O'Brien v. Brown 409 U.S. 1 (1972) (NI); Irish v. Democratic-Farmer-Labor Party, 287 F. Supp. 794 (D. Minn.), aff'd per curiam, 399 F.2d 119 (8th Cir. 1968) (NI); Smith v. State Executive Comm., 288 F. Supp. 371 (N.D. Ga. 1968) (NI); but see Maxey v. Washington State Democratic Committee, 319 F. Supp. 673 (W.D. Wash. 1970) (I); Doty v. Montana State Central Committee, 333 F. Supp. 49 (D. Mont. 1971) (I); Seergy v. Kings County Republican County Committee, 459 F.2d 308 (2d Cir. 1972) (I); cf. Bode v. National Democratic Party, 452 F.2d 1302 (D.C. Cir. 1971) (I). See also the following law review articles favoring intervention: Note, "One Person—One Vote: The Presidential Primaries and other National Delegate Selection Processes," 24 Hastings L. J. 257 (1973); Comment, "Judicial Intervention in the Presidential Selection Process: One Step Backward," 47 N.Y.U. L. Rev. 1184 (1972); Comment, "Legal Issues of the 1972 Democratic Convention and

(continued)

Footnotes to Table 9. *(continued)*

Beyond," 4 *Loyola L. J.* 137 (1973); Comment, "O'Brien v. Brown: The Politics of Avoidance," 58 *Iowa L. Rev.* 432 (1972); Segal, "Delegate Selection Standards," 38 *Geo. Wash. L. Rev.* 873 (1970); Note, "Regulation of Political Parties: Vote Dilution in the Presidential Nomination Procedure," 54 *Iowa L. Rev.* 471 (1968); Comment, "Constitutional Reform of State Delegate Selection to National Party Conventions," 64 *Nw. U. L. Rev.* 915 (1970); Note, "The Presidential Nomination: Equal Protection at the Grass Roots," 42 *S. Cal. L. Rev.* 169 (1969); Note, "One Man—One Vote in the Selection of Presidential Nominating Delegates by State Party Convention," 5 *U. Rich. L. Rev.* 349 (1971); Note, "Constitutional Safeguards in the Selection of Delegates to Presidential Nominating Conventions," 78 *Yale L. J.* 1228 (1969). *Contra:* Note, "One Man, One Vote and the Selection of Delegates to National Nominating Conventions," 37 *U. Chi. L. Rev.* 536 (1970).

hGrey v. Sanders, 372 U.S. 368 (1963) (I); Smith v. Allwright, 321 U.S. 757 (1944) (I).

iWilliams v. Rhodes, 394 U.S. 814 (1968) (I); Moore v. Ogilvie, 394 U.S. 814 (1969) (I).

j"Court Voids a Law Giving Incumbents Top Ballot Spot," *New York Times*, June 6, 1970, p. 1, col. 6 (city ed.) (I).

kBaker v. Carr, 369 U.S. 186 (1962) (I); Hadley v. Junior College District, 397 U.S. 50 (1970) (I).

lStokes v. Fortson, 234 F. Supp. 575 (N.D. Ga. 1964) (NI); Buchanan v. Rhodes, 249 F. Supp. 860, 865 (N.D. Ohio 1966) (NI); New York State Association of Trial Lawyers v. Rockefeller, 267 F. Supp. 148, 153–54 (S.D.N.Y. 1967) (NI); Romiti v. Kerner, 256 F. Supp. 35 (N.D. Ill. 1966) (ducked question); Wells v. Edwards, 93 S.Ct. 904 (1973), aff'g 347 F. Supp. 453 (M.D. La. 1972) (NI); Holshouser v. Scott, 409 U.S. 807 (1972), aff'g 335 F. Supp. 928 (M.D.N.C. 1971) (NI).

mPowell v. McCormack, 395 U.S. 486 (1969) (I); Bond v. Floyd, 385 U.S. 116 (1966) (I).

nSailors v. Board of Ed., 387 U.S. 105 (1967) (NI).

oFortson v. Morris, 385 U.S. 231 (1966) (NI).

PBunton v. Patterson, 393 U.S. 544 (1969) (I) (holding new Alabama law permitting appointment of county officers where office was traditionally elective subject to Civil Rights Act of 1965).

qMcPherson v. Blacker, 146 U.S. 1 (1892) (NI) (refused to allow attack on election of delegates to electoral college by district); Ray v. Blair, 343 U.S. 214 (1952) (NI) (refused to allow attack on electoral college delegates' pledge to party to support party candidates); Delaware v. New York, 385 U.S. 895 (1966) (rejecting small state attack on electoral college for favoring big states); Williams v. Virginia Bd. of Elections, 393 U.S. 320 (1969), aff'g 288 F. Supp. 622 (E.D. Va. 1968) (NI) (refused to allow attack on statute committing state's entire electoral college vote to candidate with greatest number of popular votes).

174

choice along two axes, a stages-of-choice axis, running from prenomination through nominations, campaigns, and elections to postelectoral choices, and a degree-of-intervention axis, ranging from areas of high perceived public involvement where the courts have already intervened (for example, general malapportioned elections) through areas currently in doubt (for example, elected judges) to areas like advisory boards which do involve public choices but do not seem currently ripe to be put under the one-man-one-vote rule.

Even readers who hate charts might do well to look at the categories. They cover an enormous amount of ground, and they afford some notion of the ground already covered by the Court since 1937. In 1937 only one of the categories, general elections and referenda (1E on the chart) was thought to be open to constitutional protection, and that only under the Fifteenth and Nineteenth Amendments. In those days you could not constitutionally keep blacks from the polls in general elections, though you could keep them from virtually every other public choice that counted. By 1944, constitutional protection had been extended to primary elections; by 1953, to preprimary elections; by 1966 to the seating of delegates after the elections. From 1962 to 1970, most of the doubtful area 2 and even some of area 3 had been opened up to judicial consideration in the lower courts, though even these seemed to find the ground less secure than area 1. The expansion of jurisdiction, from the middle of the chart to top and bottom, and from left to right, has been so explosive that one cannot help surveying the *terra irredenta* around the boggy right-hand periphery and wondering whether the Court could resist the temptation to push on and take it all.

The word *boggy* of course, is used to suggest to the reader that most of the unconquered territory is in the quagmire. As long as any distinction is recognized between the various stages of public choice, and between areas of high perceived public involvement and low perceived public involvement, the courts must face an arduous task of constitutional discrimination with very little by way of workable judicial standards for guidance. By 1970 the Court had abandoned its original option of staying out of the gray areas, but neither the Supreme Court nor the lower courts had shown much inclination to follow the other simplifying option of going all the way with one man, one vote. Lower courts resisted demands to homogenize state party committees,[106] delegates to presidential nominating conventions,[107] and delegates to constitutional conventions,[108] declaring that party decisions were not state action,[109] nor were "judicially discoverable and manageable standards" available.[110] They likewise declined intervention to equalize the constituencies of elected judges, on the ground that judges were "not representative in the same sense as are legislatures or the executive. Their function is to administer the law, not to espouse the cause of a particular constituency."[111]

The law reviews, however, were unimpressed with the courts' refusal to push on with the Fundamental Principle. Two staffers for Eugene McCarthy in the 1968 campaign complained in the *Harvard Law Review* that Mc-Carthy's supporters had been disfranchised by party rules which enabled Hubert Humphrey to corner delegates in state conventions without risking a contest with McCarthy in any of the few states with popular primary elections.[112] Had the parties deprived the McCarthyites of some kind of constitutional right to an elective arena in this area of public choice? On the Republican side, supporters of Nelson Rockefeller complained of party rules allocating extra voting power to delegations from states, mostly southern, which had favored the party in the 1964 elections. Were the votes of Rockefeller's northern supporters unconstitutionally "debased" by these rules? The *Yale Law Journal* saw a constitutional right in both cases: "In a political system which places the greatest emphasis on openness and inclusiveness it is simply inconsistent to permit a state to exclude the great mass of voters from one of the most important of the traditional mechanisms of political expression."[113] "The principle underlying all these [reapportionment and other recent voting rights] decisions seems to be that a state may not create or tolerate a political structure which gives any group of the electorate disproportionate weight in influencing the outcome of vital political decisions."[114]

Despite such sweeping language suggesting that the Court should go all the way with one man, one vote wherever a vital political decision was involved, one might wonder whether the law review writers themselves would wish to follow the suggestion to its logical conclusion—popularly elected cabinet secretaries and Supreme Court justices, plus popular referenda on policy decisions like building ABMs and SSTs or cracking down on Jehovah's Witnesses or Black Panthers. Like the farmer who wanted only the land adjoining his farm, the law reviews were willing enough to urge the next step with no great concern as to where the path was leading.[115]

Oddly enough, though, it was not the courts in the post-Warren years, nor the executive, nor even Congress who took the lead in fastening the Fundamental Principle to the nomination process but a minority faction within the Democratic party itself, with the full cooperation of the party's national leadership, and ultimately with the acquiescence of its rank and file as well.[116] The reader, recalling how a decade of Guardian impatience with perceivedly unresponsive institutions blossomed into outrage over the triumph of the old politics over the new at the 1968 Chicago Democratic convention, should not be surprised that the Democrats established a Commission on Party Structure and Delegate Selection to open the party to wider rank-and-file participation, with the intention of making it stronger and more representative. Nor, perhaps, should he be surprised that the commission's reforms had precisely the opposite effects, making the party weaker and less representative. By rights, however, he should be astonished at the willingness of old-guard Democrats to go along with reforms that threatened to cripple their party in national politics.

176

Though the commission was set up by Fred Harris, chairman of the Democratic National Committee and nominee of Hubert Humphrey, and though it included a number of moderates in its twenty-eight members (including two distinguished political scientists, Samuel Beer of Harvard and Austin Ranney of Wisconsin), it operated from the outset as an instrument of the new politics wing of the party.[117] Its chairman was Senator George McGovern, later to become the party's first newpolitics (and second political scientist) nominee for the presidency. Its vice-chairman was Senator Harold Hughes, who, as a McCarthy supporter frustrated by the old guard's control of procedural regulations, had organized a commission on the Democratic Selection of Presidential Nominees to warn the 1968 convention delegates that state delegate selection procedures "display considerably less fidelity to basic democratic principles than a nation which claims to govern itself can safely tolerate."[118] The McGovern Commission's staff director, Robert Nelson, had been McCarthy's administrative assistant, and his two principal subordinates, Chief Counsel Eli Segal and Director of Research Kenneth Bode, were both militant reformers.

The commission began quietly enough in March 1969 to undertake its charge of giving all Democratic voters "full and timely opportunity to participate" in nominating candidates through eliminating the unit rule (winner-take-all elections) and making "all feasible efforts . . . to assure that delegates are selected through party primary, convention, or committee procedures open to public participation within the calendar year of the national election."[119] It set about analyzing delegate selection procedures in each state and taking testimony from large numbers of Democrats over its objectives of aiding black participation in the South, clarifying party rules, and abolishing the unit rule. The commission's language was tentative, consistently referring to its objectives as "recommendations."

"A sudden and sweeping change," however, wrote commentators Penn Kemble and Josh Muravchik, occurred in the fall of 1969 after Edward Kennedy, the leading contender for the party's 1972 nomination, had skidded off a bridge, simultaneously drowning his companion and his chances of the nomination and throwing the race open to otherwise improbable candidates such as McGovern.[120] The commission abruptly dropped its tentative language about "recommendations" and started to speak of "requirements" and "mandates"—and the claimed mandate went far beyond the 1968 resolutions to drop the unit rule and facilitate wider public participation to require something which was not in the resolutions and had, in fact, been expressly rejected by the Hughes Commission in 1968: quotas for three of the new politics' favorite minority groups—blacks, young people, and women—in proportion to their numbers in the state. The quota proposal was sprung on the commission with virtually no advance notice at its November 1969 meeting, couched in gentle language requiring state parties "to encourage" participation of blacks, women, and youth; it was adopted by the margin of a single vote. Later, in the commission's official interpretation of the guideline to state Democratic chairmen, the phrase "to encourage" was dropped, leaving a "requirement" which state parties had to meet. McGovern and the most militant quota advocates on the commission artfully added a footnote reminiscent of faculty-meeting resolutions of the same time at the more socially conscious campuses: "It is the understanding of the Commission that this [mandatory imposition of quotas] is not to be accomplished by the mandatory imposition of quotas."[121]

Having exceeded their charge from the 1968 convention and slickered the moderate members of the commission with soft talk, the reformers worried that their mandate might be vetoed by the Democratic National Committee. Audaciously, they decided not to report to the committee at all but to proclaim themselves responsible to none but the defunct 1968 convention, and their proposals reversible, or, for that matter, debatable, only by the then nonexistent 1972 convention. In essence, they claimed to be responsible to no one then extant. "We view ourselves as the agent of that [1968] convention," they announced, "on all matters related to delegate selection. Unless the 1972 convention chooses to review any steps the commission has taken, we regard our guidelines for delegate selection as binding on the states."[122] While admitting that "we have no direct enforcement power," the reformers warned that their Guidelines were "not . . . merely suggestions to the state Parties," since they could "recommend that the Credentials Committee [of the 1972 convention] declare the seats of nonconforming delegations to be vacant and fill those seats with a delegation broadly representative of the Democrats of the state." The commission stopped short of claiming that its guidelines superseded contrary state laws, in effect suspending the one specific charge it had, namely, dropping the unit rule, in the case of states with a statutory unit requirement.[123] This omission applied only to four states, which later turned out McGovern's strongest support in the 1972 nomination race: his uncontested home state of South Dakota, and his three strongest states with contested primaries, Massachusetts, Oregon, and California. The extra 151 California delegates that McGovern claimed under the unit rule eventually proved decisive to his nomination.

Astonishingly, and despite known uneasiness among labor leaders, Hubert Humphrey, and others of the party's traditional bread-and-butter constituencies that the reforms were unauthorized and dangerous to the party, the party's two chief professionals embraced the commission's claimed mandate and declared that it was not reviewable by either the Democratic National Committee or the 1972 Credentials Committee that was supposed to enforce it. Joseph Califano, counsel to the Democratic National Committee, with the concurrence of National Chairman Larry O'Brien, instructed the DNC that the commission's guidelines were "not within the powers of this Committee, or anybody except the 1972 convention, to change," and therefore had to be incorporated without discussion or alteration in the committee's call for the 1972 convention. The committee members complied with some bewilderment but no protest or debate. O'Brien and Califano issued similar instructions to the 1972 Credentials Committee with similar results, and with the overall result that the new rules were never in any form brought before the 1972 convention. Kemble and Muravchik concluded, "The party had been radically transformed by an agency which through bluff and maneuver had successfully avoided all mechanisms of democratic review."[124]

Why the party's old guard and professional leadership were so acquiescent about the commission's phony and potentially destructive mandate is still not clear. Conceivably, Califano (a former protégé of old politician Lyndon Johnson) and others of the old guard were willing to let the ideological wing of the party, which had never been chastened in a general election as Republican ideologues had been in 1964, hang itself in November and cut its influence down a peg in future elections.[125] Conceivably, O'Brien, a long-time Kennedy stalwart, preferred McGovern's candidacy as best calculated to hold open the 1976 nomination for Edward Kennedy. The McGovern candidacy had great appeal from this point of view, offering to weaken Kennedy's chief centrist rivals by defeat at the convention and then to eliminate McGovern himself by his almost-certain defeat in November. To a Machiavellian strategist the only risk was that McGovern, through some blunder in the Nixon campaign, might win in November, but the odds of this happening were low in any case, and lower for McGovern than for his centrist rivals. More likely than these Machiavellian explanations, however, is a combination of three factors—the unexpected strength of McGovern's organization, the unexpected weakness of his rivals, and the cumulative force of a decade of ever-grander reformist rhetoric, which even those who stood to lose most by it somehow could not bring themselves to forswear. Both of the major centrist contenders hailed the commission report after its completion at the end of 1969—when McGovern was a 100-to-1 longshot—as a landmark of dynamic leadership and a reproach to the stodgy elitism of the Republicans. Hubert Humphrey declared the report "the most comprehensive and detailed analysis and recommendations" in the party's history and predicted that the commission's work would be "most helpful in achieving a party capable of meeting the critical issues of the 1970s."[126] Edmund Muskie commended the report as "searching and honest," insuring "maximum opportunity for meaningful participation in the democratic process," and providing "a base on which to build a more effective party, which is responsive and responsible."[127] Eugene McCarthy and Edward Kennedy stressed the need for prompt and full enforcement of the guidelines; Fred Harris welcomed the guidelines as "long overdue"; Larry O'Brien applauded the report for spotlighting the need to modernize and rehabilitate the party, "to assure the fullest participation of all in our Party who wish to associate with us, while being vigilant against the exclusion of any segment or element."[128]

The reforms favored McGovern's candidacy in a number of ways, of which the common denominator was their effect of weakening the influence of party professionals and strengthening that of amateurs. Amateurs, for the purposes of this discussion, are of two kinds, grassroots and participatory. Grassroots amateurs are average members of the general public, whose principal political characteristic is indifference to politics. They know and care enough about politics to belong to a party and vote in most general elections, but not much more. Secondary characteristics are diversity and immoderacy of views and lack of political knowledge, discipline, and predictability. The grassroots amateur, described in Herbert McClosky's "Consensus and Ideology in American Politics,"[129] is tolerably participatory and discerning in general elections, where, over a period of two or three months, he can examine and choose between two slates assembled by professionals. He is less fitted for, and less interested in, the task of choosing from several contenders a slate which is not only pleasing to him personally but is also reasonably likely to win the general election and govern effectively thereafter. Participatory amateurs are described in James Q. Wilson's *The Amateur Democrat*.[130] The participatory amateur is more interested and well versed in politics than the grassroots amateur, but, unlike the professional politician, his principal reward for political activity is the joy of joining battle for some good cause. Professional politicians, in contrast to both amateur categories, think in terms of supporting, perpetuating, or accommodating specific persons and groups more than fighting for abstract principles, at the possible cost of group interests. Though the McGovern reforms were designed to open nomination politics to grassroots amateurs, opening to grassroots amateurs in practice means opening to participatory amateurs, such as McGovern's supporters, who by definition are more likely than ordinary party members to involve themselves in nomination politics. While opening the party to amateur influence might have made the party more representative of its grassroots members in theory, its effect in practice was probably the reverse.

By requiring that at least 75 percent of delegates from states with convention systems be chosen at the district level or lower, the McGovern Commission guidelines diluted the power of state party leaders to unite behind Edmund Muskie, an early front-runner with good party connections. This and other burdensome restrictions discouraged several states from using the convention system at all; these dropped conventions in favor of primary elections, further weakening professional influence on nominations and adding extravagantly to the candidates' physical and financial campaign burdens. Like the low-level convention choice requirement, the induced switch to primaries opened the nominating process to a less centrist and disciplined constituency of amateurs, to the advantage of outspoken and populist candidates at the party's extremes—men such as McGovern, who won seven contested primaries in 1972, and George Wallace, who won five—against more cautious and moderate candidates, such as Humphrey, who won four, or Muskie, who won only one primary.

The reforms also augmented amateur influence at the convention by requiring quotas of young, black, or female delegates, categories selected expressly to "overcome the effects of past discrimination," that is to say, because they were short on people with political experience. Though reformer Ken Bode boasted that the delegates at Miami would be the "most representative group ever gathered in one spot in our party's history," the representativeness was strongly skewed by the guidelines to favor the new politics and disfavor the old. Shirley MacLaine burbled out the truth when she likened her California McGovern delegation to "a couple of high schools, a grape boycott, a Black Panther rally, and four or five politicians who walked in the wrong door." As Kemble and Muravchik observed, many voters seemed to share her impressions, if not her enthusiastic approval.[131] They went on to point out that the anti-Daley delegation from Chicago contained only three Poles and one Italian, though Chicago was an ethnic stronghold, and that the New York delegation included only three representatives of organized labor, although New York had more union members than any other state. To compensate for this omission there were at least nine persons on the New York delegation publicly identified with the Gay Liberation movement. Thirty-nine percent of the delegation had taken some postgraduate work (compared to four percent among the general population). Thirty-one percent of the delegates had incomes greater than $25,000, and another 31 percent had incomes between $15,000 and $25,000. "Most significantly," added Kemble and Muravchik, "the convention made its overwhelming choice a candidate who had won no more than 25 percent of the total votes cast in primaries—fewer than Humphrey and only slightly more than those cast for the unfinished candidacy of George Wallace—and who had shown remarkably low standing in the polls during most of the period when he was capturing majorities or near-majorities in caucuses and conventions . . . The delegates were hardly representative of the political views of the Democratic electorate. What they did represent was the views of the affluent, the educated, and the supporters of New-Politics liberalism."[132]

A final contribution of the McGovern Commission's guidelines to McGovern's victory was the fact that his followers, having promulgated the guidelines, were in the best position to interpret and enforce them to McGovern's advantage. Though the commission had been set up to curb the old politicians' practice of setting up and administering nomination rules to their own advantage, McGovern stayed on as chairman a full year after he had decided to run for the nomination. His reformist staff, far from divorcing the rule-making power from interested parties, used their own rule-making power to help McGovern. They advised the Kentucky party in early 1972 that the guidelines required proportional representation for minority candidates. This advice got McGovern ten Kentucky delegates, though proportional representation, as McGovern's people well knew, was not required by the guidelines but only recommended, and the recommendation was not enforced to protect anti-McGovern minorities in other states which used Kentucky's election system.[133]

McGovern also profited from his followers' procedural control in the credentials battles, which, under the commission's confusing and self-contradictory guidelines, extended to nearly half the delegates. He profited, as noted earlier, from the retention of the unit rule in his three strongest primary states. He also profited from the ouster, on a reform technicality, of fifty-nine Daley delegates from Illinois in favor of a delegation of McGovernites. The technical ground for challenging the Daley delegation was the Daley organization's failure to invite its opposition to participate in drawing up the slates. The opposition had easy access to the ballots and in some areas ran its own candidates; it was buried, however, under a massive vote for Daley's delegation; moreover, it was later confirmed that the challenge slate itself had been drawn up at closed meetings. While the delegations of other candidates were readily challengeable under the guidelines, McGovern's own delegates were relatively safe, having been assembled under the supervision of Eli Segal, the commission's chief counsel. Some thought they might be especially safe, since credentials challenges by the National Women's Political Caucus, which brought the majority of challenges in 1972, were handled by Segal's wife.

By convention time the candidates' eagerness to enforce the guidelines to their own advantage had risen to new heights. McGovern, who had been the first choice of only three percent of the Democratic voters in January of 1972, had shot up to a still-unimposing 30 percent, but he seemed to have won just enough delegates—if he could get them all credentialled—to win the nomination. Even as his reformist views blossomed in the party's National Platform Committee, which, under the gavel of converted Republican John Lindsay, called for abolition of the electoral college, direct election of the president, and public financing of election campaigns, talk was heard in other quarters of the party of a stop-McGovern campaign. Within a week the Credentials Committee stunned the McGovernites with a dose of their own medicine, upholding a challenge to California's winner-take-all primary law, despite its exemption in the guidelines from their general proscription of the unit rule, and ordering the transfer of 151 critically needed delegate positions from McGovern to his rivals in proportion to the rivals' share of votes cast in the California primary. The Credentials Committee also unseated the popularly elected Daley delegation from Illinois in favor of an essentially self-appointed, pro-McGovern challenging delegation which claimed that it was more in keeping with the McGovern guidelines. McGovern accepted the Illinois delegation award as a matter of course but was furious at the success of the California challenge, which he called "an incredible, cynical, rotten steal." Though he had earlier justified his commission's reforms, which called for other states to divide their delegates just as the Credentials Committee had divided California's, as necessary to keep Democrats from turning to a third party,[134] he threatened to leave the party if he were denied the nomination by an "illegitimate power play."[135] The *New York Times*, while commending the Credentials Committee for unseating the Daley delegation, despite its acknowledged divisiveness for the party, condemned the California challenge as "divisive" and "far worse than a mere tactical blunder"—even though the editors considered the winner-take-all rule "indefensible."[136] Roy Wilkins, executive director of the NAACP, joined in the hubub, charging that the Republicans were "being handed the election on a platter by the fumblers."[137]

Both sides rushed to court, presenting the curious spectacle of party counsel Califano publicly invoking the First Amendment to protect his party's right to "push the self-destruct button."[138] Within a frenzied week of litigation the federal district court had refused to intervene, the appellate court had intervened to order the return of the California delegates to McGovern, and the Supreme Court had stayed the appellate court's order, stating in a per curiam opinion that the issues presented were too important and too novel to be decided on the spur of the moment, especially since the question had not yet been resolved by the convention at large. "In the light of the availability of the convention as a forum to review the recommendations of the Credentials Committee . . . the lack of precedent to support the extraordinary relief granted by the Court of Appeals and the large public interest in allowing the political processes to function free from judicial supervision," said the Court, "we conclude the judgments of the Court of Appeals must be stayed."[139]

With the credentials challenges returned to the convention for resolution, two further pro-McGovern procedural rulings, made under pressure of threats by McGovern's staff that they would wreck the convention if the rulings went the wrong way, are considered to have been decisive for his ultimate victory. These were Larry O'Brien's decisions (1) that McGovern did not need the standard majority of 1,509 votes to win back his lost California delegates, but only 1,433 votes, a majority of the convention minus the disputed delegates, and (2) that McGovern's remaining California delegates were eligible to vote on a challenge to their own delegation. Together, these rulings made Mc-Govern's task almost 200 votes easier and were justly considered by Mc-Govern's supporter, Norman Mailer, to be "equivalent to giving the nomination to McGovern. The old pol [O'Brien] had decided for the new politics."[140]

With victory almost in his grasp, and his advisers worried that too much participatory democracy in nonessential seating disputes might cost him a prime-time TV audience for the crucial California seating vote, McGovern appeared to be more interested in consummating his own victory than in further efforts to implement his guidelines. To hasten the California vote he arranged for the quick defeat of intervening efforts to increase the number of women on the South Carolina delegation and to seat a predominantly black delegation from Alabama in place of the party regulars from that state. His pet constituencies (as they were to be again and again throughout the campaign) were stung by his preference for expediency over perceived principle. The newly established black leadership felt ignored and threatened to defect to Shirley Chisholm or to sit out the campaign. The National Youth Caucus, a McGovern front, blushed at his sudden indifference to their efforts to challenge the Connecticut delegation for excessive maturity. The women's caucus bridled at his reversals on their South Carolina challenge and on abortion reform. "These political sex objects," wrote Kemble and Muravchik, reacted like lovers betrayed. 'The miserable fact was that the women's caucus was not a caucus in any meaningful sense,' wrote Germaine Greer, 'They were in Miami as cards in McGovern's hands, to be led or discarded as he wished—not as players at the table.' "[141]

The protests of McGovern's "coalition of protest"[142] meant less to his chances of success than the less vocal protests of the party's traditional constituencies. McGovern went on to demonstrate his dominance of the convention by winning the California contest, 1,618 to 1,238, a show of power which everyone correctly recognized would also give him the Illinois votes and the nomination. He also dominated the platform vote, beating down efforts by the Wallace camp to introduce antibusing and prodefense and law-and-order planks, and also efforts of women's lib and gay lib to legalize abortion and homosexuality, and efforts of the National Welfare Rights Organization to guarantee an annual income of $6,500 per family of four at government expense. Though shorn of its most extravagant concessions to new politics rhetoric, McGovern's platform retained more than enough new politics language to offend large numbers of Democrats. The platform's introduction emphasized popular distrust of government, including some of the recent Democratic past. Its body read like a collection of editorials from college newspapers, advocating amnesty for draft evaders, immediate pullout from Vietnam, ending "complicity" with conservative governments in South Africa, Portugal, and Greece (while establishing warmer relations with Cuba, Russia, and other Communist countries), supporting transfer of Israel's capital from Tel Aviv to Jerusalem, and, of course, further electoral reforms, including abolition of the seniority system in Congress, election of committee chairmen by party caucus, cutoff of filibusters by majority vote, stricter rules of financial disclosure by congressmen, more regulation of lobbying, and federal financing of elections.

The Platform Committee's call for electoral reforms was more than matched by the Rules Commission's call for further reforms within the party. Earlier in the year McGovern's successor as chairman of the Commission on Party Structure and Delegate Selection, Representative Donald M. Fraser (Minn.) had joined with Representative James G. O'Hara (Mich.), chairman of the party's Commission on Rules, in calling for an even more drastic reshaping of the party than that which was taking place under the McGovern guidelines. They called for a new Democratic charter which would fulfill, at long last, the ancient political dream of having one's cake and eating it too. Its principal objectives were to shift control of the party from elected politicians to grassroots participants, but also to turn the party from a loose federation of state parties to a tightly structured body with more continuity and a stronger ideological identity. Members of the party were to pay annual dues and carry membership cards in the British fashion. Presidential primaries were to be protected from Republican crossover votes. Winner-take-all primaries were to be abolished for sure. Party efforts to increase the role of the poor, the young, the female, and the black on local committees and national conventions were to be further expanded and augmented with a special fund to subsidize poor participants. A study was to be made of the feasibility of holding the 1976 convention on the campus of a large university, so that needy delegates could use dormitory rooms and cafeterias. The chairperson of the 1976 convention was to be a woman, with the job to rotate between sexes thereafter. Four co-chairpersons were to be added in 1976 to represent blacks, youths, and other minorities. The party would be remolded into a tightly disciplined amalgam of the National Youth Caucus, women's lib, and Resurrection Village.

Some curmudgeonly politicians of the old stripe, including a two-to-one majority of Democratic congressmen, seemed to think that the reforms seemed more likely to remold the party in the image of George McGovern. Representative Wayne L. Hays (D, Ohio) put it bluntly: "The McGovern-O'Hara-Fraser Commissions reformed us out of the presidency, and now they're trying to reform us out of a party. Those people shouldn't run the party. Elected officials should. If they're going to run a party, let's abolish Congress and have them make the decisions. I don't think these people represent the mainstream of the party."[143] The curmudgeons were right. Though they did not prevent the O'Hara Commission from adopting the proposed charter June 24, by an overwhelming vote, they did succeed in getting a caucus of House Democrats to pass a resolution, by a 105-50 vote, that the proposals were "not in the best interests of the Democratic Party."[144] Their influence on the convention, while not strong enough to defeat the proposals, was strong enough to force McGovern, with the nomination in his pocket but over the strenuous objections of Common Cause and other reform groups, to agree to defer the party reform question till 1974 and close out the convention with the semblance of party harmony.

This he did in the early morning hours of June 14, calling the nation to "come home" to the new politics concept of democracy, which, with the parthenogenetic historical perception so chronic among political scientists, he described as rooted in the "founding ideas that nourished us in the beginning." "This is a nomination of the people," he continued, "and I hereby dedicate this campaign to the people. And next January we will restore the government to the people. American politics will never be the same again. We are entering a new period of important, hopeful change in America comparable to the political ferment released in the eras of Jefferson, Jackson, and Roosevelt."[145] Many of the old Guardian constituencies seemed to agree with McGovern's notion that the triumph of democracy in form in the party was equivalent to a triumph of democracy in substance which would rejuvenate the party by pulling in strong new constituencies. The *New York Times* hailed the reforms and applauded the convention for choosing a "sturdy" ticket of McGovern and his "excellent choice" of a running mate, Thomas Eagleton, who had been hurriedly chosen from a long list of reluctant possible candidates, under pressure of a filing deadline prescribed in the McGovern guidelines.[146] The *Times* also lauded the performance of McGovern's "coalition of protest" for not rioting.[147] Leading political scientists celebrated McGovern's victory as a response to the need to overhaul and democratize the two-party system; all that was wanting to complete the task, they said, was the extension of the same reforms to the stodgy old undemocratic Republicans.[148]

The truth of the matter, though, was that the Republicans had already gone through their grassroots period in the disastrous Goldwater nomination of 1964 and were hardly anxious to adopt rules to encourage a repeat performance. The Democrats should have paid closer attention to their own experience in New York State, since the New York party was "rejuvenated" by evangelical, reformist, issue-oriented amateur Democrats in the late 1950's. The New York reformers resembled McGovern's followers in many respects. They were young, well educated, well off, principled, idealistic, not disposed to compromise, better at protest than at coalition, disdainful of party loyalty, irreverent of any institution which stood in the way of perfect justice. Though rhetorically sympathetic to the poor and the working man, the New York reformers showed little sympathy or understanding for the actual preferences of these groups and almost no capacity to work in alliance with their representatives, whom they typically despised. Like the McGovernites they were a small minority of a large party, strong enough to incapacitate the party ever since, but not strong enough to elect candidates of their own. Like the McGovernites, they rose in outrage against a successful machine politician, cut him down, and crippled the party in the process. In New York's case, the archdevil was Carmine DeSapio, leader of the New York County Democratic organization, Tammany Hall, and of a political machine which had achieved electoral success and political influence almost unparalleled in American history. When DeSapio showed insufficient enthusiasm for Adlai Stevenson the reformers succeeded in insuring the defeat of the Tammany nominee for the U.S. Senate by withholding their support, a tactic which has since become standard. In 1963 they ousted DeSapio himself and embarked on a long series of romances with various fashionable causes—and an almost unbroken string of electoral defeats with consequent loss of state, city, and finally federal patronage. In the fifteen years since 1958, although a majority of New York's voters are Democrats and a majority of the Democrats are not reform Democrats, the reformists have dominated the primaries and lost the general elections; the party elected only two candidates to statewide office during this period: the unique Robert Kennedy, and Arthur Levitt, the perennial state controller. The success of the reformists's lavender-tinted McGovern delegation in 1972, which ran virtually unopposed in delegate races which seldom attracted a turnout larger than 25 percent of registered Democrats, was hardly evidence of a groundswell of grassroots support for McGovern; it is much more appropriately described by Peter Rosenblatt as symptomatic of the wreck of whatever semblance of party organization had survived the reform movement's early years.[149]

As noted earlier, McGovern's campaign against a Republican opponent with substantial vulnerabilities was a disaster compounded of the same elements that brought him the nomination. His appearance of forthright candor, which had won him 30 percent of his own party, buckled under the sudden strain of having to expand his appeal to the other 70 percent. Some of his forthrightness was irretrievably set forth in his platform and preserved in the memory of his sleights to once-reliable constituencies, his expulsion of Daley, his threats to bolt the party, in short, in his initial choice to base his candidacy on a coalition of disgruntled minorities. His appearance of backpeddling on abortion and other favored issues of his little following, and his ditching of his "excellent choice" of a running mate a week after announcing his "irrevocable decision" to keep him on the ticket gave a hollow ring to his promises to restore the nation's faith in public authority. The Republicans—to the extent that they followed professional rules that year—had only to sit back and watch McGovern stumble over his own past rhetoric and struggle in vain to convince the American public, as he had convinced so many opinionmakers, political scientists, and party leaders, that his feelingful little band represented a thitherto untapped mainstream of national opinion.[150] Fortunately for the Democrats—and significantly for those who still take seriously the McGovern Commission's notion that the cure for the ills of substantive democracy is more formal democracy—the massive defection of once-loyal Democrats was confined to the presidential race that most directly tested the Guardian theory of democracy. Whatever happens in the Democrats' 1974 charter conference (or the federal courts), it seems hardly likely that the Mc-

Govern guidelines will go down beside the events of the Jeffersonian and Jacksonian eras as a rejuvenating influence on the Democratic party, far less on American democracy. More properly the McGovern reforms should be regarded as a misguided attempt to impose on the Democratic party the direct democracy theories of Moisei Ostrogorski and the proportional representation theories of John Stuart Mill, both of which, though well designed to permit people to express their feelings, are very poorly designed for producing governments capable of responding to constituents' desires. Even political scientists who do not blush at the naïveté of Woodrow Wilson, our one colleague who made it to the White House, in seeking to run Congress as if it were the British parliament should properly blush at our colleague George McGovern for convincing the Democratic party that it ought to be run like the national assembly of the Fourth French Republic. Democrats should blush at their own party leadership's uncritical acceptance of Guardian rhetoric, for letting McGovern get away with it. The essence of the major McGovern reforms, and the reforms proposed for the 1974 conference, is an ill-conceived hope of improving American political institutions of the 1970's, judged wanting by the standards of the 1960's, by applying techniques which were shown to be faulty by the events of the 1920's and 1940's.

Position on Ballot and Campaign Advantages

The nomination process, of course, is only one of many stages of vital public decisions where inequality can creep in. After nomination choices are made, decisions must be made on a wide range of campaign issues. The Warren Court acknowledged a constitutional protection against unreasonable restriction of party listings on the ballot; though we do not have a precise definition of "unreasonable," this kind of protection is comprehensible, enforceable, not in the quagmire.[151] The biennial struggle for line C on the New York ballot, however, carried the ballot listing question one step further from solid ground. Surely electoral contests can hardly be equal if contestants do not have an equal chance to win. A candidate's position on the ballot is believed to affect his chances of winning:[152] should not the Fundamental Principle guarantee everyone an equal position? But if the rule requires equal ballot positions, one might expect it to require equal enjoyment of other means of persuasion: equal time, equal news coverage, equal campaign expenditures, and other equalities hopefully short of equal candidates.[153] This kind of equality has the same abstract aura of justice as proportional representation and many of the other so-called democratic innovations that reformers keep recommending: it discourages strong, organized, pragmatic, inclusive parties and encourages weak, ideological, and schismatic ones. No one expects the Court to go very far with this particular application of the Fundamental Principle, not so much because the area is rule resistant as because the available rules, if enforced, would be disastrous.

After Elections

Another category of public choice opened to judicial scrutiny was post-election choices. The Court had made it clear in the Jaybird case and in *Gray v. Sanders* that the Fundamental Principle went into operation long before elections; why should it not continue to operate after elections, as the dissenting justices in *Fortson v. Morris* insisted?[154] In that case the majority declined to invalidate the elections of Lester Maddox, governor of Georgia, in a runoff vote in the malapportioned Georgia legislature. Maddox had narrowly lost to his Republican opponent Howard "Bo" Calloway in popular votes, but, since neither candidate had a majority in the popular elections, Georgia law required a runoff in the legislature, whose heavy control by the Democrats insured that Maddox would win. Justice Black, writing for the majority, found no violation of his own Fundamental Principle in the prospective reversal of the popular vote, noting truthfully, if not quite in consonance with his reasoning in *Wesberry v. Sanders*, that "There is no provision of the United States Constitution . . . which either expressly or impliedly dictates the method a State must use to select its Governor."[155] It is more than doubtful that Black himself would have stuck to this reading of the Constitution if Georgia had taken him at his word and tried to nominate or elect its governor with a revived county-unit system, or had expressly delegated the runoff choice to the Democratic Central Committee. Yet throwing the choice of governor into the malapportioned legislature, run by the Democrats, had the same effect. What could explain his abandonment of the fundamental rule?

As always, one cannot read the minds of the justices, least of all in the written opinions of the Court, but it seems likely that they sensed a weakness in the intervention factors that had not been so obvious in the reapportionment cases. The weakness was in the area of interpretive rules, much as Frankfurter had predicted, with the Court facing the difficult choice, if it intervened, of either holding runoff elections by the legislature invalid per se or holding this particular runoff invalid for the legislature's being malapportioned. The first choice would raise two knotty questions—the question of whether there is any federal right to an elective arena, and that of a more difficult federal analogy problem than that raised in the *Reapportionment* cases, whose distinguishing arguments about the great compromise and sovereign subunits did not apply to the Twelfth Amendment.

Moreover, the return in equality for a little fudging in logic and history would have been much lower than that of the *Reapportionment* cases since most of the state legislatures had been reapportioned and might have been expected not to stray too far from the Fundamental Principle in picking a governor.[156] Finally, besides raising further difficult questions as to whether to bar write-in votes, whether to hold new nominations, whether to allow more than two runoff candidates (all of which issues were raised by the various parties in *Fortson v. Morris*), and what to do about repeated pluralties, barring legislative runoffs per se would, in effect, have promulgated a new fundamental rule, that district elections are of inferior constitutional dignity to general ones. But this rule would have reversed the Court's position in *Lucas v. 44th General Assembly*, where it had held that the general election, a referendum vote for unequal districts, had to yield to the requirement of equal districts.

Another alternative, invalidating the runoff as the act of a malapportioned legislature, would have had even more disruptive implications, raising the specter of invalidating other acts of "unconstitutionally" elected legislatures. The Court expressly declined to rule on the constitutionality of the Rhode Island government on this ground in *Luther v. Borden*, and it carefully avoided the question in the reapportionment cases.[157] In the reapportionment cases, however, it had been possible to attack the reapportionment issues directly and separately, while it would have been necessary in *Fortson v. Morris* to treat the malapportioned legislature and its assigned electoral acts as a tainted unit; and, if electoral acts are tainted by malapportionment, why not other legislative acts as well?

The Court would have had one out, had it chosen to intervene: it had sanctioned the malapportionment as a temporary expedient for the 1966 elections only. Moreover, it was not as irremediably barred from intervening by the posture of *Fortson v. Morris* as it had been by the posture of *Luther v. Borden*. *Fortson v. Morris* was argued and decided prior to the scheduled runoff, while *Luther v. Borden* was argued and decided seven years after the event at issue. The Court could have barred the runoff and limited the holding to the specific facts of the case, leaving the lower court to figure out what kind of action it should take under the new fundamental principle. But it could not have easily called back the logic of its holding had it invalidated, even prospectively, the acts of a malapportioned legislature as the fruits of a forbidden tree. Such logic would have invited too many people to ask too many unanswered and hard-to-answer questions. Anyone aggrieved by any law, or at least by any new law or act of government, could have claimed standing to attack it by attacking the mode of election of the authority that passed it.[158] New forms of electoral discrimination kept cropping up, even under the equal districts rule, and old ones were still abundantly untested. The Court could hardly have afforded to intervene in the Georgia runoff at the terrible cost of unleashing the notion that malapportionment taints a legislature's acts, least of all for the very meager return in equality and good government that intervention might have secured. *Fortson v. Morris* represented yet another attempt by the Court, in spite of its own rhetoric, to stay out of the quagmire.

Besides runoff elections, the Court intervened in two other types of postelectoral decisions: seating of elected representatives,[159] and an appointive option for Mississippi county offices which had traditionally been elective.[160] Intervention to seat an elected member of a state legislature would have seemed a gross and rash effrontery in the fifties; by the end of the sixties

it was accepted almost as a matter of course. Warren's valedictory intervention against the United States Congress in the Adam Clayton Powell case was
perhaps too circumspect to be called gross, but it did retain an odor of rash-
ness despite the fact that Congress made no direct retaliation. Neither delegate seating intervention relied on the equal protection clause; the Court relied on the First Amendment and the due process clause of the Fourteenth
Amendment to seat Julian Bond in the Georgia legislature, and on a narrow
construction of Article I, section 5, to rule that Powell should have been
seated. Neither case, therefore, necessarily pointed the Court into the quagmire, though the "fundamental principle" announced in *Powell* "that the
people should choose whom they please to govern them" had unlimited possibilities.

Other postelection discrimination, as yet untouched by the Court, is in the
quagmire to its eyebrows: committee assignments, seniority, bloc voting,
logrolling, influence peddling, and other such forms of parliamentary, executive, and judiciary maneuvering. The federal and state constitutions are drawn
up in contemplation of different factions taking advantage of these informal
modes of influence, taking care to assign different modes of election and appointment to different governmental authorities in the hope that one interest
could not control them all and tyrannize the rest. It is possible with much
effort to show how the different modes of organization can discriminate
against some interests and in favor of others, but no one has yet demonstrated a way to measure how much discrimination has taken place, even in
the past, through biases in the constitutional structure, let alone shown a way
to balance such biases prospectively. Without a usable balance the Court was,
and remains, ill-equipped to give the Fundamental Principle promulgated in
the reapportionment cases the same broad and penetrating interpretation it
gave the Fifteenth Amendment's right to vote in the white primary and
Tuskegee cases.

Options for Further Intervention

Can such a balance yet be found? Is there any way that the Court could vindicate the underlying principle of its Warren era voting rights decisions, as the
Yale Law Journal urged, by invalidating any "political structure which gives
any group of the electorate disproportionate weight in influencing the outcome of vital political decisions?"[161] The theme of this chapter is negative to
further adventures with the Fundamental Principle; nevertheless, it might be
worthwhile to capitulate some of the Court's options to see if some doctrinal
or policy gimmick might not permit further intervention. The Court had two
grand options: going all the way with the Fundamental Principle, or confining
itself to general elections with a few exceptions, such as white primaries and
primary elections for statewide office.[162] These options will be discussed
presently, and a preference expressed for the second. In the meantime, how-

ever, three petty options for covering the ground in between should be discussed. Short of total intervention and total nonintervention are these three options for limited intervention: (1) status quo—intervention to protect the status quo against antidemocratic changes; (2) southern strategy—intervention in the South, but not in the North; or (3) some kind of functional standard which would discriminate between "vital political decisions" that do serve a constitutionally protectable function and those that do not.

Vested Status Quo

The argument for a vested status quo test would run something like this: where a state or a party has undertaken an action initially within its own discretion (for example, public education, or primary elections), the action must meet federal standards and may become irrevocable, as in the cases of the Prince Edward County schools and the California fair housing law.[163] The states did not have to provide public schools, or require open housing, but, once having undertaken them, they could not afterwards abolish them. This argument would be consistent with *Gray v. Sanders* and the Jaybird case; it would find even stronger support in two cases where the Court invalidated Mississippi's attempt to abolish local elections (as it had during Reconstruction) and submerge local black majorities with at-large elections and appointive alternatives.[164] A major argument for the vested status quo rule would be its comparative ease of administration. The status quo may not be coherent, but it is concrete, and blatant antidemocratic changes like abolishing local elections are comparatively easy to perceive, though subtler ones are hard to evaluate. Status quo tests, however, are inherently messy and defensive, ill-suited for large-scale, principled intervention and repugnant to the Guardian Ethic for their tendency to preserve special, unstandardized situations. Not only does the status quo vary from one jurisdiction to the next, it also varies in the same jurisdiction from one day to the next. The status quo is a shifting foundation, on which courts rear doctrinal skyscrapers at their own and society's peril. Any standard based on the status quo must tend to freeze it into a permanent constitutional mandate, blocking both antidemocratic and prodemocratic changes. Antidemocratic changes, like hiring a city manager, would be forbidden for taking away citizens' "vested" right to vote for a mayor; prodemocratic changes, like switching to an elective mayoral system, would also be blocked for fear that they might become irreversable. *Nulla vestigia retrorsum*: the handwriting was on the wall, or at least in the pages of the California fair housing decision, warning the states not to embark on egalitarian reforms they might later regret.

A Southern Strategy of Intervention?

Looking back on the major voting rights decisions of the modern Court (post-1937, Hughes through Warren), as summarized in Table 10, one can

192

hardly escape the impression that the Court found it more convenient to intervene in cases from the South than in cases from the North.[165] The table of interventions shows a dramatic contrast between the southern boxscore of seventeen interventions versus four noninterventions and the northern score of four interventions versus seven noninterventions. Even if the southern intervention score should be cut in half to eliminate cases strongly involving racial exclusion, it still looks as if the Court was almost four times more likely to intervene in the South than it was in the North.

As a guide across the quagmire, however, the southern strategy is also a false lead. Most of the cases listed are landmark cases whose rules apply without discrimination between North and South, save in situations like white primaries and surgical racial gerrymanders, where a factual situation peculiar to the South justified laws whose major incidence was on the South. The southern strategy may have been a short-term device to strengthen the Court in making novel decisions, permitting it to introduce new ideas without offending its largely northern constituency or overcommitting itself on the first try, but no double standard could support a permanent occupation of the quagmire. The erosive action of hard facts frustrating enforcement North and South and hardnosed critics calling for universal application of received principles made the double standard untenable except as a temporary packaging aid. The Court did have some protection in striking down the blatant Tuskegee gerrymander in Alabama; because the South is supposed to be sui generis, the Court could get away with ignoring its initially announced principles in dealing with analogous but subtler situations farther north.[166] Likewise, it could step into the quagmire to invalidate racially inspired at-large elections and executive appointments in Mississippi without forfeiting its freedom to step out again in other contexts.[167] But these small incursions fell well short of the massive measures the Court would have had to take to conquer the quagmire in the South without miring itself throughout the North as well. What double standard, however mighty, could defy a siege by the standardizing cadre on the law reviews? The Court had won too many fields under the banner of equal justice in all circumstances to expose itself with a thoroughgoing southern strategy.

Functional Distinctions

As a principle for limited intervention, some kind of functional test would seem far more attractive than a vested status quo or a southern strategy. If the Court could find a way to distinguish public offices with representative functions from those with other functions, then it could apply the Fundamental Principle to the first kind and leave the second kind alone without provoking the Guardians. The trouble with this approach, as Frankfurter and Harlan pointed out, is that it seems to require a single theory of representation capable of covering a multitude of different, and often contradictory,

Table 10. A "Southern Strategy" of Intervention?

Subject of claim to Supreme Court Intervention	South	North
Candidate selection	I[a]–Smith v. Allwright (Tex.) 321 U.S. 649 (1944)	NI–Snowden v. Hughes (Ill.) 321 U.S. 1 (1944)
Racial Gerrymander	I–Gomillion v. Lightfoot (Ala.) 304 U.S. 339 (1960)	NI–Wright v. Rockefeller (N.Y.) 376 U.S. 52 (1964)
Equal districts: state legislature	I–Baker v. Carr (Tenn.) 369 U.S. 186 (1962) I–Reynolds v. Sims (Ala.)[b] 377 U.S. 533 (1964) I–Davis v. Mann (Va.)[b] 377 U.S. 678 (1964)	I–Lucas v. Colo. Gen. Assembly (Colo.)[b] 377 U.S. 713 (1964) NI–WMCA v. Lomenzo (N.Y.)[b] 377 U.S. 633 (1964)
U.S. Congress	I–Wesberry v. Sanders (Ga.) 376 U.S. 1 (1964)	NI–Colegrove v. Green (Ill.) 328 U.S. 549 (1949)
school districts		NI–Sailors v. Bd. of Ed. (Mich.)[c] 387 U.S. 105 (1967)
local government	I–Avery v. Midland Cty. (Tex.) 390 U.S. 474 (1968)	
Candidate residence requirements	NI–Dusch v. Davis (Va.) 387 U.S. 112 (1967)	
Multi-member districts; at-large elections	I–Fairley v. Patterson (Miss.) 393 U.S. 544 (1969) NI–Fortson v. Dorsey (Ga.) 379 U.S. 433 (1965) NI–Burnette v. Davis (Va.) 382 U.S. 42 (1965)	NI–Burns v. Richardson (Hawaii) 384 U.S. 73 (1966)
Appointive alternative	I–Bunton v. Patterson (Miss.) 393 U.S. 544 (1969)	
Poll tax	I–Harper v. Bd. of Elections (Va.) 383 U.S. 663 (1966)	
Municipal bond voting; school district elections	I–Cipriano v. City of Houma (La.) 395 U.S. 701 (1969)	I–Kramer v. Union Free School Dist. (N.Y.) 395 U.S. 621 (1969)
Felons vote		NI–McDonald v. Bd. (Ill.) 394 U.S. 802 (1969)
Literacy tests	NI–Lassiter v. N'hampton Cty. (N.C.) 360 U.S. 45 (1959)	I–Katzenbach v. Morgan (N.Y.) 384 U.S. 641 (1966)

	I–United States v. Mississippi (Miss.) 380 U.S. 128 (1965)	NI–Cardona v. Power (N.Y.) 384 U.S. 672 (1966)
	I–Louisiana v. United States (La.) 380 U.S. 145 (1965)	
Disequal. military transients	I–Carrington v. Rash (Tex.) 380 U.S. 89 (1965)	
Total Interventions:	17	4
Total Non-interventions:	4	7

[a]I = Court intervened; NI = Court did not intervene.

[b]The six *Reapportionment* cases of 1964 included two cases from the South, Reynolds v. Sims, 377 U.S. 533 (Ala.) and Davis v. Mann, 377 U.S. 678 (Va.). Two were from the North, WMCA, Inc. v. Lomenzo, 377 U.S. 633 (N.Y.) and Lucas v. Colorado General Assembly, 377 U.S. 713 (Colo.). Two were from border states and not included in the listings of this table. Maryland Comm. for Fair Representation v. Tawes, 377 U.S. 656 (Md.); Roman v. Sincock, 377 U.S. 695 (Del.). The six cases are identified by the one from the deepest South, which the Court printed at the head of the rest. The two northern cases produced a three-man dissent, while the rest produced only one dissenting vote.

The week after Reynolds v. Sims the Court disposed of reapportionment cases from seven northern states, one southern state, and one border state in memorandum decisions. Beadle v. Scholle, 377 U.S. 990 (Mich. 1964); Marshall v. Hare, 378 U.S. 561 (Mich. 1964); Meyers v. Thigpen, 378 U.S. 554 (Wash. 1964); Germano v. Kerner, 378 U.S. 560 (Ill. 1964); Hearne v. Smylie, 378 U.S. 563 (Idaho 1964); Pinney v. Butterworth, 378 U.S. 564 (Conn. 1964); Nolan v. Rhodes, 378 U.S. 556 (Ohio 1964); Hill v. Davis, 378 U.S. 565 (Iowa 1964); Swann v. Adams, 378 U.S. 533 (Fla. 1964); Williams v. Moss, 378 U.S. 558 (Okla. 1964).

[c]Hadley v. Junior College District, 397 U.S. 50 (Mo. 1970–I) is not listed, as Missouri is a border state and the case was decided after Warren's retirement.

functions. After centuries of trying, no one has yet devised such a theory. Most people believe that governments have functions, though experts differ as to which functions are important. Marxists see exploitation as the chief function of government; governments are supposed to exist to perpetuate the ruling class's control of the means of production.[168] Structural-functionalists' functional theories are more detailed. They tend to stress things like inputs and outputs. Deference, support, obedience, and participation go into the political system; extraction, regulation, allocation, and symbolic expression issue from it. Every political system has some species of interest articulation, interest aggregation, rule-making, rule application, rule adjudication, internal and external communication, systems maintenance and adaptation, socialization, and recruitment.[169] Representative systems have all or most of these functions common to all governments, but they also claim special representative functions, particularly in the matter of rule-making and rule application. We have a general idea that representation has to do with an individual reflecting or embodying a general category or constituency, but we have no fixed idea of what kind of reflection the word implies. Any sample from a collection of like objects can be representative in the sense that Yeats's "The Second Coming" is representative of the poems of his middle period. Or the individual may symbolically reflect the collectivity, as the Pope represents the Catholic church, or the bulldog represents Yale. Or the individual may represent a constituency virtually as a trustee, in the manner of Edmund Burke with his Bristol constituency, or directly as a delegate or agent, in the manner of Abba Eban representing Israel at the peace table.

Organicism and Mechanism

For democratic politics, the last two meanings of *representation* are probably the most pertinent: we think of a representative as a delegate, or trustee, or some combination of the two, for his constituency. Even this simplified concept of representation, however, is not a secure guide for judicial action, as it does not contend with (let alone resolve) contradictions between two traditions of political theory, mechanistic and organic.

"All speculations concerning forms of government," said John Stuart Mill, "bear the impress, more or less exclusive, of two conflicting theories respecting political institutions." For some (whom I call mechanists though Mill did not use the word), forms of government are "regarded as wholly an affair of invention and contrivance," "a problem to be worked out like any other question of business." Mechanists "look upon a constitution in the same light (differences of scale being allowed for) as they would upon a steam plough, or a threshing machine." For others (whom I call organicists though Mill did not), a people's political institutions "are considered as a sort of organic growth from the nature and life of that people" which "cannot be constructed by premeditated design."[170]

The distinction casts light on much that is usually left unsaid by political and social theorists. It deserves more attention than Mill gave it, and no doubt more attention than the bare outline I present in this section. Organicism and mechanism, at bottom, are two different ways of looking at imperfections in political systems, one tolerant and accepting, the other itching for something better. The mechanistic tradition has stressed universalism, individualism, equality, and abstract conceptual symmetry. Mechanists saw political life as simple in essence, manipulable by those with knowledge, ready to be perfected in accordance with the latest timeless paradigm. They stressed formal, rational ties and deprecated informal, affective ties. Society was held together by individuals' rational adherence to the paradigm; paradigm aside, it was a whole no greater than the sum of its parts. The golden age of mechanism began in the seventeenth century, when great thinkers like Bacon, Hobbes, Descartes, and Spinoza dropped the cautious dualism of Platonic tradition, which had distinguished the best *conceivable* system (for example, *The Republic*) from the best *practicable* ones (for example, those expounded in *The Statesman* or *The Laws*). For the seventeenth-century mechanists— yearning for the same order and clockwork symmetry in the human and moral universe that Galileo, Kepler, and Newton were finding in the physical universe—theoretically conceivable and politically practicable were one and the same. "Knowledge and human power," wrote Francis Bacon, "are synonymous, since ignorance of the cause frustrates the effect; for nature is subdued only by submission, and that which in contemplative philosophy corresponds with the cause in practice becomes the rule."[171] "The end of knowledge is power," added Hobbes; "the scope of all speculation is the performance of some action, or thing to be done."[172] Descartes had originally entitled his *Discourse on Method* "Project of a Universal Science Destined To Raise Our Nature to Its Highest Degree of Perfection."[173] Spinoza declared "I shall consider human actions and desires in exactly the same manner as though I were concerned with lines, planes, and solids."[174]

Mechanistic perfectionism shone brightly in the works of Condorcet, Voltaire, Fontenelle, and La Mettrie in the eighteenth century, and in the *idéologues* and Saint-Simon and Compte in the nineteenth.[175] In England it was discernible in the work of Locke, but it shone with solar luster in the writing of the proto-Guardian Jeremy Bentham. In the doctrinal shadowland of the New World one could detect traces of the mechanistic tradition in the thoughts of Jefferson, the Jacksonian populists, Thorstein Veblen, and the Guardians; however, American thinkers have been too relaxed intellectually, or too sophisticated politically, to attempt such mighty and well-coordinated doctrinal structures as those of Hobbes, Bentham, or the French *philosophes*.[176]

Since the eighteenth century, mechanistic thinkers have laid very heavy stress on majority rule as the cardinal source of legitimacy. Mechanism purports to provide simple, formal techniques for measuring the "will" of "the majority" and implementing it as though it were the unanimous opinion of all citizens. It presupposes popular sovereignty, equal vote, and direct, effective techniques for determining popular will.[177] The mechanistic concept of legitimacy—"if in doubt, follow the majority"—has virtues which have won it a warm place in the hearts of political theorists and a very secure place in their armory of doctrines. Older and more inclusive than the Guardian Ethic, it has many of the same attractions: universalism, undifferentiated individualism, aesthetic, even mathematical neatness, and accent on the measurable, on the operable, and on the Promethean role of reason. The mechanistic tradition is irresistible to reform-minded intellectuals, for it lends itself to "getting things done" by transcending the confusion and particularism of actual politics, while offering a reasonably concrete and comprehensible alternative.

On the other hand, there have always been thinkers of the opposite persuasion, organic skeptics who scoffed at the mechanists' constructs as crude misapprehensions of political reality. As the archetypal mechanist is Jeremy Bentham, the archetypal organicist is Edmund Burke. While both of these men should be regarded as moderate reformers in the sense that both favored reforms and neither was a revolutionary, their starting points and their philosophical goals were poles apart. Where the mechanist Bentham saw society as the creature of artifice, a formal structure of no greater value than the sum of its members' wishes, organicists like Burke, Walter Bagehot, and Alexis de Tocqueville saw society as a spontaneous, natural phenomenon, no more fit for radical manipulation than a living organism. Where the mechanists focused on the abstract and the universal in men and societies, the organicists focused on the concrete and the particular: *these* men in *this* society. Where the mechanists focused on formal systems (for example, the single-member district system) and thought them simple, the organicists focused on informal systems (for example, political parties), which they considered complex. Where the mechanists stressed conceptual symmetry, the organicists stressed practical workability. Where the mechanists sought to perfect political institutions by conforming them to a succession of timeless paradigms, the organicists thought the paradigms more in need of conformation to institutions, which they considered more stable and serviceable than any simple paradigm.[178] Organicists laid special emphasis on cultivating mutual trust and social cohesion, items which the mechanists took for granted would automatically spring from each individual's rational understanding that the paradigm would maximize his own advantage. Uncalculating loyalty, to the organicist, was what permitted political systems to function, but to the mechanist it stood in the way of perfection. Organicists wanted *Gemeinschaft*, mechanists, *Gesellschaft*.[179]

Organicists focused on specific institutions with a tender solicitude and an eye to system maintenance which has always lent a conservative tone to organic theory. Organicists favored reforms often enough, but they preferred safe, practical, preservative little reforms to grand restructuring, much in the fashion of doctors who order tonsillectomies readily enough but hesitate to order heart transplants. The mechanists have always been much bolder in calling for sweeping reforms to replace obsolete political contrivances (such as our "horse and buggy" Constitution) with some more modish contrivance (such as a political equivalent to the internal combustion engine?). Where the mechanists attacked the anomalies of English government—pocket boroughs, legal fictions, the King, and the aristocracy—as "fallacies" of government, the organicists cherished them for preserving prescriptive liberties and nourishing a sense of community. With their focus on preserving beneficial institutions, the organicists never tied their concept of natural law to a majority vote. Their natural law sanctioned plural things like liberties and property rights against the claims of majority rule and formal equality. Organicists preferred the special to the standard, liberties to equality, association, or consensus, and community to total and direct popular participation in political action. They preferred practical, long-run efficacy for maintaining the system to formal, short-run efficacy for securing this or that immediate popular desire.

Some latter-day thinkers in the organic tradition are Giovanni Sartori, Alfred De Grazia, Harry Jaffa, Edward Banfield, Bertrand de Jouvenel, and possibly Robert Dixon.[180] Sartori's blunt summary of the function of elections strikes a jarring contrast with the mechanistic presuppositions of the Guardians. Elections, said Sartori, are "not to make democracy more democratic, but to make democracy possible: that is, to make it function. In the very moment that we admit the need of having recourse to elections, we minimize democracy, for we realize that the system cannot be operated by the demos itself. Clearly, then, the purpose of elections is to select leadership, not to maximize democracy."[181] Banfield was equally blunt in dismissing critics of the American party system for valuing democratic procedure for its own sake without reference to the results it produces. If critics were willing to assign priority among the ends of government, he argued, they would not put democratic procedure at the top, but would give preference to protecting society and its members, offering periodic opportunity to change governments, promoting the welfare of the people, and restraining harmful conflict.[182] Banfield concluded that the American party system served these ends with great success. Our competition between two nonideological parties was a "lucky accident" which made possible a strong, stable government, continuity between administrations from different parties, cultivation and reward of moderate vote, sensitivity to concrete, practical desires, and discouragement of deep cleavages.[183] He was loath to tamper with such a complex and successful operation, though he feared that it might one day succumb to an excess of its own virtues through excessive preoccupation with democratic procedures.

The weakness of the organic tradition lies in its quietism if carried to its own logical extreme (an unorganic thing to do). A "pure" organicism could be assailed for excessive curtailment of the domain of rational purpose to which every government, in some measure, should respond.[184] On the other hand, if there was any support for pure quietist organicism in the Warren era, it was exceptionally well hidden. The threats of excessive purity came exclusively from the mechanist quarter, from perfectionist Guardians who (following John Stuart Mill) "think it a shame when anything goes wrong" and "rush to the conclusion that the evil could and ought to have been prevented" by a "more representative" system.[185] Even though only a few of the Guardians went to Mill's extreme of demanding proportional representation as the most perfectly representative system of all, their thinking ran in the same mechanistic channels. "More representative" meant more democracy in form, but usually less in substance. PR was the palladium of mechanistic democracy. It represented every shade of difference of individual opinion with geometrical accuracy; it represented "all the people, not just the majority"; it left no one out; it presented clear choices on many issues; it was proof against gerry-mandering and malapportionment. In form, it had everything. In practice, it was much less workable than the district system. It encouraged schismatism, discouraged compromise. It was wildly responsive to ripples of public senti-ment but unresponsive to tides. It gave everyone a voice but did nothing to pull the voices together in effective, stable coalition. It gave everyone a clear choice of alternatives, but the alternatives tended to be impracticable.

Many of the Guardians' proposed reforms of the 1960's shared PR's tend-ency to sacrifice democratic substance for democratic form. "Maximum feasi-ble participation," elective leadership of administrative agencies, faculty or student review of foreign and domestic policy, and PR for women, youth, and blacks in presidential nominating conventions all had something resem-bling PR'S comprehensive receptiveness to different viewpoints and its dimin-ished incentive for pulling the viewpoints together to permit action on any of the viewpoints. For practical purposes, several centers of leadership with weak incentives to coalesce are less capable of action, and therefore less re-sponsive, than one or two centers of leadership. A comparison between the House of Representatives in 1900, say, and the House today should illustrate the point, or a comparison of the House today with the United Nations. In each comparison the body with more centralized leadership is the more re-sponsive body.

In almost any case, a government's responsiveness to the will of the gov-erned over a long period of time depends on agencies for informal communi-cation and coordination. Chief among these agencies are political parties. Strong political parties are the essence of strong, stable, modern governments, irrespective of profound differences in the structures of the various govern-ments and parties. Parties provide regularized but adaptable political pro-cedures; they nourish a sense of political community; they absorb and some-times resolve disagreement; they encourage popular participation in certain political decision; and they provide a mutual discipline to leaders and follow-ers. They moderate the many forces that pull governments to unsupportable extremes; in general, they are the sine qua non of sustained political viability. In the words of Samuel Huntington, "Organization [in political parties] is the road to political power, but it is also the foundation of political stability and thus the precondition to political liberty."[186]

I suppose it could be argued that strong parties, however indispensible for nation building, are less well suited and less needed for maintaining a nation already built. Walter Dean Burnham and others have suggested that the rich American people may have come to regard politics as "an item of luxury con-sumption" with less claim on their time and attention than in the nineteenth century, and that "there is no Democratic or Republican way to solve highly complex policy problems" better fit for bureaucratic solutions.[187] There is no doubt some truth to this, as there is no doubt some truth for mature individuals that acting on tested habit may have more payoff than perpetual reexamination of one's course of action and beliefs. But the bureaucratic alternative buys short-term payoff by mortgaging its long-term flexibility and responsiveness. The flaw of all-input government (PR) is its incapacity for anything but symbolic action, its indiscipline in the matter of producing results. The flaw of all-output government is its rigidity, its indiscipline in the matter of conforming its actions to changing desires in the public at large. Without this discipline of continually renewed response to the will of a broad public, bureaucracies become isolated and weak.[188] They lose their operational autonomy and their ability to govern. Many become hostages of those they were set up to regulate, evolving narrow, unintegrated input functions of their own. The proper remedy for these bureaucratic inadequacies is not Herbert Gans's proposed multiplication of inputs, nor Rexford Tugwell's proposed multiplication of administration, nor the more rigid legalism of Theodore Lowi's "judicial democracy," nor yet John Gardner's "self-renewal" through constant internal reorganization of bureaus. The proper course is more moderate expectations from government than those of the Guardians and more tolerance of integrative institutions like political parties which pull inputs and outputs together and make them work better than either would by itself. Guardian dreams of turning every sow's ear into a silk purse are dangerous because people take them more seriously than they once did, and because they are no better thought out than mechanistic dreams of the past. A sow's ears may be homely, but they are also functional to the sow, who needs her hearing more than she needs the aesthetic enhancement of a silk purse.

Likewise, political parties are homely and uninspiring. "Only a romantic," said V. O. Key, "can say much for party leadership in most of the states, either now or in the good old days, although encouraging signs appear from place to place." Tocqueville had said the same thing a century before but gone on to marvel at the sense of community, voluntary participation, and mutual trust which the homely system elicited so much better than the educated humane, administrative leadership to which he had himself been trained in France. The great strength of democracy in America was Americans' "spirit of association," their willingness to organize in informal groups, cooperate with one another, pay their taxes, and submit without a murmur to the command of the pettiest magistrate. Willing cooperation makes up for many deficiencies. For legislators, for administrators, and for the general public it provides "trustworthy" information and judgment on a wide variety of issues, far wider than the most enlightened administrator, let alone the average voter, could find out on his own.[189] Parties and voluntary associations activate what Key called "attentive publics"—people especially interested and knowledgeable about certain aspects of public policy, to whom the not-so-attentive public can turn for cues as to how it should vote. All of us, including legislators, fall into the not-so-attentive category for some, if not most, issues; we must rely on others with more specialized knowledge, whom we trust, for proper guidance. Conservation-minded citizens and legislators, for instance, cannot normally keep abreast of all the committee hearings and amendments of all the hundreds of conservation (and anticonservation) bills which pass through a legislature in a given session. They can, however, count on an attentive public of conservation lobbies to bring important issues to their attention when mobilization is needed. They can seek (though they need not always follow) party guidance when sides are being chosen. The attentive public, for its part, will continue its attention as long as it believes its attention will ultimately have some bearing on what government does or does not do. So will the parties and so will the public at large which relies on the parties for leadership in forming its opinions.[190]

Where the parties defer to some transpartisan elite, however, or are bypassed, the incentives for attention are shifted to administrative or judicial arenas where the primary emphasis is on quick results and there is little need to cultivate institutionalized mutual trust or public participation. Success in the executive arena depends more on secrecy, speed, audacity, and timing and less on consultation, negotiation, consensus-building, and rule-abiding than success in the legislature. Action is possible without involving the public, and the incentives for the government, or the attentive public, to consult the public at large are much reduced—as are the incentives of the public at large to concern itself with the tedious and useless tasks of community-building. Without strong party leadership to cultivate a sense of community, representative bodies weaken and the general public is left only the options of the weak: ex post facto acquiescence in executive or judicial acts, or direct, and therefore short-term and normally ineffective, action to protest or impede the act, or quiet, individual noncompliance with the act (for example, cheating on taxes, or draft-dodging).

Daniel Patrick Moynihan put his finger on the effect of transpartisan mechanistic reforms in weakening party control and thereby eroding organic community power among the New York poor.

The "problem" of powerlessness must surely also have been compounded by the erosion of community-based power, a change especially to be noted in Manhattan where for so long local political organizations, coalescing in Tammany Hall, had wielded highly visible, even notorious power. Fifty years of municipal reform had just about put an end to that in New York . . . . much of the impulse to do something about the feeling of powerlessness among the lower-class ethnic minorities of the city came from much the same group that in previous decades had systematically stripped minorities of the very considerable power they had had, and did so in the name of their own good . . . [Tammany's] functions had for the most part been taken out of the political sector and consigned to bureaucracies—the very bureaucracies whose middle-class rigidity and putative disdain for the poor had been responsible for so much of the thinking behind community action![191]

In the case of New York, the reformers wanted to bypass Tammany with direct participation of the poor in administering antipoverty funds, a policy of democratic intent but antidemocratic effect (had the poor been so foolish as to embrace it), for it would have substituted several weak representative agencies ("rent strike coordinating committees" plus an ineffectual Tammany) for one strong one (Tammany with a monopoly of spoils). Even less harmful reforms, such as reapportionment, or abolishing poll taxes and literacy and residence tests, however, also undermine effective democracy when they are enacted over the parties' heads rather than through them. In a world of heavy mechanistic predominance, organic institutions are hard put to hold their own, and effective democracy is jeopardized by those most professedly anxious to strengthen it. As Key pointed out, a prominent place among those responsible for undistinguished party leadership "is held by those good [mechanistic] people who have discouraged partisanship as civic wickedness and have caused the diversion of vast quantities of social energy from party channels to nonpartisan activity or simply to inaction."[192]

The Guardians' perfectionism, inadequately tinctured with organic understanding, was not a very trustworthy guide for practical reform. Space age and all notwithstanding, representative politics are not an item of luxury consumption, even for the most hard-nosed proponent of administrative power, far less for those with democratic sympathies. Organic, integrative institutions may interfere with quick, decisive, executive action in the short run—as in many cases they should—but they cultivate and reward long-term public interest and support (as executive action alone cannot) and they make possible *sustained*, effective executive response, as unintegrated public sentiment cannot. Formal, democratic absolutism does not strengthen democracy, for its perspectives are too narrow. The absolutists are all too willing to starve the organic belly to save the mechanistic soul. When they wind up by weakening both, and then incongruously seek to set things right by more rigorous fasting ("maximum feasible participation"), the public should be less credulous than it was in the 1960's. Mechanism deserves a place of honor in political theory, but it does not deserve the heavy dominance of policy reserved for it in the Guardian Ethic. For the many things in politics which can and should be made better, and soon, and absolutely, perfectionism is no doubt a wise policy. But for the many things which cannot be "perfected" without dangerous neglect of long-term needs, perfectionism is a recipe for unfettered despotism, political decay, or both. Someone once scorned the good as the enemy of the best. Too few intelligent people in the Warren era recognized that in politics the reverse is often also true.

One of the few was Felix Frankfurter, whose dissent in *Baker v. Carr* challenged the majority's narrow philosophical absolutism years before the majority got around to giving it its fullest articulation:

What, then, is this question of legislative apportionment? [The reapportionists] complaint is simply that the representatives are not sufficiently numerous or powerful—in short, that Tennessee has adopted a basis of representation with which they are dissatisfied. Talk of "debasement" or "dilution" is circular talk. One cannot speak of "debasement" or "dilution" of the value of a vote until there is first defined a standard of reference as to what a vote should be worth. What is actually asked of the Court in this case is to choose among competing bases of representation—ultimately, really among competing theories of political philosophy—in order to establish an appropriate frame of government for the State of Tennessee and thereby for all the States of the Union . . .

The notion that representation proportioned to the geographic spread of population is so universally accepted as a necessary element of equality between man and man that it must be taken to be the standard of a political equality preserved by the Fourteenth Amendment—that it is, in appellants' words "the basic principle of representative government"—is, to put it bluntly, not true. However desirable and however desired by some among the great political thinkers and framers of our government, it has never been generally practiced, today or in the past. It was not the system chosen for the national government by the Constitution, it was not the system exclusively or even predominantly practiced by the States at the time of adoption of the Fourteenth Amendment, it is not predominantly practiced by the States today . . .

The stark fact is that if among the numerous widely varying principles and practices that control state legislative apportionment today there is any generally prevailing feature, that feature is geographic inequality in relation to the population standard. Examples could be endlessly multiplied . . . These figures show more than individual variations from a generally accepted standard of electoral equality. They show that there is not—as there has never been—a standard by which the place of equality as a factor in apportionment can be measured . . .

Apportionment, by its character, is a subject of extraordinary complexity, involving—even after the fundamental theoretical issues concerning what is to be represented in a representative legislature have been fought out or compromised—considerations of geography, demography, electoral convenience, economic and social cohesions or divergencies among particular local groups, communications, the practical effects of political institutions like the lobby and the city machine, ancient traditions and ties of settled usage, respect for proven incumbents of long experience and senior status, mathematical mechanics, censuses, compiling relevant data, and a host of others . . . in every strand of this complicated, intricate web of values meet the contending forces of partisan politics. The practical significance of apportionment is that the next election results may differ because of it. Apportionment battles are overwhelmingly party or intra-party contests.[193]

We know, of course, that the Court ignored Frankfurter's warnings and went on to devise and impose a theory of representation: one man, one vote "wherever a state government decides to select persons by popular election to perform governmental functions."[194] Was this a wise decision? Should it be extended throughout the spectrum of public choice? The answer depends on one's disposition to judge by organic or mechanistic standards, and the results of the reapportionment revolution so far give only doubtful support to further extension of mechanistic standards. The argument of the next chapter is that reapportionment has done very little to justify its high cost in constitutional fakery and overriding of democratic processes. At the same time, however, having fulfilled neither the hopes of its sponsors nor the fears of its opponents, it does not appear to have done serious damage to the structure and operation of American political institutions. As social critics, we are free to choose between three different assessments of this situation: (1) the mechanistic view, that we can expect reinvigorated democracy only when we complete the reapportionment revolution by Bakerizing the *terra irredenta*; or (2) the light organic view, that we are lucky the Court stopped short of gutting our most precious representative institutions; or (3) the heavy organic view, that even the *terra irredenta* is peripheral to the true workings of our representative institutions, which are therefore only superficially vulnerable to mechanistic meddling.

My own choice falls somewhere between the two organic views, but perhaps closer to the one fearing substantial harm from tampering with the system. In general, it seems to me that applying the Fundamental Principle to most of the remaining virgin areas of public choice would have the effect of turning them from *efficient* agencies of government to *dignified* agencies whose purpose is more to awe than to act. Walter Bagehot used these terms in the last century to distinguish the ruling "efficient" function of the British cabinet from the reigning or "dignified" function of the King.[195] Dignified agencies of government fulfilled an important purpose, to preserve the allegiance of the people by satisfying their appetite for symbolic representation, while keeping them from impeding the cabinet in its task of running the country. Dignified agencies, in a sense, served to fool the people for the short run by substituting formal gratification for substantive participation in government; however, in the longer run, dignified agencies were supposed to benefit the people by absorbing and diverting minor public fancies, while leaving the government free to respond to major changes in public opinion. No campaigner for expanded application of the Fundamental Principle has used the dignified-efficient distinction; historically and logically an organic concept, it could not be expected to loom large in mechanistic designs. Nevertheless, it seems that most of the prospective extensions of one man, one vote would substitute dignified functions for efficient ones, and one may reasonably wonder whether the public would benefit from the substitution and further wonder whether the irredentists' dream of democratizing every category of public choice would not destroy the preconditions for democracy.

Most categories of public choice now subject to the Fundamental Principle—general elections, primary elections in one-party jurisdictions, and certain details of campaigning for general elections—can be regarded as efficient institutions: they serve a function of *registration* of the choice of the pertinent constituencies. The categories not now subject to the Fundamental Principle also serve efficient functions, but efficient in a different sense. Their functions are *organizational* or *managerial.*[196] Party nomination, for instance, does not register public opinion (except in one-party primary elections); it furnishes alternatives for public choice. Executive appointments, for another instance, do not register public opinion; they implement the desires of the public's elected executive. Their function is managerial, not registrational. Imposition of the one man, one vote rule on party nominations or executive appointment presupposes that their primary function is, or should be registrational. When the *Yale Law Journal* calls for the invalidation of any "political structure which gives any group of the electorate disproportionate weight in influencing the outcome of vital political decisions,"[197] it calls explicitly for homogenization of structure and implicitly for homogenization of function. It suggests that every category of public choice should be organized to serve a registrational function. There is nothing inherently wrong with serving a registrational function, but one may question the wisdom of devoting every political structure to registration. Organicists, of course, would be shocked at a proposal, in effect, to increase photosynthesis in the political plant by requiring bark and roots to function as leaves, but even a mechanist might detect a note of redundancy in a proposal to redesign the vehicle of state to make the transmission and brakes function as steering wheels. The two extra wheels would add very little to the control of the mechanism, though they might help to convey an illusion of control if the driver-passenger did not miss the services of his gears and brakes. The first wheel (general elections) serves an efficient function of registration; but, if the extra wheels are to have any function at all, it would be a dignified function, not an efficient one.

More important, we can ill afford to do without the efficient functions of party nominations, executive appointments, the electoral college, and most of the other institutions for public choice which have not yet been homogenized. These institutions may be undemocratic in the sense that they do not follow the Fundamental Principle and in many cases grant no direct public participation in choices of public consequence, but they provide a working basis for democracy which more democratic procedures would deny. We know from the writing of Mancur Olson and others that large groups are structurally ill suited, if not incapable, of mobilizing their membership to take any kind of action, even action in the group's interest, so long as the members of the group are left free to further their own interests. Rational people will not normally pay taxes, union dues, and so forth to a large group on a voluntary basis, for their individual cost is great while their individual return is infinitesimal. Some kind of compulsion is necessary to bring about any kind of collective action entailing individual costs. But even this compulsion is impossible without some sort of voluntary collective action to make or change laws and enforce them. Such action is much more likely to come from small groups of a half-dozen members, whose individual stake in collective action is large enough to make them willing to pitch in and make the group perform,[198] than from larger groups, though the action may have to be approved by the larger group. One sociologist found that United States Senate subcommittees at the time of his investigation averaged 5.4 members, while House subcommittees, Oregon state government working units, and Eugene, Oregon municipal government working units averaged, respectively, 7.8, 4.7, and 5.3 members. He concluded "that committees should be small when you expect action and relatively large when you are looking for points of view, reactions, etc."[199]

American democracy works only by virtue of countless decision-making agencies which *do not* drag the public into the decision-making process, even though the decision may be of great public consequence, because the public is incapable of doing the hard work of deliberation that most decisions require. Instead, the agencies act under their own concept of proper policy and their own self-interest, subject to a periodic registration of a general public preferences at general elections. Most people accept this limitation on the democratic process in regard to the behavior of elected representatives, whom they expect to make decisions of public consequence without a formal expression of public feeling on each decision. They are much less aware, however, of the importance of decisions made prior to elections by small groups of political entrepreneurs in permitting the electorate to make an intelligent choice between alternatives carefully contrived to build and preserve consensus, preserve the system, and provide the basis for action on items of major public concern while avoiding it on items of minor public concern. Political entrepreneurs must think more carefully and farther ahead than the general public, for their careers depend not just on winning the next election but also on their ongoing potential for winning elections after the next election. They must pick candidates who can not only win, but govern effectively after they win. They must pick issues which will command public approval over a substantial period of time and avoid issues that will go sour, backfire, or alienate important elements of the electorate. Under the two-party, winner-take-all practice of American politics, they must strive to broaden their base of support by fielding moderate candidates and platforms appealing to the broadest possible spectrum of the electorate. They must seek accommodation of many interests and points of view, not intransigence on behalf of one interest or point of view against all others; they must discourage splintering, yet avoid the tyranny of one majority lest it prevent the formation of other majorities.

A working democracy must look not only to the quantity of its majority; in the longer run, it is the quality of the majority that counts. There is a world of difference between the volatile, unstructured, and absolutist majorities that spring up in the worlds of women's fashions and plebiscitary democracy and the stable, ordered, pragmatic majorities that spring from such undemocratic institutions as party conventions and the electoral college. These institutions perform critical functions. They strengthen and maintain our two-party system. They encourage strong candidates and strong, moderate programs. They protect against promiscuous and short-lived mutations, such as those demanded by the Know-Nothings, the Free Silver people, and the McCarthyites of the 1950's, while responding to broader based desires for change, such as those reflected in the election of Thomas Jefferson in 1800, Andrew Jackson in 1828, Abraham Lincoln in 1860, and Franklin Roosevelt in 1932.[200] They provide authorized, controllable channels for the assertion of interests. They filter out trivial, peripheral, and needlessly divisive issues and permit the public to choose intelligently between two workable alternatives rather than among a half-dozen or more unworkable ones. They protect democracy from a fatal overdose of little issues, thereby permitting it to act on the big issues. They build majorities which are effective, but moderated; they protect minorities. They encourage discussion and coordination but build a strong basis for action where it is most wanted. In short, they secure most of the ends of good government and are as indispensable to effective majority rule as roots and bark are to the well-being of a tree and as brakes and transmission are to the effectiveness of an automobile.

Reforms intended to democratize the parties, the electoral college, and most of the institutions for public choice not yet democratized could cripple majority rule as we know it by trading effective organization for the appearance of added legitimacy and by turning efficient agencies into dignified ones. The McGovern Commission guidelines—taking party structure out of the hands of party leaders, scrapping the unit rule, quotas, proportional representation—fit this model all too well. They wound up recreating the Democratic party in the image of Weimar Germany and the Fourth French Republic: representative-looking, but no longer operable and hence no longer representative in any meaningful sense; open to every shade of opinion, but offering little incentive to pull the various shades of opinion together into a coordinated and effective majority. Like evils might be expected from attempts to popularize the electoral college, which also derives its contributions to stability, moderation, and majority rule from undemocratic-looking anomalies like the unit rule.[201]

No one can accurately predict the long-term results of these proposed changes. The extension of "citizenship" might give a temporary boost to public confidence in the parties, provided the public were foolish enough to accept the gutted forms of citizenship in place of its former substance. Moreover, it might be that the basic structure of representation would be no more affected by homogenizing the *terra irredenta* than it was by reapportionment, that the body politic would evolve institutions to take over the functions of agencies crippled by reform. The parties might fall back on some kind of pre-primary nominating process to preserve themselves and incidentally preserve the old incentives to build consensus, field strong candidates, confine vogues and schisms to a minimal role, and provide the basis for effective government. More likely, however, the parties would be seriously weakened and broken down into their constituent factions, with no unit rule to reward their pulling back together.[202] At the very least, they would suffer the redundancy of trying to pull together for the equivalent of three general elections, rather than one. Some weakening of the parties seems inevitable from promiscuous democratization, and that is far more dangerous than anything done so far in the field of reapportionment. Weak parties tend to run weak candidates, flashy demagogues, movie stars, and passionate amateurs, whose sole test for office-holding is their ability to please, not their ability to please plus their ability to lead. If weak parties mean weak candidates, weak candidates mean weak government. The best that can be hoped from the irredentists' proposed reforms is that they will not kill the parties; but an even better hope is that someone will kill the reforms instead.

Conclusions

The net of all these considerations is that the Court has travelled and opened up many roads to vindicate the Fundamental Principle, but that it should not, and probably will not follow them much farther, for most of them lead into the quagmire. The Court was safe in equalizing districts in general elections in that this policy did not involve a radical contradiction between the simplicity of its underlying assumptions and their applicability to actual politics. Reapportionment, as the next chapter argues, did little to strengthen representative institutions, but it did little to weaken them. Despite its rhetoric purporting to get down to the nitty gritty, reapportionment in practice has been a peripheral reform. A few of the remaining potential reforms are of this nature—simple, enforceable, inconsequential—and could be enacted by the Court or some other legislative agency without seriously damaging the body politic. Electoral administration is one such subject of reform; qualification to vote is another. The Court could intervene on matters like disqualification of felons, absentee voting, and so forth. It could intervene on some seating controversies, like the Julian Bond and Adam Clayton Powell cases, but only with great circumspection. Deep inroads into legislative politics (for example, challenges to the seniority system and committee assignments) seem unlikely regardless of who is on the Court. The Court could intervene in some runoff situations, perhaps with some doctrinal embarrassment but without serious risk of damage, either to itself or to the political system it would be trying to reform. The Court's main difficulties in undertaking these modest reforms would be its longtime problems of combining the practice of legislation with the appearance of adjudication and of overriding representative institutions under the guise of strengthening them.

The Court could also continue to increase the rigor of its current equal districts rules and apply them zealously to marginal areas of state, and especially local government. Here the damage to representative institutions by chopping up communities and ignoring special needs would be somewhat more pronounced, but the appearance of adjudication would probably be enhanced. I think the Court would be much better advised to loosen its rigor than to tighten it in these matters, but this option, like the preceding ones, should be regarded as a little intervention, probably ill advised, but not unfeasible.

More fundamental applications of the Fundamental Principle, however, would be either impossible or possible, but disastrous. The two basic options are something resembling proportional representation, which would probably kill the party system as we know it, and various measures falling short of PR which might not kill the parties but could not possibly secure their purported objectives. Except in unusually blatant cases of racial gerrymandering in the South, there is no way short of PR to block gerrymanders judicially. Multimember districts and at-large elections could be abolished outright, but one should not forget that the threat of ordering at-large elections was an indispensible technical aid to the reapportionment revolution and not something which the courts would readily relinquish; moreover, their abolition would not abolish gerrymandering in single-member districts.

Party governance, executive appointments, judicial positions, legislative committee membership and seniority, and most questions of campaign resources likewise are inappropriate objects of the Fundamental Principle. Their functions are organizational and managerial, not registrational of public opinion. Though vital public choices are indeed made in these areas, direct public participation would be at best redundant and at worst incapacitating of the necessary preconditions of effective majority rule. These areas of public choice fall deep into the checks and balances category of voting rights, and, hence, deep into the quagmire. They are rule resistant and unsuited for judicial intervention under the Fundamental Principle, even with such gimmicks as vested status quo or southern strategy. Functional analysis, far from facilitating intervention, underlines its inappropriateness.

The various contenders in the reapportionment revolution have left the field littered with theories of intervention, some discarded, some still usable. The *Baker v. Carr* plaintiffs' contention that a state violation of its own constitution must violate the Fourteenth Amendment, an aborted species of vested status quo argument, is now dead. The Guardian view of the majority, that total equalized participation is the best policy (and therefore the true law), even if we have to cram it down the people's throats, has prevailed many times, but it is running out of easy fields to conquer. The solicitor general's suggested standard, forbidding only "gross inequalities" in representation which "give control of the legislature to small minorities," furnished positive impetus to several reapportionment decisions, but its moderating implications were ignored by most of the justices. Two tests deriving from the solicitor general's test were proposed, but never adopted: Justice Clark's "rational principle" test, asking whether an "identifiable and intelligent principle" had been consistently applied, and Justice Stewart's "systematic frustration" test, asking whether a system had permitted the systematic frustration of the will of the majority. These moderated standards are appealing because they correspond more closely to the facts of political life than the mathematical equality of the Fundamental Principle; however, they do raise the embarrassing question, can there possibly be any rational justification for unequal votes? The answer, if you follow the Guardian Ethic, is no; moreover, if you do not follow the Guardian Ethic, you risk winding up in the quagmire with no simple standards to keep you from bogging down. Robert Dixon followed Felix Frankfurter in connecting the problem of political realism with the unused, and possibly unusable guarantee clause:

In the area of legislative apportionment a focus on equal protection defined as a concern solely for equality in legislative district population, does provide a seemingly simple and easily administrable standard for testing constitutionality. It does so, however, at the cost of excluding, or tending to exclude, consideration of corollary problems of effective representation as an end result of the voting-apportionment processes. Reapportionment litigation under the republican guarantee clause or the due process clause would face these problems, and admittedly would be more difficult. Litigation under the equal protection clause has tended to be relatively easy only because the realistic questions, by definition, seem to become irrelevant.[203]

Foxes and Otters

In one sense, the reapportionment revolution is unfinished, for it has not yet addressed itself to major biases of the political system which continue to give unequal weight to some people's political influence in contravention of the Fundamental Principle. In another sense, however, the reapportionment revolution is almost finished, in that most the remaining forms of discriminations—gerrymanders, multi-member districts, appointed authorities, and informal modes of influence—appear to be beyond its powers to control. The Court has been asked to take many steps, big and little, to vindicate the Fundamental Principle; in general, it has taken the little ones but has so far had the good sense to avoid the big ones. It has so far succeeded in skirting the quagmire. This still leaves a question as to the substantive merits of reapportionment. Wiping out one form of discrimination might promote equal representation by reducing the grand total of discrimination; or it might frus-

211

trate equal representation by stripping one side of its structural advantages while leaving the other side fully armed by reason of biases which the Court cannot touch. John F. Kennedy stressed the point in 1956 when he warned against tampering with the electoral college for fear of unbalancing "a whole solar system of governmental power": "If it is proposed to change the balance of power of one of the elements of the solar system, it is necessary to consider all the others."[204] Kennedy's caution is still pertinent. You cannot equalize foxes and otters if you can equalize only on dry land. Any principled attempt to equalize should consider conditions in the swamp, and this the Court resolutely avoided. It was undoubtedly sound tactics to avoid the quagmire, but was it sound strategy to ignore it?

VII. Prometheus, Proteus, Pandora, and Procrustes Unbound:

The Political Consequences of Reapportionment

> In those momentous days the French Nation
> committed a deadly crime against democracy,
> which, on its knees, now utters the daily prayer:
> "Holy Universal Suffrage, pray for us!" Naturally
> enough, the believers in universal suffrage will not
> renounce their faith in a wonder-working power
> which has performed such great miracles on their
> behalf, which has transferred the second Bona-
> parte into a Napoleon, Saul into Paul, and Simon
> into Peter. The folk-spirit speaks to them through
> the ballot boxes as the god of the prophet Ezekiel
> spoke to the dry bones: *"Haec dicit dominus deus
> ossibus suis: Ecce ego intromittam in vos Spiritum
> et vivetis."*

—Karl Marx[1]

Two Kinds of Equality

The time has long passed (if it ever existed) when one could consider a constitutional examination closed upon laying the Constitution side by side with
the challenged act and comparing them, as suggested by Justice Roberts in
United States v. Butler.[2] Nor can one confine himself to the intent of the
framers at the time of drafting the provision involved, as suggested by Justice
Sutherland in *Home Building and Loan Association v. Blaisdell.*[3] To a certain
extent, the Court is expected to respond to an implied proviso that the Constitution be fudged a bit if the need is pressing enough and the issue is presented in a way that the Court can manage. The *Minnesota Mortgage* case is
one example of such fudging;[4] *Griswold v. Connecticut* is another;[5] the *Poll
Tax Case* is another.[6] The Court's summary treatment of claims by Germans
and Japanese in World War II shows that it can be fudged to take away rights
as well as to create them.[7] But a tradition of fudging is not of itself enough to
justify the practice in specific instances. If the Court fudges, it is supposed to
fudge with intelligence and justice. If it is moved to depart from the text and

213

traditional understanding of the Constitution, it must be able to come up with a rule which is not only newer but better.

This consideration inspired Justices Stewart and Clark to take a position in the reapportionment cases quite different from that of the majority. The right propounded by the majority was personal, next to absolute, and apparently tied exclusively to equal districts; Stewart and Clark asserted a more diffuse and relative right to a "rational" plan of representation which does not permit "the systematic frustration of the will of a majority of the electorate of the State."[8] Like the majority, Stewart and Clark cited a profusion of legal and political scholars, including Alfred De Grazia, Phil C. Neal, Robert Dixon, Jerold Israel, Jo Desha Lucas, Stanley Friedelbaum, Alexander Bickel, Paul Freund, Robert McCloskey, and Robert Dahl, to support their conclusion that representative government is a process of accommodating group interests through democratic institutions, which does not lend itself to equalizing everybody's personal voting but still can be scrutinized in the light of specific circumstances to see whether the tests of rationality and nonfrustration are met.[9]

Under this looser, group-oriented standard, Stewart and Clark were able to concur with the majority in four of the six 1964 *Reapportionment* cases, while dissenting in the last two on the grounds that New York and Colorado, though they had unequal districts, had them for rational purposes and not to a degree which systematically frustrated the majority.[10] New York's apportionment was rational for attempting to protect against overcentralization of power in one metropolitan area—New York City, Nassau, Rockland, Suffolk, and Westchester Counties—by reducing its majority in one house from its proportional 63.2 percent to a lesser figure still over 50 percent. "What the State has done is to adopt a plan of legislative apportionment which is designed in a rational way to ensure that minority voices may be heard, but that the will of the majority shall prevail."[11]

Colorado

The case of Colorado offers some evidence of the justice of Stewart's and Clark's flexible approach compared to the majority's; it also suggests that many of the hopes of the reapportionists and the fears of antireapportionists were much exaggerated. Stewart and Clark had little difficulty in showing that the Fundamental Principle fit Colorado like an Iron Maiden, but its application does not seem to have brought about a major change in Colorado politics, which since 1964 seem to have been more responsive to things like landslide elections, personalities, and vagaries of popular temper than to reapportionment. In the five years from Colorado's reapportionment to Warren's retirement, the state showed few signs either of revolutionized government or urban tyranny.

The majority's picture of Colorado consisted of cartographic symbols, dots and lines, people and districts. If the lines were drawn to make the dots equal, without unsightly deviances to accommodate geographical and economic peculiarities or the dots' desires as expressed in the last referendum, then the Fundamental Principle would be satisfied. To be sure, it might drown three of the state's economic regions in the Senate under the fourth region's weight of numbers, much as the town of Dillon had been drowned by the Green Mountain Reservoir to help keep the lawns green in Denver. Of course, there might have been a bit of a problem for senators from the western part of the state to keep in touch with constituencies bigger than the state of Maryland after the winter snows had sealed off the passes. True, Denver had regularly elected a squad of eight Democratic senators who tended to vote in a bloc; true, every county had rejected a 1962 proposal to equalize districts by an overall majority of 2-1. None of these could prevail against the Fundamental Principle. The Supreme Court agreed with Andrew Hacker that the people should be given the blessings of equality whether they wanted them or not, and it ordered equal districts over Stewart's and Clark's objections that the Court was miscasting its fabricated Fundamental Principle as an "uncritical, simplistic, and heavy-handed application of sixth-grade arithmetic."[12]

A look at Colorado politics at the time of the *Reapportionment* cases showed inequalities among the districts in the state Senate, but not sufficient to give any combination of the three minority regions a majority against the populous East Slope Region (Denver, Colorado Springs, and Pueblo).[13] Denver alone, with its surrounding counties, had 53 percent of the population of the state; with Colorado Springs and Pueblo, East Slope cities had 68 percent of the population. Counting all its inhabitants the East Slope had 75 percent of the population and controlled 75 percent of the seats in the House, but only 59 percent in the Senate. Table 11 shows the regional population and Senate representation of the different regions.

Table 11. Population, Area, and Senate Seats of Colorado Economic Regions

Area	Number of Seats	Seats (%)	Population (%)	Land (%)	Population per Seat
West	8	20.5	13	45.47	28,480
East	5	12.8	8.1	26.21	28,407
S. Central	3	7.7	3.8	13.99	22,185
E. Slope	23	59.0	75.1	14.33	57,283
Total	39	100.0	100.0	100.0	45,000 (average)

Source: Jurisdictional Statement and Appendices for Appellants, Appendix B, Trial Court Order, pp. 63–64, *Lucas v. Forty-fourth General Assembly*, 377 U.S. 713 (1964).

215

From a purely regional standpoint, it hardly seems that the East Slope, with 59 percent of the seats in the Senate, plus control of the House and the governorship, could have been much embarrassed by its underrepresentation in the Senate. Party organization, however, made a more complicated situation. In 1964 (as it has been since) Colorado had been remarkably evenly divided between the parties, territorially and historically. Democrats predominated in Denver, Pueblo, and a few outlying districts; Republicans controlled Colorado Springs and the remaining rural districts. Since 1896, Colorado's votes for presidents, governors, and United States senators had been almost precisely divided between the parties; from 1928 to 1963 the Republicans had controlled the legislature eight times, the Democrats six, and it was evenly divided on four occasions.[14] No one had counted all the roll calls in the Colorado legislature as David Derge had for Illinois and Missouri, but William Irwin did look through the 1961-62 journals of the House and Senate and found a typical very high cohesion of 70-93 percent in the House and 85-100 percent in the Senate for Denver Democrats—and Denver was represented through multi-member districts in both houses, assuring the Democrats a near monopoly of Denver's delegates by submerging local concentrations of Republican strength. The Democrats regularly captured all but one or two of Denver's eight Senate seats and all but three or four of its seventeen seats in the House of Representatives, with party endorsement and the alphabet apparently weighing more heavily than candidates' personalities and positions on local issues.[15]

The reader may recall that Chicago, St. Louis, and Kansas City, with no more than half the population of the respective states (and in spite of peculiarities of Illinois and Missouri politics that split the cities between two parties), regularly crushed all opposition on roll-call votes where they voted in a bloc. In Colorado, without such a definitive study as Derge's, it looked as though Denver and Pueblo might have had even more political leverage than Chicago, St. Louis, and Kansas City, thanks not only to their greater population relative to the rest of the state, but thanks also to quirks in Colorado's own representative system which tended to make the East Slope Democrats a highly strategic minority compared to every other group in the state: Denver and Pueblo Republicans, because they were submerged by the multi-member district; non-East Slope Democrats because Denver, Pueblo, and Adams County, a Denver suburb, could usually elect a majority bloc of party representatives; and non-East Slope Republicans in years of Democratic control of the legislature (for example, 1961-62) because East Slope Democrats—an overall minority of state voters—controlled a majority of the majority party in both houses.

Pyramiding successive majorities can turn an overall minority into a majority, or turn a bare majority into an unstoppable one. Public utility holding companies were at one time a prime example of pyramiding: one corporation, or holding company, might control 51 percent of the stock of another corporation, while being itself controlled by the holder of 51 percent of its own stock. Whoever controlled the top majority would have far more power than his proportional share of investment in the lower corporation would suggest, since his 51 percent of 51 percent would represent only 26 percent of investments in the bottom corporation. Pyramiding is now illegal in public utility holding companies; it is also illegal in white primaries: the Supreme Court was sophisticated enough to see that whoever could control a majority in the Jaybird primary could count on winning majorities in the Democratic primary and the general elections. The Court rightly held that the right to vote for a Republican loser in the nonstrategic general elections was not equal to the right to vote in the strategic Jaybird primary. Yet the same Court which pierced through formal equality in the Jaybird case to detect substantial discrimination was stymied in doing the same in the reapportionment cases, at least past the point where inequality could be detected, interpreted, and eliminated with simple rules. As argued in Chapter VI, simple rules can handle qualifications questions but not most districting questions beyond bare size, and certainly not most questions of checks and balances. The Court was able to remove obvious, measurable quirks in the system favoring rural voters, but it could not touch more subtle quirks favoring the cities.

How substantial are these subtle quirks? Even with a full-scale analysis of roll calls, like Derge's, it is exceedingly difficult to say, because roll calls do not always tell the whole story even within the confines of politics in the legislature,[16] and because a fast-changing spectrum of political issues and alignments makes it impossible to show the same kind of long-term, stable distortion as could be shown in the Jaybird case, where the same kind of discrimination had been going on for sixty years and was still a live and specific issue by the time of trial.

Colorado elections from 1960 to 1966 illustrate the difficulty of showing secular, specific discrimination; the Democrats swept both houses in 1960, lost them to the Republicans in 1962, gained back the House of Representatives in the Democratic landslide of 1964, and lost it again in the 1966 Republican shutout victory. With such a flux of men and issues it is hard to demonstrate a link between long-term distortions of representative power and specific instances of damage to one class of voters. It is possible to show that there are long-term distortions—bloc voting, submergence of minorities in multi-member districts. and strategic local majorities—and it is possible to cite specific instances of actual or threatened urban "tyranny," such as the Green Mountain Reservoir and the city-based Ku Klux Klan's bid to take over the state in the 1920's (which was blocked in the malapportioned Senate),[17] but it is hard to show a direct connection between the two.

On the other hand, this is also true of malapportionment; damage is assumed from the bare presence of distortion which "debases" a citizen's vote.

217

The difference between intervention to equalize districts and intervention to equalize other forms of debasement is not so much in the difficulty of showing specific damages as in the difficulty of measuring the discrimination. Yet one cannot always ignore what one cannot measure. It seems reasonable to ask whether the people of a state might not be permitted to balance their system of representation to compensate for quirks which can be felt, even if they cannot be measured. On its face, it looks as though the Colorado electoral system balanced a structural bias in favor of the East Slope with a structural bias in favor of the rest of the state; before either potentially dominant group could act, it had to seek a wider consensus. This form of balance could block only the rare kind of East Slope action that would produce a bloc vote in the three other regions—in contrast to other forms of minority protection like PR or extraordinary majorities which are still constitutionally permissible but which tend to stifle all action.

Can it be that the Colorado voters who chose unequal districts by an overwhelming majority picked an apportionment more in keeping with the principle of equal representation for equal numbers than that imposed by the Supreme Court? The question cannot be answered satisfactorily, but it does continue to nag. A bare discussion of the various considerations which might cast light on the question has a highly abstract and speculative quality when based on a few maps, briefs, and texts but not on actual political experience in Colorado. The author must admit to some embarrassment in attempting to assess Colorado politics from his desk in Claremont, California, yet surely the same kind of embarrassment should attach to the Supreme Court's attempt to do the same thing from Washington,[18] especially when the Court's prescription for equality in Colorado seemed to be exactly the same as its prescription for 49 other states of different political make-up from Colorado. The Supreme Court's logic in overruling a 2-1 majority in the name of majority rule, though tenable under its fabricated Fundamental Principle, still retains an unflattering aroma as a matter of practical politics, particularly when it seems to impose a one-dimensional kind of "equality" which can disarm one side but not the other. If Justice threw off her blindfold in the Jaybird case, she seems to have put it back on again in the Colorado case.

The Reapportionment Revolution Reconsidered

With the reapportionment revolution now in its second decade, it is possible to attempt a preliminary assessment of its accomplishments. Which of us has forgotten the brave words of the *cognoscenti*, Gordon Baker, Anthony Lewis, Andrew Hacker, Robert McKay, John F. Kennedy, and the Twentieth Century Fund, which spurred the public into indignation and the Supreme Court into action? Malapportionment was supposed to have reduced city-dwellers to second-class citizens and stifled urgently needed reforms like home rule, slum clearance, metropolitan transit, annexation, labor and welfare legislation, civil rights laws, equal tax laws, and equal expenditures on schools and roads "because of the ignorance and indifference of rural legislators." Besides giving special powers to rural intransigents, malapportionment was supposed further to have weakened federalism by splitting party control of legislatures and governorships, spawning "public cynicism, disillusionment, and apathy." Reapportionment was expected to destroy barnyard government, unshackle the cities, unleash the bottled-up legislation, strengthen local and state representation, and produce a new breed of legislator as well.

Yet Prometheus unchained seems remarkably unchanged, either in the matter of banishing public cynicism, disillusionment, and apathy or of producing an urban tyranny, as Strom Thurmond had feared. Such changes as did take place seem more directly connected with political upheavals like the Democratic landslide of 1964 or the Republican gains of 1966-68 than with reapportionment. Studies by Andrew Hacker and the *Congressional Quarterly* based on prereapportionment data showed no connection between unequal districts and Congress's reluctance to pass liberal, administration-backed legislation.[19] If anything, according to Hacker's weighting of sample roll calls, reapportionment could be expected to produce greater resistance to such measures. The most noted casualty of reapportionment in Congress was House Rules Committee Chairman Howard W. Smith, a conservative who lost to his moderate opponent, George C. Rawlings, Jr., by 645 votes in the 1966 Virginia primary after his district had been redrawn. The net effect of this change was to introduce a new breed of congressman in one district and that only with the help of a general trend toward new faces in Virginia politics, itself more connected with the revolt against the Byrd machine than with reapportionment. There was little change in the governance of the Rules Committee, since Smith was succeeded by another southern conservative, William M. Colmer of Mississippi.

In the states, there were many changes, often quite dramatic ones, in regional control of legislatures, and some individual changes in which reapportionment may have been a secondary factor; however, no overall trend of policy attributable to reapportionment can yet be perceived. On the basis of the *Congressional Quarterly*'s August 1966 survey of reapportionment it seems reasonable to conclude that control shifted from one region to another in the legislatures of five states:[20] Florida, Alabama, Maryland, California, and Nevada. In Florida, the fast-growing southern half of the state broke the northern half's traditional domination of the legislature after a bitter, eighteen-year struggle. In Alabama, power in the state senate was transferred from the agricultural south to the industrial north. In Maryland, the balance of power seemed to have shifted from the east shore, southern and western Maryland, to the suburbs of Baltimore and Washington, and to Baltimore itself. In California, power shifted from north to south. In Nevada, Reno and

Las Vegas (and Howard Hughes?) now control the legislature formerly dominated by rural interests. In five western states with regionally apportioned senates—Arizona, Montana, New Mexico, Utah, and Missouri—reapportionment brought radical augmentation of urban power in one house. Cities in Vermont, Chicago and the central Piedmont cities of North Carolina (Charlotte, Greensboro, Winston-Salem, and Raleigh) likewise gained substantially in their respective state senates. Georgia, Delaware, Texas, Kansas, Washington, and Michigan cities and suburbs made very substantial gains in both houses, such as to give them a good prospect of controlling the legislatures after the 1970 census. Apart from these nineteen states, reapportionment has brought little alterations in regional balances of power. Even in Tennessee, whose crazy quilt of unequal districts had inspired the Court to intervene in *Baker v. Carr*, the inequalities had been so haphazard that reapportionment does not seem to have brought about any major alterations in regional influence within the state.

Even in the nineteen states where there were changes in the regional balance of power, the new breed of legislator looked more like Proteus than Prometheus, with new policies much less responsive to reapportionment than to other influences. In Michigan and Vermont, the new breed followed liberal governors George Romney and Philip Hoff, but elsewhere it followed conservatives. In California it followed Ronald Reagan; in Florida it followed Claude Kirk; in Georgia, Lester Maddox; in Alabama, Lurleen Wallace. Could this be the revitalization that John F. Kennedy, Gordon Baker, and the Twentieth Century Fund had in mind? After the Democratic landslide of 1964, reapportionists pointed to signs that the "Great Breakthrough" had come (although only five states had reapportioned in time for the 1964 elections). In Colorado, for example, though party control of the legislature was divided, counter to the reapportionists' script, the reapportioned legislature did appropriate more money for education, especially in Denver and suburbs, passed a dog-leash law, an annexation law, a birth control law, and an abortion law; it provided for referenda on daylight savings and abolition of the death penalty, all of this amid the usual reapportionist hoots that "the rural bloc" had "sat on the lid too long."[21] The same kind of activity was going on all over the country, with reapportioned Vermont,[22] Delaware,[23] Michigan,[24] and Iowa[25] passing all sorts of welfare and civil rights legislation thitherto "bottled-up"—a record, however, which was matched in the unreapportioned United States Congress, which passed the Civil Rights Act of 1964 and the Voting Rights Act of 1965, both stalled under Kennedy, and the malapportioned California legislature, which had passed the Rumford Fair Housing Act in 1963 only to have it repealed by referendum in 1964.

Black political gains in the South since reapportionment have been very impressive. In 1949, V. O. Key found the possibility of victories by black candidates in the South limited to a few counties and city wards; he cited two black councilmen and one member of a junior college governing board as notable achievements by black campaigners.[26] By 1973, blacks held 2,627 elected offices nationwide, about half of them in the South.[27] These figures were far less than one percent of the estimated 500,000 elective offices in the nation, and even further short of the twelve percent that would make black officeholders proportional to the number of blacks in the population at large; nevertheless, they represented an enormous advance from prereapportionment days. When the Georgia senate was reapportioned in 1962, increasing the number of senators from its most populous county (containing Atlanta) from one to seven, one of the seven was Georgia's first black legislator since Reconstruction. By 1970 Georgia had 14 of the 33 black state legislators in the South and 173 nationwide. By 1973 blacks had 15 United States congressmen and one senator. Though only the beginnings of this trend were visible in the mid-sixties, there was general jubilation among the *cognoscenti*, who concluded from the civil rights legislation and growing black success at the polls that deliverance was at hand and that reapportionment had brought it. Hubert Humphrey spoke for all the Guardians in 1966 when he told the National Legislators Leaders Conference that "Reapportionment has brought new life, new vigor to state governments."[28]

But was it reapportionment? Or was it that the conservatives had been walloped at the polls in 1964 and that 1965 was the "Year of Civil Rights"? Was it equal districts which brought the new breed of legislator to Iowa and Colorado or the national Democratic landslide? Was it the fundamental principle that revitalized federalism in Michigan and Vermont, or was it George Romney and Philip Hoff? Were the black officeholders in the South a product of redistricting or of doubled black registration since the 1950's? Public apathy, disillusionment, and cynicism indeed seemed much diminished in the states in the middle sixties, exactly as the reapportionists had foretold, but the suspicion waxed as the decade waned that the optimism of those days was a product of popular fashion, not the fruit of *Reynolds v. Sims.*

Much cold water has flowed over the dam since the year of civil rights. The Republican-conservative resurgence in the elections of 1966 replaced moderate Democratic governors like Pat Brown of California, Carl Sanders of Georgia, and Haydon Burns of Florida with conservatives like Ronald Reagan, Lester Maddox, and Claude Kirk, while perpetuating the Wallace dynasty in Alabama. The Michigan legislature lost some of its luster when some of the new breed were charged with soliciting a Michigan State University coed for immoral purposes, drunken driving, wife-beating, and nonpayment of federal income taxes. Senate Democratic leader Raymond D. Dzendzel of Detroit was criticized for accepting an electric wristwatch as a gift from a lobbyist after he steered a watchmaker's bill into law.[29] California's first reapportioned legislature, though controlled by Democrats in both houses, cooperated with Republican Governor Ronald Reagan in slashing mental health expenditures and cutting back educational expansion. Colorado's second election of the new era was "dull, uninspired, and ignored by large numbers of voters,"[30] and it resulted, like many 1966 elections, in the ouster of many of the new Democrats of 1964. The president of the Maryland senate, asked to comment on the deliverance of that body from Barnyard government, observed that reapportionment had "changed the whole complexion of my Legislature," but he admitted, "I couldn't honestly say that this had been a great help for Baltimore. The new, younger men come mostly from Baltimore suburbs, and they ran away from the city in the first place. They seem to scorn it as much as the old Eastern Shore farmers used to."[31] Reapportionists and others watching the cities for the expected revitalization since reapportionment saw little sign of it; instead, every passing year seemed to show the cities and states less capable of dealing with their own problems; with the yoke of malapportionment thrown off, the cities' political efflorescence expressed itself in riots and garbage strikes, and the new federalism seemed to consist of appeals to the federal government for troops and money, if anything, more than the old.

National, state, and local elections in 1968 and 1969 continued the trend away from the civil rights euphoria of 1965, with the most dramatic rebuffs of the liberals taking place in the cities themselves. All three presidential candidates in the 1968 campaign vowed to bring back law and order, with the winner, Richard Nixon, promising to bring back a Supreme Court of strict constructionists. The Republicans held onto their gains of 1966 in Congress and added to them in the states. In the cities, conservative mayors like Sam Yorty of Los Angeles and Richard Daley of Chicago survived strong challenges from the liberals, while liberal mayors dropped like flies. Four liberal mayors, Joseph Barr of Pittsburgh, Jerome Cavanaugh of Detroit, Richard C. Lee of New Haven, and Arthur Naftalin of Minneapolis, withdrew from electoral politics by their own choice. New York City liberals Robert Wagner and John Lindsay succumbed to lesser-known conservative rivals in their own party primaries, though Lindsay went on to win the general election on the Liberal ticket. In Minneapolis moderate candidates of both parties lost to an ex-policeman, Charles Stenvig, running on the law-and-order ticket. George Wallace, surveying the new breed of mayor, vintage 1968-69, was not wholly unjustified in claiming vindication in the cities of the hard-line conservatism he had pressed in the 1968 presidential campaign. "My vote was only the tip of the iceberg," said Wallace. "There's others I'm responsible for: Stenvig, Mayor Yorty of Los Angeles, two mayoral candidates in New York. They were making Alabama speeches with a Minneapolis, Los Angeles and New York accent. The only thing they omitted was the drawl."[32] The few years since the great reapportionment of 1965-66 were a short basis on which to judge, but the swift change in the mood of government from the "Year of Civil Rights" to the "Year of Law and Order" did very little to vindicate the experts of 1962.

Shortly after *Reynolds v. Sims*, quantitative studies began to appear in political science literature casting doubt on the pre-*Baker* conventional wisdom that malapportionment suppressed party competition, split governments, and stifled legislation favoring urban ideals and interests.[33] The technique of the revisionist studies was to rank the states in order of their degree of malapportionment prior to *Baker v. Carr*, then rank them according to level of party competition, frequency of divided government, distribution of state funds between urban and rural users, and level of expenditure for welfare, and then see whether there was any relationship between the rank orders. Several different measures of malapportionment were tried, and several different indicators of urban-rural fund division and welfare expenditures. Correlation between malapportionment and its expected results ranged from zero to "very low."

Neither these studies nor the experience of the states since reapportionment proves the reapportionists wrong. The experience of the states has been very short, and the revisionist studies are limited by the clumsiness of their various standards of apportionment, by their aggregation of different political and social systems which may or may not be profitably comparable, and by their time frame, which was largely confined to the decade just before *Baker v. Carr*. Better data and techniques might give a different picture for individual states and other times—as a number of counter-revisionist political scientists have maintained.[34] The counter-revisionists, of course, display the correct professional spirit in shifting the burden of proof to the other side and insisting that judgment be reserved till after a massive deployment of even more sophisticated analysis; on the other hand, how significant can a reform be whose impact can only be discerned (if at all) with the assistance of a large foundation grant? The available evidence seems more than sufficient to put the reapportionists' expectations of a great revitalization of state and local governments into a more realistic perspective, which should rank reapportionment as a trivial political influence compared to such traditional forces as parties, personalities, interest groups, and the perversities of popular fashion.[35]

Reapportionment and Representative Government

Once the reapportionment revolution was substantially won, reapportionists could afford to concede that they might have exaggerated a trifle in claiming that reapportionment would free the cities, liberalize policies, unplug bottlenecks in government, and so forth; at least, they said, it strengthened federalism and implemented the Fundamental Principle of the Constitution by securing equal representation for equal numbers. But did it? An honest answer would have to be yes, but no. Reapportionment did a great deal to equalize representation in states like Florida, Alabama, California, Nevada, and Maryland, where unequal districts badly underrepresented regions with population majorities; it helped undermine white, one-party government in the Deep South; it corrected discrimination against large sectors of the populations of a dozen or so states besides the five worst examples mentioned; and it corrected more minor forms of discrimination in the rest of the country. As far as they went, these were not negligible accomplishments. But the Court did not make these corrections in a thoroughgoing or discerning way, except in the narrow sense of exacting strict adherence to its rule of equal districts as its best strategy for securing compliance without venturing into the quagmire. Because of the one-sided and Procrustean character of the Court's intervention against malapportionment, substantial questions remain as to whether the reapportionment revolution promoted equal representation in most of the states.

The Court's meddling with structural biases favoring one group or another was highly selective, for the best of tactical reasons: attacking the more subtle forms of structural discrimination would have raised the standards problem and landed the Court in the quagmire. The Court could abolish malapportionment, which favored rural voters, but it could do nothing about bloc voting, multi-member districts, strategic majorities, and other structural biases which favored the cities. Nor could it reach gerrymanders except to make sure they were all the same size. At the time of *Baker v. Carr* this was thought to be an important restriction. In 1962, for example, Democrats in California and Republicans in Michigan and New York had successfully gerrymandered districts in their respective states; with stricter adherence to equal districts in New York, the Republicans picked up fewer extra seats.[36] As a general rule, however, it appears that gerrymandering is very little hampered by having to work within equal districts. The reader may recall from Chapter VI the ease with which equal-sized districts can be gerrymandered, both *in abstracto* and, with the aid of computers, on the ground. Stephen Slingsby's computerized trial runs showed that a Republican programmer could get the party twice as many seats in the two California counties tested as a Democratic programmer, even with equal districts.[37] The Republicans' ill-fated "California Plan" to gain control of the legislature in time for the anticipated 1971 redistricting represented a wager of several million dollars that control of the redistricting might be translated into control of the legislature for at least a decade, and this not in spite of the reapportionment revolution but because of it. The Democrats had no choice but to hire their own programmers and embark on a California Plan of their own.

The California Plans were not the only indicator of what can be done with equal districts and deft cartography. In 1966 Robert J. Sickels examined ten congressional elections from 1946 to 1964 in states susceptible to gerrymandering, that is, with more than one district and a dominant party in the legislature with power to gerrymander. Comparing the votes received by the party with districting power with the median/mean average of its seats won,

Sickels found that the power to gerrymander conveyed a striking advantage of 11 to 17 percent extra seats. With 50-55 percent of the total state congressional votes, the party with districting power won 67/69.8 percent of the seats; the party without districting power, also with 50-55 percent of the total vote, won only 50/58 percent of the seats. No overall relationship could be found between equality of districts and effectiveness of the gerrymandering; in fact, "In the great majority of states with congressional gerrymanders, unequal district size either has not affected the gerrymander or has made it less effective than it would have been had the districts been equal."[38]

A Gerrymandering Revolution?

How can one explain Sickels's findings? Two theories come at once to mind: a gerrymander, to be effective, must be kept up to date, and nothing offers itself so readily to redrawing gerrymanders as a mandate to reapportion. The same populations shifts which caused unequal districts could also render the most skillfully drawn gerrymander obsolete. Yet in normal circumstances legislators prefer stable districts and safe seats to districts which are constantly being redrawn to follow population shifts, no matter whether the redrawing is intended to equalize the districts or to maximize the power of one party or one interest. Before reapportionment the balance of political motives in most legislatures frustrated radical redistricting of any kind; wedded to the status quo, it frustrated reapportionment and gerrymandering alike.

Radical reapportionment, however, overrides a legislature's instinct for leaving the districts alone yet leaves unchecked the normal disposition of legislators to consult their own interests. A majority party which is compelled to redraw its districts can be expected to draw them to its own advantage, as minority parties and groups across the country have found to their discomfiture. There is every reason to believe that the reapportionment revolution brought with it something which none of the experts had thought of—a gerrymandering revolution. Perhaps the most striking indicator of gerrymandering in the course of reapportionment was the profusion of grotesque districts which the mapmakers of the 1960's left behind. Texas legislators set up a district 250 miles long and one county wide for much of its length for Congressman Olin E. Teague.[39] Colorado's Fourth Congressional District stretched 400 miles diagonally across the state from the Nebraska border in the northeast to the southwestern tip of the state where it borders Utah, Arizona, and New Mexico.[40] New York's 148th Assembly District was 43 miles long, taking a slice of Rochester continuing through the towns of Greece, Parma, and Hamlin, and then stretching 24 miles into Orleans County; the 153rd District was laid out in two sections separated by three towns and two other districts.[41] A three-judge federal court invalidated New York's congressional apportionment of 1961, describing the wild contortions of four

225

Brooklyn Districts as "bizarre."[42] A North Carolina federal court invalidated a congressional apportionment plan whose districts varied no more than 8.9 percent from average because of the "tortuous lines" of districts drawn to protect incumbents.[43]

Cities and urban minority groups who had hoped to profit from reapportionment found themselves instead cut to pieces and tacked on to districts of different political make-up. In Texas, Dallas-Fort Worth and San Antonio were divided into eight districts, four of which were tied to expanded rural districts. Memphis, Kansas City, Kansas, Wichita, Oklahoma City, and Newark were likewise dismembered. Elizabeth, the county seat of Union County, New Jersey, was detached and joined to Hudson County on the other side of Newark Bay.[45] Black communities in Boston and New York City were divided and the pieces parceled out to districts with white majorities;[46] urban blacks in Georgia, Tennessee, and Virginia protested their submersion in specially created multi-member districts.[47] Partisan minorities in Hawaii, Iowa, New Mexico, and Pennsylvania also complained of submersion in multi-member districts or at-large elections.[48]

The reader should be extremely suspicious of a bare listing of distorted districts and constituents' complaints to support the theory that reapportionment has brought with it a wave of gerrymandering. Reapportionists used just such isolated and subjective "evidence" to support their dubious doctrine of barnyard government, and it has not held up well under closer examination. A better case for a connection, whether positive or negative, between reapportionment and gerrymandering would require techniques like those of Robert Sickels, comparing the ratio of votes won to seats won by parties with and without districting power, in elections before and after reapportionment.[49] If one could show that parties controlling reapportionment won more seats per vote than parties that did not, one could have a substantial indicator of the overall effectiveness of the power to gerrymander since reapportionment; the results could then be compared with those of prereapportionment elections to see whether reapportionment has encouraged or discouraged effective gerrymandering—though even this kind of examination would show very little about racial, ethnic, and other forms of nonparty gerrymandering.

Ideally, such a study would be addressed to state legislatures and cover several elections since reapportionment to avoid sampling error. Although detailed information on federal congressional elections is much easier to get than information on state elections, federal elections involve fewer districts than state elections and are more likely to produce sampling error. Moreover, congressional districts have always been subject to an external interstate reapportionment requirement under Article I, section 2, which may obscure the effects of the intrastate reapportionment requirement of *Wesberry v. Sanders.* Unfortunately, however, the states seldom circulate detailed election results, and few of them had more than two or three postapportionment elections in the Warren era.

The returns of congressional elections from 1966 to 1972, however, suggest very strongly that parties with reapportionment power used it to enormous advantage. In Kansas's 1965 reapportionment, for instance, the Republicans were ordered to redraw district boundaries to equalize the districts. They saw no reason not to draw the new boundaries to their own advantage and therefore split Sedgwick and Wyandotte Counties (Wichita and Kansas City) in two to strengthen their hold on two otherwise competitive districts.[50] By so doing, they were able to win four out of Kansas's five seats in Congress: 80 percent of the seats for only 57.3 percent of the vote, for a winner's extra margin of 22.7 percent. By contrast, Oregon Republicans, who had 51.7 percent of the popular vote but had not controlled the districting, won only two of Oregon's four seats for a popular winner's margin of minus 1.7 percent. A similar contrast may be drawn between North Carolina and Minnesota. North Carolina Democrats controlled the districting and won 72.7 percent of the seats with 59 percent of the votes in 1966, a winner's margin of 13.7 percent. Minnesota Democrats did not control the districting of 1961. In 1966, with 50.1 percent of the votes, they won only 38 percent of the seats, a margin of minus 12.1 percent.

If these examples were representative, they would indicate that the power to gerrymander gave its possessor a crushing 25 percent advantage over non-possessors who were also able to secure popular majorities. However, such examples are not necessarily representative, for a number of reasons. They are drawn from elections of a single year, 1966; they are taken from comparatively small states; and the figures for North Carolina and Minnesota are distorted by uncontested districts. Even Kansas and Oregon might have come out as they did whether there was gerrymandering or not; the samples of five and four seats in one election are too small to be free of the vagaries of their political surroundings. One of Minnesota's eight districts and two of North Carolina's eleven districts had unopposed candidates; the figures given here are based on the unrealistic assumption that the unopposed party had "won" 100 percent of the votes in the district. In states like Texas, where twelve or thirteen of the state's twenty-three candidates regularly ran unopposed in the 1960's, it is not possible to do anything but guess the political impact of gerrymanders—a serious obstacle to overall assessment, because such states were probably more thoroughly gerrymandered than states where the districts are all contested.

A good sample, however, must be tolerably commensurable with its universe and large enough to be representative. It would have to exclude cases where more than one or two seats were contested, and it would have to cancel out the vagaries of local and temporary factors either by covering several elections or by confining itself to large states whose many districts would tend to cancel out local factors. A large sample of elections will not be available until more elections have been held; that is, in the middle 1970's. However, it is still possible to examine the experience of large, widely contested states in the congressional elections of 1966-1972, and these suggest that parties with districting power used it to their own advantage with devastating effect. The fate of the Republicans in California in 1966 and 1968, or the Democrats in Indiana and Michigan in 1970 stands in sharp contrast to that of the Democrats in Missouri in all four elections. With 51-53 percent of the popular vote, the California Republicans won only 45 percent of the seats. With like popular majorities, the Indiana and Michigan Democrats won less than 37 percent of the seats. The Missouri Democrats, on the other hand, even under the 1970 reapportionment touted as the most equal in the country, consistently brought in 80-90 percent of the seats with only 56-58 percent of the votes. Some of this contrast may be due to happenstance, but Table 12 suggests a high degree of consistency in the electoral profits accruing to the districting party. The difference between the mean bonus of extra seats for the sixteen popular postreapportionment winners with districting power and that of the fourteen popular "winners" without districting powers was 19.1 percent— surely no great diminution from the 12 to 17 percent extra seats in Sickels's prereapportionment elections.[51]

Table 12 includes only twelve of the large states with contested districts; however, these dozen states comprised more than half the seats in Congress in the 1960s, 240 out of 435. Another six states with ten or more districts, but with more than one district uncontested, accounted for another 54 seats; 52 states with nine districts or less comprised the remaining 141 seats. Perhaps time and a detailed examination of elections for state legislatures will give firmer ground for assessing the gerrymandering consequences of reapportionment, but it is safe to say that party cartographers had never been so busy as they were in the late 1960's,[53] and the little firm evidence we have suggests strongly that their handiwork was deft and partisan.

Effect on Party and Black Power

The concurrence of the gerrymandering revolution with the reapportionment revolution tempered earlier predictions that reapportionment would increase Republican and black representation by favoring cities in the South and suburbs across the nation. Preliminary investigations by Andrew Hacker, the Republican National Committee, and the Legislative Reference Service had concluded that Republicans and blacks stood to gain from reapportionment, which would give more votes to their strongholds in southern cities and to suburbs across the nation where Republicans were strongest, provided districts were drawn at random.[54] However, except in some of the minority of states with nonlegislative redistricting,[55] it had not been the tradition to re-

228

Table 12. Votes Cast and Seats Won in Large Contested States, Congressional Elections of 1966–1972[a]

State	Year	Districting Date	Number Districts	Votes Won (%)[b]	Seats Won (%)	Bonus (%)
Popular winner controlled districting:						
Calif.	'70	1968D	38	51.4 (51.4)D	52.6	1.2 (1.2)
Ind.	'68	1968R[c]	11	53.2 (53.7)R	63.6	10.4 (9.9)
Ind.	'72	1971R	11	54.1 (54.1)R	63.6	9.5 (9.5)
Mich.	'66	1964R	19	50.0 (49.8)R	63.2	13.2 (13.4)
Mo.	'66	1965D	10	55.9 (53.6)D	80.0	24.1 (26.4)
Mo.	'68	1967D	10	56.9 (56.0)D	90.0	33.1 (34.0)
Mo.	'70	1970D	10	58.6[d] (63.2)D	90.0	31.4 (26.8)
Mo.	'72	1972D[e]	10	60.0 (59.9)D	90.0	30.0 (30.1)
N.J.	'66	1966D	15	60.0 (50.5)D	60.0	10.0 (9.5)
N.C.	'70	1966D	11	59.1[d] (53.3)D	63.6	4.5 (10.3)
Ohio	'66	1964R	24	57.1[d] (56.1)R	79.2	22.1 (23.1)
Ohio	'68	1968R	24	60.3 (60.8)R	75.0	14.7 (14.2)
Ohio	'70	1968R	24	52.0 (54.6)R	66.6	14.6 (12.0)
Va.	'70	1965D	10	54.7[d] (48.7)D	40.0	-14.7 (-8.7)
Wis.	'66	1963R	10	52.7 (53.8)R	70.0	17.3 (16.2)
Wis.	'68	1963R	10	53.8 (54.4)R	70.0	16.2 (15.6)
				Mean control bonus:		14.9 (15.3)

(continued)

229

Table 12. (Continued)

State	Year	Districting Date	Number Districts	Votes Won (%)[b]	Seats Won (%)	Bonus (%)
Divided Control:						
Calif.	'72	1972DR[f]	43	54.2 (53.0)D	53.5	-0.7 (.5)
Ill.	'66	1965DR[g]	24	53.3 (54.2)R	50.0	-3.3 (-4.2)
Ill.	'68	1965DR[g]	24	51.5 (53.6)R	50.0	-1.5 (-3.6)
Ill.	'70	1965DR[g]	24	53.5 (52.3)D	54.1	0.6 (1.8)
N.J.	'68	1967/68DR[h]	15	52.9 (49.2)D	60.0	7.1 (11.8)
N.J.	'70	1967/68DR[h]	15	54.4 (52.9)D	60.0	5.6 (7.1)
Ohio	'72	1972DR[i]	21	55.5[d] (51.9)R	76.2	20.7 (24.3)
Pa.	'66	1966DR[j]	27	51.5 (49.5)R	48.1	-3.4 (-1.4)
Pa.	'68	1966DR[j]	27	51.9 (53.5)D	51.9	0.0 (-1.6)
Pa.	'70	1966DR[j]	27	55.3 (54.6)D	50.0	-5.3 (-3.5)
				Mean divided control "bonus":		1.2 (3.1)
Popular winner did not control districting:						
Calif.	'66	1961D	38	51.8 (53.3)R	44.7	-7.1 (-8.6)
Calif.	'68	1968D	38	52.9 (55.0)R	44.7	-8.2 (-10.3)
Ill.	'72	1971R[k]	24	50.1 (50.5)D	41.7	-8.4 (-8.8)
Ind.	'66	1965D	11	56.8 (53.5)R	54.5	-2.3 (1.0)
Ind.	'70	1968R	11	51.5 (50.6)D	36.4	-15.1 (-14.2)
Mich.	'68	1964R	19	52.3 (49.1)D	36.8	-15.5 (-12.3)
Mich.	'70	1964R	19	52.3 (46.5)D	36.9	-15.4 (-9.6)
Mich.	'72	1972D[l]	19	50.9 (52.7)R	63.2	12.3 (10.5)
N.J.	'72	1972R[m]	15	51.0 (51.0)D	53.3	2.3 (2.3)
N.Y.	'66	1961R	41	56.1 (52.5)D	63.4	7.3 (10.9)

N.Y.	'68	1968R	41	55.6	(52.3)D	61.0	5.4 (8.7)
N.Y.	'72	1972R	39^n	55.6	(51.8)D	52.6	-3.0 (0.8)
Pa.	'72	1972D	25	51.0	(51.0)R	48.0	-3.0 (-3.0)
Wis.	'70	1963R	10	57.4	(56.1)D	50.0	-7.4 (-6.1)

Mean no-control "bonus": -4.2 (-4.7)
  -6.5 (-4.5)

Mean extra margin from districting control (mean "control" minus mean "no control"): 19.1 (20.0)

[a] Excludes all states with less than ten districts or more than one district unopposed.

[b] Percentage is of the two-party vote, computed by adding and averaging the percentages in each district. Figures in parentheses are computed by adding the actual votes won by each party.

[c] Indiana was redistricted in 1968 by a federal court with two Republicans and one Democrat.

[d] One candidate was unopposed and is credited with 100 percent support in his district.

[e] A Missouri three-judge federal court with a Democratic majority adopted a Democratic plan which had failed to pass the legislature.

[f] The California Supreme Court adopted, as an interim measure for the 1972 elections only, the Democrats' compromise plan designed to protect incumbents and avoid a veto by a Republican governor.

[g] Illinois was redistricted in 1965 by a federal court with two Democrats and one Republican, in collaboration with the state Supreme Court, which had five Republicans and two Democrats.

[h] New Jersey was redistricted by the Democrats in 1967; the Republicans altered two of the 15 districts for the 1968 elections.

[i] Republicans controlled the Ohio legislature, but they produced a compromise plan to avoid a veto by a Democratic governor.

[j] At the time of Pennsylvania's 1966 redistricting, Republicans controlled the state Senate, while Democrats controlled the House.

[k] An Illinois three-judge federal court with a Republican majority chose the plan offered by the Republicans.

[l] A Democratic federal judge chose the Democratic plan which failed to pass the legislature.

[m] A three-judge federal court with a Republican majority adopted the Republicans' plan.

[n] Three candidates ran on the Democratic-Republican ticket and are assigned one and a half to each party. Eliminating the three seats altogether would produce almost identical results.

district at random, but to redistrict to the advantage of whoever conducted the redistricting, which may explain Senator Dirksen's interest in stopping reapportionment. The reapportionment revolution took place at a particularly bad time for the Republicans; namely, after the elections of 1964, which had cost the Republicans 101 seats in state senates and 426 seats in state house of representatives. Only a handful of states had reapportioned in time for the 1964 elections;[56] forty-two states reapportioned in 1965 and 1966, when the Democrats controlled both houses in thirty-two states, the Republicans in only six, with control split in eight states.[57] "The result," concluded the *Congressional Quarterly*, in 1966, "may be a built-in Democratic advantage . . . for years to come."[58] The 1966 California elections, where the Democrats retained majorities in both houses and in the state's delegation of United States congressmen, though outpolled by the Republicans by substantial margins in all three elections,[59] show how reapportionment, combined with gerrymandering, took away in practice the equal representation it purported to convey on paper.

Although blacks probably gained overall from reapportionment in the South, they also suffered no less than other local minorities from constitutionally decent burial in multi-member districts, which shared in the general efflorescence of discriminatory districting. Georgia, Virginia, and Tennessee blacks found their hopes of electing black delegates swallowed in part by the mapmaker's dragon, but they appealed in vain to the Supreme Court and state courts, whose rule-making resources were not equal to dealing with such tasks.[60] Other minorities were likewise buried without hope of judicial rescue,[61] though in most cases the discriminatory districts had been created under the judicially sponsored pressure of reapportionment.

Besides the gerrymander, three other considerations suggest that reapportionment was a very qualified boon to blacks: (1) no one profited more from reapportionment than the suburbs, the natural enemies of inner city aspirations, including those of blacks; (2) most black-held offices were local ones, unaffected by reapportionment; and (3) it appears that even where blacks could elect a majority or a substantial (33 percent) minority, their ability to achieve changes in existing law was limited. The third limitation, most notably developed in William R. Keech's *The Impact of Negro Voting*,[62] seems the least apposite to reapportionment, though it does raise important questions about the "payoff" of voting rights. Keech concluded from his studies of Durham, North Carolina, and Tuskegee, Alabama, that the black vote in local elections might have secured some measure of "legal justice" by encouraging equal enforcement of existing laws; for example, garbage collection, paving, hospital bonds, and desegregation of schools and parks; however, it failed to achieve "social justice" by forcing the passage of new laws to ban private discrimination in jobs, housing, and so on, integration of schools, and elimination of the effects of past discrimination.[63] Keech's critique applies

232

generally to the ability of any democracy to fulfill the desires of its constituents; I give it only passing attention in this chapter on the assumption that any representation at all is better than none. If southern blacks gained better representation (as they did), and if some of the improvement was due to reapportionment (as it was), the alleged failure of the improvement to secure social justice should be noted for perspective but not interpreted to mean that better representation was not worth the trouble. We may criticize democracy for its failure to gratify our most profound desires, but practical politics seldom offers anyone a whole loaf, and most of us are willing to accept half a loaf as preferable to none.

The pertinent serious qualifications are those related to the migration of southern blacks to large cities throughout the nation. This migration since 1890 scattered potential statewide black majorities in the deep South, leaving only local concentrations in certain black-belt southern counties and inner cities throughout the country. Concentration of blacks in the cities was intensified by the flight of whites to the suburbs. The net effect was to dilute potential black strength at the state level in the South. With 19 percent of the population in the South, even after all the reapportionment and voter registration of the 1960's, blacks elected less than 2 percent of delegates to southern state legislatures (33 out of 1,801 delegates). Blacks did retain local majorities North and South, and they elected black candidates to local office, including the mayoralties of Cleveland, Gary, Wichita, Newark and Los Angeles; moreover, they were confident that further gains in big-city mayoralties would be made in the future. However, apart from Wichita, whose mayor was elected by the city commissioners, mayoralties are not affected by reapportionment, as they involve a popular vote for a single seat which cannot be apportioned. The same is true of many other local offices captured by blacks: sheriff, county assessor, treasurer, and so forth; they represent a gain for blacks, but not one attributable to reapportionment. Of the 1,586 blacks holding elective office in 1970, only 182 were members of state legislatures or the United States House of Representatives. Of these, a fraction probably owed their office a part to reapportionment, but the other 1,400 offices were local offices little affected by reapportionment by 1970.[64]

Against these limited gains, blacks had to reckon with the political consequences of the flight of urban whites to the suburbs. While rural population steadily declined from 58 percent of the United States population in 1900 to 35 percent in 1968, central city population peaked at 35 percent in 1930 and had sunk to less than 30 percent by 1968, while suburban population had more than doubled, from 16 percent in 1900 to 35 percent in 1968.[65] The suburbs remained steadfastly white throughout their growth in the 1960's, with only 5 percent blacks in 1960 and 5 percent in 1968; during the same period blacks increased their percentage in the central cities from 16 percent to 20 percent.[66] Central city blacks may have gained relative to rural voters from reapportionment, but they lost ground to suburban whites in the 1960's and will probably continue to do so in the 1970's. Race apart, the suburbs are a far more formidable foe of the inner city than rural areas ever were, for their conflicts with inner city interests over schools, transit systems, housing, taxes, and disbursements were far more numerous and direct than those of the rural voters. The racial polarity of city and suburb could only exacerbate these economic conflicts. Inner city blacks could take some comfort from the fraction of one percent of state legislators they may have owed to reapportionment, but they could hardly rejoice at reapportionment's much greater gifts to their natural enemies in the suburbs. In 1960 urban spokesmen groaned that the cities were hemmed in by a ring of clay in state legislatures; by 1970, thanks to reapportionment, it looked more like a ring of steel, for the new breed of legislator could not be expected to sympathize with inner city aspirations which would cost his constituents money.[67]

Having devoted so much attention to dismantling the myth of the rural roadblock, I would hesitate to proclaim the advent of a suburban roadblock on the basis of evidence no better than that invoked to support the rural roadblock thesis. We have no Derge-style roll-call analysis to measure the power and cohesiveness of suburban blocs relative to urban, nor Keech-style case studies of disputes over bussing, housing, welfare, and so forth, which could cast some light on the relative ability of urban and suburban interests to prevail in such disputes. On the other hand, it does seem plain that, if reapportionment had any effects at all, one such effect was to strengthen the rich, the white, and the suburban relative to the poor, the black, and the inner city or rural. One may therefore legitimately wonder whether the short shrift given to inner city aspirations in state legislatures of the late 1960's—which were chronically cold to bond issues, transit subsidies, and housing and welfare reforms—might not have been as much because of the new breed as in spite of it.

A further embarrassment of the reapportionment revolution was the recurrent character of its disruptions. Unlike its preapportionment forebears, the new breed of gerrymander and multi-member district could not be expected to weaken with time and population changes in fulfilling its discriminatory intention, for the districts had to be redrawn, according to the Fundamental Principle, at least once every ten years in a fresh reapportionment revolution, whose equal districts could be expected to discriminate in favor of those holding power in the early 1970's and 1980's, as in Warren's time they discriminated in favor of those who held power in 1965 and 1966, threatening, moreover, a disruptive distracting blood bath with every change in party ascendance at the polls. The reapportionment revolution brought with it more and better gerrymanders, and it can be expected to go on doing so in the future as long as the district system is there to provide the motivation to keep discrimination up-to-date.

Nonpartisan Districting

A theoretical countermeasure to gerrymandering short of PR was the bureaucratic alternative: nonpartisan districting. This had been used with success in a few states,[68] but it was not popular in state legislatures because it delegated a function of supreme importance to the legislators for its heavy bearing on their continuance in office. Such matters were deemed too important to entrust to functionaries. Courts could have treated this problem in one of two ways, neither of which was very satisfactory. They could have treated legislative redistricting as "inherently unequal," a reasonable assumption in most cases where one party or group controls the legislature, but with highly disruptive implications if extended to other acts of the same legislature which are likewise partisan and expected to be so. Alternatively, courts could have drawn their own districts, a practice which they tried to avoid because of the political sensitivity of the task. These bureaucratic and judicial alternatives raised two further considerations: the immediate recognition that courts and commissions are not necessarily nonpartisan,[69] and the larger question of whether commitment of a problem to nonrepresentative bodies can be properly regarded as a revitalization of representative government.

The reapportionment cases revitalized representative government only in the sense that amputating someone's leg and replacing it with a wooden leg revitalizes the leg; the Court's logic of intervention started from the assumption that the states' existing institutions were not worth saving (except in Oregon, the one state that met the Court's standards before 1962). The Court in *Baker v. Carr* discarded the alternative of nonintervention; in the *Reapportionment* cases it discarded the alternative of selective intervention, of attempting to distinguish between states like Alabama, which needed wooden legs, and states like Colorado that did not. Reapportionists argued that every state needed equal districts, essentially because they are more equal than unequal ones, but such arguments assumed their own conclusion; they proved, in effect, that every state needed wooden legs because they are more wooden than the flesh and blood ones. The Supreme Court bought this logic, why and at what cost or profit to itself will be examined in Chapter VIII, but the cost to representative government in the states, while it cannot be measured, seems to have been very high. Equal districts have chopped up some communities and stuck the pieces onto others; unqualified by any attempt to consider more subtle forms of structural bias like bloc voting, strategic majorities, multi-member districts, and gerrymanders, they have aggravated such biases by taking away the most workable form of counter balance; they have often jarred with geographical needs. If strictly applied at the local level they can discourage attempts to settle local problems through representative channels; moreover, radical district changes are enormously disruptive to other forms of legislation and highly productive of gerrymanders and discriminatory multi-member districts. Above all, imposing a rigid rule on people who do not want it, however dressed up with democratic rhetoric, is not democratic. Arthur Sutherland expressed as well as anyone the rationale for entrusting the justices with powers not given to other men: they are supposed to be educated, experienced, practical men. "To make inevitable distinctions between a time for judicial action and a time for judicial self-restraint, few sources of guidance can be as satisfying as the disciplined pre-possessions of an independent judge, aware of history, tolerant of the democratic process, and conscious of human limitations."[70] But this rationale is good only as long as the justices do not bungle. In the reapportionment cases, the majority's awareness of history took the form of wholesale fabrication; they "tolerated" the democratic process by overruling it; and their consciousness of human limitations did not stop them from imposing their own distorted and incomplete version of representative government upon the states. The reapportionment revolution did represent a triumph of administrative policy in the sense that it fitted almost every state with wooden legs in the space of only a few years, but it was a triumph of equal representation for equal numbers only if you like wooden legs—and that must be regarded (as Andrew Hacker told us in 1965) as a question of aesthetics.

VIII. The Court's Constituencies, Constitutional Atheism, and the Future of the Guardian Ethic

Citizens should be given the blessings of equality whether they want them or not.
—Andrew Hacker

Of course the Court legislates. Isn't it grand?
—John Veblen

. . . a monster of so frightful mien,
As, to be hated, needs but to be seen;
Yet seen too oft, familiar with her face,
We first endure, then pity, then embrace.
—Alexander Pope

The Age of Administration

In the dozen decades from Taney's time to Warren's the main voting rights issues came full circle, but the locus of the contests shifted from representative bodies to nonrepresentative ones. Apportionment, gerrymandering, and property and tax qualifications were the staple subjects of voting rights controversies in Taney's time as they were in Warren's time, but by the 1960's no one expected them to be properly resolved in legislatures. The clash of parties had not produced a legislative product which met modern tolerances, for two reasons: modern tolerances are stricter than traditional tolerances where measurable equality is involved, and representative institutions are no longer as central to the legislative process as they once were. The trend has been toward more and more democracy in form with less and less reliance in practice on elected bodies to make the laws. Robert Nisbet's 1953 commentary on the preceding century of democratic reforms seems even more penetrating from the viewpoint of the 1970's:

The collective political power of the people has increased enormously during the past century. So have available means of political participation by the common man: the referendum, the direct primary, the recall, the continuous

237

abolition of restrictions on voting, and other even more direct means of participation. Yet, along with these increases in popular democracy, it must be observed that there has been a general leveling of local, regional, and associative differences, a nationalization of culture and taste, a collectivization of mind, and a continuous increase in the real powers of government over management, labor, education, religion, and social welfare. Democracy, far from heightening human autonomy and cultural freedom, seems rather to have aided in the process of mechanization that has weakened them. It must be repeated again, however, that this is not the inevitable consequence of the democratic ideal of power vested residually in the people. It is the consequence of the systems of public administration which we have grafted onto the democratic ideal.[1]

This country may never again witness constitutional conventions like Virginia's in 1829-30, illumined by the presence of past and future presidents and senators and the chief justice of the United States Supreme Court. What chief justice could be expected to waste his time chaffering and dickering over public policy with scores of delegates in one state when he could impose the same policy on all the states with the concurrence of four of his colleagues on the bench? For all of the reapportionists' brave talk about revitalizing representative government, the reapportionment revolution was basically an administrative revolution, not a triumph of representative government but a substitute for representative government and a symptom of its breakdown.

The nineteenth century was the golden age of representative government, with great men and great issues gravitating to state and national legislatures for settlement. Party competition was intense and widespread, with perhaps more difference between the parties on major issues of policy than one would find today. Voters turned out in droves to listen to speakers like Daniel Webster (a tribute which by Earl Warren's time was normally extended only to television personalities, sports heroes, and movie stars), and they flocked likewise to the polls, with much higher turnout than was typical in the 1960's. Walter Dean Burnham, in his thoughtful essay on the changing shape of the American political universe, described nineteenth-century voting participation as "more complete and intensely party-oriented than ever before or since."[2] Party tactics almost to the end of the nineteenth century aimed at an expanded electorate; only with the collapse of the Populists in 1896 did the Democrats and Republicans settle on regional party monopolies in the South and North, and the regional "system of 1896" was broken, not by a revitalized or national Congress, but by the emergence, under Franklin D. Roosevelt, of a powerful national executive establishment. E. E. Schattschneider was probably correct in asserting that every major change in public policy (the Jefferson, Jackson, Lincoln, and Roosevelt revolutions) was associated with an enlargement of the electorate, but the later arrivals—northern blacks, women, big city ethnic minorities, southern blacks, and eighteen-year-olds—

came into a system where legislatures were of less and less importance. Reapportionment did not stop the trend toward flaccid legislatures; far from strengthening legislatures, the Supreme Court overruled them as unfit to settle their own problems under the new higher law.

In Taney's time the main players in the voting rights field were state legislators. After the Civil War the main players were the United States senators and congressmen who shaped the policies and laws of Reconstruction, then the southern politicians who overthrew Reconstruction and perfected the techniques of one-party white man's government around the turn of the century. The Supreme Court's role in these developments was extremely small. Though it had ample constitutional authority under the Fifteenth Amendment to intervene against white primaries and rigged literacy tests, it did not intervene effectively till 1944, forty years after the Jim Crow voting laws and twelve years after the commencement of the Roosevelt revolution, and then only after it had taken good measure of its own independent power in its war against economic regulation. But when the Court finally entered the voting rights field it came in with a terrific show of power. *Smith v. Allwright* was a strong decision in many respects: it was well grounded in the text of the Constitution; it provided the logical foundation for later landmark cases such as *Shelley v. Kraemer* and the school segregation cases, not to mention *Gomillion v. Lightfoot, United States v. Mississippi,* and the reapportionment cases themselves. Moreover, it displayed a far more profound and incisive egalitarianism than the reapportionment cases by defending a large, weak, and oppressed minority which had few political resources of its own. By contrast, the reapportionment cases were set on the weakest constitutional ground, they have not opened up avenues of major constitutional development, and their egalitarianism was far more shallow than that of *Smith v. Allwright.* In some instances they strengthened weak and oppressed elements, but in others they added to the powers of elements already disproportionately strong. *Smith v. Allwright* represented a triumph of equality in practice over equality in form; *Reynolds v. Sims* represented a triumph of equality in form over equality in practice.

By 1944 the Court probably had the power and technique to attack malapportionment; its very narrow 3-1-3 majority against intervention in *Colegrove v. Green* (1946) could easily have gone the other way; but there were still serious questions about the Court's authority to act, both under the traditional view of authority and the modern view. The Constitution did not forbid unequal districts, nor did it confer on the Supreme Court any power to rule on voting rights except where they were denied or abridged because of race or sex. Because it was dealing with a problem older than the Republic, the Court could not say, as it might have said when it struck down white primaries, that unequal districts were a new problem calling for a new interpretation of old constitutional provisions. It faced a serious problem in having to

show that what all those old senators had been calling cod-liver oil was really
understood to be a kind of wine. If the Court could clear that hurdle, it still
had to face the modern test: Is intervention sound policy as a legislative act?
Frankfurter had said no; Stewart and Clark said maybe; the Court said yes
but did an abominable job of supporting its assertion by either traditional or
modern standards.

Why? Tactical reasons seem the most likely answer, but tactical and strategic
considerations vary according to which of the Court's several battlefronts is at
issue. For each of its interventions to change the rules of voting rights the
Court had to devise ways to dispose of old rules, enforce the new ones, muf-
fle its own dissenters, ward off possible attack from outside, and preserve its
public stature as guardian of the higher law. Its carefully phased promulgation
of the Fundamental Principle displayed the closest attention to these matters
in timing, choice of supporting argument, and the personal and inflexible
nature of the right created. To distinguish the guarantee clause cases and to
keep out of the quagmire, the Court chose a personal right of individuals to
vote in preference to a collective right of groups to have equal representation.
To overcome Frankfurter's objections that it had not adumbrated a standard
clear enough to guide the lower courts, the Court settled on a standard so
rigid and unqualified as to leave very little doubt as to what the Fundamental
Principle required—though very substantial doubts remained as to whether
the Fundamental Principle itself, as applied by the Court, was sound policy.
It certainly secured few of the beneficial policy changes predicted for it, and
it appeared to bring about some unpredicted and injurious changes: dismem-
berment of communities, computerized gerrymanders, further frustration of
inner city aspirations, and, for lawmakers of every kind, the chronic threat of
judicial disembowelment—all of which, astonishingly, were packaged and
accepted as great victories for representative government.

The Court's Constituencies

The discussion has so far proceeded on the assumption that the Court's
policies can be treated separately from the text and original understanding of
the Constitution, and that the Court may appropriately be judged for its suc-
cesses and failures as a legislative body. This assumption is not without support in traditional constitutional jurisprudence; we may note that there are
many issues on which the Constitution gives no clear guidance, and other
issues on which it does give clear guidance, but where we accord the Court
some latitude to fudge. Most of us are generally inclined to accept the Court's
opinions as constitutional authority in their own right, often in the face of
our own contrary private opinions. Moreover, the traditions of appointing the
justices from different regions and reserving "Catholic," "Jewish," or "Ethnic" seats on the bench suggests that at least one perceived function of the

justice so appointed was somehow to "represent" the geographical or cultural sectors from which he sprang.[3] This notion of the Court as a representative and legislative body in its own right was never so widely and enthusiastically accepted as in the 1960's, possibly because the traditional American "cult of the robe" was magnified by "cult of the expert," then in the height of fashion. "Of course the Court legislates," John Veblen had said; "Isn't it grand?" He spoke for every believer in the Guardian Ethic.

Nevertheless, the notion of the Court as a representative or legislative body has a troublesome irredentism of its own. It nudges those who indulge it into areas of constitutional inquiry which as yet have been little explored. If the Court is a legislative-representative body, it might be presumed to have a constituency—but what constituency? And, if the Court has legislative powers, what are their sources and bounds?

Although individual justices, appointed for life, need never face an electorate which can put them out of office, they are not immune from lesser sanctions, like roasting in the *New Republic*, threats from the John Birch Society, long faces in the ABA, a broadside from Herbert Wechsler, a rebuke from the judges of the state supreme courts, or embarrassing discussion and investigation in Congress. Furthermore, the Court as a whole must reckon with political "constituencies," which can reward it with cooperation, support, or at least tolerance, or punish it with obstruction or persecution. These constituencies would surely include Congress, which can impeach members of the Court, refuse to appoint new justices, increase the number of justices, overwhelm them with assigned duties like riding circuit, confer or deny most forms of federal appellate jurisdiction, reverse decisions with new laws or constitutional amendments, or cut off money to run the courts.[4] Moreover, Congress can further the Court's policies by passing enabling legislation, such as the Voting Rights Act of 1965, though such legislation may also embarrass the Court by forcing issues like the eighteen-year-old vote to awkward and premature decision. Others of the Court's constituencies might be the legal profession, lower federal and state courts, press and law commentators, potential dissenting justices, parties to cases decided, the Guardians or some other such elite species, and the general public.[5]

Executive-Judicial Democracy

The premier constituency of the modern civil-rights-conscious Court has been the executive branch, not only because of the enormous influence the president has always had from his constitutional powers of appointment and enforcement, but also from the centripetal logic of his own position, which generally harmonized with that of the Court while conflicting with the centrifugal logic of Congress. The appointment and enforcement powers do carry enormous weight, for the Court is heavily dependent on the president's cooperation in carrying out its orders, and profoundly vulnerable to the impact of new appointments. As Robert Dahl pointed out, a president can normally expect to appoint two new justices during one term of office and four in two terms: enough to tip the balance on a normally divided court and form the basis of a new majority. "Presidents," he added, "are not famous for appointing justices hostile to their views on public policy."[6]

In the 1960's, when both the executive and the judiciary were under aggressive, expansive management, there were, no doubt, many areas related to the president's national security responsibilities where the interests of the two branches did not coincide, but in the area of civil rights there was a natural harmony of interest and principle between the two branches and perhaps a closer commingling of interest and principle than had been typical of the older voting rights reforms. The new interest was that of the professional manager, who measures his success by how much and how vigorously he manages. One might even hesitate to use the same word, "interest," to describe the petty, grasping efforts of an elected representative—say, one of those old radical republicans, or Chicago boss Richard Daley—to gather plums for himself, his party, or his constituency, and the high-minded, almost clinical efforts of an appointed official such as Robert McNamara, Burke Marshall, or Archibald Cox to build powerful and controllable administrative mechanisms to defend the country and the rights of its people.[7] Perhaps "mission of stewardship" would be as good as "interest" to describe the crack executive's inspiration to expand his own sphere of authority, simultaneously claiming mighty responsibilities and mighty powers necessary to fulfill the responsibilities. We associate such claims with the greatest presidents and the greatest chief justices: Washington, Lincoln, Jackson, both Roosevelts, John Marshall, and Earl Warren. The Supreme Court and the president have seldom approached greatness or power by spurning national claims in favor of local ones; Jefferson and Taney, to be sure, came to power opposing some national claims, but they quickly embraced others of greater consequence. John Marshall's success in converting his Democratic-appointed brethren from their states-rights beliefs to his own federalist nationalism says much for Marshall's persuasiveness and leadership, but it also says much about the logic of the Court's power and the nature of its constituency. The Court's constituency was national, and it could exert its most vigorous leadership on behalf of national claims. The same may be said of the executive, and above all for presidents as dedicated to greatness in the eyes of history as were Roosevelt, Kennedy, and Johnson: greatness lay not in accepting the comfortable, soft-nosed leadership patterns of a Hoover or an Eisenhower, but in taking bold federal initiative to meet a grave national crisis—and possibly even to embellish lesser crises, such as the missile-gap crisis, or the moon crisis, or the Tonkin Gulf crisis, or the malapportionment crisis, to make it appear that only a massive exercise of national power could avert disaster. Congressional and state leaders, on the other hand, had no national constituencies and took little initiative to expand the national sphere during the Warren era.

The contrast between the abstract, managerial motivations of modern voting rights reformers and the concrete, spoliatory motives of traditional reformers is quite striking. The old reformers were result-oriented, self-interested seekers of change for the purpose of securing their own convenience or advantage. They fought their battles in legislatures and party caucuses, arenas normally more responsive to interests than to principles. Modern voting rights reforms, by contrast, were not typically rooted in parties or legislatures, nor did their backers display the meticulous focus on group self-interest so conspicuous in the passage of the older reforms. In the old days competing parties were the first to insist on rigorous enforcement of the property qualifications—when it looked convenient—and then, when property qualifications proved too cumbersome, the first to abolish them. The debates on the passage of the Fourteenth and Fifteenth Amendments, casebook examples of the old sharp focus on self-interest, stood in marked contrast with twentieth-century debates, such as the 1970 congressional debates over the eighteen-year-old vote and reform of the electoral college. Where the nineteenth-century reformers had crassly counted up every vote they would win or lose by their reforms, sponsors of the post-1937 bills apparently wanted more democracy primarily for aesthetic reasons. One must take note of the twentieth-century reformers' devotion to "neutral principles," in sublime disregard for their consequences in application, with mixed admiration and alarm: admiration for the seeming liberation from the demands of political expediency, alarm at the unthinking demand for modish "democratic" measures with little concern as to whether in practice they would strengthen democracy or weaken it.

If the modern attachment to democratic reform for its own sake was conspicuous in the deliberations and nondeliberations of Congress, it seemed even more conspicuous in the thinking of the agencies that actually took the lead in modern democratic reforms, agencies (unlike Congress) well insulated from elective and partisan politics so that they might respond to the call of principle and not to the enveiglement of interest. Law review boards, political science panels, foundations, the solicitor general's office, the Supreme Court—these agencies have been described as result-oriented for bending constitutional principles to favor blacks, reapportionists, Jehovah's Witnesses, and so on, but their devotion to the Fundamental Principle was not based on any serious consideration of its anticipated results. Liberal reapportionist Andrew Hacker reaffirmed his faith in "the overriding issue of equal votes for equal citizens" even after his calculations had shown that equal votes would have strengthened the conservatives. His firm attachment to principle was unusual only in that he actually had given some serious attention to the consequences of reform and stood fast despite the discouraging prospects. Most reapportionists either bypassed the question of consequences as irrelevant or invoked the myth of barnyard government, which amounted to the same thing. Very few were willing to admit, as Hacker did, the "really aesthetic" grounds for their position.

The trained political scientist instinctively brushes aside assertions of principle and seeks the underlying interests which the principles serve. Unlike the typical American, who at the glimpse of a new constitutional issue is said to strain upon the start like a greyhound in the slips, the political scientist more resembles a truffle-hound sniffing for the partisan payoff. A man so trained might very well be tempted to interpret the voting reforms of the modern era as a series of power plays by the Democrats to mobilize more of their supporters among young people, city people, transients, poor people less likely to pay poll taxes, register, or own property for bond issues, illiterates, and southern blacks. Republican collaboration in the reforms, under this interest-sensitive view, might be explained by hopes for Republican gains in the suburbs and in the Democrats' southern salient, either among urban blacks resentful of the southern Democrats' tradition of white man's government, or among whites resentful of the northern Democrats' disposition to attack racial discrimination in the South while winking at subtler forms of discrimination in the North.

Such a partisan interpretation, however, would be far from the mark. Often enough, hard-nosed young party theoreticians would touch on diffuse and self-contradictory intimations of partisan interest, but usually in a supporting capacity, to show that the primary aesthetic aim would not have intolerable practical side effects. Unlike the old reformers, modern ones truly sought a prize of laurel, not truffles. Very little of the old scenario of a dominant party on faction nailing down its holdings by "reforming" the voting laws can be seen in the abolition of the white primary, the poll tax, literacy tests, and unequal districts, or diminutions of residency and age requirements. Despite occasional claims by the reformers, most of the reforms offered little clear or direct advantage to either of the parties or to any already dominant segment of society. Of the many disputes over voting rights reforms at the national level since 1937, only two were clearly partisan, both taking place in Congress and reflecting a clear conflict of party and personal interests. The first was the now-forgotten soldier-vote controversy of 1944, where a 60 percent pro-Roosevelt voting bloc was at issue, badly wanted by the Democrats and stoutly resisted by the Republicans. The second was the Dirksen amendment controversy of 1964-1966, where every legislator feared the reconstitution of his own district, and the Republicans particularly feared that they would be permanently hurt by Democratic mapmakers in the wave of reapportionment which happened to follow the Democrats' year of triumph, 1964. Apart from these two cases and the many furious struggles at the state level over *who* should reapportion and *how* (the question of *whether* having already been resolved by higher authority), debate over voting rights had an abstract and academic tone befitting the transpartisan bodies most influential in bringing modern reforms about, bodies like the American Political Science Association, the Kestnbaum Commission, the Supreme Court, and perhaps even the executive branch itself.

The reader should not conclude from these remarks or from subsequent remarks about executive-judiciary democracy that there was no difference between the parties, or between different presidents, solicitors general, and Supreme Court justices of the modern era. The "no-difference" interpretation would be just as misleading as the "partisan truffles" interpretation, for the three most activist Democratic presidents—Roosevelt, Kennedy, and Johnson—in their relations with Congress and in their appointments to the Court were distinctly more interventionist than the other Democrat, Truman, or the two Republican presidents, Eisenhower and Nixon. Eisenhower and Nixon, with bipartisan support, did secure the passage of three civil rights acts from Democratic Congresses; however, none of these Republican-backed acts was as sweeping in conception or execution as the two major Democratic-sponsored acts of 1964 and 1965, nor did any of the Republicans' acts require the massive doses of executive influence expended by Lyndon Johnson on behalf of his bills.

Truman and Eisenhower justices tended to favor intervention in voting rights cases involving racial discrimination, but they tended to oppose it in other voting rights cases. From the perspective of the Warren era, their center of gravity was on the nonintervention side. Of Truman's appointees, Justice Harold H. Burton (a Republican) voted against intervention in *Colegrove v. Green*, but for intervention against racial discrimination in the Jaybird case, *Terry v. Adams*. Chief Justice Fred M. Vinson and Justice Tom Clark joined Burton for intervention against the Jaybirds, but Truman's final appointee, Sherman M. Minton, dissented. Clark's subsequent record was mixed (see Epilogue, Table 13). Of Eisenhower's five appointments, two, Chief Justice Warren (a liberal Republican who had once run for Governor of California on both the Democratic and the Republican tickets) and Justice Brennan (a Democrat), consistently favored intervention. Two Eisenhower Republican justices, Harlan and Stewart, tended to oppose intervention except in some race cases. The last Eisenhower justice, Charles E. Whittaker, retired before *Baker v. Carr*, but he did concur in the Court's unanimous decision to intervene against the racial gerrymander in *Gomillion v. Lightfoot*. Nixon's first two appointments, Chief Justice Warren Burger and Justice Harry Blackmun, opposed intervention on behalf of the eighteen-year-old vote in *Oregon v. Mitchell*, a case which presented one striking illustration of the contrast between the orientations of the Democratic justices and the Republican. All four Republican justices—Burger, Blackmun, Harlan, and Stewart—opposed intervention; four of the five Democratic justices favored it—Brennan, Marshall, White, and Douglas—while the fifth—Black—favored it for congressional and presidential elections, but not for state elections.[8]

Roosevelt's appointees were generally favorable to intervention in the racial voting cases of the forties and fifties; his three most notable appointees, Frankfurter, Black, and Douglas, clashed in *Colegrove v. Green* and again in *Baker v. Carr*, with the ultimate victory, of course, going to the surviving interventionists, Black and Douglas. Kennedy's and Johnson's appointees, White, Goldberg, Fortas, and Marshall, were all strong interventionists (see Epilogue, Table 13).

The differences between Democratic and Republican justices should not be overdrawn to obscure a substratum of agreement on some kinds of intervention, nor should they be attributed to considerations of partisan advantage, for the reforms offered nothing like the concrete payoffs associated with the old tradition. The reader, like the author, may have finished Chapter VII in considerable perplexity as to which party, on a national scale, could be declared the "winner" of the reapportionment revolution years after its inception. If the payoff of reform was uncertain in the 1970's, it was doubly uncertain in the 1960's. It was easy enough to find partisan motivation in state redistricting disputes and in the controversy over the Dirksen amendment, where the anticipated payoffs to one party or the other were comparatively obvious. It is much harder, however, to see how Archibald Cox, or John F. Kennedy, or the Democratic justices on the Court in 1961-62 could have anticipated the Democrats' windfall gains of 1965-66, resulting from the party's landslide victories in 1964 after Kennedy's death. It is equally hard to explain, if professional politicians really expected substantial payoffs for the Democrats, the Republican's chronic acquiescence with, and even sponsorship of, interventionist policies. The Eisenhower administration initiated two civil rights bills to help enfranchise southern blacks; it made the original decision to intervene in *Baker v. Carr*; it appointed Justices Warren and Brennan, the authors of the two principal reapportionment decisions. Senator Barry Goldwater's applause for *Baker v. Carr* gave grounds to suppose that these reforms had a broad base of acceptance within the party. President Nixon's draft for the Voting Rights Amendments Act of 1970, far from curtailing the provisions of the Voting Rights Act of 1965, expanded its effect by suspending literacy tests nationwide, extending federal voting supervision to areas outside the South, and liberalizing residency and absentee voting requirements for presidential elections. He refused to veto the act when Congress passed it with a Democratic-sponsored rider enfranchising eighteen-year-olds, despite his well-founded doubts of the rider's constitutionality, because he wanted the rest of the bill badly enough to let the rider pass. The four Republican justices who unanimously opposed the Democratic justices on the eighteen-year-old vote in *Oregon v. Mitchell* were equally unanimous with the Democrats in upholding the extended bar on literacy tests and voted 3-1 with the Democrats in upholding liberalized residency requirements for presidential elections. The overall Republican record throughout and after the Warren years was one of tempered enthusiasm for intervention, not opposition to intervention. It may be profitably contrasted with the extravagant zeal of the Democrats in degree of scope and stress, but not in its acceptance of a larger federal role in equalizing the right to vote, nor in its transpartisan motivation. The Republicans did not participate in the reforms to help the Democrats; neither did the Democrats, to help themselves. Again, the payoff for the reformers was not concrete partisan spoils but something quite different.

The reader may recall, perhaps with some puzzlement, that all this discussion of interest and principle popped up in the middle of a discussion of the executive as the Court's premier constituency. The juxtaposition is not accidental, for the executive and the judiciary had in many respects a common style and common interests, and, in the Guardians and the Guardian Ethic, a common constituency and a common ideology. These added up, I submit, to a very special kind of executive-judicial democracy, qualitatively different from the old kind, centered in legislatures. The old democracy had been that described by Tocqueville in *Democracy in America*: it was rooted in local communities, highly participatory, and responsive to whims and vagaries of public fancy, but stable in the long run by virtue of its own adaptability. It was miserable in the quality of its leadership compared to that of other governments or other sectors of society, but magnificent in the devotion and voluntary cooperation it elicited from its constituents. Tocqueville marvelled at the American's response to their low-grade leadership: their reverence for the law, their willingness to submit without a murmur to the authority of the pettiest magistrate, their patriotism and public spirit which flourished despite—or was it because of?—the rude and untutored holders of public authority. He was likewise astonished at the benign character of American government: "In the United States, where public officers have no class interests to promote, the general and constant influence of the government is beneficial, although the individuals who conduct it are frequently unskillful and sometimes contemptible."[9] Tocqueville himself had been reared in a tradition of aristocratic leadership, of administrators well schooled in the art of statecraft and administration, "possessed of a self-control that protects them from the errors of temporary judgment," painstakingly educated in the intricacies of humane and enlightened government. The French leadership far eclipsed the American in its understanding of statecraft as a means, yet it was less effective than American democracy in choosing political ends approved by all. The flaw of the French magistracy, enlightenment and all, was its isolation from the desires of the people. In the short run it could lead, but in the longer run it could neither follow public sentiment nor elicit sustained public support, for its comparative coherence and stability in the short run translated into inflexibility, failure to adapt, and ultimately into secular instability.

If one may judge it by the voting rights reforms of the modern era, the new executive-judicial democracy more closely resembled Tocqueville's model of French administration than it did his model of democracy in America. Its

247

inspiration was unitary and centralist, not pluralist or local, elitist, not participatory; the reforms were founded on the recommendations of the decisions of intellectuals and Washington statesmen, not the choice of the communities most directly affected. Executive-judicial democracy was basically administrative, not representative. Its exponents were hypersensitive to the most trifling compromise of measurable equality, yet seemingly indifferent to the most glaring denials of freedom of political choice. Their interest in measurable equality was not wrong, for measurable equality is an important element of democracy, but it was dangerously one-sided, disproportionately mechanistic, careless of the rule of law which made liberal society possible. The mechanistic view of society is useful for reform because it gets results. It brushes aside imponderables and doubts, elbows in with clear standards, and effectively clears the way for concrete action. It is also potentially tyrannous in its oversimplification. The essence of the mechanistic view is social atomization and political centralization. Individuals, in this view, are standardized, abstract units, and the state the supreme choice-maker, manipulator, problemsolver. The powers of the state, under the mechanistic view, would be commensurate with its duties, which is to say, as the mechanist Hobbes delighted in pointing out, the powers would acknowledge no real bounds. Of course, the mechanist Bentham added, the power would really need no bounds if everyone had the vote because collective self-determination could not be expected to work against the determiners' own interests.

The blindness of such thinking lay in its acceptance of abstract, collective choice as equivalent to concrete choices by individuals, its easy assumption that ordinary citizens should understand their twenty-millionth share in the government to bind them to accept the government's acts as equivalent to their own. Such an understanding is, of course, grotesque in the telling and even more grotesque in attempted application to politics, for it acknowledges no limits to central governmental authority and substitutes the central state for all the other agencies and institutions of society whose diversity provides the practical preconditions for personal choice. Tocqueville long ago spotted the delusion and the danger of attempts to derive individual freedom from collective sovereignty and concentrated power:

Our contemporaries, are constantly excited by two conflicting passions: they want to be led and they wish to remain free. As they cannot destroy either the one or the other of these contrary propensities, they strive to satisfy them both at once. They devise a sole, tutelary, and all-powerful form of government elected by the people. They combine the principle of centralization and that of popular sovereignty; this gives them respite: they console themselves for being in tutelage by the reflection that they have chosen their own guardians. Every man allows himself to be in leading strings, because he sees that it is not a person or class of persons, but the people at large who hold the end of his chain . . .

I admit that by this means room is left for the intervention of individuals in the more important affairs: but it is not the less suppressed in the smaller and more private ones. It must not be forgotten that it is especially dangerous to enslave men in the minor details of life. For my own part, I should be inclined to think freedom less necessary in the great things than in the little ones, if it were possible to be secure of the one without possessing the other.[10]

It would be silly to describe the modern Court, the modern executive, or the Guardians as tyrannous or totalitarian in their handling of voting rights disputes. In general, their motives were far more noble than those of their predecessor reformers in Congress and state legislatures; their decisions generally touched on little things, not great things. None of them seriously impaired the operations of Congress and the states, and some, such as the white primary cases and the executive-sponsored Voting Rights Act of 1965, produced substantial and beneficial changes in the operation of southern politics. Even those most critical of the Warren Court would have some doubts about turning the clock back to 1960, or even 1964, and nobody worth mentioning wants a return to 1940. Neverhtheless, the undercurrent of executive-judicial absolutism should not pass without comment, for its impetus in the 1960's was away from individual choice and toward administrative fiat, and most of the intellectual community, normally suspicious of the aggrandizement of the state, was either oblivious to the trend or conscious of it and enamored with it.

Marshalling of Constituencies

The executive, as indicated, was a critical constituency through its resources in staff and organization and its ability to respond more effectively than Congress or the states to the wishes of urban and ethnic groups and the demands of a national economy, not to mention those arising from the country's status as a world power. It was also a critical constituency through its strength with the Guardians. When the executive became the leading national policymaker under Franklin D. Roosevelt, it came in at the head of a constellation of groups whose aspirations had been stymied in Congress and the states. The Roosevelt revolution gave new power to labor, blacks, urban ethnic minorities, and the national press, whose tolerance was essential to carry the large urban states with decisive votes in the electoral college. It also gave vast new power to the entire federal bureaucracy—including the Supreme Court and the judicial bureaucracy, which fought Roosevelt at first but shared, nonetheless, in the larger sphere of federal prerogative which he created. It also gave unprecedented power to college professors. Government bureaucracies of every land and time have offered a haven for intellectuals with political ambitions, and Roosevelt's bureaucracy gave American intellectuals a political home which they had never had before. Advisory commissions, brain trusts, panels of experts blossomed all over Washington, not only in the government itself, but also in Washington law firms, lobbies, and national councils of this and that which could provide the necessary expertise for dealing with government experts. The real new breed of policymaker of the Warren era was not found in legislatures but in and around the bureaucracy. No one expected to see men like Webster, Clay, and Calhoun swaying national destinies in Congress because the national destinies had passed out of Congress's hands and into the hands of the Guardians. Everyone knew that a handful of specialists in the action establishment could make more policy in a month than Congress could in a year; people might have listened to the cautions of Senators William Fulbright or Everett Dirksen every now and then when they were worried that action had gone too far, but when they wanted results they went to administrative braintrusters like Robert McNamara, McGeorge Bundy, Arthur Goldberg, and Nicholas deB. Katzenbach. When they wanted definitive rhetorical backing they went to Walter Lippman, William O. Douglas or the Twentieth Century Fund. These result-getters often shuttled around from one office of the executive or judiciary branches to another, as Arthur Goldberg and Nicholas Katzenbach did, but they were seldom to be found in Congress.

In practical political terms the Supreme Court often carried the ball for the executive because, as guardian of the higher law, it had powers which both the executive and Congress lacked. In most major policy areas, Congress could only block, modify, or approve measures initiated by the executive; yet the executive itself was often stymied by two factors: structural barriers in the party system to reforms like reapportionment and mixed primaries, and the general public's failure to embrace the Guardian vanguard's notions of freedom, equality, and representative government. If the Guardians had waited for groundswells of public demand for automatic right to counsel, exclusion of illegally seized evidence, desegregation, and abolition of school prayers and restrictive covenants, they would still be waiting.

Even the president—national, liberal, activist orientation and all—suffered from his status as an elected official. From the Guardians' viewpoint this was a signal weakness, for it confined the president only somewhat less than Congress and Mayor Daley to such diffident tinkering with the paramount questions of race, rights, and national management as the public and the parties would tolerate. Tinkering was not enough for the Guardians, nor for the more activist, history-conscious presidents who accepted the Guardians' moral authority and strove to win their approval. Naturally enough, presidents desiring to be included in Arthur Schlesinger, Jr.'s book of great (that is, activist) presidents joined the Guardians in seeking results from the courts, for, of the three branches of government, only the judiciary was sufficiently insulated from the direct sanctions of general public opinion to be able to take action that went against public opinion or beyond it.

Insulation and all, however, the Court could not afford to operate in a vacuum. It had seldom failed to satisfy the general public of the justice of its action once taken, provided the action was acceptable to intellectual opinion-makers,[11] but it could ill afford to provoke the public or the other political branches by forging ahead blindly with its own projects. Judicial politics, like all politics, are the art of the possible, and the Court, to intervene effectively, had to develop a third kind of technique besides the techniques of interpretation and enforcement it had used in the reapportionment cases. The courts evolved techniques to gather general information needed to promulgate rules of general effect, and they expanded the hearing process, traditionally limited to the facts of the case and the applicable laws, to include the same kind of background information that Congress would seek in a legislative hearing.

The Brandeis brief was a step in this direction. Recognizing that the judiciary was intervening against economic regulation, not as one applying a given standard but as one devising its own standard, Brandeis troubled little with extant laws but frankly addressed the courts as he would a legislature, as weighers of fact and value. The Supreme Court responded with opinions more and more frankly based on the authority of sociologists (as in the school segregation cases) and political scientists (as in the reapportionment cases) in preference to the authority of any traditional law-giving body. In the course of the desegregation controversy, federal courts came to rely more and more on techniques of group representation through joinder of various kinds of interested parties and acceptance of amicus curiae briefs, which often added as much to the court's understanding of the positions of the various interest groups as to its understanding of the legal issues involved. A. A. Berle, an enthusiastic proponent of judicial legislation, described a session of the United States Court of Appeals for the Fifth Circuit resembling in everything but name a congressional committee hearing:

A three-judge court handed down an order on December 29, 1966 directing desegregation of nine school districts in Louisiana and Alabama [adopting HEW "guidelines" for desegregation]. On appeal to the United States Court of Appeals for the Fifth Circuit, twelve judges were present; the head of the Department of Justice civil-rights division argued for a general ruling; the National Association for the Advancement of Colored People was represented, as were attorneys for various Southern cities . . .

The fact was that the Court of Appeals for the Fifth Circuit was conducting a legislative hearing. Fundamentally, they were deciding whether they should adopt as legislation the guidelines of the Department of Health, Education, and Welfare as applicable law covering a large area of the United States with the possibility that the precedent might become applicable all over the United States.

This is putting the courts pretty far into the decree-law business.[12]

The reapportionment cases brought an unprecedented display of the Court's constituencies in action: the solicitor general, farm and city lobbies, the ACLU, the ADA, the AFL-CIO, the NAACP, SCLC, Everett Dirksen, Bobby Kennedy, the intellectual establishment—everybody had some kind of spokesman except the general public, two-thirds of which seems to have been wholly unaware that the reapportionment revolution was taking place.[1 3]

The role of the solicitor general in influencing the Court has been stressed many times. From J. Lee Rankin's decision in 1960 to intervene in *Baker v. Carr* (or perhaps even from the time of Herbert Wechsler's arguments in *United States v. Classic*), through Archibald Cox's golden age of reform in the early 1960's, to the silver ages of Thurgood Marshall and Erwin Griswold, the solicitor general played a primary role in clearing the way for the Court to intervene in voting rights cases. The solicitor supplied indispensable aids to intervention: executive approval, blue-ribbon research well rooted in the moral authority of the Guardians, skillful argument, tactical organization, and strategic timing. A major difference between *Baker v. Carr* and the many cases before it where the Court had refused to intervene was a prod from the executive in the form of an amicus curiae brief from the solicitor general urging intervention and suggestions that the equal protection clause forbade "dilution" of votes by gross malapportionment. Besides giving a bare constitutional rationale, the solicitor general stressed the Guardian message that reapportionment was needed to strengthen representative government (as everybody then assumed it would do), and that the Supreme Court was the only agency which could force the states to reapportion.

In Tennessee, as in many other states, the underrepresentation of urban voters has been a dominant factor in the refusal of state legislatures to meet the growing problems of our urban areas . . . Legislatures have, in very large part, failed to adapt themselves to modern problems, and majority needs and this failure has resulted in public cynicism, disillusionment and loss of confidence . . . Numerous states have done nothing with regard to apportionment of their legislatures for 25 or 50 years. The only realistic remedy is federal judicial action.[1 4]

Archibald Cox himself believed that his intervention in *Baker v. Carr* may have determined its outcome, and the chances are that his appraisal is correct. The question of whether reapportionment, a cause which had attracted its share of cranks in the past, had really become a respectable mainstream cause could not have failed to worry some of the justices who did not relish a showdown with Felix Frankfurter—on constitutionally weak ground over a matter bound to stir up political antagonism in Congress and in state legislatures—without strong backing from the executive and reasonable assurance that the cause was worth the risk. Victor Navasky believed, on the basis of internal Justice Department memoranda and off-the-record comments, that at least two of the justices—Potter Stewart and Tom Clark—were swayed by the government's intervention to vote as they did in *Baker v. Carr*. Their votes were indispensable for the Court's intervention, since Justice Whittaker did not participate in the *Baker* decision, and the Court would otherwise have divided 4-4, leaving the lower court decision intact. Navasky reports that Stewart inquired through an intermediary whether Eisenhower's solicitor, J. Lee Rankin, had favored intervention. "He had," wrote Navasky, "and it was clear that Stewart cared."[15]

The solicitor's support may have been equally influential in the follow-up cases of 1963 and 1964, determining, step by step, the overall objectives of the reapportionment revolution. Attorney General Robert F. Kennedy contrived to argue *Gray v. Sanders* himself, though on narrow grounds approved by Cox. Cox delegated the argument of *Wesberry v. Sanders* to a subordinate, a decision not touched on by Navasky, but in the context of Cox's other intervention decisions an act almost certain to have warned the Court that he had misgivings about intervening.[16] The Court intervened anyway, by an 8-1 majority as strong in agreement on the desired political result as it was weak in providing a plausible legal rationale for it. Cox's intervention in the 1964 *Reapportionment* cases was valuable for its careful, cautious craftsmanship and tactical coordination of the various plaintiffs, as well as for its indication of continuing executive favor. As before, the caution of his rationale helped make more palatable the boldness of what he was asking for. Coming from Cox, who was well schooled in Frankfurterian jurisprudence, the call to overcome Frankfurterian doubts and excise the "cancer" of malapportionment carried special weight. So presented, the call to do a mighty deed proved as irresistible to the Court as it had been to Cox himself. Table 13 in the Epilogue shows that Cox's successors in the Warren years, Thurgood Marshall and Erwin Griswold, were likewise favorable to expansion of voting rights and likewise successful in getting the Court to intervene. Of the thirty cases in the table, the solicitor called for intervention in eighteen, opposed it in none; of the eighteen, the Court intervened as urged in all but two.[17]

By the time the Court heard argument on the *Reapportionment* cases, the parties of record and the Justice Department (which sided with the urban plaintiffs, in all six cases, though under a more flexible rationale than the one the Court adopted) were joined by fifteen states on the one hand, and the ACLU, the NAACP, and the American Jewish Congress on the other.[18] This marshalling of forces was only a beginning; in the course of the growing struggle in Congress to resist reapportionment, thirty-four states entered the fray, with forty-two states passing resolutions in at least one house to curtail reapportionment, and representatives of another hundred-odd interest groups lobbying for or against Congress's efforts to reverse the *Reapportionment* cases.[19]

The *Congressional Quarterly's* account of Congress's rebellion against reapportionment illustrated both the indispensability and the effectiveness of the Court's cultivation of its constituencies. Congressional and public reaction to *Baker v. Carr* was favorable; both parties saw opportunities for advantage; Barry Goldwater called *Baker v. Carr* "a proper decision"; the ADA, the American Municipal Association, the United States Conference of Mayors, and the Industrial Union Department of the AFL-CIO applauded it,[20] along with pioneer experts on reapportionment like Gordon Baker and Anthony Lewis. A few rural-based southern Democrats grumbled, and by the end of 1962 the General Assembly of the States, composed mostly of state legislators, proposed an amendment to take reapportionment out of federal court jurisdiction; moreover, the American Farm Bureau announced its intention to fight any effort to reapportion both houses of state legislatures on a population basis;[21] but Congress and the public seemed much more exercised over school prayers than they were over reapportionment.[22] *Wesberry v. Sanders* was likewise received with a few protests, much acclaim, and little congressional action.[23]

The Dirksen Counterrevolution

Not so the *Reapportionment* cases. Starkly legislative, Draconian of rule, invalidating by implication the apportionment of all but one or two states, these yanked off all the gauze from the Court's cure for malapportionment, revealing it to be a wooden leg. Reaction in Congress was immediate and adverse. Sixty-one Republican congressmen, eleven southern Democrats, and seven northern Democrats proposed constitutional amendments to limit the Court's powers over apportionment; forty-one Republicans, eighteen southern Democrats, and two northern Democrats proposed to curb the Court by ordinary legislation.[24] Under the leadership of Senator Everett Dirksen (R, Ill.), opponents of reapportionment embarked on a three-year, three-pronged attack on the *Reapportionment* cases aimed at blocking reapportionment immediately and temporarily while a constitutional amendment could be passed, either in the Senate or through constitutional convention, to block it for good, at least in one house of the state legislatures. Dirksen recognized that his chances of getting an amendment would be diminished by every new reapportionment; so did the Supreme Court and the reapportionists, but the reapportionists enjoyed a tactical advantage customarily enjoyed by the conservatives: they had only to delay legislation, since the burden of changing the legislative status quo was now on the opponents of reapportionment, while the courts could proceed with reapportionment free of parliamentary hindrances.

Although the antireapportionists were able to pass the Tuck Bill (HR 11926) in the House of Representatives to strip the federal courts of jurisdiction over reapportionment, efforts to get it through the Senate, along with

Dirksen's bill (S 3069) staying federal court reapportionment proceedings for two to four years, were stymied by a six-week, liberal filibuster that resulted in the emasculation and ultimate abandonment of both bills. Dirksen's votes melted away during the weeks from early August to late September 1964 as the shock of the *Reapportionment* cases began to fade. Fifteen law school deans and professors declared that Dirksen's and Tuck's measures "dangerously threatened the integrity of our judicial process" (August 10),[25] a Gallup Poll showed that those of the public who had formed an opinion backed the Court 3-2 (August 18),[26] and Dirksen found himself unable to stop the filibuster. By September 24 the liberals had changed the issue from, "Shall we preserve state representative institutions from the Court's attacks?" to "Shall we preserve the Court from Dirksen's attacks?" and a nonbinding "sense of Congress" resolution was passed, urging but not requiring courts to give legislatures six months to act before putting reapportionment orders into effect. At Dirksen's request, the resolution was then dropped as worse than useless.[27]

Despite the Democratic landslide of 1964, Dirksen accumulated a growing drawerful of requests from the states for a constitutional convention and in 1965 and 1966 mustered substantial majorities in the Senate favoring adoption of an amendment permitting the states to apportion one house of the state legislature on a nonpopulation basis, provided the apportionment was approved by referendum. However, the majorities were short of the two-thirds required for a constitutional amendment. Again the liberals were able to shift attention away from the merits of reapportionment itself by repeatedly attacking the wording of Dirksen's drafts and eventually by recasting reapportionment as a black rights issue, signalized by the transfer of the slogan "one man, one vote" from the National Municipal League to the NAACP in the summer of 1965. Again, Dirksen's votes faded away with each of many delays till he eventually lost his chance of mustering a constitutional majority. By 1966, reapportionment was well underway in most states, and Dirksen's last try for a constitutional majority in the Senate failed by seven votes. Despite a brief scare in the winter of 1967 that Dirksen's drawerful of state applications for a constitutional convention lacked only two or three states of the necessary two-thirds, continued reapportionment, fear of a runaway convention, and several doubts and withdrawals of applications rendered bootless any hopes Dirksen might have retained for stopping reapportionment by amendment.[28]

Ideology and Absolutism

Although the multitude of interest groups which have sought to influence the Court with amicus briefs or safeguard its decisions in Congress suggests a widespread feeling that expression of political sentiments through judicial channels is a worthwhile undertaking, it may be that the Court's ideological constituencies are even more important than its interest constituencies. It is very hard to escape the notion, if one considers the enthronement of the Guardian Ethic in such cases as the reapportionment cases, the poll tax case, most of the sit-in cases, the school segregation cases, and criminal justice cases like *Gideon v. Wainwright* and *Miranda v. Arizona*, that the many announcements in the early 1960's of the "end of ideology" were much exaggerated.[29] These announcements typically interpreted the abandonment of certain kinds of rhetoric connected with the cold war and the class war as an indication that ideology itself had gone out of style. The man of the 1960's, sophisticated, skeptical, educated, more attuned to economic than religious values, disillusioned alike with May-Day Marxism and scot-free enterprise, was supposed to be "transvaluational" and pragmatic, rather than ideological in his view of life. This judgment however, was a play on words; it suggested that, because we had abandoned some of the old value patterns, we were now too sophisticated to have values at all, or at least that our new values were so scientific that they could not possibly be described with the same language used to describe the old superstitions. The reasoning was dialectical. Once we have destroyed every class but one, said Marx, class is a meaningless term, and society must then be classless; likewise, when we had rejected every ideology but one, the one that was left was supposed to transcend ideologies, and society was supposed to be "transvaluational."

"Thou wast not born for death, immortal Bird!/No hungry generations tread thee down." So of nightingales, said Keats, but was it true of the Guardian Ethic? An honest answer must be yes, but no. The Ethic was immortal only so long as it was judged solely by its own standards; judged by any other standards, it had feet of clay. The justification of the Ethic, like that of any system of values, was that it pierced through forms and got to realities; yet we have seen that such "realities" as equal representation for equal numbers, as interpreted by the Supreme Court, were themselves more formal than real, and that the millennial pronouncements of the best minds in the country about revitalized representative government were a fraud when considered in the light of what actually happened. This is a serious charge by the Ethic's own standards; there was no greater sin against the Ethic than to be taken in, yet all of us who accepted our wise men's revelations on faith are wide open to the charge.

The Guardian Ethic was probably a product of modern, industrial-urban-bureaucratic life; its basic orientation was administrative, stressing uniformity but permitting and even requiring sharp distinctions of rank where rational (that is, measurable) categories can be made, as with money, education, professional accreditation, and so forth, while rejecting more subtle and unmeasurable considerations, such as multi-member districts, Martha's Vineyard, the memory of the Ku Klux Klan, local preference, and anything that smacked of special circumstances, as irrelevant or irrational. Modern man spends most of his time weighing and measuring, and he now tends to give disproportionate importance to things that can be weighed and measured. Georg Simmel described how urban man, faced with a swift and uninterrupted flow of changing stimuli, no longer has the time to make special, individual judgments and comes to judge exclusively by lowest measurable common denominators:

> Money economy and the dominance of the intellect are intrinsically connected. They share a matter-of-fact attitude in dealing with men and with things; and in this attitude, a formal justice is often coupled with an inconsiderate hardness. The intellectually sophisticated person is indifferent to all genuine individuality because relationships and reactions result from it which cannot be exhausted with logical opinions . . . All intimate emotional relations between persons are founded in their individuality, whereas in rational relations man is reckoned with like a number, like an element which is in itself indifferent. Only the objective measurable achievement is of interest.[30]

Reckoning by the lowest common denominator does meet some of the needs of modern society. By breaking society into basic units, into "building blocks" bound together only by rational attachments, it lends itself to change, manipulation, engineering, organization in large units. The modern business corporation, the modern bureaucratic or military hierarchies testify to the strengths and weaknesses of the building block system. But businesses and armies are typically single-mission concerns: their job is to make money or win wars. Governments are more diverse in their ends, and attempts to organize them around a single mission, like making the trains run on time, stamping out bolshevism, or completing the Workers' revolution, have not had happy results, for what they really stamp out is diversity, freedom, and individuality.

For all the Guardians' enlightenment, for all their transpartisan reformist zeal and their heartfelt patter about invigorating representative institutions and bringing effective participatory democracy to the little man, their work did far more to enhance their own power and participation than that of the little man or his drying husks of representative institutions. Political scientists of the late 1960's, far from rejoicing over the expanded democracy of the Warren era, howled at the growth of alienation, the decline of perceived participation in public choices, the rise of public cynicism, disillusionment, and apathy.[31] I cannot join my colleagues in proclaiming the death of democracy any more than I could join them in their earlier predictions of its coming resurrection. Democracy in America is still very much alive, but I suspect that it has lost some of its old responsiveness to pressures from the bottom, thanks in part to the Guardians' belief that democracy is better imposed from the top than from the bottom.[32]

I do think the operation of the Guardian Ethic in the 1960's casts further light on Bertrand de Jouvenel's observation in the 1940's, and Edmund Burke's in the 1790's, that mass democracy is an indicator of the growth of despotism.[33] The Guardians shared a mixture of idealism and absolutism such as we normally associate with adolescents: they were impatient of the past, sick of ambiguity and diversity, steeped in the ancient and honorable philosophic longing for unity and rationality, and chafing to pound the real world into a rationality consonant with that of the symbolic world. We owe much of the world's change and excitement to adolescent brashness, and much of its wisdom and insight as well; nevertheless, by itself it is a poor guide for action. It is shallow, heedless, pushy, absolutist, short on staying power, and blinded by excessive preoccupation with the present and the immediate future. Carefully educated and constrained, it is our hope for the long run, but left to itself it is foolish at best and despotic at worst.

The distinctive and disturbing characteristic of the 1960's was the degree to which the Guardians were not only left to themselves but encouraged to impose their theories on society. No one seemed seriously concerned that all their insistence on unity, collective necessity, action, and mobilization of large groups might impinge on diversity, individual choice, and freedom to participate in smaller groups. The Guardian Ethic demanded equality in measurables with a special vehemence because it could demand so little else, but the equality it conferred was the equality of wooden legs—a boon to some, but a devaluation for most because, in spite of all the mandates of modern living, most of us would rather be special than equal, and the Ethic could confer only the cold specialness of Making It. Older people eventually learn to bear up under this kind of standardization without complaining, but too many young people since 1960 have been opting for private coercion, anarchism, and flower power to quiet the suspicion that our rites of passage into Guardian manhood have involved a species of emotional scarification hardly less barbarous than the physical mutilations practiced by less enlightened societies. Simmel pointed out the isolation and degradation which those who rely solely on "objective" reckoning must undergo: "The self-preservation of certain personalities is bought at the price of devaluating the whole objective world, a devaluation which in the end unavoidably drags one's own personality down into a feeling of the same worthlessness."[34]

Constitutional Atheism and the Viability of the Guardian Ethic

This kind of consideration bears heavily on the Supreme Court because, as expounder of the higher law, the Court does have to reckon with whatever ideology its constituency happens to think is enshrined in the higher law. The Court's constituency was an elite body of intellectuals—managers, advisers, professionals of various hues, themselves devoted to the Ethic, in spite of its agonies, for a number of reasons: it did seem to match the conditions of modern life, and everyone who counted accepted it, possibly because it did promote them from mere persons to brigadier generals of society. The political logic of the Ethic reversed the older higher law of Madison, under which the country managed to operate for many years; Madison's higher law was respectful of authority, suspicious of ungoverned action, oriented to curb governments and protect the liberty of individuals. The new higher law was that of Bentham, impatient of traditional symbols and observances, cynical of political authority but respectful of action, especially action oriented toward uniformity, equality, and expertise—things you can measure. The reapportionment cases were as overwhelmingly right by these standards as they were wrong by the old ones. They cut through constitutional red tape to impose a measurable equality, with the approval of the APSA and the Twentieth Century Fund; and they showed how a blue-ribbon panel of philosopher kings could amend the Constitution far more quickly and neatly than Congress and the states, whose Article V credentials were no longer the hardest constitutional currency because they could not get results the way the Court did.

Intellectuals, as we have seen, hailed the reapportionment cases as a triumph of the Ethic, as indeed they were. Delivering the 1967 Charpentier Lectures at Columbia University, A. A. Berle praised the reapportionment revolution as a significant and enlightened application of the laws of power. Noting with approval that "ultimate legislative power in the United States has come to rest in the Supreme Court,"[35] Berle congratulated the country for concentrating extraordinary powers in a body so eminently qualified to use them. Berle assumed without discussion, as most Guardians did, that the times demanded revolutionary action and that the main concern of sensible men should be to make sure that the action is taken in an "orderly" fashion by the right people—otherwise, the revolution might turn out to be "French" (that is, "explosive, not to say disorderly," and worse, a failure)—presumably because it might fall into the hands of amateurs.[36] Because such action as reapportionment and equal public accommodation "had" to be taken, and Congress and the states were too mired in the unconcern of their electorates to take it quickly enough, the Supreme Court "had" to intervene to fill the action vacuum, which every Guardian abhorred. The Court's interpretation of the equal protection clause seemed more than adequate to justify such intervention and point the way for future intervention: "The 'equal protection' clause under present doctrine requires the courts not only to strike down action affirmatively denying such protection, but also to remedy the lack of action that *should have been taken* to give such protection. Abstention— avoidance of the problem—seems no longer practicable."[37]

All that the Court lacked for effective exercise of its "reserve revolutionary powers," said Berle, was better staff backup in the form of a Council of Constitutional Advisors to help the Court "educate" Congress and the states as to what was best for them, and also to help work out the difficult administrative details of such reforms as incorporating the school administrations of Maryland and Virginia suburbs into the District of Columbia school system by judicial fiat.[38] Plainly, Berle was at one with his one-time colleague in the action establishment, McGeorge Bundy, who also stressed the need, in his 1968 Godkin Lectures at Harvard, for more action and more establishment. Berle was at least forthright enough not to describe his plan as a way of strengthening representative government, perhaps because it was so widely accepted that action, not representation, was the imperative of the times. Berle's rationale was that judicial action would "safeguard the United States from an otherwise chaotic and dangerous situation which might have led to catastrophe," justifying the risk of turning the Court into "a variety of benevolent dictator."[39]

Even Justice Black shrank from Berle's overwarm embrace of the judicial revolution which had been so much Black's own handiwork. In the 1968 Charpentier Lectures, Black declared: "I deeply fear for our constitutional system of government when life-appointed judges can strike down a law passed by Congress or a state legislature with no more justification than that the judges believe the law is 'unreasonable.' "[40]

Black's reaction is understandable both as that of a man who loved the Constitution and as that of a man who wanted to preserve the power of the Supreme Court. It would be difficult to imagine a more profound repudiation of what is left of our representative institutions than Berle's proposed exercise of the Court's reserve revolutionary powers, nor a course of action more aptly designed to undermine the two major bases of the Court's long-run power; separation of powers, which permits the Court to act as umpire, and the higher law tradition itself. If the Court ever succeeded, in the course of its umpiring, in securing so crushing a triumph of itself and the executive over Congress and the states that the latter two could never thwart the Guardians' ambitions again, it would destroy the balance which permits it in some cases to hold its own against the executive.

It would be too much to say that the result-oriented Warren Court destroyed its long-run power base of public regard for the Constitution and the Court as impartial interpreter. But it would not be too much to say that the Court was working in that direction and that its constituencies were growing restless at the end. Guardians like Berle lost patience because the result-oriented justices were not coming across with enough results. Constitutional believers were indignant because the Court seemed to be trifling with the Constitution. By the time of Warren's retirement in 1969—only two years after Berle's call to arms—the Court was badly bruised by widespread public repudiation of the most cherished tenets of the Guardian Ethic. Anti-Guardian sentiment waxed in the furor over Justice Fortas's outside income, leading ultimately to his resignation. There was talk of impeaching Justice Douglas. Kennedy liberals, and even some establishment types who had so recently rallied to Lyndon Johnson's appeal for action on all fronts were now falling over one another in their haste to dissociate themselves from this most Guardian-acting of all administrations. With the firing of Fortas, the threats to Douglas, and the victory of the unGuardian Richard Nixon on a pledge to curb judicial activism, the Court had reason to consider a lesson that should have been apparent from the prior eclipse of Johnson and his Great Society: that the Ethic was strongest when it consisted of talk, as it did under the Kennedies, or when the talk was first put into action, as in Johnson's first two years, but weakest when the action was pushed beyond its initial stages, revealing its inadequacies and inconveniences.

Despite his spacious ambitions and immense political resources, Johnson withdrew from the 1968 campaign under fire from his anti-activist foes and his former activist friends. It seems hardly likely that the Court, even without its new, Nixon-appointed leadership and membership, could have carried on for the Guardians, who had themselves turned on Johnson. However interventionist such an extended Warren Court might have been, it could hardly have dared, with its tiny resources of staff, money, and patronage, to carry out Berle's mandate where Johnson had failed—or, having dared to try, to have survived the kind of attacks that brought down Johnson for not performing to Guardian specifications. Even with the greatest possible political powers the Court would have found as Johnson and others found, that there are many kinds of action which the most adroit management has been unable to accomplish: ending poverty, winning in Vietnam, making people feel cared about, ending public cynicism, disillusionment, and apathy. The Guardian Ethic imposed on the president, the Court, and anybody willing to try to take it on, an impossible task; it asked them to accomplish by bureaucracy tasks which no bureaucracy has ever been able to do.

When in history were people better managed than Americans in the 1960's? Yet the management in retrospect seems clumsy, harsh, ineffective—if anything, less responsive to people's needs than the crude administrations of prior decades. Why? Because it is the nature of bureaucracies to confine their attention to the very narrow range of short-term, superficial considerations which lend themselves to administrative supervision. The bigger the bureaucracy, the more this kind of consideration can be expected to dominate and the less the bureaucracy can be expected to respond to political leadership, the desires and needs of the general public, or anything other than its own people's desire to become brigadier generals or keep from being fired. Seymour Lipset was undoubtedly correct in saying that bureaucratization means a decline of the arbitrary power of those in authority: "By establishing norms of fair and equal treatment, and by reducing the unlimited power possessed by the leaders of many non-bureaucratic organizations, bureaucracy may mean less rather than greater need to conform to superiors."[41] But this is just another way of admitting that bureaucracies stifle and frustrate action from the top by insulating their staff from the need to conform to superiors. New, growing bureaucracies in systems which have not built up institutional insulation against bureaucratic mobilization are probably as powerful instruments of influence as could be found, because they can temporarily draw authority and power from both traditional and modern sources. For a while they can share the traditional authority of less intrusive institutions (for example, the Taney Court before Dred Scott) with the power of modern, intrusive, action-oriented institutions (for example, the draft). But the very triumph of intrusion saps the intruder's authority, as Michel Crozier has shown in examining the impact of bureaucratic patterns of action on French society: the highly centralized French bureaucracies, whose managers had almost unlimited powers on paper, produced protective cultural countermeasures in the form of social isolation, suspension of informal communication, and a willingness to cooperate to frustrate action while avoiding any initiative to take it. The only way to produce change in such a system was to precipitate a crisis, and the system could take action only rarely and at great cost.[42] In this country the draft for the war in Vietnam aroused, especially among intellectuals, a similar disposition to obstruct a government whose intrusive methods of mobilization cost it much of the loyalty it could command before it made a habit of intrusion. In Daniel Webster's day, and even in Dwight Eisenhower's day, intellectuals were concerned about loyalty to the Union; by 1968 they were worried about complicity with it. Why? It was not that the government had adopted more reactionary or flaccid policies since 1953, but that the intellectuals had become disillusioned at the sorry results even of escalated government action.

The Supreme Court was a decade or two behind the executive in embracing the role of revolutionary intendant. Unlike the executive and despite its dalliance with management in the Warren years, it did not undertake an irrevocable managerial commitment. I suppose the temptation to transform itself for some noble cause from a judicial agency to an administrative one will present itself again from time to time, but the risks of such transformation seemed more apparent in 1970 than they did in 1960, and much greater for the Court than for the executive. The Court's public image as keeper of the higher law is far more traditional and nonintrusive than that of the executive. In the words of Felix Frankfurter, "The Court's authority possessed of neither the purse nor the sword ultimately rests on sustained public confidence in its moral sanction. Such feeling must be nourished by the Court's complete detachment, in fact and in appearance, from political entanglements and by abstention from injecting itself into the clash of political forces in political settlements."[43] For such a body to undertake the kind of exercise of "reserve revolutionary powers" that Berle proposed would be little different from the Pope taking up atheism pursuant to his own duties as guardian of the higher law or ordering the worship of a golden statue of the Rolling

Stones according to the Fundamental Principle of the Bible, as expressed in section two of the First Commandment.[44] The Court and the Pope cannot afford to turn a blind eye to the fashions of the times, but both must be particularly careful about embracing fashions which destroy their traditional sources of authority because, when the fashion passes, the traditional sources of authority may have passed also. An action Court such as Berle proposed would almost certainly erode both of the two bases of judicial review: public respect for the Constitution, and public regard for the Court as a neutral interpreter of the Constitution. The reapportionment and poll tax cases, blatantly legislative, drew great applause from the illuminati, but they did nothing to enlist their long-term loyalty. "Of course the Court legislates," said John Veblen, "Isn't it grand?" It was grand only so long as the Court came across with the right results for its highly result-oriented clientele. When it failed to satisfy them in this regard, as the executive failed to satisfy them, the Court could not fall back on political reserves such as the executive retains even in its darkest moments; nor could it fall back on its own traditional reserves, having habitually treated the Constitution as a scrap of paper and long since squandered public confidence in its impartiality. The Guardian Ethic's constitutional atheism, like most brands of atheism, was a curious and volatile mixture of credulity and unbelief—credulity that experts and standardization could settle the basic problems of modern society, and disbelief that the older higher law had any relevance to modern government. We know that much of the credulity has disappeared—perhaps one day to be replaced by something resembling the polar confrontation of profound devotion to hierarchic order and intense antihierarchical mysticism found in other systems where administration has won out over representation[45]—but can we expect the old belief to come back once it has been repudiated by the Court which gave it its greatest glory?

Those of us who retain a fondness for representative government and a sense of loyalty to the Supreme Court and the Constitution can draw little comfort from the Court's great tactical success in the reapportionment cases because it was so fraught with strategic dangers. I suppose the Court has almost always had an ideological constituency; John Marshall's was the Federalist party; Taney's was the Democratic party; the Taft and Hughes Courts responded to big business, the ABA, and certain influential law writers. The Warren Court responded often very appropriately to the ideological views of the Guardians, but it responded on an incomparably grander scale than any Court had before. The danger to Court and country was correspondingly greater. The temptation has always existed for the Court to lash itself to some ideological mast as it did in the *Dred Scott* case, *Hepburn v. Griswold*, and *Lochner v. New York*,[46] confident that the intellectual vogue of some one period was transvaluational, chagrined to find out, as it sometimes did to its cost, that such a posture was uncomfortable when the ship went down. The last years of the Warren era gave us intimations of the Guardian Ethic's mortality, if not of its final demise. The Burger Court has not yet lashed itself to the Guardian Ethic, and I hope when future Guardians clamor for extra-constitutional adventures, however noble in inspiration, that future Courts will resist their Napoleonic urging to press on to Moscow. Justice Holmes warned the Court that the Fourteenth Amendment did not enact Herbert Spencer's *Social Statics*; neither did it enact Jeremy Bentham's *Resolutions on Parliamentary Reform*; and least of all did it enact Vladimir Ilyich Lenin's *What Is to Be Done.*

Epilogue: Was There a Better Way to Do It?

No lines can be laid down for civil or political wisdom.
They are a matter incapable of exact definition. But,
though no man can draw a stroke between the confines of
day and night, yet light and darkness are upon the whole
tolerably distinguishable.
—Edmund Burke

If the reader has detected an air of brashness about this book, an appearance of excessive assurance about questions that most of us are (or should be) still struggling to answer, I should admit that much of my criticism of the Guardian approach has been emboldened by my dissenting viewpoint on most Warren era interventions. Every student of constitutional jurisprudence knows that the dissenter can speak with a freedom and vivid assurance seldom available to the writer of majority opinions. The dissenter is his own man, at least temporarily free of the burdens of power; he has no need to blur his words or compromise his logic to keep the concurrence of others; he can forget questions of tactics; he is less bound to caution and qualification than a majority which has taken responsibility for an affirmative action, for the dissent abjures responsibility for the majority's action but takes no action of its own. His alternative usually sounds good, but he is not as strongly motivated as most majorities to offer a constructive alternative or, having offered one, to make sure it would work. Every man who has tried his hand at both knows that it is normally easier to be firm in the negative and the abstract than in the affirmative and the concrete. Firmness, however, is not necessarily to be equated with justice to the subject. We do live in a world of the affirmative, the concrete, and the ambiguous, and I would feel remiss in pausing in my speculations without some consideration of whether there was not a better way for the Court to have handled the voting rights issues of the 1960's.

Going into the 1960's, the Court had three options for dealing with voting rights questions: nonintervention, massive intervention, and selective intervention. Nonintervention could be roughly equated with the opinions of Justices Harlan and Frankfurter, who were willing enough to back intervention under the Fifteenth Amendment in cases involving racial discrimination, but very reluctant to follow the other justices' expansive reading of the Fourteenth Amendment. Massive intervention is what the Court actually did in the 1960's, pushing the Fundamental Principle almost to the limit of its practical applicability. Selective intervention is represented by the concurring and dissenting opinions of Justices Clark and Stewart, and also by the language of Solicitor General Archibald Cox, all of whom appeared to favor intervention subject to some kind of limiting rule of reason. My own choice of these options wavers between the Harlan-Frankfurter position and the Stewart-Clark position, both of which I believe preferable to massive intervention under both modern and traditional views of constitutional interpretation. The great strength of the noninterventionists, Harlan and Frankfurter, was their fidelity to the framers' specific text and intent. I am not unmindful of the compromises and crass calculations of political interest which often went into the making of the Constitution. Nevertheless, I have not been able to suppress my suspicion that there is a great and abiding strength of principle in the Constitution, possibly the greater and the more abiding for its political winnowing through the representative process. I believe the framers' prescriptions have been generally sounder than those emanating from changing fads of conventional wisdom. I believe that there is a deeper wisdom in careful and specific consultation of the text of the Constitution and the original understanding of its framers. Frankfurter and Harlan were rock solid in their adherence to this fundamental principle, and the fundamentalist in me rejoices in their reasoning.

They were perhaps less solid by the modern test of balancing considerations of policy, for nonintervention did signal a willingness to tolerate the most egregious forms of malapportionment. I must own to a certain embarrassment about embracing such tolerance in the case of the half-dozen worst states, and also in view of the possibility that Court-sanctioned malapportionment might add to southern white mapmakers' powers, already great, to gerrymander to neutralize the newly widened franchise of southern blacks.[1] Reapportionment did strengthen representative government in these situations, and a rounded assessment of nonintervention versus massive intervention would weigh the benefits of reapportionment, properly discounted (Chapter VII), against its costs: for example, its tendency to disrupt sound representative institutions as well as sick ones, to chop up communities, update gerrymanders, and plunge legislatures into needlessly frequent and bloody battles for individual and party survival—not to mention the violence done to legislatures and Constitution alike by judicial override, or the legitimacy crises elicited by opening up new categories of public choice to the possibility of judicial intrusion. The reader may make his own assessment of whether reapportionment was worth it as legislative policy; I remain skeptical that its rather modest benefits were worth its costs.

Justices Stewart and Clark, and Solicitor General Cox, in their separate ways, suggested a third alternative—selective intervention—which strikes me as superior to massive intervention in fidelity to constitutional text and intent, though not as strong as nonintervention, and better than nonintervention on policy grounds. If selective intervention is judicially administrable (which I believe it to be), it appears to be preferable to both of the polar alternatives as a statesmanlike guide to action. The advocates of selective intervention suggested that the Court would do well to intervene against "gross inequities" (Cox) resulting in the "systematic frustration of the will of a majority" (Stewart), while staying its hand in the case of "rational" discrimination which was neither capricious nor egregious. Less closely tied to an absolute, personal right to vote than the Fundamental Principle, selective intervention may be grounded on a "right to reasonably equal representation," arguably protectable by the equal protection clause, broadly construed (or the due process clause or the guarantee clause), though subtler and more difficult to administer than the Fundamental Principle. As an instrument of policy, selective intervention might have spared us the most flagrant examples of judicial overkill—the Colorado and New York cases, the poll tax case, the junior college district case, *Katzenbach v. Morgan*, and *Kirkpatrick v. Preisler*—while preserving the power to knock out gross discrimination in the worst states—for example, Florida, Nevada, Maryland, Alabama, Georgia, California, and Delaware—and also to combat racial discrimination and one-party dominion in the South. At some cost in administrative convenience, selective intervention offered greater accommodation of the political facts of life.

Selective intervention presents a very attractive alternative in one respect dear to scholars: it has never been tried, and its side-effects in application are still unknown. Unlike nonintervention, which was applied with mixed results before reapportionment, and massive intervention, which has been applied with mixed results since reapportionment, the Stewart-Clark-Cox approach was all "ought," and no "is." It shone in comparison with doctrines where the "ought" had suffered the dislocations of transformation into "is." If one may judge from its adoption by the solicitor general, and also from the fact that Frankfurter in *Baker v. Carr* chose it as his primary target, selective intervention is the approach that Smart Money would have backed in 1961. Frankfurter was attempting to silence what he thought was the enemy's main battery. One cannot help wondering in retrospect whether he did not silence it only too well. He so masterfully assailed the "best" approach for equalizing representation without overkill that the majority may well have chosen overkill to sidestep his attack on selectivity. In any case, the majority left open Frankfurter's question whether coherent standards could be found for selective intervention, such as was suggested by the solicitor general and ultimately chosen by Stewart and Clark as their own basis for intervention.

Table 13, which summarizes the positions of the solicitor general and the votes of the justices on voting rights cases from just after *Baker v. Carr* to the

Table 13. Voting Records of the Justices and Solicitor General in Voting Rights Cases, 1963–1969

Case	Vote	Harlan	Stewart	Clark	Black	White	Marshall	Fortas	Warren	Brennan	Goldberg	Douglas	Solicitor General
Gray v. Sanders (Ga.) 372 U.S. 368 (1963)	8–1	NI	I	I	I	I	—	—	I	I	I	I	I
Wesberry v. Sanders (Ga.) 376 U.S. 1 (1964)	8–1	NI	I	I	I	I	—	—	I	I	I	I	I
Reynolds v. Sims (Ala.) 377 US 533 (1964)													
Roman v. Sincock (Dela.)	8–1	NI[4]	I[4]	I[4]	I[4]	I[4]	—	—	I[4]	I[4]	I[4]	I[4]	I[4]
Md. Cmee. v. Tawes (Md.)													
Davis v. Mann (Va.)													
Allen v. Board (Va., Miss.) 393 U.S. 544 (1969)	8–1	I[3]	I[3]	I[3]	NI[3]	I[3]	I[3]	—	I[3]	I[3]	—	I[3]	I[3]
Gaston Cty. v. US (N.C.) 395 U.S. 285 (1969)	7–1	I	I	—	NI	I	—	—	I	I	—	I	I
Powell v. McCormack (N.Y.) 395 U.S. 486 (1969)	7–1	I	NI	—	I	I	—	X	I	I	—	I	I
Carrington v. Rash (Tex.) 380 U.S. 89 (1965)	7–1	NI	I	I	I	I	—	—	X	I	—	I	—
Katzenbach v. Morgan (N.Y.) 384 U.S. 641 (1966)	7–2	NI	NI	I	I	I	—	I	I	I	—	I	I
Swann v. Adams (Fla.) 385 U.S. 440 (1967)	7–2	NI	NI	I	I	I	—	I	I	I	—	I	—
Moore v. Ogilvie (Ill.) 394 U.S. 814 (1969)	7–2	NI	NI	—	—	I	—	I	I	I	—	I	—
Hadnott v. Amos (Ala.) 394 U.S. 358 (1969)	6–2	I	NI	—	X	NI	—	—	I	I	—	I	I
Lucas v. Colo. Assy. (Colo.) 377 U.S. 713 (1964)	6–3	NI[2]	NI[2]	NI[2]	I[2]	I[2]	—	—	I[2]	I[2]	I[2]	I[2]	I[2]
WMCA v. Lomenzo (N.Y.) 377 U.S. 633 (1964)													

Case	Vote												
Harper v. Bd. (Va.) 383 U.S. 663 (1966)	6-3	NI	NI	—	NI	I	NI	I	I	I	—	—	—
Williams v. Rhodes (Ohio) 393 U.S. 23 (1968)	6-3	—	NI	—	I	I	—	—	I	NI	—	—	—
Wells v. Rockefeller (N.Y.) 394 U.S. 526 (1969)	6-3	NI	—	—	I	NI	—	—	I	I	—	NI	—
Kirkpatrick v. Preisler (Mo.) 394 U.S. 526 (1969)	6-3	NI[2]	NI[2]	—	I[2]	I[2]	I[2]	I[2]	NI[2]	I[2]	—	I[2]	I[2]
Avery v. Midland (Tex.) 390 U.S. 474 (1968)	5-3	NI	NI	—	—	I	NI	NI	I	I	—	NI	—
Kramer v. Union (N.Y.) 395 U.S. 621 (1969)	5-3	NI	—	—	—	I	X	X	I	—	—	I	I
Fortson v. Morris (Ga.) 385 U.S. 231 (1966)	4-5	NI	NI	NI	NI	NI	I	I	I	I	—	I	—
Wright v. Rockefeller (N.Y.) 376 U.S. 52 (1964)	2-7	NI	NI	NI	NI	NI	—	—	NI	I	I	I	—
Fortson v. Dorsey (Ga.) 379 U.S. 433 (1965)	1-8	NI	NI	NI	NI	NI	—	—	NI	NI	—	NI	—
Burns v. Richardson (Hawaii) 384 U.S. 73 (1966)	0-8	NI	NI	NI	NI	NI	X	X	NI	NI	—	NI	—
Sailors v. Bd. (Mich.) 387 U.S. 105 (1967)	0-9	NI[2]	NI[2]	NI[2]	NI[2]	NI[2]	NI[2]	NI[2]	NI[2]	NI[2]	NI	NI[2]	NI
Dusch v. Davis (Va.) 387 U.S. 112 (1967)	0-9	NI[2]	NI[2]	NI[2]	NI[2]	NI[2]	NI[2]	NI[2]	NI[2]	NI[2]	—	NI[2]	I[2]
Total		I: 7 NI: 23	I: 11 NI: 19	I: 13 NI: 8	I: 7 NI: 12	I: 20 NI: 10	I: 9 NI: 0	I: 9 NI: 2	I: 23 NI: 6	I: 25 NI: 5	I: 10 NI: 1	I: 27 NI: 3	I: 18 NI: 0

I = Voted/Urged to Intervene
NI = Voted/Urged not to Intervene
— = Not on Court
X = Did not vote or take position
2 = Vote applies to 2 cases
3 = Vote applies to 3 cases
4 = Vote applies to 4 cases

end of the Warren era, may furnish some insights not available in Frankfurter's time as to how selective intervention might have fared.[2] The first insight, suggested by the contrast between the solicitor general's positions and the voting records of Clark and Stewart, is that moderate language does not necessarily result in a moderate position. Despite the selective-sounding language of his briefs in *Baker* and *Reynolds*, the solicitor general never submitted a brief which did not call for intervention. Though, like the Court itself, the solicitor general had once called for "due recognition of geographic and other minority interests" as a "comprehensible reason for reducing the weight of votes in great cities,"[3] he nevertheless called for intervention in *Lucas v. Colorado, WMCA v. Lomenzo*, and also *Avery v. Midland County*. His overall record on the thirty cases in the table was: for intervention, eighteen; no brief, twelve; against intervention, none—in contrast to Stewart's record of eleven votes for intervention, eighteen against. This contrast should not be overdrawn. The solicitor general was not clinging to his own 1961 standards but building on successively more rigorous standards developed by the Court (this, however, was also true of Stewart). Most of the solicitor general's calls for intervention after *Reynolds v. Sims* had to do with qualifications for the franchise, rather than reapportionment. Moreover, the solicitor general was free to stay out of borderline cases and often did so, never vouchsafing a no, or even a maybe, but leaving the Court and the public free to speculate as to the reasons for the poignant silences between the yeses. His track record with the Court was remarkably good in the Warren era, with only one brief calling the Court beyond its inclination to intervene.[4] The solicitor general's dearth of noes, however, translates into a dearth of selectivity. It gives us little basis to evaluate the viability of selective intervention as an alternative to the Fundamental Principle.

Stewart's voting record, more complete than that of Clark, who retired in 1967, and more selective than that of the solicitor general, does give us some notion of how selective intervention might have worked in practice. Stewart early demonstrated his willingness to intervene against gross examples of all three of the major patterns of malapportionment: unusually low Dauer-Kelsay score, large population variance between districts, and large maximum detrimental deviation.[5] A low Dauer-Kelsay score, showing that a small fraction of the voters could elect a majority in the legislature, indicated general inequality of districts. Stewart voted for intervention in Alabama, Maryland, and Delaware, all of which had exceptionally low (26 percent or lower) Dauer-Kelsay scores.[6] These states also flunked the other two standards relating to specific inequalities: they had a large variance between the largest and smallest districts and a large detriment to one or more exceptionally large districts.[7] Stewart, moreover, voted to intervene in Virginia, whose 1962 Dauer-Kelsay scores were quite high (41.1 percent in the Senate, 40.5 percent in the House) but which discriminated against a few exceptionally large districts in northern Virginia.[8] He did not, however, leave a clear-cut indication as to how he would vote on the mildest indicator of malapportionment, population variance between the largest and smallest district.[9] Stewart's votes for intervention against malapportionment had two things in common: they involved southern or border states, and their discrimination appeared to be more the fruit of population shifts plus inertia than a conscious design approved by the voters.

Stewart voted against intervention in Colorado, whose voters had approved a tolerably consistent pattern of unequal districts, and in New York, which followed a constitutional formula guaranteeing minimum representation to each county.[10] He also voted not to intervene against an Illinois law requiring candidates from new parties to secure a petition of 25,000 signatures, including 200 signatures from any 50 of the state's 102 counties.[11] He opposed intervention to require rigorous mathematical equality of districts,[12] to impose the fundamental principle on local government units,[13] to invalidate a state run-off election for governor,[14] to attack alleged partisan and racial gerrymanders,[15] or to invalidate "pyramidal" appointments to school boards and candidates' residential requirements in districts of unequal population.[16]

In voting rights cases not involving territorial discrimination, Stewart opposed intervention under the Voting Rights Act of 1965 to override a New York state language requirement and to invalidate an Alabama law tightening deadlines for independent candidates to get their names on the ballot.[17] On the other hand, he favored intervention under the act to require federal review of three southern states' new voting laws: a Virginia law forbidding stick-on write-in labels; Mississippi laws permitting appointive offices and at-large elections in certain counties; and a North Carolina literacy test "impartially" administered, where black schools had been poorer than white.[18] The only other case in which Stewart favored intervention was *Carrington v. Rash*,[19] where the Court invalidated a Texas residency requirement barring military personnel from acquiring residence while on duty in the state. He opposed intervention in the Adam Clayton Powell case, in the poll tax case, in an Ohio case placing heavy restrictions on third party access to ballot positions, and in a New York case where the franchise in certain school district elections was restricted to property owners and parents of school children in the district.[20]

One could argue that some of Stewart's votes were inconsistent: for example, voting to intervene against Virginia's stick-on label law but not to intervene against Alabama declaration deadlines disadvantageous to black candidates,[21] or voting to intervene against the Texas no-residence-for-military law but not to intervene against the Virginia poll tax law.[22] One might also cavil at his propensity to back intervention in the South while opposing it in the North. A recurrence to Table 13 (with the addition of *Baker v. Carr*) shows that Stewart voted to intervene in ten southern situations, two border state situations, and no northern situations; he voted not to intervene in all eleven northern situations, six southern situations, and one border state situation.[23] His vote to intervene against moderately unequal districts in Virginia while not intervening against slightly less equal districts in New York might be cited as a specific indicator of a pro-northern bias.[24]

On the other hand, when all the cavilling is registered, most of the so-called inconsistencies may be reasonably ascribed to differences between the facts of the different cases. There are differences between stick-on labels and candidate registration requirements; one has to do with voting, the other with running for office. A special discrimination against military personnel is arguably unreasonable, while discrimination against nonpayers of poll taxes is arguably reasonable. A special propensity for intervening in the South may be ascribed to special circumstances of southern politics: one-party rule, gross malapportionment, and a history of blatant racial discrimination in voting rights questions. Southern states, as noted in Chapter VI, did present especially juicy factual backgrounds for pioneering efforts at intervention, and we have no way of knowing whether the hint of regional bias in Stewart's pioneering opinions would have been any more viable in general application than that of the majority's Fundamental Principle, which did not turn out to show serious bias against the South, despite initial appearances. I do not mean to worry the question of inconsistency beyond its proper due. Most cases which come before the Court could be argued in all sorts of different ways, and no one should be surprised if a given justice—especially one arguing for an intermediate position of selective intervention—does not line all of his opinions down the same axis. It seems to me that Stewart's opinions compared very favorably in the matter of consistency with those of such unflagging champions of intervention as Douglas and Goldberg and could even hold their own against the opinions of Harlan, leading champion of careful judicial craftsmanship.

As a matter of legislative policy, I conclude that selective intervention would have been a better choice for the country than either the Fundamental Principle or nonintervention. It seems to me that Stewart's Warren era opinions did show a way the Court could intervene selectively without bogging down in the breadth of its own discretion. His votes did suggest reasonable and comprehensible rules for intervention: gross malapportionment, low Dauer-Kelsay scores, large detrimental deviation of a few districts—courts should intervene; medium malapportionment, variance between largest and smallest districts—maybe intervene; mild malapportionment deriving from a constitutional plan, especially one approved by a majority of voters—no intervention. Voting qualifications involving racial discrimination or discrimination against servicemen—intervention; state poll tax and candidate qualifications—no intervention. No intervention against Congress under the circumstances of the *Powell* case, or against unequal districts in local or special purpose situations, or against gerrymanders, except exceptionally blatant racial gerrymanders. Without retracing all the arguments of Chapter VII, I should note that the interventions against gross malapportionment and racial discrimination at the polls were highly desirable; without retracing the arguments of Chapter VI, I should note that most of the interventions Stewart shunned were high-cost, irredentist adventures, dangerous in their implications to Court and country but offering little compensatory return in fairer or more effective representation. I am inclined to think (with due caution over the fact that it was never tried in general application) that Stewart did make a case for selective intervention, in spite of Frankfurter's warnings, as a practicable way to combat real malapportionment with a minimum of overkill.

A practical flaw in this argument is the fact that it is all in the past subjunctive. We can discern in retrospect the wisdom of selective intervention, but we cannot ask the Court to turn the clock back to 1963 and take a more moderate path—though we can hope that future Courts will be more sympathetic to the selective approach. Those most critical of the Warren Court's approach to voting rights questions tend to those most wedded to old-fashioned notions of legitimacy, suspicious of tearing down constitutional structures, however grotesque, unless there is clear evidence that they will do serious harm if left standing. This cannot really be said of the Warren Court's handiwork in voting rights cases, which produced a few changes for the better, a few for the worse, and many with no discernible result at all. For the conservative of the organic tradition, solicitous of the Constitution as an encouragement to consensus, community, and mutual trust, it is no doubt sad that the Warren Court took unnecessary liberties with the Constitution, for these must surely have aggravated the bruises to consensus at the end of the sixties, but tearing up the Court's work could hardly be expected to remedy the matter.

As for the liberal reformer, I suppose that the dearth of practical benefits from reapportionment, relative to what was promised, might still be held preferable to the festering resentment of unequal districts which would probably still be with us if the reapportionment revolution had not taken place to show us how little difference equalizing the districts actually made. Conceivably, had it not been for the reapportionment revolution, deterioration of the cities in the late 1960's, still supposedly attributable to malapportionment, would have generated such a furor against malapportionment among the *illuminati* as to inject into the body politic an even more virulent strain of Fundamental Principle than Warren's or, failing that, would have left the Guardians in an even deeper state of frustration and despair than they were at the end of the Warren era. In this sense, the voting rights revolution may not have aggravated the legitimacy crisis of the late 1960's among the Court's constituencies, but tempered it—though my own conclusion is the reverse. In any case, the experience of the Fundamental Principle may have been of some value in showing its backer's hopes to have been ill founded, permitting the redirection of attention to more productive channels. I do think that

273

Court and country would profit from a more careful effort to distinguish between light and darkness in cases bearing upon our freedom to choose our own leaders and laws. I think that there is more light in the text and intent of the Constitution than was commonly supposed in the 1960's, and less in the dictates of the Guardian Ethic, and I cannot help thinking, as Burke did, that if you look hard enough, light and darkness are indeed tolerably distinguishable.

Appendix

Bibliography

Index

Appendix

Voting and Electoral Provisions

of the Constitution

Article I

Section 2. The House of Representatives shall be composed of members chosen every second year by the people of the several States, and the electors in each State shall have the qualifications requisite for electors of the most numerous branch of the State legislature.

Section 3. The Senate of the United States shall be composed of two Senators from each State [chosen by the legislature thereof] [1] for six years; and each Senator shall have one vote.

Section 4. The times, places, and manner of holding elections for Senators and Representatives shall be prescribed in each State by the legislature thereof; but the Congress may at any time by law make or alter such regulations, except as to the places of choosing Senators.

Section 5. Each house shall be the judge of the elections, returns, and qualifications of its own members . . .

Article II

Section 1. The executive power shall be vested in a President of the United States of America. He shall hold his office during the term of four years, and together with the Vice-President, chosen for the same term, be elected as follows:

Each State shall appoint, in such manner as the legislature thereof may direct, a number of electors, equal to the whole number of Senators and Representatives to which the State may be entitled in the Congress; but no Senator or Representative or person holding an office of trust or profit under the United States, shall be appointed an elector.

[The electors shall meet in their respective States and vote by ballot for two persons, of whom one at least shall not be an inhabitant of the same State with themselves. And they shall make a list of all the persons voted for, and of the number of votes for each; which list they shall sign and certify, and transmit sealed to the seat of government of the United States, directed to the President of the Senate. The President of the Senate shall, in the presence of the Senate and House of Representatives, open all the certificates, and the votes shall then be counted. The person having the greatest number of votes shall be the President, if such number be a majority of the whole number of electors appointed; and if there be more than one who have such majority, and have an equal number of votes, then the House of Representatives shall immediately choose by ballot one of them for President; and if no person have a majority, then from the five highest on the list the said House shall in like manner choose the President. But in choosing the President the votes shall be taken by States, the representation from each State having one vote; a quorum for this purpose shall consist of a member or members from two thirds of the States, and a majority of all the States shall be necessary to a choice. In every case, after the choice of the President, the person having the greatest number of votes of the electors shall be the Vice-President. But if there should remain two or more who have equal votes, the Senate shall choose from them by ballot the Vice-President.][2]

The Congress may determine the time of choosing the electors and the day on which they shall give their votes, which day shall be the same throughout the United States.

Article IV

Section 4. The United States shall guarantee to every State in this Union a republican form of government, and shall protect each of them against invasion, and on application of the legislature, or of the executive (when the legislature cannot be convened), against domestic violence.

Fourteenth Amendment

Section 1. All persons born or naturalized in the United States, and subject to the jurisdiction thereof, are citizens of the United States and of the State wherein they reside. No State shall make or enforce any law which shall abridge the privileges or immunities of citizens of the United States; nor shall any State deprive any person of life, liberty, or property, without due process of law; nor deny to any person within its jurisdiction the equal protection of the laws.

Section 2. Representatives shall be apportioned among the several States according to their respective numbers, counting the whole number of persons in each State, excluding Indians not taxed. But when the right to vote at any election for the choice of electors for President and Vice-President of the United States, Representatives in Congress, the Executive and Judicial officers of a State, or the members of the Legislature thereof, is denied to any of the male inhabitants of such State, being twenty-one years of age, and citizens of the United States, or in any way abridged, except for participation in rebellion, or other crime, the basis of representation therein shall be reduced in the proportion which the number of such male citizens shall bear to the whole number of male citizens twenty-one years of age in such State.

Section 5. The Congress shall have power to enforce, by appropriate legislation, the provisions of this article.

Fifteenth Amendment

Section 1. The right of citizens of the United States to vote shall not be denied or abridged by the United States or by any State on account of race, color, or previous condition of servitude.

Section 2. The Congress shall have power to enforce this article by appropriate legislation.

Seventeenth Amendment

The Senate of the United States shall be composed of two Senators from each State, elected by the people thereof, for six years; and each Senator shall have one vote. The electors in each State shall have the qualifications requisite for electors of the most numerous branch of the State legislatures.

When vacancies happen in the representation of any State in the Senate, the executive authority of such State shall issue writs of election to fill such vacancies: Provided, that the legislature of any State may empower the executive thereof to make temporary appointments until the people fill the vacancies by election as the legislature may direct.

This amendment shall not be so construed as to affect the election or term of any Senator chosen before it becomes valid as part of the Constitution.

Nineteenth Amendment

The right of citizens of the United States to vote shall not be denied or abridged by the United States or by any State on account of sex.

Congress shall have the power to enforce this article by appropriate legislation.

Twenty-Third Amendment

Section 1. The District constituting the seat of Government of the United States shall appoint in such manner as the Congress may direct:

A number of electors of President and Vice-President equal to the whole number of Senators and Representatives in Congress to which the District would be entitled if it were a State, but in no event more than the least populous State; they shall be in addition to those appointed by the States, but they shall be considered, for the purposes of the election of President and Vice-President, to be electors appointed by a State; and they shall meet in the District and perform such duties as provided by the twelfth article of amendment.

Section 2. The Congress shall have power to enforce this article by appropriate legislation.

Twenty-Fourth Amendment

Section 1. The right of citizens of the United States to vote in any primary or other election for President or Vice-President, for electors for President or Vice-President, or for Senator or Representative in Congress, shall not be denied or abridged by the United States or any State by reason of failure to pay any poll tax or other tax.

Section 2. The Congress shall have power to enforce this article by appropriate legislation.

Twenty-Sixth Amendment

Section 1. The right of citizens of the United States, who are eighteen years of age or older, to vote shall not be denied or abridged by the United States or by any State on account of age.

Section 2. The Congress shall have power to enforce this article by appropriate legislation.

Bibliography

Books

Almond, Gabriel, and Sidney Verba. *The Civic Culture.* Princeton: Princeton University Press, 1963.

Aron, Raymond. *The Opium of the Intellectuals.* New York: Norton, 1962.

Avins, Alfred, ed. *The Reconstruction Debates.* Richmond: The Virginia Commission on Constitutional Government, 1967.

Bain, Henry M., and Donald S. Hecock. *Ballot Positions and Voter's Choice: The Arrangement of Names on the Ballot and Its Effect on the Voter.* Detroit: Wayne State University Press, 1957.

Baker, Gordon, E. *Rural versus Urban Political Power.* New York: Random House, 1963.

Ball, Howard. *The Warren Court's Conceptions of Democracy: An Evaluation of the Supreme Court's Apportionment Opinions.* Rutherford, N.J.: Fairleigh Dickinson University Press, 1971.

Banfield, Edward C. *The Unheavenly City: The Nature and the Future of Our Urban Crisis.* Boston: Little, Brown, 1968.

———and James Q. Wilson. *City Politics.* Cambridge, Mass.: Harvard University Press, 1963.

Baran, Paul, and Paul Sweezy. *Monopoly Capital: An Essay on the American Economic and Social Order.* New York: Monthly Review Press, 1966.

Bazelon, David T. *Power in America: The Politics of the New Class.* New York: New American Library, 1967.

Beard, Charles. *An Economic Interpretation of the Constitution of the United States.* New York: Macmillan, 1913.

Becker, Theodore. *Political Behavioralism and Modern Jurisprudence.* Chicago: Rand McNally, 1961.

Bell, Daniel. *The End of Ideology.* New York: Free Press, 1962.

Benda, Julien. *The Betrayal of the Intellectuals.* Boston: Beacon Press, 1955.

Benson, Lee. *Turner and Beard.* Glencoe, Ill.: Free Press, 1960.

Berle, Adolf A. *The Three Faces of Power: The Supreme Court's New Revolution.* New York: Harcourt, Brace and World, 1967.

Berman, Daniel. *A Bill Becomes a Law: The Civil Rights Act of 1960.* New York: Macmillan, 1962.

Bernstein, Barton J., and Allen Matusow, eds. *Twentieth-Century America: Recent Interpretations.* New York: Harcourt, Brace and World, 1969.

Bickel, Alexander, M. *Politics and the Warren Court.* New York: Harper and Row, 1965.

281

_____ *The Least Dangerous Branch.* New York: Bobbs-Merrill, 1962.

_____ *The New Age of Political Reform: The Electoral College, the Convention, and the Party System.* New York: Harper Colophon Books, 1968.

_____ *The Supreme Court and the Idea of Progress.* New York: Harper and Row, 1970.

Binkley, Wilfred E. *President and Congress.* New York: Random House, 1962.

Birch, David C. *The Economic Future of City and Suburb.* New York: Committee for Economic Development, 1970.

Boulding, Kenneth. *The Impact of the Social Sciences.* New Brunswick, N.J.: Rutgers University Press, 1966.

Boyd, William D., and Ruth C. Silva. *Selected Bibliography on Legislative Apportionment and Districting.* New York: National Municipal League, 1963.

Brown, Robert E. *Charles Beard and the Constitution.* Princeton: Princeton University Press, 1956.

_____ *Middle-Class Democracy and the Revolution in Massachusetts, 1691-1780.* Ithaca: Cornell University Press, 1955.

_____ and Katherine Brown. *Virginia 1705-1716: Democracy or Aristocracy?* East Lansing: Michigan State University Press, 1964.

Bundy, McGeorge. *The Strength of Government.* Cambridge, Mass.: Harvard University Press, 1968.

Buni, Andrew. *The Negro in Virginia Politics, 1903-1965.* Charlottesville: University of Virginia Press, 1967.

Burnham, Walter Dean. *Critical Elections and the Mainsprings of American Politics.* New York: Norton, 1970.

Burns, James M. *The Deadlock of Democracy: Four-Party Politics in America.* Englewood Cliffs, N.J.: Prentice-Hall, 1963.

Butler, D. E. *The Electoral System in Britain Since 1918*, 2d ed. New York: Oxford University Press, 1963.

Chambers, William, and Walter Burnham. *The American Party Systems: Stages of Political Development.* New York: Oxford University Press, 1967.

Chomsky, Noam. *American Power and the New Mandarins: Historical and Political Essays.* New York: Pantheon, 1969.

Chute, Marchette. *The First Liberty: A History of the Right to Vote in America, 1619-1850.* New York: Dutton, 1969.

Claude, Richard. *The Supreme Court and the Electoral Process.* Baltimore: Johns Hopkins Press, 1970.

Conference of Research Scholars and Political Scientists. *One Man—One Vote.* New York: Twentieth Century Fund, 1962.

Congressional Quarterly, *Representation and Apportionment,* Washington, D.C., 1966.

Cortner, Richard C. *The Apportionment Cases.* Knoxville: University of Tennessee Press, 1970.

Corwin, Edward S. *Court over Constitution.* Princeton: Princeton University Press, 1938.

Coser, Lewis. *Men of Ideas: A Sociologist's View.* New York: Free Press, 1965.

Cox, Archibald. *The Warren Court: Constitutional Decision as an Instrument of Reform.* Cambridge, Mass.: Harvard University Press, 1968.

Crozier, Michel. *The Bureaucratic Phenomenon.* Chicago: University of Chicago Press, 1964.

Cummings, Homer, and Carl MacFarland. *Federal Justice: Chapters in the History of Justice and the Federal Executive.* New York: Macmillan, 1937.

Dahl, Robert A. *A Preface to Democratic Theory.* Chicago: University of Chicago Press, 1956.

_____ *Who Governs?* New Haven: Yale University Press, 1963.

David, Paul T., and Ralph Eisenberg. *Devaluation of the Urban and Suburban Vote,* 2 vols. Charlottesville: Bureau of Public Administration, University of Virginia, 1961-1962.

De Grazia, Alfred. *Apportionment and Representative Government.* New York: Praeger, 1963.

_____ *Public and Republic: Political Representation in America.* New York: Knopf, 1951.

Democratic National Committee, Commission on Party Structure and Delegate Selection, *Mandate for Reform.* Washington, D.C., 1970.

Diamond, Martin, Winston Fisk, and Herbert Garfinkel. *The Democratic Republic: An Introduction to American National Government.* Chicago: Rand McNally, 1970.

Dietze, Gottfried. *America's Political Dilemma: From Limited to Unlimited Democracy.* Baltimore: Johns Hopkins Press, 1970.

Dinsmore, Herman. *All the News That Fits.* New Rochelle: Arlington House, 1969.

Dixon, Robert G., Jr. *Democratic Representation: Reapportionment in Law and Politics.* New York: Oxford University Press, 1968.

Domhoff, William G. *The Higher Circles: The Governing Class in America.* New York: Random House, 1970.

Dorr, Thomas W. [attrib.]. *An Address to the People of Rhode Island from the Convention to Promote the Establishment of a State Constitution.* Providence, 1834.

Douglas, William O. *Points of Rebellion.* New York: Random House, 1970.

Dupré, J. Stefan, and Sanford A. Lakoff. *Science and the Nation: Policy and Politics.* Englewood Cliffs, N.J.: Prentice-Hall, 1962.

Dye, Thomas R. *The Politics of Equality.* Indianapolis: Bobbs-Merrill, 1971.

_____ and Harmon Ziegler. *The Irony of Democracy: An Uncommon Introduction to American Politics.* Belmont, Calif.: Wadsworth, 1970.

Elliot, Jonathan. *Debates on the Adoption of the Federal Constitution.* Washington, D.C., 1845.

Elliott, Ward E. Y. "Ideology and Intervention: Supreme Court Intervention in Voting Rights Disputes from Taney to Warren." Ph.D. diss., Harvard University, Cambridge, Massachusetts, 1968.

Elliott, William Y. *The Need for Constitutional Reform: A Program for National Security.* New York: McGraw-Hill, 1935.

_____ *The Pragmatic Revolt in Politics: Syndicalism, Fascism, and the Constitutional State.* New York: Macmillan, 1928. Repr. New York: Howard Fertig, 1968.

Ellul, Jacques. *The Technological Society.* New York: Knopf, 1964.

Flack, Horace E. *The Adoption of the Fourteenth Amendment.* Baltimore: Johns Hopkins Press, 1908.

Faulkner, Harold G. *The Quest for Social Justice, 1898-1914.* New York: Macmillan, 1931.

Flexner, Eleanor. *Century of Struggle: The Woman's Rights Movement in the United States.* Cambridge, Mass.: Harvard University Press, 1959.

Ford, Henry Jones. *The Rise and Growth of American Politics.* New York: Macmillan, 1903.

Galbraith, John Kenneth. *The New Industrial State.* Boston: Houghton Mifflin, 1967.

Gardner, John. *Self-Renewal: The Individual and the Innovative.* New York: Harper and Row, 1964.

Gillette, William. *The Right to Vote: Politics and the Passage of the Fifteenth Amendment.* Baltimore: Johns Hopkins Press, 1965.

Goldwin, Robert, ed. *Political Parties, U.S.A.* Chicago: Rand McNally, 1964.

———— ed. *Representation and Misrepresentation.* Chicago: Rand McNally, 1968.

Green, Fletcher M. *Constitutional Development in the South Atlantic States, 1776-1860: A Study in the Evolution of Democracy.* New York: Norton, 1966.

Griffith, Elmer C. *The Rise and Development of the Gerrymander.* Chicago: Scott, Foresman, 1970.

Grimes, Alan P. *Equality in America: Religion, Race, and the Urban Majority.* New York: Oxford University Press, 1964.

———— *The Puritan Ethic and Woman Suffrage.* New York: Oxford University Press, 1967.

Gusfield, Joseph. *Symbolic Crusade: Status Politics and the American Temperance Movement.* Urbana: University of Illinois Press, 1963.

Hacker, Andrew. *American Political Institutions and Public Policy.* Boston: Little, Brown, 1969.

———— *Congressional Districting: The Issue of Equal Representation.* Rev. ed. Washington, D.C.: Brookings Institution, 1964.

Hallett, Benjamin F. *Mr. Hallett's Arguments in the Rhode Island Causes.* Boston: Beals and Greene, 1848.

Hallett, George, Jr. *Proportional Representation–The Key to Democracy.* Washington, D.C.: National Home Library Foundation, 1937.

Handlin, Oscar. *The Uprooted.* Boston: Little, Brown, 1951.

Harris, Robert J. *The Quest for Equality.* Baton Rouge: Louisiana State University Press, 1960.

Hartz, Louis. *The Liberal Tradition in America.* New York: Harcourt, Brace and World, 1955.

Haskins, George Lee. *Law and Authority in Early Massachusetts: A Study in Tradition and Design.* New York: Macmillan, 1960.

Havard, William C., and Loren P. Beth. *The Politics of Misrepresentation.* Baton Rouge: Louisiana State University Press, 1962.

Hoffman, Ross J. S., and Paul Levack, eds. *Burke's Politics.* New York: Knopf, 1949.

Hofstadter, Richard. *Anti-Intellectualism in America.* New York: Knopf, 1963.

———— *The Age of Reform: From Bryan to F.D.R.* New York: Knopf, 1955.

Holcombe, Arthur N. *Our More Perfect Union: From Eighteenth-Century Principles to Twentieth-Century Practice.* Cambridge, Mass.: Harvard University Press, 1958.

Horn, Robert A. *Groups and the Constitution.* Stanford: Stanford University Press, 1956.

Huntington, Samuel. *Political Order in Changing Societies.* New Haven: Yale University Press, 1968.

Hyneman, Charles S. *The Supreme Court on Trial.* New York: Atherton Press, 1963.

Jackson, Luther P. *Free Negro Labor and Property Holding in Virginia, 1830-1860,* New York: Appleton Century, 1942.

Jacob, Herbert, ed. *Law, Politics, and the Federal Courts.* Boston: Little, Brown, 1967.

Jacobs, Clyde E. *Law Writers and the Courts: The Influence of Thomas M. Cooley, Christopher Tiedemann, and John F. Dillon upon American Constitutional Law.* Berkeley and Los Angeles: University of California Press, 1954.

Jaffa, Harry V. *Equality and Liberty: Theory and Practice in American Politics.* New York: Oxford University Press, 1965.

James, Joseph R. *The Framing of the Fourteenth Amendment.* Urbana: University of Illinois Press, 1956.

Jewell, Malcolm E., ed. *The Politics of Reapportionment.* New York: Atherton Press, 1962.

Kariel, Henry. *The Decline of American Pluralism.* Stanford: Stanford University Press, 1961.

Keech, William R. *The Impact of Negro Voting: The Role of the Vote in the Quest for Equality.* Chicago: Rand McNally, 1968.

Keller, Suzanne. *Beyond the Ruling Class: Strategic Elites in Modern Society.* New York: Random House, 1963.

Kendrick, Benjamin B. *Journal of the Joint Committee of Fifteen on Reconstruction.* New York: Columbia University Press, 1914.

Key, V. O., Jr. *Politics, Parties, and Pressure Groups.* 5th ed. New York: Crowell, 1964.

———— *Public Opinion and American Democracy.* New York: Knopf, 1961.

———— *Southern Politics in State and Nation.* New York: Knopf, 1949.

Kraditor, Aileen S. *The Ideas of the Woman Suffrage Movement, 1890-1920.* New York: Columbia University Press, 1965.

Krislov, Samuel. *The Supreme Court in the Political Process.* New York: Macmillan, 1965.

Kurland, Philip B. *Politics, the Constitution, and the Warren Court.* Chicago: University of Chicago Press, 1970.

Ladd, Everett Carl, Jr. *American Political Parties: Social Change and Political Response.* New York: Norton, 1971.

La Palombara, Joseph, and Myron Weiner, eds. *Political Parties and Political Development.* Princeton: Princeton University Press, 1966.

Lakeman, Enid, and James D. Lambert. *Voting in Democracies: A Study of Majority and Proportional Elections Systems.* London: Faber and Faber, 1955.

Lakoff, Sanford A. *Equality in Political Philosophy.* Cambridge, Mass.: Harvard University Press, 1964.

Lamb, Karl A., William J. Pierce, and John P. White, *Apportionment and Representation Institutions: The Michigan Experience.* Washington, D.C.: Institute of Social Science Research, 1963.

Larson, James E. *Reapportionment and the Courts.* Tuscaloosa: University of Alabama Press, 1962.

Lee, Calvin B. T. *One Man One Vote: WMCA and the Struggle for Equal Representation.* New York: Scribner's, 1967.

Lewinson, Paul. *Race, Class, and Party*. New York: Oxford University Press, 1932.

Lewis, Anthony. *Gideon's Trumpet*. New York: Random House, 1964.

Lieberman, Jethro K. *The Tyranny of the Experts: How Professionals Are Closing the Open Society*. New York: Walker, 1970.

Lipset, Seymour Martin. *Political Man: The Social Bases of Politics*. Garden City, N.Y.: Doubleday, 1963.

Llewellyn, Karl. *The Common Law Tradition: Deciding Appeals*. Boston: Little, Brown, 1960.

Lockard, Duane. *The Politics of State and Local Government*. New York: Macmillan, 1963.

Lovejoy, David S. *Rhode Island Politics and the American Revolution, 1760-1776*. Providence: Brown University Press, 1958.

Lowi, Theodore. *The End of Liberalism: Ideology, Policy, and the Crisis of Public Authority*. New York: Norton, 1969.

Mannheim, Karl. *Ideology and Utopia*. New York: Harcourt, Brace and World, 1936.

Mason, Alpheus T. *Harlan Fiske Stone, Pillar of the Law*. New York: Viking Press, 1956.

_____ *The Supreme Court from Taft to Warren*. Baton Rouge: Louisiana State University Press, 1958.

Mathews, John M. *Legislative and Judicial History of the Fifteenth Amendment*. Baltimore: Johns Hopkins Press, 1909.

Matthews, Donald R., and James W. Prothro. *Negroes and the New Southern Politics*. New York: Harcourt, Brace and World, 1966.

Matson, Floyd W. *The Broken Image: Man, Science, and Society*. New York: Braziller, 1964.

Merriam, Charles E., and Louise Overacker. *Primary Elections*. Chicago: University of Chicago Press, 1928.

Merton, Richard L. "The Negro in Virginia Politics, 1865-1902." Ph.D. diss., University of Virginia, 1918.

Mill, John Stewart. *Considerations on Representative Government*. 2d ed. London: Parker, Son and Bourne, 1861.

Miller, Charles A. *The Supreme Court and the Uses of History*. Cambridge, Mass.: Harvard University Press, 1969.

Mills, C. Wright. *The Power Elite*. New York: Oxford University Press, 1956.

Mowry, Arthur M. *The Dorr War: The Constitutional Struggle in Rhode Island*. Providence: Preston and Rounds, 1901.

Moynihan, Daniel Patrick. *Maximum Feasible Misunderstanding: Community Action in the War on Poverty*. New York: Free Press, 1969.

Murphy, Walter F. *Congress and the Court*. Chicago: University of Chicago Press, 1962.

_____ *Elements of Judicial Strategy*. Chicago: University of Chicago Press, 1964.

McCloskey, Robert G. *The American Supreme Court*. Chicago: University of Chicago Press, 1960.

McConnell, John P. *Negroes and Their Treatment in Virginia from 1865 to 1867*. Pulaski, Va.: B. D. Smith and Brothers, 1910.

McCulloch, Albert J. *Suffrage and Its Problems*. Baltimore: Warwick and York, 1929.

McKay, Robert B. *Reapportionment and the Federal Analogy*. New York: National Municipal League, 1962.

_____ *Reapportionment: The Law and Politics of Equal Representation.* New York: Twentieth Century Fund, 1965.

McKelvey, Blake. *The Urbanization of America.* New Brunswick, N.J.: Rutgers University Press, 1963.

McKinley, Albert E. *The Suffrage Franchise in the Thirteen English Colonies in America.* Philadelphia: University of Pennsylvania, 1905.

National Municipal League. *Compendium on Legislative Apportionment.* New York, 1962.

_____ *Court Decisions on Legislative Apportionment.* 13 vols. New York, 1962-1965.

_____ *Reapportionment: A Year in Review.* New York, 1963.

_____ *State Constitutional Reapportionment.* New York, 1962.

Navasky, Victor S. *Kennedy Justice.* New York: Athenaeum, 1971.

Nevins, Allan. *The American States During and After the Revolution.* New York: Macmillan, 1924.

Nisbet, Robert A. *Community and Power.* New York: Oxford University Press, 1953.

Ogden, F.D. *The Poll Tax in the South.* University: University of Alabama Press, 1958.

Olson, Mancur, Jr. *The Logic of Collective Action: Public Goods and the Theory of Groups.* Cambridge, Mass.: Harvard University Press, 1965.

Orfield, Lester B. *The Amending of the Federal Constitution.* Chicago: Gallaghan, 1942.

O'Rourke, Terry B. *Reapportionment: Law, Politics, Computers.* Washington, D.C.: American Enterprise Institute, 1972.

Peltason, Jack W. *58 Lonely Men: Southern Federal Judges and School Segregation.* New York: Harcourt, Brace and World, 1961.

Pennock, J. Roland, and John Chapman. *Representation: Nomos X.* New York: Atherton Press, 1968.

Pierce, Neal R. *The People's President: The Electoral College in American History and the Direct-Vote Alternative.* New York: Simon and Schuster, 1968.

Pole, J. R. *Political Representation in England and the Origins of the American Republic.* New York: St. Martin's Press, 1966.

Polsby, Nelson W., ed. *Reapportionment in the 1970s.* Berkeley: University of California Press, 1971.

Porter, Kirk H. *A History of Suffrage in the United States.* Chicago: University of Chicago Press, 1918.

Post, Charles G. *The Supreme Court and Political Questions.* Baltimore: Johns Hopkins Press, 1936.

Pranger, Robert. *The Eclipse of Citizenship: Power and Participation in Contemporary Politics.* New York: Holt, 1968.

President's Commission on Registration and Voting Participation. *Report of the President's Commission on Registration and Voting Participation.* Washington, D.C., 1963.

Public Administration Service, *State Legislative Redistricting.* Chicago, 1962.

Report of the Trial of Thomas Wilson Dorr for Treason. Providence: B. F. Moore, 1844.

Rhode Island House of Representatives. *Report to the Committee on the Subject of an Extension of Suffrage.* Providence, 1829.

Roche, John P. *The Early Development of United States Citizenship.* Ithaca: Cornell University Press, 1949.

Rodell, Fred. *Nine Men: A Political History of the Supreme Court from 1790 to 1955.* New York: Random House, 1955.

Rogin, Michael Paul. *The Intellectuals and McCarthy.* Cambridge, Mass.: M.I.T. Press, 1967.

Rose, Arnold. *The Power Structure: Political Process in American Society.* New York: Oxford University Press, 1967.

Rovere, Richard H. *The American Establishment.* New York: Harcourt, Brace and World, 1962.

Rourke, Francis, ed. *Bureaucratic Power in National Politics.* Boston: Little, Brown, 1965.

Sartori, Giovanni. *Democratic Theory.* New York: Praeger, 1965.

Scammon, Richard, and Ben Wattenberg. *The Real Majority.* New York: Coward, 1970.

Schattschneider, E. E. *The Semi-Sovereign People.* New York: Holt, Rinehart and Winston, 1960.

Schmidhauser, John R., and Larry L. Berg. *The Supreme Court and Congress: Conflict and Interaction, 1945-1968.* New York: Free Press, 1972.

Schmidhauser, John. *The Supreme Court: Its Politics, Personalities, and Procedures.* New York: Holt, Rinehart and Winston, 1963.

Schubert, Glendon, ed. *Reapportionment.* New York: Scribner's, 1965.

Schumpeter, Joseph A. *Capitalism, Socialism, and Democracy.* 3d ed. New York: Harper and Brothers, 1942.

Shapiro, Martin. *Law and Politics in the Supreme Court.* New York: Free Press, 1964.

Sinclair, Andrew. *The Better Half: The Emancipation of the American Woman.* New York: Harper and Row, 1965.

Shils, Edward. *The Intellectuals and the Powers.* Chicago: University of Chicago Press, 1972.

Slingsby, Stephen D. "The Gerrymander: Its Rise, Use, and Potential." Ph.D. diss., Claremont Graduate School, Claremont, California, 1967.

Smith, Constance E. *Voting and Election Laws.* New York: Oceana, 1960.

Strong, Donald S. *Negroes, Ballots, and Judges: National Voting Rights Legislation in the Federal Courts.* University, Ala.: University of Alabama Press, 1968.

Sutherland, Arthur S. *Constitutionalism in America: Its Origins and the Evolution of Its Fundamental Ideas.* New York: Blaisdell, 1965.

Talese, Gay. *The Kingdom and the Power.* New York: World Publishing Co., 1969.

Taper, Bernard. *Gomillion versus Lightfoot: Apartheid in Alabama.* New York: McGraw-Hill, 1962.

TenBroek, Jacobus. *Equal Under Law.* New York: Collier Books, 1965.

Timberlake, James S. *Prohibition and the Progressive Movement, 1900-1920.* Cambridge, Mass.: Harvard University Press, 1963.

Toennies, Ferdinand. *Community and Society (Gemeinschaft und Gesellschaft).* East Lansing: Michigan State University Press, 1957.

Toffler, Alvin. *Future Shock.* New York: Random House, 1970.

Tompkins, Dorothy C. *State Government and Administration: A Bibliography.* Berkeley: Bureau of Public Administration, University of California, 1954.

Truman, David, ed. *The Congress and America's Future.* Englewood Cliffs, N.J.: Spectrum Books, 1965.

Twiss, Benjamin. *Lawyers and the Constitution*. Princeton: Princeton University Press, 1942.

U.S. Advisory Commission on Intergovernmental Relations. *A Report to the President for Transmittal to Congress*. Washington, D.C.: Government Printing Office, 1955.

_____ *Report on Apportionment of State Legislatures*. Washington, D.C.: Government Printing Office, 1962.

U.S. Senate, *Hearings . . . on S.J. Res.* 7, 19, 32, 34, 38, 73, 87, 102, 105, 141, 147 (Lowering the Voting Age to 18) 91st Cong., 2nd sess., 1970.

_____ *Hearings . . . on S.J. Res.* 2, 37, 38, 44 (Reapportionment of State Legislatures), 89th Cong., 1st sess., 1965.

U.S., The Library of Congress, *Guide to the Study of the United States of America*, Washington, D.C., 1960.

U.S., The Library of Congress Legislative Reference Service, *Action with Respect to Apportionment of State Legislatures and Congressional Districting*, Washington, D.C., 1964, 1965.

_____ *Apportionment of Local Political Subdivisions and Judicial Districts*, Washington, D.C., 1965.

_____ *Apportionment of State Legislatures*, Washington, D.C., 1965.

_____ *Congressional Districting and Legislative Apportionment: Selected References*, Washington, D.C., 1965.

_____ *Congressional Districting and the Wesberry Case*, Washington, D.C., 1965.

_____ *Legislative Apportionment: A Study of the Issues*. Washington, D.C., 1965.

_____ *Legislative Apportionment: Statistics*, Washington, D.C., 1965.

_____ *Recent Supreme Court Decisions on Apportionment: Their Political Impact*. Washington, D.C., 1964.

_____ *State Constitutional and Statutory Provisions for Popular Initiative and Referendum with Particular Reference to Legislative Apportionment*. Washington, D.C., 1964.

_____ *State Conventions as Instrumentalities for Considering Ratification of Constitutional Amendments*, Washington, D.C., 1964.

_____ *State Petitions and Memorials to Congress on the Subject of Apportionment of State Legislatures*, Washington, D.C., 1965.

_____ *Withdrawal of Jurisdiction of Federal Courts over Questions of State Legislative Apportionment*, Washington, D.C., 1965.

University of Chicago Law School Library, *Federal and State Legislative Apportionment: A Selected List of References*, Chicago, 1962.

Vose, Clement E. *Caucasians Only*. Berkeley and Los Angeles: University of California Press, 1959.

Westin, Alan F., ed. *Freedom Now! The Civil Rights Struggle in America*. New York: Basic Books, 1964.

Wilson, Logan. *The Academic Man*. New York: Oxford University Press, 1942.

Williamson, Chilton. *American Suffrage: From Property to Democracy, 1760-1860*, Princeton: Princeton University Press, 1960.

Woodward, C. Vann. *The Strange Career of Jim Crow*. 2d rev. ed. New York: Oxford University Press, 1966.

Yellowitz, Irwin. *Labor and the Progressive Movement in New York State*. Ithaca: Cornell University Press, 1965.

Zeller, Belle, ed. *American State Legislatures: Report of the Committee on American Legislatures, American Political Science Association.* New York: Crowell, 1954.

Articles

Adiches, Roland. "California Reapportionment: A New Testament." 40 *S. Cal. L. Rev.* 696 (1967).

Anderson, Totten G., and Eugene C. Lee. "The 1966 Election in California." 20 *Western Pol. Q.* 535, 551 (June 1967).

Andrews, William G. "American Voting Participation." 19 *Western Pol. Q.* 639 (1966).

"Apportionment and the Courts—A Synopsis and Prognosis." 59 *Nw. U. L. Rev.* 500 (1964).

Auerbach, Carl A. "Proposal II and the National Interest in State Legislative Apportionment." 39 *Notre Dame Law* 628 (1964).

_____ "The Reapportionment Cases: One Person, One Vote—One Vote, One Value." 1964, *S. Ct. L. Rev.* 1.

Aylsworth, Leon E. "The Passing of Alien Suffrage." 25 *Am. Pol. Sci. Rev.* 114 (1931).

"Baker v. Carr and Legislative Apportionment: A Problem of Standards." 72 *Yale L.J.* 968 (1963).

"Baker v. Carr—Malapportionment in State Governments Becomes a Federal Constitutional Issue." 15 *Vand. L. Rev.* 985 (1962).

Baldwin, Fletcher N., Jr., and Stanley K. Laughlin, Jr. "The Reapportionment Cases: A Study in the Constitutional Adjudication Process." 17 *U. Fla. L. Rev.* 301 (1964).

Banfield, Edward C. "In Defense of the American Party System." In Robert Goldwin, ed., *Political Parties, U.S.A.* Chicago: Rand McNally, 1968.

Banzhaf, John E. "Multi-member Electoral Districts—Do They Violate the 'One Man, One Vote Principle'?" 75 *Yale L.J.* 1309 (1966).

Barclay, Thomas. "The Reapportionment Struggle in California in 1948," 4 *Western Pol. Q.* 317 (1951).

Bebout, John E., and John P. Wheeler. "After Reapportionment." 51 *Nat'l Civ. Rev.* 246 (1962).

"Beyond Wesberry: State Apportionment and Equal Protection." 39 *N.Y.U. L. Rev.* 264 (1964).

Bickel, Alexander, M. "Reapportionment and Liberal Myths." 6 *Commentary* 483 (1963).

_____ "The Durability of Colegrove v. Green." 72 *Yale L. J.* 39 (1962).

_____ "The Voting Rights Laws." 1966 *S. Ct. L. Rev.* 79.

Black, Charles, L., Jr. "Inequalities in Districting for Congress: Baker v. Carr and Colegrove v. Green." 72 *Yale L. J.* 13 (1962).

Blair, George S. "Cumulative Voting: Patterns of Party Alliance and Rational Choice in Illinois State Legislature Contests." 52 *Am. Pol. Sci. Rev.* 123 (March 1958).

Blume, Ralph R. "Use of Literacy Tests to Restrict the Right to Vote." 31 *Notre Dame Law.* 251 (1956).

Bondurant, Emmet J. "A Stream Polluted at its Source: The Georgia County Unit System." 12 *J. Pub. Law,* 86 (1963).

Bone, Hugh A. "States Attempting to Comply with Reapportionment Requirements." 17 *Law & Contemp. Prob.* 387 (1952).

Bonfield, Arthur E. "Baker v. Carr: New Light on the Constitutional Guarantee of Republican Government." 50 *Calif. L. Rev.* 245 (1962).

———— "The Guarantee Clause of Article IV, Section 4: A Study in Constitutional Disuetude." 46 *Minn. L. Rev.* 513 (1962).

———— "The Right to Vote and Judicial Enforcement of Section Two of the Fourteenth Amendment." 46 *Cornell L. Q.* 108 (1960).

Bryan, Frank M. "Who is Legislating?" 56 *Nat. Civic Rev.* 627 (December 1967).

Brzezinski, Zbigniew. "America in the Technetronic Age." 30 *Encounter* 16-26 (January 1968).

Burnham, Walter Dean. "The Changing Shape of the American Political Universe." 59 *Am. Pol. Sci. Rev.* 7 (1965).

Caruso, Lawrence R. "The Proper Role of the Federal Courts in the Reapportionment of State Legislatures." 36 *Miss. L.J.*, 300 (1965).

———— "Lucas Case (Lucas v. Forty-Fourth Gen. Assembly of Colorado, 84 Sup. Ct. 1459) and the Reapportionment of State Legislatures." 37 *U. Colo. L. Rev.* 433 (1965).

"Case for District Court Management of the Reapportionment Process." 114 *U. Pa. L. Rev.* 504 (1966).

"Challenges to Congressional Districting: After Baker v. Carr Does Colegrove v. Green Endure?" 63 *Col. L. Rev.* 99 (1963).

Celler, Emanuel. "Congressional Apportionment—Past, Present, and Future." 17 *Law & Contemp. Prob.* 268 (1952).

Chafee, Zechariah, Jr. "Congressional Reapportionment." 42 *Harv. L. Rev.* 1015 (1929).

"City Government in the State Courts." 78 *Harv. L. Rev.* 1596 (1965).

Claude, Richard. "Constitutional Voting Rights and Early U.S. Supreme Court Doctrine." 51 *J. Negro Hist.* 114 (April 1966).

Clem, Alan L. "Guidelines for Solving the Representation Riddle." 8 *S.D. L. Rev.* 109 (1963).

"Comprehensive Survey of Redistricting or Reapportionment Law." 48 *Marquette L. Rev.* 516 (1965).

"Congressional Apportionment: The Unproductive Search for Standards and Remedies." 63 *Mich. L. Rev.* 374 (1964).

"Congressional Exclusion and the Adam Clayton Powell Case." 14 *How. L. J.* 162 (1968).

"Congressional Quarterly Census Analysis: Congressional Districts of the United States." 22 *Cong. Q.* 1787-1798 (August 21, 1964).

"Congressional Reapportionment: The Theory of Representation in the House of Representatives." 39 *Tul. L. Rev.* 286 (1965).

Conron, Michael A. "Law, Politics, and Chief Justice Taney: A Reconsideration of the Luther v. Borden Decision." 11 *Am. J.L. Hist.*, 377 (1967).

Comment, "Constitutional Reform of State Delegate Selection to National Political Party Conventions." 64 *Nw. U. L. Rev.* 915 (1970).

"Courts and Legislative Reapportionment after Baker v. Carr." 1963 *U. Ill. L. Forum* 75 (1963).

Cox, L., and J. H. Cox. "Negro Suffrage and Republican Politics, The Problem of Motive in Reconstruction Historiography." 33 *J. Southern Hist.* 303 (August 1967).

Crosskey, William W. "Charles Fairman, 'Legislative History,' and the Constitutional Limitations on State Authority." 22 *U. Chi. L. Rev.* 1 (1954).

Dahl, Robert A. "Decision-Making in a Democracy: The Supreme Court as a National Policy-Maker." 65 *J. Publ. Law* 279, 284 (1958).

Dauer, Manning J. "Multi-Member Districts in Dade County: A Study of a Problem and a Delegation." 28 *J. Politics* 617 (August 1966).

Davis, J. W. "Implications of Baker v. Carr on the County Commissioner's Court in Texas." 17 *Baylor L. Rev.* 41 (1965).

Dawson, R. E., and J. A. Robinson. "Inter-Party Competition, Economic Variables, and Welfare Policies in the American States." 25 *J. Politics*, 265 (May 1963).

De Grazia, Alfred. "General Theory of Apportionment." 17 *Law & Contemp. Prob.* 257 (1952).

_____ "Righting the Wrongs of Representation." 38 *State Gov't.* 113 (1965).

Derge, David R. "Metropolitan and Outstate Alignments in Illinois and Missouri Legislative Delegations." 52 *Am. Pol. Sci. Rev.* 1051 (December 1958).

Dixon, Robert G., Jr. "Apportionment Standards and Judicial Power." 38 *Notre Dame Law.* 367 (1963).

_____ "New Constitutional Forms for Metropolis: Reapportioned County Boards; Local Councils of Government." 30 *Law and Contemp. Prob.* 57 (1965).

_____ "Reapportionment in the Supreme Court and Congress: Constitutional Struggle for Fair Representation." 63 *Mich. L. Rev.* 209 (1964).

_____ "Reapportionment Perspectives: What is Fair Representation?" 51 *A.B.A.J.* 319 (1965).

_____ "The Reapportionment Amendments and Direct Democracy." 38 *State Gov't.* 117 (1965).

_____ "The Warren Court Crusade for the Holy Grail of One Man—One Vote," 1969 *S. Ct. L. Rev.* 219.

Durfee, Elizabeth. "Apportionment of Representation in the Legislature: A Study of State Constitutions." 43 *Mich. L. Rev.* 1091 (1945).

Dye, Thomas R. "Malapportionment and Public Policy in the States." 27 *J. Politics* 586 (August 1965).

Easton, David. "The New Revolution in Political Science." 63 *Am. Pol. Sci. Rev.* 1051, 1059 (December 1969).

Edwards, Charles P. "Theoretical and Comparative Aspects of Reapportionment and Redistricting: With Reference to Baker v. Carr." 15 *Vand. L. Rev.* 1265 (1962).

Comment, "Effective Representation and Multi-Member Districts," 68 *Mich. L. Rev.* 1577 (1970).

Eisenberg, Ralph. "Legislative Reapportionment and Congressional Redistricting in Virginia." 23 *Wash. & Lee L. Rev.* 295 (1966).

Elliott, Ward E. Y. "Guilt and Overguilt: Some Reflections on Moral Stimulus and Paralysis." 78 *Ethics* 247-254 (July 1968).

_____ "The 18-Year-Old Vote: Constitutional Crisis in the Fall?" Mimeograph. Claremont Men's College, Claremont, California (June 1970).

Elliott, William Y. "The Constitution as the American Social Myth." In Read Conyers, ed., *The Constitution Reconsidered.* New York: Columbia University Press, 1938.

Emerson, Thomas I. "Malapportionment and Judicial Power: The Supreme Court's Decision in Baker v. Carr." 72 *Yale L. J.* 64 (1962).

Engle, Robert H. "Weighting Legislators' Votes to Equalize Representation." 12 *Western Pol. Q.* 442 (1959).

"Extraordinary Voting Requirements." 58 *Geo. L. J.* 426 (1969).

Fairman, Charles. "Does the Fourteenth Amendment Incorporate the Bill of Rights? The Original Understanding." 2 *Stan. L. Rev.* 5 (1949).

Farrelly, David G., and Ivan Hinderaker. "Congressional Reapportionment and National Political Power." 17 *Law & Contemp. Prob.* 338 (1952).

Finegold, Alan H. "Julian Bond and the First Amendment Balance." 29 *U. Pitt. L. Rev.* 167 (1967).

Flinn, Thomas A. "The Outline of Ohio Politics." 13 *Western Pol. Q.* 702 (1960).

Ford, Maurice. "Segregation in Northern Schools: Boston Is Forced to Look." 15 *Public Policy* 52, 73 (1966).

Frank, John P., and Robert F. Munro. "The Original Misunderstanding of Equal Protection of the Laws." 50 *Colum. L. Rev.* 131 (1950).

Frantz, Laurent B. "Congressional Power to Enforce the Fourteenth Amendment Against Private Acts." 73 *Yale L. J.* 1353 (1964).

Freund, Paul. "New Vistas in Constitutional Law." 112 *U. Pa. L. Rev.* 631 (1964).

Friedelbaum, Stanley H. "Baker v. Carr: The New Doctrine of Judicial Intervention and Its Implications for American Federalism." 29 *U. Chi. L. Rev.* 673 (1962).

Friedman, Robert. "The Urban-Rural Conflict Revisited." 14 *Western Pol. Q.* 481 (June 1961).

Frost, Richard T. "On Derge's Metropolitan and Outstate Delegations." 53 *Am. Pol. Sci. Rev.* 792 (1959).

Goldberg, Arthur L. "The Statistics of Malapportionment." 72 *Yale L. J.* 90 (1962).

"Government Litigation in the Supreme Court: The Role of the Solicitor General." 78 *Yale L. J.* 1442 (1969).

Graham, Howard J. "Our 'Declaratory' Fourteenth Amendment." 7 *Stan. L. Rev.* 3 (1954).

———— "The Conspiracy Theory of the Fourteenth Amendment." 47 *Yale L. J.* (1938).

———— "The Early Antislavery Background of the Fourteenth Amendment." 1950 *Wis. L. Rev.* 479, 610.

Hacker, Andrew. "Votes Cast and Seats Won." *Trans-Action* 7 (September-October 1964).

Hagan, Charles B. "The Bicameral Principle in State Legislatures." 11 *J. Pub. L.* 310 (1962).

Hakman, Nathan. "Lobbying the Supreme Court—An Appraisal of 'Political Science' Folklore." 35 *Fordham L. Rev.* 15 (1966).

Hamilton, Howard D. "Legislative Constituencies: Single Member Districts, Multi-Member Districts, and Floterial Districts." 20 *Western Pol. Q.* 321 (June 1967).

Hanson, Royce. "Courts in the Thicket: The Problem of Judicial Standards in Apportionment Cases." 12 *Am. U. L. Rev.* 51 (1963).

Harvey, Lashley G. "Reapportionment of State Legislatures—Legal Requirements." 17 *Law & Contemp. Prob.* 364 (1952).

Hatheway, Gordon W., Jr. "Political Gerrymandering: The Law and Politics of Partisan Districting." 36 *G. W. L. Rev.* 144 (1967).

Hofferbert, R. I. "Relations Between Public Policy and Some Structural and

Environmental Variables in the American States." 60 *Am. Pol. Sci. Rev.* 73 (March 1966).

Holls, F. W. "Compulsory Voting." 1 *Annals of the Am. Acad. of Polit. and Soc. Sci.* 546 (April 1891).

Irvine, William P. "Representation and Election: The Reapportionment Cases in Retrospect." 67 *Mich. L. Rev.* 748 (1969).

Israel, Jerold. "Nonpopulation Factors Relevant to an Acceptable Standard of Apportionment." 38 *Notre Dame Law.* 499 (1963).

_____ "On Charting A Course Through the Mathematical Quagmire: The Future of Baker v. Carr." 61 *Mich. L. Rev.* 107 (1962).

Jacob, Herbert. "The Consequences of Malapportionment: A Note of Caution." 27 *Soc. Forces* 256 (December 1964).

Jaffa, Harry V. "The Nature and Origin of the American Party System." In Robert Goldwin, ed., *Political Parties, U.S.A.* Chicago: Rand McNally, 1964.

Jewell, Malcolm E. "Minority Representation: A Political or Judicial Question." 53 *Ky. L. J.* 267 (1965).

Jones, Charles E. "Interparty Competition for Congressional Seats." 17 *Western Pol. Q.* 461 (September 1964).

Kauper, Paul G. "Some Comments on the Reapportionment Cases." 63 *Mich. L. Rev.* 243 (1964).

Kelly, Alfred. "The Fourteenth Amendment Reconsidered." 54 *Mich. L. Rev.* 1049 (1956).

_____ "The Congressional Controversy over School Segregation, 1867-1875." 64 *Am. Hist. Rev.* 537 (April 1959).

Kendall, Wilmoore. "John Locke and the Doctrine of Majority Rule." *Illinois Studies in the Social Sciences*, vol. 26, no. 2 (1941).

Kendregan, Charles P. "The Case of Adam Clayton Powell, Jr., and Julian Bond: The Right of Legislative Bodies to Exclude Members-elect." 2 *Suff. L. Rev.* 58 (1968).

Kennedy, Cornelius, B. "The Reapportionment Decisions: A Constitutional Amendment is Needed." 51 *A.B.A.J.* 123 (1965).

Klain, Maurice. "A New Look at the Constituencies: The Need for a Recount and a Reappraisal." 39 *Amer. Pol. Sci. Rev.* 1105 (1955).

Krastin, Karl. "The Implementation of Representative Government in a Democracy." 48 *Iowa L. Rev.* 549 (1963).

Kurland, Philip B. "The Supreme Court 1963 Term, Foreword: Equivalent in Origin and Title to the Legislative and Executive Branches of the Government." 78 *Harv. L. Rev.* 143 (1964).

Lancaster, Robert. "What's Wrong with Baker v. Carr?" 15 *Vand. L. Rev.* 1247 (1962).

La Palombara, Joseph. "Decline of Ideology: A Dissent and an Interpretation." 60 *Am. Pol. Sci. Rev.* 5 (March 1966).

Larson, James E. "Awaiting the Other Shoe." 52 *Nat'l. Civ. Rev.* 189-193 (1963).

Laughlin, Charles V. "Proportional Representation: It Can Cure Our Apportionment Ills." 49 *A.B.A.J.* 1065 (1963).

"Legal Problems of Ward Realignment in Philadelphia." 38 *Temple L. Q.* 174 (1965).

"Legislative Apportionment: A Judicial Dilemma?" 15 *Rutgers L. Rev.* 82 (1960).

Lerner, Max. "Constitution and Court as Symbols." 46 *Yale L. J.* 1290, 1319 (1938).

Lewis, Anthony. "Legislative Apportionment and the Federal Courts." 71 *Harv. L. Rev.* 1057 (1958).

Longaker, Richard P. "Andrew Jackson and the Judiciary." 71 *Pol. Sci. Q.* 341 (September 1956).

Longley, Lawrence, and John Yunker. "Who is Really Advantaged by the Electoral College—And Just Who Thinks He Is?" Paper delivered at APSA conference, Chicago, September 1971.

Lucas, Jo Desha. "Legislative Apportionment and Representative Government: The Meaning of Baker v. Carr." 61 *Mich. L. Rev.* 711 (1963).

———— "Of Ducks and Drakes: Judicial Relief in Reapportionment Cases." 38 *Notre Dame Law.* 401 (1963).

Marshall, Burke. "The Pattern of Southern Disenfranchisement of Negroes." In Alan F. Westin, ed., *Freedom Now! The Civil-Rights Struggle in America.* New York: Basic Books, 1964.

Merrill, Maurice H. "Blazes for a Trail Through the Thicket of Reapportionment." 16 *Okla. L. Rev.* 59 (1963).

Miller, Warren E., and Donald E. Stokes. "Contituency Influence in Congress." 57 *Am. Pol. Sci. Rev.* 45 (1963).

Mitchell, Stephen R. "Judicial Self-Restraint: Political Questions and Malapportionment." 39 *Wash. L. Rev.* 761 (1964).

Montague, Robert L. "The Role of Federal Courts in the Reapportionment of State Legislatures." 24 *Wash. & Lee L. Rev.* 227 (1967).

Murphy, Walter F. "Lower Court Checks on Supreme Court Power." 53 *Am. Pol. Sci. Rev.* 1018 (1959).

———— and Joseph Tanenhaus. "Constitutional Courts and Political Representation." In Michael Danielson and Walter Murphy, eds. *Modern American Democracy: Readings.* New York: Holt, Rinehart and Winston, 1969.

McBride, Conrad L. "The 1966 Elections in Colorado." 20 *Western Pol. Q.* 555 (June 1967).

McCloskey, Robert G. "Reflections on the Warren Court." 51 *Va. L. Rev.* 54 (1965).

———— "Foreword: The Reapportionment Case." 76 *Harv. L. Rev.* 54 (1962).

McDermott, John. "Overclass/Underclass: Knowledge is Power." 208 *Nation* 458 (April 14, 1969).

———— "Technology: The Opiate of the Intellectuals." 13 *New York Review of Books* 25 (July 31, 1969).

McKay, Robert B. "Court, Congress, and Reapportionment." 63 *Mich. L. Rev.* 255 (1964).

———— "Don't Amend the Constitution." 38 *State Gov't.* 121 (1965).

———— "Political Thickets and Crazy Quilts: Reapportionment and Equal Protection." 61 *Mich. L. Rev.* 645 (1963).

———— "Reapportionment Decisions: Retrospect and Prospect." 51 *A.B.A.J.* 128 (1965).

———— "Reapportionment: The Success Story of the Warren Court." 67 *Mich. L. Rev.* 226 (1968).

———— "The Federal Analogy and State Apportionment Standards." 38 *Notre Dame Law.* 487 (1963).

Nagel, Stuart S. "Applying Correlations Analysis to Case Prediction." 42 *Tex. L. Rev.* 1006 (1964).

Nahstoll, R. W. "The Role of the Federal Courts in the Reapportionment of State Legislatures." 50 *A.B.A.J.* 842 (1964).

Neal, Phil C. "Baker v. Carr: Politics in Search of Law." 1962 *S. Ct. Rev.* 252.

Newland, Chester A. "Legal Periodicals and the United States Supreme Court." 3 *Midwest J. Pol. Sci.* No. 1 (1959).

———— "Press Coverage of the United States Supreme Court." 62 *Western Pol. Q.* (1964).

"Nonpolitical Remedies of the People." 20 *N.Y.U. Intra. L. Rev.* 274 (1965).

O'Brien, F. William, "Baker v. Carr Abroad: The Swiss Federal Tribunal and Cantonal Elections." 72 *Yale L.J.* 46 (1962).

Oden, W.E., and R. L. Meek. "Implications of Baker v. Carr on the County Commissioner's Court in Texas, by J. W. Davis: A Rebuttal." 18 *Baylor L. Rev.* 15 (1966).

"One Man, One Vote and Selection of Delegates to National Nominating Conventions." 37 *Chi. L. Rev.* 536 (1970).

Parsons, Talcott. "On the Concept of Political Power." In his *Sociological Theory and Modern Society*. New York: Free Press, 1967.

Paschal, Joel F. "The House of Representatives: Grand Depository of the Democratic Principle?" 17 *Law & Contemp. Prob.* 276 (1952).

Perrin, Noel. "In Defense of Country Votes." *Yale Rev.* 23 (Fall 1962).

Peter, Roger P. "Molar Motions in Supreme Court Decisions." 37 *Notre Dame Law.* 128 (1961).

———— "Political Factors and Voter Registration in the South." 57 *Am. Pol. Sci. Rev.* 355 (June 1963).

"Political Gerrymandering: The Law and Politics of Partisan Districting." 36 *Geo. Wash. L. Rev.* 144 (1967).

Pollak, Louis H. "Judicial Power and 'The Politics of the People.' " 72 *Yale L. J.* 81 (1962).

"The Power of a House of Congress to Judge the Qualifications of Its Members." 81 *Harv. L. Rev.* 673 (1968).

Prendergast, William B. "Memorandum on Congressional Redistricting." Republican National Committee, Jan. 8, 1963.

"The Presidential Nomination: Equal Protection at the Grass Roots." 42 *S. Cal. L. Rev.* 169 (1969).

Pulsipher, Allen G., and James L. Weatherby. "Malapportionment Party Competition, and the Functional Distribution of Governmental Expenditures." 62 *Am. Pol. Sci. Rev.* 1207, 1919 (December 1968).

Rankin, J. L. "High Price Exacted for not Entering the Political Thicket." 15 *Am. U.L. Rev.* 1 (1965).

"Reapportionment." 79 *Harv. L. Rev.* 1228 (1966).

"Reapportionment of the California County Central Committees." 18 *Stan. L. Rev.* 742 (1966).

"Reflections of the Electoral College." 13 *Vill. L. Rev.* 303 (1968).

"Regulation of Political Parties: Vote Dilution in the Presidential Nomination Procedure." 54 *Iowa L. Rev.* 471 (1968).

Rodell, Fred. "For Every Justice, Judicial Deference is a Sometime Thing." 50 *Geo. L. J.* 700 (1962).

Roeck, Ernest G., Jr. "Measuring Compactness as a Requirement of Legislative Apportionment." 5 *Midwest J. Pol. Sci.* 70 (1961).

"Role of State and Federal Courts in State Legislative Reapportionment—the New York Conflict." 50 *Minn. L. Rev.* 714 (1966).

Roll, Charles W., Jr. "We, Some of the People: Apportionment in the 13 State Conventions Ratifying the Constitution." 56 *J. Am. Hist.* 21 (June 1969).

Rourke, F. E. "Urbanism and the National Party Organization." 18 *Western Pol. Q.* 149 (March 1965).

Rudolph, W. M. A. "A Conservative Defense of Individual Rights." 45 *Neb. L. Rev.* 854 (1964).

Sandalow, Terrance. "The Limits of Municipal Power under Home Rule: A Role for the Courts." 48 *Minn. L. Rev.* 643 (1964).

Scanlan, Alfred L. "Problems of Pleading, Proof, and Persuasion in a Reapportionment Case." 38 *Notre Dame Law.* 415 (1963).

Schaar, John, and Wolin Sheldon. "Education in the Technological Society." 13 *New York Review of Books* 3 (Oct. 9, 1969).

Scharpf, Fritz W. "Judicial Review and the Political Question: A Functional Analysis." 75 *Yale L. J.* 517 (1966).

Schattschneider, E. E. "Urbanization & Reapportionment." 72 *Yale L. J.* 7 (1962).

Schmeckbier, Laurence F. "The Method of Equal Proportions." 17 *Law & Contemp. Prob.* 302 (1952).

Schmidhauser, John. "Judicial Behavior and the Sectional Crisis of 1837-1860." 23 *J. Politics* 615 (November 1961).

Schmidt, John R., and Wayne W. Whalen. "Credentials Contests at the 1968—and 1972—Democratic National Conventions." 82 *Harv. L. Rev.* 1438 (1969).

Schubert, Glendon, and Charles Press. "Measuring Malapportionment." 58 *Am. Pol. Sci. Rev.* 302, 966-970 (1964).

Seagull, Louis. "The Youth Vote and Change in American Politics." Paper delivered at APSA Conference, Chicago, September 1971.

"Selection of Delegates to Conventions." 78 *Yale L. J.* 1228 (1969).

Sentell, R. Perry, Jr. "Reapportionment and Local Government." 1 *Ga. L. Rev.* 596 (1967).

Sharkansky, Ira. "Voting Behavior of Metropolitan Congressmen: Prospects for Changes with Reapportionment." 28 *J. Politics* 774 (1966).

Shils, Edward. "The End of Ideology." 5 *Encounter* 52 (1955).

Short, Lloyd M. "States That Have Not Met Their Constitutional Requirements." 17 *Law & Contemp. Prob.* 377 (1952).

Shull, Charles W. "Political and Partisan Implications of State Legislative Apportionment." 17 *Law & Contemp. Prob.* 417 (1952).

Sickels, Robert J. "Dragons, Bacon Strips, and Dumbbells—Who's Afraid of Reapportionment?" 75 *Yale L. J.* 1300 (1966).

_____ "Power Index and the Electoral College: A Challenge to Banzhaf's Analysis." 14 *Vill. L. Rev.* 87 (1968).

Silva, Ruth C. "Compared Values of the Single- and Multi-Member Legislative District." 17 *Western Pol. Q.* 504 (1964).

_____ "Reapportionment and Redistricting." 213 *Scientific American* 20 (November 1965).

Sindler, Alan P. "Baker v. Carr: How to 'Sear the Conscience' of Legislators." 72 *Yale L. J.* 23 (1962).

Snyder, L. B., and Pearson, R. N. "Effect of Malapportionment Cases on

Political Subdivisions of the State." 39 *Conn. Bar J.* 1 (1965).

"Social and Economic Factors and Negro Voting Registration in the South." 57 *Am. Pol. Sci. Rev.* 24 (March 1963).

Sokolow, Alvin D. "After Reapportionment: Numbers of Policies." 19 *Western Pol. Q.* Supp. 21 (September 1966).

Srb, Hugo F. "The Unicameral Legislature—A Successful Innovation." 40 *Neb. L. Rev.* 626 (1961).

"The Strange Career of State Action Under the Fifteenth Amendment." 74 *Yale L. J.* 1448 (1965).

Starzinger, Vincent E. "The British Pattern of Apportionment." *Va. Q. Rev.*, vol. 41, no. 3 (1965).

Sterling, Carleton W. "The Failure of Bloc Voting in the Electoral College to Benefit Urban Liberal and Ethnic Groups." Paper delivered at APSA Convention, Los Angeles, September 1970.

Sutherland, Arthur S. "Establishment According to *Engel.*" *Harv. L. Rev.* 25, 40 (1962).

Swindler, William F. "Reapportionment: Revisionism or Revolution." 43 *N. C. L. Rev.* 55 (1964).

Swinney, Everette. "Enforcing the Fifteenth Amendment, 1870-1877." 28 *J. Southern Hist.* 202 (May 1962).

Symposium. "Comments on Powell v. McCormack." 17 *U.C.L.A. L. Rev.* 1 (1969).

Tabor, Neil. "The Gerrymandering of State and Federal Legislative Districts." 16 *Md. L. Rev.* 277 (1956).

Taylor, William L. "Legal Action to Enjoin Legislative Malapportionment: The Political Question Doctrine." 34 *So. Cal. L. Rev.* 179 (1961).

"The Apportionment Cases: An Expanded Concept of Equal Protection." 1965 *Wis. L. Rev.* 606 (1965).

"The Equal-Population Standard: A New Concept of Equal Protection in State Apportionment Cases." *U. Cinc. L. Rev.* 483 (1964).

Todd, James E. "The Apportionment Problem Faced by the States." 17 *Law & Contemp. Prob.* 314 (1952).

Tollett, K. S. "Political Questions and the Law." 42 *U. Det. L. J.* 439 (1965).

Tyler, Gus. "Court Versus Legislature." 27 *Law & Contemp. Prob.* 390 (1962).

Van Alstyne, William. "The Fourteenth Amendment, the Right to Vote, and the Understanding of the 39th Congress." 1965 *S. Ct. L. Rev.* 33.

Velvel, Lawrence. "Suggested Approaches to Constitutional Adjudication and Apportionment." 12 *U.C.L.A. L. Rev.* 1381 (1965).

Vickery, William. "On the Prevention of Gerrymandering." 76 *Pol. Sci. Q.* 105 (1961).

Vose, Clement E. "Interest Groups, Judicial Review, and Local Government." 19 *Western Pol. Q.* 83 (1966).

Waldron, E. "100 Years of Reapportionment in Montana." 28 *Montana L. Rev.* 1 (1966).

Wallace, L. H. "Legislative Reapportionment in Indiana: A Case History." 42 *Ind. L. J.* 6 (1966).

Weaver, James B., and Sidney W. Hess. "A Procedure for Nonpartisan Districting: Development of Computer Techniques." 73 *Yale L. J.* 289 (1963).

Weaver, James B. "Districting by Machine." 53 *Nat'l Civ. Rev.* 293 (1964).

Wechsler, Herbert. "The Political Safeguards of Federalism: The Role of the States in the Composition and Selection of the National Government." 54 *Colum. L. Rev.* 543 (1954).

———— "Toward Neutral Principles of Constitutional Law." 73 *Harv. L. Rev.* 1 (1959).

Weeks, Stephen B. "The History of Negro Suffrage in the South." 9 *Pol. Sci. Q.* 671 (1894).

Weinstein, Jack B. "The Effect of the Federal Reapportionment Decisions on Counties and Other Forms of Municipal Government." 65 *Colum. L. Rev.* 21 (1965).

Weiss, Jonathan. "Analysis of Wesberry v. Sanders." 38 *So. Cal. L. Rev.* 67 (1965).

Westin, Alan F. "The Supreme Court and Group Conflict: Thoughts on Seeing Burke Put Through the Mill." 52 *Am. Pol. Sci. Rev.* 665 (September 1958).

Willcox, Walter F. "Last Words on the Apportionment Problem." 17 *Law & Contemp. Prob.* 290 (1952).

Wilson, James Q. "Crime and the Liberal Audience." 51 *Commentary* 71 (January 1971).

"WMCA v. Lomenzo (84 Sup. Ct. 1418): A Case Study of Politics in Reapportionment Litigation." 1 *Colum. J. L. & Soc. Prob.* 1 (1965).

Wolfinger, Raymond E., and Joan Heifetz. "Safe Seats, Seniority, and Power in Congress." 59 *Am. Pol. Sci. Rev.* 337 (June 1965).

Wood, Forrest G. "On Revising Reconstruction History: Negro Suffrage, White Disenfranchisement, and Common Sense." 51 *J. Negro Hist.* 98 (April 1966).

Wright, Benjamin F., Jr. "American Interpretation of Natural Law." 20 *Am. Pol. Sci. Rev.* 525 (1926).

Young, George D. "The 1958 Special Session of the Missouri General Assembly." *Missouri Political Science Newsletter*, no. 3 (1958).

Zuckerman, George D. "A Consideration of the History and Present Status of Section 2 of the Fourteenth Amendment." 30 *Ford L. Rev.* 93 (1961).

Notes

Notes to Chapter I

1. Alexander Bickel, *The Supreme Court and the Idea of Progress* (New York: Harper and Row, 1970).

2. *Political Man: The Social Bases of Politics* (New York, Doubleday, 1960), epilogue, p. 403.

3. William Gillette, *The Right to Vote: Politics and the Passage of the Fifteenth Amendment* (Baltimore: Johns Hopkins Press, 1965); Alan P. Grimes, *The Puritan Ethic and Woman Suffrage* (New York: Oxford University Press, 1967); Chilton Williamson, *American Suffrage: From Property to Democracy, 1760-1860* (Princeton: Princeton University Press, 1960).

4. See E. E. Schattschneider, *The Semi-Sovereign People* (New York: Holt, Rinehart and Winston, 1960), p. 101.

5. Strictly speaking, a voting right is a right to choose between people or policies in an election. Felix Frankfurter distinguished questions involving group rights—reapportionment, gerrymandering, etc.—as "representation" questions, for having no bearing on who gets to vote. The majority of the Court, however, has consistently treated such matters as "voting" rights, for tactical reasons, but also because they do bear on how much people's votes count. Thus, in *Reynolds v. Sims*, 377 U.S. 533 (1964), the sections of the opinion (II and III) in which the Court set out to describe what rights it was trying to protect, it mentioned the right to vote thirty-six times and the right of equal representation only five times. The broader usage of the majority will be used in this book, comprehending not only the right to make a choice, but also the right to make one's choices effective.

6. Perhaps the greatest victory of the proponents of reapportionment was the public acceptance of the term *malapportionment*, even by opponents of reapportionment. The term is handy, but loaded, as it implies that all inequality of districts—which can be good or bad according to political context—is "bad apportionment."

7. 238 U.S. 347 (1915); 321 U.S. 649 (1944).

8. 369 U.S. 186 (1962).

9. See Arnold Rose, *The Power Structure: Political Process in American Society* (New York: Oxford University Press, 1967), chap. 2; Samuel Huntington, *Political Order in Changing Societies* (New Haven: Yale University Press, 1968), chap. 1; Talcott Parsons, "On the Concept of Political Power," in his *Sociological Theory and Modern Society* (New York: Free Press, 1967).

10. Max Lerner, "Constitution and Court as Symbols," 46 *Yale L.J.* 1290, 1319 (1938).

11. Adolf A. Berle, *The Three Faces of Power: The Supreme Court's New Revolution* (New York: Harcourt, Brace and World, 1967), p. 3.

12. See Theodore Lowi, *The End of Liberalism: Ideology, Policy, and the Crisis of Public Authority* (New York: Norton, 1969).

13. Samuel Huntington, "Congressional Responses to the Twentieth Century," in David Truman, ed., *The Congress and America's Future* (Englewood Cliffs, N.J.: Spectrum Books, 1965), p. 7.

14. Lowi, *End of Liberalism*, chap. 5.

15. Lowi, *End of Liberalism*, p. 144.

16. Rule interpretation itself loses its focus when the rules are cast in terms of "fair trade practices," "fair labor standards," "public convenience and necessity," "public interest," or "reasonable return on value." Is it any wonder that a Court habitually called on to make head or tail of such Delphic standards might be more cavalier than a nineteenth-century court with standards like "due process" and "equal protection of the laws?"

17. Belle Zeller, ed., *American State Legislatures: Report of the Committee on American Legislatures, American Political Science Association* (New York: Crowell, 1954).

18. Interest groups, such as the NAACP, the National Municipal League, and various liberal groups, did figure in many of the most important modern voting rights cases, but more by way of marshalling evidence to persuade the Court of the justice of their cause than by way of crushing opposition with weight of numbers. Even in marshalling evidence, the interest-group attorneys were often overshadowed by the solicitor general.

19. The Gallup poll showed that 52 percent of the sample (having been told the Supreme Court had ordered it) favored reapportionment; 23 percent favored a return to the old system; 25 percent were undecided. *New York Times*, July 17, 1969, p. 55. Kenneth M. Dolbeare, "The Public Views the Supreme Court," in Herbert Jacob, ed., *Law, Politics, and the Federal Courts* (Boston: Little-Brown, 1967), pp. 199-200.

20. Nor, as a general rule, was it a mandate of the Constitution, though this rule was not invariable (see Epilogue). Constitutional text and intent were a major consideration in abolishing white primaries, but most of the leading voting rights decisions of the Warren era were delivered in spite of the Constitution, not because of it.

21. The phrase "guardians of the civilized, humane values" is from Professor David Easton's 1969 presidential address to the APSA. It was addressed to political scientists but could easily be extended to include the many other reformist professors, press commentators, etc., who shared the same commitment to the "passionate truths" of the time. David Easton, "The New Revolution in Political Science," 63 *Am. Pol. Sci. Rev.* 1051, 1059 (December 1969).

More than the reformers of the old stamp, the Guardians spoke from a doctrinal consensus so broad and so unchallenged that monolithic organization and definition were not needed, or even thought of. The idea of the Guardians as a separate and definable body emerged, not in their heyday in the Warren era, but in the 1970's, when skeptical works like James Q. Wilson's "Crime and the Liberal Audience" (51 *Commentary* 71 [January 1971]), and the present work appeared, and also John Gardner's "Common Cause," which had the look of an attempt to organize a lobby of neo-Guardians. Wilson's "liberal audience" consisted of "activist professors whose advice—and more important, whose blessing—is valued; friendly syndicated columnists and key editors and reporters in the 'national' press (the New York *Times*, the Washington *Post, Newsweek*, etc.); wealthy individuals, mostly in New York (and some in Los Angeles) . . . and volunteer workers." While the liberal audience was not to be confused with the "Eastern Liberal Establishment" that "dictates" policy and "selects" candidates, it did have a principal hand between elections in determining the "standing" of various political figures. I suspect that Wilson's liberal audience is the direct descendant of my Guardians but ranged around issues of the early 1970's—crime, violence, etc.—rather than those of the 1960's, and is farther left of center (as of 1971) and more exclusively associated with the Democratic party than the Guardians.

Perhaps a summary of what the Guardians were *not* would help define what they were. They were not quite Wilson's liberal audience, being more closely tied to 1960's issues, more politically moderate, less closely identified with the Democratic party. They were not the New Left for the first two reasons, only more so. No one has been quite so ferocious in attacking the Guardians' policies and pretensions in the Kennedy-Johnson years as the radical-chic *New York Review*. See John McDermott, "Technology: The Opiate of the Intellectuals," *New York Review of Books* (July 31, 1969), pp. 25-35; John Schaar and Sheldon Wolin, "Education in the Technological Society," *New York Review of Books* (October 9, 1969), pp. 3-6. See also, John McDermott, "Knowledge Is Power," *Nation* (April 14, 1969); Noam Chomsky, *American Power and the New Mandarins: Historical and Political Essays* (New York: Pantheon, 1969); William O. Douglas, *Points of Rebellion* (New York: Random House, 1970); William G. Domhoff, *The Higher Circles: The Governing Class in America* (New York: Random House, 1970).

Nor were the Guardians the same thing as the American establishment, though the establishment might have been considered the conservative wing of the Guardians. "The American Establishment" was a term used in the 1960's to describe a perceived body of exceptionally seasoned and respected men of affairs, whose reputation for liberal moderation and enlightened judgment carried great weight on the East coast and among intellectuals. If there was any such thing as an establishment, it was best described in Richard Rovere's tongue-in-cheek (but trenchant) *The American Establishment* (New York: Harcourt, Brace and World, 1962). Rovere believed that the establishment accommodated a wide range of moderate views "from about as far left as, say, Walter Reuther to about as far right as, say, Dwight Eishenhower." "It may be said," he added, "that those principles and policies that have editorial support of the New York *Times* are at the core of Establishment doctrine. And those irregularities and eccentricities that receive sympathetic *consideration* in the *Times* (not only on the editorial page but in the Sunday Magazine and the Book Review) are within the range of Establishment doctrinal tolerance" (pp. 11, 13). The Guardians as a whole were less established than the establishment, less seasoned, less well known, less rooted in the East, more impatient for reform, more passionate about the passionate truths of a highly reformist era.

Finally, the Guardians bore only a superficial resemblance to Plato's

Guardians. Though they did seek to guide power with knowledge, their notion of knowledge was quite different from Plato's, being intensely pragmatic and even antiphilosophical, where Plato's was quite the reverse.

22. An ideology is a pattern of abstract beliefs by which men evaluate political aims and events. Sociologists Daniel Bell, Seymour Martin Lipset, and Edward Shils thought we were too sophisticated for such things. Bell, *The End of Ideology* (Glencoe, Ill.: Free Press, 1960); Lipset, *Political Man*, epilogue; Shils, "The End of Ideology," 5 *Encounter* 52 (1955).

23. "Like the wealth of an economy," said Samuel Huntington, "power in a polity exists in two dimensions not just one. It can be expanded and contracted as well as concentrated and dispersed. . . . The amount of power in a society depends upon the number and intensity of the influence relationships within the society, that is, relationships in which action by one person or group produces changes in the behavior of another person or group." *Political Order in Changing Societies* (New Haven: Yale University Press, 1968), p. 143.

24. 328 U.S. 549 (1946).

25. Zeller, *American State Legislatures*, pp. 45-46.

26. 128 *Nation* 389 (May 1, 1954); 296 *Annals of the American Academy* 172 (November 1954); *Christian Science Monitor* (May 8, 1954), p. 9.

27. Charles Hyneman, 48 *Am. Pol. Sci. Rev.* 864, 865-868 (1954).

28. Respectively, United States Commission on Intergovernmental Relations, *A Report to the President for Transmittal to Congress* (Washington, D.C.: Government Printing Office, 1955); Baker, *Rural versus Urban Political Power* (New York: Random House, 1955); Lewis, "Legislative Reapportionment and the Federal Courts," 71 *Harv. L. Rev.* 1057 (1958); David and Eisenberg, *Devaluation of the Urban and Suburban Vote*, 2 vols. (Charlottesville: Bureau of Public Administration, University of Virginia, 1961).

29. 52 *Am. Pol. Sci. Rev.* 1051 (Dec. 1958).

30. Robert Friedman, "The Urban-Rural Conflict Revisited," 14 *Western Pol. Q.* 781 (June 1961).

31. Robert G. McCloskey, "Foreword: The Reapportionment Case," 76 *Harv. L. Rev.* 54 (1962); Phil C. Neal, "Baker v. Carr: Politics in Search of Law," 1962 *S. Ct. Rev.* 252; Alexander Bickel, "The Durability of Colegrove v. Green," 72 *Yale L.J.* 39 (1962); Robert G. Dixon, "Legislative Apportionment and the Federal Constitution," 27 *Law & Contemp. Probs.* 329 (1962); Philip B. Kurland, "The Supreme Court 1963 Term, Foreword: Equivalent in Origin and Title to the Legislative and Executive Branches of the Government," 78 *Harv. L. Rev.* 143 (1964); Martin Shapiro, *Law and Politics in the Supreme Court* (New York: Free Press, 1964).

32. Alfred De Grazia, *Apportionment and Representative Government* (New York: Praeger, 1963).

33. Herbert Jacob, "The Consequences of Malapportionment: A Note of Caution," 43 *Soc. Forces* 256 (1964); Thomas R. Dye, "Malapportionment and Public Policy in the States," 27 *J. Politics* 586 (August 1965); Alvin D. Sokolow, "After Reapportionment: Numbers or Policies?" mimeograph, University of California, Davis (March 1966); Richard I. Hofferbert, "The Relation Between Public Policy and Some Structural and Environmental Variables in the American States," 60 *Am. Pol. Sci. Rev.* 73 (March 1966). See Duane Lockard, *The Politics of State and Local Government* (New York: Macmillan,

1963), p. 319 on finding Massachusetts legislature with cities overrepresented no more responsive to urban needs than Connecticut, where cities were underrepresented. See also chapter VII for summary of these studies.

34. Robert G. Dixon, *Democratic Representation: Reapportionment in Law and Politics* (New York: Oxford University Press, 1968).

35. For example, Baker, *Rural versus Urban Political Power*; Andrew Hacker, *Congressional Districting: The Issue of Equal Representation*, rev. ed. (Washington, D.C.: Brookings Institution, 1964); William C. Havard and Loren P. Beth, *The Politics of Misrepresentation* (Baton Rouge: Louisiana State University Press, 1962); Malcolm E. Jewell, ed., *The Politics of Reapportionment* (New York: Atherton Press, 1962).

36. And one professor of English, Noel Perrin. Perrin, "In Defense of Country Votes," 52 *Yale Review* 16 (Autumn 1962).

37. "The Shame of the States," *New York Times Magazine* (May 18, 1958), p. 12.

38. *New York Times*, Nov. 25, 1960, p. 26, col. 4.

39. "On the Trail of the Fierce Gerrymander," *New York Times Magazine* (February 19, 1961), pp. 17, 20.

40. *New York Times*, Dec. 27, 1961, p. 26, col. 3.

41. "Voice of 90 Million Americans," *New York Times Magazine* (Mar. 4, 1962), p. 11.

42. Letter to the Editor, *New York Times Magazine* (Mar. 18, 1962), p. 24. A year later, under the sponsorship of the Brookings Institution, a repentant Andrew Hacker joined a triumphant Guardian host in demanding "equal votes for equal citizens" in the House—even though his computations showed no relationship between malapportionment and the defeat of Kennedy's liberal programs. Hacker, *Congressional Districting*, pp. 89-91.

43. Conference of Research Scholars and Political Scientists (CRSPS), *One Man—One Vote* (New York: Twentieth Century Fund, 1962), pp. 3-8, 17. See Dixon, *Democratic Representation*, pp. 286-288. Dixon wrote: "In retrospect, this leaflet may have been as influential as all of the briefs and arguments in the Supreme Court in the 'big six' cases [*Reynolds v. Sims*]. Interestingly, there was no counter-document, issued by a foundation of differing orientation and based on conclusions of other scholars, seeking to set forth counter-views. Possible counter-views could include the role of consensus in representation theory, the de minimis nature of an occasional deviant district to give a separated community a voice, the possible viability of a modified federal plan, or even an argument for proportional representation as the only logical answer to 'one man-one vote.' " The fifteen signers of the conference paper included ten political science professors, one journalist, one representative of the National Municipal League, one trade union official, one representative from the Ford Foundation, and one free-lance reporter. There was only one dissenter, political philosopher Alfred De Grazia.

44. CRSPS, *One Man, One Vote*, p. 17; *Wesberry v. Sanders*, 376 U.S. 1, 7-8 (1964); Dixon, *Democratic Representation*, p. 286.

45. "Historic Change in the Supreme Court," *New York Times Magazine* (June 17, 1962), p. 7.

46. "Also on The Bench: 'Dominant Opinion,' " *New York Times Magazine* (Oct. 21, 1962), p. 30. "By 'dominant opinion,' " Westin wrote, "we mean the active consensus of our era as represented in the passionate truths held by the majority of elected state and Federal officials[!], the leaders of the most

influential civic and religious groups, and those mass media trusted by the general public."

47. Commentators who seem to prefer to distinguish intellectuals from experts include: Joseph A. Schumpeter, *Capitalism, Socialism, and Democracy*, 3d. ed. (New York: Harper and Brothers, 1950), p. 145; Lewis Coser, *Men of Ideas: A Sociologist's View* (New York: Free Press, 1965), preface; Richard Hofstadter, *Anti-Intellectualism in America* (New York: Knopf, 1963), p. 25; Julien Benda, *The Betrayal of the Intellectuals* (Boston: Beacon Press, 1955), p. 30.

48. McGeorge Bundy, *The Strength of Government* (Cambridge, Mass.: Harvard University Press, 1968); Berle, *The Three Faces of Power*; John Kenneth Galbraith, *The New Industrial State* (Boston: Houghton Mifflin, 1967); Zbigniew Brzezinski, "America in the Technetronic Age," 30 *Encounter* 16-26 (January 1968); Lipset, *Political Man*, chap. 13. But see, Jethro K. Lieberman, *The Tyranny of the Experts: How The Professionals and Specialists Are Closing the Open Society* (New York: Walker and Co., 1970).

49. Even this scholarly solid ground, however, owes much of its solidity to professional convention, to shared perceptual preferences which facilitate agreement on what is true, what is false, what is important, and what is trivial. Accepted professional paradigms change from time to time, partly in accordance with better empirical observations, but also partly in accordance with intellectual vogues and volatile, quasi-aesthetic criteria. Thomas Kuhn, in his *Structure of Scientific Revolutions* (Chicago: University of Chicago Press, 1962), argues that consensus on explanatory paradigms has been the essence of scientific understanding. Scientists would choose a paradigm—say, the Ptolemaic universe, the phlogiston theory, or the periodic table of elements—on the basis of quasi-aesthetic criteria (economy, symmetry, simplicity, manageability, emotional appeal) as well as on the more strictly scientific criteria of internal consistency and consonance with observed facts. Thus, the Ptolemaic, earth-centered universe may have won out over the Aristarchan, sun-centered universe by virtue of its superior emotional appeal. It was more secure, more conceptually comfortable, more man-centered. As planetary observations became more precise, reputable astronomers had to fudge on some aspects of the Ptolemaic model to keep it "factual," but still earth-centered. They added epicycles and epi-epicycles to account for errant planetary orbits; Tycho Brahe was driven by his own precise observations to admit that the *other* planets might revolve around the sun, while insisting that the sun, planets, stars, and all still revolved around the earth, at tremendous speed, once a day. So qualified, the Ptolemaic system continued to accord with observed facts, but it lost its simplicity and symmetry. Scientists dropped it in favor of the now more elegant and manageable Copernican system. Thus also, molecular theorist James D. Watson knew by its elegance and economy that he had hit on the right theory for the structure of DNA: "It was so simple it had to be right." Watson, *The Double Helix* (New York: New American Library, 1968), p. 77.

Thus also, political scientists have found great attraction in the conceptual elegance of proportional representation, equal districts, compulsory voting, etc. These were prescriptive paradigms closely approximating a simple, symmetrical norm; moreover, they postulated a manageable political universe that was, or should have been, political-science-centered, which is to say, political-scientist-centered. "It was so simple it had to be right," except it was wrong because social sciences are different from natural sciences, which have no prescriptive dimensions and have lent themselves much more easily to paradigmatic summation. The political world has never been shown to be conceptually simple in the same sense as the Newtonian universe. As far as we can see, it does not repeat itself as invariably and exactly as planets and atoms do; it does not confirm and deny theories as readily as the natural world. Social and political theorists have written books, sometimes great ones, on the assumption that the social world is much simpler than it actually is. But the social theorist's greatness is perceptual, like that of an artist, not practical, like that of a doctor or a politician. Theorists' perceptions often do guide the actions of practical men, but they are seldom as directly suitable for the governance of society as practical men's decisions. Practical men are less bound to paradigms that are comfortable to theorists but not so comfortable to a public, which may (unless it is too carefully indoctrinated to the contrary) prefer a conceptually messy but responsive government to a neat but less workable one.

50. "Science as a Vocation," in Hans Gerth and C. Wright Mills, eds., *From Max Weber: Essays in Sociology* (New York: Oxford University Press, 1968), pp. 152-153.

51. Case studies: Dixon, *Democratic Representation*; Calvin B. T. Lee, *One Man One Vote: WMCA and the Struggle for Equal Representation* (New York: Scribner's, 1967); Bernard Taper, *Gomillion v. Lightfoot: Apartheid in Alabama* (New York: McGraw-Hill, 1963).

Statistical analyses: David and Eisenberg, *Devaluation of the Urban and Suburban Vote*; Glendon Schubert and Charles Press, "Measuring Malapportionment," 58 *Am. Pol. Sci. Rev.* 302, 966-970 (1964).

Grand theories: Walter F. Murphy, *Elements of Judicial Strategy* (Chicago: University of Chicago Press, 1964); S. Sidney Ulmer, "Mathematical Models for Predicting Judicial Behavior," in Jahnige and Goldman, eds., *The Federal Judicial System: Readings in Process and Behavior* (New York: Holt, Rinehart and Winston, 1968); Charles Black, *The People and the Court* (New York: Macmillan, 1960).

Critical analyses: Philip B. Kurland, "The Supreme Court 1963 Term, Foreword: Equivalent in Origin and Title to the Legislative and Executive Branches of the Government," 78 *Harv. L. Rev.* 143 (1964); Shapiro, *Law and Politics in the Supreme Court.*

Conveniently ideological: Hacker, *Congressional Districting*; Baker, *Rural versus Urban Political Power*; Richard Claude, *The Supreme Court and the Electoral Process* (Baltimore: Johns Hopkins Press, 1970).

Miscellaneous: Dixon, *Democratic Representation.* Dixon's book, which encompassed more than 400 cases with 21 chapters and ten major themes, is the magistral text on voting rights. Dixon did full justice to almost every item, at some cost in coherence, but with a thoroughness that will not soon be matched.

Ideological and miscellaneous: Robert B. McKay, *Reapportionment: The Law and Politics of Equal Representation* (New York: Twentieth Century Fund, 1965). I suppose the present book might also fall into this category.

52. *Ideology and Utopia* (New York: Harcourt, Brace and World, 1936), p. 156. Mannheim believed that intellectuals could take a more "total" view than ordinary mortals, being "to a large degree unattached to any social

class," and "recruited from an increasingly inclusive area of social life." More recent studies support Mannheim's belief that intellectuals—or at least college professors in certain disciplines—are less influenced than ordinary people by their class origins as indicated by the education and occupation of their parents. On the other hand, the professors seemed to be so homogeneous in their political views on a wide range of subjects, "from Vietnam to the hiring of black faculty, from busing on behalf of integration to the proper student role in setting course content," that two eminent analysts marvelled at the "intensely ideological character of the political thinking of American college and university professors." One of the analysts was Seymour Martin Lipset, who had joined in heralding the end of ideology a decade earlier. Everett Carll Ladd and Seymour Martin Lipset, "The Politics of American Political Scientists," 4 *PS* 135, 138-139 (Spring 1971). Sixty-one percent of American political scientists in the Ladd-Lipset sample were rated "very liberal or liberal," and doctrinal homogeneity within age groups and religious categories was even more pronounced. Seventy-three percent of the political scientists under 30 were rated "very liberal or liberal" (versus 40 percent over 50), and 81 percent of the political scientists of Jewish background (versus 56 percent Catholics, 60 percent Protestants). Ladd and Lipset also found a high correlation between scholarly achievement and liberalism. "Political scientists committed to research, currently publishing at a high level and teaching at major universities are, in each age stratum, the most liberal" (pp. 141-143). While not as liberal as sociologists (72 percent "very liberal or liberal"), political scientists (61 percent) held their own with psychologists (62 percent), anthropologists (64 percent), and economists (57 percent). Social scientists generally were more liberal (63 percent) than professors in the humanities (55 percent), law (51 percent), physical and biological sciences (38 and 35 percent), business (20 percent) and engineering (24 percent) (p. 139). Charles Spaulding and Henry Turner had roughly similar findings: 74 percent of political scientists in their sample were Democratic identifiers; only 10 percent rated "conservative." Spaulding and Turner, "Political Orientation and Field of Specialization Among College Professors," 41 *Sociology of Education* 247, 253 (Summer 1968).

   Why should social scientists be so much more consistently liberal on matters of public and academic policy than, say, engineers, or the public at large? Do they know something that the others don't? Or is there something in the logic of their position that conduces to a certain point of view? Lipset leaned toward the latter interpretation, speculating that orientation toward social problems should encourage, or be encouraged by, a liberal, critical feeling that the problems ought to be solved. Seymour Martin Lipset and Mildred A. Schwartz, "The Politics of Professionals," in Howard M. Vollmer and Donald L. Mills, eds., *Professionalization* (Englewood Cliffs, N.J.; Prentice-Hall, 1966), p. 304. And, if solved, how better than by the application of the methods one knows best? More detailed study, which might confirm or deny these speculations, would be a very welcome addition to our presently very sketchy stock of knowledge about professional perspectives.

   53. The question of the origins of the urban riots of the 1960's might illustrate this point. As far as I know, no one really knows what caused them, yet one could easily select which of the various potential responses to the question would be respectable and which not. Among the nonrespectable responses would be: (1) we don't know; (2) riots were in vogue; (3) rioters

wanted fun; (4) rioters wanted beer and TV sets; (5) rioters were genetically
aggressive; (6) police did not stop rioters; (7) lots of reasons. None of these
responses offered the specialist a preferred policymaking role. "Don't know"
and "lots of reasons" were respectively defeatist and pantheistic. "Police"
accorded the solution to a nonacademic profession. "Vogue," "fun," "beer
and TV," and "genes" were all unacceptable because none was subject to
rational manipulation or accountable to scholarly paradigms. Political scientists know less about vogues than dress designers. Sociologists and economists
know less about fun, beer, and TV than most of their students. Discussion of
genetic traits in regard to human beings was bad taste in the 1960's, since
Hitler had done it, and also because human genes could not be professionally
managed.

More respectable explanations for the riots were, in ascending order of
respectability: (1) rioters' family upbringing; (2) rioters' economic situation;
(3) rioters' school situation; and (4) white racism. All of these offered the
specialist a piece of the action, especially "economic situation," "school situation," and "white racism." "Family upbringing" presented difficult problems of expert management, though not insuperable: regardless of whether
the specialist tried to reform the family or bypass it, he had to think in terms
of doing it for a generation or more, a next-to-impossible task for the activists
of the time. "Economic situation" and "school situation" looked much better, readily lending themselves to static, quantitative evaluation, immediate
use of research talent, and solution with doses of money. Experts would be
center-stage and well funded, too.

"White racism," however, was the best of all the explanations by far,
for it combined a seemly appearance of modesty with an implied arrogation
of sole moral agency, such as in simpler times was reserved for the Deity. By
claiming the rioters as their own responsibility the Guardians were able to
reduce the rioters to a dependent variable and reaffirm their claim to the
master role, while noting that the situation called above all for the commitment of more technique and more money. From the evidence available, there
was very little reason to pick white racism over the other possible explanations of the riots, yet white racism was the stock explanation of the riot commissions, possibly because it whispered what the Guardians most wanted to
hear: that they were indeed Guardians, and that they needed fact-finding
commissions, advisory panels, lectures, courses, fellowships, monographs,
secretaries, books, money, and public recognition to finish off the problem
once and for all. The Guardians were known to be more high-minded than
ordinary people, but it strains credulity to think that they found much difficulty in choosing between a world view that offered them a secretary and one
that did not.

A good evaluation of the recommendations of federal commissions—by
someone other than another federal commission—is badly needed to help
show which recommendations are based on good evidence, which on a bare
canvass of conventional wisdom by the panelists and their staff, and which
are based on the appointing agency's desire to build academic legitimacy for
some policy or other. Much of the best thinking so far along these lines can
be traced to two maverick political scientists from Harvard, Edward Banfield
and James Q. Wilson. See Banfield, *The Unheavenly City: The Nature and
Future of Our Urban Crisis* (Boston, Little, Brown, 1968), *passim*, but especially chapter 9, "Rioting Mainly for Fun and Profit" (Crime Commission,

Riot Commissions); Wilson, "Violence, Pornography, and Social Science," *The Public Interest* (Winter 1971), p. 45 (Violence Commission, Obscenity and Pornography Commission).

For a consideration of the pretentiousness of affluent white intellectuals" claims of their own guilt, see my "Guilt and Overguilt: Some Reflections on Moral Stimulus and Paralysis," 78 *Ethics* 247 (July 1968).

54. Zeller, *American State Legislatures*, p. vi.

55. Bickel, *Supreme Court and the Idea of Progress*, p. 173. See also, Philip Kurland, *Politics, The Constitution, and the Warren Court* (Chicago: University of Chicago Press, 1970), especially chap. 4. For a more enthusiastic assessment of the Warren Court's accomplishment, see Archibald Cox, *The Warren Court: Constitutional Decision as an Instrument of Reform* (Cambridge, Mass.: Harvard University Press, 1968).

56. "America in the Technetronic Age," 30 *Encounter* 16, 23 (January 1968).

57. Alfred De Grazia, *Public and Republic: Political Representation in America* (New York: Knopf, 1951), p. 149.

58. Wilson's program was temporarily successful but ultimately a failure, perhaps because he tried to push it too far by appealing for a Democratic Congress in 1918. See Wilfred E. Binkley, *President and Congress* (New York: Random House, 1962), chap. 11.

59. Daniel Patrick Moynihan, *Maximum Feasible Misunderstanding: Community Action in the War on Poverty* (New York: Free Press, 1969).

60. Herbert Gans, "We Won't End the Urban Crisis Until We End 'Majority Rule,' " *New York Times Magazine* (Aug. 3, 1969), p. 12. Gans also called for one man, one vote at all levels of government, free television time to third, fourth, and *n*th parties, free postage and publicly financed polls to let legislators know exactly what the public wants, tax deduction for lobbying organizations, and strengthening of courts and cabinet departments which "represented" minority interests.

61. Liberal academics of the late 1960's, having lost faith in the presidency and Congress to fulfill the commitments of the early 1960's in the desired manner, turned to a kind of intellectual's populism, designed to use academic institutions as instruments to register and propagate their collective opinions. Organizations like the Caucus for a New Political Science and the Sociology Liberation Movement demanded that their staid old disciplinary associations take action to democratize their own procedures and end injustice in the outside world. Several professional associations transferred their 1969 conventions from Chicago to other cities to chastise Mayor Richard Daley and his police for interfering with the attempts of antiwar students to establish Participatory Democracy at the 1968 Democratic National Convention. At the better universities the air rang with demands for more faculty and student power and for collective stands on this or that issue: abolishing ROTC, government funding, investment in war-related industries, and correspondence with the draft authorities, providing housing and jobs for the poor, and stopping military intervention in Cambodia. Earnest young men, and old, rose at faculty meetings to demand academic freedom in both the old sense and the Guardian sense: insulation from the world combined with dominion over it; power, but without responsibility. All too often the rest of the faculty listened and agreed, somehow persuaded that converting the universities and the professional associations into representative institutions would add to the

responsiveness of the government without detracting from the autonomy of the universities. Perhaps they were attracted to Macaulay's vision of the American Constitution as "all sail and no anchor"—with each sail trimmed to catch a different wind and a committee of political scientists, sociologists, professors of English literature, and social gospel theologians at the helm (including, of course, a significant percentage of students, women, and blacks).

62. Democratic National Committee, Commission on Party Structure and Delegate Selection, *Mandate for Reform* (Washington, D.C., 1970).

63. Statement of former United States Attorney General Ramsey Clark, 27 *Congressional Q.* 4 (January 3, 1969). Since its vogue among political scientists in the 1890's, compulsory voting has popped up every so often, during periods of anxiety over the legitimacy of various governmental policies, in the thoughts of those subscribing to the silly notion that "the more nearly our citizenship turns out a 100 percent vote the better entitled we are to call ourselves a self-governing democracy." See *New York Times*, Editorial, Oct. 18, 1944, p. 20, col. 2 (calling for maximum, but not compulsory, mobilization of soldier vote).

64. Rexford G. Tugwell, *Model for a New Constitution for a United Republics of America* (Palo Alto: James E. Freel, 1971).

65. Proposal of Senator Walter Mondale, *New York Times*, Dec. 25, 1969. p. 28, col. 3.

66. Proposals of Professors Emmanuel Mesthene, of the Harvard Program on Technology, and Zbigniew Brzezinski, Columbia political scientist. *New York Times*, Jan. 18, 1969; Brzezinski, "America in the Technetronic Age"; Bundy, *The Strength of Government.*

67. Berle, *Three Faces of Power*, part 3.

68. The Guardians' faith in modernity and action combined to encourage them to look on political life as a succession of short-term crises, each in urgent need of a quick administrative solution. They had almost no sense of the longer run, scorning both past and future as unrelated to the nitty-gritty talk of getting the current job done. They lived in the present and the immediate future, protected from the past by Henry Ford's dictum that history is bunk, and from the more distant future by Lord Keynes' assurance that in the long run we are all dead. As Alexander Bickel pointed out in *The Supreme Court and the Idea of Progress,* they were infatuated with progress and resentful of old and persistent things like the Constitution for being "horse-and-buggy," and also for still being around. Some of the more perspicuous actually touted the planned ephemerality of their own "improvements" as an advantage for meeting the fast-changing conditions of modern life. Rexford Tugwell's disposable constitution accorded with this view (which also paralleled the vogue for situation ethics, then in full flower among theologians). John Gardner, Secretary of Health, Education, and Welfare under Lyndon Johnson and founder of the Guardian revival movement, Common Cause, also firmly believed in constant reorganization. Gardner, *Self-Renewal: The Individual and the Innovative* (New York: Harper and Row, 1964); see also, Alvin Toffler, *Future Shock* (New York: Random House, 1970), chap. 7, "The Coming Ad-Hocracy."

Trendy people that they were, and lacking in long-term perspective, the Guardians found it especially difficult to comprehend either John Marshall Harlan's preoccupation with the original understanding of the Fourteenth Amendment or Felix Frankfurter's appeals to the Court to think beyond the immediate problem in the light of the Court's capabilities for the longer run. Such long-run perspectives seemed unrelated to the overbearing need to solve the perceived crises of the time of which there were a great many.

Our faith in action has a long and honorable history, being deeply imbedded in our cultural heritage through the Greek myth of Prometheus, the Protestant and Hebrew concept of justification by deeds, and the Judaeo-Christian tradition of man as master of nature. See David McClelland, *The Achieving Society* (New York: Free Press, 1961), chap. 8, "The Spirit of Hermes"; Talcott Parsons, *The Social System* (Glencoe, Ill.: Free Press, 1951), pp. 58-67; Lynn White, "The Historical Roots of Our Ecological Crisis," 155 *Science* 1203 (March 10, 1967). It lent itself admirably to the Enlightenment, the Industrial Revolution, and the conditions of American politics during the heyday of the Roosevelt Consensus. All right-thinking men could join in hailing action in the public sphere for the betterment of man, as they had once hailed it in the private sphere. The Warren Court's judicial activism no doubt reflected a larger activism in a Guardian constituency which could not bear to see things left alone. By the same token, however, the Court also shared much of the opprobrium heaped on the Promethean powers of the 1960's who had raised high expectations of salvation through public action and then failed to fulfill them. Many of the crises of the 1960's were merely manifestations of secular forces which could not be settled with a single massive wallop of federal money and commitment, no matter how amply fortified with the Guardians' latest techniques of "crisis management." By the end of the 1960's, sobered by the government's failure to win quick victories in its wars on poverty and in Vietnam, people were more critical of things like action and commitment, recognizing them as means, not ends in themselves, and subject to judgment according to laws higher than action.

69. Even after the Guardian Ethic had fallen into popular disfavor for the executive and judiciary branches, it found new vigor in Congress (which passed the eighteen-year-old vote law and came very close to restructuring the electoral college) and also in the Democratic party, which actually carried out a resolution calling for something resembling proportional representation in its presidential nominating convention. These reformist efforts were Guardian to the core, even though they originated in agencies historically not greatly concerned with the Ethic. Their backers sought abstract, conceptual justice with little regard to political or institutional effects.

70. Hacker, *Congressional Districting*, p. 120.

71. 377 U.S. 713 (1964).

72. 27 *Congressional Q.* 4 (Jan. 3, 1969).

73. The curious ideal of democracy without consent, so popular among intellectuals of the 1960's, and among politicians and judges sensitive to intellectual vogues, had overtones of colonial administration. The Guardians, like their namesakes in the Indian Civil Service during the heyday of the British Raj, meant business about bettering the lot of the public, and they could not afford to tolerate the natives' attachment to their outmoded ideas and institutions. See Philip Woodruff, *The Men Who Ruled India* (New York: St. Martin's Press, 1954), II, *The Guardians*. I suspect that the Supreme Court's habit of intervening in the South had some reference to this feeling. The Guardians have always regarded the South, if not as a conquered province, at least as a province that ought to be conquered at earliest opportunity. Judicial innovations like reapportionment, right to free counsel, and ending poll

taxes and de facto segregation had a special savor of righteousness when visited on a people who preferred watching football to reading the *New York Times*. When it appeared that this and other benighted southern preferences were not confined to the South, it seemed only natural to treat the rest of the country as a conquered province also, ripe for the imposition of a federal rule.

74. Banfield, "In Defense of the American Party System"; Richard Scammon and Ben Wattenberg, *The Real Majority* (New York: Coward, 1970).

75. Bertrand de Jouvenel used the growth of formal democracy as one measure of the growth of tyrannous, centralized power. *On Power: Its Nature and the Origin of Its Growth* (New York: Viking Press, 1948), chap. 14, "Totalitarian Democracy."

76. *Smith v. Allwright*, 321 U.S. 649 (1944); *Terry v. Adams*, 345 U.S. 461 (1953).

77. 334 U.S. 1 (1948).

78. The half decade is compared with the twenty-six years it took to subdue white primaries, including seventeen years from the first white primary case, *Nixon v. Herndon*, 273 U.S. 563 (1927) to the main one, *Smith v. Allwright* (1944), and another nine years to end state arrangements which circumvented *Smith v. Allwright* (1944), and another nine years to end state arrangements which circumvented *Smith v. Allwright*.

79. *Gomillion v. Lightfoot*, 364 U.S. 399 (1960). See *Wright v. Rockefeller*, 376 U.S. 54 (1964).

Notes to Chapter II

1. Jonathan Elliot, *Debates on the Adoption of the Federal Constitution* (Washington, D.C., 1845), V, 385-386; *Federalist*, No. 52 (Madison). There is some reason to believe that the constitution would not have been ratified, had it not been for malapportionment in the ratifying conventions. Supporters of the constitution tended to come from overrepresented districts of small population; opponents tended to come from larger underrepresented districts. Charles W. Roll, Jr., "We, Some of the People: Apportionment in the Thirteen State Conventions Ratifying the Constitution," 56 *J. Am. Hist.* 21 (June 1969).

The Constitution has fourteen provisions related to the electoral process, reprinted in the Appendix and summarized below. Those bearing on the right to vote limit its abridgement by the states but confer no right directly.

> Article I, sections 2 and 3, and the Seventeenth Amendment provide for the election of Senators and Representatives, the current provisions requiring only that electors in each state shall have the qualifications requisite for electors of the most numerous branch of the state legislature. Article I, section 2 also requires that Representatives shall be apportioned among the several states "according to their respective numbers."
>
> Article I, section 4 authorizes the states to prescribe the times, places, and manner of holding elections for Senators and Representatives, subject to alteration by Congress.
>
> Article I, section 5 makes each house judge of the election of its own members.

Article II, section 1 and the Twelfth Amendment provide for the election of the President.

Article IV, section 4 guarantees to each state a republican form of government.

The Fourteenth Amendment requires the states to provide due process and equal protection of the laws; section 2 reduces the basis of representation of states denying or abridging the voting rights of adult males.

The Fifteenth, Nineteenth, Twenty-sixth, and Twenty-fourth Amendments bar abridgement of voting rights based on race, sex, age (above 18), and failure to pay poll tax in federal elections.

The Twenty-third Amendment permits Congress to appoint Presidential electors for the District of Columbia.

2. S. E. Morison, *The Oxford History of the American People* (New York: Oxford University Press, 1965), pp. 434-435, 491. The public not only endured but demanded political speeches hours long. In one of Morison's examples of the public's appetite for mighty orations "so many favorite sons preceded Webster at an evening rally that he did not come on until 2:00 a.m.; he talked for over an hour, 'and you could have heard a pin drop,' the audience was so entranced" (p. 491).

3. Chilton Williamson, *American Suffrage, from Property to Democracy, 1760-1860* (Princeton: Princeton University Press, 1960), chap. 2. Williamson's conclusion that few people were excluded from voting in late colonial times represents the modern consensus on an old question. Other works supporting this position are Forrest McDonald, *We the People* (Chicago: University of Chicago Press, 1958), p. 359, n. 1, and three books by Robert and Katherine Brown: Robert E. Brown, *Charles Beard and the Constitution* (Princeton: Princeton University Press, 1956), and *Middle Class Democracy and the Revolution in Massachusetts, 1691-1780* (Ithaca: Cornell University Press, 1955); and Robert and Katherine Brown, *Virginia 1705-1786: Democracy or Aristocracy?* (East Lansing: Michigan State University Press, 1964). The Browns' figures for Virginians voting in one county ranged from 44 percent of the adult white males to 63 percent; actual voters as a percentage of adult males in seventeen Massachusetts cities and towns ranged from 53 percent to 97 percent. *Virginia*, p. 146; *Massachusetts*, p. 50. The older view of Charles Beard, *An Economic Interpretation of the Constitution of the United States* (New York: Macmillan, 1913), p. 242, that as many as a third of adult males were disfranchised is defended by Lee Benson in *Turner and Beard* (New York: Free Press, 1960). For a tabular sketch of suffrage developments in the colonies, see Appendix II of the dissertation on which this book is based, "Ideology and Intervention: Supreme Court Intervention in Voting Rights Disputes from Taney to Warren," Ph.D. diss. Harvard University, Cambridge, Massachusetts, 1968.

4. Relaxed property qualifications by 1793: Pennsylvania, 1776; South Carolina, 1778; New Hampshire, 1784; Georgia, 1789; Delaware, 1792. By 1812: New Jersey, 1797, Maryland, 1810. By 1822: Connecticut, 1818; New York, 1821; Massachusetts, 1822. After 1822: Rhode Island, 1842; Virginia, 1850; North Carolina, 1854. Special provisions for militia: Mississippi, 1817; Connecticut, 1818; New York, 1821; Florida, 1838; Rhode Island, 1842. See Appendix II of Elliott, "Ideology and Intervention."

5. Paul Studenski and Herman Kroos, *Financial History of the United States*, 2d ed. (New York: McGraw-Hill, 1963), p. 54. Depreciation of paper money during the Revolution virtually nullified property requirements in Georgia, Maryland, New Jersey, and Rhode Island. Williamson, *American Suffrage*, p. 121.

6. Studenski and Kroos, *Financial History*, p. 131.

7. Fletcher M. Green, *Constitutional Development in the South Atlantic States, 1776-1860: A Study in the Evolution of Democracy* (New York: Norton, 1966), p. 212. Among the members of this notable and conservative convention were two ex-presidents, one a member of the conventions of 1776 and 1887; a future president; the chief justice of the Supreme Court; seven men who had been or were to be United States senators; fifteen representatives; four judges, four governors; and many members of the state legislature (p. 211).

8. As when Thomas Dorr slyly used the antiforeign sentiments of his opponents to press for abolition of the freehold: "while some of the descendents of the early settlers of the State have no vote in the places of their fathers, anyone may come in from abroad, and upon the purchase of real estate, and being propounded three months previously, may become a voter. We welcome strangers, but not to greater privileges than are enjoyed by the majority of our own citizens." *An Address to the People of Rhode Island from the Convention to Promote the Establishment of a State Constitution* (Providence, 1834), p. 53. This address is unsigned but attributed to Dorr.

9. Harper v. Virginia State Board, 383 U.S. 663 (1966) (abolishing poll tax in state elections).

10. Albert J. McCulloch, *Suffrage and Its Problems* (Baltimore: Warwick and York, 1929), p. 80.

11. James Kent, *Commentaries on American Law*, 10th ed. (1860), II, 278, cited by Stephen B. Weeks, "The History of Negro Suffrage in the South," 9 *Pol. Sci. Q.* 671, 679 (1894).

12. *Lynchburg Patriot*, May 23, 1850, quoted by Williamson, *American Suffrage*, p. 240.

13. Elmer C. Griffith, *The Rise and Development of the Gerrymander* (Chicago: Scott, Foresman, 1907), 16-19, 67-73.

14. Kirk H. Porter, *A History of Suffrage in the United States* (Chicago: University of Chicago Press, 1918), p. 117.

15. T. H. McKee, *Party Conventions*, p. 100, quoted by Porter, *History of Suffrage*, p. 129.

16. Porter, *History of Suffrage*, p. 116.

17. Porter, *History of Suffrage*, pp. 118, 131-132; Williamson, *American Suffrage*, p. 287. Several of the midwestern states, however, tried to attract foreigners by allowing prospective citizens to vote. See Appendix III of Elliott, "Ideology and Intervention."

18. 7 How. 1 (1849).

19. Dorr, *Address*, pp. 20-25. A Dauer-Kelsay score is the minimum number necessary to elect a majority in a legislature.

20. Dorr, *Address*, pp. 24, 55, 27, 32, 40-43, 27, and 29, respectively.

21. Dorr, *Address*, p. 26.

22. Arthur May Mowry, *The Dorr War, or the Constitutional Struggle in Rhode Island* (Providence: Preston and Rounds, 1901), pp. 113-114.

23. *Providence Journal* (March 3, 1842), quoted by Mowry, *Dorr War*, pp. 128-129.

24. *Burke's Report*, pp. 706-717, cited by Mowry, *Dorr War*, pp. 134-135.

25. *Report of the Trial of Thomas Wilson Dorr, for Treason* (Providence: B. F. Moore, 1844), pp. 37-42.

26. *Report*, p. 38.

27. *Report*, p. 39 (Justice Staples concurring).

28. *Ex parte* Dorr, 3 How. 103 (1845) dismissed for want of federal habeas corpus jurisdiction, because Dorr was confined under state authority.

29. As it happened, however, three justices—Catron, Daniel, and McKinley—were absent when the case was finally argued.

30. Article IV, section 4 of the United States Constitution: "The United States shall guarantee to every State in this Union a republican form of government, and shall protect each of them against invasion, and on application of the legislature, or of the executive (when the legislature cannot be convened), against domestic violence."

31. In fact, Tyler had done no such thing. His letter of April 11, 1842 to Governor King treated the Dorr controversies as "questions of municipal regulation . . . with which this Government can have nothing to do." He refused to aid the charter government on the ground that no actual insurrection existed but did accept it as his duty in the event of an actual insurrection "to respect the requisitions of that government which has been recognized as the existing government of the State through all time past [i.e., the charter government] until I am advised, in regular manner, that it has been altered and abolished, and another substituted in its place, by legal and peaceable proceedings." *Burke's Report*, House Reports, 28 Cong., 1st sess., no. 546, pp. 658-659. In other words, Tyler undertook to consider supporting the charter government, if need be, at a later date unless advised in regular manner that it was no longer legitimate. Tyler's letter was not nearly so much a gesture of support for the charter government as an attempt to stay out of the argument.

32. The Court had long since refused to review presidential authority to call out militia in *Martin v. Mott*, 12 Wheat. 19, 29-31 (1827); likewise, in *Foster v. Neilson*, 2 Pet. 253, 309 (1829), it had refused to challenge the president's position on a boundary question.

33. This principle had not been decided at the time of *Luther v. Borden* (1849); however, it was the same Court in 1851 which decided in *Cooley v. Board of Wardens*, 12 How. 299, that the commerce power could be exercised concurrently by the states.

34. *Mr. Hallett's Argument in the Rhode Island Causes on the Rights of the People* (Boston: Beals and Greene, 1848), p. 7. The Supreme Court, in *Swift v. Tyson*, 16 Pet. 1 (1842), had decided that federal courts were not required to follow the decisions of state courts in questions of general jurisprudence, but could make their own interpretations of the Common Law. This holding was reversed a century later in *Erie RR. v. Tompkins*, 304 U.S. 64 (1938).

35. Hallett's crowning authority was Webster himself, who had thundered against the Holy Alliances' claims to Divine responsibility in the *Laybach Circular* (1821). "Society, upon this principle," said Webster, "has no rights of its own . . . Its whole privilege is to receive the favors that may be dispensed by the sovereign power, and all its duty is described in the single word

submission . . . I want words to express my abhorrence of this abominable principle!" *Hallett's Argument*, p. 48.

36. *Hallett's Argument*, pp. 8-9.

37. Even if one counts James M. Wayne a Whig, as John Schmidhauser does despite his appointment by Jackson ("Judicial Behavior and the Sectional Crisis" 23 *J. Politics* 621 [1961]), and excludes the three Democrats, Catron, Daniel, and McKinley, who did not hear the case, the Democrats retained a majority of 4-2.

38. Arthur E. Bonfield, "Baker v. Carr: New Light on the Constitutional Guarantee of Republican Government," 50 *Calif. L. Rev.* 245 (1962); "The Guarantee Clause of Article IV, section 4: A Study in Constitutional Disuetude," 46 *Minn. L. Rev.* 513 (1962).

39. A similar line of reasoning later proved successful in *Ex parte Milligan*, 4 Wall. 2 (1866), which invalidated a United States Army court-martial conviction rendered under martial law in Indiana, where there had been no fighting.

40. Cherokee Nation v. Georgia, 5 Pet. 1 (1831); Worcester v. Georgia, 6 Pet. 515 (1832).

41. 5 Pet., p. 20.

42. The retroactive posture of the case also permitted Taney to treat the sovereignty question as one outside the Court's physical power to influence, much as questions of sovereignty in foreign countries—long recognized as political questions—were removed from the Court's jurisdiction by territorial space. Thus, in *United States v. Palmer*, 3 Wheat. 610, 635 (1818), the Court had refused to choose between two sides claiming sovereignty in a civil war in Spain.

43. See Douglas's disavowal of retroactive effect in his concurrence in *Baker v. Carr*, 369 U.S. 186, 250, n. 5 (1962); Fortson v. Morris, 385 U.S. 231 (1966).

44. *Ex parte* Young, 209 U.S. 123 (1908). This principle had been recognized much earlier in *Osborn v. Bank*, 9 Wheat. 738, 848-59, 868 (1824), but it had never been used independently to support an injunction.

45. 28 U.S.C. 2201 (1964).

46. Aetna Life Insurance Co. v. Haworth, 300 U.S. 227 (1937).

47. 376 U.S. 1 (1964).

Notes to Chapter III

1. William Gillette, *The Right to Vote: Politics and the Passage of the Fifteenth Amendment* (Baltimore: Johns Hopkins Press, 1965), pp. 26-27. Gillette's book is much the best available reference for the political undercurrents of post-Civil War voting reform. Also important are William Van Alstyne's attempt to show that section one of the Fourteenth Amendment could be used to protect voting rights, "The Fourteenth Amendment, the Right to Vote, and the Understanding of the 39th Congress," 165 *S. Ct. L. Rev.* 33; Edward M. Goldberg's "Mr. Justice Harlan, the Uses of History, and the Congressional Globe," 15 *J. Publ. Law* 181 (1966); Charles A. Miller, *The Supreme Court and the Uses of History* (Cambridge, Mass.: Harvard University Press, 1969), chap. 7, and John M. Mathews' early work *Legislative and Judicial History of the Fifteenth Amendment* (Baltimore: Johns Hopkins Press, 1909).

For a blistering assault on the motives of northern opponents of slavery before, during, and after the Civil War, see C. Vann Woodward's "White Racism and Black Emancipation," 12 *New York Review of Books*, no. 4, p. 5 (Feb. 27, 1969), also, Leslie H. Fischel, Jr., "Northern Prejudice and Negro Suffrage, 1865-1870," 39 *J. Negro Hist.* 8 (1954).

2. *Congressional Globe*, 38th Cong., 1st sess. (1864), p. 302.

3. For example, Robert J. Harris, *The Quest for Equality* (Baton Rouge: Louisiana State University Press, 1960); Joseph R. James, *The Framing of the Fourteenth Amendment* (Urbana: University of Illinois Press, 1956); Jacobus Ten Broek, *Equal Under Law* (New York: Collier Books, 1965), originally published as *The Antislavery Origins of the Fourteenth Amendment*; Benjamin B. Kendrick, *Journal of the Joint Committee of Fifteen on Reconstruction* (New York: Columbia University Press, 1914); Horace E. Flack, *The Adoption of the Fourteenth Amendment* (Baltimore: Johns Hopkins Press, 1908); Laurent B. Frantz, "Congressional Power to Enforce the Fourteenth Amendment Against Private Acts," 73 *Yale L. J.* 1353 (1964); Charles L. Black, Jr., "The Lawfulness of the Segregation Decisions," 69 *Yale L. J.* 421 (1960); Alexander Bickel, "The Original Understanding and the Segregation Decision," 69 *Harv. L. Rev.* 1 (1955); Alfred Kelly, "The Fourteenth Amendment Reconsidered: The Segregation Question," 54 *Mich. L. Rev.* 1049 (1956); "The Congressional Controversy over School Segregation, 1867-1875," 64 *Am. Hist. Rev.* 537 (April 1959); Howard J. Graham, "Our 'Declaratory' Fourteenth Amendment," 7 *Stan. L. Rev.* 3 (1954), "The Early Antislavery Background of the Fourteenth Amendment," 1950 *Wis. L. Rev.* 479, 610 and "The Conspiracy Theory of the Fourteenth Amendment," 47 *Yale L. J.* 371 (1938); Charles Fairman, "Does the Fourteenth Amendment Incorporate the Bill of Rights? The Original Understanding," 2 *Stan. L. Rev.* 5 (1949); William W. Crosskey, "Charles Fairman, 'Legislative History,' and the Constitutional Limitations on State Authority," 22 *U. Chi. L. Rev.* 1 (1954); John P. Frank and Robert F. Munro, "The Original Understanding of Equal Protection of the Laws," 50 *Colum. L. Rev.* 131 (1950); Louis Boudin, "Truth and Fiction about the Fourteenth Amendment," 16 *N.Y.U. L.Q.* 19 (1938).

4. U.S. Constitution, Art. I, sec. 2.

5. *Congressional Globe*, 39th Cong., 1st sess. (1865), p. 73 (hereafter, *Globe*, 39th).

6. *Globe*, 39th, p. 74.

7. Section two of the Fourteenth Amendment reads: "Representatives shall be apportioned among the several States according to their respective numbers, counting the whole number of persons in each State, excluding Indians not taxed. But when the right to vote at any election for the choice of electors for President and Vice President of the United States, Representatives in Congress, the Executive and Judicial officers of a State, or the members of the Legislature thereof, is denied to any of the male inhabitants of such State, being twenty-one years of age, and citizens of the United States, or in any way abridge, except for participation in rebellion, or other crime, the basis of representation therein shall be reduced in the proportion which the number of such male citizens shall bear to the whole number of male citizens twenty-one years of age in such State."

8. *Globe*, 39th, p. 141.

9. *Globe*, 39th, pp. 362, 702; 1287; Gillette, *Fifteenth Amendment*, p. 23 (proposals of John B. Henderson [R, Minn.] and Charles Sumner [R, Mass.]).

10. *Globe*, 39th, p. 1289.

11. Gillette, *Fifteenth Amendment*, p. 24.

12. *Globe*, 39th, p. 2766. Howard spoke on May 23, 1866, after the Fourteenth Amendment was consolidated (April 9) but before it passed in the Senate (June 8). His final understanding should be contrasted with his earlier insistence on Negro suffrage: "The Negro *must* vote. It is our *only* security and means of making emancipation effectual. He *must* vote." Letter to Charles Sumner, 22 June 1865, quoted in James, *Framing of Fourteenth Amendment*, p. 13, n. 3.

13. 377 U.S. 533, 589-632 (1964).

14. 400 U.S. 112 (1970).

15. *Globe*, 39th, p. 2542.

16. 377 U.S. 593-594, 611-612 (1964).

17. Van Alstyne, "Fourteenth Amendment."

18. Respectively, John A. Bingham (R, Ohio) and Thaddeus Stevens (R, Pa.). Though Van Alstyne did not say so outright, he leaves us to conclude that Harlan was also in error for treating the Fourteenth Amendment as a unit with the rest of the Constitution, specifically the Fifteenth, Seventeenth, Nineteenth, and Twenty-Fourth Amendments, which would be superfluous, like section two of the Fourteenth, if section one controlled the vote.

19. Van Alstyne, "Fourteenth Amendment," pp. 49-51.

20. *Globe*, 39th, 432, 25 January 1866.

21. *Globe*, 39th, 536, 31 January 1866.

22. Van Alstyne, "Fourteenth Amendment," pp. 63-64.

23. Ibid., p. 64; *Congressional Globe*, 40th Cong., 2d sess., 1966-67 (1868).

24. Gillette, *Fifteenth Amendment*, p. 24, n. 6.

25. Alexander Bickel, "The Original Understanding and the Segregation Decision," 69 *Harv. L. Rev.* 1 (1955).

26. See, for example, Van Alstyne, "Fourteenth Amendment," pp. 55-56, 73, 78.

27. Technically the understanding of the ratifiers, not that of the drafters, should determine the original intent of constitutional language, since it is the ratifiers who give the language its final effect. The understanding of the drafters, however, can cast light on the understanding of the ratifiers; moreover, drafters' debates are more accessible and come closer to representing a national consensus than states' debates; hence, they have always received the most attention from historians.

28. In the House only. The broad language had passed the Senate on the strength of the same denials that civil rights included political rights.

29. Van Alstyne, "Fourteenth Amendment," pp. 75-78. However, the 40th Congress did consider apportionment in connection with the readmission of Florida, whose constitution apportioned its representatives "in such a manner as to give the sparsely populated portions of the State the control of the legislature. The sparsely populated parts of the State are those where there are very few negroes, the parts inhabited by the white rebels." Arch-Radical Benjamin F. Butler of Massachusetts silenced these objections voiced by Congressman John Farnsworth of Illinois: "All these arguments . . . have been submitted to the Judicial Committee of the Senate . . . this Constitution has been submitted to the Senate, and they have found it republican and proper. It has been submitted to your own Committee on Reconstruction, and they have found it republican and proper and have reported it to the House."

Globe, 40th Cong., 2d sess., pp. 3090-3092 (1868). There is little force in Van Alstyne's argument that the Radicals' failure to amend section one to deny its pertinence to voting rights "could scarcely have been inadvertent," leaving themselves free later to put through "such further civil rights provisions (including voting) as they thought the country could take in the future." No such express denial appeared in the Civil Rights Act, nor anywhere in the rest of the Constitution (as might be expected in a Constitution of enumerated powers). The Radicals resented bitterly their repeated defeats on the suffrage question, but their failure to memorialize them in terms hardly amounts to converting them into final victory.

30. Apportionment is slightly less suspect than poll taxes as a legitimate subject for the protection of section one since, as Van Alstyne pointed out, it was not considered by the 39th Congress which framed the Fourteenth Amendment. Although twenty-one of the thirty-three ratifying states apportioned their legislatures without exclusive regard to population and might not be expected to have intended to invalidate their own constitutions *sub silentio*, a framers' and ratifiers' understanding of zero on apportionment translates more easily into a blank check than a clear framers' understanding of "no" to the question of suffrage; moreover, apportionment could be distinguished from the voting provisions pre-empted by section two if it were considered a question of representation instead. The Court avoided this approach for reasons to be discussed in Chapter V.

31. Gillette, *Fifteenth Amendment*, pp. 29-31; First Reconstruction Act of March 2, 1867, 14 Stat. 429 (1867).

32. Gillette, *Fifteenth Amendment*, p. 32.

33. *Ibid.*, table 1, pp. 82-83.

34. *Congressional Globe*, 40th Cong., 3d sess., p. 904 (1869) (hereafter, *Globe*, 40th).

35. *Globe*, 40th, p. 728.

36. *Ibid.*

37. *Ibid.*, p. 686.

38. Gillette, *Fifteenth Amendment*, pp. 50-76.

39. For example, *Globe*, 40th, pp. 1012, 1029, 1226.

40. *Globe*, 40th, 1012. Western politicians like William M. Stewart, Cornelius Cole, and Henry W. Corbett were willing to let blacks vote, but drew the line at Chinese; Rhode Island Republicans like Henry B. Anthony were more interested in excluding Irish. Gillette, *Fifteenth Amendment*, pp. 54-58, 151-153.

41. *Globe*, 40th, p. 1029.

42. *Ibid.*, p. 862. Ratification politics in the states were hardly less emancipated from board principles, or less ruled by prospects of immediate gain or loss than drafting politics in Congress. Democrats uniformly fought ratification except in Connecticut and Rhode Island, where they thought to gain Irish voters. Republicans supported ratification except in Rhode Island, where they feared the Irish vote, and in Georgia, where they hoped to get an amendment with more stringent protections for southern black votes. Southern states accepted the amendment as a cheap price for readmission to the Union, since black voting was already a fact in the occupied states and the amendment had obvious loopholes for later disfranchisement. Unreconstructed border states fought ratification tooth and nail; so did anti-Chinese Pacific Coast states. Woman suffragists were split according to different read-

ings of advantage to their own cause: Susan B. Anthony and Elisabeth Cady
Stanton believed, with their National Women Suffrage Association, that
blacks should not vote before women; Lucy Stone and the American
Woman's Suffrage Association believed that opposing black suffrage might
damage their own claims to impartial suffrage. See Gillette, *Fifteenth Amendment*, chapters 3-9.

43. 16 Stat. 140-146 (1870).
44. 16 Stat. 433-440 (1871).
45. 17 Stat. 13-15 (1871).
46. 92 U.S. 542 (1876).
47. Homer Cummings and Carl McFarland, *Federal Justice: Chapters in the History of Justice and the Federal Executive* (New York: Macmillan, 1937), p. 243; Everette Swinney, "Enforcing the Fifteenth Amendment, 1870-1877," 28 *J. Southern Hist.* 202, 207-208 (May 1962).
48. Swinney, "Enforcing the Fifteenth Amendment," p. 209.
49. *Ibid.*, p. 210.
50. *Ibid.* Federal habeas corpus for persons in state custody was authorized by statutes passed in 1833 and 1837 (4 Stat. 634 [1850]; 14 Stat. 385 [1862], but their constitutionality was not established till 1890. *In re* Neagle, 135 U.S. 1 (1890); cf., Ex parte Dorr, 3 How. 103 (1845).
51. Cummings and McFarland, *Federal Justice*, chap. 12; Swinney, "Enforcing the Fifteenth Amendment," pp. 210-211.
52. Williams claimed a victory over the Klan in 1874 but felt the need to "suspend these prosecutions except in some of the worst cases in the hope that the effect will be to produce obedience to the law and quiet and peace among the people." Cummings and McFarland, *Federal Justice*, p. 238. Between 1870 and 1896, 7,372 cases were tried under the enforcement acts (in contrast with less than a hundred cases tried from 1957 to 1967 under the civil rights acts of 1957, 1960, and 1964) Swinney, "Enforcing the Fifteenth Amendment," pp. 204-205.
53. United States v. Cruikshank, 92 U.S. 542 (1876); United States v. Reese, 92 U.S. 214 (1875).
54. C. Vann Woodward, *The Strange Career of Jim Crow*, 2d rev. ed. (New York: Oxford University Press, 1966), pp. 52-53.
55. 28 Stat. 36 (1894).
56. Justices Miller, Swayne, Davis, and Field were Lincoln appointees, Waite, Hunt, Strong, and Bradley Grant appointees. James G. Blaine described the remaining Justice, Nathan Clifford (who had argued for intervention in *Luther v. Borden*) as "an in-grown, hungry Democrat, double dyed and dyed in the wool, and coarse wool at that." Though he wrote separate or dissenting opinions in three of the four voting rights cases on which he sat, Old Democrat Clifford voted against intervention every time. Minor v. Happersett, 21 Wall. 162 (1875); United States v. Reese, 92 U.S. 214, 222 (1875); United States v. Cruikshank, 92 U.S. 542, 559 (1876); Ex parte Siebold, 100 U.S. 371, 404 (1880).
57. Cummings and McFarland, *Federal Justice*, pp. 243-244.
58. 12 Wall. 457 (1871), *overruling* Hepburn v. Griswold, 8 Wall. 603 (1870).
59. Ex parte Merryman, Fed. Cas. no. 9487 (1861) (Lincoln's general successfully refused to obey Taney's writ of habeas corpus); Ex parte McCardle, 7 Wall. 506 (1869) (Court submitted to Congress' repeal of habeas corpus appeal statute); see Fred Rodell, *Nine Men: A Political History of the Su-*

preme Court of the United States from 1790 to 1955 (New York: Random House, 1955), p. 153 for an account of the Court's surrender to obstruction by the state of Iowa over railroad subsidies.

60. Dred Scott v. Sanford, 19 How. 304 (1857).

61. 21 Wall. 162 (1875).

62. 92 U.S. 214 (1875).

63. 92 U.S. 542 (1876).

64. *Id.*, p. 556. Cummings and McFarland describe the background of the case, *Federal Justice*, pp. 241-247.

65. Ex parte Siebold, 100 U.S. 371 (1880); Ex parte Clarke, 100 U.S. 399 (1880); United States v. Gale, 109 U.S. 65 (1883); Ex parte Yarbrough, 110 U.S. 651 (1884); In re Coy, 127 U.S. 731 (1888); United States v. Mosley, 238 U.S. 383 (1915); United States v. Classic, 313 U.S. 299 (1941); United States v. Saylor, 322 U.S. 385 (1944).

66. McPherson v. Blacker, 146 U.S. 1 (1892) (refusing to allow attack on election of delegates to electoral college by districts); Ray v. Blair, 343 U.S. 214 (1952) (refusing to allow attack on required pledges of electoral college delegates to support party's national candidates). See Walker v. United States, 93 F.2d 542 (8th Cir. 1937) (holding right to vote for presidential electors dependent "exclusively upon state legislation").

67. United States v. Reese, 92 U.S. 214 (1875); United States v. Cruikshank, 92 U.S. 542 (1876).

68. Williams v. Mississippi, 170 U.S. 213 (1898) (barring attack on jury panel appointed from voting lists with literacy test); Pope v. Williams, 193 U.S. 621 (1904) (barring attack on residence requirement); Giles v. Harris, 189 U.S. 475 (1903) (denying injunction for refusal to register Negro); Mason v. Missouri, 179 U.S. 308, 335 (1900) (barring attack on special registration requirements for St. Louis).

69. Ex parte Yarbrough, 110 U.S. 651 (1884). This case, in which Justice Miller attempted to invoke the Fifteenth Amendment, as well as Art. I, sec. 4, against private coercion, is the one exception to the Court's early practice of intervening only when state action *and* a federal election were involved.

70. United States v. Harris, 106 U.S. 629 (1882) (Fourteenth Amendment does not protect Negroes in custody of law from being beaten up by private gang); Baldwin v. Franks, 120 U.S. 678 (1887) (nor Chinese from being driven out of their homes).

71. James v. Bowman, 190 U.S. 127 (1903); United States v. Bathgate, 246 U.S. 220 (1918).

72. Now 18 U.S.C.A. §§ 241-242 (1969).

73. United States v. Mosley, 238 U.S. 383 (1915); United States v. Saylor, 322 U.S. 385 (1944); see Donald Kommers, "The Right to Vote and its Implementation," 39 *Notre Dame Law.* 365, 368-371 (1964).

74. United States v. Saylor, 322 U.S., 385, 391 (1944).

75. Wiley v. Sinkler, 179 U.S. 58 (1900); Swafford v. Templeton, 185 U.S. 487 (1902).

76. Giles v. Harris, 189 U.S. 475 (1903); Giles v. Teasley, 193 U.S. 146 (1904).

77. 189 U.S., p. 487. Justices Harlan, Brown, and Brewer dissented.

78. 193 U.S., p. 165. Justice Harlan dissented without opinion.

79. Norton v. Shelby County, 118 U.S. 428, 442 (1886); cf. Chicot County Drainage Dist. v. Baxter Bank, 308 U.S. 371 (1940).

80. Ex parte Young, 209 U.S. 123 (1908). Justice Harlan, who had dis-

sented in both Giles cases, nevertheless dissented in *Ex parte Young*, 209 U.S. pp. 175-176: "I cannot suppose that the great men who framed the Constitution ever thought the time would come when a subordinate Federal Court, having no power to compel a State in its corporate capacity, to appear before it as a litigant, would yet assume to deprive a State of the right to be represented in its own courts by its regular law officer [through enjoining the officer in a federal court]." The *Young* case aroused concern that state governments might be disrupted by injunction suits against state officials in federal courts. This concern led to the passage of the three-judge court acts, 36 Stat. 557 (1910); 37 Stat. 1013 (1913); 28 U.S.C.A. § 2281 (1965).

81. The rise of industry and finance in the South changed the old pattern of sectional rivalry by giving the plantation vote strong new allies, as the up-country agrarians found to their cost. V. O. Key, Jr., *Southern Politics* (New York: Vintage Books, 1949), pp. 544, 548. Key's book is still indispensible for state-by-state analysis of post-Reconstruction politics in the South.

82. Key, *Southern Politics*, p. 541. From 1874 to 1900 16 of 20 Virginia congressional elections were contested for fraud, arousing Republican pressures to bring back federal supervision of southern elections. *Ibid.*, p. 540. Southerners blamed the blacks for lowering the tone of elections by inspiring whites to fraud to discount their votes. The *Richmond Times* fumed: "I would rather see the Democrats take shot guns and drive the Negroes from the polls than to see our young men cheat." Quoted in Andrew Buni, *Negro in Virginia Politics, 1903-1965* (Charlottesville: University of Virginia Press, 1967), p. 12.

83. Key, *Southern Politics*, p. 538. According to the census of 1900, illiteracy among southern blacks ranged from 39.4 percent in Florida to 61.3 percent in Louisiana. Among southern whites, illiteracy ranged from 5.3 percent in Texas to 20.3 percent in Louisiana. *Id.*, p. 550. There were potential black majorities in South Carolina, Mississippi, and Louisiana, and Alabama, Georgia, Virginia, and Florida were more than 40 percent black. Forrest G. Wood, "On Revising Reconstruction History: Negro Suffrage: White Disenfranchisement, and Common Sense," 51 J. *Negro History* 98, 102 (April 1966).

84. Virginia Constitutional Convention, 1901-02, vol. II, p. 3076, quoted in Buni, *Negro in Virginia Politics*, pp. 17-18.

85. Florida, Tennessee, Arkansas, and Texas, however, limited their suffrage reforms of this period to the poll tax. Two northern states had passed literacy tests during earlier periods of concern over immigrants' voting: Connecticut in 1855, and Massachusetts in 1857. Variations of the Jim Crow voting laws were property alternatives, adopted in Georgia, South Carolina, Louisiana, and Alabama but dropped in the latter two states for making it too easy for blacks to qualify. Louisiana, North Carolina, South Carolina, and Oklahoma had grandfather clauses permitting registration of 1867 voters and their descendants who did not pass the literacy tests. All of these but Oklahoma had early deadlines for registration, rendering them thereafter relatively safe from constitutional attack. Oklahoma's statute was invalidated in *Guinn v. United States* (238 U.S. 347 [1915]). Georgia, Virginia, and Alabama had provisions to exempt ex-soldiers from the test; Georgia, Louisiana, and Alabama had "good character" alternatives. See Elliott, "Ideology and Intervention," Appendix IV; Key, *Southern Politics*, pp. 556-559.

86. Letter of registrar to Rep. Harry D. Flood (D, Va.), quoted in Buni, *Negro in Virginia Politics*, p. 21.

87. *Richmond Times*, July 10, 1907, quoted in Buni, *Negro in Virginia Politics*, p. 19.

88. Key, *Southern Politics*, pp. 539-550.

89. C. Vann Woodward, *The Strange Career of Jim Crow*, 2d rev. ed. (New York: Oxford University Press, 1966), p. 72.

90. *Ibid.*

91. Quoted in Alan P. Grimes, *Equality in America: Religion, Race, and the Urban Majority* (New York: Oxford University Press, 1964), p. 62.

92. *New York Times*, May 10, 1900, quoted in Woodward, *Strange Career*, p. 73.

93. Woodward, *Strange Career*, p. 73, 74.

94. For example, Ex parte Siebold, 100 U.S. 371 (1880); United States v. Mosley, 238 U.S. 383 (1915).

95. Strauder v. West Virginia, 100 U.S. 303 (1880); Ex parte Virginia, 100 U.S. 339 (1880).

96. Civil rights cases, 109 U.S. 3 (1883); Hall v. de Cuir, 95 U.S. 485 (1877); Plessy v. Ferguson, 163 U.S. 537 (1896).

97. Davis v. Beason, 133 U.S. 333, 345-347 (1890) (upholding age, residence, criminal record tests); In re Green, 134 U.S. 377 (1890) (upholding petty larceny test); Lassiter v. Northampton County Board, 360 U.S. 45 (1959) (upholding literacy test, absent showing of racial discrimination).

98. 238 U.S. 397 (1915).

99. The Court's logic in *Guinn v. United States* was foreshadowed in *Yick Wo v. Hopkins* (118 U.S. 356 [1886]), *Ex parte Yarbrough* (110 U.S. 651 [1884]), and Justice Harlan's dissent in *Plessy v. Ferguson* (163 U.S. 537 [1896]).

100. With a unanimous holding written by Chief Justice Edward D. White, once of the Confederate Army, the Court anticipated its strategy in the school segregation cases by taking a strong stand in principle while making sure that the principle would not be endangered by immediate and general application.

101. *Ex parte Yarbrough* (110 U.S. 651 [1884]) might be considered modern in terms of its penetrating logic, but it was decided three decades too soon and was not followed by the Court during its Jim Crow period from the late 1880's to the early 1900's.

102. Lane v. Wilson, 307 U.S. 268, 275 (1939) (striking down a replacement to Oklahoma's grandfather law exempting from the literacy test all those who had voted in the 1914 election—which itself was held under the grandfather law).

103. 71 *Harv. L. Rev.* 1057 (1959).

104. 26 *Harv. L. Rev.* 42 (1912).

105. *Ibid.*, pp. 62-63.

106. Arthur Machen, "Is the Fifteenth Amendment Void?" 23 *Harv. L. Rev.* 169 (1910), cited to the Court in *Myers v. Anderson*, 238 U.S. 368 (1915). Machen argued that the Fifteenth Amendment in effect deprived the states of representation in the Senate and was therefore not a permissible amendment under Article V.

107. Forrest G. Wood, "Revising Reconstruction History," pp. 106-107. Wood estimated on the basis of fragmentary figures from the southern states that some 200,000 of 612,000 blacks registered were disfranchised.

108. United States v. Mississippi, 380 U.S. 128, 132 (1965); Louisiana v.

United States, 380 U.S. 145, 147-149 (1965). For state-by-state percentages of registered Negro voters, see table 2 at the end of this chapter.

109. Burke Marshall, "The Pattern of Southern Disfranchisement of Negroes," in Alan F. Westin, ed., *Freedom Now! The Civil Rights Struggle in America* (New York: Basic Books, 1964), pp. 95-96.

110. Key demonstrated that voter turnout increased where there was local two-party competition as in North Carolina, or, as in Louisiana under Huey Long, where there was a stir over local or state issues. Key, *Southern Politics*, chap. 23. Donald R. Matthews and James W. Prothro concluded that low political participation among blacks resulted more from social and economic factors, such as low income, limited education, or residence in Black Belt counties, than from direct political discrimination by the white community, though the latter did have a noticeable effect in the minority of jurisdictions where it was practiced at the time of the study (1958-1961). *Negroes and the New Southern Politics* (New York: Harcourt, Brace and World, Inc., 1966). Matthews and Prothro found that black registration was more closely related to percentage of blacks in the county than to anything else, with lowest registration in Black Belt counties. Low black registration was also associated with high educational level of whites but urbanization, industrialization, and rate of white registration had little independent effect on black registration. Individuals with high income and education were more likely to vote than those without these advantages.

Having established predictable levels of participation in terms of social and economic variables, Matthews and Prothro then compared the predicted levels with actual levels in states with various different voting requirements and discovered only moderate (10.5 percent) deficiencies of actual registration in states with both poll taxes and literacy tests (Mississippi, Alabama, and Virginia) from predicted registration as compared with 46 percent negative correlation between percentage of blacks in the county and registration of blacks. Poll taxes and literacy tests alone seemed to make even less difference on a statewide basis, but discriminatory administration of literacy tests made a big difference (29 percent) between counties where they were practiced and other counties in the same state (North Carolina) where they were not. Factional competition made some difference, but party competition seemed to make little difference when social and economic factors were controlled. Actual racial violence seemed to make little difference in black registration, though many respondents in one of Matthews and Prothro's sample counties said that fear of violence or (more often) of losing their job kept them from voting.

111. Key, *Southern Politics*, pp. 504-505. Overall voter turnout was still low by Warren's time in all of the southern states but North Carolina, ranging from 13.7 percent in Mississippi to 28.6 percent in Tennessee in the 1962 general elections, and from 33.2 percent in Mississippi to 51.2 percent in Tennessee in 1964. 24 *Cong. Q. Weekly Rev.* 2657 (28 October 1966).

112. Poll tax, 1904; white primary, 1923. Key, *Southern Politics*, p. 534.

113. Paul Lewinson, *Race, Class, and Party* (New York: Oxford University Press, 1932), app. 3; West v. Bliley, 33 F. 2d 177 (E.D. Va. 1929) *aff'd*, 42 F. 2d 101 (4th Cir. 1930).

114. Newberry v. United States, 256 U.S. 232 (1921).

115. 273 U.S. 536 (1927); 286 U.S. 73 (1932).

116. Note, "Nixon v. Condon—Disfranchisement of the Negro in Texas," 41 *Yale L. J.* 1212, 1216 (1932).

117. 273 U.S. 536, 540 (1927).

118. 21 Wall. 162 (1875).

119. *New York Times*, March 8, 1927, p. 1.

120. *Ibid.*; also May 3, 1932, p. 2, col. 4.

121. Note, Nixon v. Condon, 41 *Yale L. J.* 1212, 1215 (1932). Holmes had indulged in a like ironic aside a quarter-century earlier, when, having denied relief to a black plaintiff who had been refused registration, he advised the plaintiff to seek redress from the state government or Congress. Giles v. Harris, 189 U.S. 475, 488 (1903).

122. Note, Nixon v. Herndon, 28 *Mich. L. Rev.* 613 (1930).

123. Note, Nixon v. Condon, 41 *Yale L. J.* 1212, 1218-1219 (1932). One of the longer and bolder of the law review comments on the Nixon cases was Morton Milman's casenote on the district court opinion in *Nixon v. Condon*, 34 F.2d 464 (W.D. Tex. 1929), 15 *Cornell L. Q.* 262 (1930). Milman put forth the Fourteenth Amendment argument later adopted by the Supreme Court in *Nixon v. Condon*, that the white primary had been "adopted, regulated, and made compulsory by the State of Texas." He also propounded the Fifteenth Amendment argument later adopted by the Court in *Smith v. Allwright*: "The primary has become an inseparable part of the electoral machinery and therefore a vote in the primary comes within the purpose of the Fifteenth Amendment. . . . It is to be hoped that our highest court will once for all assert the proposition that the right to vote at primary elections is as sacred as the right to vote at the general elections which follow." *Id.*, pp. 267-269.

124. 295 U.S. 45 (1935).

125. *New York Times*, April 2, 1935, p. 15, col. 1.

126. Note, "Control of Party Membership," 33 *Mich. L. Rev.* 955 (1935). Other casenotes on *Grovey v. Townsend* are: 35 *Colum. L. Rev.* 607 (1935); 48 *Harv. L. Rev.* 1436 (1935); 2 *U. Chi. L. Rev.* 640 (1935); 83 *U. Pa. L. Rev.* 1027 (1935); 22 *Va. L. Rev.* 91 (1935).

127. Norris v. Alabama, 294 U.S. 587 (1935).

128. For example, *New York Times*, Sept. 18, 1941, p. 24, col. 5.

129. For example, *New York Times*, Jan. 13, 1944, p. 20, col. 3.

130. For example, *New York Times*, May 27, 1941, p. 1, col. 2.

131. For example, Smith v. Allwright, 321 U.S. 649 (1944).

132. For example, *New York Times*, May 27, 1941, p. 1, col. 2.

133. For example, *New York Times*, Oct. 20, 1944, p. 20, col. 5.

134. For example, *New York Times*, Sept. 21, 1944, p. 26, col. 4.

135. *New York Times* editorials, Jan. 13, 1944, p. 20, col. 3; Oct. 18, 1944, p. 20, col. 2.

136. The National Negro Council and the Chicago Citizen's Committee urged blacks to back Republicans in the 1944 elections to punish the Democrats for concessions to discriminatory labor unions.

137. *New York Times*, Jan. 27, 1944, p. 1, col. 3; Jan. 28, 1944, p. 16, col. 3.

138. 328 U.S. 549 (1946). See the *New York Times Index* (New York: New York Times Pub. Co., 1942, 1944), "elections." Soldier vote items in the index for other years were: 1864: 28; 1918: 8; 1940: 0.

The state control faction was endorsed by the Republican party and the Presbyterian church in the USA. Though the Democrats did not succeed in nationalizing the soldier ballot, soldier balloting in the 1944 elections did succeed in focusing public attention on the soldier vote, both in the field and on the home front. Soldier balloting shot up from half of one percent in the 1942 off-year elections to 35 percent in the 1944 elections. An estimated 2.8 million soldier ballots were cast in 1944, out of some 8 million eligible soldiers. Total national vote was 42 million. The *Times Index* for 1944 lists 400 articles touching on every aspect of the soldier vote: whether pictures of FDR in the *Official Guide to the Army Air Force* were political propaganda; whether the army should show two pro-Democratic movies, *Wilson* and *Heavenly Days*, in service theaters; how the troops on the Italian front felt about the vote, as compared to those in France; instructions on opening ballot envelopes affected by heat; transport of the ballots by elephant, oxcart, and parachute at risk of life and limb; speculation as to how the soldier vote affected the election; and estimates of its size. In the end, though it appeared that the Democrats did get 60 percent of the service vote, there is little evidence that it affected the outcome of the election, which was Democratic by a comfortable margin. Roosevelt won the presidency with no difficulty, and the Democrats picked up 22 more seats in Congress.

139. 313 U.S. 299 (1941).

140. Richard Claude gives many details of the background of the *Classic* case in *The Supreme Court and the Electoral Process* (Baltimore: Johns Hopkins Press, 1970), pp. 31-36.

141. 313 U.S. 299, 301-302 (1941).

142. 313 U.S. 299, 311, 314 (1941). To round out the list of anomalies, the three most liberal members of the Court, Justices Douglas, Black, and Murphy dissented vigorously, arguing that Congress, having repealed the conspiracy provisions of the old enforcement acts, did not intend to have vote fraud regulated under the general conspiracy statute, 35 Stat. 1092, 18 U.S.C. 51, 52 (1927). Douglas snorted: "This Court is legislating!" Had either Roberts or Stone voted with the dissenters, Classic would have gone free because his acquittal by the district court would then have been affirmed by a 4-4 tie vote.

143. 313 U.S. 299, 314, n. 2.

144. *Colum. L. Rev.* 1101 (1941).

145. 321 U.S. 649 (1944).

146. Ex parte Yarbrough, 110 U.S. 651 (1884); Guinn v. United States, 238 U.S. 347 (1915); Nixon v. Herndon, 256 U.S. 232 (1927); Nixon v. Condon, 286 U.S. 73 (1932).

147. 321 U.S., 649, 663-664 (1944).

148. Arthur Krock, "Self Re-examination Continues in the Court," *New York Times,* Apr. 4, 1944, p. 20, col. 5.

149. Quoted in Key, *Southern Politics,* p. 627.

150. Elmore v. Rice, 72 F. Supp. 516 (E.D.S.C. 1947), aff'd, 165 F. 2d 387 (4th Cir. 1947), *cert. denied,* 333 U.S. 875 (1948).

151. Key, *Southern Politics,* p. 638.

152. Brown v. Baskin, 78 F. Supp. 933, 937 (E.D.S.C. 1948).

153. Key, *Southern Politics,* p. 637, 639. However, Virginia, Louisiana, and Mississippi had separate primaries for state and local officers and for federal ones.

154. 345 U.S. p. 461 (majority opinion of Justice Black).
155. *Id.*
156. *Id.*, p. 475 (Frankfurter concurrence).
157. *Id.*, p. 476. The logic used suggests that the Court might not find state action in the case of racial exclusion by parties like the Black Panther party which lack the monopoly power of the Democrats.
158. Alabama, Georgia, Louisiana, Mississippi, North Carolina, South Carolina, and Virginia; Louisiana and Alabama required capacity to understand and explain the Constitution, understand the duties and obligations of citizenship under a republican form of government, and be of good character. Both states' requirements have since been held unconstitutional.
159. Virginia and North Carolina blacks registered freely in most cities and upcountry counties but suffered discrimination in Black Belt counties; Georgia and South Carolina registrars often discouraged black registration but seemed willing to yield to various forms of legal and other pressure.
160. Key, *Southern Politics*, pp. 563–567. Davis v. Schnell, 81 F. Supp. 872 (S.D. Ala. 1949).
161. United States v. Mississippi, 380 U.S. 128 (1965); Louisiana v. United States, 380 U.S. 145 (1965). Absent a showing of racial discrimination, literacy tests were still technically permissible though subject to the Civil Rights Act of 1965/70. Lassiter v. Northampton County Board, 360 U.S. 45 (1959); Cardona v. Power, 384 U.S. 672 (1966); *but see*, Gaston County v. United States, 395 U.S. 285 (1969) (invalidating "impartial" literacy test where black schools were inferior).
162. Harper v. Board of Elections, 383 U.S. 663 (1966); Kramer v. Union Free School District, 395 U.S. 621 (1969).
163. 71 Stat. 634 (1957).
164. 74 Stat. 86 (1960).
165. 78 Stat. 241 (1964).
166. 79 Stat. 437 (1965).
167. Public Law 91-285, 91st Cong. H.R. 4249, June 22, 1970.
168. Residency requirements longer than 30 days have since been held unconstitutional. Dunn v. Blumstein 405 U.S. 330 (1972), but see Burns v. Fortson, 410 U.S. 686 (1973) (permitting 50-day registration cutoff).
169. The Court invalidated a New York language test under the Voting Rights Act of 1965 in *Katzenbach v. Morgan* (384 U.S. 641 [1966]) and dealt a serious blow to all literacy tests in *Gaston County v. United States*, 395 U.S. 285 (1969), by invalidating a North Carolina literacy test, though impartially administered, in the context of inferior black schools.
170. Key, *Southern Politics*, p. 579; Matthews and Prothro, *Negroes and the New Southern Politics*, p. 154.
171. 364 U.S. 349 (1960).
172. 328 U.S. 549 (1946).
173. 328 U.S., p. 556.
174. Wright v. Rockefeller, 376 U.S. 52 (1964). Members of the Court in Gomillion grazed the standards problem in oral argument but never focused on it head on. Bernard Taper's book *Gomillion v. Lightfoot: Apartheid in Alabama* (New York: McGraw-Hill, 1962), gives a journalistic view of the background of the case.
175. Korematsu v. United States, 323 U.S. 214 (1944); Hirabayashi v. United States, 320 U.S. 81 (1943).

Notes to Chapter IV

1. Walter Dean Burnham, "The Changing Shape of the American Political Universe," 59 *Am. Pol. Sci. Rev.* 7 (1965); Everett Carl Ladd, *American Political Parties: Social Change and Political Response*, New York, Norton, 1970, Chap. 4.

2. F. W. Holls, "Compulsory Voting," *Annals of the Am. Acad. of Polit. and Soc. Science* 546 (April 1891). North Dakota's constitution of 1898 authorized laws for the punishment of qualified nonvoters. Charles Kettleborough, *State Constitutions*, Indianapolis, F. Bowen & Co., 1918, p. 1034; Ward Elliott, "Ideology and Intervention: Supreme Court Intervention in Voting Rights Disputes from Taney to Warren," Ph.D. diss, Harvard University, Cambridge, Mass., 1968, appendix IV.

3. Between 1855 and 1924 eleven northern and western states adopted literacy tests: Connecticut, 1855; Massachusetts, 1857; Wyoming, 1889; Maine, 1892; California, 1894; Washington, 1896; Delaware, 1897; New Hampshire, 1902; Arizona, 1913; New York, 1921; and Oregon, 1924. Of these, all but Wyoming required voters to read or write English. California, Oregon, Idaho, and Nevada retained constitutional provisions excluding Chinese from voting. See Elliott, "Ideology and Intervention," appendix IV.

4. "Is there any room for reasonable doubt," asked Strong, "that this race, unless devitalized by alcohol and tobacco, is destined to dispossess many weaker races, assimilate others, and mold the remainder, until, in a very true and important sense, it has Anglo-Saxonized mankind?" Josiah Strong, *Our Country* (New York: Baker and Taylor, 1885), p. 175, quoted Alan P. Grimes, *The Puritan Ethic and Woman Suffrage* (New York: Oxford University Press, 1967), p. 112. Grimes's interpretation of progressivism as a native, middle-class, Yankee movement follows the view of the most eminent historians; e.g., Oscar Handlin, *The Uprooted* (Boston: Little, Brown, 1951), pp. 209-217; Richard Hofstadter, *The Age of Reform: From Bryan to FDR* (New York: Knopf, 1955), p. 318; George E. Mowry, *The Era of Theodore Roosevelt, 1900-1912* (New York: Harper, 1958), p. 86. But see J. Joseph Huthmacher, "Urban Liberalism and the Age of Reform," 49 *Miss. Valley Hist. Rev.* 231 (September 1962) (arguing some representatives of Irish, Jewish, and Italian working-class district supported direct democracy, corrupt practice laws, and woman suffrage). Though non-Yankee Democrats like Louis D. Brandeis, Robert F. Wagner, and even James Michael Curley have been called progressive by virtue of their support for certain measures favored by the Progressives, I think they should more properly be considered precursors of FDR liberalism than as representative figures of the Progressive movement. Huthmacher's conclusions have been challenged both for their limited evidentiary basis, confined to two states, and for misinterpretation of the evidence as to one of those two states. Barton J. Bernstein and Allen J. Matusow, eds., *Twentieth-Century America: Recent Interpretations* (New York: Harcourt, Brace and World, 1969), p. 24; Irwin Yellowitz, *Labor and the Progressive Movement in New York State* (Ithaca: Cornell University Press), 1965.

Samuel P. Hays, in "The Politics of Reform in Municipal Government in the Progressive Era," 55 *Pacific Northwest Q.* 157 (October 1964), persuasively argues that municipal reforms followed an ideology of efficiency and rationality purveyed by upper-middle-class, chamber-of-commerce-type sponsors. These eminent business and professional men felt that a good government should be organized like a good business, with expert management, sound planning and accounting, and centralized decision-making. Lower-class voters and the ward politicians who represented them fought the reforms tooth and nail, preferring to run their own affairs at the price of some corruption and inefficiency. The reformers used initiative and referendum where these were tactically expedient and avoided them where they were inexpedient. Hays's portrayal of Progressive reformers strongly foreshadows the Guardians in the stress on centralized "rational" administration. There were also, however, some differences. The Progressives were still fighting in a legislative arena and could not rely as exclusively as the Guardians on a bare appeal to constitutional or professional principles. They were also oriented to turn-of-the-century local issues—city machines and corruption—more than to the national questions of equal rights (especially race rights) and court prerogative favored by the Guardians. For a discussion of progressive indifference to black rights, see Dewey W. Grantham, Jr., "The Progressive Movement and the Negro," 54 *S. Atlantic Q.* 461 (October 1955). This article, and the articles by Huthmacher and Hays, are reprinted in Bernstein and Matusow, *Twentieth-Century America.*

5. Seymour M. Lipset, *Political Man: The Social Bases of Politics* (Garden City, N.Y.: Doubleday, 1960), pp. 207-208.

6. Grimes, *Puritan Ethic*, chap. 2.

7. *Ibid.*, chap. 1.

8. Kansas rejected woman suffrage by referendum in 1867, Michigan in 1874, Colorado in 1877, Nebraska in 1882, Oregon in 1884, Washington in 1889, and South Dakota in 1890. *Ibid.*, pp. 21-22.

9. Of the ten western states which adopted woman suffrage between 1893 and 1914—Colorado, Idaho, Utah, Washington, California, Oregon, Arizona, Kansas, Nevada, and Montana—all but Kansas, Nevada, and California had adopted Prohibition by 1917 (see Table 3). Of the eleven southern states which adopted literacy or poll tax laws from 1890 to 1908, all but four—Georgia, Tennessee, Florida, and Texas—had passed Prohibition by 1915. James H. Timberlake, *Prohibition and the Progressive Movement, 1900-1920* (Cambridge, Mass.: Harvard University Press, 1963), p. 166.

10. Albert J. McCulloch, *Suffrage and Its Problems* (Baltimore: Warwick and York, 1929), p. 127.

11. Grimes, *Puritan Ethic*, pp. 137, 142.

12. Charles E. Merriam and Louise Overacker, *Primary Elections* (Chicago: University of Chicago Press, 1928), p. 62.

13. Initiative and referendum: South Dakota, 1898; Utah, 1900; Nevada, 1904 (initiative, 1912); Montana, 1906; Oklahoma, 1907; Maine and Missouri, 1908; Michigan, Arkansas and Colorado, 1910; California, New Mexico, Arizona, 1911; Idaho, Nebraska, Ohio and Washington, 1912. Recall: Oregon, 1908; California, 1911; Arizona, Idaho, Washington, Colorado, and Nevada, 1912; Michigan, 1913; Louisiana and Kansas, 1914. Harold G. Faulkner, *The Quest for Social Justice, 1898-1914*, New York, Macmillan, 1931, pp. 85-86.

14. F. W. Holls, "Compulsory Voting,"; Edward W. Shepard, "Compulsory Voting," pamphlet (New York, 1891); even opponents of compulsory voting agreed that "abstention is a very serious evil." Albert Bushnell Hart, "The Exercise of the Suffrage," 7 *Pol. Sci. Q.* 311, 317 (1892).

15. Holls, "Compulsory Voting," pp. 596-597.

16. George H. Hallett, Jr., *Proportional Representation—the Key to Democracy* sponsored by the National Municipal League and the Citizens Union of the City of New York (Washington, National Home Library Foundation, 1937), chap. 4.

17. Quoted in *ibid.*, p. 74.

18. George S. Blair, "Cumulative Voting: Patterns of Party Alliance and Rational Choice in Illinois State Legislature Contests," 52 *Am. Pol. Sci. Rev.* 123 (March 1958).

19. 223 U.S. 118 (1912) (refusing to review a challenge to a law passed by referendum for violating the guarantee clause, on the ground that such challenges raised a political question.)

20. Equal, contiguous, and compact: 17 Stat. 128 (1872); 5 Stat. 491 (1842); 31 Stat. 733 (1901). Dropped: 46 Stat. 21 (1929); Wood v. Broom, 287 U.S. 1 (1932).

21. Malcolm E. Jewell, ed., *The Politics of Reapportionment* (New York: Atherton Press, 1962), pp. 11-12; Gordon E. Baker, "The California Senate," in Jewell, *Politics of Reapportionment*, pp. 52-57; Karl A. Lamb, "Michigan Legislative Apportionment," Jewell, *Politics of Reapportionment*, p. 268; *Lucas v. 44th Gen. Assembly*, 377 U.S. 713 (1964) (Colorado, 1962). In Michigan, 1952, Colorado, 1962, and California, 1926, the voters had a choice between two initiative proposals and chose the one less favorable to the urban centers. In Colorado, 1962, and California, 1948, the urban-proposed initiatives were defeated in every district, including urban. In California, 1928, only Los Angeles and San Francisco mustered majorities for the initiative; in 1960, only Los Angeles, Arkansas established an apportionment board by initiative in 1936, but froze its districts by another initiative in 1956. Oregon, Washington, and Colorado voters accepted apportionment initiatives in 1952, 1930 and 1956, and 1932 respectively. The Washington 1956 initiative was thwarted by legislative repeal—see *State ex. rel. O'Connell v. Myers*, 319 P. 2d 828 (Washington, 1956); a similar attempt by the Colorado legislature was stopped in the state courts. See Armstrong v. Mitten 95 Colo. 425, 37 P.2d 757 (1934).

A rash of referenda in the 1962 elections showed a greater urban interest in securing more of the blessings of equality since *Baker v. Carr*—a possible example of the educational effect ascribed to the Supreme Court by Judge Wyzanski. Florida, Mississippi, and Maryland voters defeated plans giving populous districts some additional representation but retaining a heavy basic imbalance. North Carolina and Oklahoma voters approved automatic and/or board-controlled apportionment, respectively; Washington approved of a population standard; West Virginia rejected a county standard. At the same time, however, California and Colorado voters rejected proposals with population standards, and Georgia, Nebraska, and Tennessee voters approved departures from population standards. See National Municipal League, *Reapportionment: A Year in Review, 1963* pp. 18-19.

22. Thomas Barclay, "The Reapportionment Struggle in California in 1948," 4 *Western Pol. Q.* 317 (1951); Andrew Hacker, *Congressional Districting: The Issue of Equal Representation*, rev. ed. (Washington, D.C.: Brookings Institution, 1964), p. 112.

23. Alfred De Grazia, *The Politics of Reapportionment* (New York: Praeger, 1963), pp. 70-82.

24. Second ed., National Municipal League (July 1962), updated in appen-

dix A of Arthur Goldberg, "The Statistics of Malapportionment," 72
Yale L. J. 90, 100-91 (1962).

25. Manning J. Dauer and Robert G. Kelsay, "Unrepresentative States," 44
National Munic. Rev. 515, 587 (1955); Thomas Dorr, *An Address to the People of Rhode Island from the Convention to Promote the Establishment of a State Constitution,* Providence, 1834, pp. 20-25.

26. Glendon Schubert and Charles Press, "Measuring Malapportionment,"
58 *Am. Pol. Sci. Rev.* 302 (June 1964), *revised to correct a technical oversight, ibid.,* pp. 966-970. The revised figures, which found Ohio to be the best apportioned of the states and Minnesota the worst, suggest that further refinements are still in order. "Well apportioned," in Schubert's language, meant both houses equally apportioned, "unapportioned" meant equal Senate, unequal House, "misapportioned" meant equal House, unequal Senate, and "malapportioned" meant both houses unequal. See also Alan L. Clem, "Measuring Legislative Malapportionment: In Search of a Better Yardstick" 7 *Midwest J. Pol. Sci.* 125 (May 1963); James B. Weaver and Sidney W. Hess, "A Procedure for Nonpartisan Districting: Development of Computer Techniques," 73 *Yale L. J.* 288 (1963).

27. *Compendium on Legislative Reapportionment,* New York, 1962; Gordon Baker, *Rural versus Urban Political Power* (New York: Random House, 1955), pp. 4, 27; "The Eighth American Assembly Participants' Findings," *The 48 States: Their Tasks as Policy Makers and Administrators* (New York: American Assembly, Graduate School of Business, Columbia University, 1955), p. 139; National Municipal League, *A Year in Review, 1962,* p. 12; United States Advisory Comm. on Inter-Governmental Relations, *Apportionment of State Legislatures* (Washington, D.C., 1962); Twentieth Century Fund, *One Man—One Vote,* New York, 1962; Andrew Hacker, *Congressional Districting;* John F. Kennedy, "The Shame of the States," *New York Times Magazine* (May 18, 1958), p. 12.

28. Baker, *Rural versus Urban,* pp. 27-39.

29. Jewell, *Politics of Reapportionment,* pp. 18-19.

30. Anthony Lewis, "Legislative Apportionment and the Federal Courts,"
71 *Harv. L. Rev.* 1057, 1063 (1958).

31. Baker, *Rural versus Urban,* p. 21.

32. *Ibid.,* pp. 28-29.

33. *Ibid.,* p. 49.

34. "Urban," according to different Census Bureau standards, could mean incorporated places with 2,500 or more inhabitants, or with 50,000 or more, with or without suburban fringes, or places with 100,000 or more.

35. Reapportionists relied almost exclusively on legislator's opinions, usually self-serving (e.g., Baker, *Rural versus Urban,* pp. 28-29), or on showing that cities paid more tax and got less return than the rest of the state, although this was also true of equally apportioned states like Massachusetts and probably was more directly related to greater urban wealth and costlier rural services than to malapportionment. See Chapter VII for post-*Baker v. Carr* studies, based on pre-*Baker* data, showing very little relationship between unequal apportionment and its supposed consequences.

36. See Chapters VI and VII for discussion of these questions.

37. See note 26.

38. For example, Anthony Lewis, "Legislative Apportionment in the Federal Courts," 71 *Harv. L. Rev.* 1057 (1958); William L. Taylor, "Legal Action

to Enjoin Legislative Malapportionment: The Political Question Doctrine," 34 *So. Cal. L. Rev.* 179 (1961); Alexander M. Bickel, "The Durability of Colegrove v. Green," 72 *Yale L. J.* 39 (1962); Louis H. Pollak, "Judicial Power and 'The Politics of the People,' " 72 *Yale L. J.* 81 (1962); Robert B. McKay, "Political Thickets and Crazy Quilts: Reapportionment and Equal Protection," 61 *Mich. L. Rev.* 645 (1963); Malcolm E. Jewell, "Minority Representation: A Political or Judicial Question?" 53 *Ky. L. J.* 267 (1964-65).

39. For example, United States Advisory Commission on Intergovernmental Relations, *Apportionment of State Legislatures* (Washington, 1962); Robert G. Dixon, Jr., "Reapportionment in the Supreme Court and Congress: Constitutional Struggle for Fair Representation," 63 *Mich. L. Rev.* 209, 239-242 (1964); Robert G. Dixon, Jr., "Apportionment Standards and Judicial Power," 38 *Notre Dame Law.*, 367 (1963); Robert B. McKay, *Reapportionment: The Law and Politics of Equal Representation* (New York: Twentieth Century Fund, 1965), pp. 459-475; Glendon Schubert, ed., *Reapportionment* (New York: Scribner's, 1965), pp. 67-78.

40. McKay, *Reapportionment*, pp. 273-458; Congressional Quarterly, *Representation and Apportionment* (Washington, D.C., 1966).

41. Karl A. Lamb et. al., *Apportionment and Representative Institutions: The Michigan Experience* (Washington, D.C.: Institute for Social Science Research, 1963); Gilbert Steiner and Samuel Gove, *Legislative Politics in Illinois* (Urbana, University of Illinois Press, 1960); Murray C. Havens, *City vs. Farm* (Bureau of Public Administration, University of Alabama, 1957); William C. Havard and Loren P. Beth, *The Politics of Misrepresentation* (Baton Rouge: Louisiana State University Press, 1962); Jewell, *Politics of Reapportionment*; David R. Derge, "Metropolitan and Outstate Alignments in Illinois and Missouri Legislative Delegations," 52 *Am. Pol. Sci. Rev.* 1051 (December 1958); George D. Young, "The 1958 Special Session of the Missouri General Assembly," *Missouri Political Science Newsletter* No. 3 (1958).

42. Baker, *Rural versus Urban*, p. 27 (Ill.); p. 29 (Mo.); Hacker, *Congressional Districting*, p. 19 (Ill.).

43. Only a small proportion of the 19,000 votes (from 1949 to 1957 in the Missouri House of Representatives and both houses of the Illinois legislature) were contested at all; contested votes were much more likely to produce party blocs than regional blocs. Derge, *Politics of Reapportionment.*

44. George D. Young reached similar conclusions in his study of voting patterns in the Missouri Senate; see his "1958 Special Session."

45. Derge, *Politics of Reapportionment*, pp. 1058-1059.

46. St. Louis was Democratic, Kansas City Republican; Chicago was dominated by the Democrats but split by Illinois's cumulative voting system, which tends to give the majority party two of three representatives from a three-member district, instead of one from a one-member district. Blair, "Cumulative Voting."

47. Havens, *City vs. Farm*; Thomas A. Flinn, "The Outline of Ohio Politics, 13 *Western Pol. Q.* 702, 717 (1960); three studies in Jewell, *Politics of Reapportionment*; William P. Irwin, "Colorado: A Matter of Balance," pp. 64-74. Edward P. Cooke and William J. Keefe, "The Limits of Power in a Divided Government," pp. 149-154 (Pa.) David W. Minar, "Equilibrium in Illinois, Frustration, and Accommodation of the Parties," pp. 134, 146; Robert Friedman, "The Urban Rural Conflict Revisited," *Western Pol. Q.* 481 (June 1961) (Tennessee). See Richard T. Frost, "On Derge's Metropolitan and Outstate

Delegations," 53 *Am. Pol. Sci. Rev.* 792 (1959); Derge's reply, *ibid.*, p. 1097.

48. 377 U.S. 533 (1964).

49. Herbert Jacob, "The Consequences of Malapportionment: A Note of Caution," 27 *Soc. Forces* 256 (December 1964); Thomas R. Dye, "Malapportionment and Public Policy in the States," 27 *J. Politics* 586 (August 1965); Alvin D. Sokolow, "After Reapportionment: Numbers or Policies," 19 *Western Pol. Q.* Supp. 21 (September 1966) (summary).

50. James M. Burns, *The Deadlock of Democracy: Four-party Politics in America* (Englewood Cliffs, N.J.: Prentice-Hall, 1963).

51. Table 6 shows that rural electors had something less than 20 percent more "representation" in the House of Representatives than urban and suburban ones through unequal districts. Rural interests were underrepresented in the Senate if "urban" means 2,500 inhabitants because only 11 states had rural majorities by that standard. The 22 Senate seats allotted to these states gave rural voters—30.0 percent of the population by the 1960 census—only 22 percent of the seats. However, if "urban" means 50,000 inhabitants, 30 states had rural majorities, and rural voters were overrepresented with 60 percent of the seats for only 46.8 percent of the population. United States Census Bureau, *Statistical Abstract of the United States* (Washington, D.C., 1964), p. 16; *Cong. Q. Census Analysis: Congressional Districts of the United States, August 21, 1964,* 22 *Cong. Q.*, pp. 1787-1798. One indicator of the rural-urban balance of power at the time of the *Reapportionment* cases was the attempted passage of the Tuck Bill (H.R. 11926) to remove the Supreme Court's appellate jurisdiction over reapportionment actions. The bill passed the House, 218-175, but the Senate changed its language from mandatory to advisory, 44-38, to leave the Court's power intact. 22 *Cong. Q. Weekly Report,* pp. 1895, 2206 (1964).

Rural interest groups had been at a substantial disadvantage in lobbying expenditures. Only two of the twenty-one largest spending lobbies in 1963, the National Farmer's Union and the American Farm Bureau Federation, ranked fifth and sixth respectively, could be identified with rural interests. 1963 lobbying expenditures of rural groups were $405,000—less than a tenth of total lobbying expenditures for that year, $4.1 million. Of the balance, much the greater part was spent by urban-oriented categories such as business ($1.5 million), labor ($1.1 million), citizens' groups ($707,000), and professional groups ($86,000). The remaining category, military and veterans' groups, would seem to be no more urban than the general population, but its share of expenditures was quite small ($140,000). 22 *Cong. Q. Weekly Report,* pp. 2691, 2696 (September 25, 1964). Arthur Holcombe's summary of 1950 was still descriptive in the 1960's: "The organized urban industrial interests are much more numerous and complex than the agrarian organizations . . . and much more formidable competitors of the official representative bodies under the Constitution." *Our More Perfect Union: From Eighteenth Century Constitutional Principles to Twentieth Century Practice* (Cambridge, Mass.: Harvard University Press, 1950), p. 56.

Despite a slight rural bias in the representation formula of the electoral college, the presidency was considered an urban seat. A successful candidate had to be acceptable to a majority in some or all of the eleven most populous states—New York, California, Pennsylvania, Texas, Illinois, Ohio, Michigan, New Jersey, Florida, Massachusetts, and North Carolina by the 1960 census— or he would lose the election. That majority was urban, and it was the cities that a presidential candidate had to woo most vigorously. The only presidential election since the time of Wilson that the rural vote had been decisive was Truman's surprise victory over Dewey in 1948, where the farm vote gave Truman his margin of victory. Wesley McCune, "Farmers in Politics," 319 *Annals* 45 (1958). Since the president appointed the justices of the Supreme Court, only slightly confined by having to seek the advice and consent of the Senate, it seems not unlikely that the urban point of view prevailed there also. See John Schmidhauser, *The Supreme Court: Its Politics, Personalities, and Procedures* (New York: Holt, Rinehart, and Winston, 1963), *passim*, but especially pp. 11-14, 16. For a 1970 retort to the "urban seat" concept of the presidency, see Carleton W. Sterling, "The Failure of Bloc Voting in the Electoral College to Benefit Urban Liberal and Ethnic Groups," paper delivered to the APSA Convention, Los Angeles, California, September 1970.

52. 20 *Cong. Q. Weekly Rev.* 153 (Feb. 2, 1962). The roll calls involved legislative action on feed grains, minimum wages, area redevelopment, water pollution, housing, New England Water Compact, aid to education, juvenile delinquency, public works, and the AEC-Hanford atomic reactor. Although the study found no major difference between urban and rural congressmen generally as to degree of liberality, it did find that the liberal scores of ranking Democratic committee members of major committees was substantially lower (55 percent) than the national Democratic average of 78 percent. It may well be that the predominance of rural southern conservatives in the committees was a block on free play of executive power, but the predominance of such legislators seemed more attributable to seniority than to malapportionment.

53. *Cong. Q. Census Analysis*, p. 1788 (Aug. 21, 1964). However, Andrew Hacker and William B. Prendergast, research chairman of the Republican National Committee, 1960-1964, both believed that the Republicans, with strong appeal in the suburbs, would benefit more from reapportionment than the Democrats. Hacker, "Votes Cast and Seats Won," *Trans-Action* 7 (Sept.-Oct. 1964); Prendergast, "Memorandum on Congressional Districting," Republican National Committee (Jan. 8, 1963). A revised version of Prendergast's memorandum is printed in Glendon Schubert's *Reapportionment* (New York: Scribner's, 1965), p. 201.

54. Hacker, *Congressional Districting*, p. 89. The bills, respectively, were H.R. 530, carried 271 to 156, disapproving creation of Department of Urban Affairs; H.R. 8890, defeated 251-179, giving federal aid to education; H.R. 11222, defeated 222-212, Administration's Agriculture Bill; and H.R. 127, passed 219-214, adding three members to the Rules Committee.

55. *Ibid.*, pp. 89-91.

56. *Ibid.*

57. *Ibid.*

58. E-Day is commonly reckoned at June 15, 1964, when the Court decided *Reynolds v. Sims.*

59. 295 U.S. 45 (1935).

60. Section two of the Fourteenth Amendment, which penalizes states for abridging the right to vote in specified state and federal elections by reducing their basis of representation in Congress offered a possible theoretical ground to attack unequal districts, but the Court could not have tried to enforce this section against Congress without risking a fight which it was bound to lose. See George D. Zuckerman, "A Consideration of the History and Present

Status of Section 2 of the Fourteenth Amendment," 30 *Ford. L. Rev.* 93 (1961); Arthur E. Bonfield, "The Right to Vote and Judicial Enforcement of Section Two of the Fourteenth Amendment," 46 *Cornell L. Q.* 108 (1960).

61. Edward Corwin, *Court over Constitution* (Princeton: Princeton University Press, 1938).

62. Walter F. Murphy and C. Herman Pritchett, *Courts, Judges, and Politics: An Introduction to the Judicial Process* (New York: Random House, 1961), p. 8.

63. Ex parte Young, 209 U.S. 123 (1908).

64. 28 U.S.C. 2281 (1964).

65. 28 U.S.C. 2201 (1964).

66. Aetna Life Ins. Co. v. Haworth, 300 U.S. 227 (1937).

67. "Legislative Reapportionment and the Federal Courts," 71 *Harv. L. Rev.* 1057 (1958).

68. Att'y. Gen. v. Suffolk County Apportionment Commissioners, 224 Mass. 598, 113 N.E. 581 (1916). In 1962, thirteen states had nonlegislative apportionment bodies, seven—California, Illinois, Michigan, North Dakota, Oregon, South Dakota, and Texas—providing for apportionment if the legislature should fail to apportion, six—Alaska, Arizona, Arkansas, Hawaii, Missouri, and Ohio—leaving apportionment entirely to the nonlegislative body. Seven states—Alaska, Arkansas, Hawaii, New York, Oklahoma, Oregon, and Texas—provided for court review of apportionment plans. Advisory Commission on Intergovernmental Relations, *Report on Apportionment of State Legislatures*, pp. 21-22 (1962).

69. Donovan v. Suffolk County Apportionment Comm'rs., 225 Mass. 55, 113 N.E. 740 (1916); Brophy v. Suffolk County Apportionment Comm'rs. 225 Mass. 124, 133 N.E. 1040 (1916).

70. Fergus v. Marks, 321 Ill. 510, 152, N.E. 557 (1926).

71. State *ex rel.* Martin v. Zimmerman, 249 Wis. 101, 23 N.W. 2d 610 (1946).

72. Fergus v. Kinney, 333 Ill. 437, 164 N.E. 665, *cert. denied*, 279 U.S. 854 (1929).

73. People *ex rel.* Fergus v. Blackwell, 342 Ill. 223, 173 N.E. 750 (1930).

74. Waid v. Pool, 255 Ala. 441, 51 So. 2d 869 (1951); Burns v. Flynn, 155 Misc. 742, 281 N.Y. Supp. 494, *aff'd mem.*, 245 App. Div. 799, 281 N.Y. Supp. 497, *aff'd mem.*, 268 N.Y. 601, 198 N.E. 424 (1935); Romang v. Cordell, 200 Okla. 369, 243 P.2d 677 (1952); Latting v. Cordell, 197 Okla. 369, 172 P.2d 397 (1946).

75. Ragland v. Anderson, 125 Ky. 141, 100 S.W. 865 (1907); Stiglitz v. Schardien, 239 Ky. 799, 40 S.W. 2d 315 (1931).

76. Adams v. Bosworth, 126 Ky. 61, 102 S.W. 861 (1907).

77. Note, 32 *Ind. L.J.* 489, 513014 (1957).

78. Brown v. Saunders, 159 Va. 28, 166 S.E. 105 (1932).

79. People v. Clardy, 334 Ill. 160, 165 N.E. 638 (1929).

80. *New York Times*, Jan. 14, 1936, p. 3 (late city ed.).

81. 285 U.S. 355, 375, 380 (1932).

82. 287 U.S. 1 (1932).

83. 37 Stat. 13 (1911).

84. 328 U.S. 549 (1946).

85. *Ibid.*, p. 556.

86. The Court lacked two justices, Chief Justice Stone having died in April, 1946, and Justice Jackson being absent during the entire term.

87. 328 U.S., p. 566.

88. Cook v. Fortson, 329 U.S. 675 (1946); Colegrove v. Barrett, 330 U.S. 804 (1946); MacDougall v. Green, 335 U.S. 281 (1948); South v. Peters, 339 U.S. 276 (1950); Tedesco v. Board of Supervisors, 339 U.S. 940 (1950); Remmey v. Smith, 342 U.S. 916 (1952); Cox v. Peters, 342 U.S. 936 (1952); Anderson v. Jordan, 343 U.S. 912 (1952); Kidd v. McCanless, 352 U.S. 920 (1956); Radford v. Gary, 352 U.S. 991 (1957); Hartsfield v. Sloan, 357 U.S. 916 (1958); Matthews v. Handley, 361 U.S. 127 (1959).

89. 330 U.S. 804 (1947).

90. 335 U.S. 281, 284 (1948).

91. 339 U.S. 276 (1950).

92. United States Conference of Mayors, Pamphlet, "Of the People, By the People, For the People," 1948.

93. Belle Zeller, ed., *American State Legislatures: Report by the APSA Committee on American Legislatures* (New York: Crowell, 1954).

94. Commission on Intergovernmental Relations, *A Report to the President for Transmittal to Congress* (Washington, D.C.: Government Printing Office, 1955).

95. New York: Random House, 1955.

96. "Legislative Reapportionment and the Federal Courts," 71 *Harv. L. Rev.* 1057 (1958).

97. "The Shame of the States," *New York Times Magazine*, May 18, 1958, p. 12.

98. Charlottesville: Bureau of Public Administration, University of Virginia, 1961 (2 vols.).

99. Brief for the United States as amicus curiae on Reargument, *Baker v. Carr*, 369 U.S. 186 (1962), quoted and discussed, Congressional Quarterly, *Representation and Apportionment*, p. 4. Cf. Baker, *Rural versus Urban Political Power*, pp. 28-29.

100. Reply to Appellee's Statement in Opposition and Motion to Dismiss, Baker v. Carr, 369 U.S. 196 (1962), p. 2. See Robert G. Dixon, *Democratic Representation: Reapportionment in Law and Politics* (New York: Oxford University Press, 1968), pp. 128-129.

101. Brief for the United States, p. 24.

102. *Id.*, pp. 29-30.

103. *Id.*, p. 78.

104. For example, McKay, *Reapportionment*, p. 67.

Notes to Chapter V

1. Alexander Bickel and Harry Wellington, "Legislative Purpose and the Judicial Process: The Lincoln Mills Case," 71 *Harv. L. Rev.*, 1, 3 (1957); Herbert Wechsler, "Toward Neutral Principles of Constitutional Law," 73 *Harv. L. Rev.* 1, 5-6 (1959); Philip Kurland, "The Supreme Court, 1963 Term. Foreword, Equivalent in Origin and Title to the Legislative and Executive Branches of the Government," 78 *Harv. L. Rev.* 143 (1964).

2. Bickel and Wellington, "Legislative Purpose," n. 145.

3. 369 U.S. 186 (1962).

4. Kurland, "Equivalent in Origin and Title," n. 1.

5. 3 Wheat. 610 (4 U.S. 314) (1818).

6. Martin v. Mott, 12 Wheat. 419 (1827); Cherokee Nation v. Georgia, 5

336

Pet. 1 (1831); Ex parte McCardle, 7 Wall. 506 (1869); Korematsu v. United States, 323 U.S. 214 (1944); Ex parte Quirin, 317 U.S. 1 (1942); Banco Nacional de Cuba v. Sabbatino, 376 U.S. 398 (1964). The Sabbatino case, where the Court refused to rule on the merits of an act of state of a recognized foreign government, was modified in part by the Sabbatino Amendment to the Foreign Assistance Act of 1961, 22 U.S.C. s 2370 (e) (2), without objection by the Court. In less heated cases than Korematsu, McCardle, and Quirin, the Court has intervened with some success to bar court-martial jurisdiction over civilians. Ex parte Milligan, 4 Wall. 2 (1866); Duncan v. Kahanamoku, 327 U.S. 304 (1946); Kinsella v. United States ex rel. Singleton, 361 U.S. 234 (1960). In the 1967 term, the Court refused to hear an action to enjoin the secretary of defense from sending conscripts to fight an "unconstitutional" war in Vietnam; Mora v. McNamara, 373 F. 2d 664 (D.D.C.), *cert. denied*, 389 U.S. 934, *rehearing denied*, 389 U.S. 1025 (1967). It also denied certiorari on a Roman Catholic's unsuccessful claim to conscientious objector status on the ground that the war was "unjust," and therefore forbidden to members of his faith. Spiro v. United States, 390 U.S. 956 (1968); cf., United States v. O'Brien, 391 U.S. 367 (1968) (upholding law against draftcard burning).

7. *Defied and lost*: Ex parte Merryman, 17 Fed. Cas. No. 9487 (1861); Worcester v. Georgia, 6 Pet. 515 (1832). *Defied and won*: Youngstown Sheet and Tube Co. v. Sawyer, 343 U.S. 579 (1952). Ex parte Milligan might be regarded as an instance of the Court intervening successfully against a strong desire of Congress not strongly supported by the president; however, Milligan's success was considerably dampened by its reversal for practical purposes in Ex parte McCardle, 7 Wall. 506 (1869).

8. 262 U.S. 447, 484-831 (1923). *But see*, Flast v. Cohen, 392 U.S. 83 (1968).

9. See Tileston v. Ullman, 318 U.S. 44 (1943).

10. 287 U.S. 1 (1932).

11. 223 U.S. 118 (1912). See also, *In re* Duncan, 139 U.S. 449 (1891) (upholding murder conviction against claim that relevant codes were invalidly enacted); Taylor & Marshall v. Beckham (No. 1), 178 U.S. 548 (1900) (claim that Kentucky's resolution of contested gubernatorial election deprived voters of republican government held nonjusticiable); Kiernan v. Portland, 223 U.S. 151 (1912) (claim that municipal charter amendment per municipal initiative and referendum negated republican government held nonjusticiable); Marshall v. Dye, 231 U.S. 250 (1913) (claim that Indiana's constitutional amendment procedure negated republican government held nonjusticiable); O'Neill v. Leamer, 239 U.S. 244 (1915) (claim that delegation to court of power to form drainage districts negated republican government held "futile"); Ohio ex rel. Davis v. Hildebrant, 241 U.S. 565 (1916) (claim that invalidation of state reapportionment statute per referendum negates republican government held nonjusticiable); Ohio ex rel. Bryant v. Akron Metropolitan Park District, 281 U.S. 74 (1950) (claim that rule requiring invalidation of statute by all but one justice of state court negated republican government held nonjusticiable); Mountain Timber Co. v. Washington, 243 U.S. 219 (1917) (claim that workmen's compensation violated republican government held nonjusticiable); Highland Farms Dairy v. Agnew, 300 U.S. 608 (1937) (claim that delegation to agency of power to control milk prices violated republican government, rejected); Coleman v. Miller, 307 U.S. 433 (1939) (rati-

fication of U.S. Constitution Amendment by tie-breaking vote by lieutenant governor, after previous rejection held not justiciable); Snowden v. Hughes, 321 U.S. 1 (1944) (Illinois candidate's action against party official for refusal to list him as candidate held not justiciable). See Fritz W. Scharpf, "Judicial Review and the Political Question: A Functional Analysis," 75 *Yale L. J.* 517 (1966) for a general consideration of the philosophy of political questions.

12. 369 U.S. pp. 244-245. Douglas also was of the opinion that intervention against unequal districts would not invalidate acts of malapportioned legislatures. *Id.*, p. 250, n. 5.

13. Gray v. Sanders, 372 U.S. 368, 381 (1963).

14. 377 U.S. 251, 254.

15. 339 U.S. 376 (1950).

16. 369 U.S. pp. 258-259. Clark stuck to this view in his dissent in Lucas v. 44th Gen. Assembly, 377 U.S. 713 (1964).

17. 369 U.S. p. 267.

18. *Id.*, pp. 307-323. "The notion that representation proportioned to the geographic spread of population is so universally accepted as a necessary element of equality between man and man that it must be taken to be the standard of a political equality preserved by the Fourteenth Amendment—that it is, in appellants' words 'the basic principle of representative government'—is, to put it bluntly, not true. However desirable and however desired by some among the great political thinkers and framers of our government, it has never been generally practiced, today or in the past. It was not the English system, it was not the colonial system, it was not the system chosen for the national government by the Constitution, it was not the system exclusively or even predominantly practiced by the States today." *Id.*, p. 307. For a useful discussion of the court's treatment of historical intent in the reapportionment cases, see Charles A. Miller, *The Supreme Court and the Uses of History* (Cambridge, Mass.: Harvard University Press, 1969), chap. 7.

19. 369 U.S., p. 323.

20. Jack Peltason, *58 Lonely Men: Southern Federal Judges and School Segregation* (New York: Harcourt, Brace and World, 1961), p. 245.

21. 369 U.S. p. 226.

22. *Id.*, p. 268.

23. Congressional Quarterly, *Representation and Apportionment*, (Washington, D.C., 1966), p. 18.

24. *Ibid.*

25. One unsuccessful attempt at painless reapportionment was weighted voting, giving extra votes to representatives with large constituencies without risking the upheaval of redrawing districts. Weighting votes made it much too obvious that a representative's vote was only a small part of his activities as a representative. He had also to service the grievances of his constituents, act on committees, do his part for the party—none of which lent themselves to weighting. Only a few courts considered weighting for statewide elections and only one actually threatened to impose it, only to drop the threat later as unworkable. Thigpen v. Myers, 231 F. Supp. 938 (W.D. Wash. 1964); *aff'd per curiam*, 378 U.S. 554 (1964). See Robert G. Dixon, "Reapportionment in the Supreme Court and Congress: Constitutional Struggle for Fair Representation," 63 *Mich. L. Rev.* 209, 226 (1964); John E. Banzhaf, III, "Weighted Voting Doesn't Work: A Mathematical Analysis," 19 *Rutgers L. Rev.* 317 (1965); Note, "Reapportionment," 79 *Harv. L. Rev.* 1226, 1256-1258

(1966); Carl Auerbach, "The Reapportionment Cases: One Person, One Vote–One Vote, One Value," 1964 *Supreme Court Rev.* 1, 44. Two New York courts permitted weighting at the county level on an interim basis, one noting that it had been used in Nassau County for many years without undue difficulties. Shilbury v. Board of Supervisors, 46 Misc. 2d 837, 260 N.Y.S. 2d 931 (Sup. Ct. 1965); Seaman v. Fedourich, 47 Misc. 2d 26, 262 N.Y.S. 2d 591 (Sup. Ct. 1965).

26. Voters in California, Colorado, and Washington, however, chose "federal plans" with unequal districts in one house by huge margins in 1962 referenda.

27. Congressional Quarterly, *Representation and Apportionment*, p. 27. Goldwater opposed *Reynolds v. Sims* in the 1964 electoral campaign.

28. 372 U.S. 368 (1963).

29. Brief for Appellee, Gray v. Sanders, 372 U.S. 368 (1963), p. 10.

30. Brief for the United States as amicus curiae in Gray v. Sanders, pp. 3-4, 39-41; see Robert G. Dixon, Jr., *Democratic Representation: Reapportionment in Law and Politics* (New York: Oxford University Press, 1968), pp. 179-181. The case was actually briefed and argued by the attorney general, Robert F. Kennedy, on grounds specified by the solicitor general. See pp. 368-370 *infra*.

31. 377 U.S. 533 (1964).

32. 369 U.S. 186, 250 n. 5, 258-259.

33. *San Francisco Chronicle*, Oct. 16, 1948; see Thomas S. Barclay, "The Reapportionment Struggle in California in 1948," 4 *Western Pol. Q.* 319 (June 1951); "I have never been in favor of redistricting the representation in the senate to a strictly population basis. *U.S. News and World Report* (June 6, 1964), p. 34.

34. 372 U.S. p. 381. The Court had upheld the county unit system in three prior per curiam decisions: Cook v. Fortson, 329 U.S. 675 (1946); South v. Peters, 339 U.S. 276 (1950); Cox v. Peters, 342 U.S. 936 (1956), and Hartfield v. Sloan, 357 U.S. 916 (1958). All of these differed from *Gray v. Sanders* in that they involved more than one district.

35. 376 U.S. 1 (1964).

36. 376 U.S. pp. 15-17. Black's reliance on the phrase "by the people" in Article I, section 2 appeared to contradict his earlier admission that "the Constitution contains no express provision requiring that congressional election districts established by the states must contain approximately equal populations." Colegrove v. Green, 328 U.S. 549, 570 (1946) (dissenting opinion).

In the 1920's, Black, then-senator, had insisted that redistricting was a congressional prerogative which could not be constitutionally delegated to the executive even by act of Congress. Opposing the 1929 redistricting act, which he felt embodied a principle "which the Anglo-Saxon race has been fighting since its beginning," Black declared: "I claim that it is a violation of the spirit of the Constitution to attempt to take it [redistricting] out of the hands of Congress and place it in the hands of the President." 71 *Congressional Record* 1612 (1929). He found the Constitution much more pliant three decades later in permitting taking redistricting out of the hands of Congress and placing it in the hands of the Supreme Court.

37. 376 U.S. pp. 15-17.

38. 376 U.S. p. 18.

39. Reynolds v. Sims, 377 U.S. 533; WMCA, Inc. v. Lomenzo, U.S. 633;

Maryland Committee for Fair Representation v. Tawes, 377 U.S. 656; Davis v. Mann, 377 U.S. 678; Roman v. Sincock, 377 U.S. 695, and Lucas v. Forty-fourth Gen. Assembly, 377 U.S. 713 (1964).

40. The solicitor general did not take the lead in *Wesberry v. Sanders*, 376 U.S. 1 (1964) as he did in *Baker v. Carr, Gray v. Sanders*, and *Reynolds v. Sims*, whether from wariness of a brush with Congress, diffidence at tackling an exceptionally difficult task of historical fabrication, or some other reason. In *Wesberry*, where the district court, citing *Colegrove v. Green*, had dismissed the plaintiffs' action to equalize United States congressional districts in Georgia "for want of equity," the solicitor instructed his subordinate to urge remand to the district court "for argument on the merits." Both of the parties of record, and the Supreme Court, felt the merits had been reached, so nobody was interested in the solicitor's strategy for technical postponement of the plaintiffs' case. As a result, the case was decided with no help on the merits from the solicitor, perhaps unfortunately, if one may judge from comments on the quality of the Court's opinion. Alfred H. Kelly, "Clio and the Court: An Illicit Love Affair," 1965 *S. Ct. L. Rev.* 119; Dixon, *Democratic Representation*, pp. 182-195.

41. Dixon, *Democratic Representation*, pp. 250-251.

42. Brief for the United States, Maryland Committee for Fair Play v. Tawes, 377 U.S. 656 (1964), pp. 29-49, summarized and discussed in Dixon, *Democratic Representation*, pp. 250-260.

43. 377 U.S. 713 (1964).

44. "The Government is not prepared to reject the rule of 'per capita' equality, but it does not presently urge it. Such an interpretation would press the Equal Protection Clause to an extreme, as applied to State legislative apportionment, would require radical changes in three-quarters of the State governments, and would eliminate the opportunities for local variation. *On the other hand, to reject the interpretation at this early stage of the development under Baker v. Carr would prematurely close an important line of constitutional evolution.*" Brief for the United States as amicus curiae, Lucas v. Colorado Assembly, 377 U.S. 713 (1964), p. 32 (italics mine).

45. Dixon, *Democratic Representation*, p. 256.

46. 21 Wall. 162 (1875).

47. 377 U.S. 593-632.

48. Robert G. Dixon, "Reapportionment in the Supreme Court and Congress: Constitutional Struggle for Fair Representation," 63 *Mich. L. Rev.* 209, 239-242 (1964).

49. Besides invoking Lincoln, Jefferson, and the Declaration of Independence, the Court relied heavily on modern reapportionist commentators and groups, citing Robert McKay, Arthur Goldberg, Maurice Merrill, Robert Dixon, Paul David, and Ralph Eisenberg, 377 U.S. 556, 572, 579, 582, notes 30, 50, 60, 62, and the Advisory Commission on Intergovernmental Relations, 377 U.S. p. 572, n. 52. Justice Warren's catchphrase "people, not land or trees or pastures, vote" (377 U.S. p. 580), derives from the Twentieth Century Fund's Conference of Research Scholars and Political Scientists, *One Man—One Vote* (New York: Twentieth Century Fund, 1962), p. 5.

50. Frankfurter himself distinguished personal suffrage rights (under sections of the Constitution mentioning the right to vote) from rights of representation, involving group interests. Rights of representation were protectable, if at all, by the guarantee clause, and the Court had made it clear in *Pacific States Tel. Co. v. Oregon* and in other cases that guarantee-clause

claims were not justiciable. 369 U.S. 267, 297. Arthur Bonfield argued that apportionment was a guarantee-clause question but that the Court should have intervened anyway: "Baker v. Carr: New Light on the Constitutional Guarantee of Republican Government," 50 *Calif. L. Rev.*, 245 (1962); see also, Arthur E. Bonfield, "The Guarantee Clause of Article IV, Section 4: A Study in Constitutional Disuetude," 46 *Minn. L. Rev.* 513 (1962).

51. 369 U.S. p. 267 (Frankfurter dissenting opinion): The relation between population and legislative representation was "a wholly different matter from denial of the franchise to individuals because of race, color, religion, or sex."

52. Another consideration favoring the use of a broad definition of voting rights in preference to a right of representation limited to reapportionment was its greater potential for future intervention. If the Court had tried to limit the coverage of the equal protection clause to problems of the district system it could have used it to attack problems of qualifications, such as those presented in the poll tax case, *Harper v. Board of Electors*, 383 U.S. 663 (1966), only with great difficulty, and probably only with the same kind of historical fabrication it pioneered in the reapportionment cases.

Notes to Chapter VI

1. However, once the slightest irregularity creeps in, measurements problems creep in as well. See Robert G. Dixon's plentifully documented *Democratic Representation* (New York: Oxford University Press, 1968), pp. 535-543.

2. *Bolling v. Sharpe*, 347 U.S. 497, 500 (1954), read the equal protection clause into the Fifth Amendment with these words: "It would be unthinkable that the same Constitution would impose a lesser duty on the Federal Government."

3. Delaware v. New York, 385 U.S. 895 (1966); cf. Gray v. Sanders, 372 U.S. 368 (1963). The numerical bias of the Senate and the electoral college against the larger states derived from the allocation, in both cases, of two senatorial votes to each state, regardless of population. The operational bias favoring voters in the larger states derived from the "winner take all," or unit rule practice among the states, giving all their electoral college votes to the statewide winner rather than giving the loser a proportional share. The unit rule made it theoretically possible for the candidate carrying the eleven largest states, by however small a margin, to carry the whole country, perhaps with a popular minority of nationwide votes. The unit rule was therefore supposed to guarantee that no candidate could win whose views were unacceptable to large-state voters. It was thought to favor urban voters, especially Democrats, workers, and ethnic minorities.

In practice, there has never been an election where one candidate carried almost all the big states and the other carried almost all the smaller ones. Big and small states alike followed nationwide preferences closely, voting together for national landslide winners, dividing on close contests. Since 1824 there has been only one clear case of a candidate with a plurality of popular votes losing a majority in the electoral college. That case was Grover Cleveland's loss to Benjamin Harrison in 1888. Though it is undoubtedly true that most presidential candidates come from large, urban states and that a candidate must carry most of the big states to win, this would also be true (though perhaps to a lesser extent) with other systems than the electoral college.

Since the electoral college had multi-member delegations of varying size, there was a mathematical bias favoring voters from large states. See Dixon, *Democratic Representation*, pp. 575-571, and John F. Banzhaf, III, "One Man, 3.312 Votes: A Mathematical Analysis of the Electoral College," 13 *Vill. L. Rev.* 304 (1967). See also Robert J. Sickels, "Power Index and the Electoral College: A Challenge to Banzhaf's Analysis," 14 *Vill. L. Rev.* 87 (1968). Perhaps the best argument for direct election may be found in Neal R. Pierce, *The People's President: The Electoral College in American History and the Direct-Vote Alternative* (New York: Clarion Books, 1968). Excellent argument against direct election may be found in the supporting material for the minority views of Senators Eastland, McClellan, Ervin, Hruska, Fong, and Thurmond, "Direct Popular Election of the President," Calendar No. 1135, Report No. 91-1123, 91st Cong. 2d sess., August 14, 1970. See also Alexander M. Bickel, *The New Age of Political Reform: The Electoral College, the Convention, and the Party System* (New York: Harper Colophon Books, 1968).

4. Carleton W. Sterling, "The Failure of Bloc Voting in the Electoral College to Benefit Urban Liberal and Ethnic Groups," paper delivered at APSA Convention, Los Angeles, September 1970. Sterling's views were shared by Lawrence Longley and John Yunker: "Who is Really Advantaged by the Electoral College—and Just Who Thinks He Is?" paper delivered at APSA Convention, Chicago, September 1971.

5. "Electing the President," Hearings Before the Senate Subcommittee on Constitutional Amendments, 91st Cong., 1st sess., January-May 1969, p. 66.

6. An electoral system should be chosen with an eye to the quality of the majorities it is expected to elicit, as well as the quantity. A system which produces stable, cohesive, center-seeking majorities should be preferred to one which produces volatile or extremist majorities, as primary elections are said to do. Paul T. David, "Experimental Approaches to Vote-Counting Theory in Nominating Choice," 56 *Am. Pol. Sci. Rev.* 673 (September 1963). The existing electoral system is of the first type. It is heavily insulated against short-term political fads and tunnel-visioned zealots seeking quick and utter justice on a single grand issue with no particular regard to its effect on other values and needs. It shrugs off third and fourth parties; it discourages Napoleonic leadership and short-term virtuosity at the very top, while cultivating the sustained and disciplined attention in the middle and participatory cooperation at the bottom which have been the greatest strength of democracy in America. America has never had an executive of the transpartisan brilliance of a Napoleon or a de Gaulle. She has never needed one, and, if she is lucky, she never will.

Nor does she need the raw, plebiscitary majorities on which Napoleon and de Gaulle relied while they lasted, nor the intransigent multiplicity of parties which have tended in France to fill the gaps between one transpartisan leader and the next. If the examples of France and such large states as New York and California in the television age provide any guidance, they suggest that direct election of major officers with very large constituencies goes together with weak parties and candidates long on glamor (or *grandeur*, in the French case) but not necessarily long on political experience, organizational talent, seasoned judgment and ability, or party loyalty. The new generation of image candidates in New York and California in the late 1960's and early 1970's sparkled with new faces, but it was remarkably innocent of party loyalty or discipline, with a Democrat-turned-Republican here, a Republican-turned-Democrat there, and a Republican-turned-Conservative yonder. The new faces no doubt refreshed the tired spirit of their respective parties, and some turned out to have leadership talent comparable to that of more experienced professionals (though others did not). The sudden success of shortcut candidates, however, could hardly be expected to strengthen the parties, for it sapped the expected rewards of party regulars while increasing those of the irregulars, a dangerous effect in the long run.

Direction election of the president would encourage such shortcutting at the national level, enhancing the chances that a third- or fourth-party candidate could successfully play a spoiling role, or possibly come out a winner in a political universe hospitable to third and fourth parties, as third-party candidates John Lindsay and James Buckley did in New York. Even with a 40-percent-plurality-or-runoff requirement, a third- or fourth-party candidate would find it much easier to marshall a formidable minority by sweeping up all his potential supporters in the country than by winning separate majorities in a substantial block of states, as he must do under the present system. Direct national primaries, called for by several of the bills before Congress in 1969, would likewise raise the prospects for success outside of party channels and weaken the incentives to bother with the tedious tasks of coalition building, negotiation, ticket balancing, interest aggregation, and careful, professional assessment of candidates, which the parties—in their own interest—have traditionally performed with devotion and skill. American democracy depends very heavily on *someone's* willingness and ability to perform these tasks, and the indirect, state-by-state arrangement of the present presidential nominating and electing processes has fortunately supplied strong incentives to party professionals to do them on a sustained basis. Direct national presidential primaries would surely weaken the parties, as direct primaries did in the states; so, in all likelihood, would direct election of the president by increasing the potential rewards to shortcutters and diminishing those of party regulars.

7. Powell v. McCormack, 395 U.S. 486, 547 (1969). See Note, "The Power of a House of Congress to Judge the Qualifications of Its Members," 81 *Harv. L. Rev.* 673 (1968); Comment, "Legislative Exclusion: Julian Bond and Adam Clayton Powell," 35 *U. Chi. L. Rev.* 151 (1967); "Comments on Powell v. McCormack," 17 *U.C.L.A. L. Rev.* 1 (1969).

8. Powell v. McCormack, 395 F. 2d 577 (D.C. Cir. 1968).

9. The Court applied the Twenty-Fourth Amendment in *Harman v. Forsenious*, 380 U.S. 528 (1965), but rendered it superfluous in *Harper v. Board of Elections*, 383 U.S. 663 (1966).

10. The Voting Rights Act of 1965, 79 Stat. 437, came into play by a "trigger" provision in states and districts where less than 50 percent of adult blacks were registered for the 1964 elections. It authorized suspension of state literacy tests and substitution of federal examiners to register blacks where discrimination was found. Under the act, a sixth-grade education in an American-flag school was presumptive evidence of literacy. The Court upheld the act against assertions that the trigger provision was unconstitutional, *South Carolina v. Katzenbach*, 383 U.S. 301 (1966), and against New York's claim that the act did not preempt its language requirement, *Katzenbach v. Morgan*, 384 U.S. 641 (1966). State language tests, however, did not violate the equal protection clause where the Voting Rights Act did not apply. *Cardona v. Power*, 384 U.S. 672 (1966). Although the Court in 1959 upheld

a literacy test where no discrimination was shown, in *Lassiter v. Northampton Cty. Board*, 360 U.S. 45, it decided ten years later that literacy tests in Gaston County, N.C., however impartially administered, were racially discriminatory because of historically inferior black schools in the county. *Gaston County v. United States*, 395 U.S. 285 (1969).

11. *In re* Gault, 387 U.S. 1 (1967).

12. Thomas E. Spencer, "A Proposal for Voting Reform," 78 *Ethics* 289, 292-294 (July 1968): "The logic of the total situation demands that we take immediate and bold steps, as we head into history's most bewildering age, to get the best possible electorate. I believe that one giant step in this direction would be to lower the voting age at both ends of the scale, particularly at the top. *The old have had their say; now let them depart in peace.*" (Emphasis original.)

13. *Congressional Quarterly* (May 23, 1969), pp. 824-826.

14. *New York Times*, Mar. 2, 1970, p. 36, col. 1 (city ed.).

15. *Ibid.* Sixty-eight senators had favored securing a constitutional amendment.

16. Between the Senate's passage of the voting rights package and the House's, a curious debate between several giants of constitutional jurisprudence took place in the letters pages of the *New York Times*. The debate notably failed to display the customary polarity of liberal, activist, broad constructionists on one side and conservative, anti-activist, strict constructionists on the other. Instead, constitutional commentators were somewhat taken aback to find six Yale law school professors of widely varying views—including the liberal, activist, broad constructionist Charles Black and the moderate proponent of the "passive virtues" of constitutional construction Alexander Bickel—joining in a letter which blasted the eighteen-year-old vote provision as unconstitutional. Noting that section two of the Fourteenth Amendment penalized state denial or abridgment of the right to vote of "any of the male inhabitants of such state, being twenty-one years of age, and citizens of the United States," the Yale professors found it hard to imagine how the twenty-one-year-old standard could be found irrational and invidious when it seemed to be presented in the next section as a constitutional standard. "It surpasses belief," they warned, "that the Constitution authorizes Congress to define the Fourteenth Amendment's equal protection clause so as to outlaw what the Amendment's next section approves." *New York Times*, April 15, 1970, pt. IV, p. 13, col. 1 (city ed.). The other professors were Robert H. Bork, John Hart Ely, Louis H. Pollack, and Eugene W. Rostow.

Two Harvard law professors, neither noted for his sympathy for loose construction, joined the debate with a defense of Congress's authority, based on a rationale of loose construction. Paul Freund, a moderate proponent of judicial restraint, joined with Archibald Cox, the liberal activist architect of the reapportionment cases, in supporting the statute. The Harvard professors believed that the equal protection clause did indeed forbid irrational discrimination in voting rights and that the twenty-one-year-old standard in section two, which penalized state restrictions on the franchise, had "nothing to do with enlargement" by Congress, leaving Congress free to order the eighteen-year-old vote by statute under the equal protection clause. *New York Times*, Apr. 12, 1970, pt. IV, p. 13, col. 2 (city ed.).

17. 384 U.S. 641 (1966).

18. *Id.*, p. 653. Despite this dictum, the case was not clear authority to

support the eighteen-year-old vote. It could be limited on its facts, as the Yale professors suggested, to the protection of ethnic minorities (thereby perhaps falling more appropriately under the Fifteenth Amendment). Or it might have been limited to situations involving Congress's power to protect inhabitants of the Commonwealth of Puerto Rico from invidious discrimination based on their linguistic differences from inhabitants of the states. Or, as the dissenting Justices Harlan and Stewart maintained, the Court may have been wrong in holding that literacy tests could be irrational discrimination. *Katzenbach v. Morgan* was an arguable foundation for the eighteen-year-old statute, but not a strong one.

19. McGowan v. Maryland, 366 U.S. 420, 425-426 (1961).

20. Kramer v. Union Free School District, 395 U.S. 621, 626-630 (1969). See also Shapiro v. Thompson, 394 U.S. 618, 634 (1969); United States v. Jackson, 390 U.S. 570, 582-583 (1968); Sherbert v. Verner, 374 U.S. 398, 406-409 (1963); Bates v. City of Little Rock, 361 U.S. 516, 524 (1959); Speiser v. Randall, 357 U.S. 513, 525-526 (1958).

21. Puishes v. Mann, No. 25, 401 (9th Cir. 1970); WMCA Vote at 18 Club v. Board of Elections, No. 70 Civ. 1814 (S.D.N.Y. 1970); Greenspun v. Nevada, No. 24087, 9th Cir. 1970 (also invoking Article IV, section 2, and the Ninth, Fifteenth, and Nineteenth Amendments, as well as the privileges and immunities clause of the Fourteenth). Cf. Ward Elliott, "The 18-Year-Old Vote: Constitutional Crisis in the Fall?" mimeograph, Claremont Men's College (June 22, 1970).

22. 400 U.S. 112 (1970).

23. Black's argument from Article I, section 4, was not very convincing, as qualifications for voting in federal elections are specified in Article I, section 2: "The Electors in each State shall have the Qualifications requisite for Electors of the most numerous branch of the State Legislature."

24. Article II, section 1, paragraph 2, gives the states power to determine the manner of appointing members of the electoral college: "Each State shall appoint in such manner as the legislature thereof may direct, a number of Electors . . . "

25. Youth-vote partisans, of course, can still apply most of the arguments for enfranchising eighteen-year-olds to the task of enfranchising those under eighteen. See, for example, Gaunt v. Brown 341 F. Supp. 1187 (S.D. Ohio) aff'd. per curiam, 93 S. Ct. 69 (1973) (unsuccessful effort by seventeen-year-old who would be eighteen for general election to vote in primary under the equal protection clause).

26. Richard M. Scammon and Ben J. Wattenberg, *The Real Majority: An Extraordinary Examination of the American Electorate* (New York: Coward, McCann, and Geohegan, 1971), pp. 50, 46-53, and *passim*.

27. For example, Michael A. Rappeport, "The Kids Will be More than Just Younger," *The Washington Monthly* (September 1970); Louis M. Seagull, "The Youth Vote and Change in American Politics," 391 *Annals* 83 (September 1971); William G. Carleton, "Votes for Teenagers," 58 *Yale Review* 45 (October 1968).

28. Daniel Patrick Moynihan, " 'Peace'—Some Thoughts on the 1960s and 1970s," *The Public Interest* (Summer 1973), pp. 3, 6-12. The youth boom, like the baby boom which produced it, will soon level off and decline as the smaller cohorts of the 1960's replace the large ones of the 1950's.

29. Congressional Quarterly, *Current American Government* (Washington,

D.C., Spring 1973), p. 24. Political commentators Rowland Evans and Robert Novack report that this misconception was also prevalent among top Republican strategists on the White House staff. According to Evans and Novack, President Nixon's signing of the Voting Rights Amendments of 1970 was reluctant and done "over ardent protests of the President's top political advisor, Attorney General John Mitchell, and the entire White House Congressional liaison staff," who "had not the slightest doubt . . . that the eighteen-, nineteen-, and twenty-year-olds would vote Democratic en masse." Nixon's decision to sign the bill, which Evans and Novack supposed might have been made "for fear of an anti-Nixon youth rebellion" if he did not (!) or possibly out of concern over his role in history, was regarded by one White House aide as "one that will go down as Richard Nixon's major political blunder." Rowland Evans and Robert D. Novack, *Nixon in the White House: The Frustration of Power* (New York: Random House, 1971), pp. 129-132.

30. See the *Congressional Quarterly*'s skeptical assessment of the youth vote's impact in the 1972 elections, *Current American Government* (Washington, D.C., Spring 1973), p. 24. The nearest approximations the *Quarterly* could find to a youth impact on congressional elections were two races where the candidate carried the college student vote in his district but lost, plus one where the candidate carried the college vote but would have won without it, albeit narrowly.

31. Respectively, Carrington v. Rash, 380 U.S. 89 (1965) and Harper v. Virginia Board of Elections, 383 U.S. 663 (1966) ("In determining what lines are constitutionally discriminatory, we have never been confined to historic notions of equality.").

32. Kramer v. Union Free School District, 395 U.S. 621 (1969) (New York): Cipriano v. Houma, 395 U.S. 701 (1969) (Louisiana).

33. 395 U.S., pp. 632-633 (1969).

34. See, besides the Harper, Kramer, and Cipriano cases, Williams v. Rhodes, 393 U.S. 23 (1968); Evans v. Cornman, 398 U.S. 419 (1970); Phoenix v. Kolodziejski, 399 U.S. 204 (1970); Dunn v. Blumstein, 405 U.S. 331 (1972).

35. Evans v. Cornman, 398 U.S. 419 (1970).

36. Phoenix v. Kolodziejski, 399 U.S. 204 (1970).

37. Salyer Land Co. v. Tulare Lake Basin Water Storage District, 93 S.Ct. 1224, 1236 (1973).

38. Alvin Toffler, *Future Shock* (New York: Bantam Books, 1971), p. 75.

39. In 1967-68, twenty-to-twenty-four-year-olds were the most mobile of all general age categories. As many as 41.5 percent of them had changed addresses with the year, a figure exceeded only that (44.2 percent) of married males twenty-five to thirty-four years old, not living with their wives. The latter category was high almost by definition, including young husbands separated from their wives but not divorced, and married servicemen on hardship tours without dependents. Married men twenty-five to thirty-four living with their wives, at 31 percent, were the third highest category, followed by all eighteen- and nineteen-year-olds (25.2 percent). The national average for mobility was 18.8 percent. United States Bureau of the Census, Department of Commerce, *Current Population Reports*, ser. P-20 No. 188, p. 1 (1969).

40. *Newsweek* (August 30, 1971), p. 27.

41. Paul R. Rentenbach, "Student Voting Rights in University Communities," 6 *Harv. Civil Liberties L. Rev.* 397, 399 (1971).

42. Richard Claude, *The Supreme Court and the Electoral Process* (Baltimore: Johns Hopkins Press, 1970), pp. 254-257.

43. Reynolds v. Sims, 377 U.S. 533, 567 (1964).

44. Shapiro v. Thompson, 394, U.S. 618 (1969); Carrington v. Rash, 380 U.S. 89 (1965). It also rejected an apportionment scheme which was ostensibly based on total population but whose unequal districts could be explained only by exclusion of transient military personnel. Davis v. Mann, 377 U.S. 678, 691 (1964). See Wilkins v. Davis, 139 S.E. 2d 849, 852 (Va. 1965). However, it did allow a voter-based (as opposed to population-based) apportionment in Hawaii, despite its discrimination against temporary residents and nonvoting military personnel. Burns v. Richarson, 384 U.S. 73 (1966).

45. Oregon v. Mitchell, 400 U.S. 112 (1970).

46. 405 U.S. 330, 346 (1972).

47. 405 U.S., p. 360.

48. See, for example, Alan F. Westin, *Privacy and Freedom* (New York: Athenaeum, 1968), chap. 12, "Pulling All the Facts Together."

49. Sweezy v. New Hampshire, 354 U.S. 234, 262 (1957) (Frankfurter, J., concurring).

50. The dormitory vote can have significant impact only where dormitory registration is high to begin with, and turnout is high, politically homogeneous, and contrary to the surrounding public. These are almost impossible requirements for influencing elections in most county-sized or larger districts; they are stiff requirements even for most smaller districts. By definition they eliminate commuter colleges, whose students are local residents anyway. As a matter of numbers, they minimize the potential impact of small, resident colleges and larger ones located in heavily populated voting districts. Inundation by a *majority* of students is possible only in small places—like Amherst, Massachusetts (with 7,000 registered voters in 1971 and 15,000 college students), New Paltz, New York (3,270 voters; 7,000 students), and Norman, Oklahoma (15,000 voters; 17,000 students)—with large numbers of students. Even in such places, and others where college students are a minority too large to ignore, the students must register and turn out, both of which they are more likely to do than nonstudents of the same age, but less likely to do than older voters. A Gallup poll in the spring of 1972 showed 66 percent of the student population registered to vote (not necessarily on campus), as opposed to 41 percent of nonstudents of the same age and 74 percent of the total eligible adult population. Minus a substantial fraction for those who registered but did not vote, these figures probably give a reasonable indication of relative turnout among the three categories for the presidential elections of 1972. An even larger fraction should be subtracted for all categories for local elections, which attract less turnout than presidential elections.

51. Paul Seabury, "Berkeley: A Tale of One City," *Commentary* (August 1971), pp. 66-70.

52. Mary Ellen Leary, "It's Radicals vs. Liberals in Tuesday's Berkeley Vote," *Los Angeles Times*, April 15, 1973, p. VII-1, col. 1.

53. *Ibid.* "The striking thing about these rival slates," observed Ms. Leary, "is the degree of similarity in their objectives. They share an impatience for change and agree on the specifics of where to begin: more local health services, far more child-care centers, tougher zoning controls, public transit, more low-cost housing. All candidates approve rent control, favor the new Affirmative Action program."

54. *Los Angeles Times*, August 23, 1973, p. I-3, col. 3.

55. *Congressional Quarterly Guide, Current American Government* (Washington, D.C.: Fall 1972), p. 48. Four states—Utah, Arkansas, Minnesota, and Virginia—allowed students to vote on campus in some cases where they could show intention of permanent residence. Five states—Hawaii, New York, South Carolina, Tennessee, and Texas—did not allow students to register at their colleges under any circumstances. In Arizona, Missouri, and Montana the rules were not clarified and were being tested in court.

56. Marston v. Lewis, 410 U.S. 679 (1973): Burns v. Fortson, 410 U.S. 686 (1973).

57. Rosario v. Rockefeller, 410 U.S. 752 (1973).

58. Vlandis v. Kline, 412 U.S. 441 (1973): cf., Starns v. Malkerson, 326 F. Supp. 234 (D. Minn. 1970), *aff'd per curiam,* 401 U.S. 985 (1971); Kirk v. Board of Regents, 273 Cal. App. 2dx 430, 78 Cal. Reptr. 260 (1969), appeal dismissed, 396 U.S. 554 (1970) (upholding tuition discrimination between in-state and out-of-state students).

59. 412 U.S. pp. 454-455.

60. 412 U.S. pp. 456-459.

61. 412 U.S. pp. 459-469. A residual cluster of minor qualifications issues surrounds the question of disfranchisement for crimes, insanity, and miscellaneous laws still on the books in some states, though no longer enforced, barring blasphemers, subversives, prostitutes, paupers, vagrants, or tax delinquents. Laws barring insane people from voting are still common and still enforced to some degree. Though these laws have not been challenged in court they could arguably contravene Section 4 (c) of the Voting Rights Act of 1965, which suspends tests or devices requiring the prospective voter to "demonstrate the ability to read, write, understand, or interpret any matter." Most of the states bar convicted felons from voting, both during and after confinement. Some bar misdemeanants; some bar only those convicted of voting law violations. The Supreme Court long ago acquiesced in the disfranchisement of Mormons, not for practicing bigamy themselves, but for being members of orders upholding bigamy. Davis v. Beason, 133 U.S. 333 (1890). A much stricter standard would be expected today, and a few lower courts have struck down or questioned laws disfranchising former felons, under the Equal Protection Clause; for example, Stephens v. Yeomans, 327 F. Supp. 1182 (D.N.J. 1970); Ramirez v. Brown, 107 Cal. Reptr. 137, 9 Cal. 3d. 199 (1973); Dillenburg v. Kramer, 469 F. 2d. 1222 (9th Cir. 1972). Neither the Warren Court nor the Burger Court, however, has followed these leads. McDonald v. Board of Elections Commissioners, 394 U.S. 802 (1969) (upholding absentee ballot statute whose alleged effect was to deny the vote to those in jail awaiting trial); *but see,* Goosby v. Osser, 93 S. Ct. 854 (1973) (reversing dismissal of jailed person's suit for absentee ballot on ground that it was not necessarily frivolous or insubstantial under McDonald v. Board); O'Brien v. Skinner, 42 U.S. L. Week 4151, Jan. 16, 1974 (statute denying absentee ballot to jailed person awaiting trial in county of residence violated equal protection clause). Lower courts have rejected arguments that disfranchising felons, besides violating the equal protection clause, was also a cruel and unusual punishment or a bill of attainder or a violation of the First Amendment. Fincher v. Scott, *supra;* Green v. Board of Elections, 380 F. 2d 445 (2d Cir. 1967); Kronlund v. Honstein, 327 F. Supp. 71 (N.D. Ga. 1971).

The Supreme Court's neglect to apply the compelling state interest test to the disfranchisement of felons and exfelons seems logically out of line with its other decisions on voting qualifications, especially in the Warren and early Burger years. It must be applauded, however, from the standpoints of traditional constitutional jurisprudence, and, in the case of convicts still in prison, must be particularly applauded from the public policy standpoint as well, since the prisoners, once franchised, would meet residency requirements easily and might well want, like students, to exercise the resultant right to become a force in local politics.

A tabular summary of state franchise laws up to 1968 may be found in Ward Elliott, "Ideology and Intervention: Supreme Court Intervention in Voting Rights Disputes from Taney to Warren," Ph.D. diss. (Harvard University, Cambridge, Mass., 1968), App. II-IV.

62. D. E. Butler, *The Electoral System in Britain Since 1918* (London: Oxford University Press, 1963), pp. 213-220; Charles P. Edwards, "Theoretical and Comparative Aspects of Reapportionment and Redistricting," 15 *Vand. L. Rev.* 1265 (1962); Arthur Goldberg, "The Statistics of Malapportionment," 72 *Yale L. J.* 90, 95 (1962).

63. National Municipal League, *A Year in Review*, 1962, p. 12.

64. Gordon W. Hatheway, Jr., "Political Gerrymanders: The Law and Politics of Partisan Districting," 26 *G.W.L. Rev.* 1144, 148 (1967); H.R. 2508, 90th Cong., 1st sess., H.R. Report No. 191, 90th Cong., 1st sess. (1967).

65. Kirkpatrick v. Preisler, 394 U.S. 526 (1969). A proper apportionment should meet three kinds of tests: a *population variance* test considering the ratio between the largest and smallest district; a *maximum detrimental deviation* test to keep states from singling out one large district for underrepresentation in an otherwise equal system; and a *Dauer-Kelsay* score of the minimum fraction of the population necessary to control the legislature to show overall equality of districts. See Note, "Reapportionment," 79 *Harv. L. Rev.* 1228, 1248-1254 (1966).

66. Gong v. Kirk, 278 F. Supp. 133 (S.D. Fla. 1967), *aff'd per curiam* 389 U.S. 574 (1968); Lucas v. Rhodes, Civil No. 65, 264 (N.D. Ohio 1967), *rev'd per curiam* 389 U.S. 212 (1967). See Robert G. Dixon, "The Warren Court Crusade for the Holy Grail of One Man—One Vote," 1969 *S. Ct. L. Rev.* 219.

The Burger Court, while holding to the Warren Court's rigid standards for U.S. congressional districts (e.g., *White v. Weiser*, 412 U.S. 783 [1973]), has been more permissive for state and local districts. In *Abate v. Mundt*, 403 U.S. 182 (1971) it upheld a 12 percent maximum population variance between districts in Rockland County, New York, owing to the "extensive functional interrelation" of county governmental agencies and lack of systematic "built-in bias" against larger or smaller units. In *Mahan v. Powell*, 410 U.S. 315 (1973), it upheld a plan with 16.4 percent maximum variance for Virginia's House of Delegates, since the variation resulted from the rational objective of avoiding fragmentation of political subdivisions. See also White v. Regester, 412 U.S. 755 (1973); Gaffney v. Cummings, 412 U.S. 735 (1973).

67. Congressional Quarterly, *Representation and Apportionment* (Washington, D.C., 1966), pp. 57-58.

68. *Ibid.*

69. Dinis v. Volpe, 264 F. Supp. 425 (D. Mass. 1967) *aff'd per curiam* 289 U.S. 570 (1968).

70. Holt v. Richardson, 238 F. Supp. 468, 476-477 (D. Hawaii 1965),

modified on other grounds, 240 F. Supp. 724, *vacated and remanded on other grounds*, 384 U.S. 73 (1965).

71. Lucas v. Forty-fourth Gen. Assembly, 377 U.S. 713, 736 (1964); Note, Reapportionment, 79 *Harv. L. Rev.* 1228, 1247-1248 (1966).

72. Mann v. Davis, 377 U.S. 678 691 (1964).

73. Burns v. Richardson, 384 U.S. 73 (1965).

74. Kirk v. Cong, 278 F. Supp. 133 (S.D. Fla. (1967), *aff'd per curiam*, 389 U.S. 574 (1968).

75. Once an apportionment basis has been chosen, changes are suspect. WMCA v. Lomenzo, 238 F. Supp. 916, 924-925 (S.D.N.Y.), *aff'd.* 382, U.S. 4 (1965). See Dixon, *Democratic Representation*, pp. 501-503.

76. Gordon v. Lance, 403 U.S. 1 (1971) (upholding West Virginia 60 percent majority requirement for bond issues and tax increases).

77. The difficulties were practical, not constitutional. It was well established that subdivisions of states are agents of the states, subject to the provisions of the Fourteenth and Fifteenth Amendments. Hunter v. Pittsburgh, 207 U.S. 161 (1907); Reynolds v. Sims, 377 U.S. 503, 575 (1964) (dictum); Gomillion v. Lightfoot, 304 U.S. 339 (1960).

78. Avery v. Midland County, 390 U.S. 474, 499-500 (1968) (Fortas, J., dissenting).

79. Robert G. Wood, *1400 Governments: The Political Economy of the New York Metropolitan Area* (New York: Doubleday, 1964).

80. See Manning J. Dauer, "Multi-member Districts in Dade County: A Study of a Problem and a Delegation," 28 *J. Politics* 617 (Aug. 1966); Jack B. Weinstein, "The Effect of the Federal Reapportionment Decisions in Counties and Other Forms of Municipal Government," 65 *Colum. L. Rev.* 21 (1965); 52 *Nat'l Civic Rev.* 505 (1963); Note, "Reapportionment," 79 *Harv. L. Rev.* 1228, 1278-80 (1966). New York was formed as a federation of once independent boroughs; its Board of Estimates and City Council were apportioned to favor smaller boroughs. Both were challenged under *Reynolds v. Sims.* McMillan v. Wagner, 234 Supp. 32 (S.D.N.Y. 1964); *New York Times*, Apr. 4, 1965, p. 85, col. 3; *New York Times*, May 26, 1965, p. 1, col. 2.

81. 377 U.S. 533, 573 (1964).

82. 390 U.S. 474 (1968).

83. Dixon, *Democratic Representation*, pp. 551-557.

84. For example, Augostini v. Lasky, 46 Misc. 2d 26, 262 N.Y.S. 2d 594, 604 (Sup. Ct. 1965) (overruling two recent referenda). See R. Perry Sentell, Jr., "Reapportionment and Local Government," 1 *Ga. L. Rev.* 596 (1967); Note, "Reapportionment," 79 *Harv. L. Rev.* 1228, 1272 (1966).

85. 387 U.S. 105 (1967).

86. 387 U.S. 112 (1967).

87. Hadley v. Junior College District, 397 U.S. 50 (1970); cf., Salyer Land Co. v. Tulare Lake Basin District, 93 S. Ct. 1224 (1973) (upholding water district board vote weighted by value of land owned).

88. The Hadley case also suggested that school district elections would be subject to the equal districts requirement, though school districts do present questions about variances in student turnout (say, because of parochial schools, or different age profiles) between one district and another that have not yet been brought before the Supreme Court. See Note, "Reapportionment," 79 *Harv. L. Rev.* 1228, 1275-78 (1966). Other special purpose districts might also be distinguishable.

The reapportionment cases have been invoked as precedent for court-ordered redrawing of school districts across municipal and even state boundaries to achieve a more standardized mixture of students of different races. Maurice Ford, "Segregation in Northern Schools: Boston is Forced to Look," 15 *Public Policy* 52, 73 (1966); A. A. Berle, *The Three Faces of Power* (New York: Harcourt, Brace, and World, 1967), pp. 65-66, citing comments by Judge J. Skelly Wright in preliminary argument in *Hobson v. Hansen*, 269 F. Supp. 401 (D.D.C. 1967), 40 *N.Y.U. L. Rev.* 285, 305-06 (1965). Such a move might counteract a major political effect of reapportionment, which was to strengthen suburban elements opposed to sharing the racial and educational problems of the inner cities. It could not, however, be described as strengthening local representative government, for, like most of the voting rights reforms of the Warren era, it would be a substitution of federal administrative judgment for local representative judgment.

89. Dixon, *Democratic Representation*, p. 462.

90. 376 U.S. 52 (1964).

91. Gordon W. Hatheway, Jr., "Political Gerrymandering: The Law and Politics of Partisan Districting," 36 *G.W. L. Rev.* 114 (1967). State and federal courts have found reasons not to intervene against partisan gerrymandering. WMCA v. Lomenzo, 238 F. Supp. 916, 925-926 (S.D.N.Y.), *aff'd per curiam*, 382 U.S. 4 (1965); Badgley v. Hare, 385 U.S. 114 (1966) (dismissed for "want of substantial federal question"), *In re* Apportionment of the Michigan Legislature, 377 Mich. 396, 140 N.W. 2d 436 (1966); Honeywell v. Rockefeller, 214 F. Supp. 897 (E.D.N.Y. 1963), *aff'd per curiam*, 376 U.S. 222 (1964) (failure of proof); Sincock v. Gately, 262 F. Supp. 739 (D. Del. 1967) (found gerrymander, but held "not cognizable under the Fourteenth Amendment"); Jones v. Falcey, 48 N.J. 25, 22 A. 2d 101 (1966); Graham v. Board of Supervisors, No. C-86010 (N.Y. Sup. Ct. Jan. 30, 1967); See also Dixon, *Democratic Representation*, pp. 458-499.

92. Robert Dixon suggests that courts have tended to maintain a double standard for the reconstruction amendments: strict for the deep South, lenient for the rest of the country. School segregation and literacy test decisions seem to bear him out. Though an Alabama federal district court "operating more on judicial notice than on proof of record" has twice sustained charges of racial gerrymandering, the intervention, like the Supreme Court's in *Gomillion v. Lightfoot*, may be *sui generis*. Sims v. Baggett, 247 F. Supp. 96, 109 (M.D. Ala. 1965); Smith v. Paris, 157 F. Supp. 901 (M.D. Ala. 1966); Dixon, *Democratic Representation*, p. 472-474.

Early decisions of the Burger Court also seem consonant with Dixon's theory. Whitcomb v. Chavis, 403 U.S. 124, 141-150 (1971) (dismissing attack on Indiana multi-member district for failure to show "real life impact" of discrimination against blacks apart from the fact that they almost never got representatives of their own); cf., White v. Regester, 93 S. Ct. 2332 (1973) (upholding attack on Dallas MMD where lower court found history of systematic racial discrimination); Amos v. Sims, 409 U.S. 942 (1972), aff'g 336 F. Supp. 924 (M.D. Ala. 1972) (rejecting Alabama MMD).

93. Lucas v. Forty-fourth Gen. Assembly, 377 U.S. 713 (1964).

94. Burnette v. Davis, 382 U.S. 42 (1965); Fortson v. Dorsey, 379 U.S. 433 (1965). See also Burns v. Richardson, 384 U.S. 73 (1966); Kilgarlin v. Hill, 386 U.S. 120 (1967); cf. note 92, above.

Robert Lineberry noted that urban blacks almost never supported metropolitan expansion for fear that their own proportional voting strength would be diluted—even though expansion might broaden the cities' tax bases and equip them better to deal with poverty problems. Suburban whites, of course, were happy to be spared inner-city problems for the time being. Lineberry likened the situation to the "prisoner's dilemma," where individually rational decisions worked to collective detriment. "Reforming Metropolitan Governance: Requiem or Reality," 58 *Georgetown L.J.* 675, 691-696 (1970).

95. Congressional Quarterly, *Representation and Apportionment*, p. 25.

96. John F. Banzhaf, III, "Multi-Member Districts: Do They Violate the 'One Man, One Vote' Principle?" 75 *Yale L. J.* 1309, 1323 (1966); cited, Kilgarlin v. Hill, 386 U.S. 120, 125 N. 3 (1967); Dixon, *Democratic Representation*, pp. 535-543. In *Whitcomb v. Chavis*, 403 U.S. 124, 141-150 (1971), the Court admitted Banzhaf's mathematics but rejected the plaintiffs' attack on a large Indiana multi-member district for not showing "actual discrimination." Justice Harlan, concurring, hailed the Court's decision as "nothing short of a complete vindication of Mr. Justice Frankfurter's warning nine years ago of the mathematical quagmire . . . into which this Court today catapults the lower courts of the country." 403 U.S., p. 170.

97. Banzhaf, "Multi-Member Districts," pp. 1324-1335; "One Man 3.312 Votes: A Mathematical Analysis of the Electoral College"; but see Sickels, "Power Index and the Electoral College," p. 87. 98. Howard D. Hamilton, "Legislative Constituencies, Single-Member Districts, Multi-Member Districts, and Floterial Districts," 20 *Western Pol. Q.* 321 (June 1967).

99. Hamilton concluded from examining multi-member districts in Indiana, Michigan, and Ohio that most of the expected bad effects were to be found in all three jurisdictions but that the distortion of multi-member districts had varied effect on the states' overall balance of representation, depending on distribution of population. He concluded that multi-member districts made little difference in Michigan, counterbalanced distortions of single-member districts in Ohio, and magnified single-member district distortions in Indiana. *Ibid.*, p. 327.

100. Some floterial districts were extravagantly big. Hamilton cited one with a potpouri of districts comprising one-sixth of the population of Indiana, "more conducive to schizophrenia than to good representation." *Ibid.*, p. 336.

   Residence requirements added another complication to those endemic to multi-member and floterial districts: does it make any difference whether "your" representative lives in your subdistrict? The Supreme Court seemed to think not, since it permitted a Virginia Beach multi-member district with equal votes for representatives but a requirement that representatives reside in subdistricts of unequal population. Dusch v. Davis, 387 U.S. 112 (1967). But it is still open to question whether one is as well represented by someone who lives in another neighborhood as by one's own neighbor.

101. Ruth Silva, "Reapportionment and Redistricting," 213 *Scientific American* 20 (Nov. 1965).

102. I would not think of burdening my readers, far less myself, with a detailed review of the technical niceties. A short, useful review may be found in Robert Dixon's section of the "New Mathematics of Effective Representation," *Democratic Representation*, pp. 537-543.

103. *Ibid.*, pp. 534, 527-535.

104. Circular to California Republican State Committee, quoted, Stephen
D. Slingsby, "The Gerrymander: Its Rise, Use, and Potential," Ph.D. diss.
(Claremont Graduate School, Claremont, Calif., 1967), pp. 115, 155.

105. In fairness to the reapportionists, it must be conceded that the prospects of judicial rescue had increased considerably by the summer of 1973 after two years of bitter deadlock between the Democratic-controlled legislature and Republican Governor Ronald Reagan. Three special masters assigned to recommend redistricting plans to the state supreme court disregarded the state's tradition of districting to protect incumbents and, with the help of a computer, redrew boundaries to preserve the integrity of communities and geographical regions. The plan (which was subsequently approved by the state supreme court) appeared likely to cost a substantial number of legislators their seats but also to give black and Mexican-American districts greater representation. Legislature of the State of California v. Reinecke, Sac. 7917, 7919, 7923 (1973); *Los Angeles Times*, Sept. 2, 1973, p. I-1, col. 5.

106. For example, Lynch v. Torquato, 343 F. 2d 370 (3d Cir. 1965); Rogers v. State Committee of Republican Party, 96 N.J. Super 265, 232 A. 2d 852 (1967); Kyle v. Adams, Cause No. 66-321-CIV-EC (S.D. Fla., Miami Div. 1966); Davis v. Sullivan, 47 Misc. 2d 60, 261 N.Y.S. 2d 697 (1965); Dahl v. Republican State Committee, 319 F. Supp. 682 (W.D. Wash. 1970).

107. Irish v. Democratic-Farmer-Labor Party, 287 F. Supp. 794 (D. Minn.), *aff'd per curiam*, 399 F. 2d 119 (8th Cir. 1968); Smith v. State Executive Comm., 288 F. Supp. 371 (N.D. Ga. 1968); *contra*: Maxey v. Washington State Democratic Committee, 319 F. Supp. 673 (W.D. Wash. 1970); Doty v. Montana State Central Committee, 333 F. Supp. 49 (D. Mont. 1971); Seergy v. Kings County Republican County Committee, 459 F. 2d 308 (2d Cir. 1972); cf., Bode v. National Democratic Party, 452 F. 2d 1302 (D.C. Cir. 1971).

108. Livingston v. Ogilvie, 43 Ill. 2d 9, 250 N.W. 2d 138 (1969); West v. Carr, 212 Tenn. 367, 370 S.W. 2d 469 (6th Cir. 1963) (NI); Blunt v. Board of Electors, 247 Md. 342, 230 A. 2d 639 (1967).

109. Lynch v. Torquato, 343 F. 2d 370, 372 (3d Cir. 1965); Irish v. Democratic-Farmer-Labor Party, 287 F. Supp. 794, 801 (D. Minn. 1968); Smith v. State Exec. Comm., 288 F. Supp. 371, 376 (N.D. Ga. 1968).

110. Stokes v. Fortson, 234 F. Supp. 575, (N.D. Ga. 1964); Buchanan v. Rhodes, 249 F. Supp. 860, 865 (N.D. Ohio 1966); New York State Assn. v. Rockefeller, 267 F. Supp. 148, 153-154 (S.D.N.Y. 1967); Romiti v. Kerner, 256, F. Supp. 35 (N.D. Ill. 1966). But see Berle, *Three Faces of Power*, chap. 3 (Court as constitutional convention to help direct coming revolution); David T. Bazelon, *Power in America: The Politics of the New Class* (New York: New American Library, 1967), chap. 9, esp. p. 321 (Court as voice of "the people who yelled '*Adlai!*' and meant it" [emphasis original]).

111. Stokes v. Fortson, 234 F. Supp. 575, 577 (N.D. Ga. 1964).

112. John R. Schmidt and Wayne W. Whalen, "Credentials Contests at the 1968—and 1972—Democratic National Conventions," 82 *Harv. L. Rev.* 1438 (1969).

113. Note, "Selection of Delegates to Conventions," 78 *Yale L. J.* 1228, 1252 (1969).

114. *Ibid.*, p. 1247.

115. For other irredentist commentaries, see the citations in note g, Table 9. For an able, and solitary rebuttal, see Note, "One Man, One Vote and

Selection of Delegates to National Nominating Conventions," 37 *Chi. L. Rev.* 536 (1970).

116. The courts' immediate contribution to this process was largely confined to the post-1970 cases cited in note 107 above, requiring party officials in three circuits to apportion delegates in primary elections according to population or party strength.

The States' contribution was to have more primaries than before, 23 in 1972 as opposed to 15 in 1968, arabesque in their variety of different rules and regulations, spread out over 15 grueling and expensive weeks of rushing from one state to another, and attended with dark intimations that there would be 30 or more primaries for the 1976 elections. Political analysts worried at the heavy physical and financial strain the system put on candidates, and also at the degree to which the outcome appeared to be influenced by the vagaries of television coverage to the disadvantage of centrist candidates. Congressional Quarterly Guide, *Current American Government* (Fall 1972), p. 29; Alternative Educational Foundation, *Report on Network News' Treatment of the 1972 Democratic Presidential Candidates.*

Congress responded to these problems with a flurry of unsuccessful attempts to reform the nominating process, the most comprehensive of which, had they succeeded, would almost certainly have made the problems much worse. The principal proposal was that of Senators Mike Mansfield (D, Mont.) and George Aiken (R, Vt.), and House Republican Leader Gerald Ford (Mich.) and Silvio Conte (R, Mass.), to establish a national primary with a runoff between the two top candidates if no candidate received more than 40 percent of the vote. A less radical variant of this concept was the proposal of Senator Robert Packwood (R, Oreg.) to establish five regional primaries, to be held once a month between March and July, with proportional (rather than winner-take-all) allocation of delegates. Congressional Quarterly, *Current American Government*, pp. 31-33. Both of these proposals, had they been implemented, would have favored splinter candidates by making it easier for them to gather a nationwide factional following at the expense of centrist candidates. Both proposals, by vastly enlarging the target constituencies, implicitly offered to make nomination politics more TV-sensitive, and hence more expensive, more responsive to name recognition and image approval, and less responsive to the traditional influences of party regularity and personal contact.

117. The reformers claimed that Harris had promised them not to appoint any people to the commission who would be opposed to reform, though nearly half of the 1968 delegates had opposed one of the key reform resolutions. See Penn Kemble's and Josh Muravchik's illuminating article, "The New Politics and the Democrats," *Commentary* (December 1972), p. 78; this essay has been a primary reference for my discussion of the political history of the McGovern reforms.

118. *Mandate for Reform: A Report of the Commission on Party Structure and Delegate Selection to the Democratic National Committee* (Washington, D.C.: Democratic National Committee, April 1970), p. 14.

119. *Ibid.*, p. 15.

120. "New Politics and the Democrats," p. 79.

121. *Ibid.*, pp. 78-79; *Mandate for Reform*, pp. 34, 40. McGovern later explained, "The way we got the quota thing through was by not using the word 'quotas.' " "New Politics and the Democrats," p. 80.

122. *Mandate for Reform*, p. 36.

123. *Ibid.*, pp. 36-37.

124. "New Politics and the Democrats," pp. 80-81.

125. Califano admitted in court, during the convention, that the convention's decisions to unseat the Daley delegation and seat McGovern's disputed California delegates—both of which he defended—were indicative of the party's wish to "push the self-destruct button." *New York Times*, July 5, 1972, p. 30, col. 3.

126. *Mandate for Reform*, p. 6.

127. *Ibid.*

128. *Ibid.*, pp. 6-7.

129. 58 *Am. Pol. Sci. Rev.* 361 (1964).

130. Chicago: University of Chicago Press, 1962.

131. "New Politics and the Democrats," p. 83.

132. *Ibid.*

133. *Ibid.*, p. 82.

134. *Mandate for Reform*, p. 49.

135. *New York Times*, July 2, 1972, p. 28, col. 6.

136. *New York Times*, editorial, July 3, 1972, p. 16, col. 1.

137. *Ibid.*, p. 15.

138. Note 125 above.

139. O'Brien v. Brown, 409 U.S. 1 (1972). Justices White, Douglas, and Marshall dissented.

140. "New Politics and the Democrats," p. 80.

141. *Ibid.*, p. 84.

142. See note 147 below.

143. Congressional Quarterly Guide, *Current American Government* (Fall 1972), p. 11.

144. *Ibid.*

145. *Ibid.*, p. 13.

146. Editorial, *New York Times*, July 16, 1972, pt. IV, p. 10, col. 1. The appearance of participatory democracy was preserved for Eagleton's ratification by permitting more than 60 other candidates, including Eleanor McGovern, the Berrigan brothers, and Martha Mitchell, to be considered also.

147. Editorial, *New York Times*, July 13, 1972, p. 34, col. 1.

148. See, for example, *New York Times*, July 16, 1972, p. 20, col. 2; August 1, 1972, p. 35, col. 2.

149. This paragraph is drawn from Peter Rosenblatt, "New York's Lesson for Democratic Reform," *Los Angeles Times*, Sept. 10, 1972, sec. G, p. 3, col. 1.

150. Unfortunately for the Republicans, the Republican presidential campaign turned out also to be run by a feelingful little band of amateurs, separated from broad party concerns, lacking professional political experience and party discipline. Some members or associates of the Committee to Reelect the President could not bear to sit back and watch McGovern lose but found it necessary to break into the Democratic National Committee's Watergate office, plant bugs, read papers and indulge in other scandalous activities whose disclosure, within a half year after the Republican presidential landslide, so reduced public confidence in the Nixon administration that polls at one point indicated that the public would rather have had McGovern as president.

151. Williams v. Rhodes, 393 U.S. 23 (1968).

152. Henry M. Bain and Donald S. Hecock, *Ballot Positions and Voter's Choice: The Arrangement of Names on the Ballot and Its Effect on the Voter* (Detroit: Wayne State University Press, 1957); *New York Times*, June 6, 1970, p. 1, col. 6 (city ed.).

153. See Gorman v. Lukowski, F. 2d (6th Cir. 1970) (court dismissed suit protesting as a "violation of the Civil Rights Act" a Kentucky bar association poll indicating plaintiff was an inferior candidate for election as a judge).

154. 385 U.S. p. 231 (1966).

155. *Id.*, p. 234.

156. There was very little difference in the qualifications and views of the two candidates Lester Maddox and "Bo" Callaway.

157. The question of invalidating the acts of a malapportioned legislature could arise in three contexts: acts prior to the reapportionment cases, acts after the reapportionment cases or after a court has found malapportionment but before the court has expressly enjoined the legislature from doing any act but apportioning; and acts after such injunction. No court has ever invalidated a legislative act prior to the reapportionment cases for failure to reapportion, even in the presence of state reapportionment laws, and it is highly unlikely that the Supreme Court would invalidate such acts. People v. Clardy, 334 Ill. App. 160, 165 N.E. 638 (1929); Cedar Rapids v. Cox, 252 Iowa 948, 964, 108 N.W. 2d 253, 262-263 (1961); Kidd v. McCanless, 200 Tenn. 273, 292 S.W. 2d 40 (1956); Baker v. Carr, 369 U.S. 186, 250, n. 5 (1962) (dictum in Douglas concurring opinion); *but cf.*, Norton v. Shelby County, 118 U.S. 428, 442 (1886): an "unconstitutional statute is, in legal contemplation, as inoperative as though it had never been passed." Acts after the announcement of the Fundamental Principle or after a specific finding of malapportionment might not be so secure as prior ones since the legislatures would stand warned, but there should be a very strong presumption against completely disabling a legislature even for the clearest of reasons, and reapportionment is still far from settled in many areas. Only in the last case, where the court had enjoined the legislature from doing anything till it has reapportioned, would it be likely that the act would be invalidated, and even there a blanket invalidation is not likely.

158. Claiming standing, of course, is not the same as having standing. The claimant could be required to show that he personally had been denied equal representation, either at the time the offending law was passed or afterwards, so that he was denied an equal chance to get it repealed, or he might be required to bring or have brought a reapportionment action himself or be connected with a reapportionment class action. This kind of distinction, however, would raise equal protection problems of its own by giving standing to people in large underrepresented districts to object to certain laws, while denying it to people from smaller districts.

159. Bond v. Floyd, 385 U.S. 116 (1966); Powell v. McCormack, 395 U.S. 486 (1969).

160. Bunton v. Patterson, 393 U.S. 544 (1969).

161. Note, "Selection of Delegates to Conventions," 78 *Yale L. J.* 1228, 1247 (1969).

162. See Snowden v. Hughes, 321 U.S. 1 (1944) (declining to rule on an Illinois candidate's action against his party for refusal to list him as party's nominee). If *Snowden v. Hughes* is the rule against intervention in party actions, then *Terry v. Adams*, 345 U.S. 461 (1953), *Smith v. Allwright*, 321

U.S. 757 (1944), and *Gray v. Sanders*, 372 U.S. 368 (1963), are the exceptions.

163. Griffin v. County School Board, 377 U.S. 218 (1964); Reitman v. Mulkey, 386 U.S. 970 (1967).

164. Bunton v. Patterson, 393 U.S. 544 (1969); Fairley v. Patterson, 393 U.S. 544 (1969).

165. Compare Dixon, *Democratic Representation*, pp. 472-473: "It is hard to down the feeling that the real distinction between the two Alabama cases and *Wright v. Rockefeller* is geographical. In regard to racial discrimination in education we have tended to devise two Fourteenth Amendments, a mild one for the North, a strict one for the South: racial legislative district allegations may fit this same pattern."

166. See the commentary on Frankfurter's opinion in *Gomillion v. Lightfoot*, 364 U.S. 339 (1960), CH. III, Sec. 6; Wright v. Rockefeller, 376 U.S. 52 (1964).

167. Bunton v. Patterson, Fairley v. Patterson, 393 U.S. 544 (1969).

168. For example, Paul Baran and Paul Sweezy, *Monopoly Capital: An Essay on the American Economic and Social Order* (New York: Monthly Review Press, 1966); C. Wright Mills, *The Power Elite* (New York: Oxford University Press, 1956); cf. Thomas Dye and Harmon Ziegler, *The Irony of Democracy: An Uncommon Introduction to American Politics* (Belmont, Calif.: Wadsworth Publishing Co., 1970).

169. David Easton, "An Approach to the Analysis of Political Systems," *World Politics* (Apr. 1957), p. 383; Gabriel Almond and G. Bingham Powell, *Comparative Politics: A Developmental Approach* (Boston: Little, Brown, 1966), chap. 1.

170. John Stuart Mill, *Considerations on Representative Government*, 2d ed. (London, 1861), pp. 1-3.

171. *Novum Organum*, Aph. 3.

172. *De Corpore*, Sir William Molesworth, ed., *English Works of Thomas Hobbes* (London, 1839), I, 7.

173. Floyd W. Matson, *The Broken Image: Man, Science and Society* (New York: Braziller, 1964), pp. 29-36.

174. Spinoza, *Opera* (The Hague: Martinus Nijhoff, 1882), I, 125 (*Ethics*, Part 3).

175. Matson, *Broken Image*, chaps. 1, 2. Among the closest intellectual antecedents of the anti-ideological Guardians were the original *ideologues* of postrevolutionary France. These were moderate, liberal bourgeois disciples of the Enlightenment, dedicated to the creation of a just and enlightened social order by turning the educational system, and then the state, to the service of "rational and scientific principles." The *ideologues* had some prominence in the French Revolution but saw their greatest ascendancy during Thermidor and the early Napoleonic years when they had great, but temporary influence on the emperor-to-be. They founded the Ecole Normale, the Ecole Centrale, and the Ecole Polytechnique; their major spokesman was Antoine Destutt de Tracy, who coined the word "ideology." Their rise and fall is briefly and well described in Lewis Coser, *Men of Ideas: A Sociologistic View* (New York: Free Press, 1965), chap. 15.

176. See Louis Hartz, *The Liberal Tradition in America* (New York: Harcourt, Brace, and World, 1955).

177. Wilmoore Kendall, *John Locke and the Doctrine of Majority Rule*,

Illinois Studies in the Social Sciences, vol. 26, no. 2 (Urbana, University of Illinois Press, 1941), p. 134.

178. Attitudes toward change may be another matter on which organicists differ with mechanists, though such attitudes are seldom spelled out as explicitly as the more static perceptions, especially in the case of mechanists. In general, organicists accept change as part of the natural order of things, but not necessarily for the better. Organicism admits of a cyclic, growth-and-decay view of history as readily, or perhaps more readily, than a growth-only view of history as unilinear progress. Institutions are best preserved by a continuing succession of little adaptations. As Burke observed, "A State without the means of some change is without the means of its conservation." Mechanists tend to prefer one last big change to a long succession of little ones, perhaps with the notion that if their change is big enough, further change will not be necessary. In general, mechanists have little interest in past and future. If they have any notion of history whatsoever, it tends to be a vague assumption of unilinear progress toward their own consummatory reforms, perhaps to be followed by an indefinite static period during which the reforms may be savored to their fullest. I suspect that the same perceptual biases which inspire the boldest reformers—exaggerated confidence in the perfection of their own paradigms, contempt for the blundering efforts of those who have gone before—also explain the successful reformer's often noted intolerance of the next generation's efforts to improve on "perfection." The greatest reformers are usually those who focus with tunnel vision on a particular goal and then plough through all opposition and doubt to achieve the goal. Such single-mindedness does not yield readily to abandoning the goal afterward to pursue a different one, and the most creative reformers of one generation are often the most rigid conservatives of the next. John Marshall, who combined creativity and conservatism in fighting for federalist aims while he was chief justice, leaned in the mechanistic direction in describing the Constitution as "designed to approach immortality as nearly as human institutions can approach it." Cohens v. Virginia, 6 Wheat. 264, 387 (1821). Oliver Wendell Holmes, on the other hand, spoke of "organic, living institutions," and insisted that "the case before us must be considered in the light of our whole experience, not merely in that of what was said a hundred years ago." See Gompers v. United States, 233 U.S. 604, 610 (1914); Missouri v. Holland, 252 U.S. 416, 433 (1920); Charles Miller, *The Supreme Court and the Uses of History* (Cambridge: Harvard University Press, 1969), pp. 167-168.

179. See Ferdinand Toennies, *Community and Society (Gemeinschaft und Gesellschaft)* (East Lansing, Mich.: Michigan State University Press, 1957).

180. Giovanni Sartori, *Democratic Theory* (New York: Praeger, 1965); Alfred De Grazia, *Public and Republic* (New York: Knopf, 1951); Harry Jaffa, "The Nature and Origin of the American Party System" in Robert Goldwin, ed., *Political Parties, U.S.A.* (Chicago: Rand McNally, 1964); Edward Banfield, "In Defense of the American Party System," in Goldwin, *Political Parties*, U.S.A.; Bertrand de Jouvenel, *On Power: The Nature and History of Its Growth* (New York, Viking Press, 1948); Dixon, *Democratic Representation*.

181. Sartori, *Democratic Theory*, p. 108.

182. Banfield, "In Defense of the American Party System," p. 24-25.

183. *Ibid.*, pp. 29-30.

184. See my essay on "The Militant Blockhead," chap. 7 in "Bertrand de

Jouvenel and the Organic Tradition" (Honors Thesis, Harvard University, 1959). An example of extreme organicism may be found in Lucian Pye's brilliant description of Burmese politicians in *Politics, Personality, and Nation Building: Burma's Search for Identity* (New Haven: Yale University Press, 1962), chap. 12, esp. pp. 170-171: "Possibly the most striking characteristic of the calculations of Burmese politicians [said Pye] is their extreme sensitivity to the possibility of numberless complexities in any political situation. Every political relationship, event, or issue is seen as having so many dimensions and endless possibilities that only the sophisticated can fully appreciate them. . . . The ability to find endless complications in what would seem the simplest of problems in other political cultures constantly leads the Burmese politician astray from the purpose for which he began his calculations. In particular there is a strong likelihood that, by the time he has elaborated in his own mind all that might or could be done with respect to a particular problem, he has become so sensitive to all the possibilities of offending and provoking others that he suffers a complete paralysis of effort, usually followed by a feeling that others with malicious intentions have been frustrating his desires and making his life difficult. Pye ultimately concluded, however, that the Burmese were held back from "nation-building" for a very organic reason; Burmese intellectuals' repudiation of their own traditions in favor of modern British modes which turned out not to fit. *Ibid.*, pt. 5.

William Y. Elliott's "co-organic theory of the state" holds both "organic" and "purposive" functions to be essential to just government: systems maintenance (in modern jargon) and moral goals. *The Pragmatic Revolt in Politics: Syndicalism, Fascism, and the Constitutional State* (New York: Macmillan, 1928; repr. New York: Howard Fertig, 1968), pts. 4 and 5. *The Pragmatic Revolt*, which is probably the greatest of the senior Elliott's many great books, protested the pragmatism of the time as lacking in rational moral perspective, while granting the pragmatists' assertion that "organic and functional" institutions were needed to avoid social breakdown and retrogression (e.g., pp. 416-417). See also his "The Constitution as the American Social Myth," in Conyers Read, ed., *The Constitution Reconsidered* (New York: Columbia University Press, 1938) (calling for combined reverence to constitutional symbols with freedom of revision to meet modern needs). As it turned out, the Guardians and the Supreme Court followed Elliott's lead a step too far, clinging to the rhetoric of pragmatism but losing sight of organic needs in their preoccupation with abstract moral goals.

185. J. S. Mill, *Representative Government* p. 64.

186. *Political Order in Changing Societies* (New Haven: Yale University Press, 1968), p. 461. See also, Joseph La Palombara and Myron Weiner, eds., *Political Parties and Political Development* (Princeton: Princeton University Press, 1966, esp. Giovanni Sartori, "European Political Parties: The Case of Polarized Pluralism"; William N. Chambers and Walter Dean Burnham, *The American Party Systems* (New York: Oxford University Press, 1967), esp. chaps. 1 and 10.

187. Burnham, "Party Systems and the Political Process," in Chambers and Burnham, *American Party System*, p. 305.

188. Samuel Huntington, "The Marasmus of the I.C.C.," 61 *Yale L.J.* 467 (1952), reprinted as chap. 7 in Francis Rourke, ed., *Bureaucratic Power in National Politics* (Boston: Little, Brown, 1965).

189. Most empirical scholars of the legislative process stress trust, informal

personal contacts, and mutual cooperation in reducing uncertainty and minimizing conflict as essential to legislative effectiveness. See, e.g., Richard Fenno, "The Internal Distribution of Influence: The House," in David Truman, ed., *The Congress and America's Future* (Englewood Cliffs, N.J.: Prentice-Hall, 1965), p. 74: "Most of the time the two kinds of leaders [party leaders and committee chairmen] cooperate—sometimes on the basis of a policy agreement, but always on the basis of a mutual need. The party leaders need the support of the committee leaders if they want any bill at all to get to the floor; the committee leaders need the support of the party leaders if they want procedural assistance and sufficient supporting votes on the floor. . . . Sanctions and the threat of sanctions are, of course, available on both sides and may be used. But knock-down, drag-out battles within the majority party are events to be avoided at nearly any cost. The committee leaders risk a loss of influence inside and outside their committees and the party leaders risk the permanent loss of sources of support which they may need on later issues." See also, Richard Fenno, *The Power of The Purse: Appropriations Politics in Congress* (Boston: Little, Brown, 1966), esp. pp. 303-312; Allan Fiellin, "The Functions of Informal Groups in Legislative Institutions," 24 *J. Politics* 72 (February 1962), reprinted in Heinz Eulau, ed., *Political Behavior in America* (New York: Random House, 1962); William Keefe and Morris Ogul, *The American Legislative Process: Congress and the States* (Englewood Cliffs, N.J.: Prentice-Hall, 1968), chap. 9.

190. V. O. Key, *Public Opinion and American Democracy* (New York: Knopf, 1961), chap. 21.

191. *Maximum Feasible Misunderstanding*, pp. 108-109.

192. *American State Politics: An Introduction* (New York: Knopf, 1956), p. 131.

193. Baker v. Carr, 369 U.S. 186, 299-302 (1962) (dissenting opinion).

194. Hadley v. Junior College Dist., 397 U.S. 50, 56 (1970).

195. See Eric Nordlinger, "Representation, Governmental Stability, and Decisional Effectiveness," in J. Roland Pennock and John W. Chapman, eds., *Nomos X, Representation* (New York: Atherton Press, 1968), p. 124; Walter Bagehot, *The English Constitution* (New York: Oxford University Press, 1933).

196. See Note, "One Man, One Vote, and Selection of Delegates to National Nominating Conventions," 37 *U. Chi. L. Rev.* 536, 551-558 (1970).

197. Note, "Selection of Delegates to Conventions," 78 *Yale L. J.* 1228, 1247 (1969).

198. Mancur Olson, Jr., *The Logic of Collective Action: Public Goods and the Theory of Groups* (Cambridge: Harvard University Press, 1965), esp. chap. 2.

199. John James, "A Preliminary Study of the Size Determinant in Small Groups Interaction," 16 *Am. Sociological Rev.* 474 (Aug. 1951). This and other studies drawing similar conclusions are summarized in Olson, *Logic of Collective Action*, p. 54.

200. See Jaffa, "Nature and Origin of American Party System."

201. See the "Statement of the Minority Members of the Senate Subcommittee on the Judiciary," 91st Cong., 2d sess., Senate Cal. no. 1135, Rep. no. 91-1123, Aug. 14, 1970. This document gives an excellent summary of arguments on the value of the electoral college in maintaining the two-party system, discouraging splinter parties, maintaining the federal system and separa-

tion of powers, moderating the expression of public opinions, and minimizing incentives for electoral fraud and challenge to electoral results.

202. Note, "Selection of Delegates," 37 *U. Chi. L. Rev.* 536, 554-556. (1970).

203. Dixon, *Democratic Representation*, p. 137.

204. 102 *Congressional Record* 5150 (1956).

Notes to Chapter VII

1. Marx's quote is from the first edition of the 18th *Brumaire of Louis Bonaparte*, deleted from subsequent editions but quoted in J. P. Mayer, ed., *The Recollections of Alexis de Tocqueville* (New York: Columbia University Press, 1949), pp. xx-xxi.

2. 297 U.S. 1, 62 (1936).

3. 290 U.S. 398, 453 (1934) (dissenting opinion).

4. "Fudging" refers to a reasonably plain contradiction of the text or intent of the Constitution. It differs from "traduction" and "desecration" in that no one gets very excited about it. In the mortgage moratorium case, *Home Building and Loan Association v. Blaisdell*, 290 U.S. 398 (1934), the Court upheld a statute suspending mortgage foreclosures for two years against objections, well founded in the text and history of the contract clause, that it impaired the obligation of the mortgage contract. Moved by the desperate economic hardships which had produced the statute, the Court was willing to make believe that the statute did not impair the obligation of the contract, but only removed the "remedy" of foreclosure. Memoranda by Justices Cardozo and Stone, urging a more straightforward approach than the remedy fiction, were only partially adopted in the majority opinion. See Alpheus T. Mason, *Harlan Fiske Stone: Pillar of the Law* (New York: Viking Press, 1956), pp. 360-365.

5. 381 U.S. 479 (1965), "discovering" a "right of privacy older than the Bill of Rights" somewhere in the "penumbra" of the Bill of Rights, or in the Ninth Amendment, to invalidate a state law against contraceptives. See Tileston v. Ullman, 318 U.S. 44 (1943).

6. Harper v. State Board of Elections, 383 U.S. 663 (1966) (outlawing poll taxes in state elections).

7. *Ex parte* Quirin, 317 U.S. 1 (1942); Korematsu v. United States, 323 U.S. 214 (1944).

8. Lucas v. Forty-fourth Gen. Assembly, 377 U.S. 713, 754-765 (1964) (dissenting opinion).

9. *Id.*, p. 746, notes 9, 10, pp. 749-750.

10. *Id.*; WMCA v. Lomenzo, 377 U.S. 633 (1964).

11. Lucas v. Forty-fourth Gen. Assembly, 377 U.S. 713, 765 (1964).

12. *Id.*, p. 750.

13. Colorado's four regions were the urban East Slope of the Rampart Range, the agricultural plains region running from the East Slope eastward to Kansas, the thinly populated, mountainous west, with a mining-tourist economy, and the south central region, fruit-raising with a large Spanish-American ethnic minority. William Irwin described Colorado politics up to the time of *Baker v. Carr* in his article, "Colorado, A Matter of Balance," in Malcolm Jewell, ed., *The Politics of Reapportionment* (New York: Atherton Press, 1962).

14. *Ibid.*, p. 64, n. 10.

15. One observer, a long-time Democratic precinct captain in Denver, noted that, besides having party and lobby support, a successful candidate had to rank high on the ballot list. Since ranking was alphabetical, most of the eight Denver senators had names beginning with A, B, or C. Appendix to Brief for Appellees and Added Appellees, Lucas v. Forty-fourth Gen. Assembly, 377 U.S. 713 (1964), p. 12. First District (Denver) senators in the 43d General Assembly: Allen, Bennett, Bishop, Brown, Byrne, Chenoweth, Cleary, and Saunders.

16. Richard T. Frost, "On Derge's Metropolitan and Outstate Delegations," 53 *Am. Pol. Sci. Rev.* 792 (1959); Derge's reply, *ibid.*, p. 1097 (1959).

17. See the testimony of James Grafton Rogers, ex-dean of the University of Colorado Law School, and Edwin C. Johnson, former governor of the state, United States senator, and member of the Colorado General Assembly. Appendix to Brief for Appellees and Added Appellees, Lucas v. Forty-fourth Gen. Assembly, 377 U.S. 713 (1964), pp. 81, 203. Rogers believed that urban influence was much better organized and powerful in Colorado history than rural: "Most of the striking organization of Colorado which has occurred . . . has centered around Denver. The corrupt Big Mint organization, here fifty or sixty years ago . . . the Ku Klux Klan, which made the most troublesome, the darkest period in Colorado history, centered around Denver. I am not conscious of any movement . . . of any importance that has occurred in Colorado that was truly rural." *Ibid.*, p. 81. Johnson explained how Colorado's Madisonian arrangement of checks and balances had restrained the Ku Klux Klan: "When I was a member of the Colorado Legislature in 1925, the Ku Klux Klan had taken over political power in the major portions of the state measured by population. This was mostly an urban movement. By reason of their control of a bare majority of the votes in large cities, the Klan dominated the legislature. I well remember that the House Leader had a small flagpole on his desk down front in the Assembly. When it was erect, his gang all voted "aye," and when it was tipped they voted "no." Their majority in the House was three to one. Had it not been for the fact that senators were elected from districts representing different interests, and had a different approach to state problems, the damage to this state and its future development which the Klan could have inflicted would have been enormous." *Ibid.*, p. 203.

18. An exception might be made in the case of Justice White, who was raised in rural Wellington, Colorado, and practiced law in Denver.

19. 20 *Cong. Q. Weekly Report* 153-154, Feb. 2, 1962; *Cong. Q. Census Analysis*, p. 1788, Aug. 21, 1964; Andrew Hacker, *Congressional Districting: The Issue of Equal Representation* (Washington, D.C., Brookings Institution, 1964), p. 89.

20. Congressional Quarterly, *Representation and Apportionment* (Washington, D.C., 1966), *passim*, but especially pp. 45-49, 62-93.

21. Robert B. McKay, *Reapportionment: The Law and Politics of Equal Representation* (New York: Twentieth Century Fund, 1965), p. 268; Alan Dines, "A Reapportioned State," 55 *Nat. Civic Rev.* 70 (Feb. 1966).

22. Frank M. Bryan, "Who is Legislating?" 56 *Nat. Civic Rev.* 627 (Dec. 1967).

23. McKay, *Reapportionment*, p. 267.

24. *Ibid.*; Note, "Reapportionment," 79 *Harv. L. Rev.* 1228, 1240 (1966).

25. Congressional Quarterly, *Representation and Apportionment*, pp. 41-42.

26. Key, *Southern Politics*, p. 639.

27. *Los Angeles Times*, July 29, 1973, p. VI-4, col. 2.

28. Congressional Quarterly, *Representation and Apportionment*, p. 41.

29. *Ibid.*

30. Conrad L. McBride, "The 1966 Elections in Colorado," 20 *Western Pol. Q.* 555 (June 1967).

31. 27 *Cong. Q. Weekly Report* 2341 (Nov. 21, 1969).

32. *Newsweek* (Oct. 6, 1969), p. 65.

33. Herbert Jacob, "The Consequences of Malapportionment: A Note of Caution," 43 *Soc. Forces* 256 (1964); Thomas R. Dye, "Malapportionment and Public Policy in the States," 27 *J. Politics* 586 (August 1965); Alvin D. Sokolow, "After Reapportionment: Numbers or Policies?" mimeograph (University of California, Davis, March 1966); Richard I. Hofferbert, "The Relation Between Public Policy and Some Structural and Environmental Variables in the American States," 60 *Am. Pol. Sci. Rev.* 73 (March 1966); David Brady and Douglas Edwards, "The Effects of Malapportionment on Policy Output in the American States," The Laboratory for Political Research, Report No. 3, Department of Political Science, University of Iowa, paper for the meeting of the Midwest Conference of Political Scientists, April 1966, revised and published under the title, "One Man, One Vote—So What?" 4 *Trans-Action* 41 (March 1967); see Duane Lockard, *The Politics of State and Local Government* (New York: Macmillan, 1963), p. 319 (finding Massachusetts legislature with cities overrepresented no more responsive to urban needs than Connecticut, where cities were underrepresented).

34. See Allan G. Pulsipher and James L. Weatherby, Jr., "Malapportionment, Party Competition, and the Functional Distribution of Governmental Expenditures," 62 *Am. Pol. Sci. Rev.* 1207 (1968) ("Study much more ambitious than ours . . . is required"); Robert E. Crew, Jr., and Roger A. Hanson, "Reapportionment's Impact upon Public Policy: A Comparative Analysis of Intra-State Variations in State Spending," unpub., Political Science Departments of University of Minnesota and University of Georgia, 1970; William E. Bicker, "The Effects of Malapportionment in the States—A Mistrial," in Nelson W. Polsby, ed., *Reapportionment in the 1970s* (Berkeley: University of California Press, 1971) (much more rigorous analysis needed to show reapportionists wrong). Yong H. Cho and H. George Frederickson, "Apportionment and Legislative Responsiveness to Policy Preferences in the American States," paper presented at the New York Academy of Sciences Conference on Democratic Representation and Apportionment, November 1972 (adequate before-after test needed); William R. Cantrall and Stuart S. Nagel, "The Effects of Reapportionment on the Passage of Non-Expenditure Legislation," paper presented at the New York Academy of Sciences Conference on Democratic Representation and Apportionment, November 1972 (finding significant but low correlations between some measures of malapportionment and some liberal laws in areas of racial equality, labor rights, highway safety, women's liberation, and aid to parochial schools).

35. The effects of reapportionment on congressional policymaking appear to have been minimal. See Milton C. Cummings, "Reapportionment in the 1970s: Its Effect on Congress," with commentary by Charles O. Jones, both in Polsby, *Reapportionment in the 1970s*. The 1960's saw no change in the 1950's pattern of party division in the House of Representatives: 200 or so safe Democratic seats, 130 or so safe Republican seats, and 90 or so seats which changed hands from one election to the next. Where the House had

averaged 96 new faces at each election from 1940 to 1948, the average dropped to 68 from 1950 to 1958, then to 64 from 1960 to 1970, with fewer new faces after reapportionment than before. See Charles O. Jones, "Inter-Party Competition for Congressional Seats," 17 *Western Pol. Q.* 461 (Sept. 1964). There were 63 new faces in the House after the 1960 elections; 65 after 1962; 86 after 1964; 73 after 1966; 39 after 1968; 56 after 1970. In 1972 the newcomer count rose to 73, primarily as a result of retirements, of which there were 21, and the decennial redistricting, which created sixteen new districts.

36. 20 *Cong. Q. Weekly Report* 2163, 2165-66 (Nov. 16, 1962).

37. Stephen D. Slingsby, "The Gerrymander," Ph.D. diss., (Claremont Graduate School, Claremont, Calif. 1969), pp. 115,155. The Missouri redistricting which followed *Kirkpatrick v. Preisler*, 394 U.S. 526 (1969) was hailed for bringing the "closest balance in the United States" with an average population deviation among districts of a tiny .0674 percent. It was also one of the most shrewdly gerrymandered, splitting St. Louis County up among five different districts, one of which was compared in outline to a flying turkey, another to a moose with antlers. Chief Justice Warren during the arguments in *Kirkpatrick v. Preisler* noted that the moose district "looks most unusual and what might ordinarily be called a gerrymandered district. Why do you have to go in that circuitous way?" On redrawing, however, the moose remained intact, with only minor alterations in its antlers. The Democrats, with 58 percent of the votes, continued to retain 90 percent of the seats in the 1970 elections. See also, Terry O'Rourke, *Reapportionment: Law, Politics, Computers* (Washington, D.C.: American Enterprise Institute, 1972), chap. 3.

38. Robert J. Sickels, "Dragons, Bacon Strips, and Dumbbells—Who's Afraid of Reapportionment?" 75 *Yale L. J.* 1300, 1303, (1966). Double figures are median/mean percentages of seats won.

39. *New York Times*, May 25, 1967, p. 3, col. 3 (city ed.).

40. Congressional Quarterly, *Representation and Apportionment*, p. 87.

41. *In re* Orans Petition, 45 Misc. 2d 616, 257 N.Y.S. 2d 839.

42. *New York Times*, May 11, 1967, p. 1, col. 8 (city ed.).

43. Congressional Quarterly, *Representation and Apportionment*, p. 57.

44. *Ibid.*, pp. 57, 89 (Dallas-Fort Worth, San Antonio, Memphis, Kansas City, Wichita); 26 *Cong. Q. Weekly Report* 23 (Jan. 5, 1968) (Oklahoma City); Jones v. Falcey, 48 N.J. 25, 222 A. 2d 101 (1966) (Newark).

45. *Id.*

46. *New York Times*, March 29, 1967, p. 34, col. 1 (city ed.).

47. Fortson v. Dorsey, 379 U.S. 433 (1965); Burnette v. Davis, 382 U.S. 42, *aff'g per curiam*, Mann v. Davis, 245 F. Supp. 241 (E.D. Va. 1965); CQ, p. 25.

48. Burns v. Richardson, 384 U.S. 73 (1966) (Hawaii); Congressional Quarterly, *Representation and Apportionment*, p. 25 (Iowa); Gordon W. Hatheway, "Political Gerrymanders," 36 *G. Wash. L. Rev.* 144, 148 (1967) (New Mexico); Drew v. Scranton, 279 F. Supp. 310 (M.D. Pa.), *vacated and remanded*, 379 U.S. 40 (1964) (Pennsylvania).

49. Sickels, "Dragons, Bacon Strips, and Dumbbells."

50. 24 *Cong. Q. Weekly Report* 2084 (1966). The Republicans swept all five Kansas congressional districts in the 1966 and 1968 elections; however, the Democrats did win one seat in 1970 and 1972.

51. Note, however, that the basis for the 19.1 figure in the 1968-1972 elections is not commensurable with Sickels's basis for the 1946-1964 elections. Sickels excluded all elections where any district was uncontested and all elections where one party won more than 55 percent of the popular vote. His mean margin of advantage for all contested elections in all states was 11.8 percent, median margin, 17.0 percent. For states of ten or more districts, all districts contested, the mean margin of advantage was 16.9 percent, median, 14.5 percent. Sickels, "Dragons, Bacon Strips, and Dumbbells," pp. 1300, 1302-1303. If all elections in Table 12 with popular majorities in excess of 55 percent, or with one district unopposed, were dropped, the basis of the margin of advantage in the large states would be the same as Sickels's, though it is not clear how Sickels would have handled the states with divided control. If the "divided control" states are not counted, the mean advantage to the districting party in the post reapportionment elections cited would be higher—18.3 percent—than Sickels's prereapportionment mean of 16.9 percent. If the "divided control" states are all counted as "no control," then the postreapportionment figure—12.1 percent—would be lower than Sickels's prereapportionment figure. Comparison with Sickels is further complicated by the greater frequency with which redistricting has been performed (or threatened to be performed) by courts in the 1970's, leaving doubt in some cases as to which party controlled the districting.

52. These states were: Florida (12 seats); Georgia (10); Massachusetts (12); and Texas (20).

53. All the states but Oregon had some kind of redistricting under *Baker v. Carr* during Warren's tenure. Some states went through repeated redistricting as parties struggled to replace each other's gerrymanders with their own. Thus, Missouri redistricted in 1961, 1965, 1967, 1970, and 1972; New Jersey in 1961, 1966, 1968, and 1972, with each redistricting battle diverting the legislators' attention from more substantive matters.

54. *Cong. Q. Census Analysis*, p. 1788 (Aug. 21, 1964); Legislative Reference Service, Library of Congress, *Recent Supreme Court Decisions on Apportionment: Their Political Impact* (Washington, D.C., 1964), pp. 11-12, 22-23.

55. Only six states, Alaska, Arizona, Arkansas, Hawaii, Missouri, and Ohio, had nonlegislative reapportionment in 1962; seven others, California, Illinois, Michigan, North Dakota, Oregon, South Dakota, and Texas, provided for nonlegislative apportionment if the legislature failed to act within a specified time. Seven states, Alaska, Arkansas, Hawaii, New York, Oklahoma, Oregon, and Texas, provided for court review of apportionment plans. Advisory Commission on Intergovernmental Relations, *Report on Apportionment of State Legislatures*, n. 45, pp. 21-22 (1962).

See Congressional Quarterly, *Representation and Apportionment*, pp. 49-50, for a description of the three-year fight in Illinois over which "nonpartisan" body—the United States District Court in Chicago (with two Democratic judges and one Republican), or the state supreme court (Republican, 5-2), or the senate redistricting commission—should redistrict. Most of the issues were eventually settled by compromise between the parties themselves. State and federal courts in Indiana, Missouri, Illinois, Michigan, and New Jersey dutifully rendered judgments in 1967-72 redistricting cases in accord with the party background of the judges. See notes to Table 12. Republicans called for a congressional investigation when district court Judge

John W. Oliver, a longtime Democrat, consulted with Democratic Governor Warren E. Hearnes prior to rendering the Court's decision. 36 *Cong. Q.* 448 (Mar. 1968).

56. Note, "Reapportionment," 79 *Harv. L. Rev.* 1228, 1239 (1964); Congressional Quarterly, *Representation and Apportionment*, pp. 68-69.

57. *Ibid.*, pp. 59, 69. The Republicans had lost control of both houses in six states, one house in another seven states.

58. *Ibid.*, p. 44.

59. Totten G. Anderson and Eugene C. Lee, "The 1966 Election in California," 20 *Western Pol. Q.* 535, 551 (June 1967). The effect of the California gerrymandering was to create so many safe seats that California politics are more and more centered in party primaries, as in the South. "In all three chambers, Senate, Assembly, and House of Representatives, well over half the seats are so heavily registered for one party or another that general election offers little chance of success." *Ibid.*

60. Fortson v. Dorsey, 379 U.S. 433 (1965); Burnette v. Davis, 382 U.S. 42 (1965); Congressional Quarterly, *Representation and Apportionment*, p. 25; But see Fairley v. Patterson, 393 U.S. 544 (1969).

61. Drew v. Scranton, 279 F. Supp. 310 (M.D. Pa.), *vacated and remanded*, 379 U.S. 40 (1964); Burns v. Richardson, 384 U.S. 73 (1966); but see White v. Regester, 42 *U.S.L. Week* 4885 (June 19, 1973) section III (sustaining lower court in invalidating Texas multimember districts where record showed evidence of intent to discriminate against blacks).

62. William R. Keech, *The Impact of Negro Voting: The Role of the Vote in the Quest for Equality* (Chicago: Rand McNally, 1968).

63. *Ibid.*, chap. 6.

64. *U.S. News and World Report* (July 13, 1970), p. 41.

65. David C. Birch, *The Economic Future of City and Suburb*, CED Supplementary Paper No. 30 (New York: Committee for Economic Development, 1970), p. 19.

66. *Ibid.*, p. 29.

67. See "Many Cities Struggling in Suburban Strangle-Hold," *New York Times*, Dec. 6, 1970, p. 72, col. 1.

68. See note 55, above.

69. Note 55, paragraph 2.

70. Arthur Sutherland, "Establishment According to *Engel*" 79 *Harv. L. Rev.* 25, 40 (1962).

Notes to Chapter VIII

1. Robert Nisbet, *Community and Power*, (New York: Oxford University Press, 1953), pp. 258-259.

2. Walter Dean Burnham, "The Changing Shape of the American Political Universe," 59 *Am. Pol. Sci. Rev.* 7, 22 (1965). In 1896 almost 80 percent of the enfranchised population came to the polls for presidential elections; between 1920 and 1968 the figure varied between 49 percent and 63 percent.

3. See Walter Murphy and Joseph Tanenhaus, "Constitutional Courts and Political Representation," chap. 72 in Michael Danielson and Walter Murphy, eds., *Modern American Democracy: Readings* (New York: Holt, Rinehart, and Winston, 1969).

Conservative Senator Roman Hruska (R, Neb.) appeared to share the quasi-representative image of the Court in attempting to refute charges that Richard Nixon's nominee, G. Harrold Carswell, was "mediocre" and therefore did not belong on the Court. "Even if he were mediocre," said Hruska, "there are a lot of mediocre judges and people and lawyers, and they are entitled to a little representation, aren't they? We can't have all Brandeises, Frankfurters and Cardozos." *New York Times*, Mar. 17, 1970, p. 21.

4. See Walter Murphy, *Congress and the Court* (Chicago: University of Chicago Press, 1962); Walter Murphy, *Elements of Judicial Strategy* (Chicago: University of Chicago Press, 1964), chap. 3. The Constitution forbids cutting the justices' salaries, but Congress can legally cut other parts of the Court's budget; moreover, it is doubtful that the Court could force even a salary appropriation from an unwilling Congress.

5. Legal profession: John Schmidhauser, *The Supreme Court: Its Politics Personalities, and Procedures* (New York: Holt, Rinehart and Winston, 1960), pt. 2; Theodore Becker, *Political Behavioralism and Modern Jurisprudence* (Chicago: Rand McNally, 1961).

Lower courts: Walter Murphy, "Lower Court Checks on Supreme Court Power," 53 *Am. Pol. Sci. Rev.* 1018 (1959); Note, "Evasion of Supreme Court Mandates in Cases Remanded to State Courts Since 1941," 67 *Harv. L. Rev.* 1251 (1954); Murphy, *Elements*, chap. 4.

Law reviews and press commentators: Chester A. Newland, "Press Coverage of the United States Supreme Court," 62 *Western Pol. Q.* 15 (1964); Chester A. Newland, "Legal Periodicals and the United States Supreme Court," 3 *Midwest J. Pol. Sci.* No. 1 (1959); Benjamin Twiss, *Lawyers and the Constitution* (Princeton: Princeton University Press, 1942); Clyde E. Jacobs, *Law Writers and the Courts: The Influence of Thomas M. Cooley, Christopher G. Tiedeman, and John F. Dillon upon American Constitutional Law* (Berkeley and Los Angeles: University of California Press, 1954).

Dissenting justices: Murphy, *Elements*, chap. 3.

Parties to the case and friends of the Court: Samuel Krislov, *The Supreme Court in the Political Process* (New York: Macmillan, 1965), chap. 2; Nathan Hakman, "Lobbying the Supreme Court—An Appraisal of 'Political Science' Folklore," 35 *Fordham L. Rev.* 15 (1966); Clement Vose, *Caucasians Only* (Berkeley and Los Angeles: University of California Press, 1959).

Elites: Adolf A. Berle, *The Three Faces of Power* (New York: Harcourt, Brace and World, 1967).

General public: Kenneth Dolbeare, "The Public Views the Supreme Court," in Herbert Jacob, ed., *Law, Politics, and the Federal Courts* (Boston: Little, Brown, 1967); John Kessel, "Perceptions of the Supreme Court," in Theodore Becker, ed., *The Impact of Supreme Court Decisions* (New York: Oxford University Press, 1969).

6. Robert A. Dahl, "Decision-Making in a Democracy: The Supreme Court as a National Policy-Maker," 65 *J. Publ. Law* 279, 284 (1958). In the eleven years from Dahl's writing to Warren's retirement, five new justices were appointed, one by Eisenhower, two by Kennedy, and two by Johnson. Johnson was prevented by senatorial opposition from filling two additional vacancies left by the retirement of Justice Clark and the prospective retirement of Chief Justice Warren. Samuel Krislov noted that turnover since 1870, when the Court's membership was stabilized at nine members, had been faster than Dahl's twenty-two-month average for the Court's entire history; from 1937 to

1963 the average was seventeen months. Samuel Krislov, *The Supreme Court in the Political Process* (New York: Macmillan, 1965), p. 10. For discussion of the political influences bearing on the appointment of federal justices and judges, see also Schmidhauser, *Supreme Court*; Joel Grossman, *Lawyers and Judges* (New York: John Wile, 1965); and David Danelski, *A Supreme Court Justice Is Appointed* (New York: Random House, 1964).

7. Victor Navasky's *Kennedy Justice* (New York: Athenaeum, 1971) provides a valuable illustration of the degree to which top Justice Department figures in the crucial Kennedy-Cox years perceived reapportionment as a cause in its own right, rather than a means of changing the rules to take seats away from the Republicans. Navasky's sixth chapter describes how Attorney General Robert F. Kennedy and his activist staff enticed his eminent and Frankfurterian solicitor general to overcome his legal scruples and devote the full range of his talents to ending malapportionment. All of the principals, including Cox, who later declared that malapportionment was a "cancer" that "would continue to grow unless the Court excised it," shared the then-prevalent conviction that malapportionment was terribly unfair, that it was holding up progress, and that it needed to be eliminated to get Congress and the state legislatures "working right" (pp. 303, 315). See Archibald Cox, *The Warren Court: Constitutional Decision as an Instrument of Reform* (Cambridge, Mass.: Harvard University Press, 1968), pp. 117-119. For Kennedy, the perceived need of action settled the matter. He was equally impatient of Cox's qualms over legal niceties and political strategist Larry O'Brien's worries that reapportionment might cost the Democrats some seats in the suburbs. He cut short a Cox lecture on the juridical hazards of intervening in *Reynolds v. Sims*, demanding, "Archie—isn't the real issue should some people's vote count more than other people's vote?"

Cox is said to have assented grudgingly, later muttering to his assistant, "You know these guys don't really understand what this is all about" (pp. 314-315). By Navasky's account, almost all of Cox's amicus curiae briefs asking for further intervention against malapportionment were submitted with reluctance only after the cautious and professorial Cox, carefully prompted by his superiors and subordinates, came down to the question which carried its own answer: "How would we look coming out against reapportionment?" (p. 318). "Awful" was the correct political answer, and Cox always acceded, though never as fully as his colleagues wanted him to, nor as fully as the Supreme Court eventually did in *Reynolds v. Sims*. When he became solicitor general he considered retracting his Republican predecessor's decision to intervene in *Baker v. Carr* or delegating argument to a subordinate. He decided to go ahead with the brief, and to argue the case himself, only after consultation with Kennedy, justice-to-be Byron White, and *New York Times* man Anthony Lewis indicated that any decision not to attack malapportionment, or even not to attack it in person, would be interpreted as a decision that it was legitimate. Though Cox later concluded with pride that his intervention in *Baker* "played the most important role" and "may even have determined the result," he is nonetheless said to have admitted on leaving the courtroom after oral argument, "Frankfurter was right" (pp. 299,304).

After *Baker*, Navasky relates, Kennedy and his lieutenants redoubled their efforts to coax their still-reluctant champion (he was too big a man to be ordered) to urge the Court to order the states to reapportion. Cox's assistant for reapportionment, Bruce Terris (who, like Anthony Lewis, appears to have been one of Navasky's major informants), prepared memoranda emphasizing that reapportionment would "significantly benefit the country," and that the decision of whether and how to intervene further was not a legal one but "a political decision properly made at the highest levels of government"— that is, by Robert or John Kennedy, both of whom wanted to smash malapportionment by whatever means were available (pp. 308-309). Several young attorneys in the Civil Rights Division, primed by Terris and Anthony Lewis, prepared a memo questioning whether land and cows should be represented in a legislature, noting that reapportionment was inseparable from black rights, since large numbers of blacks live in underrepresented urban areas, and concluding that it was "extremely important for the court to formulate a standard which is clear and forthright" and based predominantly, although not necessarily exclusively, on population (pp. 309-310).

Deputy attorney general Nicholas Katzenbach and Burke Marshall, chief of the Civil Rights Division, joined zestfully into the game of "engineering" Cox into pushing the "true-blue view on reapportionment" (p. 302) by convincing him of the political need to have Robert Kennedy argue the first post-*Baker* reapportionment case himself. They needed a case which was not in the fields of civil rights or crime, not too complicated, but important and winnable. *Gray v. Sanders* was their chosen vehicle, and they got Cox to agree by eliminating all other possibilities; Cox was able to hold Kennedy to arguing the case on narrow grounds, but he did not prevent the logical blurring in the brief, nor Kennedy's exuberance in oral argument, which forecast further and bolder government intervention. "Archie was a prince of a fellow," Katzenbach glowed. "We pushed the lobster into the trap but he did everything possible to help" (p. 305).

This manipulatory groundwork may or may not have influenced Cox's accession—at a meeting which included not only Kennedy and his Justice Department staff but also a phalanx of White House staff and Kennedy clansmen—to Kennedy's rhetorical question whether the true issue was not the political one: whether some people's votes should count more than others'. It may or may not have influenced his eventual decision to intervene in all six of the 1964 *Reapportionment* cases, including the Colorado case, despite his own belief (pp. 318-319) that the Colorado plaintiff's position was "at variance with our entire Constitutional history," that it "would ask the Supreme Court to fasten upon the people of every state a doctrinaire system of representation regardless of their wishes," that it would "risk a severe constitutional crisis," and that for the government to adopt it would "be going back on the position which it urged . . . in *Baker v. Carr*" and endanger the prospects of favorable court response to the other five of the *Reapportionment* cases. It may or may not have led him to ask for the states to be held to stricter standards than he otherwise might have asked, or to countenance changes in the brief for *Reynolds v. Sims* after Anthony Lewis (who had read the brief in galley proof) drove to Cox's home and told him that he was "giving too many hostages" to those skeptical of the one man, one vote rule (p. 317).

Cox himself, contrary to Navasky, maintained that he had known all along where he was going to come out (p. 299), leaving the onlooker to suppose that his many doubts and demurrances did not represent his own fears that intervention would be constitutionally sloppy and hazardous to the Court but merely were professorial nods to give the opposing side its due, or tactical indirections to give a false appearance of caution and moderation to a program intended from the start to extirpate malapportionment. Whether real or false, his cautions and doubts could hardly have been improved on as tactical facilitators to the Court's intervention. From most appearances, Navasky's position seems more convincing than Cox's, but regardless of whether or how much Cox was engineered to intervene, the contest for his endorsement was not between partisan interests and transpartisan principles, but between two sets of transpartisan principles, one legal, one political. If he attacked malapportionment, he would risk criticism in the law reviews for losing track of the Constitution and risking immersion in the quagmire; if he failed to attack it, he would face that all-too-easily answered question, "How would we look" to the reading public?

The task of choosing between the two sets of principles and trying to resolve the differences between them did not fall to professional political strategists like Larry O'Brien, but to a university professor with a reputation of craftsmanship to uphold, surrounded by bright young administrators (one of them, Terris, a holdover from the Eisenhower administration), all impatient to get into the history books on the good side. No doubt these young reformers, and perhaps the old professor, too, loved power no less than party regulars—more, maybe, because their time of power was measured in months (or was it days?), while that of party regulars is measured in years. Their thoughts of self-perpetuation (and hence their regard for existing political institutions) may have been correspondingly less than that of party regulars and their thoughts of doing great things while they had the chance correspondingly greater. Their relationship with power was more that of a love affair than that of a marriage. Despite having a stronger grounding in long-term institutional needs than Kennedy's whiz kids, neither Archibald Cox nor the Warren Court could resist the call to greatness so blandishing to the younger men. When greatness beckoned, Cox invariably responded with misgivings, but he never failed to respond. Even in his moment of triumph, however, when the Court announced its opinion in *Reynolds v. Sims* and the ubiquitous Anthony Lewis asked him, "How does it feel to be present at the second American Constitutional Convention?" Cox retained enough of his old perspectives to answer, "It feels awful."

8. Oregon v. Mitchell, 400 U.S. 112 (1970).

9. *Democracy in America* (New York: Knopf, 1945), I, 241.

10. *Ibid.*, II, 337-338.

11. Robert McCloskey cited opinion polls as illustrations of the Court's opinion leadership. In 1942, 45 percent of white adults in the North favored integration, 2 percent in the South; by 1963, 75 percent of northern whites and 30 percent of southern whites favored integration, with much of the increase probably attributable to the Court's "finding" the Fourteenth Amendment to bar segregation. "Reflections on the Warren Court," 51 *Va. L. Rev.* 1229, 1258 (1965).

12. Berle, *Three Faces of Power*, p. 53.

13. A 1966 cross-sectional survey of Wisconsin adults conducted by the University of Wisconsin Survey Research Laboratory indicated that 56 percent of the sample did not know whether the Supreme Court had recently decided any cases involving reapportionment; another 9 percent believed that it had not. Kenneth M. Dolbeare, "The Public Views to Supreme Court," in Jacob, *Law, Politics, and the Federal Courts*, p. 200.

14. Brief for the United States as Amicus Curiae on Reargument, Baker v. Carr, 369 U.S. 186 (1962), Congressional Quarterly, *Representation and Ap-*

portionment (Washington, D.C., 1966) pp. 14-15. The reference to "public cynicism and disillusionment" was taken from Gordon Baker, *Rural versus Urban Political Power* (New York: Random House, 1955), pp. 28-29.

15. Navasky, *Kennedy Justice*, p. 299.

16. According to Navasky, Cox had decided *not* to delegate argument in *Baker v. Carr* after conversations with colleagues indicated that the delegation "would have been a dead giveaway [of lukewarm endorsement] and would have undermined the government's case." *Kennedy Justice*, p. 302; see also note 7 above.

17. The NAACP, whose Legal Defense Fund was organized about the same time as the Justice Department's Civil Rights Division (late 1930's) could not provide the assurance of executive support available from the solicitor general, but it did provide comparable resources of legal skills, strategic management of litigation, information gathering, and organized pressure for reform, both on the Supreme Court and on the lower courts.

18. Congressional Quarterly, *Representation and Apportionment*, p. 19. Arizona, Colorado, Georgia, Hawaii, Idaho, Indiana, Kansas, Louisiana, New Jersey, North Carolina, North Dakota, Pennsylvania, Rhode Island, South Dakota, and Vermont joined in the brief. For discussion of the use of amicus briefs as instruments of interest group policy, see Krislov, "The Amicus Curiae Brief: From Friendship to Advocacy," 72 *Yale L. J.* 694 (1961), and Vose, *Caucasions Only*.

19. Congressional Quarterly, *Representation and Apportionment*, pp. 32-35; Berle, *Three Faces of Power*, p. vii. Lobbying against reapportionment were the National Grange, National Farmer's Union, the American Farm Bureau Federation, local affiliates of the National Association of Manufacturers, the Chamber of Commerce of the United States with constituent local groups, the American Retail Federation, the National Commission on Constitutional Government, the Citizens Committee for Balanced Legislative Representation, itself sponsored by the California Agricultural Council, the California Farm Bureau Federation, the California Manufacturers Association, the California Chamber of Commerce, the California Grape and Tree Fruit Association, the League of California Cities, the California county supervisors organization, the California State Automobile Association, and the California Retailers Association.

Backing reapportionment were the NAACP, Robert F. Kennedy, the United States Council of Mayors, and the National Committee for Fair Representation, with the following affiliates: Amalgamated Clothing Workers of America (AFL-CIO); American Civil Liberties Union; American Ethical Union; American Federation of State, County and Municipal Employees (AFL-CIO); American Jewish Congress; American Newspaper Guild (AFL-CIO); American Veterans Committee; Americans for Democratic Action; B'nai B'rith Women; Committee on Political Education (COPE) of the AFL-CIO; Delta Sigma Theta; AFL-CIO Industrial Union Department; International Ladies Garment Workers Union (AFL-CIO); Jewish War Veterans; Labor Zionists; National Jewish Welfare Board; National Council of Jewish Women; Textile Workers of America (AFL-CIO); United Presbyterian Church, Office of Church and Society; Union of American Hebrew Congregations; United Auto Workers (AFL-CIO); Women's International League for Peace and Freedom; YWCA National Board; and Southern Christian Leadership Conference.

In late June 1965, the Leadership Conference on Civil Rights, with the support of one hundred organizations interested in civil rights, took over lobbying responsibility from the National Committee for Fair Representation; the *Congressional Quarterly* does not list the one hundred groups. Congressional Quarterly, *Representation and Apportionment*, p. 35.

20. *Ibid.*, p. 27.

21. *Ibid.*

22. *Ibid.*

23. *Ibid.*, p. 28.

24. *Ibid.*

25. Calvin B. T. Lee, *One Man One Vote: WMCA and the Struggle for Equal Representation* (New York: Scribners, 1967), p. 108.

26. Congressional Quarterly, *Representation and Apportionment*, p. 30.

27. *Ibid.*, p. 29. In spite of his favorable reaction to *Baker v. Carr*, Barry Goldwater had opposed reapportionment in the 1964 presidential campaign; Lyndon Johnson had refused to take a stand.

28. Another congressional reaction to the reapportionment cases, distinct from Dirksen's efforts, was Congress's attempt to enact its own standards of apportionment in the form of the Celler Bill, H.R. 2508, 90th Cong. 1st sess., H.R. Rep. No. 191, 90th Cong., 1st sess. (1967). This bill was to limit district variance from average to 10 percent and forbid at-large elections in states with more than one representative; it seems to have been inspired partly by the reforming example set by the Supreme Court, partly by fears that the Court would impose even stricter standards if Congress did not come up with standards of its own. The bill was emasculated in conference by removing provisions for court review and postponing all action till the election of the 93rd Congress in 1972. See Gordon W. Hatheway, "Note, Political Gerrymandering: The Law and Politics of Partisan Districting," 36 *G. W. L. Rev.* 144 (1967). If the bill was meant as a hint to the Court to settle for 10 percent variance, the Court ignored it, choosing much stricter standards in *Kirkpatrick v. Preisler*, 394 U.S. 526 (1969).

29. Daniel Bell, *The End of Ideology* (Glencoe, Ill.: Free Press, 1960; Seymour Martin Lipset, *Political Man: The Social Bases of Politics* (Garden City, N.Y.: Doubleday, 1960), chap. 13; Edward Shils, "The End of Ideology," 5 *Encounter* 52 (Nov. 1955).

30. Georg Simmel, "The Metropolis and Mental Life," in Paul K. Hatt and Albert J. Reiss, Jr., eds., *Cities and Society: The Revised Reader in Urban Sociology*, Glencoe, Ill.: Free Press of Glencoe, 1957), p. 636.

31. See Robert Pranger, *The Eclipse of Citizenship: Power and Participation in Contemporary Politics* (New York: Holt, 1968); Theodore Lowi, *The End of Liberalism* (New York: Norton, 1969); Gottfried Dietze, *America's Political Dilemma: From Limited to Unlimited Democracy* (Baltimore: Johns Hopkins Press, 1970); Thomas Dye and Harmon Ziegler, *The Irony of Democracy: An Uncommon Introduction to American Politics* (Belmont, Calif.: Wadsworth, 1972).

32. See Eric A. Nordlinger, "Representation, Governmental Stability, and Decisional Effectiveness," chap. 8 in J. Roland Pennock and John W. Chapman, eds., *Nomos X, Representation* (New York: Atherton Press, 1968).

33. Bertrand de Jouvenel, *On Power: Its Nature and the History of Its Growth* (Boston: Beacon Press, 1962) chap. 14, "Totalitarian Democracy"; Edmund Burke, "Reflections on the French Revolution," chap. 7 in Ross Hoffman and Paul Levack, eds., *Burke's Politics* (New York: Knopf, 1949).

34. Simmel, "Metropolis and Mental Life," p. 639.

35. Berle, *Three Faces of Power*, p. 3.

36. *Ibid.*, pp. 55, 56. Symptomatic of the Guardians' tendency to trust experts first and the public last was their horror at the prospect of a constitutional convention to qualify *Reynolds v. Sims* because it "might enter areas other than those proposed by Senator Dirksen." Entering new areas of extraordinary legislation, of course, is exactly what Berle wanted for the Supreme Court; the real source of his uneasiness was not the prospect of revolutionary change but the thought that it might be unduly influenced by party politics or, worse, by the untutored desires of the general public.

37. Berle, *Three Faces of Power*, p. 54.

38. *Ibid.*, pp. 61-70.

39. *Ibid.*, p. 10, 77.

40. *U.S. News and World Report* (Apr. 1, 1968), p. 16.

41. Lipset, *Political Man*, p. 414.

42. Michel Crozier, *The Bureaucratic Phenomenon* (Chicago: University of Chicago Press, 1964), chaps. 8, 9.

43. Baker v. Carr, 369 U.S. 186, 267 (dissenting opinion). A 1966 Wisconsin survey indicated that adults in that state trusted the Supreme Court less than any other branch of government, with 39 percent having no confidence in the Court's actions, as opposed to 33 percent mistrusting the president and only 16 percent mistrusting Congress. Twenty-eight percent of the sample expressed confidence in the Court, 35 percent trusted the president, and 50 percent trusted Congress, the rest being undecided. Kenneth Dolbeare, "The Public Views the Supreme Court," in Jacob, *Law, Politics, and the Federal Courts*, p. 197.

44. Exodus 20:4. "Thou shalt not make unto thee any graven image, or any likeness of any thing that is in heaven above, or that is in the earth beneath, or that is in the water under the earth."

45. The classic example of polar philosophies for and against bureaucratic values is Confucianism and Taoism. Confucianism embraced hierarchy, deference, and the application of a "prescribed path" to every part of life; Taoism stressed spontaneous individuality and independence from the claims of civilization. A similar, but much more fragmented polarity may be found in French political philosophy, France having produced in thinkers like de Maistre and Bonald a highly doctrinaire priesthood of order, and in thinkers like Proudhon a highly refined doctrine of anarchism. I suppose these contrary trends may have been foreshadowed in the late 1960's and early 1970's by A. A. Berle's *Three Faces of Power* and Rexford Tugwell's constitution on the Confucian side, and, for the Taoists, the counterculture literature of Herbert Marcuse, *Eros and Civilization: A Philosophical Inquiry into Freud* (Boston: Beacon Press, 1966); Theodore Rozhak, *The Making of a Counter-Culture: Reflections on the Technocratic Society and Its Youthful Opposition* (Garden City, N.Y.: Doubleday, 1968); and Charles Reich, *The Greening of America* (New York: Random House, 1970).

46. Respectively, 19 How. 393 (1857); 8 Wall. 603 (1870); and 198 U.S. 45 (1905).

Notes to Epilogue

1. The Court could have dealt with flagrant racial malapportionment in the South under the Fifteenth Amendment, as it had with the racial gerrymander in *Gomillion v. Lightfoot*, without having to resort to the Fourteenth Amend-

ment "authority" of *Baker v. Carr*. This approach would have raised difficult questions of further applications (as was true of Gomillion), and it would not have been very effective against partisan gerrymandering. But neither was reapportionment.

2. I suppose all three positions could be described as selective in the sense that even Harlan and Frankfurter would intervene in some cases, and even the most irredentist of the justices, Douglas and Brennan, drew the line at some forms of intervention; however, for the purposes of this argument, the middle is presumed to be more selective than the extremes.

3. Brief for the United States as *amicus curiae* on reargument, Baker v. Carr, pp. 29-30.

4. The solicitor general called unsuccessfully for the Court to intervene in *Sailors v. Board*, 387 U.S. 105 (1967), and its companion case, *Dusch v. Davis*, 387 U.S. 112 (1967). To the surprise of many observers, the Court held positions on a school-board-above-school-boards to be "pyramidally appointed," not elected, and also upheld a law requiring candidates for a multi-member district to reside in unequal subdistricts.

5. See Note, "Reapportionment," 79 *Harv. L. Rev.* 1228, 1248-1254 (1966).

6. Reynolds v. Sims, 377 U.S. 533 (1964); Maryland Committee for Fair Representation v. Tawes, 377 U.S. 656 (1964); Roman v. Sincock, 377 U.S. 695 (1964). Dauer-Kelsay scores for these states were as follows: Alabama—Senate, 25.1 percent; House, 25.7 percent; Maryland—Senate, 14.2 percent; House, 25.3 percent; Delaware—Senate, 22.0 percent; House, 18.5 percent. Stewart excluded the Maryland Senate from his concurring opinion finding it based on an "intelligible principle" of one seat per county, six seats for Baltimore. He voted to remand the case for a finding whether the Senate worked "systematically to prevent ultimate majority rule." 377 U.S. p. 677.

7. See Robert G. Dixon, *Representative Government*, app. A and B.

8. Davis v. Mann, 377 U.S. 678 (1964).

9. Population variance between the largest and smallest district is considered a milder form of discrimination than detrimental variance because it also measures variances favorable to specific districts. Though favorable variance for a few districts means unfavorable variance for the many, the discrimination is comparatively innocuous in the same sense that enforcing a will benefiting a minority (e.g., the testator's own descendents, or needy black students) is considered innocuous compared to enforcing a will which excludes a protectable minority (e.g., blacks). If the few are favored, the individual cost to the many is low; if the few are disfavored, the cost to them is high.

10. Lucas v. Forty-Fourth General Assembly, 377 U.S. 713 (1964); WMCA v. Lomenzo, 377 U.S. 633 (1964).

11. Moore v. Ogilvie, 394 U.S. 814 (1969).

12. Swann v. Adams, 385 U.S. 440 (1967); Kirkpatrick v. Preisler, 394 U.S. 526 (1969).

13. Avery v. Midland County, 390 U.S. 474 (1968).

14. Fortson v. Morris, 385 U.S. 231 (1966).

15. Wright v. Rockefeller, 372 U.S. 52 (1964); Fortson v. Dorsey, 379 U.S. 433 (1965); Burns v. Richardson, 384 U.S. 73 (1966).

16. Sailors v. Board of Election, 387 U.S. 105 (1967); Dusch v. Davis, 387 U.S. 112 (1967).

17. Katzenbach v. Morgan, 384 U.S. 641 (1966); Hadnott v. Amos, 394 U.S. 358 (1969).

18. Respectively, Allen v. Board, 393 U.S. 544 (1969) (Va. and Miss.); Gaston County v. United States, 395 U.S. 486 (1969) (N.C.).

19. 380 U.S. 89 (1965).

20. Powell v. McCormack, 395 U.S. 486 (1969); Harper v. Board of Elections, 383 U.S. 663 (1966); Williams v. Rhodes, 393 U.S. 23 (1968); Kramer v. Union School District, 395 U.S. 621 (1969).

21. Allen v. Board of Election 393 U.S. 544 (1969); cf. Hadnott v. Amos 394 U.S. 358 (1969).

22. Carrington v. Rash, 380 U.S. 89 (1965); cf. Harper v. Board of Elections, 383 U.S. 663 (1966).

23. Stewart voted for intervention in the following ten cases involving southern states: *Baker v. Carr* (Tenn.); *Gray v. Sanders* (Ga.); *Wesberry v. Sanders* (Ga.); *Reynolds v. Sims* (Ala.); *Davis v. Mann* (Va.); *Carrington v. Rash* (Tex.); *Allen v. Board* (Va.); *Fairley v. Patterson* (Miss.); *Bunton v. Patterson* (Miss.); and *Gaston County v. United States* (N.C.). He opposed intervention in two border-state cases, *Roman v. Sincock* (Dela.) and *Maryland Committee v. Tawes* (Md.). In no case during the Warren era did he vote for intervention against a northern state.

He voted not to intervene in six southern-state cases: *Swann v. Adams* (Fla.); *Hadnott v. Amos* (Ala.); *Harper v. Board* (Va.); *Fortson v. Morris* (Ga.); *Fortson v. Dorsey* (Ga.); and *Dusch v. Davis* (Va.). He opposed intervention in one border-state case, *Kirkpatrick v. Preisler* (Mo.), and in eleven northern-state cases: *Powell v. McCormack* (N.Y.); *Katzenbach v. Morgan* (N.Y.); *Lucas v. Colorado* (Colo.); *WMCA v. Lomenzo* (N.Y.); *Williams v. Rhodes* (Ohio); *Moore v. Ogilvie* (Ill.); *Wells v. Rockefeller* (N.Y.); *Wright v. Rockefeller* (N.Y.); *Kramer v. School District* (N.Y.); *Burns v. Richardson* (Haw.); and *Sailors v. Board* (Mich.).

24. Stewart voted to invalidate Virginia malapportionment while upholding that of New York, despite the fact that Virginia had higher Dauer-Kelsay scores in both houses (S, 41.1 percent; H, 40.5 percent) than New York (S, 38.1 percent; H, 37.5 percent). Davis v. Mann, 377 U.S. 678 (1964) (Va.); WMCA v. Lomenzo, 377 U.S. 633 (1964) (N.Y.). The Virginia discrimination, however, appeared to be the result of failure to redistrict, rather than the result of a constitutional plan. Frankfurter in *Gomillion v. Lightfoot* had thought planned discrimination was more invidious than unplanned, but Stewart seemed to entertain the opposite view. See Dixon, *Democratic Representation*, pp. 275-277.

Notes to Appendix

1. Bracketed section superseded by Seventeenth Amendment.
2. Bracketed section superseded by Twelfth Amendment.

Table of Cases

Index

Absentee ballot, 77
Academic freedom, *see* College professors; Dormitory vote
Adams County, Colo., 216
Administrative abuses of voting rights, 3, 66–67, 81, 84, 133, 209
Advisory Commission on Intergovernmental Relations, 10, 97. *See also* Kestnbaum Commission Report
AFL-CIO, 138, 252, 254
Alabama, 66, 69, 70, 81, 83, 86, 87, 99, 121, 193, 219, 220, 221, 222, 223, 232, 235, 251, 267, 270, 271
Algerine laws, 46–48
Amateurs, 11, 259; in Democratic Party, 1972, 180–188. *See also* Guardian Ethic; McGovern Commission
American Academy of Political and Social Science, 90
American Assembly, 97
American Bar Association, 135, 136, 138, 241, 263
American Civil Liberties Union (ACLU), 138, 252, 253
American Establishment, 260, 302
American Farm Bureau, 254
American Good Government Society, 135, 138
American Jewish Congress, 253
American Political Science Association, 10, 13–16, 23, 31, 90, 97, 110, 134, 137, 162, 245, 259. *See also* Political science
American Proportional Representation League, 90
Americans for Democratic Action, 138, 141, 252, 254
Appointive office, 190
"April Coalition," 156, 157, 158, 159
Aristotle, 37
Arizona, 93, 143, 150, 159, 220, 225
Arkansas, 81, 86, 87

Article I, *see* Constitution
At-large elections, 107, 169. *See also* Multi-member districts
Atlanta, Ga., 169, 221

Bacon, Francis, 196, 197
Bagehot, Walter, 198, 205
Bailey, D'Army, 157
Baker, Gordon, 10, 16, 18, 31, 110–112, 139, 218, 220, 254
Ballot box stuffing, *see* Administrative abuses
Ballot, position on, 172, 188, 271
Baltimore, Md., 98, 219, 222
Banfield, Edward, 199, 308
Banzhaf, John F., 136, 137, 169, 352
Barnyard government, *see* Rural-urban conflict
Barr, Joseph, 222
Bayh amendment, 137, 138
Beard, Charles, 94
Bedsheet ballot, 107, 112
Beer, Samuel, 177
Behavioralism, 7
Bentham, Jeremy, 23, 197, 198, 248, 259, 264
Berkeley, Calif., 156, 157, 158, 159
Berle, Adolf A., 6, 251, 259, 260, 261, 262
Beveridge, Albert, 70
Bickel, Alexander, 1, 24, 60–61, 114, 214, 310, 344
Bingham, John A., 58–59, 61, 143
Bischoff, Charles W., 136, 137
Black, Hugo, 66, 85, 88, 108, 111, 144, 189, 245, 246, 260, 268–269, 326, 339, 344
Blackmun, Harry, 58, 144, 160, 245
Blackstone, William, 39
Black vote, 62–63, 105, 151, 226, 228–234, 238, 323–327; registration, 31, 72, 86–87. *See also* Gerrymanders;

381

Harvard Political Studies

*Out of print

*John Fairfield Sly. *Town Government in Massachusetts (1620–1930).* 1930.
*Hugh Langdon Elsbree. *Interstate Transmission of Electric Power: A Study in the Conflict of State and Federal Jurisdictions.* 1931.
*Benjamin Fletcher Wright, Jr. *American Interpretations of Natural Law.* 1931.
*Payson S. Wild, Jr. *Sanctions and Treaty Enforcement,* 1934.
*William P. Maddox. *Foreign Relations in British Labour Politics.* 1934.
*George C. S. Benson. *Administration of the Civil Service in Massachusetts, with Special Reference to State Control of City Civil Service.* 1935.
*Merle Fainsod. *International Socialism and the World War.* 1935.
*John Day Larkin. *The President's Control of the Tariff.* 1936.
*E. Pendleton Herring. *Federal Commissioners: A Study of Their Careers and Qualifications.* 1936.
*John Thurston. *Government Proprietary Corporations in the English-Speaking Countries.* 1937.
*Mario Einaudi. *The Physiocratic Doctrine of Judicial Control.* 1938.
*Frederick Mundell Watkins. *The Failure of Constitutional Emergency Powers under the German Republic.* 1939.
*G. Griffith Johnson, Jr. *The Treasury and Monetary Policy, 1933–1938.* 1939.
*Arnold Brecht and Comstock Glaser. *The Art and Technique of Administration in German Ministries.* 1940.
*Oliver Garceau. *The Political Life of the American Medical Association.* 1941.
*Ralph F. Bischoff. *Nazi Conquest through German Culture.* 1942.
*Charles R. Cherington. *The Regulation of Railroad Abandonments.* 1948.
*Samuel H. Beer. *The City of Reason.* 1949.
*Herman Miles Somers. *Presidential Agency: The Office of War Mobilization and Reconversion.* 1950.
*Adam B. Ulam. *Philosophical Foundations of English Socialism.* 1951.
*Morton Robert Godine. *The Labor Problem in the Public Service: A Study in Political Pluralism.* 1951.
*Arthur Maass. *Muddy Waters: The Army Engineers and the Nation's Rivers.* 1951.
*Robert Green McCloskey. *American Conservatism in the Age of Enterprise:*

A Study of William Graham Sumner, Stephen J. Field, and Andrew Carnegie. 1951.

*Inis L. Claude, Jr. *National Minorities: An International Problem.* 1955.

*Joseph Cornwall Palamountain, Jr. *The Politics of Distribution.* 1955.

*Herbert J. Spiro. *The Politics of German Codetermination.* 1958.

Harry Eckstein. *The English Health Service: Its Origins, Structure, and Achievements.* 1958.

*Richard F. Fenno, Jr. *The President's Cabinet: An Analysis in the Period from Wilson to Eisenhower.* 1959.

Nadav Safran. *Egypt in Search of Political Community: An Analysis of the Intellectual and Political Evolution of Egypt, 1804–1952.* 1961.

*Paul E. Sigmund. *Nicholas of Cusa and Medieval Political Thought.* 1963.

Sanford A. Lakoff. *Equality in Political Philosophy.* 1964.

*Charles T. Goodsell. *Administration of a Revolution: Executive Reform in Puerto Rico under Governor Tugwell, 1941–1946.* 1965.

Martha Derthick. *The National Guard in Politics.* 1965.

Bruce L. R. Smith. *The RAND Corporation: Case Study of a Nonprofit Advisory Corporation.* 1966.

David R. Mayhew. *Party Loyalty among Congressmen: The Difference between Democrats and Republicans, 1947–1962.* 1966.

Isaac Kramnick. *Bolingbroke and His Circle: The Politics of Nostalgia in the Age of Walpole.* 1968.

Donald W. Hanson. *From Kingdom to Commonwealth: The Development of Civic Consciousness in English Political Thought.* 1970.

Ward E. Y. Elliott. *The Rise of Guardian Democracy: The Supreme Court's Role in Voting Rights Disputes, 1845–1969.* 1974.